Personalizing
Music Education
A PLAN FOR IMPLEMENTATION

Contains a complete handbook for developing your own
GAMES, ACTIVITIES, and CHALLENGES.

JOAN Z. FYFE

D1298652

Published by Alfred Publishing Co., Inc.
15335 Morrison Street, Sherman Oaks, CA 91403

Copyright © 1978 by Alfred Publishing Co., Inc.
All Rights Reserved.

Printed in the United States of America

Library of Congress Cataloging in Publication Data

Fyfe, Joan.
    Personalizing music education.

    Bibliography: p.
    Includes index.
    1. School music—Instruction and study.   I. Title.
MT1.F96   780'.72   78-52356
ISBN 0-88284-063-0

CONTENTS

SECTION ONE

SECTION TWO

DEDICATION

"The arts play a radically different role in the open classroom than in the traditional school. Painting, sculpture, music, dance, crafts—these are not frills to be indulged in if time is left over from the real business of education; they are the business of education as much as reading, writing, math, or science."

Charles E. Silberman
The Open Classroom Reader

PROLOGUE

When I finally realized and accepted the fact that I was going to have to come forth with a workable and realistic plan for teaching music in a multi-age organizational setting, I began a journey that has been exciting and exhilarating if not, at times, frustrating and frenzied; an obstacle course that, quite frequently, seemed insurmountable. Yet, the whole experience, to date, has enabled me to grow far beyond the boundaries one might envision for a good elementary music teacher.

The experience has forced me to evaluate the role of music in a child's total educational life and my role in his continuing growth pattern. It has made it imperative for me to be completely knowledgeable about how a child learns: the sequential development of psychomotor as well as cognitive skills and the more subtle but, nonetheless, important aspect of his affective development as he interracts within a musical setting and reacts to music. It has forced me to evaluate the music program in terms of the individual child and his needs, both immediate and long term, in a much more realistic, if not less conservatory-type approach.

Most rewarding for me is the fact that I have been removed from a rather-segregated position as a "special" and placed in the role of a viable and contributing member of the total educational team.

My first challenge came in a philosophical guise. How easy is it to put aside those "sacred truths and traditions" that one has held dear for lo, how many years? In my case, it was eighteen! Yes, I had always tried to provide satisfying experiences for the slow child and motivationally exciting ones for the more able and talented student but, in reality, was I not always teaching to the whole class, right down the middle?

And, notice all the "I's," the personalization. Was I going to be able to re-linquish my exalted position and accept the fact that the children might just possibly achieve as much, maybe even learn more, if I got out of their way? Could I accept "we" and "they"? Even that large desk; I never used it, but wasn't it, too, a symbol of my authority?

The goal of our organizational plan was to have the special subjects completely integrated into the school day, thus breaking down the traditional time barriers. But, at the same time, contractual obligations still had to be met as to provision of preparation periods for classroom teachers. This presented the second challenge: organization through scheduling.

The third problem to be overcome was that of the learning environment. For classroom teachers there is a plethora of materials available for individualizing all aspects of curricular life; programs already implemented can be observed and evaluated and experts by the score are ready to serve as consultants, provide guidance through workshops, and so on. But, for the special subject teacher, the enriched environment, within which boys and girls could learn at their own rate, according to needs and interests, was one I would have to provide through my own creation, for when I looked to the market, the market was virtually bare.

Now, how was I going to evaluate pupil progress? Certainly class tests given at periodic intervals were no longer consonant with an educational philosophy bent on personalization but, in this day, when accountability is on the lips of school boards, taxpayers, and administrators everywhere, could I rely solely on my instincts, my expertise, my intuitions? Believe me, I was rather shocked to discover that my judgments alone had not always provided a sound basis for an objective evaluation and had occasionally fallen short of the mark.

I had to devise the means for testing pupil progress though, as you will discover, this was not always to be through the formal test per se. Also, the diagnostic and pretest became important in joint planning and prescribing with individual students. This then was the fourth step in the development of a program for which I could be held accountable.

My purpose in writing this book has been to assist those of you who wish to move in the direction of an individualized approach to music teaching. I have attempted to be as practical as possible, offering alternatives and providing answers to the more cogent problems. However, keep in mind that this can only be a guide and, hopefully, will facilitate the implementation of your program in your school with your students. This is the key to its use, for we are as unique as our individual students, as our school sizes and community personalities, as our administrators and supervisors, as our funding and our physical layout, but we share a common concern in that those students with whom we come in contact will improve their basic skills through music and attain the foundation for a lifelong satisfaction in music.

SECTION
ONE

1 The Philosophical Evolution

The philosophical considerations of an open program of music instruction have to be viewed in terms of the total educational philosophy of the school or, once again, the special subject teacher will find himself in an isolated position. It is mutually productive when a sense of direction is developed in conjunction with one's colleagues even though there may be differences in process.

The "openness" which we sought implied a desire to offer alternative styles of instruction to children and to personalize each child's acquisition of basic skills. That process of internalization was to come about through peer and professional interaction within whatever physical environment the child found himself at any given time. In other words the barriers were down at this point, at least in a philosophical sense.

In order to clarify my thinking, I found it helpful to explore current research and alternative programs, both in special subject areas and in general education. For those of you whose time is limited, I suggest as a starting point, *Open Education: A Sourcebook for Parents and Teachers,* edited by Ewald P. Nyquist and Gene R. Hawes and published by Bantam Books, Inc., 1972. It is a compilation of current thinking as to philosophy and methodology and will lead to further inquiry. Also, the editors of *Music Educators Journal,* Music Educators National Conference, have been publishing articles dealing with both specifics and generalities in this evolving program of music education since 1965.

No one author, no single article, provided the blueprint for a procedural reorganization but, at the very least, each established a pattern for inquiry and, at best, enriched the field of thought from which one could depart.

In its most practical terms, here are objectives and a subsequent rationale for the implementation of an individualized program of music instruction; a blending of the traditional with the confluent (cognitive and affective), a fusion of creative and academic thought, a realization of and reconciliation with our role in public education and, most hopefully, a framework upon which you can build and present your program.*

OBJECTIVE: To develop a music program that is child-centered.

RATIONALE FOR IMPLEMENTATION: As a child develops musically, his needs will be continually diagnosed, his interests observed, his progress evaluated, so that a specific curriculum may be designed to ensure his continued growth. A child may find the reading of music to be abstract when approached vocally but, when presented with activities at the keyboard, the abstract may become concrete and quite possible.

OBJECTIVE: To consider the needs and interests of each child in determining his curriculum in music.

RATIONALE FOR IMPLEMENTATION: Activities, games, and projects are to be designed specifically to interest and challenge every child. Learning styles differ, modes of learning change periodically for individuals; therefore, a variety of approaches to any behavioral objective is needed.

*Cooperative Area Programs, Jericho Public Schools, *Multi-Age Grouping,* Summer 1973. Professional Staff of the Robert Williams School.

OBJECTIVE: To provide an environment in which children can and will learn through discovery.

RATIONALE FOR IMPLEMENTATION: The environment should be enriched with a multiplicity of vehicles which will invite discovery. It should include task cards, activities, games, tapes, recordings, keyboard instruments, pitched, non-pitched, and indefinite pitched percussive instruments, recorder, guitar, and any other devices that a child may find motivationally satisfying.

OBJECTIVE: To provide opportunities for individual investigation based upon a transfer of knowledge.

RATIONALE FOR IMPLEMENTATION: Once a child has developed a skill or a set of skills, it is quite possible for him to pursue an individualized project/-activity through a transfer of knowledge. Internalization of a concept has taken place when this kind of satisfying activity can occur.

OBJECTIVE: To provide an environment for interaction between children of varying ages, interests, and skill levels.

RATIONALE FOR IMPLEMENTATION: While this objective is specifically designed for the multi-age plan of organization, there are many opportunities possible for interaction between children of varying emotional, intellectual, physical, and psychological levels within a traditionally organized class. The greater the opportunities for intermingling, the wider the range of possibilities for growth and development.

OBJECTIVE: To provide for a perception and understanding of music within a totality of disciplines: correlation.

RATIONALE FOR IMPLEMENTATION: The interrelationship of music with all subjects is predicated upon the sincere belief that we teach children *through* music, not in music. Therefore, when we consider correlation, it is at two levels. The first is one of enrichment. A child wants to know more about life in the Middle Ages and investigates it through music. The second level is functional and should be the essence of our purpose and focus in elementary education. It is one of process. For the child described, it is not so much the enrichment of his social studies curriculum and the knowledge gained as it is the act of investigating and discovering relationships. It is this which should be inherent in all pursuits.

OBJECTIVE: To provide activities which will facilitate and reinforce acquisition of developmental skills.

RATIONALE FOR IMPLEMENTATION: The activities of music are all designed to reinforce basic learning skills in one way or another. It becomes incumbent upon the teacher to know and prescribe those activities which will foster acquisition of specific skills, be they psychomotor or cognitive, in a developmental sequence.

OBJECTIVE: To provide an enriched environment for cultivation of creative behavior in children.

RATIONALE FOR IMPLEMENTATION: The creative act, the creative thought process should be built into as many activity situations as possible. In the acquiring of concepts, this can be the motivating force.

OBJECTIVE: To provide for the continuous progress of each child through a systematic but diverse exploration of experiences.

RATIONALE FOR IMPLEMENTATION: Throughout the teaching-learning process, no matter how diverse, the scope and sequence of the music curriculum must be a significant factor in determining the alternatives confronting an individual student.

OBJECTIVE: To provide for continuous diagnosis and evaluation of needs and progress.

RATIONALE FOR IMPLEMENTATION: Specifically designed diagnostic tests should be administered to aid in the planning and implementation of the direction of the curriculum. Each child's progress should be evaluated and recorded systematically.

In the last fifteen years each of us has seen if, indeed, not felt a significant change in our whole approach to music education. Who among us could escape or deny the impact of Dalcroze, Orff, and Kodaly, whose efforts have played a paramount role in breaking down the barriers of traditional music education? And, certainly not to be overlooked are the responses of all those music educators who brought the singular efforts of these men into concert and made possible the pedagogy for American children.

In no way is this book attempting to "Americanize" or set forth another implementation for what has been so outstandingly accomplished; the purpose is to show how one may utilize the precepts of current thinking in music education in a personalized approach. However, it will still remain for the general music teacher to adapt and interpret the theories of these educators, in his own plan for individualizing the music program.

In the adaptation and interpretation, you will find many significant experience-oriented activities based upon the philosophical objectives previously outlined. These can be most easily incorporated into a personalized approach to music education if you accept the premise that a child grows and develops at his own rate, according to his own needs, abilities, and interests, at the same time that he maintains an interdependent relationship with others.

While this relationship may be in small groups of two or three, the communicative nature of music lends itself to larger group activities through choruses, bands, orchestras, ensembles, and the like.

There may be occasions when preparation for performance will cause time lapses in personalized instruction, depending on the teacher-pupil ratio. Yet, in any such program, time must be provided for these activities, for it is through interaction with others that students will attain the most growth, be it cognitive, affective, or even psychomotor, because, a significant motivational force is dominant at these moments of group effort for a common goal.

Productions may also take new forms. Some might be of the showcase type in which small groups present the culmination of activities in which they have been involved. Others will be of a spontaneous nature, a result of open and integrated activity between disciplines and, still others, a recital type of presentation.

Philosophically, large group activities do have a meaningful role in the program of instruction for they are simply an extension of the personalized plan for each child, the moment when he can communicate what he has internalized, the time for contributing his share.

2 Scheduling – the Organization Plan

The matter of scheduling and the overall organizational plan for a personalized program of instruction is a key issue to be settled before implementation. Solutions and alternatives will be predicated upon school size and pupil-teacher ratios as well as physical layout and facilities. The teacher in a small school with a designated room is certainly in a different position from one who services a whole building in half-hour blocks of time with no unscheduled periods and, in addition, must push a cart from room to room. However, no matter how insurmountable the problems may seem and even if all possibilities have been exhausted, it is still possible to individualize to some degree, even if you are "stuck" with last year's very traditional, locked-in time schedule.

Ideally, there should be no set all-class music periods. Children should have the freedom to spend greater or lesser amounts of time in the music area, depending upon needs and interests. However, the following "practicalities/realities" demand otherwise:

1. Contractual commitments to preparation time for classroom teachers.

2. The need for total school structure, careful planning, and organization, so that all teachers and students can experience an atmosphere of freedom with responsibility.

3. The need for basic skills in music (or art or physical education) to be taught in developmental sequence. (The ideal may be to teach the skills when needed, but this is not always possible due to time considerations.)

4. The fact that some children need more motivation than others to become involved in music, art, or physical education and, in an unscheduled organizational plan, may miss even minimum exposure.

The basic scheduled time blocks should be minimally thirty minutes, twice a week for Grades One through Six. The approximate division of time within a given class period might be ten to fifteen minutes for a group meeting in which a particular skill is presented, the initial steps of an instrumentation pursued, or a song learned. The skills presentations are simply exposures and should be followed up by activities at appropriate interest/grade levels, whenever the developmental sequence demands. These exposures will be repeated in many ways throughout the elementary years and elaborated upon at the moment of readiness for each child.

The overall purpose of the group meeting is to provide a time for dissemination of information, a sharing of ideas, a presentation of completed projects, and a unity of effort. It gives direction and focus in a general way and sets the tone for the day's work. Occasionally, it may be deleted, but it is as important as the personalized aspects of the program because it establishes a mutuality of purpose.

During the remaining time, within any given class period, the children pursue their prescribed activities. The matter of the prescription will be covered at length but, as a general introduction, it is a work plan for each child, based upon where he is developmentally with consideration given to his learning style and including experiences related to skills work presentation of the group meeting, whenever appropriate.

Ideally, Grades Three through Six should have longer time periods; in fact, if no other options are possible, choose one forty-five minute period, once a week, rather than the two half-hour periods. Many children become frustrated because they are unable to complete an activity within the shorter time frame. Any remaining minutes should be left open and unscheduled as enrichment periods which allow for guitar, piano, advanced recorder, ensembles, and the like, as well as extended involvement in activities and integrated learnings predicated upon prescribed assignments.

Kindergarten has not been mentioned in prior discussion because all Kindergarten music experiences should be initiated by the class teacher with the music teacher providing materials and suggestions for activities in consultation. Music is inherent in every aspect of a Kindergarten class, and should not be segregated into single blocks of time.

However, to return to realities; in most situations the music teacher is now expected to provide approximately one half hour of instruction per week for Kindergarten. What form should this take? This must be determined in conjunction with the class teacher, and for the experience to be meaningful, it should provide for follow through by the class teacher. These sessions should focus on initial conceptual experiences, giving the children a broad base to draw on in meeting new challenges.

The enrichment periods mentioned earlier are an extra dividend in a personalized program and allow for many more experiences than the traditionally closed class. The terminology is simply one of semantics. The following are a variety of functions of this period to which the reader may add many more:

1. Extending work in basic concepts. After diagnosing gaps
    in conceptual internalization (high/low, up/down. fast/slow,
    changing meter and tempo, aural, oral, visual skills of music
    reading, and the like), activities are set up for children to
    work on their own in the acquisition of these skills.

2. Extending basic music skills. Using a wide variety of activities as a base, children may continue to work on their prescribed tasks alone or with friends.

3. Providing for individual (not group) instruction in piano, guitar, soprano, alto, and tenor recorder.*

4. Providing for ensemble work: pitched, nonpitched, and indefinite pitched instruments. Materials should always be available.

5. Providing additional time for project work in music. In this plan it takes the form of I.T.T.'s (integrated tasks and topics), which will be discussed further on.

6. Providing an atmosphere for additional experiences in body movement from free response and problem solving through movement to ballet, modern dance, folk, and square dancing.

7. Extending the child's scope of classroom work in any given subject/project area through correlated music involvement.

8. Becoming a music lab for creativity and discovery.

9. Performing the function of an extended class, tutorial, in which the child is working on his basic cognitive skills while using music as the medium. One example: Children may need help with blends and the music teacher may provide specific speech chant activities to this end or may direct children in building word chains based on specific blends. These can be rhythmically notated, chanted, given a melody, and instrumented.

10. Providing for extended work with children on psychomotor and perceptual development through a wide variety of musical experiences.

11. Providing a time for quiet, meaningful, purposeful, guided listening.

*In no way does this replace private instruction. More children are studying privately since implementation because appetites have been "whetted."

Should it be impossible to schedule for this kind of involvement, there is an alternative to regularly scheduled enrichment periods. Children can pursue these activities even while a whole class session is in progress and do, quite successfully and satisfactorily. But how?

The key here, and, in fact, the key to the success of the entire program is *structure*, and its importance cannot be overstated. If the environment is rich with materials and devices, if rules for operating in that environment are systematically and carefully set and agreed to by the children, and if the children always come with a purpose in mind, they can operate in the various work areas of the room, take materials outside the room, and proceed on their own. Just keep in mind that most students can work without a teacher, at least some of the time, as long as the ground rules are fully understood.

Another possibility is paraprofessional or parent volunteer staffing. I have left a responsible adult in charge while I am working in another school. The results have been excellent. He or she need not be a musician or even musically inclined — simply someone who is interested in children and sensitive to their needs. This person can monitor the environment and actually become involved with the children. I use a "sign-in" book for these times and children must include a sentence or two as to their purpose for coming. This gives the music teacher a means for monitoring the progress of these experiences. This procedure has proven to be a "plus" for public relations; the volunteer participant sees the process instead of always the product.

In the initial chapter on philosophy, the importance of retaining large group activities — chorus, band, orchestra, was mentioned. Ideally, they should be scheduled within the school day if we sincerely believe in their importance. However, many schools have found it impossible and therefore, here are alternatives, with comments:

1. Before school. This is possible if your school day does not begin too early and you meet with no parental objections.

2. After school. This is even more difficult due to the myriad of commitments our students have.

3. During recess. This has been found to be the most acceptable. If the activity is exciting and the experience satisfying and goal seeking, children will readily forego the play period twice or even three times a week.

Quite obviously, the operational aspects of this type of program necessitate many different things happening simultaneously in and around the music area. Therefore, the ground rules mentioned before are all-important.

1. Each child must be responsible for his own materials, all of which are kept in his folder in the spot designated for his class. He may take his folder from the area, but he must return it when finished.

2. Each child must be responsible for the environment, replacing all materials when finished.

3. Each child is responsible for the keeping of a record of his activities and charting his progress on piano, guitar, and so forth.

4. Each child must be considerate of others, sharing materials and facilities and keeping the sound level within tolerable bounds.

5. Each child must respond to the sound of the gong; one strike means silence for a necessary announcement, two strikes mean clean up the area. (Because the signal system is used with great discretion, it is usually observed quickly.)

The major problem in implementing a program of this scope is one of teacher time. There just is never enough. The following suggestions may offer the reader some possible solutions:

1. Peer teachers. Older children enjoy helping younger ones; advanced students willingly assist beginners. Who was it that said you really have learned a concept when you can teach it to someone else!

2. Interested high school students who are participating in community involvement programs and receive permission to assist for a scheduled number of hours per week.

3. Student teachers from nearby universities.

4. Student interns from universities who participate in observation-assistance type programs during their sophomore and junior years.

5. Parent volunteers. Invaluable for record keeping, filing, resetting the environment, and listening to children's efforts, even if their knowledge of music is limited.

6. Paraprofessionals. To be used in the same ways as parent volunteers.

For those who are teaching in large schools and have no open periods of time and must move from room to room, the following possibilities are offered:

1. Shortening the length of the regularly scheduled music periods, even by five minutes, to allow for at least half an hour per day for open activities. (This may become a matter of weighing options and employing value judgments.)

2. Combining two classes each day, on a rotating basis, thereby freeing a period for open activities.

3. Setting up activity centers in hallways adjacent to classrooms. Usually all classes of a grade level are housed within a circumscribed area of the building. The materials in the center would be chosen for the interests and abilities of that grade level, and children would be free to use them whenever their classroom teacher permitted.

4. Using the stage of the auditorium to house the activity centers, all of which could be on tables and in cases which can be easily moved when the area is needed for another purpose. (After all, just how often is the auditorium used during the year?)

5. Locating a large supply closet which can house the activities. Children could sign out equipment at will. Perhaps it might be large enough for two or three children to work in for short periods of time.

6. Setting up a music activity corner in each classroom with the assistance of the classroom teacher. Rather than having to duplicate activities for each room, they could be rotated from class to class on a regular basis. Children could be encouraged to contribute to this corner.

Lacking a room or an area of your own and/or being inhibited by antiquated scheduling will undoubtedly limit the program but, with creative use of existing facilities and some time adjustments, one can begin to provide an open, extended musical environment and make an inroad toward personalization. The prime consideration throughout the organizational planning must be the most effective use of available time for each child.

3 Curriculum and Sequence

If one accepts the philosophical premise upon which this program is based, it then becomes necessary to examine what was, in the past, called the music curriculum. Most curriculums included a myriad of skills which were to be mastered at each grade level, together with numerous listening experiences; with a "hard sell" and a hearty constitution, the best one could ever hope for was exposure to all. Then, too, in order to "cover" everything, there were times when the teaching had to occur in isolation, without regard to need or practical and functional application for the child. We taught; did everyone really learn, internalize what was so diligently and courageously offered? Is it any wonder that some children immediately shut off the intake valve on music, no matter how much we motivated or cajoled?

And what of the organization of the content of music, the units or whatever else they may have been called? Remember the Community Helpers in Grade One, the Indians in Grade Three and again in Grade Five? While the school was organized in a traditional way, it was possible, perhaps even necessary at times, to rely on this system of imparting content, thereby ensuring some kind of surface correlation with the total curriculum.

But, here we are, committed to a personalized program for each child in which we offer alternatives for total growth. How do we go about choosing the materials and organizing the content through which the skills of music will be learned and, at the same time, keep in mind that music is another medium through which children acquire the basic learning skills?

The most important factor in this planning process is the person for whom we are doing the planning, the child. Talking with him, observing him, asking him about his preferences is a good way to begin. A simple example: Joseph has never enjoyed group singing, never understood nor wanted to understand decoding of those abstracts of music, but now he wants to play guitar. If his initial steps in guitar are immediately gratifying, he could be self-motivated to learn how to decode and then to find satisfaction in singing as he plays.

The classroom teacher who sees the child for longer periods of time and is more intimately involved with him is most essential in assisting you to know each student. Conferring and planning with the teacher is a tremendous asset. Not only can he diagnose and request your help in planning the child's total academic program, but he can direct the child to and encourage him in music. For example: Some children are researching presidents of the United States and have become interested in their life styles, the times in which they lived, and the cultural influences in their lives. The classroom teacher suggests that they find out what kind of music they enjoyed, what steps they danced, what songs they sang. I need go no further because here is the direction for the content of a child's program in whatever depth you and the student find mutually satisfying and beneficial.

The content of the curriculum, its focus and direction, must now be with the child and his world, past, present, and future. What are his needs? What does he need to know? How does he see himself and in what relationship to this world? No matter what content or social area we consider, there is a role that music can play in expanding and enriching that environment.

It is well at this point to consider the matter of Rock because there will be those among you who will argue that this is where we find the child of today, this is his world, his music, his environment. Perhaps, but I am not quite sure that our children have been given enough significant alternative experiences to arbitrarily decide that this is it! When one evaluates media programming and the resultant exposures, it is quite evident that what a child hears in his out-of-school hours has been predetermined by adults and that his choices are really limited. Therefore, because children have become "sold" on the idea that this is their music, it is necessary for the music teacher to deal with its positive aspects.

My only point of contention is that as educators, we cannot allow the child to remain in a static position. We can expand upon all the positive aspects of each experience, but we must also include additional exposure in electronic music, aleatory music, neoromantic music, or whatever may be the music of today. These exposures should bear reference to the music of yesterday, and children can be led to discover the relationships. In addition, they can lead to interests in ethnic music and nationalistic influences; they can project to a futuristic conceptualization. However, they should be handled with the same goal standards that are brought to bear upon the more traditional aspects of our program. The rhythms are to be read, the melodies are to be analyzed and internalized as written, the form should be perceived.

The overriding influence in each of these contemporary experiences (as with everything we do) should be of value to the child and significant in the developmental process. There will be times when it becomes necessary to suggest and even pedantically prescribe content for a child. It remains incumbent upon the music teacher to offer a broad base of exposures. How can one know and have feelings about that which has never been experienced?

However, as the music teacher becomes more skilled in this process of perception and prescription, the alternatives offer many possibilities for pursuing and fulfilling mutually satisfying goals. In order to become adept at prescribing for children then, the teacher must know them and the fabric that makes up their educational experiences. But, in addition, in order to foster and promote growth in music, it is necessary to continually keep in mind the skill sequences. Those which are the basis for prescribing in the personalized program have been included. They are formulated upon experiences with many children and how they learn, many educators and their works and, ultimately, assimilated into a practical step-by-step approach.

You may argue that one cannot isolate skills in this way, that there are crossovers and duplications as well as skills you do not consider absolutely necessary. However, in dealing with so many factors, it is very helpful to have some logical order in mind. It is far easier to delete, make substitutions, and even augmentations when one knows generally where he is going. Then, too, the parameters are wide. You might ask how many children finish Grade Twelve never having been exposed to, let alone acquiring skills in half the sequences. But, for the one or two children we may encounter in a year or even a lifetime who can achieve more than the average elementary school child, one must be ready for their extraordinary talents.

MELODY:

Introduction of SOL.

Introduction of MI.

The rule for SOL-MI placement.

Introduction of LA.

The rule for placing LA in relation to SOL.

Introduction of DO_1. (Low DO.)

The rule for SOL-MI-DO placement.

Presentation of term: Interval. (Simple form, as distance from one pitch to the next in a melody.)

Intervals:

SOL-MI	MI-SOL
MI-DO_1	DO_1-MI
SOL-DO_1	DO_1-SOL
MI-LA	LA-MI
SOL-MI-LA	LA-MI-SOL

Any and all combinations of DO_1, MI, SOL, LA.

Presentation of term: Chord. (Basic concept of two or more notes sounded at the same time.)

Presentation of term: Triad. (Basic concept: chord of three notes.)

Presentation of term: Tonic Triad.

Triads:

DO_1-MI-SOL patterns, melodically and harmonically.

Introduction of RE.

Rule for placement of RE in relation to DO_1 and MI.

Patterns:

DO-RE-MI
MI-RE-DO
DO-SOL-RE

Presentation of Pentatonic Major Scale. Placement in many positions.

Introduction of DO^1. (High DO.)

Interval: DO_1-DO^1

Extension of interval concept to include each new interval encountered.

Letter names of lines and spaces, treble staff. (Letter names of lines and spaces, bass staff, are to be presented functionally.)

Recognition of repeated note patterns, steps and skips, ascending and descending.

Perception of melodic shapes.

Introduction of LA_1. (Low LA.)

Presentation of Pentatonic Minor Scale. (LA_1-DO_1-RE-MI-SOL.)

Introduction of SOL_1. (Low SOL.)

Introduction of FA.

Rule for placement of FA.

Presentation of whole and half step concepts.

Use of keyboard to reinforce whole and half step concepts.

The sharp, flat, and natural signs.

Introduction of TI.

Rule for placement of TI.

Presentation of Diatonic Major Scale.

Building a Major Scale.

Key Signatures: C, G, and F Major.

Simple transposition through these keys.

Alternative forms of notation.

Extension of the triad concept through C, G, and F Major.

Presentation of Chromatic Scale, ascending and descending.

Continued extension of interval concept to include each new interval encountered.

Melodic sequences.

Building Major Scales: D and B-flat Major.

Simple transposition through these keys.

Natural minor as Aeolian mode. (LA_1 to LA^1).

Major-Minor intervals in scales.

Chords: I, IV, V, and V7 in C, G, F, D, and B-flat. Naming according to root designations.

Building melodies on given chord patterns.

Choosing appropriate chords for given melodies.

Presentation of concept: Parallel minor, Relative minor.
        Forms: Natural (reviewed), Harmonic, and Melodic.

Extending the whole and half step concepts through the minors.

Key Signatures: A, E, B, E-flat, A-flat, D-flat Major. (Includes parallel and related minors when functional.)

Chords through the above signatures.

Presentation of concept: Inverting a chord.

Key Signatures: G-flat, C-flat, F-sharp and C-sharp Major. (Includes parallel and related minors when functional.)

Reading and composing in the modes.

Recognition of and composition with tone clusters.

Atonality.

Polytonality.

RHYTHM AND METER:

Introduction of the basic beat. (| = ta.)

Presentation of the concept of meter as the ongoing, underlying basic beat.

Placing basic beats in sets:
    2 (Conducting in 2.)
    4 (Conducting in 4.)
    3 (Conducting in 3.)
    5 (Conducting in 5)

Introduction of the equivalent concept.

Presentation of the quarter rest. (Quarter rest = 1 basic beat.)

Presentation of the eighth note in a pair, 2 eighth notes = ti-ti. (Eighth note pair = 1 basic beat.)

Presentation of the half note. (Half note = 2 quarter notes = 2 basic beats.)

Half rest = 2 quarter rests = 2 basic beats.

Reading, reacting to, and taking rhythmic dictation of patterns which include quarter notes and rests, eighth notes in pairs, half notes and half rests.

Introduction of concept of rhythm as sounds and silences of varying lengths arranged in patterns.

Introduction of the tie.

Presentation of the whole note. (Whole note = 2 half notes = 4 quarter notes = 4 basic beats.)

Presentation of the dotted half note. (Dotted half note = half note and quarter note, tied = 3 quarter notes, tied = 3 basic beats.)

Extension of patterns to include whole note, whole rest, and dotted half note in a functional setting.

Presentation of concept of accenting; strong and weak beats.

Presentation of the anacrusis; splitting the measure, the pickup beat.

Introduction of ties over bar lines.

Placing basic beats in sets of 6 and 7. (Quarter note remains the basic beat note.)

Presentation of concept: Differentiation between rhythm and meter.

Splitting the eighth note "twins" into single eighth notes. (Single eighth note = ti.)

Presentation of the eighth rest.

Placing the single eighth note and eighth rest in various positions for recognition and reading in a functional setting.

Introduction to traditional counting.

Developing and encouraging alternate forms of rhythmic notation.

Introduction to syncopation: Eighth note, quarter note, eighth note and quarter note, half note, quarter note.

Presentation of the triplet concept.

Learning the names of notes and rests in order of value, including the sixteenth note and the sixteenth rest.

Presentation of four sixteenth notes in a group. (Four sixteenth notes = 1 basic beat.)

Developing an extended concept of equal values to include facility with all notes and rests.

Decoding note values through time signatures: $\frac{2}{4}\frac{3}{4}\frac{4}{4}\frac{5}{4}\frac{6}{4}$
(NOTE: This is done through the system of equal values and the value of the whole note is always derived from the bottom number; all other values always are in relationship to the whole.)

Presentation of the dotted quarter note. (Dotted quarter note = quarter note and eighth note, tied = 1½ basic beats.)

Presentation of rule for dotted notes.

Presentation of eighths and sixteenths in combination, the eighth followed by 2 sixteenths and 2 sixteenths followed by the eighth.

Presentation of the dotted eighth note followed by the sixteenth note.

Extension of patterns to include each new notated rhythm in a functional setting. Whenever a new combination is encountered, it is hoped that the child will be able to read it through a transfer of knowledge. If not, specific instruction must be given.

Introduction of $\frac{6}{8}$ through speech and movement.

Presentation of $\frac{6}{8}$ rhythm sounds:

♪ ti (1 basic beat)
| ta (2 basic beats)
|. ta-i (3 basic beats)
♫ ti ti ti (3 basic beats)
|♪ ta ti (3 basic beats)
♪| ti ta (3 basic beats)

♩.=|.|. ta-i-a-i (6 basic beats) or ♩.= ⌣⌣⌣⌣⌣⌣ ti-i-i-i-i-i

Extension of decoding of note values through $\frac{3}{8}\,\frac{6}{8}\,\frac{9}{8}\,\frac{12}{8}$.

   a. First, as related to the whole note.

   b. Second, for those children who can mathematically grasp the concept, in compound terms.

$$\frac{3}{8} = \frac{3}{♪} = \frac{1}{♩.} \qquad \frac{6}{8} = \frac{6}{♪} = \frac{2}{♩.} \qquad \frac{9}{8} = \frac{9}{♪} = \frac{3}{♩.} \qquad \frac{12}{8} = \frac{12}{♪} = \frac{4}{♩.}$$

In either case, the concept of groupings of 3 is essential for true internalization of compound time.

Presentation of C, Common Time as relating to $\frac{4}{4}$.

Presentation of $\frac{2}{2}$ and ₵ with note value decoding.

Introduction to changes in meter. (Example, $\frac{2}{4}$ to $\frac{5}{4}$ and $\frac{2}{4}$ to $\frac{6}{8}$.)

Introduction to polyrhythms.

Extension of set numbers to whatever point is deemed functional.

FORM:

Presentation of the phrase and relating it in musical terms.

Recognition of like and unlike phrases. (Repetition and contrast.)

Recognition of phrases of varying lengths.

Identifying by sight and sound, AB form.

Identifying by sight and sound, ABA form.

Creating speech patterns, movement patterns, artistic representations, songs, and instrumental pieces in AB and ABA forms.

Recognition of variant forms of AB and ABA.

Creating speech patterns, movement patterns, artistic representations, songs, and instrumental pieces in AB and ABA variant forms.

Recognition of verse and refrain and analysis of phrase structure within.

Presentation of Introduction and Coda.

Presentation of the Rondo.

Creating speech patterns, movement patterns, artistic representations, songs, and instrumental pieces in Rondo form.

Recognition of phrases with slight variations as opposed to like and unlike phrases. (Repetition, Variant, and Contrast.)

Facility in use of letters in analysis and planning of form.

Presentation of the Theme and Variations.

Creating speech patterns, movement patterns, artistic representations, songs, and instrumental pieces in Theme and Variations form.

Introduction to the Suite.

Creating speech patterns, movement patterns, artistic representations, songs, and instrumental pieces, singularly or in concert as a representation of the Suite.

Introduction of through composed music.

Experiences with creating through composed music.

Introduction to, recognition of, and experiences with the larger musical forms as they occur functionally, including:

Symphony	Concerto
Sonata Allegro	Fugue
Musical Comedy	Dance Forms
Operetta	Rhapsody
Opera	Scherzo
Oratorio	Fantasia
Ballet	

(These are not mentioned in any particular order, nor is the list to be limited to just these forms. Presentation should occur at the moment of impact and in relation to interest, needs, and motivation. In some instances, one should trigger interest in another; for example, Musical Comedy to Operetta to Opera to Oratorio.)

HARMONY:

Chants in concert.

Ostinati, vocal and instruments.

Rounds; two parts.

Instrumental accompaniments.

Concept: Music may consist of a single melody used in a variety of ways to create harmony. Parts of the melody may be used in accompaniment.

Reinforcement of monophonic melodic concept.

Concept: Melodies (exact repetition) may be repeated at different intervals to create harmony. The Round becomes a simple example of polyphony.

Concept: Music may consist of two or more different melodies sounded simultaneously (an extension of the polyphonic concept).

Concept: Melodies may be accompanied by an additional melody or melodies above to create harmony. The Descant becomes another example of polyphony.

Concept: Melodies may be accompanied by dissonant and consonant notes.

Introduction to homophonic concept.

Sequential development of harmonic concepts vocally and/or instrumentally as follows:

a. Melodies (Monophonic)

b. Rounds, 2, 3, and 4 part (Polyphonic)

c. Canons (Polyphonic)

d. Partner Songs (Polyphonic)

e. Songs with descants (Polyphonic)

f. Two-part songs, chordal harmony, vertical (Homophonic)

g. Three-part songs, chordal harmony, vertical (Homophonic)

h. Chordal accompaniments to melodies (Homophonic)

Recognition and analysis of depth and kind of harmonic texture, vocally and instrumentally.

The sequencing in tone color (sound and its concommitant parts) has not been included as have not the elements of interpretation and the specifics of signs, symbols, and terms. The time for presentation of all of these elements will be readily perceived by the teacher and should be taught at that moment. In fact they may, in part, be considered as enrichment of the music skills per se.

Each step in this sequencing needs reinforcing, drill, and review. We are not only building upward but outward as well, and we must provide many and varied experiences to ensure internalization of skills and concepts. Nothing can, nor should, happen in isolation and, in many instances, the child will have to call upon more than one skill to complete a task or participate in an activity; this includes both musical skills and basic learning skills. It is important that you, as the teacher, can clearly define those skills, not necessarily for the child, but so that you can foresee any problems, instruct when instruction is called for, and prescribe in such a way that the child will be confronted with just the right amount of frustration to make the experience challenging, yet satisfying and educationally profitable.

There will be times when a child needs to know a skill in order to complete an activity, even though the skill may be beyond the level at which he is working. Knowing the child and his abilities will help you to decide on the best course to follow. In some instances, it will be better to simply supply the missing fact or step; in others, provide the child with the means to discover what he needs and, in still other instances, give instruction in that skill. For example, some first- and second-grade children had written a speech chant and were working out the rhythmic notation. They had most of it completed correctly, using the quarter and eighth notes and quarter rests, but had great difficulty with one spot. Nothing seemed to work and — they were right! What they needed was the eighth note triplet. Rather than discard or change what they had done, I taught them "triple-ti" which they could understand at that point because the problem was functional. They had discovered the need; I provided the instruction. From then on, these particular children used the triplet quite naturally.

So, once again, these sequences are not meant to be the last word to be followed in lock-step fashion. This, in itself, would be defeating the flexibility and openness of purpose. Instead, they are a structure from which one can depart in achieving a freedom of environment within a framework of accountability.

4 *The Physical Environment*

The implementation of this program necessitates changes in the physical environment of the music room. Since I could not break down any walls or move to a larger area, it became necessary to expand what I already had. This will, most probably, be similar to the situations experienced by many readers.

The first step was to physically empty the room of everything that could be considered nonessential. This included the teacher's desk, all chairs, most project tables, and whatever else was in the way. Immediately, a large, open area was available (this might have been "undiscovered" for years).

As one goes about this process, it is important to view the environment realistically. If there is a piece of furniture about which you are in doubt, think seriously about how much use it has had in the past and whether it will have a place in the evolving program. Don't give it away if you're not sure; you may want it back again, but do try to rid yourself of cumbersome objects so that you can have flexibility in setting the environment.

The next step was to evaluate every other piece of equipment, clean out closets, bookshelves, file cabinets, and so forth, to determine what should be kept on hand, what could be stored until needed, and just how much area would remain. Most of the full set basal music books were removed except for five copies of each which would be used for reference, enrichment, small group activities, and basal text prescriptions. Full sets of two series were retained for group singing. Full sets of one/two level songbooks were placed in the primary wing for children to use in their home classes for enrichment purposes. All others were placed in storage, but readily available. This created many free bookshelves.

Upon careful review of the supply of traditional rhythm instruments, many were removed from the area and placed in the primary wing also. After all, how many times would a whole class be playing woodblocks together, if ever? All closets and the file cabinet were emptied of personal materials, professional books, and the like to allow for the children's materials.

Once this process has been completed, it becomes necessary to decide one's needs in terms of the physical layout in order to carry out the program. Therefore, we will consider each essential in turn.

1. SEATING

Some chairs will be needed for writing and arts activities and, at certain instruments (bass metallophone and xylophone, chord organ, piano, and so on). Work surfaces will also be required.

Chairs were kept to a minimum and were the least cumbersome of those available. Step stools and low stools which not only were comfortable, but proved to be most versatile were also added. A donated wicker sofa completed the seating requirements.

Other seating possibilities are the small squares of carpet (samples from carpet stores) and floor cushions which can be stacked for storage when not in use. One might also encourage the children to make "sit upons" from woven strips of newspaper or from vinyl squares. In general, however, most children are perfectly content to sit on the floor and prefer it.

A word of caution: unless your room is very large, avoid area carpets. They are excellent for seating and for absorbing sound but inhibit freedom in body movement and use up floor space where you may wish to tape large staves and game squares. If this is the case, and carpets cannot be avoided or removed, perhaps these activities could take place in an adjoining corridor.

2. WORK SURFACES

Work tables and desks provide the writing and work surfaces required and become tables for instruments. Kind, size, and number are again dependent on the area with which you have to work.

Opening an unused coat closet at the back of the room provided two sections large enough to take a standard desk with chair, an ideal place for quiet contemplation and work. The third section, smaller in size, provided storage space for six guitars.

Other desks might be added in "out of the way" places either singly or grouped to accommodate other students. It is best to search out the nooks and corners so as not to break up large areas.

As mentioned before, bar instruments may be placed on standard sized desks; they are the right height, can be moved about with ease, and provide for storage of the chromatic bars. Each of these desks and instruments should be labeled with a large name card for two reasons: it teaches the children the instrument's name and, should the instrument be removed from the desk, reminds them where to replace it.

When choosing the larger work tables, it is essential to consider both size and shape. Round tables are difficult to place unless situated in the center of the room because they take up too much area. The rectangular ones seem to fit better within the ordinary room contour. Placing of tables should be viewed as semipermanent since they are quite heavy to move about and will mar taped floor surfaces.

Consider adding a formica-topped rectangular kitchen table and chairs. I have one set in a listening corner and it has proved to be the most popular spot in the room. For younger children, a discarded child's picnic table or tea table with chairs can provide a good work area for four or five. It is easily moved, and, because of its structure, an excellent place for small group activities.

If you use your imagination, you will probably come up with many other kinds of seating/writing surfaces, some of which will serve a dual purpose. For example, one teacher used the small cable spools, discards of the telephone company, to create an exciting work environment. Another added picnic tables and benches both inside and directly outside her room.

At any rate be alert for "friendly" discards, neighborhood sales, and refuse collections. A gold mine in equipment may be right behind a nearby discount house on the night before the pickup truck comes.

3. THE LISTENING AREA

Because I chose to have a listening center to which children might go at any time, I found the corner of the room the farthest removed from activity and view, yet with storage area for records and an outlet for the record player. Here was placed the kitchen table and chairs, the record player on a separate desk, head sets for undisturbed listening, recordings, and a task card file which directed the listening experiences. Around this was placed a folding wooden screen to provide a private area for this most personal kind of activity. Just as a footnote, this has become a favorite lunch/recess area. The children can eat and listen at the same time and, because of the interest, the area is frequently kept open during the noon hour.

In setting up the listening area, the prime considerations will have to be where outlets are placed and how utilization of this area is envisioned. Of all the places in the room, this should be the most inviting since this seems to be one activity requiring maximum motivation.

4. THE ARTS AREA

The nature of the activity required that it be in close proximity to the sink, should the room have one. If not, another secluded spot will suffice as long as children may bring in water for washing paint brushes. Buckets should be provided for this purpose.

The arts corner should contain every media possible in large, labeled boxes or on adjoining shelves. A nearby supply closet may hold paper and poster board of all sizes and colors. Crayons, scissors, markers, and so on may be within the central supply area or inside desks. Needles, thread, embroidery cotton, compass, protractors, rulers, fabric, egg cartons, containers, meat trays and all sorts of "junk" materials should be included. Perhaps you may have an easel or two to add. These will serve a dual purpose: the first for the artist, the second as an area divider.

Should it be impossible to include an arts area in the room, some arrangements may be made with the art teacher for an open exchange of students. Even if the range of related art activities must be limited, it is most important that minimum provision be made.

5. PLACEMENT OF INSTRUMENTS

This becomes quite a challenge to the teacher with a small room because many of the instruments are large and heavy, need a certain amount of protection and concern, and must be readily accessible and out of the pathway of children who are involved in activities within the open floor space.

I chose to keep the bar/Orff instruments and tympani within half of the peripheral area of the room, on desks, when necessary, as previously described. They are completely mobile and may be moved, with and without the desks, in and out of the room.

One studio/upright piano was housed on the opposite side of the room, quite close to the door, since it is frequently moved out into the hall for keyboard work and/or to cut down on the sound level.

The standard rhythm instruments, along with the orchestra bells, hand bells, and so forth acquired over a period of time, need to be accessible and, at the same time, cannot clutter the environment. Therefore, I chose to use the top portion of the now free bookshelf area to display them and provide for their continued accessibility.

Coffee cans can hold mallets, rhythm sticks, jingle clogs, shakers, and the like; a little self-stick paper goes a long way toward decorating the holders and adding a bit of color to the room. *An added note:* it is good to label each holder. Again, it teaches names and reminds children where to replace equipment.

6. UTILIZATION OF FLOOR, CEILING, AND WALL AREAS

I am sure that at first glance this heading met with a look of incredulity; but, remember, we are stretching, bending, and making the given environment as elastic as possible. So it is at this point that one must look up, down, and all around.

The ceiling, depending upon its composition, can provide an arena for both instructional and communicative materials, teacher and student-produced. If you have a ceiling composed of soundproof material with holes, you can "hook up" anything of a relatively lightweight nature on a paper clip, wire, or hanger. If your lighting fixtures afford you the luxury of clips through which you can secure a hanger, you are, again, in luck.

Should the room be without these joys of modernity, do not be dismayed. There are "push pins" which will go through just about anything or you might string lines across the room and have a kind of "washline" for you and your students to display meaningful materials.

Now, the floor. My first concern was to keep the floor area as free as possible to allow for maximum mobility. However, there are activities that can be "programmed" from the floor. With white plastic tape, often referred to as gym tape, two floor staves were set out with the lines far enough apart to accommodate a child as either a line or a space note. In addition, the floor may be a magic square, a musical people checkers board, or whatever else one chooses. This tape is easily applied and removed and stands up to much wear and tear.

The bulletin board areas will be utilized instructionally and motivationally, but there may not be enough area because children wish to make many contributions. How about all that blank wall space above the bulletin boards? It is an excellent spot for those instructional charts to be used throughout the year. They will stay permanently affixed with masking tape.

In a personalized program only a small chalkboard area is required. The excess may be treated as bulletin board space for whatever materials one finds worthwhile. Lightweight objects may also be attached to window blinds with tape or pins. And, check out the doors. What will they hold? I placed a dart game on the bathroom door!

Look all around your area. Make it stretch to fit your needs.

7. SHELVES, FILES, AND CLOSETS

The bookshelves, files, and closets which were emptied of nonessentials are now ready to house the materials necessary to the program. First, you will need a section of shelves for those recordings necessary to an indivualized listening program. If the bookshelf space is limited, do not keep "out" those recordings which are only for group activity or for prescribed remediation. Instead, utilize the area to its fullest potential; eliminate confusion.

Allow an area of bookshelf space for the music song texts, including all the "oldies" as references. They still contain songs, activities, challenges, and opportunities for prescribed invoivement which continue to interest, motivate, and educate children. The remai.der of the bookshelf area will be taken up with program materials, including the books from the library which are about some aspect of music and receive far greater circulation when housed in the music room.

If you are in the average-sized classroom, you will not have enough book-shelf space. In addition to the aforementioned materials, provision must be made for the consumables such as staff paper, composition paper, "scratch" paper, art supplies, and the like. The children will need these materials constantly and they must be accessible.

It may be possible to have the district carpenter, school custodian, industrial arts department, or the children themselves build additional shelves. Many elementary schools now have a woodworking area for children. If not, you may improvise with bricks supporting slats, cubicles built from vegetable crates, or cartons of like sizes piled one upon the other. The children will be most anxious to paint or cover them as their contribution to the aesthetics of the environment.

Bookshelves may be placed against the walls under chalkboards or under bulletin boards. Both are out of the way and these areas are wasted wall spaces. The shelves may also be used as room dividers, sectioning off and designating specific areas. Smaller boxes or cartons of the same size may be stacked and secured with paper fasteners. These provide adequate storage for paper, dittos, worksheets, and pre- and post-tests. Although makeshift, I have found them to be quite substantial.

Not to be ignored are discards. Since becoming involved in this program, I am always ready for a bargain at a garage/yard sale and have become a specialist in surveying the morning refuse deposits. This has produced two book-shelves and a small file with drawers and closet in which I keep prepared tapes, blank tapes, filmstrips, and slides.

The large file cabinets found in most elementary classrooms may not be very attractive, but they are quite useful. Here one can file worksheets, piano music at different instructional levels, guitar music, and so on — anything the children will need. It is an invaluable aid in organizing materials.

One personal note before leaving this subject. This aspect of the personalized process does take considerable effort on the part of the teacher and will probably entail some expense, but it is worth it. Not only will it make your job easier and allow you to spend your hours with the students in a really effective way, but it will also be pleasing to you aesthetically. When you consider the number of hours spent in the music room, you deserve to have it as comfortable, functional, and lovely as possible.

8. EXTENDING THE ROOM "WITHOUT"

Look beyond your four walls. Can you use the corridor outside your room? Are you near the front lobby? Does your room have a door which leads out to a play area? Are you close to the auditorium? Are there soundproof practice rooms nearby? Do you have a media center? Is your library "open" in the sense that children may use it anytime?

If the sound level can be tolerated by your immediate neighbors, the corridor is an excellent area for the upright pianos. They do not extend very far into the passageway, and children can be relatively undisturbed and undisturbing as they go about their keyboard work. The corridor is also a good place for guitarists and for groups of children working on ensembles with the bar instruments. Should the sound level be a major consideration, the area could be used for quiet activities and games.

Some buildings have lobbies or larger foyers which are infrequently used once the school day has begun. These areas may also be used individually or by small groups. I have even utilized the wall area for balance in working with children on simple ballet movements.

How do visitors and administrators view this extended usage? In general, I think you will find them supportive and in accord with total utilization of the building as long as it is handled with respect and consideration.

If the music room has a door which leads to the play area, children can work there, weather permitting. The teacher can still see and monitor their activities, materials can be easily moved in and out, and you've added that much more working space. Perhaps a picnic table or two might be placed outside for work surface.

The auditorium usually has a piano which is seldom used. It is an excellent place for individual keyboard work. The stage area can be used by small groups for projects, games, activities, and ensembles, as well as provide space for working out problems in movement or a series of dance steps. The seating area, even the aisles, can be places where children work individually or together. Even the offstage "wings" provide private places for work, with the curtains muffling the sound.

The auditorium is so large that many things may occur there simultaneously. Children have a tremendous capacity for shutting out extraneous noises and simply concentrating on their own pursuits, much more so than adults.

I need say little about soundproof practice rooms; great, if you have them. Certainly they are better used by the children than as storage areas for building supplies, as I observed in one school!

There may not be enough area within the music room to set up a listening center. A listening station could be situated in the corridor if outlets are accessible, but consider the media center. Children may take recordings from the music room for listening in this area or might obtain them from the media center aide. They could also use the center for viewing filmstrips, loops, slides, television programs, closed circuit television lessons, and the like as long as they have been guided and prepared as to purpose.

If the library is unscheduled, children may go from the music room to this area for research projects, reading and writing, especially if they require a more quiet, tranquil setting.

In this discussion of the physical environment, I have presented the reader with many problem situations. Yours may very well be different, if not unique. However, it is hoped that the solutions or alternatives which were considered will lead to further investigation of possible answers. Musicians are creative people, and it is this creative force which you will bring to bear upon those problems of physical environment which may seem insurmountable.

5 The Materials of the Environment

The discussion of materials is presented before the chapter on the specifics of prescribing to acquaint the reader with the possible aspects of the environment upon which one may draw when formulating a work plan for each child. The task of stocking the environment will seem overwhelming in the initial stages. It did to me and I sometimes wonder how I was able to cull together as many different materials as I did. The cliche, begin where you find the child, may be applied to the teacher who is implementing a personalized approach to music education: begin with what you already have and adapt and adopt.

A key formula in devising games and activities is as follows: *break down each problem, concept, or skill into its simplest components.* Try to perceive each challenge in its simplest form, eliminating the network of complexities in even the most basic of song activities. Certainly, in the more advanced level activities, this will not be possible but, for acquiring beginning developmental skills and concepts, one must look to clarity and simplicity as prime considerations.

The place to begin is with the basal music texts. Even if you have only one copy of a particular series, it may be of use. Using the following set of headings, I examined each book in my possession and programmed it for prescribing from a master worktext. What follows is a detailed offering of the workings of this method of adaptation.

The first step was to establish a workable code which the students and I could understand. I chose to use publisher initials (for example, ABC—American Book Company) and grade level. I then proceeded as follows:

1. **COMPOSITION**
   a. Title of Activity
   b. Source
   c. Page
   d. Contents
   e. Basic Learning Skills

2. **ENRICHMENT—SCIENCE**
   a. Title of Activity
   b. Source
   c. Page
   d. Basic Learning Skills

3. **ENRICHMENT—SOCIAL STUDIES**, listed as follows with descriptive titles, sources, and pages:

a. Africa
b. Alaska
c. American Indians
d. Asia
e. Central and South America
f. Europe
g. United States
h. Time Line for Exploring Music

4. **FAMOUS COMPOSERS**
   a. Composer
   b. Source
   c. Page
   d. Composition/Contents

5. **FORM**
   a. Title of Activity
   b. Source
   c. Page
   d. Contents
   e. Basic Learning Skills

6. **HARMONY**
   a. Title of Activity
   b. Source
   c. Page
   d. Contents
   e. Basic Learning Skills

7. **IMAGINATION/CREATIVITY**
   (These activities, artistic representations, prose and poetry offerings are included as stimuli for children's imaginative and creative expressions.)
   a. Stimulus
   b. Source
   c. Page
   d. Contents

8. **INSTRUMENTAL MUSIC AND FAMILIES**
   (These activities develop aural perception, foster an understanding of instrumental tone color, provide instruction about family groupings and give experiences in creating a mood or communicating a meaning through the discriminating use of sound.)
   a. Title of Activity
   b. Source
   c. Page
   d. Contents

9. INTERPRETATION

(While inherently the elements are subjective, one may prescribe for enrichment involving degrees of sound, vocal inflection, mood and its subtleties, speed and its subtleties, speed and its variations, and individualism in style.)

a. Title of Activity
b. Source
c. Page
d. Contents

10. MELODY

a. Title of Activity
b. Source
c. Page
d. Contents
e. Basic Learning Skills

11. MOVEMENT

a. Title of Activity
b. Source
c. Page
d. Contents
e. Basic Learning Skills

12. PERFORMING INSTRUMENTALLY

(The basic learning skills will vary only in level of difficulty; they include left to right progression, simultaneous reading of symbols, reading in phrases, scanning, eye-to-hand coordination, and small muscle motor development.)

a. Title of Activity
b. Source
c. Page
d. Contents

13. POETRY

(These activities are to be prescribed on the basis of topic interest as well as reading comprehension and relating to facility with language, syllabication, phrasing, form, meter/-sets, scanning, and style.)

a. Title of Activity
b. Source
c. Page
d. Contents and Suggestions for Prescribed Activities

14. PROGRAM MUSIC
(Music which tells a story, directly or indirectly, lends itself to the extension of basic learning skills. Other than reading, comprehending "the program," the child will need to use his ability to follow sequence and draw inferences from the facts presented. He will have opportunities to select main ideas and should be motivated to create original programs with musical implementation.)

a. Title
b. Source
c. Page
d. Program/Contents

15. RHYTHM AND METER

a. Title of Activity
b. Source
c. Page
d. Contents
e. Basic Learning Skills

16. SOUND

a. Title of Activity
b. Source
c. Page
d. Contents
e. Basic Learning Skills

17. TERMS, SIGNS, AND SYMBOLS
(Each activity is designed to expand the child's ability to recognize, decode, and give meaning to terms, signs, and abstract symbols.)

a. Title of Activity
b. Source
c. Page
d. Contents

18. TONE COLOR

a. Title of Activity
b. Source
c. Page
d. Contents
e. Basic Learning Skills

Once you have set up an initial program based upon the texts, look to source books and workbooks on hand. The personalized program will mean a diversity of use and different time schedules for utilization, so make the most of these sources.

1. Take apart all workbooks at the seam. Choose the side of the page with the activity that you think will be most beneficial. Paste on oak tag or poster board. Write answers on back of card. Cover with self-stick paper or, preferably, have laminated. Children may now write on the cards with grease pencils or pens with washable ink.

2. Follow the same procedure for books which may be cut up and utilized for activity/skill work.

3. Set up a file in a cabinet or sturdy cardboard box designating categories such as *Rhythm, Meter, Compound Time, Instruments,* and so forth. Then color code. For example, *Rhythm* may be *Blue.* All Rhythm activity/skill cards and the Rhythm separator will have a Blue mark in the corner. This may be accomplished with colored tape after laminating or with colored pen before laminating. Students will know exactly where to replace materials.

4. Following this same idea, cut out poems, riddles, and so on for speech chants which may be notated by children, given a melody, instrumented, dramatized, or put into ensemble. Include a wide variety such as fun poems, brain teasers, jump rope chants, and math poems. Once again, color code by categories and file for ease in replacement.

5. Using the same procedure, arrange a file of single copies of songs in your possession. The simplest ones, which I call "Let's Begin," will be at the beginning of the melodic sequence and are color coded melodically so that the primary child can experience immediate success. The bars on all instruments, as well as the keyboards, are also color coded to correspond to the application of colored tape. (Key of C only.)*

The categories proceed through the melodic sequence from the simple to the more advanced materials.

The reader may look upon melodic color coding as a crutch, unnecessary, and uneducational. If so, simply eliminate it, but the following are my reasons for its use:

It insures success and aids in reinforcement and aural/visual perception for beginners.

*The Code: DO-Black, RE-Green, MI-Blue, FA-Orange, SOL-Red, LA-Yellow, TI-Purple.

It allows the older, less able, minimally motivated child to join in with his peers when he is unsure and can provide the stimulus for his wanting to learn.

It provides for a wider variety of experiences.

It permits the new child entering the school system to participate immediately and easily even if his background is sparse and knowledge very limited.

As soon as the child is ready, he is moved from this point and reads solely by syllables and letters. I must admit that some children are simply lazy and would stay in C Major, pentatonic or diatonic, forever, but this is where the teacher intervenes and encourages movement forward or, if necessary, insists upon it. No child should ever be permitted to remain "status quo" in a spiraling educational process.

The method or methods (singularly or a compilation) you choose for piano/- guitar/recorder instruction will need to be purchased from publishers unless you develop a system which is *uniquely* your own and can then be set on dittoed sheets. Purchase enough books at each level so that at any given time there will be one book for each child. Children may wish to purchase a book of their own, especially if they have a guitar, piano, or recorder at home, and they should be encouraged to do so. In addition, gather together as many supplementary materials as possible so that your file will contain many other experiences for study at each level of development.

A word on guitar! I chose to use a melody approach, rather than a chord method, with elementary school children for the following reasons:

1. Physically, the hands of the younger and smaller children work with greater ease. After a period of time, movement into simple form, then full form chords becomes natural.

2. This method requests children to sing along, right from the very beginning, thereby reinforcing their reading of music.

3. The success rate has been good, progress steady, little "leveling off," dropout rate minimal when compared to those children who began with a chord method.

This, then, is the basic "stock" for the material environment and should take a minimum amount of time to assemble. With this, the teacher has a definite base upon which to build, as the need arises and time permits. Given a little direction, children will add their contributions also.

LISTENING CORNER

Stocking the listening corner is a more time-consuming task because the ultimate goal is to provide a listening work card for each and every selection. In the beginning, the options are:

> Put out all recordings with one simple plan, a set of general questions, which will cover all listening experiences.

> Put out a limited number of recordings for which you have prepared directed listening work cards and rotate or add to the collection as materials are prepared.

I would choose the former plan in this instance because my first goal is to get children to *listen* and then react in some verbal or nonverbal way to what they hear. Perhaps this is the most difficult of all skills to teach, not only for music teachers, but for all teachers in this multi-media era. Therefore, I feel it is necessary to provide for greater freedom of choice in order to personalize each experience.

Once you are able to set up the specific tasks, you may use a card file (in addition to its musical purpose, it reinforces the skill of catalogue usage) or a pocket envelope may be attached to each recording with the appropriate card inside. I keep a "recipe box" accessible, really an information file, to which children may refer when confronted by terms in their listening experiences which create a cognitive obstacle. This may also be accomplished by having a music dictionary on hand, containing definitions that are simple and easy to comprehend.

If any of the recordings include slides for accompanying viewing, a viewer may be kept in the listening corner also. It will suffice and save the space problem of a larger projector. Some recordings come with a corresponding ditto-master worksheet. These may be run off and kept available too, each in its separate folder, together with an answer key. Children may then check their own work.

A word here about children checking their own work. Once the spirit of trust, responsibility, and mutuality of goals has been established, children will not cheat. There are no 100 percents, no prizes; the only reward comes from one's own sense of satisfaction in growth and achievement. Therefore, it is to everyone's benefit to provide answer keys, self-correcting devices, and the like to save time and to allow the child to instantly see his strengths and weaknesses.

Listening may take place through tapes. We use cassette tape recorders for this purpose as well as for listening to directed skill activities prepared by the teacher and for recording student performance, integrated tasks, and the like. A file of prepared tapes and blanks is kept in a small file cabinet, clearly labeled for easy replacement of materials.

Tapes with accompanying filmstrips are also set up in another section of the listening corner. Those which are always accessible, together with a filmstrip viewer, deal with the instruments of the orchestra since this is one subject most children can learn about on their own. Once again, there are prepared dittos for self-checking factual information.

An interesting comment was made to me on this use of recordings, tapes, slides, and so on. After having viewed the program in operation, a music teacher said, "My goodness, you can use these things all the time. I'm lucky if I use half the materials a few times a year." Interesting comment, because when one considers the traditional versus the personalized approach, it is possible to see greater utilization of materials and closer student contact with those materials.

Children enjoy challenges in all guises. They provide just the right amount of competition for motivation without becoming discriminatory or frustrating. Children may challenge themselves or others. I have found that when a child challenges someone else, it is usually someone at a similar skill level. In general, the children use very good judgment. To set the stage for challenges, individual or in small groups, I use an ordinary three-minute egg timer and a sixty-minute kitchen timer. Many activities can be devised for this purpose. For example:

Challenge a friend. Who can write the most three-beat measures in three minutes? Use the egg timer.

Set the kitchen timer. How long does it take you to tell the letter names of all the notes on the treble staff? Use the flash cards. The answers are on the back. Try again. Can you beat your own time?

The possibilities are endless. Without any intricate preparation, this can be implemented with sets of flash cards, pictures of instruments, and so on, all of which most teachers have on hand.

Magnetic boards and flannel boards serve many purposes in skills work. Most flannel boards come prepared with a permanent staff and a complete supply of signs, symbols, notes, and rests. Magnetic boards may be used in the same way, taping on the staff and cutting notes, rests, signs, and symbols from felt and magnetizing them with a small piece of magnetic tape which is now readily available. The note heads for either may be color coded for beginners in melody reading, and activities may be set up sequentially. I find this device excellent for "spelling words" with music note heads as well. Patterns may be played and sung, by syllable or letter, once again depending upon purpose. Both devices are also good for children who are having perceptual problems with lines and spaces and numbering *up* the music staff ladder instead of *down*.

Additional activities in line and space perception, simple melodic reading, and notation and experiencing letter names can also be accomplished in the following ways:

1. The large floor staff, painted on permanently, taped, or, when the area is limited, taped on a large sheet of heavy vinyl or oil cloth which can be rolled up and stored. Children themselves may become the note heads to be placed about or moved on the staff. Large cardboard discs, color coded and laminated to save wear and tear, may become the note

heads with rhythm sticks forming the rhythmic notation. (Be sure diameter of discs allows for fitting in a space. Children want these to be exact.) Beanbags may also provide the basis for games in line and space recognition.

2. Large cards, 12" x 18" oak tag sheets upon which are drawn music staves. Poker chips become note heads, toothpicks become sticks for forming the rhythmic notation.

3. Lick 'Em, Stick 'Em's. Using a large dittoed staff, children may place note heads which are color coded and cut out, in proper size, from gummed paper. These may be glued in place and sticks drawn for rhythmic notation.

I always work from these larger type staffs and continue for as long as necessary. I have found that frustration and error in children's work, even on the wider-lined staff paper, occurs because developmentally the children are not ready to perceive the closeness of lines and spaces. Even when children do work with conventional staff paper, I find I must occasionally return to what is more perceptually concrete, simply for clarity.

Another use for the floor has been the magic squares. The squares are taped boxes on the floor. Accompanying are two sets of notation card squares, one simple in stick notation, the other more advanced, using notes with heads as well as rests. The task is to create, across and down, measures of equal value. For example, 5.
4:

SEE DIAGRAM

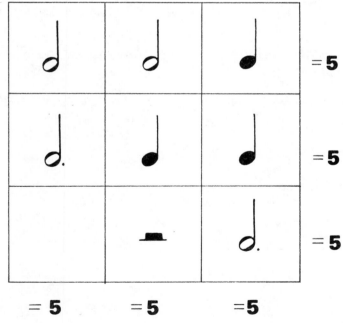

There are possible variations for the magic squares as well as challenges. The biggest accomplishment is to have a balance horizontally, vertically, and diagonally.

In the prologue to this book, I stated that I looked to the market and the market was bare insofar as purchasable games, activities, and devices were concerned. Now, in all fairness, there are some things available; the self-correcting devices for naming and locating notes, treble, and bass staff, are excellent. Some of the bingo-type games are good. However, in general, I have found that I had to adapt other games that I purchased. This situation comes about because they are too complex. They have not been broken down into simplest components and require a multiplicity of factual knowledge and skills before they can be utilized by the children. Also, many of the instructions for play are difficult to comprehend. We want and need games and activities that will instruct developmentally and sequentially as well as reinforce and clarify.

I have purchased some commercial music games and then adapted them. For example, one game might be played in three or four different ways based upon the level of skill development. Also, many of these games are not based upon the Orff system of reading rhythmic notation or the Kodaly system of reading melodic notation, and this aspect must be altered, unless my purpose is to take the more advanced child through a transition process to traditional skills of reading.

I do not mean to discourage the reader. Just be prepared to do some reworking before presentation of games to the children. This can pay dividends when you multiply the uses of just one game.

Other nonmusical, commercially produced games and devices can be adapted for your purposes. For example:

Scrabble. The words spelled must all be musical words and can include proper names of composers, conductors, musicians, and titles of compositions.

Twister. Use just as is. Helps reinforce knowledge and use of left and right.

Ants in the Pants. Substitute any set of skills or a different series of skills to provide games at different levels, using the same set of "pants." Skills are glued on to the ants.

Nuts! Substitute reading skills for the marbles inside the nuts.

Barbie's Electric Drawing Set. Use as a device to teach drawing of clefs and drawing of notes and rests.

Etch a Sketch. To be used with listening activities to relate music, mood, and design.

The library, which was briefly mentioned in the chapter on the physical environment, will provide many more possibilities as you set up your materials. I brought in many of the books on all aspects of music from the "how-to" types (making instruments) to books on theater, dance, recording artists, musicians, composers, etc., as well as biographies, music encyclopedias, dictionaries, and other references. For many books a series of work cards with questions for directed reading and comprehension was devised. For some, there are extended and follow-up activities, including map work. A sign-out book is used for record keeping and even though I seldom have time to be a librarian per se, no books have been lost to date. However, should a loss occur, this would not alter the method of operation since it is far better to have the books used and read and chance the losses than all neatly stacked on shelves, gathering dust.

Charts which are teacher made and accumulated through the years, including everything from kinds of notes and rests to building a chromatic scale, should now be permanently displayed around the room, preferably on the upper levels, or hung on racks for instructional purposes, for quick check references, and for constant environmental exposure. They should not be moved throughout the year so that the students may know the exact place to look for help.

I keep all scale charts on hanging racks for easy reference, the sharps on one, flats on the other. Each chart includes the major diatonic with syllables, letters, and numbers, the relative minor, the parallel minor, and the triads.

The commercially produced charts which accompany Grace Nash's "Today With Music" books, (Alfred Publishing Company), the Mary Helen Richards' "Threshold to Music," (Fearron Publishing Company), and the Aden Lewis "Listen, Look and Sing," (Silver Burdett Company), are intended for large group instruction, but these very excellent materials may also be programmed for individual and small group activity instructionally and for reinforcement. I have also used them to help new students fill in conceptual gaps on their own. In addition, Aden Lewis includes many excellent supplementary games and activities in his teacher's guides which may be put on work cards for students to pursue individually or in small groups. Have you ever played "Jack Jump Over the Bar Lines"?

Another source for musical activities may be found outside the music area and brought within. Many of the science series and systems have units on sound, building instruments, and so forth. In addition to those work cards you may make pertaining to these subjects, you may choose to bring these units to your room, along with copies of old science books containing correlated activities. I have gathered many of the materials for implementation in a large, closeted area under the sink which we call the Science Supply, and additional materials may be found elsewhere in the school or brought in from home. Sometimes children choose to bring the activity home, working on it with a parent, sibling, or friend.

Having accumulated a collection of good prints by major artists as well as clipped reproductions from calendars and the like, I have utilized them in the following ways:

> The smaller works have been set up in folders in categories such as *Repetition and Contrast, Unity and Balance, Color, Texture, Line,* and so on. The folder includes musical activities relating to the student's perceptions.

> The larger works are hung from the ceiling all around the room and include the activities which relate artistic, visual representations to musical, aural perceptions.

Most, if not all, of the bulletin boards in an active music area should be working bulletin boards. The following are possibilities:

1. Guided listening bulletin board which includes forms to be completed and filed in personal folders upon completion of each listening activity.

2. Teaching bulletin board or boards. For example, you expose an entire class to a particular skill — perhaps the function of a dot. You then set up a bulletin board with envelope pockets for activities which begin with basic perceptions (perceiving the difference between notes with and without dots) and continue to activities which require reading patterns which include the dotted eighth followed by the sixteenth note to be played with a partner.

3. Correlated/integrated boards. For example, mine is called "Pick-a-Pocket" and is ruled over by Fagin of "Oliver" fame. I have four levels of dittoed sheets which may span the parameters from the number of basic beats in each set to writing maths in music notes. The children "pick" at will and deposit in the IN box. I correct and place papers in the PICK-UP box for children to collect.

4. Project board. This is designed to invite exploration and interest in integrated tasks and topics and includes a plan which children may follow when designing their own projects.

I use dittos in this program, but try to keep their use to a minimum. I choose not to rely upon the paper-and-pencil-type activities, except when necessary, for pre- and post-testing, remediation, or reinforcement of a particular skill. However, certain exposures may be facilitated by prepared activity booklets. I rely upon these only because of time limitations and preponderance of knowledge which one hopes to impart, the fact of which occasionally closes in. I find that, in general, activity booklets tend to circumscribe learning and may be closed-ended. Presently, I am using one on *Form*, simply because there are so many larger forms to which one should traditionally expose children. One may question the validity of this packaging which, to the reader, might seem in direct opposition to the sequencing premise, but the booklet is never prescribed before the child is ready to deal with its contents, options are offered within, and opportunities are provided for interaction with fellow students.

For the beginner in individualization, learning packages can serve the purpose of a broad introduction to general areas, not unlike the unit approach, but with choices and options. They provide the teacher with a point of departure and may facilitate further personalization.

A general outline for a learning package might be:

1. General Statement — Introductory

2. Behavioral Objective, Number One
    A. Activity One
    B. Activity Two   } CHOICE
    C. Activity Three

3. Behavioral Objective, Number Two
    A. Activity One
    B. Activity Two   } CHOICE
    C. Activity Three

4. Behavioral Objective, Number Three
    A. Activity One
    B. Activity Two   } CHOICE
    C. Activity Three

5. General Statement — Summary

6. Suggestions for Further Inquiry and Activity.

It is best to keep the learning package short since children perceive goals in short terms. Instead, have a number of packets available on the same subject based on sequential levels of conceptualization. At the conclusion of each, or upon completion of each behavioral objective, the teacher may include a short quiz, general and/or specific in nature, to monitor progress and cognitive learning. To provide for an open-ended aspect in the learning package, the suggestions for further inquiry and activity are included and should be encouraged.

The project work in music is a very important aspect of the individualized program since it is this which both correlates and integrates learning. The child uses skills acquired in a relationship to other disciplines and begins to perceive music in a totality, rather than as a segregated segment of knowledge. The form developed for project work is called the "I.T.T.". It is an Integrated Task or Topic. This dimension was added to the program after the author's attendance at a summer workshop at C. W. Post College, Long Island. The workshop dealt with the British Infant School and credit is to be given here to the English instructors, Harvey Norton, William Perry, and Fred Skinner who are advocates of and experts in the integrated approach. However, the focus was not on music, so once again it was adopt and adapt.

A series of work cards was set up as samples or starting points which directed experiences for children, considering varying interests and levels of skill proficiency. The subjects included anything and everything from *The Planet, Jupiter* to *Mozart, Sounds in Nature, The Color, Red,* and *Tie Dyeing.* It is possible to develop almost any topic into an I.T.T., following this general outline:*

*See Appendix for actual samples.

1. **Center of Interest** — The topic to be investigated.

2. **Research** — Four or five good, concise, closed-ended questions for research. The purpose here is not to elicit volumes of written answers, but rather thoughtful statements of knowledge acquired. The emphasis should be on the research process.

3. **Musical Discovery** — Listening to music which has been composed, based upon a related program or topic.

4. **Musical Creativity** — Creating and notating in the style of the music heard. Writing a program, then creating and notating. Creating dance movements to the original music or the composer's music. (CHOICE.)

5. **Creative Writing** — Poetry or prose, related to the subject.

6. **Related Art Work** — May take any form in relation to the center of interest.

7. **Related Math Work** — Using math in a creative way to enrich some aspect of the topic. Most usually, it takes the form of a survey, the results of which are graphed. (*Note:* Sometimes this portion is deleted because it is not relevant.)

Included with the project work cards is one which shows children how to set up their own subject choice in I.T.T. form, and dittoed outline forms are provided for this purpose. All children *must* submit a written work plan *before* proceeding and must show each completed segment of work before going on to the next step. This is mutually beneficial; I can monitor progress and the children receive ongoing constructive criticism and direction.

All the work cards can and should be colorful, well-designed, and aesthetically pleasing, the teacher's best effort, as is everything in the environment. The most important reason is that we expect and, in fact, should only accept a child's best efforts, therefore, he must see ours! Because attention is continually focused herein, I find the quality of work improving in relation to a child's developmental level and individual ability. One cannot expect the impossible; one must not accept less than the possible.

At this point you will find that the environment is quite rich with a diversity of materials from which one can prescribe for many learning styles and a wide range of skill and interest levels. Now the teacher may choose to begin to create games, activities, and challenges (homespuns).*

Using categories similar to those suggested when programming basal texts for prescribed activities, the following type game/activities may be devised:

---

*See Part 2 for a complete handbook containing specifics for preparing homespuns, which provides details for constructing and directions for playing games and using activities. Homespuns is a term used for teacher-made, teacher-devised materials.

1. CARD GAMES

a. *Old Maid* — For any quick recall, perception, or identification skill.

b. *Musicnochle* — Played like pinochle with a prepared deck of cards which relates measures in sets to meters. Can be developed for simple or compound time signatures.

c. *Rummy* — For identification and execution of rhythm patterns. More than one set of *Rummy* cards may be created, each set progressing in difficulty.

d. *Hearts* — For identification and reading of melodic patterns in syllables or letters. Set one: DO in a space. Set two: DO on a line.

e. *Concentration* — For any quick recall, perception, or identification skill. May match like notes, notes with rests, notes and rests with values, notes with names, notes with letter names, and so on.

f. *War* — For recalling note/rest values: the higher value wins each challenge. Also, for note/staff recognition, treble and bass: highest note wins each challenge.

g. *Go Fish* — For any rhythmic or melodic reinforcement.

2. BOARD GAMES

a. *Rhythm Scrabble* — Set up with a similar game board as regulation Scrabble with the bonus points but, instead of making words, the children build measures. A roll of a "die" controls the number of beats to be placed by each player.

b. *Value Checkers* — Using regulation checkers and board but securing to each checker a note or rest, same for black and red. Rule change: checker of higher value may jump checker of lower value, in any direction.

c. *Music Land* — Played like the traditional "Candy Land," but the board requires identification of notes and rests or drawing of notes and rests to move forward. A similar idea may be used for performing rhythms or melodic skill work.

d. *Bingo* — Special Bingo cards may be made for identifying notes by letter names, kinds of notes and rests, identification of signs and symbols, instrument identification, and rhythms identification.

e. *Lotto* — Same as above; can also include composers, conductors, and musicians.

f. *Rhythm Football* — Board is a football field. Playing cards include rhythm patterns which must be properly executed before player can advance. Can also be used for computing note values.

g. *Rhythm Basketball* — Plays are made through the reading of rhythm patterns.

h. *Rhythm Baseball* — Sets of cards are graduated in difficulty for single, double, triple, and home run. The playing board is a baseball field.

i. *Measure Magic* — Building measures from a variety of note/rest cards, whole to sixteenth. Player drops a coin on game board and must build a measure with correct number of beats as designated by the coin. Time signatures include: $\frac{2}{4}$ $\frac{3}{4}$ $\frac{4}{4}$ $\frac{5}{4}$. Can also be devised for compound time.

3. **GAMES OF SKILL OR CHANCE**

a. *Go Fishing* — One "pond" can be used for many different sets of fish, each set designed to reinforce a skill level. The fish may be magnetized with a piece of magnetic tape or paper clips. A regular horseshoe magnet tied to a pole becomes the fishing rod.

b. *Darts* — Magnetic or Velcro darts are safe! Point score on each round corresponds to numbered pockets, one through ten, from which children draw question cards which must be answered or executed correctly in order to receive full point value.

c. *Marble Rolling-Bowling* — Using a shoebox, cut five openings (and number from two through five). Child rolls three marbles. Must build a measure to correspond to point score of each marble to receive full point value. Can also be used with sets of question cards, each of which has a point designation.

d. *Beanbag Toss* — Same as above but the construction must have holes large enough to accommodate the beanbags.

e. *Dice Games* — A roll of a conventional "die" may be the chance factor in a variety of games from perceiving lines and spaces to designating the value for a measure which is to be written.

Other dice may be constructed in the same way that a square box is made. Three of these dice may have a note or rest drawn on each side, the fourth, an activity on each side. The first three dice are rolled, then the fourth, telling what must be done with the other three. For example, clap in order of the roll as you step the basic beat, step in order of the roll while clapping the basic beat, play on an instrument, say in rhythm sounds, and so forth.

Dice can be set up for varying degrees of difficulty and for melody skills as well.

f. *Dominoes* — Constructed so that a measure must be matched to its appropriate time signature or a note/rest matched to its value. Many variations are possible, but the usual rules of Dominoes apply.

g. *Sprinkle Notes and Rests* — Tiny note/rest squares are made. Player sprinkles them over an egg carton, then picks a cup and must name each note and rest in it. He scores one point for each correct identification.

4. DEVICES

a. *Weigh-a-Note* — Using a balanced scale and correctly weighted notes, rests, and values, the child uses work cards to direct him in balancing equations and discovering two, three, four, and five beat combinations. Also, this can be used for teaching compound time, but with a different set of value weights. Metal washers are excellent weights.

b. *Pendulum* — Attach a simple pendulum device to a wall. Children may clap, step, or play an instrument with each swing of the pendulum to reinforce meter and sense of basic beat. More advanced students can play or clap rhythm patters, using the swing of the pendulum as the meter.

c. *Reveal Boards* — Simple devices which reveal answers to children, these are fun to use and can be devised for building major scales, minor scales, triads, inversions, and so on.

	FIFTH	
	THIRD	
	ROOT	
I II III IV V VI VII		

Index
Card
6″ x 8″

d. *Self-Correcting Devices* — Quick and easy to construct, these devices can be designed for skills which require drill or for instructional purposes. The self-correcting device may take this form:

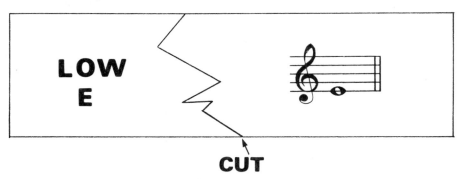

The child makes the match, records his answer on music staff paper and goes on to the next one.

e. *Jig Saw Puzzles* — Another quick and simple way to provide reinforcement, especially for rules. When puzzle is assembled, it may be a familiar melody or rhythm to be played or sung, clapped or stepped.

In this, as in all devices, the difficulty in degree of assembling should be in direct relationship to the skill level being taught. Simple skill, simple assembly.

Index
Card
6″ x 8″

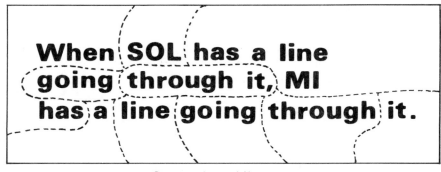

Cut on dotted lines.

As the reader ponders this compilation, he will undoubtedly have many suggestions and ideas of his own. The more creative, the more innovative, the better. Keep in mind the keyword, simplicity; complexity may lead to confusion and result in frustration.

To make best use of your time, try to have one "homespun" serve more than one purpose. For example, one set of rhythm cards may be used for three different games but each game should have its own, singular objective.

And, remember the words of Ewald B. Nyquist, New York State Commissioner of Education: "Make haste slowly." This process of stocking the environment cannot be accomplished in a day, a month, one summer, or even one year. It will be a gradual evolution and will always require constant renewal and reevaluation.

6 Diagnosing and Prescribing

The title sounds formidable; within certain systems of individualization, it is. But for those of us dealing with a personalized program of music education, diagnosing and prescribing is, quite simply, knowing and directing. Knowing is being aware of each child's level in the sequential spiral. At the beginner level, the initial check is done on a one-to-one basis with diagnostic testing of basic concepts.* I do believe that each child must have a firm foundation in the concepts upon which all musical understandings rely. These include:

1. **Up and Down** — This involves being able to hear an ascending or descending melody. Some children do not know what up and down means and need many experiences in this area before being able to apply the concept to music.

2. **High and Low** — At the first level, the differences in pitches are wide; ultimately, and after many experiences in dealing with high and low, the interval is a second.

3. **Loud and Soft** — Initially, for many children, loud is low and soft is slow, though I really don't know why. Later testing should focus on subtle changes, again, after many activities which lead to this conceptualization.

4. **Fast and Slow** — When dealing with tempi, some children confuse fast with loud. The goal is to be able to discern slight differences.

5. **The Basic Beat** — Internalization of the basic beat is most essential to all understandings of both rhythm and meter.

6. **Reacting to Changing Tempi** — At the first level, the changes are quite marked; later, they become more subtle.

7. **Placing Basic Beats in Sets** — For the child who has difficulty with math, this is a problem and so work in this area serves an obvious dual purpose.

8. **Echo Clapping Simple Patterns** — These include quarter, twin eighth notes, and the quarter rest at level one.

9. **Echo Clapping Extended Patterns** — The length of the pattern will correspond to the level of proficiency being evaluated and may also include a spiraling of difficulty in the rhythms.

*See Appendix for sample copies of diagnostic tests.

10. **Providing an Answer to a Rhythmic Question** — The complexity depends upon the level. Each "correct" answer should retain some element of the question.

11. **Providing an Answer to a Melodic Question** — The complexity depends upon the level. Again, each correct answer should retain some element of the question.

12. **Sensing Meter** — At level one, this involves differentiating between and knowing two, three, four, and five beats in a measure. Ultimately, it is sensing meter from rhythm, including changes in meter.

13. **Echo Singing** — Initially, this involves the child's "finding" of his singing voice; then, he can echo and sing in tune.

14. **Perceiving Lines and Spaces** — This is included to ensure understanding of the "up the ladder" concept as related to the staff and to check on perception of lines and spaces which is confusing to young children. First, the floor staff is used; the taped lines are wide apart. Then the magnetic board and oak tag staves are used and, finally, conventional music staff paper is provided as the testing medium for perception. Even at grade levels five and six, some children cannot work with staff paper.

15. **Placing SOL/MI/LA in Various Positions on Five-Line Staff** — When a child can demonstrate his ability to do this, all other placements are ensured, but these may also be tested, right through the diatonic major and minor scales.

16. **Duration** — This involves the child's ability to hear differences in duration from the obvious to the finite. Again, this depends upon the level being tested.

For every other skill level and area of emphasis, the process of diagnosing may proceed as follows:

1. **FORMAL**

   a. *The Pre-test* — Before a new skill is taught, the student is given a written pre-test, designed to discover strengths and weaknesses. Depending upon the degree of proficiency, the teacher will prescribe at different levels, within the frame of reference, or not at all. (It is understood that many skills will have been introduced through class instruction. For some children, this exposure will be all that is necessary, but must be checked for purposes of accountability.)

b. *The "On-the-Spot" or Performance Pre-test* — The teacher has a set of skill cards which are designed for quick evaluation. The emphasis is on quality of elicited responses, not quantity.

2. INFORMAL

a. *Knowing the Student* — Because the teacher is monitoring student progress and evaluating the work of the students continually, he can direct, i.e., prescribe upon the basis of that which he has perceived.

b. *Monitoring Need* — This means being sensitive to the needs of children, the imperatives which arise within their day to day involvements, intervening, reacting to, and directing their activities to satisfy the needed skill acquisitions.

I use all modes for diagnosing but consider knowing each student to be the most important factor. The subjective relationship which the teacher has with each child will be the best information upon which to base a personalized work plan but should be used in conjunction with objective methods.

As you examine the prescription form itself, it is my sincere hope that you sense STRUCTURE. If I have not made this point clear before, may I restate it for emphasis. The teacher and the students must have direction, focus and purpose. For this reason the term "open" has been avoided because, for so many people, lay and tutored alike, it connotes freedom without responsibility. There is no such thing as freedom without responsibility nor internalization without structure, all of which comes from explicit direction and planning, teacher initiated and mutually conceived, whenever possible. The teacher who chooses to implement a personalized program must accept the fact that the program must be structured, structured for facility of operation, structured for building a responsible attitude toward work within each student and structured for overall accountability. From this will come true freedom in the creative pursuit of knowledge.

The written prescription form is initiated at the third grade level for most children because they can now read and comprehend simple directions. The form devised appears on the next page.

NAME: _____

CLASS: _____ MARKING PERIOD: _____

SKILL WORK: _____

I.T.T: _____

CURRENT EVENTS: One article about music. It can be about any part of the musical world. Check newspapers and periodicals. Read, write a summary of your article, and put it in your folder.

LISTENING: 3 listenings. You can substitute attendance at concerts, approved television programs, or other live performances. Be sure to submit a listening form or a summary review.

FREE CHOICE: _____

BONUS:
1. Make a musical game or puzzle.
2. Read a book or a section of a book on a musical subject. See our library.
3. Do any of the art activities which you see all around the room.
4. Plan a special project, but see me first.

SIGNED: _____

DATE: _____

Children receive one prescription form per marking period, approximately every ten weeks and, within the given time frame, additions and deletions are made on the basis of need. On the reverse side of the form, the child lists the activities, games, skill sheets, and whatever else he has participated in or completed. It is important that he does so at each session because he may forget about some aspect of his work from one week to the next.

The prescription may take any form and be devised to fit your needs; even a personal checklist will fill the requirement, but it must clearly indicate to the child his responsibilities and allow you to check progress easily and efficiently.

Specifically, each part of the prescription works as follows:

1. SKILLS

After diagnosing, specific tasks are assigned which the child is to do. Upon completion of each task or activity, he is given a post-test or evaluation of his work, and together teacher and student decide upon the next step which is then listed. The child also keeps his list of what he has done to complete the task.

For example, I may list five different activities on letter names because I know the child needs much reinforcement in this area and that he is a child who requires a very highly structured work plan.

For another child, I may simply state "letter name activies," and he will do as few or as many as he feels necessary to accomplish the goal. He will list each one. When he feels he is ready, he will come for a post-test check.

Obviously, the first child's directions are more specific because this is the way he works best. The second child is given more freedom because he has evidenced self-direction and has a good perception of his own strengths and weaknesses.

2. I.T.T.

Space is provided for the child to write in his choice of integrated task or topic. For example, he may list RED which is a prepared I.T.T. and requires no written plan since it has already been formalized. I then know he will follow the step-by-step sequence on the work card.

Children who are choosing their own center of interest will write in the title, then submit the formal plan as discussed in the chapter on materials.

Some children will not be required to do an integrated task because, for any number of reasons, they are not ready. Without a minimum of cognitive and musical skills, it can become a meaningless chore. For children who have spent too much time on an I.T.T. during one marking period, I may delete it the next if I feel that progress in the skill area has been unsatisfactory. Interestingly, children in the latter case find this punitive; they really enjoy the integrated experiences and will not have this situation occur twice. An added dividend here is that the child learns how to budget and make optimum use of his time.

3. CURRENT EVENTS

I require each child to "read" one article from a newspaper or periodical and write a summary each ten weeks. I place "read" in quotes because some children cannot decode all the words and comprehend what they have read. Then I expect them to ask a parent or older member of the household for assistance or, when all else fails, to come to me for help.

This requirement is included because I want students to know the many aspects of today's music world, performers, performances, theater, new compositions, and the like. They need to become aware of what is happening around them.

4. LISTENING ACTIVITIES

I require three "listenings" per marking period, together with a written statement about what was heard. For this purpose, I keep a simple form in the listening center to be completed after each experience and placed in the child's folder. If I find, upon reading the child's statements, that he has not done his best work, I require that the experience be repeated and I give personal directed assistance to ensure success. Some children need more than a listening task card in the beginning stages.

Children may substitute attendance at concerts or other live performances and viewing of television programs for "listenings." I require prior approval of concerts and distribute a weekly listing of television programs which have been approved for credit. The child writes a summary or a review of the experience and this, too, is placed in the folder. You may find, as I did, that more children and their parents are making an effort to attend concerts and that quality television programs are being viewed. Children become concerned when the television offerings for a given week are sparse or nonexistent. Perhaps it is possible to develop audiences who are more discerning and demanding of quality if we begin early enough to cultivate awareness.

By keeping the requirement for listenings minimal within the ten-week period, it is possible for all children to fulfill the responsibility. Many children do much more for the simple reason that they are finding enjoyment in and through listening.

5. FREE CHOICE

This gives the child an opportunity to explore areas which are unprescribed or to have additional experiences alone or with friends in a frame of reference in which he feels knowledgeable and secure. The only requirement is that the child pursue purposeful activities.

6. BONUS

In addition to those possibilities listed, a child may devise his own bonus or earn bonus credit through outstanding contributions. This is indicated by a comment on the report card.

All prescriptions are dated and signed by student and teacher to give emphasis to the aspect of joint planning and mutual understanding of the requirements.

From time to time, I find some students who cannot work in the skill area of the prescription in the way that I have described for the following reasons:

Lack of self-control.

Little self-motivation or direction.

Abuse of freedom and infringement on rights of other students.

Emotionally disturbed or possessing extreme psychomotor and/or perceptual deficiencies.

For the child who lacks self-control, I require that he remain in the music room in one designated spot and that he show me exactly what he has accomplished at the end of each work period. Should he finish one task before it is time to leave, he is immediately presented with another. Once the pattern is established, I work with this child in the same manner that I work with any child. His program is not treated negatively, but considered his learning style.

From time to time, I present the child with an experience that requires a measure of self-control and gives him more freedom. If he shows growth and can handle himself well, additional experiences are given. If not, we return to the original style of learning until I feel he is ready to try again. For some children, self-control is a slow process, and they are actually happier with the teacher in the role of imparter of knowledge and ruler of the roost.

The child with little self-direction or motivation will need to be given a specific set of lock-step tasks to be completed at each work period. Again, as with the first case, it is treated as his learning style and requires his daily accountability. As soon as he shows any indication of ability to produce with less formal direction, he too may do so.

The key to both types of situations is in accepting the child as he is and continually giving him opportunities for growth and development in an atmosphere of trust.

The third child, the one who abuses freedom and infringes upon the rights of the other children, is given a chance to correct the situation himself after a discussion of the ways in which he has been "undemocratic." If the problem continues, he must be given a highly structured set of tasks which requires him to work alone and allows no interaction whatsoever. These problems are usually short-lived because work at this point does have a punitive connotation. There is no fun and little sense of satisfaction in continually pushing a pencil on a piece of paper and knowing *why* you are required to work in this way.

The less able child, no matter what his malfunction, must be handled sensitively at all times and will need a great deal of your attention. Much of his skill work, if not all, is geared to treating the malfunction. It may be anything from finger painting to music to performing sets of rhythms, over and over again, on a favorite drum. It may be tossing a beanbag to the basic beat set on a metronome or walking lines and spaces on a floor staff. It is essential that these children feel worthy in their work and that they are treated without discrimination by their peers. Children can be understanding and show empathy when given the opportunity.

So, it is knowing and directing, diagnosing and prescribing which is the process in personalizing music as it provides the framework within which individual growth and development does occur.

7 Evaluation

The bottom line on any personalized program of instruction is the process of evaluation, measuring pupil progress. It is this which furnishes us with a concrete record indicating our work with and the growth of each child; it is this for which we are accountable.

As with diagnosing, evaluation will take various forms but, as was stated in the prologue, testing cannot always be based upon teacher judgment, as astute as it might be. Other more formal types of testing must also be included for the following reasons:

1. Objectivity.
2. Learning how to take tests.
3. Producing written evidence of progress.
4. Having written or recorded accounts of strengths and weaknesses.

Therefore, the following types of testing take place:

1. **FORMAL**

   a. Objectively designed written quizzes to test one particular skill area or concept. These should be short and concise. Once again, it is the quality of questioning, not the quantity. These may be termed post-tests.

   b. Written quizzes which test the child's ability to work with and interrelate two or more skills, for example, decoding rhythmically and melodically simultaneously.

   c. Prepared performances in which the child demonstrates his achievement of a skill or skills; for example, playing on a bar instrument and singing a song that has been learned through syllables and letters. These performances may be taped for later evaluation by both teacher and student.

   d. Transference of knowledge. Testing whether the child can use the knowledge acquired in one set of activities in another similar objective situation. For example, after working with the C Major Pentatonic, can the child sight sing a new exercise or song in the same key with accuracy?

2. **INFORMAL**

   a. Monitoring and observing. Watching the child as he plays a particular game or works with an activity to check progress and acquisition of the skill.

    b.   On the spot post-testing. Using another set of skill cards, similar to those used in the pre-test, to check the child's level of achievement or using elements from the activity itself such as matching the pairs in an Old Maid Game.

    c.   Team contests involving numbers of children who have been working on the same skill. Observing each child's ability to perform successfully.

The written record may be kept in a variety of ways:

The child keeps a compiled record through his folder file. Initially, each activity as it is recorded means that the teacher has accepted it as being satisfactorily completed. Guitar and piano students keep another progress chart in the notebooks provided for this purpose, indicating page completed and listing supplementary work.

A checklist may be devised, based upon the skill sequences and prepared for each child as an ongoing record of his progress.

Anecdotal records may be kept in a class notebook or file, indicating strengths, weaknesses, and significant points of progress.

Whatever the method or methods one chooses, it is important that the record keeping itself not become more important than the child or his work. It should be kept simple so as not to take up too much of the teacher's time. Otherwise, there is the danger of one becoming a checklist monitor, always walking around with clipboard in hand.

There are other aspects of the personalized program to be evaluated and these fall within the affectual domain. For example: How well does the child work with others? Does he work more effectively by himself, with one other child, or in a small group? What is his frustration level? Has he learned to share? Does he wait his turn? How does he handle materials within the environment? Does he exhibit a responsible attitude toward work? Does he use his time wisely? What changes have occurred in his perception of himself?

The list could go on, but the important aspects to note are the positive and negative changes in attitude. The latter should be few but, should one become aware of negativism in any child, this is a top priority situation and should be dealt with immediately.

The affectual aspects are best recorded in anecdotal style and might be as concise as one or two words.

Methods for reporting to parents are quite varied from one school district to the next; some have extensive lists of skills and attitudes dealing with music and the music learning environment, while others are vary vague. Therefore, it is recommended that at the end of each marking period or at each reporting time a thorough appraisal be given each child's work. Then, an informal, verbal evaluation should be offered each student and a short, written evaluation be given each classroom teacher for each member of his group. The classroom teacher may include the comment on the child's report card or mention it to the parent in conference, the parent then contacting the music teacher for further enlightenment if he feels the need.

Admittedly, this is time-consuming, but it is worthwhile for the following reasons:

1. It provides for four-way communication: child, music teacher, classroom teacher, and parent.

2. It gives added importance and dimension to the student's work in music.

3. It gives status to the music program and draws attention to the fact that music is an important aspect of the total curriculum.

4. It individualizes the evaluation process and makes it personally more meaningful.

Together, the cognitive and affectual evaluations, when viewed in totality, should serve the music teacher as a good indicator of the success or lack of success of the program or some aspect of its implementation.

I have found self-evaluation to be quite important, a chance to step back and look at the workings of personalization with a critical eye. From my own experience, I know how worthwhile this is, in spite of the occasional "pain" it may cause, because it is sometimes necessary to make deletions, substitutions, or changes in process. Sometimes a game just doesn't work or does not fulfill the objective, an activity is too complex, or a child has been incorrectly diagnosed and must be reevaluated. In other words, I goofed! To err is human; to make the corrections immediately absolutely essential, even if it means admitting momentary failure to the children. However, there is even a benefit in making mistakes and applying remedies because, while improving the situation, the children are afforded the opportunity to see you realistically and know that we all have failings.

We will be evaluated formally or informally by our fellow classroom teachers as we confer with them and as we see how much they encourage and assign children to extended learnings in music. This will serve as comment on the effectiveness of the program. In addition, the music teacher may devise a survey to be returned without signature, eliciting reactions to aspects of the program and inviting constructive criticism and suggestions.

We will also be evaluated formally and informally by the building administrator, music coordinator, curriculum supervisor, and the like. Whether or not they are knowledgeable in the content area, they are conversant with personalized education and are in an excellent position to give objective evaluations and suggest procedural alternatives.

Parents will evaluate the program through their children: Are they happy? What is their attitude toward music? Are they involved? Does their work show growth and development, affectively and cognitively?

In conclusion, the best measure of success, the most meaningful implement for program evaluation, will be the child, for he *is* the program.

8 The End as a Beginning

After viewing the personalized program in operation, many teachers have made a commitment to implement a similar process. But where to begin? Therefore, I have chosen to end this book with specific suggestions for beginning a similar program, taking into consideration its scope and the variables of school size, scheduling, and funding.

STEP ONE: OBSERVING

Visit as many alternate style programs as possible. Should none be available in music, observe in any nontraditional classroom because it is plan of organization and process which are important; content is secondary.

Keep a notebook in which you list all positive and negative aspects of what you observe. Include a drawing of room layout, learning centers, furnishings, and so on. Do not trust your memory since there will be so much to absorb at once.

Take a camera and, if permission is given, snap pictures of the environment, displays, bulletin boards, activity centers, and whatever else appears to be especially worthwhile.

Look at everything in the room and *in* everything in the room. Looking at a contained activity is far different from opening it up and finding out how it works.

Ask children questions about what they are doing. Ask individual children to see their prescriptions, contracts, work folders, and the like. Children enjoy this experience.

Take the class teacher to lunch! I say this only because every adult is busy with students 100 percent of the time in an individualized program of instruction. In fact, the children will probably involve any visitor immediately, which is another excellent way to acquire a feeling for the program. Therefore, save your questions for the lunch break. At this time the classroom teacher may also be able to direct you to specifics for your afternoon of observation.

At some time later in the day, write out your conclusions from the observation and list all those aspects which you might be able to adopt and adapt.

After a few observations, you will have begun to formulate a general plan, together with some specifics for your own program.

STEP TWO: READING AND DEVELOPING A PHILOSOPHY

At the very outset of this book, the importance of knowing why you are implementing a personalized program of instruction was emphasized. I restate it again, in conclusion, since it is this which provides the rationale and gives direction to all that you do.

I suggest readings from the bibliography or from whatever sources you find meaningful. As you agree or disagree with the authors, you will come to grips with the more important questions in education today as well as become conversant with divergent and conflicting points of view.

Again, take notes. Reread significant statements and you will emerge with your personal philosophy of individualized music education.

STEP THREE: CHANGING THE PHYSICAL ENVIRONMENT

Make a scale drawing of your room. Mentally empty the room of everything. Then experiment with layout: learning centers, shelves for storing activities, games, records, basal books, a library, instruments, and so forth. Don't forget to check for outlets and door access.

Day by day remove nonessentials from your room. Invite children to help. Ask them for suggestions because you want them to feel that the environment is "ours," not "theirs" or "yours." This feeling of mutual ownership is an important foundation for the development of responsible attitudes toward room management and upkeep.

Experiment! What is uncomfortable or nonfunctional should be rearranged immediately, but try to think through the placement of heavy pieces of equipment first.

STEP FOUR: STOCKING THE ENVIRONMENT

Following the plan as outlined in Chapter 5 on materials, the environment will evolve gradually. Keep in mind the following:

1. Begin with what is on hand: a. basal texts; b. flash cards, charts, games; c. records, filmstrips, slides, tapes; d. library books, and make them work for you with a simple adaptation to personalization.

2. Look to the media center, school library, and reading and science labs for additional materials.

3. Gradually add homespuns as time permits and need arises. (Keep a notebook of homespuns in which you list all your ideas. Then when you begin to work on games and activities, you will only spend time on execution, not planning. Catalogue all those that have been completed in a card file together with a short description and objective for which devised.)

STEP FIVE: WORKING WITH COLLEAGUES

Discuss your plans with fellow teachers and supervisors to elicit their suggestions and support. Since one of the program's goals is to bring music into the mainstream of each child's educational life, classroom teachers need to be aware of your objectives and what you can offer children in correlated, integrated, and extended learning experiences.

From time to time, attend grade level meetings with classroom teachers to become familiar with total curriculum. Join in case conferences with school psychologists and specialists in remediation of individual students. You have much to offer, since you see each child in another environment, operating within a musical frame of reference. Attend in-service courses when possible, even if the content is totally divorced from music. You will become familiar with the current trends in curriculum and, perhaps, come away with ideas for program organization and activities that you can adapt.

Join together with fellow music teachers to share ideas and exchange materials on a regular basis.

STEP SIX: IMPLEMENTING

Gradually move your classes in the direction of a personalized program in any of the following ways:

1. Involve the whole class in small group activities on a limited basis so that the children can get a feel for working on their own. For example, the class has been working with syncopation (quarter, half, quarter note, and eighth, quarter, eighth note). Group One will play given patterns in ensemble. Group Two will play a game based upon reading syncopated patterns. Group Three will do speech chants in syncopation. At subsequent lessons, groups will change activities.

   Children will begin to learn how to handle materials and replace them in designated areas, work independent of direct teacher control, see a need for sharing, and begin to monitor sound levels so that everyone can work effectively.

2. Within every class there are some children who already possess those affective work habits and character traits that are effectual goals of the program. These children can be assigned activities, tasks, and/or project work and be allowed to proceed on their own while the teacher works with the remainder of the class as a group. Soon, other children will want to do likewise when they see the

fun and excitement in the personalized approach. The teacher will gradually be able to add more students to the program until it is possible to fully implement a diagnosing and prescribing procedure.

3. The teacher may choose to implement with those classes in which the subject work has already been personalized. These children will transfer work habits and processes from home class to music class.

   In many elementary schools there are a variety of teaching styles from the very traditional to a highly personalized approach. Also, classes may be homogeneous, heterogeneous, or integrated in various interaging plans. It is to your advantage to initially work with those groups familiar with individualization.

4. The teacher may choose to implement for certain skills. A simple one with which to begin is naming notes and rests. A pre-test is given. Through exposure and constant repetition, some children will know them well enough to go on to working with games and activities requiring this prior knowledge and will reinforce the skill, or they may proceed to working with equal values activities.

   A few children will have no prior knowledge of the subject, not even remembering that notes are circles. Therefore, this will be the group with which the teacher will work directly in instructing and providing game-type drills.

   The other students will have some knowledge of notes and rests and can play the games and participate in the activities and challenges designed to both reinforce instruction and provide for facility of utilization.

You are now on your way to full implementation of a personalized program of music instruction which is unique because it was conceived and designed by you, for your students, in your school, in your community which is unlike any other except in its desire to provide the best, most meaningful education for all of its children.

Epilogue

Someone once said that teaching in an individualized program is only for the "stouthearted." There are days and times when I would agree because, as with any program, there are pluses and minuses, successes and failures.

The minus factor, at least at the beginning stages, involves time. Personalization requires many hours of preparation, certainly more than the traditional programs. There always seems to be one more thing to be done. Therefore, set realistic goals and reasonable limits. One classroom teacher told me that for one month she set herself a goal of two activities each weekday night, and at the end of the month she had an excellent store of materials.

The failures, if they can really be considered failures, would be with individual students for whom you might have incorrectly prescribed or whose learning needs have yet to be met. These are easily reversed when the situation is reevaluated and adjusted.

However, the benefits to all definitely outweigh the negative aspects. I speak from experience. I am a working teacher, dealing with personalization in an ongoing program, every day. This book was not written in isolation, but as a direct result of personal involvement and with a sincere desire to assist and guide colleagues over the rough areas and around the pitfalls.

It works! All that I have included in this book has been tested by experts — the children.

The problems will always be there. Whenever we deal in human relationships there will be problems, but they do become fewer and easier to handle and discipline problems become virtually nonexistent.

The reward for you, the teacher, is the excitement that you find in each new and creative endeavor you undertake, in the interest, joy, and measurable growth you see in the children with whom you *do business*, and the constant renewal you feel as you interact within the environment that you created.

To all who opt for the experience, I wish you the ongoing feeling of satisfaction and fulfillment that is mine.

Bibliography

Brearley, Molly, and Hitchfield, Elizabeth. *A Guide to Reading Piaget.* New York: Schocken Books, 1966.

Featherstone, Joseph. *Schools Where Children Learn.* New York: Liveright, 1971.

Fowler, Charles B. "The Discovery Method: Its Relevance for Music Education." In *Perspectives in Music Education, Source Book III.* Washington, D.C.: Music Educators National Conference, 1966.

Holt, John. *How Children Fail.* New York: Dell Publishing Company, Inc., 1964, 1970.

—————. *How Children Learn.* New York: Dell Publishing Company, Inc., 1967, 1970.

Nyquist, Ewald B., and Hawes, Gene R., ed. *Open Education: A Sourcebook for Parents and Teachers.* New York: Bantam Books, Inc., 1972.

Pulaski, Mary Ann Spencer. *Understanding Piaget: An Introduction to Children's Cognitive Development.* New York: Harper & Row, Publishers, 1971.

Rogers, Vincent R. *Teaching in the British Primary School.* London: The Macmillan Company, 1970.

Silberman, Charles E., ed. *The Open Classroom Reader.* New York: Vintage Books, 1973.

Stark, Charles John. "Creativity: Its Application to the Theory and Practice of Music Teaching." In *Perspectives In Music Education, Source Book III.* Washington, D.C.: Music Educators National Conference, 1966.

Woodruff, Asahel D. "Concept Teaching in Music." In *Perspectives in Music Education, Source Book III.* Washington, D.C.: Music Educators National Conference, 1966.

PERIODICALS

Vail, Thomas. "Implementing Music Education in Open Education." *The School Music News.* Little Falls, N.Y.: New York State School Music Association (May-June 1973), vol. 36, no. 9.

The remaining articles are from *Music Educators Journal,* Music Educators National Conference, Washington, D.C.

Barth, Roland S. "First We Start with Some Different Assumptions." (April 1974), vol. 60, no. 8.

Cornell, Helen Loftin. "Drums and Dumpsters, Puppets and Pods." (April 1974), vol. 60, no. 8.

Duckworth, Eleanor. "The 'Bat-Poet' Knows: Evaluation in Informal Education." (April 1974), vol. 60, no. 8.

Earl, Janet C. "Recognizing the Individual: It's Important in Music, Too." (November 1972), vol. 59, no. 3.

—————. "The 'I's' Have It." (November 1972), vol. 59, no. 3.

—————. "Some Thoughts." (November 1972), vol. 59, no. 3.

Eddins, John M. "Two Trends in Teaching Music: The Comprehensive and the Cross-Cultural." (September 1969), vol. 56, no. 1.

Evenson, Flavis. " . . . And How They Are Applied." (February 1970), vol. 56, no. 6.

Fowler, Charles B. "Discovery: One of the Best Ways to Teach a Musical Concept." (October 1970), vol. 57, no. 2.

Goldiamond, Israel, and Pleskoff, Stanley. "Music Education and the Rationale Underlying Programmed Instruction." (February-March 1965), vol. 51, no. 4.

Guenther, Annette R. "Open Education Places the Arts in the Core of the Curriculum." (April 1974), vol. 60, no. 8.

Haynes, Carrie A. "Grape Street Elementary School, Los Angeles." (April 1974), vol. 60, no. 8.

Haynes, Margaret S. "The Open Classroom — Its Structure and Rationale." (November 1972), vol. 59, no. 3.

Jensen, Eric. "Creativity and Its Sources." (March 1969), vol. 55, no. 7.

Kunhardt, Barbara. "Shady Hill School, Cambridge, Massachusetts." (April 1974), vol. 60, no. 8.

Landon, Joseph W. "Music in Britain's Informal Classrooms (What Does It Suggest for American Education?)" (May 1973), vol. 59, no. 9.

—————. "Strategies for Opening the Traditional Classroom." (April 1974), vol. 60, no. 8.

Lathrop, Robert L. "The Psychology of Music and Music Education." (February 1970), vol. 56, no. 6.

Neidlinger, Robert J. "Dimensions of Sound and Silence: The Basis of a Liberal Education in Music." (April 1973), vol. 59, no. 8.

Potter, Jean. "Contracts." (February 1975), vol. 61, no. 6.

Rathbone, Charles H. "No Longer Just a Knowledge Pusher." (April 1974), vol. 60, no. 8.

Rausch, Kathy. "Olive School, Arlington Heights, Illinois." (April 1974), vol. 60, no. 8.

Redding, Frances S. "Individualization Is a State of Mind." (November 1972), vol. 59, no. 3.

—————. "Team Planning in Broward County." (November 1972), vol. 69, no. 3.

Regelski, Thomas A. "A Ride on the Dialectic Seesaw." (March 1975), vol. 61, no. 7.

Rogers, Vincent R. "Open Education: Where Is It Now? Where Is It Heading?" (April 1974), vol. 60, no. 8 .

Schmidt, Lloyd. "The Process of Music Education." (February 1975), vol. 61, no. 6.

Spodek, Bernard. "Preparing Music Teachers for Open Education." (April 1974), vol. 60, no. 8.

Springer, Virginia F. "Campus Laboratory School, Cortland, New York." (April 1974), vol. 60, no. 8.

Thiebe, Edward H. "Somewhere the Child Has Been Lost." (November 1972), vol. 59, no. 3.

Thompson, Keith P. "Music Cannot be Locked in a Closet." (April 1974), vol. 60, no. 8.

Uhl, Gladys C. "Singing Helps Children Learn How To Read." (December 1969), vol. 56, no. 4.

Westervelt, Marie J. "Involvement and Integration." (April 1974), vol. 60, no. 8.

Wilkey, Jay W. "Marshall McLuhan and Meaning in Music." (September 1969), vol. 56, no. 1.

Willour, Judith. "Beginning with Delight, Leading to Wisdom: Dalcroze." (September 1969), vol. 56, no. 1.

Woodruff, Asahel D. "How Music Concepts Are Developed." (February 1970), vol. 56, no. 6.

Zimmermann, Marilyn Pflederer. "Percept and Concept: Implications of Piaget." (February 1970), vol. 56, no. 6.

Appendix

Conceptual Diagnostic Test, Level One

NAME: CLASS

CONCEPT   **COMMENT**

1. **UP AND DOWN**
   Given an ascending melody and a descending melody, the child can identify the melodic direction. (The leaps in each melody are wide.)

2. **HIGH AND LOW**
   Given two notes on the keyboard, the child can identify the higher note. (Use the extremes; very low, very high.)

3. **LOUD AND SOFT**
   Given a melody, the child will differentiate between the fff execution and the ppp execution.

4. **FAST AND SLOW**
   Given a basic beat on a drum, the child will differentiate between the pattern that is very fast and the pattern that is very slow. (The difference must be marked.)

5. **BASIC BEAT**
   Given a basic beat on a drum, the child will clap or step with the basic beat.

6. **REACTING TO CHANGING TEMPO**
   Given a basic beat that markedly changes from very slow to very fast, the child will clap or step with the beat.

7. **PLACING BASIC BEATS IN SETS**
   Given a number of rhythm sticks (multiples), each of which represents the quarter note, the basic beat (ta), the child will place them into sets, as directed by the teacher. (2, 3, 4, or 5.)

8. **ECHO CLAPPING**
   Given three rhythm patterns containing quarter note, eighth notes, and quarter rest, the child will accurately clap back each pattern. (One measure each, maximum five beats.)

9. **ECHO CLAPPING EXTENDED PATTERNS**

   Given one pattern containing quarter note, eighth notes, and quarter rest, extended to two measures, the child will accurately clap back the pattern.

10. **PROVIDING A RHYTHMIC ANSWER TO A RHYTHMIC QUESTION**

    Given a one-measure rhythmic question containing quarter note, eighth notes, and quarter rest, the child will provide a rhythmic answer, one measure in length, containing some element of the question.

11. **PROVIDING A MELODIC ANSWER TO A MELODIC QUESTION**

    Given a melodic question containing the notes SOL-MI-LA, the child will provide an answer of the same length and containing elements of the question. (One measure, maximum five beats.)

12. **SENSING METER**

    Given a recurring set of basic beats, the child will be able to discern the number in each set.

13. **ECHO SINGING**

    Given the pattern SOL-MI-LA, the child will echo sing accurately and in tune.

14. **PERCEIVING LINES AND SPACES**

    Given a floor staff, the child will be able to identify lines and spaces by number, in ascending order.

15. **PLACING SOL/MI/LA ON A FIVE-LINE STAFF**

    Given the position of SOL, the child will place SOL-MI-LA in proper relationship, using the floor staff and large circles.

16. **DURATION**

    Given two notes sounded on the keyboard, the child will be able to identify the longer of the two sounds. (The difference is marked.)

Conceptual Diagnostic Test, Level Two

NAME: CLASS:

CONCEPT   **COMMENT**

1. **UP AND DOWN**
    Given an ascending melody and a descending melody containing steps and skips, the child can identify the melodic direction.

2. **HIGH AND LOW**
    Given two notes on the keyboard, the child can identify the higher note. (The notes are from one to two octaves apart.)

3. **LOUD AND SOFT**
    Given a melody, the child will differentiate between the ff execution and the pp execution.

4. **FAST AND SLOW**
    Given a basic beat on a drum, the child will differentiate between the pattern that is fast and the pattern that is slow.

5. **BASIC BEAT**
    Given a basic beat on a drum, the child will clap and step with the basic beat.

6. **REACTING TO CHANGING TEMPO**
    Given a basic beat that markedly changes from slow to fast, the child will clap and step with the beat.

7. **PLACING BEATS IN SETS**
    Given a written rhythm pattern containing multiples of quarter notes, eighth notes, and quarter rests, the child will place them into sets (measures), as designated by the teacher.

8. **ECHO CLAPPING**
    Given three rhythm patterns containing quarter note, eighth notes, quarter rest, and half note, the child will accurately clap back each pattern. (One measure, maximum five beats.)

9. **ECHO CLAPPING EXTENDED PATTERNS**

   Given one pattern containing quarter note, eighth notes, quarter rest, and half note, extended to two measures, the child will accurately clap back the pattern.

10. **PROVIDING A RHYTHMIC ANSWER TO A RHYTHMIC QUESTION**

    Given a two-measure rhythmic question containing quarter note, eighth notes, quarter rest, and half note, the child will provide a rhythmic answer, two measures in length, containing some element of the question.

11. **PROVIDING A MELODIC ANSWER TO A MELODIC QUESTION**

    Given a melodic question containing the notes SOL-MI-LA-DO$_1$, the child will provide an answer of the same length and containing elements of the question. (Two measures in length.)

12. **SENSING METER**

    Given a set of basic beats, the meter of which changes, the child will be able to discern and identify the numbers (changes) as they occur. (One change, 2 to 4 or 3 to 5.)

13. **ECHO SINGING**

    Given a pattern containing SOL-MI-LA-DO$_1$, the child will echo sing accurately and in tune.

14. **PERCEIVING LINES AND SPACES**

    Given a large oaktag staff and poker chips, the child will place the chips on the line or in the space, as designated by the teacher, by number.

15. **PLACING SOL/MI/LA/DO$_1$ ON A FIVE-LINE STAFF**

    Given the position of DO$_1$, the child will place SOL-MI-LA-DO$_1$ in proper relationship, using the large oak tag staff and poker chips.

16. **DURATION**

    Given two notes sounded on the keyboard, the child will be able to identify the longer of the two sounds. (The difference is less marked than at Level One.)

Conceptual Diagnostic Test, Level Three

NAME: CLASS:

CONCEPT   COMMENT

1. **UP AND DOWN**
   Given an ascending melody and a descending melody, each of which moves in steps, the child can identify the melodic direction.

2. **HIGH AND LOW**
   Given two notes on the keyboard, the child can identify the higher note. (The notes are within one octave.)

3. **LOUD AND SOFT**
   Given a melody, the child will differentiate between the f execution and the p execution.

4. **FAST AND SLOW**
   Given a basic beat on a drum, the child will differentiate between the pattern that is fast and the pattern that is slow. (Difference is slight: medium fast to medium slow.)

5. **BASIC BEAT**
   Given a simple notated rhythm pattern, the child will clap it as he steps the basic beat that has been set by the teacher.

6. **REACTING TO CHANGING TEMPO**
   Given a basic beat that changes from medium slow to medium fast, the child will clap and step with the beat.

7. **PLACING BEATS IN SETS**
   Given a written rhythm pattern containing multiples of quarter notes, eighth notes, quarter rests, half notes, and half rests, the child will place them into sets (measures), as designated by the teacher.

8. **ECHO CLAPPING**
   Given three rhythm patterns containing quarter note, eighth notes, quarter rest, half note, and whole note, the child will accurately clap each pattern. (One measure, maximum five beats.)

9. **ECHO CLAPPING EXTENDED PATTERNS**

Given one pattern containing any combination of notes/rests, whole through eighths (no dotted notes), extended to two measures, the child will accurately clap back the pattern.

10. **PROVIDING A RHYTHMIC ANSWER TO A RHYTHMIC QUESTION**

Given a two-measure rhythmic question containing any combination of notes/rests, whole through eighths (no dotted notes), the child will provide a rhythmic answer, two measures in length, containing some element of the question.

11. **PROVIDING A MELODIC ANSWER TO A MELODIC QUESTION**

Given a melodic question in the pentatonic scale, the child will provide an answer of the same length and containing elements of the question. (Two measures in length.)

12. **SENSING METER**

Given a set of basic beats, the meter of which changes, the child will be able to discern and identify the numbers. (More than one change, 2 through 5.)

13. **ECHO SINGING**

Given a pattern in the pentatonic scale, the child will echo sing accurately and in tune.

14. **PERCEIVING LINES AND SPACES**

Given a magnetic board staff or a flannel board staff, the child will place the note heads on the line or in the space, as designated by the teacher, by number.

15. **PLACING NOTES OF THE PENTATONIC SCALE ON A FIVE-LINE STAFF**

Given the position of DO_1, the child will place the notes of the pentatonic scale in proper relationship, using the magnetic board staff or the flannel board staff.

16. **DURATION**

Given two notes sounded on the keyboard, the child will be able to identify the longer of the two sounds. (The difference is less marked than at Level Two.)

Conceptual Diagnostic Test, Level Four

NAME: CLASS:

CONCEPT   **COMMENT**

1. **UP AND DOWN**
   Given a melody that ascends, descends, and stays in the same place, the child can identify the melodic direction.

2. **HIGH AND LOW**
   Given two notes·on the keyboard, the child can identify the higher note. (The notes are an interval of a second.)

3. **LOUD AND SOFT**
   Given a melody, the child will differentiate between the mf execution and the mp execution.

4. **FAST AND SLOW**
   Given a drum, the child will play three basic beat patterns, each eight beats long. The first will be played at a fast tempo, the second at a medium tempo, the third at a slow tempo, the tempi to be set by the child.

5. **BASIC BEAT**
   Given a notated rhythm pattern that includes all notes within the child's reading vocabulary, the child will clap it as he steps the basic beat that has been set by the teacher.

6. **REACTING TO CHANGING TEMPO**
   Given a basic beat that changes from degrees of slow to degrees of fast to degrees of slow, the child will clap and step with the beat.

7. **PLACING BEATS IN SETS**
   Given a written rhythm pattern containing multiples of quarter notes, eighth notes, quarter rests, half notes and rests, whole notes and rests, and dotted half notes, the child will place them into sets (measures), as designated by the teacher.

8. **ECHO CLAPPING**

Given three rhythm patterns containing notes/ rests, whole through the sixteenth note set, the child will accurately clap back each pattern. (One measure, maximum five beats.)

9. **ECHO CLAPPING EXTENDED PATTERNS**

Given one pattern containing any combination of notes/rests, whole through sixteenths, extended to four measures, the child will accurately clap back the pattern.

10. **PROVIDING A RHYTHMIC ANSWER TO A RHYTHMIC QUESTION**

Given a two-measure rhythmic question containing any combination of notes/rests, whole through sixteenths, the child will provide a rhythmic answer, two measures in length, containing some element of the question.

11. **PROVIDING A MELODIC ANSWER TO A MELODIC QUESTION**

Given a melodic question in the diatonic scale, the child will provide an answer of the same length and containing the elements of the question. (Two measures in length.)

12. **SENSING METER**

Given a clapped rhythm pattern, the meter of which changes, the child will be able to discern and identify the changes by numbers.

13. **ECHO SINGING**

Given a pattern in the diatonic scale, the child will echo sing accurately and in tune.

14. **PERCEIVING LINES AND SPACES**

Given staff paper, the child will draw note heads on the line or in the space, as designated by the teacher, by number.

15. **PLACING NOTES OF THE DIATONIC SCALE ON A FIVE-LINE STAFF**

Given the position of DO_1, the child will place the notes of the diatonic scale in proper relationship on staff paper.

16. DURATION

Given two notes sounded on the keyboard, the child will be able to identify the longer of the two sounds. (The difference is less marked than at Level Three.)

An Integrated Topic

RED...

Read this poem about
RED.

Read it out loud.
Can you make your
voice sound like
RED?

You may tape
your reading
of the poem.

How does RED
make you feel?
Can you move
like RED?

Red is a sunset
Blazy and bright.
Red is feeling brave
With all your might.
Red is a lipstick
Red is a shout,
That says: "Watch out!"

Red is a show-off
No doubt about —
But can you imagine
Living without it?

Which instruments can make
RED sounds? Can you create
a RED song for instruments?
Write it down using pictures,
symbols, or music notes. Now
your friends can play it, too!

Can you paint
with RED?
Add BLUE
paint to the
RED, measuring
each amount.
What happened?
Keep experimenting
until you like the
color.

Do the same thing
adding YELLOW
to RED.
What happened?

Add some WHITE to each. What
happened? Now try some BLACK.

Write about the NEW
color you like best.

Make a painting
with all
your new colors!

"WHAT IS RED" from Halestones and Halibut Bones by Mary O'Neill
Copyright © 1961 Mary LeDuc O'Neill reprinted by permission of the publisher Doubleday & Co., Inc.

SOUNDS IN NATURE...

1. Listen to the sounds in nature. Sit out-of-doors and listen to the sounds of trees, birds, animals, insects, the wind and so on for five minutes. Make a list of everything you hear.

2. Do the first activity again on another day at a different time.

3. Try to find instruments that will sound like some of the things you heard. Record your ideas on tape.

4. Write a song about nature. Begin with the words. Then add a melody.

5. Make a picture collage of the sounds you heard.

An Integrated Topic

DISCOVER:

1. Who he was.

2. When and where he lived and worked.

3. What kind of life he led.

4. What important events happened during his lifetime.

5. What kind of music he wrote.

EXPERIENCE:

1. His music for orchestra.

2. A song he wrote. Learn to sing it and/or play it.

You may use this general outline to study any composer.

Insert a picture of Mozart here when preparing this work card. (It will focus attention on the center of interest.)

MOZART

BE AN ARTIST:

1. Make an illustration (picture) of your poem/song.

2. Make a scene showing Mozart's world.

3. Make a map of the country in which he lived.

(Choose one.)

CREATE:

1. A poem in the same form as the song you learned.

2. A melody for the poem. (Be sure to notate your song so others may sing and play it.)

JUPITER, the BRINGER of JOLLITY*

The Planet Jupiter is named after the god, Jupiter, who is known as the Bringer of Jollity.

1. Find out 4 facts about the planet, Jupiter.

2. Read about the god, Jupiter. What was he like?

3. Listen to "Jupiter, the Bringer of Jollity" from *The Planets* by Gustave Holst. How many different themes (melodies) do you hear? What is the mood?

4. Creat a set of themes, each of which has the same mood as "Jupiter" OR create a set of dance movements to the music.

5. Do a piece of art work about Jupiter, the planet or god.

6. Write a story or a poem about "Jolly Jupiter."

*Title from *The Planets* by Gustave Holst.

SECTION
TWO

PREFACE

The activities and games that are included are simple to make and require no special skills. However, the reader may find the following general instructions helpful.

1. Materials

Have on hand lined index cards in all sizes, 3''x5'', 4''x6'', and 5''x8'' in white and colors, if you so choose. If you intend to make many of the activities requiring index cards, buy in quantity.

Poster board may be purchased in different weights and colors. Weight will depend upon the function. Heavier poster board is preferred for large circle note heads, game boards, and cubes. Heavy cardboard may be substituted for poster board. This may be purchased or saved from packaging.

Save all scraps! You can use them for small cards, markers, circles for note heads, and so forth.

Use permanent ink pens for all marking, both wide tipped and fine point. Have on hand a supply of all colors. Permanent ink will not fade as rapidly as washable colors.

It is recommended that good equipment be purchased: scissors, ruler, compass, hole punch, stapler, and a small paper cutter. Also purchase top-quality clear, plastic, cloth, and masking tapes. Quality equipment and materials will facilitate production of activities and games as well as save you time.

2. Laminating

All materials should be laminated; even the cubes can be covered before folding and taping. If the reader does not have access to a laminating machine, clear adhesive-backed paper may be used.

When applying the adhesive-backed paper, place it sticky side up on a table and put the article to be laminated on the paper. This has proven to be the best method for eliminating "bubbles" and "wrinkles."

When laminating a series of cards, circles, or other small objects, cut apart *after* laminating to save duplication of processes.

In any case, *Do Laminate Everything!* Don't yield to the temptation of using a game or activity before this process has been completed.

3. Special Notes

a. **Scoring:** Place ruler on fold line of poster board or cardboard and, using closed scissors, mark on this line for ease in folding.

b. **Writing:** Print everything in large, clear letters. Those activities designed for younger children should be large in both size and writing for ease in perception.

c. **Cutting:** Use paper cutter for preparing sets of cards. The paper cutter will cut multiples of poster board.

d. **Colors:** Vary colors for both emphasis and aesthetics.

e. **Decorations:** Cartoon figures, caricatures, pictures, and the like motivate children and invite them to pick up the activity. If you cannot draw, use pictures from periodicals.

4. Packaging

Every activity should be clearly labeled and in its own folder, container, or box together with directions. Each one may also be coded so that the child knows to which shelf the activity should be returned.

Example: Rhythm and Meter — All activities coded with a RED circle.

Save and collect boxes in varying shapes and sizes from small to very large. Egg cartons, coffee cans, candy boxes, foil tins, and any unusual container may be just what you need for a particular activity.

5. Adapting Commercial Games

It is suggested that you request from students those games which they no longer are using. You may wish to invite the children to become involved in adapting the games for music.

In addition to organizing your ideas in a notebook so that they will be available when you are ready to work, having your materials on hand and set up in working order will save you many unnecessary shopping trips and much time.

And finally, it is suggested that you make everything as permanent as possible. It is more rewarding for you and your students to have you spend your available time developing new materials rather than remaking old ones.

Cubes

Many of the games and activities require cubes; therefore, general instructions for construction are included here.

(Note: Size may be scaled up or down, but it is recommended that none be smaller than 1-1/2" cubed for facility of both construction and perception. Make cubes of poster board or heavy cardboard.

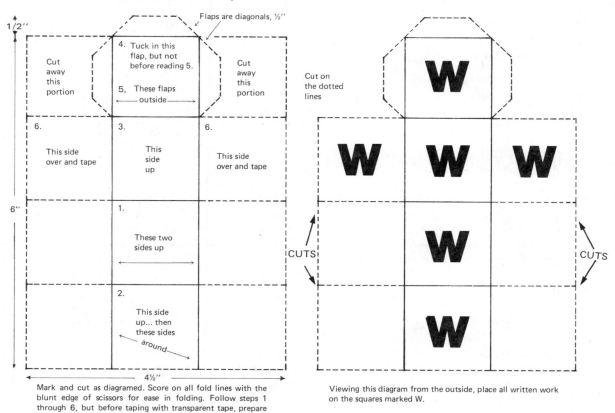

Mark and cut as diagramed. Score on all fold lines with the blunt edge of scissors for ease in folding. Follow steps 1 through 6, but before taping with transparent tape, prepare the outer sides of each cube with whatever signs, symbols, or directions are required for the game.

Viewing this diagram from the outside, place all written work on the squares marked W.

Activities for:

FLOOR STAFF with LARGE NOTE HEADS
STAFF CARDS and POKER CHIPS
MAGNETIC BOARD and MAGNETIC NOTES
"LICK 'EM, STICK 'EM"
WRITING on a STAFF

Objectives:

1. To provide for instruction in melodic notation.
2. To reinforce and remediate in melodic notation.
3. To provide activities in visual perception and discrimination.
4. To reinforce skill of reading from left to right.

Materials, Contents, and Preparation:

1. Floor Staff with Large Note Heads.

Use white Mystik Plastic tape for the floor staff. It is suggested that the lines be 8" apart. Be sure to accommodate for the width of the tape as you apply it. Place a single bar line at the beginning of the staff, a double bar line at the end, and the treble clef sign at the left if you can handle the tape. Be sure children know position of line one.

Cut note heads from heavy cardboard, 8" in diameter. (If you are color coding, use colored poster board or color each circle with permanent ink markers.) Laminate the circles.

Should you wish to add sticks to the note heads for simple rhythmic/melodic notation, you may use rhythm sticks or flat pieces of balsa wood which are available in most craft shops and are easily cut to the desired length.

To preserve the floor staff, apply a coat of clear vinyl liquid floor wax.

2. Staff Cards and Poker Chips

Use oaktag or poster board for the staff cards, each 18" x 12". Draw staff on each card as follows:

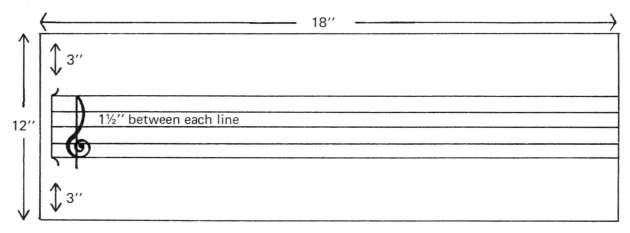

The distance between lines is very important since it must exactly accommodate poker chips which will be used as note heads. Cards should be laminated or covered with clear adhesive-backed paper.

3. Magnetic Board and Magnetic Notes.

The board is available from Child Guidance Toys, Inc., and may be adapted as follows: Beginning at 1-1/2 inches from the top, make five lines for the staff using narrow black Mystik tape (plastic is preferable to cloth). Each space between the lines should be 1''. Once again, remember to accommodate for the width of the tape. Add a single bar line at the beginning and a double bar at the end of the staff. You may also add a treble clef sign if you are clever with the tape, but this is not necessary since children will work from left to right automatically in most cases and will become accustomed to the double bar being the end.

Cut note heads from felt in 1'' diameter. Adhere to heavy cardboard which is also cut in 1'' circles. Magnetize with a small piece of Scotch Magnetic Strips (The 3M Company) affixed to the back of each cardboard circle. (If you are color coding use colored felt.)

(Note: The Child Guidance Magnetic Board comes with a stand which makes it a good device for instructional purposes as well as personalized work.)

4. "Lick 'Em, Stick 'Em."

This activity can be used instructionally and creatively or when children wish to keep their work or the teacher requires a sample of students' efforts. It is a permanent example that can be exhibited, sent home, or filed for future reference.

The staff should be prepared on a ditto lengthwise with 1'' between lines. The note heads, again color coded if the teacher so chooses, are 1'' circles cut from gummed craft paper. These should be prepared in quantity before introducing "Lick 'Em, Stick 'Em" because children enjoy using them to create melodies that they sing and play for fellow students. Sticks may be added to note heads with crayon or felt-tipped pen for simple rhythmic notation.

5. Writing on a Staff

The author recommends preparation of dittoed staff paper for written notation, with lines 1/2'' apart and 1/4'' apart. This allows for a gradual transition from floor staff to card and/or magnetic board staves to "Lick 'Em, Stick 'Em" sheets to 1/2'' and 1/4'' width staves and, finally, to standard staff paper.

This will eliminate the frustration that seems to be inherent in melodic notation, especially for those children who have perceptual problems and those younger students who are not developmentally ready to use the standard prepared staves.

The Activities:

Make a Melody

Cards are arranged in sets according to level of difficulty within the melodic sequence. Children "make a melody" as designated. They may use the floor staff, card or magnetic staff, "Lick 'Em, Stick 'Em" sheets, or staff paper. The teacher will direct the child to that which is appropriate for his level of development. Answers are placed on the back of each card. The child may sing and/or play his melody on any instrument of his choice after he has notated it correctly.

Using a 3" x 5" index card, the activity is set up as follows:

Blank side of index card:

SOL: LINE 2

MAKE THIS MELODY

SOL MI SOL LA

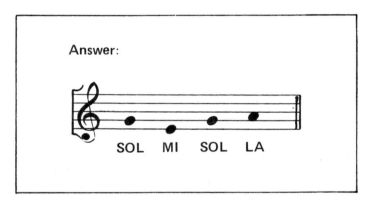

Answer:

SOL   MI   SOL   LA

Suggestions for sets:

Set One — SOL, Line 2.
1. SOL MI SOL
2. SOL SOL MI SOL
3. SOL MI SOL MI
4. SOL MI LA
5. SOL LA SOL MI
6. SOL MI SOL LA
7. SOL MI LA SOL MI
8. MI SOL LA SOL

Set Two — SOL, Space 3.
(Same as Set One except new key.)

Set Three — SOL, Line 3.
1. SOL MI DO_1
2. SOL MI DO_1 MI
3. SOL LA SOL MI DO_1
4. MI SOL DO_1 MI
5. MI SOL LA SOL DO_1
6. MI DO_1 MI
7. DO_1 MI SOL LA SOL MI DO_1

Set Four — SOL, Space 4.
(Same as Set Three except new key.)

Set Five — DO, Line 1.
1. DO_1 RE MI SOL LA
2. LA SOL MI RE DO_1
3. DO_1 RE MI LA SOL
4. RE DO_1 MI SOL LA
5. SOL LA MI RE DO_1
6. DO_1 RE DO_1 MI DO_1 SOL DO_1 LA
7. LA SOL LA ME RE RE DO_1
8. DO_1 LA SOL MI RE DO_1

Set Six — DO, Space 1.
(Same as Set Five except new key.)

What's in a Word? Spell and Play

Provide children with cards that spell a word within the music alphabet system, A through G. On reverse side of each card, provide all possible answers.

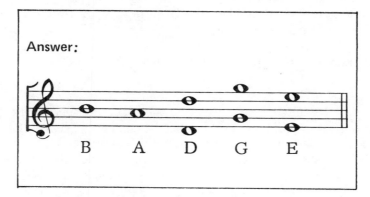

Directions for children:

1. Place note heads on the lines or in the spaces to spell out each word.
2. What word have you spelled?
3. Check your answers on the back of each card.
4. Play each word on a bar instrument after you have spelled it correctly in note heads.

Line or Space Game (2, 3, or 4 players)

This game is recommended for children who are in the initial stages of working with the five-line staff and for those students who experience difficulty in perception of lines and spaces.

Prepare two cubes as per general directions.

Write on one cube as follows:
    Side 1 — Line 1
    Side 2 — Line 2
    Side 3 — Line 3
    Side 4 — Line 4
    Side 5 — Line 5
    Side 6 — Bonus: Score 1 point

Write on the other cube as follows:
    Side 1 — Space 1
    Side 2 — Space 2
    Side 3 — Space 3
    Side 4 — Space 4
    Side 5 — Bonus: Score 1 point
    Side 6 — Penalty: Take away 1 point.

This game may be played using any of the following staves as designated by the teacher:

1. Floor Staff — Child stands on the line or in the space or places the large circle prepared for this staff.

2. Large Card Staff — Child places the poker chip on the line or in the space.

3. Magnetic Board — Child places the magnetized note on the line or in the space.

4. Staff Paper — Child draws the note as designated.

(**Note:** It is impractical to use the Lick 'Em, Stick 'Em's for this purpose.)

Game Directions:

Round One

Player One rolls the LINE die. He finds the line number shown on the die and places himself or a note head on the line. If correct, he scores *the number of the line.* For example, line 3, score 3 points. If he rolls the Bonus, he scores 1 free point.

Each player then rolls the LINE die in turn.

Round Two

Player One rolls the SPACE die. He finds the space number shown on the die and places himself or a note head in the space. If correct, he scores *the number of the space.* For example, Space 2, score 2 points. If he rolls the Bonus, he scores 1 free point. If he rolls the Penalty, he loses 1 point. Each player then rolls the SPACE die in turn.

Play continues in this way, alternating from line to space until one player reaches 20 points. He is the winner.

ACTIVITIES FOR THE PENDULUM

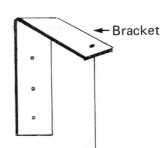

Bracket

Objectives:
1. To make the concept of meter concrete through visualization.
2. To remediate and reinforce concept of basic beat.
3. To provide experiences with placing beats in sets and accenting.
4. To provide experiences with clapping rhythms to a basic beat.

Materials:
A shelf bracket, string, weight, 5'' x 8'' index cards, a set of rhythm flash cards.

Contents:
The pendulum, activity cards and rhythm flash cards.

Preparation:
Place shelf bracket on a wooden frame of a bulletin board or in any spot where it is possible to permanently affix it. Suspend string from bracket, approximately 48'' or whatever length is at a convenient level for the children and will be accessible. Place weight at lower end of string.

(Place each activity on 5'' x 8'' index cards.)

Activity One:
Start the pendulum in motion. Clap with each swing of the pendulum.
Can you keep a steady beat?

Activity Two:
Start the pendulum in motion. Clap with each swing of the pendulum, accenting the first beat in each set of 2.

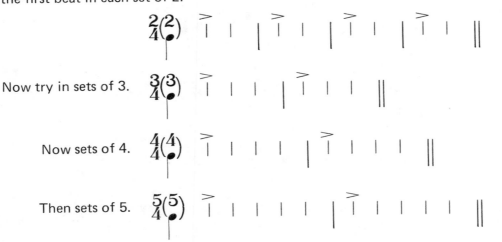

Now try in sets of 3.

Now sets of 4.

Then sets of 5.

Activity Three:
Start the pendulum in motion.
1. Count the swings. Count out loud.
    OR
2. Chant the alphabet aloud to each swing of the pendulum.

Activity Four:

(**Note:** If you have a set of rhythm flash cards available that includes simple combinations of notes/rests, these will be adaptable to this activity. It is suggested that the more difficult and extended note/rest patterns be prescribed for this activity when children have attained facility with rhythms at the beginning and intermediate levels of the sequencing.)

1. Get the Rhythm One flash cards.
2. Start the pendulum in motion.
3. Clap each pattern with the swings of the pendulum. Work for a steady TEMPO!

ALGEBRA MUSIC MATHS
(A series of work cards.)

Objectives:

1. To facilitate the computation of note values in $\dfrac{2}{4}$, $\dfrac{3}{4}$, $\dfrac{4}{4}$, $\dfrac{5}{4}$, $\dfrac{3}{8}$, $\dfrac{6}{8}$, $\dfrac{9}{8}$, $\dfrac{12}{8}$, and $\dfrac{2}{2}$.

2. To relate math and music math.

Materials:

5'' x 8'' index cards.

Contents:

One instruction card, 12 "Algebra Music Maths" cards.

Preparation:

Prepare index cards as work cards.

Directions Card:

1. Do cards in a group, in numerical order, 1-4, green, aqua, and purple.

$\dfrac{2}{4}$, $\dfrac{3}{4}$, $\dfrac{4}{4}$, $\dfrac{5}{4}$	Green 1
	Green 2
	Green 3
	Green 4
$\dfrac{3}{8}$, $\dfrac{6}{8}$, $\dfrac{9}{8}$, $\dfrac{12}{8}$	Aqua 1
	Aqua 2
	Aqua 3
	Aqua 4
$\dfrac{2}{2}$	Purple 1
$\dfrac{2}{2}$	Purple 2
	Purple 3
	Purple 4

2. Do all of your work on a separate sheet of paper. When your answers don't match the teacher's, try to find out why. If you can't, bring the teacher the worksheets to work out the problem together.

GREEN 1 (**Note:** Use green marker.)

These are ♩, ♩, ♩, ♪, and ♪ values in $\frac{2}{4}$, $\frac{3}{4}$, $\frac{4}{4}$, $\frac{5}{4}$ time.

Given: x = 4

𝅝 = x   ♪ = 1/8 of x

♩ = 1/2 of x   ♪ = 1/16 of x

♩ = 1/4 of x

(Answers on back.)

GREEN 1 ANSWERS

𝅝 = 4
♩ = 1/2 of 4 = 2
♩ = 1/4 of 4 = 1
♪ = 1/8 of 4 = 1/2
♪ = 1/16 of 4 = 1/4

GREEN 2 (**Note:** Use green marker.)
These are ♩ and ♩. values in $\frac{2}{4}$, $\frac{3}{4}$, $\frac{4}{4}$, $\frac{5}{4}$ time.

Given: x = 2

♩ = x
♩ = x + 1/2 of x

(Answers on back.)

GREEN 2 ANSWERS

♩ = 2
♩. = 2 + 1/2 of 2 = 2 + 1 = 3

GREEN 3 (**Note.** Use green marker.)
These are ♩ and ♩. values in $\frac{2}{4}$, $\frac{3}{4}$, $\frac{4}{4}$, $\frac{5}{4}$ time.

Given: x = 1

♩ = x
♩. = x + 1/2 of x

(Answers on back.)

GREEN 3 ANSWERS

♩ = 1
♩. - 1 + 1/2 of 1 = 1 + 1/2 = 1 1/2

GREEN 4 (**Note:** Use green marker.)
These are ♪ and ♪ values in $\frac{2}{4}, \frac{3}{4}, \frac{4}{4}, \frac{5}{4}$ time.

Given: x = 1/2

♪ = x
♪. = x + 1/2 of x

(Answers on back.)

GREEN 4 ANSWERS

♪ = 1/2
♪. = 1/2 + 1/2 of 1/2 = 1/2 + 1/4 = 2/4 + 1/4 = 3/4

AQUA 1 (**Note:** Use aqua marker.)
These are ○ , ♩ , ♩ , ♪ , and ♪ values in $\frac{3}{8}, \frac{6}{8}, \frac{9}{8}, \frac{12}{8}$ time.

Given: x = 8

○ = x   ♪ = 1/8 of x
♩ = 1/2 of x   ♪ = 1/16 of x
♩ = 1/4 of x

(Answers on back.)

AQUA 1 ANSWERS

○ = 8
♩ = 1/2 of 8 = 4
♩ = 1/4 of 8 = 2
♪ = 1/8 of 8 = 1
♪ = 1/16 of 8 = 1/2

AQUA 2 (**Note:** Use aqua marker.)
These are ♩ and ♩. values in $\frac{3}{8}, \frac{6}{8}, \frac{9}{8}, \frac{12}{8}$ time.

Given: x = 4

♩ = x
♩. = x + 1/2 of x

(Answers on back.)

AQUA 2 ANSWERS

♩ = 4
♩. = 4 + 1/2 of 4 = 4 + 2 = 6

AQUA 3 (**Note:** Use aqua markers.)
These are ♩ and ♩. values in $\frac{3}{8}, \frac{6}{8}, \frac{9}{8}, \frac{12}{8}$ time.

Given x = 2

♩ = x
♩. = x + 1/2 of x

(Answers on back.)

AQUA 3 ANSWERS

♩ = 2
♩. = 2 + 1/2 of 2 = 2 + 1 = 3

AQUA 4 (**Note:** Use aqua marker.)
These are ♪ and ♪. values in $\frac{3}{8}, \frac{6}{8}, \frac{9}{8}, \frac{12}{8}$ time.

Given x = 1

♪ = x
♪. = x + 1/2 of x

(Answers on back.)

AQUA 4 ANSWERS

♪ = 1
♪. = 1 + 1/2 of 1 = 1 + 1/2 = 1 1/2

PURPLE 1 (**Note:** Use purple marker.)
These are ○ , ♩ , ♩ , ♪ , and ♬ values in $\frac{2}{2}$ time.

Given: x = 2

○ = x   ♪ = 1/8 of x
♩ = 1/2 of x   ♬ = 1/16 of x
♩ = 1/4 of x

(Answers on back.)

PURPLE 1 ANSWERS

○ = 2
♩ = 1/2 of 2 = 1
♩ = 1/4 of 2 = 1/2
♪ = 1/8 of 2 = 1/4
♬ = 1/16 of 2 = 1/8

PURPLE 2 (**Note:** Use purple marker.)
These are ♩ and ♩. values in $\frac{2}{2}$ time.

Given x = 1

♩ = x
♩. = x + 1/2 of x

(Answers on back.)

PURPLE 2 ANSWERS

♩ = 1
♩. = 1 + 1/2 of 1 = 1 + 1/2 = 1 1/2

PURPLE 3 (**Note:** Use purple marker.)
These are ♩ and ♩. values in $\frac{2}{2}$ time.

Given: x = 1/2

♩ = x
♩. = x + 1/2 of x

(Answers on back.)

PURPLE 3 ANSWERS

♩ = 1/2
♩. = 1/2 + 1/2 of 1/2 = 1/2 + 1/4 = 2/4 + 1/4 = 3/4

PURPLE 4 (**Note:** Use purple marker.)
These are ♪ and ♪. values in $\frac{2}{2}$ time.

Given: x = 1/4

♪ = x
♪. = x + 1/2 of x

(Answers on back.)

PURPLE 4 ANSWERS

♪ = 1/4
♪. = 1/4 + 1/2 of 1/4 = 1/4 + 1/8 = 2/8 + 1/8 = 3/8

ANTS IN THE PANTS®
(Adaptation of a game by Schaper Manufacturing Company, Inc.)

"Green" Objectives . . . the Rhythm Game:
1. Facility with reading rhythms . . . beginning of rhythm sequence.
2. Remediation for older student who has not achieved this skill.
3. Left to right progression.

"Black" Objectives . . . the Notes/Rests Game:
To reinforce identification of notes/rests.

Materials:
The "Ants in the Pants" Game which consists of a pair of molded plastic pants and 4 sets of ants, 4 in each set. Sets are red, yellow, blue and green. Poster board. Duco Cement.

Preparation:
Cut 16 pieces of poster board, 3/4" x 1-1/4". Fold each one in half lengthwise. Bond cards to the backs of the ants with Duco Cement. Hold firmly to set.

With green pen, draw rhythm patterns on one side of each ant. I chose to adapt this part of the game for beginning levels, so confined rhythms to ♩, ♩, ♫♩𝄾

With black pen, draw notes and rests on the other side of each ant.

Game Directions:
A. Green . . . Rhythms. (2 to 4 Players)
Each player chooses one color set, red, yellow, blue and green. On the word "GO," each player tries to get his "ants" into the "pants" as per the standard game directions. The first player to get all his ants into the pants calls "Stop!" All other players stop shooting.

Now, the winning player must clap the rhythm on each of his "ants." He scores 5 points for every rhythm he claps correctly.

Then, each of the other players claps the rhythm of each of the "ants" they got into the "pants." They score 1 point for each correct rhythm.

Second round, change colors.

Play 4 rounds . . . . once for each color with each player. Player with the highest score at the end of the game is the WINNER.

B. Black . . . Notes and Rests. (2 to 4 Players)
Each player chooses one color set, red, yellow, blue and green. On the word "GO," each player tries to get his "ants" into the "pants." The first player to get all his ants into the pants calls "Stop!" All other players stop shooting.

Now, the winning player must name the notes and rests on each of his "ants." He scores 5 points for every correct answer.

Then, each of the other players must name the notes and rests on each of the "ants" they got into the "pants." They score 1 point for each correct answer.

Second round, change colors.

Play 4 rounds . . . . once for each color with each player.

Player with the highest score at the end of the game is the WINNER.

(Note: May substitute giving note/rest values for identification.)

® Registered trademark of the Schaper Manufacturing Company.

ART AND MUSIC

Objectives:
1. To encourage interest in works of art.
2. To reinforce and extend skills of visual perception.
3. To relate the visual elements of line, color, texture, unity and balance, and repetition and contrast to their aural counterparts.
4. To encourage creativity with an awareness of these elements.

Materials:
Containers for the pictures (suggest using pocket folders), reproductions of works of art which may be purchased or collected from various sources, including art magazines and calendars.

Contents:
The art reproductions arranged and packaged in sets.

Preparation:
Examine each picture and decide upon the category to which it belongs:
1. Line
2. Color
3. Texture
4. Unity and Balance
5. Repetition and Contrast

Prepare each folder as follows, placing the directions on the covers.

A. LINE
Choose one picture you like.
1. How many different kinds of lines do you see in the picture? Draw some of these lines.
2. Musical line is MELODY. Create some melodies on a pitched instrument that will "sound" like each of the lines you saw and drew.
3. Create a dance movement for each of your melody lines.

B. COLOR
Choose one picture you like.
1. Choose an instrument whose sound is like one of the colors you see in the picture. Then do the same thing for each color. Be able to tell *why* you made these choices.
2. How would you make each instrument show a darker shade of its color? a lighter shade?
3. What mood do you get from looking at your picture? How does it make you feel? What kind of music makes you feel the same way?
4. Write a story or a poem about your picture and create background music for it.
5. Create a dance movement about your picture.

C. TEXTURE (**Note:** For this activity, simple ensembles which utilize Orff instruments, recorder, and so on, should be available to students with notated parts.)

Choose one picture you like.

1. How is it an example of texture?
2. How do we create texture in music?
3. Play an ensemble with your friends. This is an example of *musical texture.*
4. Create an ensemble for 2 or more players. Use a Pentatonic scale. You have created a *musical* texture.
5. Listen to J. S. Bach's, "Little Fugue in G minor." How would you describe its texture?

D. UNITY and BALANCE

Choose one picture you like.

1. Go to the dictionary and look up the words *unity* and *balance.* What does each word mean?
2. Look at your picture. How does it show unity?
3. How does it show balance?
4. Create a musical composition that has unity and balance.
5. Create a dance movement that shows unity and balance.

E. REPETITION and CONTRAST

Choose one picture you like.

1. Go to the dictionary and look up the words *repetition* and *contrast.* What does each word mean?
2. How does your picture show repetition?
3. How does your picture show contrast?
4. How does a composer create repetition in music?
5. Make a list of all the ways you can think of in which a composer creates contrast in music.
6. Create a piece of music that shows repetition and contrast.
7. Create a dance movement that shows repetition and contrast.
8. Why is it important to have both repetition and contrast in art, music, and the dance?

BE A . . .

Objectives:
1. To motivate creativity through movement.
2. To communicate through movement.
3. To create music that communicates an idea.

Materials:

5'' x 8'' index cards, a variety of magazines.

Contents:

The picture cards and the task card.

Preparation:

Cut 25 pictures of interesting objects from magazines. Paste the pictures on index cards and laminate.

Prepare side one of the task card as follows:

BE A . . .

Place all the picture cards on the floor so that everyone can see them. The first player chooses one card but doesn't tell anyone which card he has chosen. He leaves it right where it is, on the floor. Then he moves like the object in the picture would move. Everyone tries to guess which picture he has chosen. The first player to guess the correct picture gets to keep the card. Play until there are only 3 cards left. The player with the most cards is the WINNER!

OR

Deal out all picture cards face down. (Everyone should have the same number of cards so leave out any extras.) The first player chooses one of his cards to act out in movement. The other players try to guess the object on his card. If they do, he keeps the card in his own discard pile because he has "communicated." If not, it goes into the discard pile in the center of the playing area. Continue taking turns until all the cards are played. Player with the most cards in his pile is the WINNER!

Prepare side two of the task card as follows:

OR

Each player receives one picture card and has five minutes to make up a chant, a song, or an instrumental piece about his object. Then each player performs his work for the group.

BINGO GAMES

General Objective:

To reinforce identification skills within a specific center of interest or subject area.

Materials:

White or colored poster board.

Contents:

Bingo cards, calling squares, bingo markers.

Preparation:

Prepare as many Bingo cards for each game as you will have players. (May be designated as a small group activity or for a whole class.) The dimensions of each Bingo card are 5'' x 9'' and follow this general form:

B	I	N	G	O
		F R E E		

Within each square on the Bingo card, write in the specific item to be identified as per each game. Cut calling square for every B, I, N, G, and O item. Make Bingo card markers for all players.

BINGO ONE: Identifying Notes and Rests

All B, N, and O squares have drawings of notes and rests. All I and G squares have the names of notes and rests. The calling squares to be used by the Game Leader have the names of notes and rests on the B, N, and O squares and the pictures of notes and rests to be *drawn* on the chalkboard for identification on the I and G squares.

Sample card:

B	I	N	G	O
𝄽	sixteenth note	𝄼	triplet	♪.
♩.	half rest	♪	whole rest	𝅗𝅥
𝅝	set of sixteenth notes	F R E E	quarter note	♪
♫	dotted eighth note	𝅗𝅥.	whole note	𝄾
𝄻	eighth rest	𝄿	half note	♩

Sample calling squares:

B - quarter rest, B - dotted quarter note, B - whole note, B - set of eighth notes, B - half rest.

I - ♪, I - 𝄼, I - ♫♫, I - ♪., I - 𝄿.

N - whole rest, N - eighth note, N - dotted half note, N - sixteenth rest.

G - ⌒3 ♫, G - 𝄼, G - ♩, G - 𝅝, G - 𝅗𝅥.

O - dotted eighth note, O - half note, O - sixteenth note, O - eighth rest, O - quarter note.

BINGO TWO: Terms, Signs, and Symbols

All B, N, and O squares have the term written on them or the sign or symbol drawn. All I and G squares have the function or definition written out. The calling squares to be used by the Game Leader have the function or definitions on the B, N, and O squares and the term written or sign or symbol drawn on the I and G squares. Drawings will be done on chalkboard. (Sample card on following page.)

B	I	N	G	O
tempo	natural	cresc.	music staff	*ff*
‖: :‖	second ending	*pp*	smooth & connected	♩.
1.⌐	walking tempo	F R E E	med. soft	▷
mf	accent	𝄞	return to the sign	Fine
rit.	soft	♯	very loud	♭

Sample calling squares:
B - speed, B - repeat, B - first ending, B - medium loud, B - to get slower little by little.

I - ♮ , I - 2.⌐ , I - andante, I - ▷ , I - *p* .

N - to get louder, little by little, N - very soft, N - G clef or treble clef sign, N - sharp.

G - 𝄞 , G - legato, G - *mp* , G - D.S., G - *ff* .

O - very loud, O - staccato, O - decrescendo, O - the end, O - flat sign.

BINGO THREE: Instruments of the Orchestra

All squares on Bingo cards have names of instruments. Calling squares also have names of instruments whose pictures the Game Leader holds up as he draws each name.   Sample card:

B	I	N	G	O
clari-net	timpani	English horn	viola	tuba
harp	bells	bass	trumpet	cymbal
tri-angle	cello	F R E E	piccolo	French horn
claves	bass-oon	flute	bass drum	oboe
trom-bone	saxo-phone	gong	piano	violin

BINGO FOUR: Rhythm Bingo

BINGO FOUR: Rhythm Bingo

All squares on Bingo cards have rhythm patterns. Calling squares also have the rhythm patterns which the Game Leader claps out as he draws each square.
Sample card:

BINGO FIVE: Letter Names Bingo

All B, N, and O squares have staves on which are drawn note heads. All I and G squares have the letter names of notes. The calling squares to be used by the Game Leader have the letter names of notes on the B, N, and O squares and staves with note heads to be *drawn* on the chalkboard for identification on the I and G squares.

Sample calling squares:

B - low E, B - high C, B - A, B - high F, B - low C.

N - high D, N - low C, N - low F, N - high G.

O - low D, O - high F, O - low G, O - high E, O - B.

103

CHALLENGES

Objectives:
(These will depend upon the purpose for which each set is designed. However, they may be generally stated.)
1. To provide for experiences with identification: instruction and/or reinforcement.
2. To provide for remediation.

Materials:
Construction paper or oak tag, 5" x 8" index cards, adhesive-backed paper.

Contents:
Work/task cards, egg timer, flash cards or picture cards when required.

Preparation:
Challenges may be written on index cards. These work/task cards may be taped to a table upon which are the materials for the challenges and the egg timer. Cover the cards with clear, adhesive-backed paper. You may use a three-sided "invitation" to the challenge which is constructed as follows:

1. Use a sheet of paper or oak tag, 18" x 12". Fold in thirds.

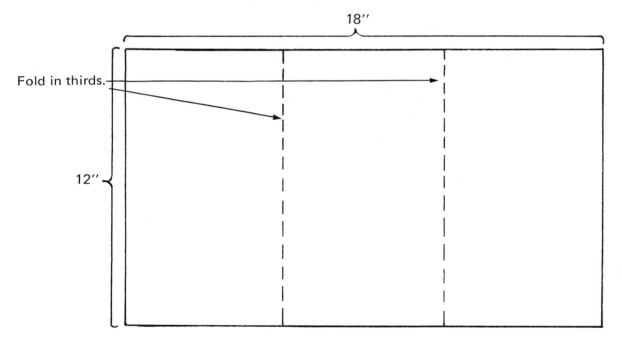

2. On the outside, write on each part as you choose, or as follows:

Tape open side closed with clear tape.
(**Note:** This three-sided sign may be hung and can be adapted for other activities in the room and to designate activity/learning centers.)

Possible challenges:

1. How many different notes and rests can you draw in 3 minutes? Use the egg timer. Keep score.

2. How many different kinds of notes and rests can you name in 3 minutes? Use the egg timer. Keep score.
   (**Note:** Have notes/rests flashcards available.)

3. How many different music signs and symbols can you draw in 3 minutes? Use the egg timer. Keep score.
   Example: *ff*

4. How many instruments of the orchestra can you name in 3 minutes? Use the egg timer. Keep score.
   (**Note:** Have pictures of the orchestra instruments available.)

5. How many 2 beat rhythm patterns can you write in 3 minutes? Use the egg timer. Keep score. Be sure to make each one different.
   Example:

6. How many 3 beat rhythm patterns can you write in 3 minutes? Use the egg timer. Keep score. Be sure to make each one different.
   Example:

7. How many 4 beat rhythm patterns can you draw in 3 minutes? Use the egg timer. Keep score. Be sure to make each one different.
   Example:

8. How many 5 beat rhythm patterns can you write in 3 minutes? Use the egg timer. Keep score. Be sure to make each one different.
   Example:

COMBO-CUBE

Objectives:
1. To reinforce knowledge of note/rest values in 2, 3, 4, 5 meters.
   $$\frac{}{4} \quad \frac{}{4} \quad \frac{}{4} \quad \frac{}{4}$$
2. To provide experiences with building measures in 2, 3, 4, 5 meters.
   $$\frac{}{4} \quad \frac{}{4} \quad \frac{}{4} \quad \frac{}{4}$$
3. To provide extended learning in math (addition).

Materials:
Poster board or heavy cardboard.

Contents:
One number (meter) cube and a set of notes/rests playing cards.

Preparation:
Prepare the cube as in the general directions. Before taping, write on the squares as shown in the following example:

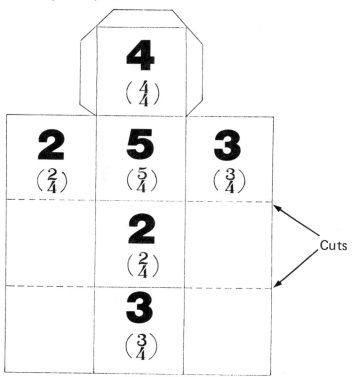

Using a regulation playing card as a pattern, cut out 60 playing cards. Write on each card as follows: Laminate the playing cards.

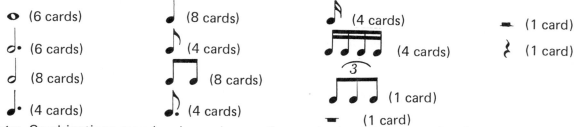

(Note: Combinations may be changed according to the level in sequencing from beginning to full facility with all note/rest values.)

Game Directions: (2, 3, or 4 Players)

Shuffle and deal out 7 cards to each player. Players arrange the cards in a hand. Remaining cards are placed in a pile in the center of the table, face down. Each player rolls the cube. Player who rolls the highest meter (number) will be first.

Player One rolls the cube. He melds the number of cards needed to total this number of beats. He then replaces these cards from the center pile so that he still has 7. If he is unable to meld, he loses his turn.

Play continues in this way until one player has melded all his cards. He is the winner. (In order to go out, the player must be able to meld the exact number of beats of the roll.) If any player melds all his cards on one roll, he is an *instant winner.*

Scoring:

Winner of game receives 25 points.

Instant Winner of game receives 50 points.

Subtract 5 points for each card left in a player's hand at the end of each game.

Add 2 points for each card melded in each game.

Play as many games as time permits.

200 points wins COMBO-CUBE.

CONCENTRATION LETTER MATCH

Objectives:
  1. To provide instruction and reinforcement of letter names (𝄞).
  2. To provide remediation for older students who have not acquired this skill.

Materials:
  Index cards.

Contents:
  The playing cards.

Preparation:
  Make 24 cards the size of regulation playing cards from index cards, to facilitate the drawing of staves. Make 2 cards of each of the following:

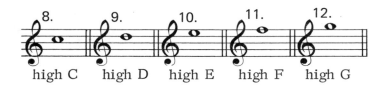

I have included the letter name on each card for purposes of reinforcement and remediation. This is optional.

Laminate each card.

Game Directions: (2 Players)
  Shuffle cards and place face down in rows, 4 rows of 6 cards each. Player One turns up two cards. If they match, he keeps the pair and continues until he can make no more matches. If the two cards do not match, he turns them face down again.
  Player Two continues in the same way. Game is over when all matches have been made. Player with the most cards wins.

CONCENTRATION LETTER NAMES

This game is exactly like Concentration Letter Match, but the pairs are made as follows:

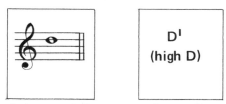

This game is recommended as a reinforcement for students who have attained the skill.

CONCENTRATION NOTES-RESTS MATCH

Objectives, Materials, Contents, Preparation, and Game Directions are the same as for previous Concentration games with the following exceptions:
1. It is specifically designed for instruction and remediation.
2. Make 30 playing cards of white poster board. Make two each of the following:

    A. whole note o
    B. whole rest ▬
    C. half note ♩
    D. half rest ▬
    E. quarter note ♩
    F. quarter rest 𝄽
    G. eighth note ♪
    H. eighth rest 𝄾
    I. sixteenth note ♬
    J. sixteenth rest 𝄿
    K. dotted half note 𝅗𝅥.
    L. dotted quarter note ♩.
    M. dotted eighth note ♪.
    N. set of eighth notes ♫
    O. set of sixteenth notes ♬♬

Matches are made like this:

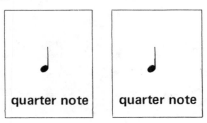

CONCENTRATION NOTES-RESTS NAMES

This game is exactly like Concentration Notes-Rests Match, but the pairs are made as follows:

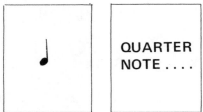

This game is recommended as a reinforcement for students who have attained the skill.

CONCENTRATION

Objectives:
1. To provide reinforcement of 1/2 step concept—sharps.
2. To facilitate matching the natural note with its corresponding sharp.

Materials:
   Index cards.

Contents:
   The playing cards.

Preparation:
   Cut 24 cards from index cards, the size of regulation playing cards. Write on each card as follows:

Laminate all cards.

Game Directions:
   This game is exactly like Concentration Letter Match, but the pairs are made, natural to sharp.

CONCENTRATION ♭

   Objectives, Materials, Contents, Preparation and Game Directions are the same as for Concentration ♯ , with a substitution of flats for sharps.

CONTINENTS

Objectives:
1. To provide experiences with identification, letter names 𝄞
2. To provide Social Studies enrichment.

Materials:
3″ x 5″ lined index cards.

Contents:
Index cards on which have been written the continent names in note heads and letters.

Preparation:
Prepare one card for each continent like the following example.

(Place answer on the back of each card.)

Game Directions:

Challenge yourself or a friend!

How many of the continents can you name and spell correctly in 3 minutes? Use the egg timer.

Try again. Can you beat your own time?

DANCE-A-SHAPE

Objectives:
1. To provide experiences in visual perceptions.
2. To provide experiences in communicating through movement.
3. To motivate body movement activities.

Materials:
4" x 6" cards.

Contents:
A set of cards upon which have been drawn "the shapes."

Some examples:

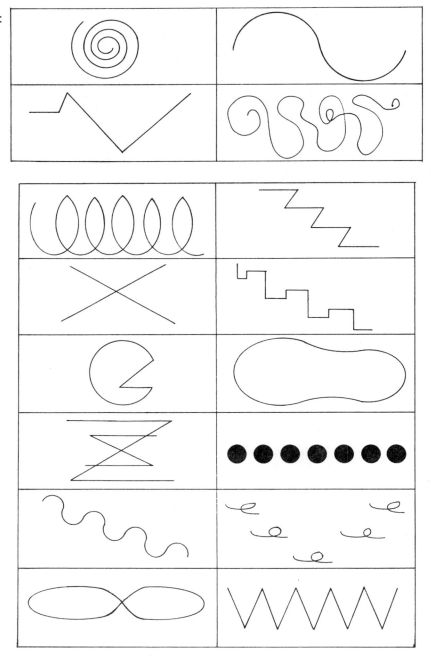

Game Directions: (2, 3, or 4 Players)
1. Place all shape cards, face up, in front of all players.
2. Player One looks at all the cards and chooses one, but he leaves it in place.
3. Player One "dances-the-shape"; he moves like the shape.
4. Each of the other players tries to guess which of the shape cards was being danced.
5. If they guess it, Player One gets 1 point.
6. Play continues in this way until one player gets 10 points.

OR

Play the game in teams; 2 teams, 2 or 3 players on a team. Play the same way, but the teammates of the "dancer" must guess the shape in 60 seconds in order to score.

Again, 10 points wins.

ALSO

Try "dancing-a-shape" with a partner. Can you "dance-a-shape" with two people?

Make up some shapes of your own. Put them on cards for others to use.

DARTS

Objectives:
1. To review and reinforce the overall concepts and skills of music, general and specific.
2. To provide extended learning in math (addition).

Materials:
A conventional Dart Board, covered with Velcro, Velcro darts; poster board; 3'' x 5'' index cards (200); cloth or plastic Mystik tape.

Contents:
Darts and Dart Board, "pockets," and task cards.

Preparation:
Make 10 "pockets" from poster board as follows.

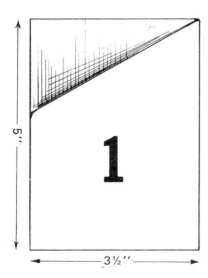

Cut 10 pieces of poster board, 3-1/2'' x 10''. Score at 5'' and fold. Cut diagonal slash in front half. (This will facilitate using the task cards.) Tape closed on sides. Place pocket number on front.

Attach pockets to the Dart Board wall with tape or tack to Dart Board bulletin board.

Prepare index cards as task cards in 10 sets, 20 in each set. Sets should be in categories such as:
1. Kinds of Notes/Rests Identification
2. Letter names ($\begin{smallmatrix}\mathcal{G}\end{smallmatrix}$)
3. Note Values, $\frac{2}{4}$ $\frac{3}{4}$ $\frac{4}{4}$ $\frac{5}{4}$
4. Instruments
5. Composers
6. Reading Rhythms
7. Short Melodies to Sight Sing
8. Chromatics
9. Signs and Symbols
10. Key Signatures

Write the question, task or statement to be answered on the front of each card, and the answer on the back, together with the set number to which the card belongs. This will facilitate the replacement of cards in the proper pockets.

Game Directions: (2 Players)

Player One throws all 3 darts. He adds up his score. Then he takes a game card from the pocket that has his score number. If he can answer his question he gets his score for the round. If not, he gets a zero. Card goes to the bottom of the pocket after it has been used.

Player Two then takes his turn. Play continues until one player gets 50 points. He is the winner. Then, begin a new game.

Examples:

1. Your score is 5 — take a card from the "5" pocket.
2. Your score is 12 — take a card from the "10" pocket and the "2" pocket. If you answer both correctly, you get 12 points. If you get the 2 question correct and the 10 question wrong, you get 2 points. Suppose you get the 10 question correct and the 2 question wrong, how many points would you receive?

DISCOVERING YOUR SPACE . . . THE SPACE AROUND YOU!

Objectives:
1. To provide experiences in self-awareness.
2. To explore space in relationship to one's self.
3. To motivate creative thinking.
4. To provide extended learning in estimating and measuring.

Materials:
5" x 8" index cards.

Contents:
The task cards. Prepare the task cards as follows:

DISCOVERING YOUR SPACE . . . THE SPACE AROUND

YOU!

1. Find a spot YOU like . . . one you would like to call YOURS.

2. Sit right down on the floor, on YOUR spot.

3. Pretend you are GLUED there. Wow! You better find out all you can about this spot, especially if you have to stay there.

4. Stretch your arms as high as you can. Can you feel the space above you?

5. Stretch your arms to each side. Stretch as far as you can in front of you and behind you. Can you feel the space around you?

6. How far can you stretch at floor level?

7. Can you estimate (guess) how much space is yours?

8. Can you estimate (guess) in inches and feet?

9. Now, use a yardstick and try to get an accurate answer.

10. Is there another way to measure the space that is yours?

11. Make a picture (a diagram) that shows you, the space above you and all the space around you.

DOMINOTES

Objectives:
1. To provide experiences with identification of notes, rests, signs and symbols.
2. To reinforce skills of identification.

Materials:
Poster board.

Contents:
The dominotes.

Preparation:
Cut 35 cards, 1" x 2" from poster board. Divide each card in half with a line.

Write on the cards as follows:

1.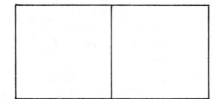
2. quarter rest/eighth rest
3. First ending/Music Staff
4. quarter note/eighth note
5.
6.
7. Music Staff/FREE
8. G-clef sign/repeat
9.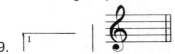
10. eighth note/quarter note
11. sixteenth note/triplet
12. half note/quarter note
13. eighth note/sixteenth note
14.
15.
16. FREE/FREE (Make 2)
17. eighth rest/sixteenth rest
18.
19. sixteenth note/half note

20.
21. triplet/whole rest
22.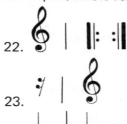
23.
24.
25.
26. repeat sign/First ending
27.
28. whole note/half note
29.
30.
31. whole rest/half rest
32. FREE
33. sixteenth rest/G-clef sign
34. half rest/quarter rest
Laminate all cards.

Game Directions: (2, 3, or 4 Players)

Place all cards face down in box. Each player chooses 3 DOMINOTES cards, sight unseen.

Player One puts one DOMINOTE card in center of play area, face up. Then he chooses another DOMINOTE to replace the one he played.

Player Two must build on the card that Player One put down. If he can, he replaces his DOMINOTE. If not, he loses his turn.

(Note: If a player cannot build 2 turns in a row, he may replace one of his DOMI-NOTE cards and then play if he can.

Play continues in this way until all DOMINOTES have been played or no one can go. Player with fewest cards left is the winner.

Special Instructions:

1. You may use free boxes anywhere.
2. You may build in any direction, symbol to definition, definition to symbol.
3. You may not build symbol to symbol, or definition to definition.

Examples of possible plays:

DOTS AND TIES

Objectives:

1. To provide experiences with visual perception of notes, with and without dots.

2. To provide experiences with identifying kinds of dotted notes and relating corresponding rhythm sounds.

3. To relate and equate "ties" and "dots."

4. To learn the rule for dotted note rhythms.

5. To provide experiences with reading, writing, and performing dotted rhythms.

6. To provide experiences with polyrhythms.

7. To review standard song repertoire.

8. To provide extended learning in math (addition of fractions).

9. To provide experiences with measure completion in different meters.

10. To provide experiences with reading, writing, and performing in compound time.

Materials:

5" x 8" index cards.

Contents:

Activities set on work cards dealing with dots and ties, working from the simple to the more complex, levels one through seven.

(**Note:** These activities may be part of a working bulletin board, the teacher prescribing those sets for which the individual students are ready. Each set is placed in a poster board envelope.)

Preparation:

Prepare each card as per specific examples:

Level 1:

How many dotted quarter notes can you find in this picture?
What else do you see?

Answers: 𝅘𝅥𝅭 — ‖   Also... 1 quarter rest... 𝄽   1 half note... 𝅗𝅥

1 set sixteenth notes... 𝅘𝅥𝅯𝅘𝅥𝅯𝅘𝅥𝅯𝅘𝅥𝅯

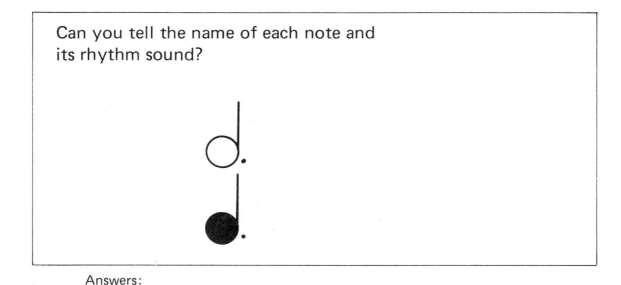

Can you tell the name of each note and
its rhythm sound?

Answers:

𝅗𝅥. Dotted half note ... ta-a-a   𝅘𝅥𝅭 Dotted quarter ... ta-i

How many dotted half notes can you find in this picture?
What else do you see?

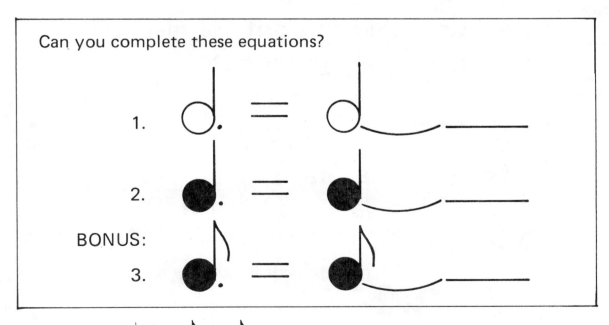

Answers: ♩. 12 Also . . . 1 whole rest . . . ▬
1 half rest . . . ▬

Can you complete these equations?

1. 𝅗𝅥. = 𝅗𝅥 ⌣ _____

2. ♩. = ♩ ⌣ _____

BONUS:

3. ♪. = ♪ ⌣ _____

Answers: 1 ♩ 2 ♪ 3 ♬

121

What are the missing words? _____

Whenever a _____ follows a note,

it sounds the same as if that _____

were _____ to a note of just _____

its value.

Answers on back.

Answers:
dot
tied
half

Level 2:

Cut on black lines for a jigsaw puzzle.

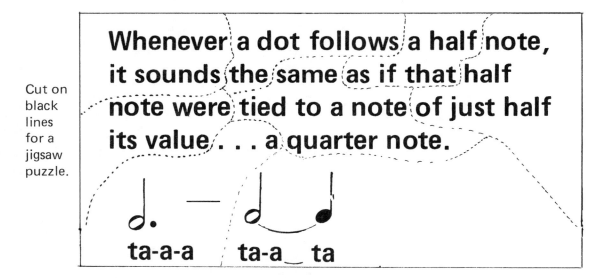

Whenever a dot follows a half note, it sounds the same as if that half note were tied to a note of just half its value . . . a quarter note.

ta-a-a   ta-a_ ta

Place in an envelope with these directions:
Put the "rule" puzzle together. Try to remember it. Can you apply it to your music reading and writing?

A Music Menu. Each "item" on the menu includes a dotted half note (𝅗𝅥.). Say each item. Then clap and say it. Write it in music notes on a piece of scrap paper. Check answers on back.

Example: Strawberry pie.   3/4 ♩ ♩ ♩ | 𝅗𝅥. ‖

1. Jelly roll and TUMS.   3/4 | ‖

2. Cornbread and fish.   3/4 | ‖

3. Hot hamburgers.   3/4 | ‖

4. Pizza pie and milk.   3/4 | ‖

5. Catsup and bread.   3/4 | ‖

Answers:

3/4 ♫ ♩ ♩ | 𝅗𝅥. ‖
Jel - ly roll   and   tums.

3/4 ♩ ♩ ♩ | 𝅗𝅥. ‖
Corn   bread   and   fish.

3/4 𝅗𝅥. | ♩ ♩ ♩ ‖
Hot   ham - bur - gers.

3/4 ♫ ♩ ♩ | 𝅗𝅥. ‖
Piz - za pie   and   milk.

3/4 ♩ ♩ ♩ | 𝅗𝅥. ‖
Cat - sup   and   bread.

Read in rhythm sounds and clap each pattern.

Now try each one on an instrument.

(See back.)

Answers:

Fun with a Partner

(2)

Say It with a Dot

(2)

Say and clap each pattern as it is written. Then say it again with a dot (dotted half note 𝅗𝅥.). (See back for answers.) Can you write out each dotted example?

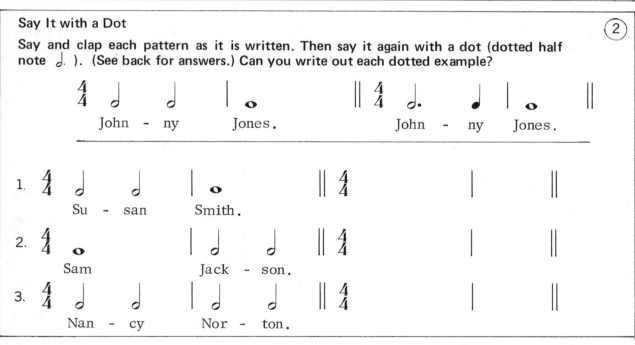

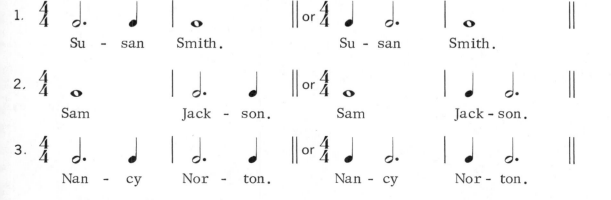

Level 3:

③

Cut on black lines for jigsaw puzzle.

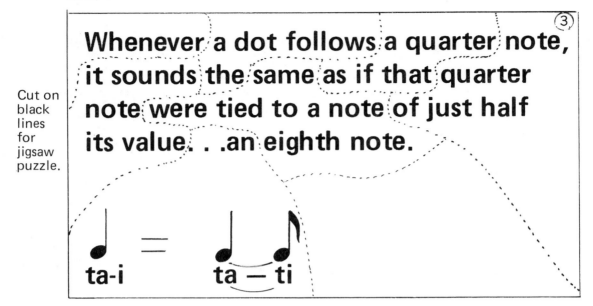

Whenever a dot follows a quarter note, it sounds the same as if that quarter note were tied to a note of just half its value. . .an eighth note.

♩. = ♩ ♪
ta-i   ta — ti

Place in an envelope with these directions:

Put the "rule" puzzle together. Try to remember it. Can you apply it to your music reading and writing?

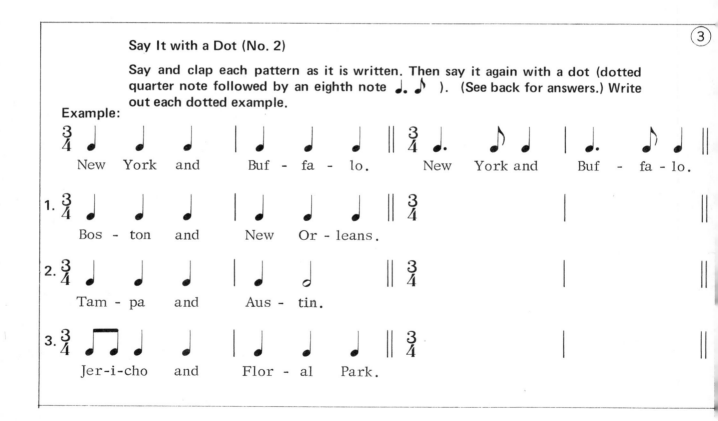

③

Say It with a Dot (No. 2)

Say and clap each pattern as it is written. Then say it again with a dot (dotted quarter note followed by an eighth note ♩. ♪). (See back for answers.) Write out each dotted example.

Example:

New York and Buf - fa - lo.   New York and Buf - fa - lo.

1. Bos - ton and New Or - leans.

2. Tam - pa and Aus - tin.

3. Jer-i-cho and Flor - al Park.

Answers:

1. 3/4 𝅘𝅥𝅭 𝅘𝅥𝅮 𝅘𝅥 | 𝅘𝅥𝅭 𝅘𝅥𝅮 𝅘𝅥 ‖
Bos - ton and   New   Or- leans.

2. 3/4 𝅘𝅥𝅭 𝅘𝅥𝅮 𝅘𝅥 | 𝅘𝅥 𝅗𝅥 ‖
Tam - pa and   Aus - tin.

3. 3/4 𝅘𝅥𝅮𝅘𝅥𝅮 𝅘𝅥 𝅘𝅥 | 𝅘𝅥𝅭 𝅘𝅥𝅮 𝅘𝅥 ‖
Jer -i- cho and   Flor - al Park.

Say It with a Dot (No. 1)   ③

Say and clap each pattern as it is written. Then say it again with a dot (dotted quarter note followed by an eighth note 𝅘𝅥𝅭 𝅘𝅥𝅮). (See back for answers.) Write each dotted example.

Example:

4/4 𝅘𝅥 𝅘𝅥 𝅘𝅥 𝅘𝅥 | 𝅘𝅥 𝅘𝅥 𝅘𝅥 𝅘𝅥 ‖ 4/4 𝅘𝅥𝅭 𝅘𝅥𝅮 𝅘𝅥𝅭 𝅘𝅥𝅮 | 𝅘𝅥𝅭 𝅘𝅥𝅮 𝅘𝅥𝅭 𝅘𝅥𝅮 ‖
Pe - ter, Pe - ter,   pump- kin eat - er.   Pe - ter, Pe - ter, pump- kin eat - er.

4/4 𝅘𝅥 𝅘𝅥 𝅘𝅥 𝅘𝅥 | 𝅘𝅥 𝅘𝅥 𝅘𝅥 𝅘𝅥 ‖ 4/4 | ‖
Al - ly, Al - ly,   Al - ly - ga - tor.

4/4 𝅘𝅥 𝅘𝅥 𝅘𝅥 𝅘𝅥 | 𝅘𝅥 𝅘𝅥 𝅗𝅥 ‖ 4/4 | ‖
Croc - y, Croc - y,   Croc - y - dile.

4/4 𝅘𝅥 𝅘𝅥 𝅘𝅥 𝅘𝅥 | 𝅘𝅥 𝅘𝅥 𝅘𝅥 𝅘𝅥 ‖ 4/4 | ‖
Min - nie Muf - fet   on   a   tuf - fet.

Answers:

1. 4/4 𝅘𝅥𝅭 𝅘𝅥𝅮 𝅘𝅥𝅭 𝅘𝅥𝅮 | 𝅘𝅥𝅭 𝅘𝅥𝅮 𝅘𝅥𝅭 𝅘𝅥𝅮 ‖
Al - ly, Al - ly,   Al - ly - ga - tor.

2. 4/4 𝅘𝅥𝅭 𝅘𝅥𝅮 𝅘𝅥𝅭 𝅘𝅥𝅮 | 𝅘𝅥𝅭 𝅘𝅥𝅮 𝅗𝅥 ‖
Croc - y, Croc - y,   Croc - y-dile.

3. 4/4 𝅘𝅥𝅭 𝅘𝅥𝅮 𝅘𝅥𝅭 𝅘𝅥𝅮 | 𝅘𝅥𝅭 𝅘𝅥𝅮 𝅘𝅥𝅭 𝅘𝅥𝅮 ‖
Min - nie Muf - fet   on   a   tuf - fet.

Fun with a Partner ③

Rewrite each pattern replacing ♩. with ♩♪ and each ♩♪ with a ♩. . Do this on a piece of paper. Check answers on back. Then clap and/or play each one on a nonpitched instrument.

Answers:

Level 4:

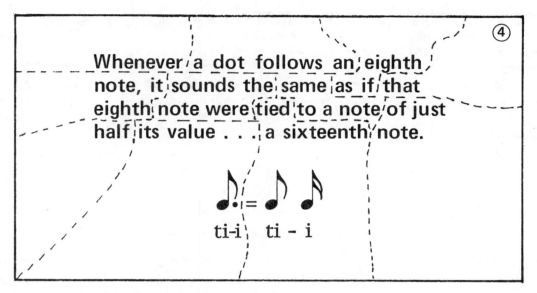

④

Whenever a dot follows an eighth note, it sounds the same as if that eighth note were tied to a note of just half its value . . . a sixteenth note.

ti-i   ti - i

Place the puzzle in an envelope with the following directions:

Put the "rule" puzzle together. Try to remember it. Can you apply it to your music reading and writing?

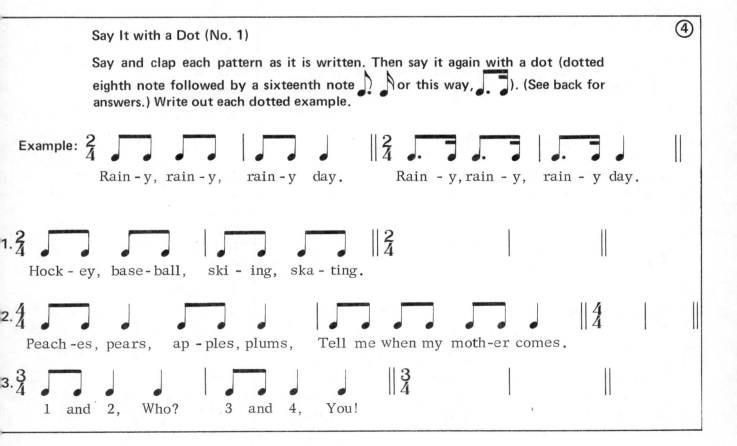

Say It with a Dot (No. 1)   ④

Say and clap each pattern as it is written. Then say it again with a dot (dotted eighth note followed by a sixteenth note ♪. ♪ or this way, ♩. ♪). (See back for answers.) Write out each dotted example.

Example: 2/4

Rain - y, rain - y, rain - y day.   Rain - y, rain - y, rain - y day.

1. 2/4

Hock - ey, base - ball, ski - ing, ska - ting.

2. 4/4

Peach - es, pears, ap - ples, plums, Tell me when my moth - er comes.

3. 3/4

1 and 2, Who? 3 and 4, You!

Answers:

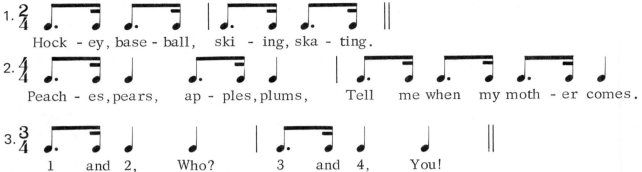

1. Hock - ey, base - ball, ski - ing, ska - ting.

2. Peach - es, pears, ap - ples, plums, Tell me when my moth - er comes.

3. 1 and 2, Who? 3 and 4, You!

Read in rhythm sounds and clap each pattern.

Answers:

ti-i - di ti-i - di ta rest ta-a ta-a ta ti-i - di, ti-i - di ta ta ti - ti ta ta

ta ti-i - di ta ti-ti ti-ti ta ta ti-i - di ta ta ti-ti ta

ta ti-i-di ta ta ta ta-a ta ti-i-di ta ta ti-i-di ti-i-di ta ta ta rest ta ti-ti

ta ti-i-di ta ta ti-i-di ti-i-di ti-i-di ta ta ti-i-di ti-i-di ta ta ta ta ta

130

Fun with a Partner ④

Rewrite each pattern, replacing ♪· with ♪ ♪ and each ♪ ♪ with a ♪· . Write on a sheet of paper. Then clap and/or play each one on an instrument. Check answers on back. ④

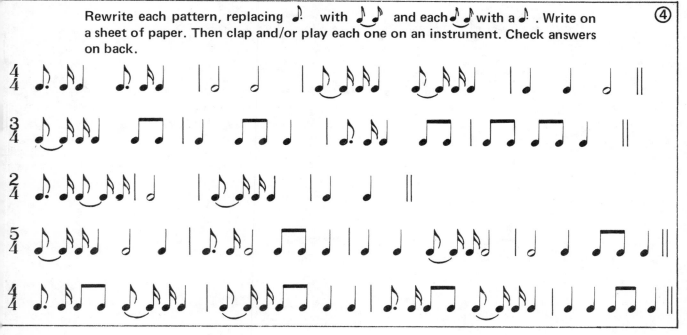

Answers:

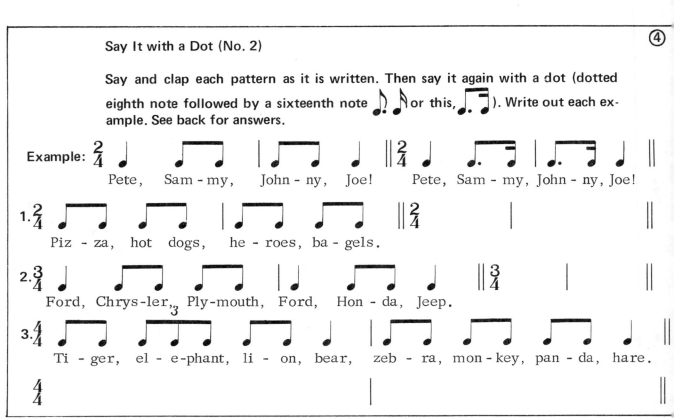

Say It with a Dot (No. 2) ④

Say and clap each pattern as it is written. Then say it again with a dot (dotted eighth note followed by a sixteenth note ♪. ♪ or this, ♪. ♪). Write out each example. See back for answers.

Example: Pete, Sam - my, John - ny, Joe!   Pete, Sam - my, John - ny, Joe!

1. Piz - za, hot dogs, he - roes, ba - gels.

2. Ford, Chrys - ler, Ply - mouth, Ford, Hon - da, Jeep.

3. Ti - ger, el - e-phant, li - on, bear, zeb - ra, mon - key, pan - da, hare.

Answers:

1. Piz - za, hot dogs, he - roes, ba - gels.

2. Ford, Chrys - ler, Ply - mouth, Ford, Hon - da, Jeep.

3. Ti - ger, el - e-phant, li - on, bear, ze - bra, mon - key, pan - da, hare!

Level 5:

⑤

The Case of the Missing Dot!

There is a dot missing in each measure. Copy each example, add the dot where it belongs, and clap each pattern. (Check answers on back.)

Answers:

Answers:

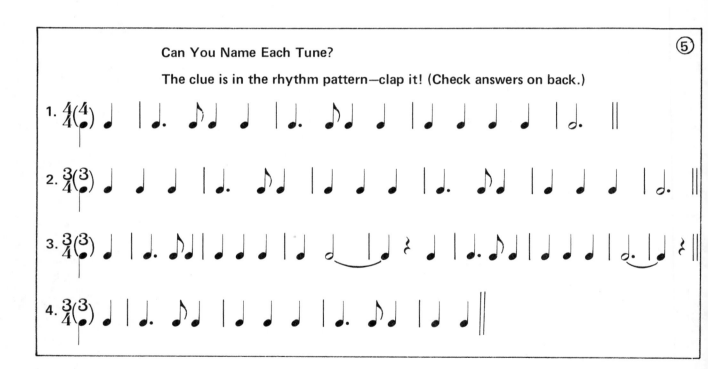

Answers:

1. "America, the Beautiful"
2. "America"
3. "My Bonnie"
4. "We Gather Together" ("Harvest Hymn")

Read in rhythm sounds and clap each pattern. ⑤

Answers:

Fun with a Partner ⑤

Level 6:

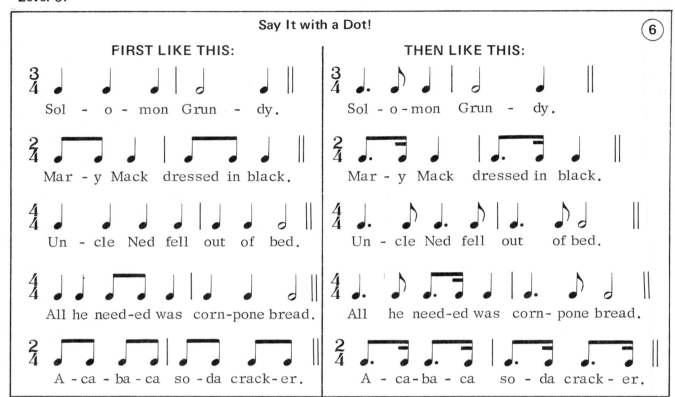

Say It with a Dot! ⑥

FIRST LIKE THIS:

Sol - o - mon Grun - dy.

Mar - y Mack dressed in black.

Un - cle Ned fell out of bed.

All he need-ed was corn-pone bread.

A - ca - ba - ca so - da crack-er.

THEN LIKE THIS:

Sol - o - mon Grun - dy.

Mar - y Mack dressed in black.

Un - cle Ned fell out of bed.

All he need-ed was corn- pone bread.

A - ca - ba - ca so - da crack- er.

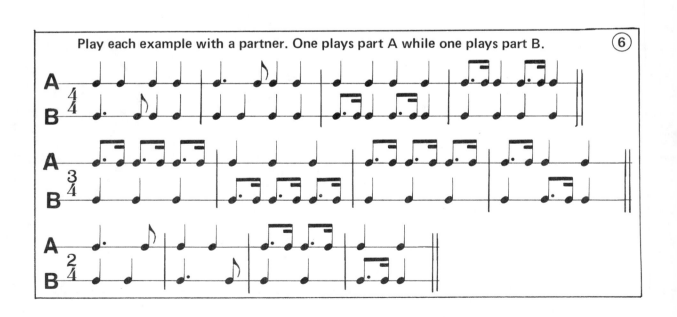

Play each example with a partner. One plays part A while one plays part B. ⑥

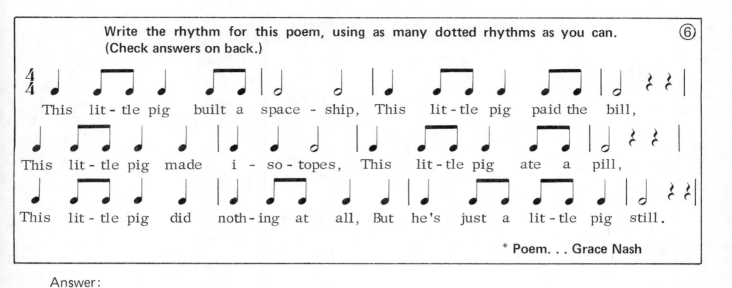

Write the rhythm for this poem, using as many dotted rhythms as you can. (Check answers on back.) **6**

This lit - tle pig built a space - ship, This lit - tle pig paid the bill,

This lit - tle pig made i - so - topes, This lit - tle pig ate a pill,

This lit - tle pig did noth - ing at all, But he's just a lit - tle pig still.

* Poem. . . Grace Nash

Answer:

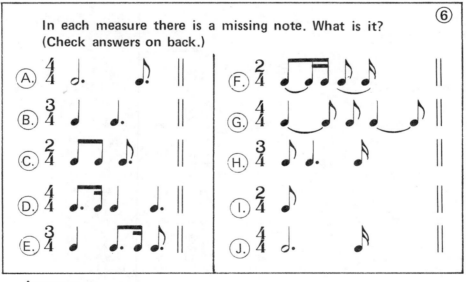

In each measure there is a missing note. What is it? (Check answers on back.) **6**

A.
B.
C.
D.
E.
F.
G.
H.
I.
J.

Answers:

A. B. C. D. E. F. G.

H. I. J.

*by special permission; "The Five Little Pigs", from Series III, "Music With Children" by Grace C. Nash, Nash Publications. Verse from "Space Child's Mother Goose" by Winsor & Parry, copyright 1958. Simon & Schuster, Publisher.

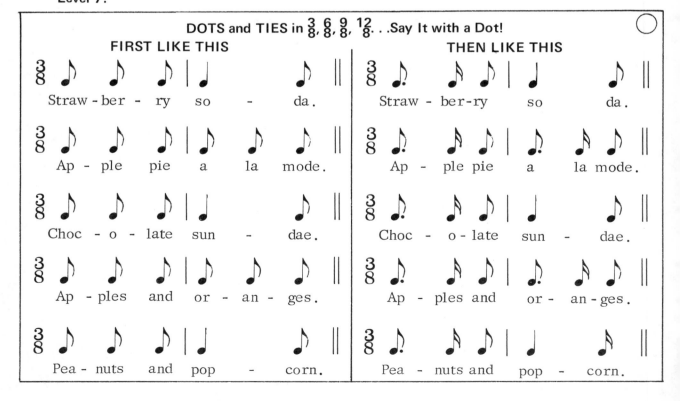

Write these "maths" in music notes. (Check answers on back.) ⑥

4/4   3/4 + 1/4 + 1 + 1 1/2 + 1/2

2/4   1 + 1 1/2 + 1/2

3/4   1/2 + 1/2 + 3/4 + 1/4

4/4   3 + 3/4 + 1/4

3/4   3/4 + 1/4 + 1 1/2 + 1/2

Answers:

Ⓐ 4/4 $\frac{3}{4} + \frac{1}{4} + 1 + 1\frac{1}{2} + \frac{1}{2}$ = 4

Ⓓ 4/4 $3 + \frac{3}{4} + \frac{1}{4}$ = 4

Ⓑ 3/4 $1 + 1\frac{1}{2} + \frac{1}{2}$ = 3

Ⓔ 3/4 $\frac{3}{4} + \frac{1}{4} + 1\frac{1}{2} + \frac{1}{2}$ = 3

Ⓒ 2/4 $\frac{1}{2} + \frac{1}{2} + \frac{3}{4} + \frac{1}{4}$ = 2

Level 7:

DOTS and TIES in 3/8, 6/8, 9/8, 12/8 . . . Say It with a Dot!

FIRST LIKE THIS   **THEN LIKE THIS**

3/8   Straw - ber - ry so - da.   3/8   Straw - ber-ry so da.

3/8   Ap - ple pie a la mode.   3/8   Ap - ple pie a la mode.

3/8   Choc - o - late sun - dae.   3/8   Choc - o - late sun - dae.

3/8   Ap - ples and or - an - ges.   3/8   Ap - ples and or - an - ges.

3/8   Pea - nuts and pop - corn.   3/8   Pea - nuts and pop - corn.

Dots and Ties in $\frac{3}{8}$, $\frac{6}{8}$, $\frac{9}{8}$, $\frac{12}{8}$

This card is for practice. Clap and say each measure.

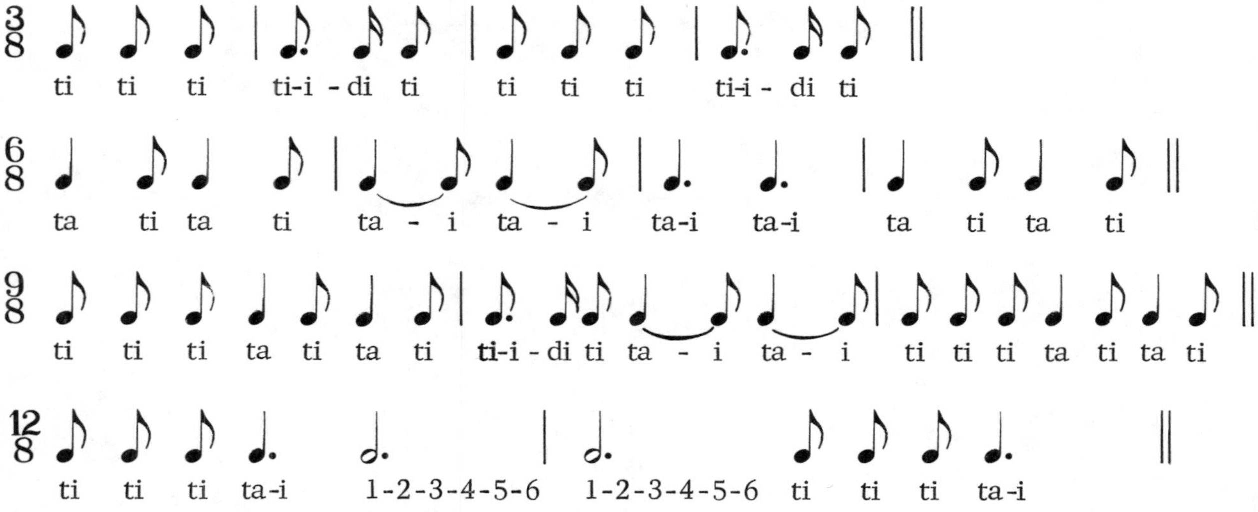

Write these "maths" in music notes. (Check answers on back.) ⑦

Ⓐ $\frac{3}{8}$ 1 + 1 1/2 + 1/2

Ⓑ $\frac{6}{8}$ 3 + 3

Ⓒ $\frac{9}{8}$ 1 + 1 + 1 + 6

Ⓓ $\frac{12}{8}$ 3 + 6 + 3

Ⓔ $\frac{6}{8}$ 1 1/2 + 1/2 + 1 + 3

Answers:

Ⓐ $\frac{3}{8}$ ♪ ♪. ♪ = 3
  1 + 1½ + ½

Ⓑ $\frac{6}{8}$ ♩. ♩. = 6
  3 + 3

Ⓒ $\frac{9}{8}$ ♪ ♪ ♪ ♩. = 9
  1 + 1 + 1 + 6

Ⓓ $\frac{12}{8}$ ♩. ♩. ♩. = 12
  3 + 6 + 3

Ⓔ $\frac{6}{8}$ ♪. ♪ ♪ ♩. = 6
  1½ + ½ + 1 + 3

139

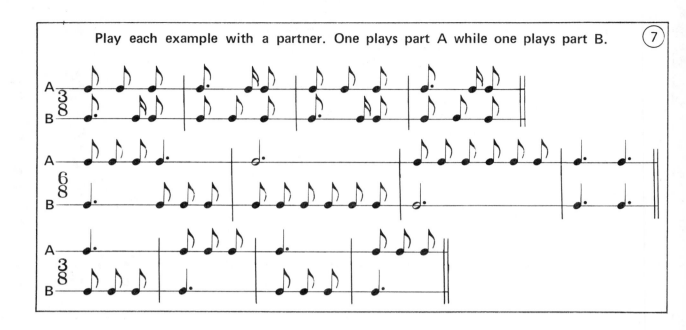

Play each example with a partner. One plays part A while one plays part B.

⑦

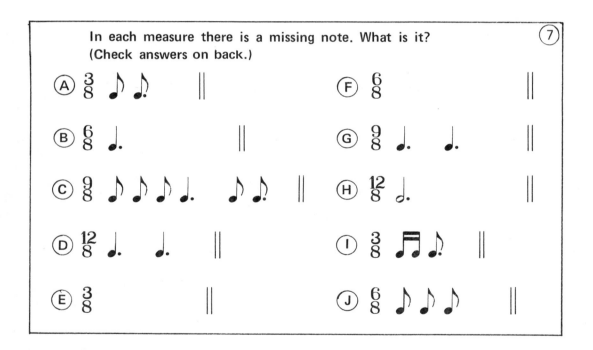

In each measure there is a missing note. What is it?
(Check answers on back.)

⑦

Ⓐ $\frac{3}{8}$ ♪ ♪. ‖

Ⓑ $\frac{6}{8}$ ♩. ‖

Ⓒ $\frac{9}{8}$ ♪ ♪ ♪ ♩. ♪ ♪ ‖

Ⓓ $\frac{12}{8}$ ♩. ♩. ‖

Ⓔ $\frac{3}{8}$ ‖

Ⓕ $\frac{6}{8}$ ‖

Ⓖ $\frac{9}{8}$ ♩. ♩. ‖

Ⓗ $\frac{12}{8}$ ♩. ‖

Ⓘ $\frac{3}{8}$ ♫ ♪. ‖

Ⓙ $\frac{6}{8}$ ♪ ♪ ♪ ‖

Answers:

Ⓐ ♪ Ⓑ ♩. Ⓒ ♪ Ⓓ ♩. Ⓔ ♩. Ⓕ ♩. Ⓖ ♩.

Ⓗ ♩. Ⓘ ♪ Ⓙ ♩.

140

EVEN STEVEN—AN EQUAL VALUES GAME

Objective:
To reinforce concept of equal values to the whole note.

Materials:
White poster board or index cards.

Contents:
The playing cards.

Preparation:
Cut 52 cards, the size of regulation playing cards. On the back of each one write the game name, "Even Steven." Prepare the faces as follows:

𝅝 - ten cards

𝅗𝅥 - ten cards

♩ - ten cards

♫ - ten cards

♬ - ten cards

JOKER - two cards

Game Directions: (2, 3 or 4 Players)

Shuffle the cards and deal out 7 cards to each player. Place remaining cards in the center of the table, FACE DOWN. Turn up the TOP card and place it next to the pile. All Players arrange their 7 cards in a hand. Then they MELD (put down in front of them) all whole note cards and *like* combinations of note cards which equal the value of the whole note. For example: 𝅗𝅥 𝅗𝅥 or ♩ ♩ ♩ ♩ or ♫ ♫ ♫ ♫

 The JOKER may be used as 𝅝, 𝅗𝅥, ♩, ♩ or ♬

Player One then picks up the TOP card of the FACE DOWN pile or the card which has been turned FACE UP. He then melds, if he can and discards one card, placing it face UP next to the pile in the center of the table.

Each player continues in this way until one player has melded all his cards.

WINNING a ROUND: The player who melds all his cards first wins the round and scores 1 "WIN POINT." Because he is going out, he may or may not discard, as he chooses.

A BLITZ: If a player melds ALL his cards WITHOUT a DISCARD before play has begun, he "Blitzes" and scores 5 "Win Points." This ends the round and a new hand is dealt.

WINNING the GAME: Play as many rounds as time allows. The Player with the most "WIN POINTS" at the end of the time period wins "Even Steven."

Note: When picking up the FACE UP card, the player must pick up every card in the FACE UP pile!

FEELINGS

Objectives:
1. To motivate creativity through movement.
2. To express feelings through music and movement.
3. To listen to music that expresses a mood.
4. To create music that expresses a mood.
5. To provide extended learning in language arts (vocabulary).

Materials:
5'' x 8'' index cards, a variety of magazines.

Contents:
The picture cards and the task card.

Preparation:
Cut 25 pictures that show a variety of emotions from magazines. Paste the pictures on index cards and laminate.
Prepare the task card as follows:

FEELINGS

Choose a picture that you like. How does the picture make you feel? Think of some words that tell how you feel. Write the words on a piece of paper and show them to the teacher.

Write a poem about the picture. Create a melody for your poem. Sing it for the teacher.

Find a recording that "sounds" your feelings.

Create dance movements to show your feelings.

"FILL-IT-IN" GAMES . . . NATIONAL SONGS
"America"
"America, the Beautiful"
"The Star-Spangled Banner"

Objectives:
1. To build and reinforce the song repertoire.
2. To reinforce phrase concepts.
3. To provide Social Studies enrichment.
4. To provide language arts experiences (phrasing and punctuation).

Materials:
3" x 5" lined index cards.

Contents:
A set of cards for each song on which one word phrase from the song has been written, with one word left out.

Preparation:
On each card write one phrase from the song being prepared, leaving out one significant word. On the back of each card, write the song title and the missing word.

Example:

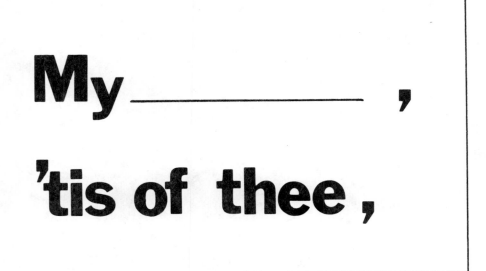

Note: The same phrase may be included more than once leaving out a different word.

Game Directions:
(Same game directions for each song set.)

Game One (2 Players)
Deal cards, face up. Each player arranges his pile, face up, in front of him.

Player One tells the word that is missing on his top card. If correct, he discards it to center discard pile. If not, he places it on bottom of his own pile, face up.

Play continues in this way until one player has no more cards. He is the winner. **(Note:** Depending on the number of cards in each game, the deal should be equal. Leave out the unequal amount.)

Game Two (2, 3, or 4 Players)
Shuffle all cards; place in pile in center of table, face up.

Player One takes the top card. He tells the missing word. If correct, he keeps the card. If not, he puts it on the bottom of the pile, face up.

Play continues in this way until all cards are played. Player with the most cards wins.

Game Three (Alone or 2 Players)
Challenge yourself or a friend. How quickly can you call out all the missing words? Time yourself. You may use the kitchen timer.

Game Four "The Super Game" (2 to 6 Players)
Put together the "Fill-It-In" cards from "America," "America, the Beautiful," and "The Star-Spangled Banner." Shuffle them. Place all cards face up in the center of the table. Play as in Game No. Two, but each player must name the song *and* tell the missing word.

(Note: *Please* replace cards in separate decks according to song titles when you have finished playing.)

FISHING GAMES

Objectives:
(A different game should be devised for each objective.)
1. To provide experiences with identification.
    a. Letter names, 𝄞, and/or 𝄢 .
    b. Kinds of notes and rests.
    c. Signs and symbols.
    d. Terms.
    e. Key signatures.
    f. Spelling words with note heads
2. To provide experiences with sight reading.
    a. Short melodies to be sung and/or played.
    b. Short rhythms to be clapped or performed on a non-pitched instrument.

Materials:

Small cardboard carton, string, pointer, horseshoe magnet, colored poster board, paper fasteners.

Contents:

A fishpond, fishing pole, sets of different colored fish for each game.

Preparation:

The fishpond is made from the small cardboard carton. Shape the top to resemble waves. Paint the carton blue or cover with bright blue adhesive-backed paper.

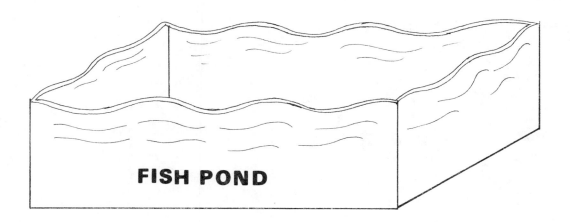

FISH POND

The fishing pole is made from a pointer. Cut a length of string and tie one end to the eye on end of pointer. (Add a screw eye to end of pointer if it does not have one.) Attach the horseshoe magnet to the other end of the string.

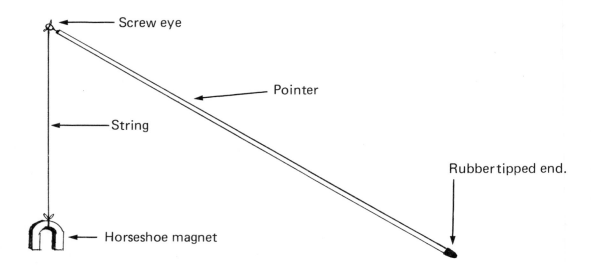

Make fish from colored poster board, approximately 5″ long, 2-1/2″ wide. You will need one fish for each task in each game. The task is written on the body of the fish. It is then laminated and magnetized with a paper fastener or a paper clip.

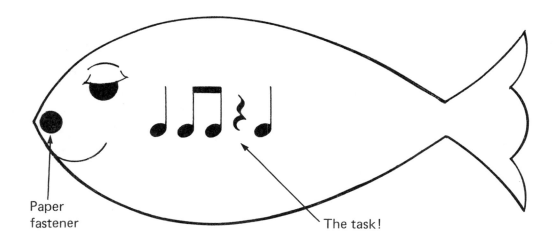

Game Directions: (2, 3, or 4 Players)

Player One "fishes" and must perform the task, be it identifying or sight reading. If correct, he keeps the fish. If not, the fish goes back into the pond to be caught again. Game continues in this way until all the fish are caught. Player with the largest catch wins.

FUN WITH MOVEMENT

Objectives:
1. To provide opportunities for creativity through movement.
2. To create awareness of spatial relationships.
3. To foster awareness of self in relation to others.
4. To provide extended learning in math (estimating, graphing and ratio).

Materials:

5'' x 8'' index cards.

Contents:

Task cards, each one stating a "Fun With Movement" problem.

Preparation:

Write one problem on each index card. It is suggested that an appropriate illustration or design be drawn on each card to motivate the students.

The Problems:
1. Stand in front of the room. Using *big* steps, walk to the back of the room. How many big steps did you take? Try again using *little* steps. How many little steps did you take? (Can you write the ratio of big steps to little steps?)
2. Stand at the door. Using *big* steps, walk to the other side of the room. How many big steps did you take? Try again using *little* steps. How many little steps did you take? (Can you write the ratio of big steps to little steps?)
3. Think of things that bend and stretch! How many different "bendable-stretchables" can you be?
4. Be a rag doll. How many different ways can you flop?
5. Be a jumping bean. How far can you jump until you have no jumps left? How high can you jump?
6. Gallop! Make your hands, head, shoulders, and arms a part of the gallop.
7. How many different ways can you move while you are sitting?
8. How high can you skip? Keep trying. What's your highest level? Can you make a drawing or a graph showing your different skipping levels?
9. How would you move if you were in a tiny box? a big box?
10. Move on all three levels; high, middle, and low. Keep changing. Can you move on two levels at the same time? three?
11. Put yourself into a little box. Pretend the box is growing taller and taller, until it is a box filled with giant sunflowers.
12. Put yourself into a tall, skinny box. Now, break out! How many different ways can you do it?
13. How heavy can you make yourself? Think of the heaviest thing in the world. Can you be that heavy? Now be the opposite — the lightest thing you can imagine. How did you feel when you were heavy? How did "light" make you feel?

General Directions
1. You can work by yourself or you can work with a partner.
2. Pick a problem and try to solve it.
3. Write it up! (Write a few sentences about your problem and how you solved it. Perhaps you can draw a picture about it.)
4. Try another one.
5. Can you set the problem to an accompaniment?

GAME OF HISTORICAL EVENTS

Objectives:
1. To provide experiences with identification, letter names, (𝄞)
2. To reinforce note values, concept: $\frac{2}{4}$, $\frac{3}{4}$, $\frac{4}{4}$, $\frac{5}{4}$
3. To provide Social Studies enrichment.
4. To provide extended learning in math (addition).

Materials:
3'' x 5'' lined index cards.

Contents:
Index cards on which the year and date of important historical events have been written in notes and rests in combination and the month and missing word from the event have been written out in note heads and letters.

Preparation:
Prepare one card for each event like the following example.

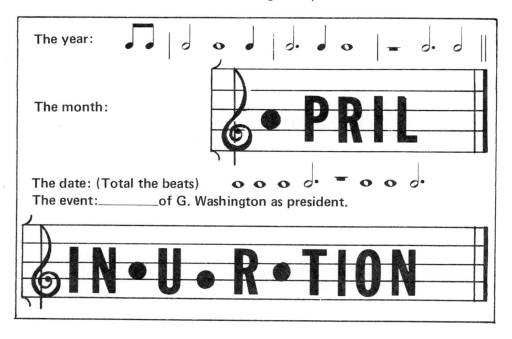

(Place answers on the back of each card.)

Game Directions:

Game One (Alone or 2 Players)

Challenge yourself or a friend. How long does it take for you to "decode" a history card? Keep a record of your own time or, if 2 people are playing, the one who is first to "decode" the playing card keeps it. Player with most cards at the end of the game is the winner. (See the back of each card for the answers.)

Game Two (2, 3, or 4 Players)

Deal out all cards, face up. (Each player should have an equal number of cards. Leave out any extras.) Each player places his cards in a pile in front of him as they are dealt, face up.

Player One "decodes" each problem on his top card. If he is correct, he discards the card to the pile in the center of the table. If not, he puts the card on the bottom of his pile.

Play continues in this way until one player has no more cards. He is the winner.

Game Three (2, 3, or 4 Players)

Shuffle all cards and place in a pile, face up, in the center of the table.

Player One takes the top card. He receives 1 point for each problem correctly solved. (See back of each card for answers.)

Play continues in this way until all cards have been played. The player with the highest score wins.

THE GAME OF OPPOSITES

Objectives:

1. To motivate creativity through movement.
2. To integrate language arts (antonyms), and body movement.
3. To bring about increased awareness of self.

Materials:

Eighteen 3'' x 5'' index cards.

Contents:

The antonym cards.

Preparation:

Divide each index card in half. Use red marker to write on left side, black marker to write on right side.

RED	BLACK	RED	BLACK
1. BLACK	WHITE	10. HOT	COLD
2. DARK	LIGHT	11. HEAVY	LIGHT
3. NIGHT	DAY	12. FAST	SLOW
4. TALL	SHORT	13. IN	OUT
5. SMOOTH	BUMPY	14. LOUD	SOFT
6. OPEN	CLOSED	15. LITTLE	BIG
7. LONG	SHORT	16. OVER	UNDER
8. AWAKE	ASLEEP	17. UP	DOWN
9. HIGH	LOW	18. STRONG	WEAK

Laminate each card.

Game Directions:

Game One: (2 Teams of 2, 3, or 4 Players)

All cards are placed face down in the center of the playing area.

Team One is "up" first. One member of the team takes the top card and shows through body movement only both words on the card. The team members have 60 seconds to guess the pair of words. If they do, they score 10 points. If not, they do not score.

Then Team Two is up. The same procedure is followed. First team to score 50 points wins.

(Note: Children may add additional antonyms to the game and should be encouraged to do so.)

Game Two: (2 players)

Using instruments, show the antonyms through sound, one child "playing" his impression of the "red" word, the partner playing his impression of the "black" word. (Children might be encouraged to choose the antonym with which they are most comfortable — quality rather than quantity.) A challenge — can both words sound together? Are they harmonious? Are they unharmonious? In other words, how well do they sound together? Should antonyms sound well together?

GAME OF THE NINES AND EIGHTS AND SEVENS
GAME OF THE SIXES AND FIVES AND FOURS
GAME OF THE THREES AND TWOS AND ONES

Objectives:

1. To rhyme in rhythm.
2. To provide experiences with rhythmic chanting.
3. To develop meter concepts.
4. To provide extended learning in math (reinforcing multiplication skills).

Materials:

Poster board or index cards.

Contents:

A set of 27 cards for each game, and 1 card for instructions.

Preparation:

For each game cut 27 cards, 3" x 2-1/2". On each card write an example from the multiplication tables, one through nine. Put the answer on the back of each card. Also, write the name of the game on the back of each card.

Example:

2 x **3** is . . . . _____ .	**GAME** **of the** **THREES** **and TWOS** **and ONES**
Front	Back

Game Directions: (3 or 4 Players; when 4 are playing, remove 1 card.)

Shuffle all cards. Place in pile, face up, in center of the table.

Player One takes the top cards, solves the "math," and adds a rhyming line. If correct, he keeps the game card. If not, it is put face up on the bottom of the pile in the center of the table.

Play continues in this way until all cards are gone. The player with the most cards wins.

Example:

3x3 is 9.

Walk the silver line.

GAME OF THE PRESIDENTS

Objectives:
1. To provide experiences with identification, letter names (𝄞).
2. To reinforce note values concept 2, 3, 4, 5
  4 4 4 4.
3. To provide Social Studies enrichment.
4. To provide extended learning in math (addition).

Materials:
3'' x 5'' lined index cards.

Contents:
Index cards on which the name of each president has been written in note heads and letters and his place in the presidential order has been written in notes and rests in combination.

Preparation:
Prepare one card for each president like the following example.

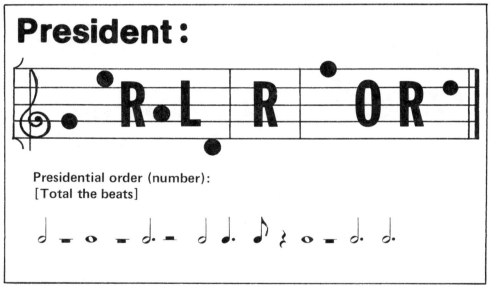

(Put answers on back of each card.)

Game Directions:

Game One (2, 3, or 4 Players)
Deal out all cards, face up. (Each player should have the same number of cards. Leave out any extras.) Each player places his cards in a pile in front of him as they are dealt face up.

Player One calls out the name of the president on his top card and spells it. Then he adds the note/rest values to find out the "number" president he is. If correct, he places the card in the discard pile in the center of the table. If not, he puts the card on the bottom of his pile.

Play continues in this way until one player has no more cards. He is the winner.
Note: Answers are on the back of each card.

Game Two (2, 3, or 4 Players)

Shuffle cards. Place in pile, face up, in center of the table.

Player One takes the top card. He calls out and spells the name of the president. Then he adds the note/rest values to find out the ''number'' president he is.

Score 1 point for every letter name correctly called and 1 point for the correct ''number.'' Continue playing until all cards have been used. Player with the highest score wins.

Game Three (Alone or 2 Players)

Challenge yourself or a friend. How many presidents and ''numbers'' can you call out in 3 minutes? Use the egg timer.

GAME OF THE STATES

Objectives:
1. To provide experiences with identification, letter names,
2. To provide Social Studies enrichment.

Materials:
50 3'' x 5'' lined index cards.

Contents:
Index cards on which have been written the names of each state with its capital in note heads and letters.

Preparation:
Prepare one card for each state like the following example.

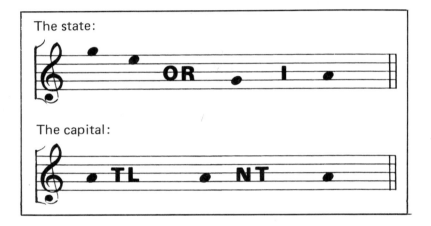

(Place answers on the back of each card.)

Game Directions:

Game One (2 to 4 Players)

Deal out all cards face up. (Leave out any extra cards so that each player has the same number.)

Player One calls out and spells the name of the state and capital on his top card. If he is correct, he puts the card in the discard pile in the center of the table. If not, he has to put it on the bottom of his pile.

Each player follows in turn. The winner is the player who is first to discard all his cards. (Answers are on the back of each card.)

Game Two (2 to 4 Players)

Shuffle the cards. Place them in a pile in the center of the table, face up.

Player One calls out and spells the name of the state and capital on the top card. He scores 1 point for each correct note letter.

Player Two follows in turn. The winner is the player with the most points. (Answers are on the back of each card.)

HIGH ROLLERS

Objectives:
1. To reinforce and motivate recall of general and/or specific information regarding all aspects of music.
2. To provide opportunities for planning a strategy.
3. To provide extended learning in math (working with all possible combinations through 12).

Materials:
Poster board or oak tag, 100 3'' x 5'' index cards, two small triangles with strikers, one pair of dice.

Contents:
Number cards, "note prize" cards, question cards, triangles with strikers, and one pair of dice.

Preparation:
Make 10 large number cards, 4-1/2'' x 6''.
Place one numeral on the face of each card, 1 through 10.
Example:

Make 10 "note prize" cards 4'' x 5-1/2''. Write on face of each as follows:
1. 𝅝 (Back of card — 4 beats.)
2. 𝅗𝅥. (Back of card — 3 beats.)
3. 𝅗𝅥 (Back of card — 2 beats.)
4. ♩. (Back of card — 1-1/2 beats.)
5. ♩ (Back of card — 1 beat.)
6. ♪. (Back of card — 3/4 beat.)
7. ♪ (Back of card — 1/2 beat.)
8. ♪ (Back of card — 1/4 beat.)
9. ♫ (Back of card — 1 beat.)
10. ♬ (Back of card — 1 beat.)

Using 3'' x 5'' index card, write out a question on each one pertaining to any aspect of music you choose. It is suggested that the questions be short and specific. Place answers on the back of each card.

Game Directions: (Game Leader and 2 Players or Game Leader and two teams of Players — 2, 3, or 4 Players on each team. When playing in teams, players take turns "being up.")

(You will need paper and pencil for scoring, a pair of dice and 2 triangles with strikers.)

Game Leader sets up number cards as follows:

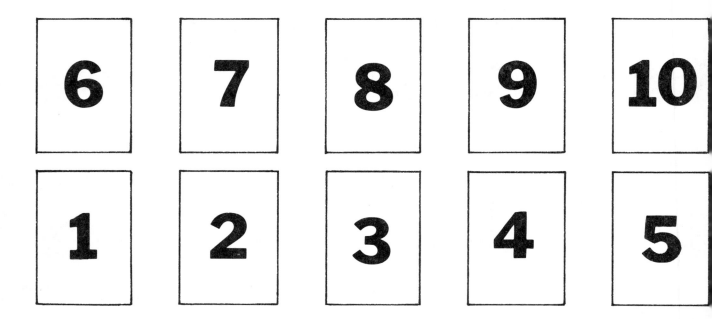

Under each number card, he places one "note prize" card. Only he must know what is under each number.

Each player holds a triangle and striker and is ready to strike it when he knows the answer to the first question asked by the Game Leader. (In teams, it will be the first player on each team.)

Game Leader shuffles the question cards and reads out first question. The player who knows the answer strikes his triangle. Then he answers the question. If correct, he gets control of the dice. This means he may roll them or pass them to his opponent who will *have to take the roll.* If incorrect, his opponent gets control of the dice and he may roll them or pass them back to the player who did not answer correctly and *that player will have to take the roll.* If *both players* strike triangles at exactly the same time, the question doesn't count and a new question will be asked.

After a player rolls the dice, he then picks any number cards which will equal his roll.

For example:

Roll	Possibilities
2	2
3	2&1 or 3
4	3&1 or 4
5	1&4, 2&3 or 5
6	1-2-3, 1&5, 2&4 or 6.
7	1-2-4, 3&4, 2&5, 1&6 or 7.
8	1-2-5, 1-3-4, 2&6, 3&5, 1&7 or 8
9	1-2-6, 1-3-5, 1&8, 2&7, 3&6, 4&5 or 9
10	1-2-3-4, 1-2-7, 1-3-6, 2-3-5, 1-4-5, 1&9, 2&8, 3&7, 6&4 or 10
11	1-2-3-5, 1-2-8, 1-3-7, 2-3-6, 1-4-6, 2-4-5, 1&10, 2&9, 3&8, 4&7, or 5&6
12	1-2-3-6, 1-2-4-5, 1-2-9, 1-3-8, 2-3-7, 1-4-7, 2-4-6, 3-4-5, 1-5-6, 2&10, 3&9, 4&8, 5&7.

Game Leader should *read* the possible combinations for his roll.

After picking his number cards, the player gets the "note prizes" that are under the numbers. Then these numbers are taken out of the game.

Game Leader then asks the next question and the same procedure follows, rolling the dice, receiving "note prizes," and removing number cards from the game until the player who has rolled cannot make his roll in number cards. He loses the round and his opponent is the winner of the round.

Keeping Score: The winner receives as many points as he has in note cards.

For example:

$$\mathbf{o}, \, \mathbf{d} \cdot, \, \mathbf{\square} \quad \text{and} \quad \mathbf{\flat} = 4+3+1+\tfrac{1}{4} = 8\tfrac{1}{4} \text{ points.}$$

(Values are on the back of each note card.)

The loser of the round receives *zero.*

Play as many rounds as time permits. Player or Team with highest score wins.

INTERVAL RACES

Objectives:
1. To reinforce concept of ascending and descending movement on the treble staff.
2. To gain facility with interval recognition.

Materials:
White poster board, 3" x 5" index cards.

Contents:
Game board, game cards, and four markers.

Preparation:
Cut poster board 14" x 22" for game board. (See below.)

Make 4 circular player markers of poster board, each 2" in diameter and marked as follows:

     Red = Player 1
     Blue = Player 2
     Yellow = Player 3
     Green = Player 4

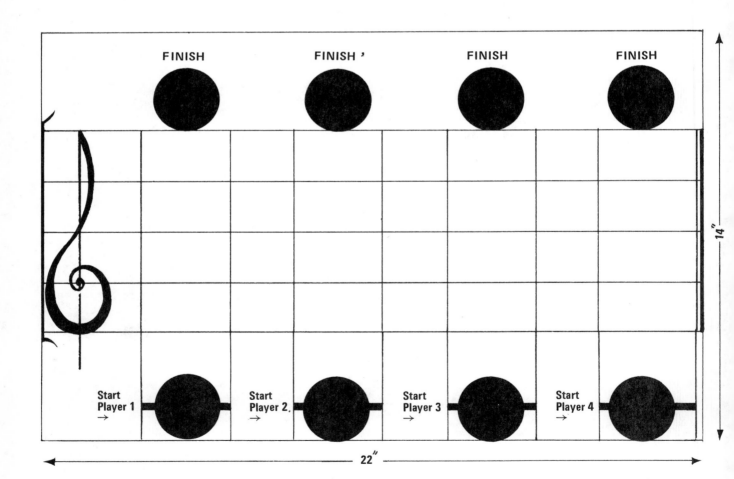

Cut 15 3" x 5" index cards in half (3" x 2-1/2") for game cards and prepare two of each as follows:

Unison (Stay where you are.)
Up an interval of a 2nd.
Down an interval of a 2nd
Up an interval of a 3rd.
Down an interval of a 3rd.
Up an interval of a 4th.
Down an interval of a 4th.
Up an interval of a 5th.
Down an interval of a 5th.
Up an interval of a 6th.
Down an interval of a 6th.
Up an interval of a 7th.
Down an interval of a 7th.
Up an interval of an octave.
Down an interval of an octave.

Game Directions: (For 2, 3, or 4 Players.)

2 Players = Use positions one and two, red and blue.
3 Players = Add position 3, yellow.
4 Players = Add position 4, green.

Each player takes a colored disc he has chosen and places it on START. The cards are shuffled and placed face down next to the playing board.

Player One takes the top card and moves as indicated on the card. If he cannot, he loses his turn and places his card face down on the bottom of the pile. If he can move, he does so and places the card face down on the bottom of the pile.

(**Note:** No player may move *below* the START position or *above* the FINISH position.)

Play continues in this way until one player enters the FINISH circle. **To Win:** Player must draw the *exact* interval number to enter the WINNING/FINISH circle.

JIGSAW PUZZLES . . . NATIONAL SONGS
"America"
"America, the Beautiful"
"The Star-Spangled Banner"

Objectives:
1. To build and reinforce the song repertoire.
2. To provide experiences with reading and chanting rhythmically.
3. To provide language arts experiences (phrases and syllabication).
4. To provide Social Studies enrichment.

Materials:
5" x 8" lined index cards.

Contents:
A jigsaw puzzle of each song.

Preparation:
On each card, write out the words of each song, phrase by phrase, changing the color for each word for perceptual clarification. Laminate or cover with clear adhesive-backed paper. Cut as for a jigsaw puzzle, being careful to cut between words or syllables.

Example:

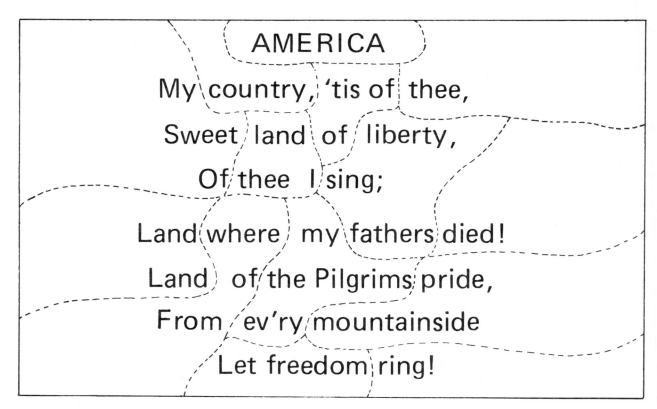

*Cut on the dotted lines.

Directions:
Using the words as clues, how quickly can you put the puzzle together? When you finish, read the words aloud, in rhythm.

THE LADYBUG AND THE ELEPHANT

Objectives:
1. To motivate creativity through movement.
2. To relate concepts of large and small to sound.
3. To provide for extended learnings in comparing sizes.

Materials:
5" x 8" index cards.

Contents:
The task cards, A and B and C. The task cards are set up as follows:

The LADYBUG and the

    ELEPHANT . . .

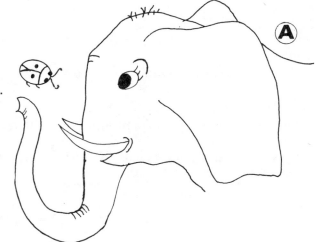

1. The ladybug is small . . . . so very small.

2. The elephant is big . . . so very big.

3. Some things are small.
   Some things are big.

4. How small can you make yourself? Move around in this tiny, small shape.

5. How big can you make yourself? Move around in this very big shape.

The LADYBUG and the

    ELEPHANT

B

1. When you were a small shape, how did you feel?
   a. Go to an instrument and make the sounds of "small." Why did you choose this instrument?
   b. Draw a picture of how you felt when you were small.
   c. Would you like to write about being small? You may.

2. When you were a big shape, how did you feel?
   a. Go to an instrument and make the sounds of "big." Why did you choose this instrument?
   b. Draw a picture of how you felt when you were big.
   c. Would you like to write about being big? You may.

The LADYBUG and the

ELEPHANT

S
M
A
L
L

1. Cut out pictures of other things that are small. Put them together in a collage.

2. Make a word chain of "small" words. Write the rhythm sounds for your word chain.
   (Example:

   sand, ants, peas, pebbles)

3. Make a melody for your word chain.

B
I
G

1. Cut out pictures of other things that are big. Put them together in a collage.

2. Make a word chain of "big" words. Write the rhythm sounds for your word chain.
   (Example:

   jets, giants, trucks, skyscrapers)

3. Make a melody for your word chain.

LIKE ME

Objectives:

1. To provide experiences with perceptual recognition of like objects — notes and rests.
2. To provide a beginning level of instruction or remediation in perceiving and knowing notes and rests by name.

Materials:

5" x 8" index cards.

Contents:

The "Like Me" puzzle cards.

Preparation:

Divide each card in half with a light pencil mark. On each side draw a note or rest. On one side include its name also. For example.

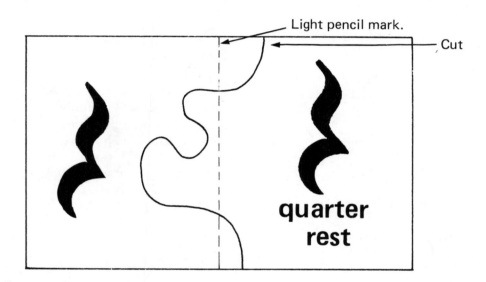

Laminate each card and cut in 2 parts as a puzzle.

Directions for use:

Children will make matches, then draw the note or rest and write its name.

LOTTO GAMES

Objectives:
1. To provide experiences with identification related to a general subject or a particular skill.
2. To provide instruction and/or reinforcement of a general subject or a particular skill.

Materials:
Oak tag or poster board; pictures (optional).

Contents:
Lotto boards, and calling cards.

Preparation:
Make Lotto boards from poster board. Example:

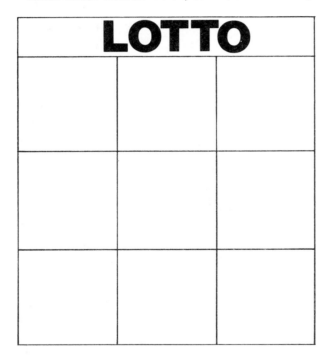

In each square place one of the things to be identified. Possibilities are:
a. Instruments (pictures)
b. Composers (pictures)
c. Conductors (pictures)
d. Performers (pictures)
e. Notes and rests
f. Notes on staves for letter name identification.

Make 6 to 8 boards. If you have repeats on any cards, be sure to repeat when preparing the individual "calling" cards.

Make a "calling" card for each square on your Lotto board. It should be the exact dimension of one square on the board.

(6 boards — 54 cards; 7 boards — 63 cards; 8 boards — 72 cards.)

Game Directions: (For 3, 4, 5, 6, 7, or 8 Players and a Game Leader)

Each player takes one Lotto Board. (3 players, each may take 2 boards; 4 players, each may take 2 boards.) The Game Leader holds up the first "calling" card and says its name. (For example: "Violin" as he shows its picture.) Each player looks for the object and the player who has it raises his hand and receives the "calling" card. He then covers this square on his Lotto board with the "calling" card.

Game continues in this way until one player has filled his board(s). He is the winner.

MACHINES

Objectives:
1. To motivate creativity through body movement.
2. To bring about awareness of self and relation to others.

Materials:
5" x 8" index cards.

Contents:
Set of picture cards.

Preparation:
On each card, paste a picture of a machine. Following are some suggestions.

1.	Ferris Wheel	15.	Record Player
2.	Escalator	16.	Computer
3.	Elevator	17.	Pinball Machine
4.	Pencil Sharpener	18.	Roller Coaster
5.	Sewing Machine	19.	Toaster
6.	Washing Machine	20.	Steam Shovel
7.	Egg Beater	21.	Steam Roller
8.	Garbage Truck	22.	Coke Machine
9.	Washing Machine	23.	Popcorn Maker
10.	Cement Mixer	24.	Blender
11.	Traffic Light	25.	Clock
12.	Tractor	26.	Merry-Go-Round
13.	Television Set	27.	Typewriter
14.	Tape Recorder		

Game Directions: (Two teams, 2, 3, or 4 players on each team)
Machines. How do they work? What jobs do they do?

Place all cards face up so that both teams may see them. One Player from Team One chooses one machine card to act out, but he does not take the card from where it is placed. He whispers his choice to one player from Team Two. Then player from Team One shows his machine through body movements to the other players on his team. They have 60 seconds to guess it. If they are correct, they get 5 points.

Team Two then follows the same procedure. Game continues until one team has 30 points.

Activity Directions:
Two or three people may work together. They choose one machine and find out how it works and what it does. Then they create a movement and an instrumental accompaniment for the machine. Some questions: How many machines can you have working at once? Same ones? Different ones? Does your machine change speed? How many different directions does it go in? Does it ever break down? Can you fix it?

MAGIC SQUARES

Objectives:
1. To practice reinforcement of notes/rests values concept — $\frac{2}{4}$, $\frac{3}{4}$, $\frac{4}{4}$, $\frac{5}{4}$.
2. To provide experiences with building measures.
3. To provide extended learning in math (addition).

Materials:
Mystik plastic tape; oak tag or poster board; 5″ x 8″ index cards.

Contents:
The Magic Squares playing area (taped on floor or constructed as a game board), the notes/rests squares, work cards.

Preparation:
Tape Magic Squares on floor as follows:

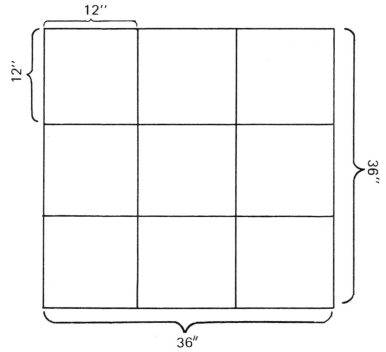

(**Note:** Game board may be used instead of floor squares.)

Cut 35 cards from oak tag or poster board, 12″ x 12″. Write on each card as follows:

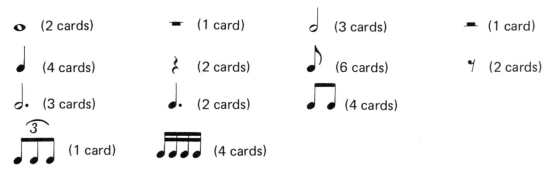

Prepare work cards from 5" x 8" index cards as follows:

Magic Squares for Two:
1. Decide which time signature you will use — $\frac{2}{4}$, $\frac{3}{4}$, $\frac{4}{4}$, $\frac{5}{4}$. Decide who will go first.
2. Place all cards face up.
3. First player chooses one card and places it on any square.
4. Second player follows the same procedure.

Object of the Game: To be the first player to get the chosen number of beats in a row, across, down, or diagonally.

Play as many rounds as time permits. You may add to the difficulty by taking out the notes/rests cards which have been used.

Magic Square Work Card — $\frac{2}{4}$ (Alone or 2 Players)
1. Using note/rest cards, make each row across equal 2 beats ($\frac{2}{4}$ time).
2. Then check each row down. These must equal 2 beats also.
3. Try to make each measure different.
4. Can you make a Magic Square that equals 2 beats across, 2 beats down, and 2 beats diagonally?
   Example:

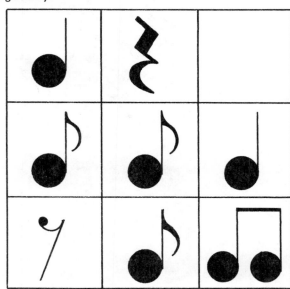

$1 + 1 = 2$

$\frac{1}{2} + \frac{1}{2} + 1 = 2$

$\frac{1}{2} + \frac{1}{2} + 1 = 2$

$\frac{1}{2} + \frac{1}{2} + 1 = 2$ $\frac{1}{2} + \frac{1}{2} + 1 = 2$ $1 + 1 = 2$

5. Remove the cards you used in the round and try again.
6. When two people are working together, one may challenge the other.
7. Try to block your opponent.

Set up work cards for $\frac{3}{4}$, $\frac{4}{4}$, & $\frac{5}{4}$ in the same manner.

Note: This activity may be adapted for younger children who are working at the beginning level of the rhythm sequence. Use stick notation (suggest,). The placement of beats is controlled by the roll of a die or a number cube (2-3-4-5). When using a die, exclude 1 and 6; should they appear, roll again.

MEASURE MAGIC I (2, 3, 4, 5)
(4 4 4 4)

Objectives:

1. To build measures in 2, 3, 4, and 5 using
   4   4   4   and 4

2. To provide extended learning in math (addition of whole numbers and fractions).

Materials:

Poster board or oak tag; a penny.

Contents:

Game board, game cards, and a penny.

Preparation:

Cut game board from poster board, 8″ x 8″, and write on it as follows:

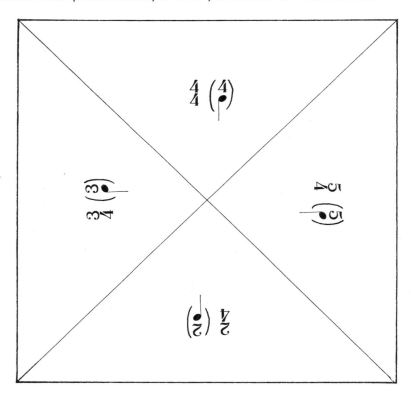

Cut 24 cards, 3″ x 4″ and draw on as follows:

1. 𝅝

2. ▬

3. 𝅗𝅥.

4. 𝅗𝅥 (2)

5. ▬

6. ♩ (5)

7. 𝄽 (2)

8. ♪ (5)

9. 𝄾

10. ♫ (3)

11. ♬ (2)

Game Directions: (2, 3 or 4 Players)

Player One tosses a penny on the game board. Using the note/rest cards, he must build a complete measure containing the same number of beats as the TOP NUMBER of the time signature.

If he builds his measure correctly, he receives as his point score, the number of beats in his measure. If he does not build his measure correctly, he receives ZERO for this round.

Play continues in this way. The first player to reach 20 points WINS! One person may keep score for all players.

(Note: After each play, all cards are put back in the Pot!)

Variation:

Spread out all the note/rest cards. Follow the same procedure as before, only this time, the cards are NOT returned to the pot after they have been used. If the player cannot build his measure from the note/rest cards available, he must forfeit his turn. Play continues until all cards have been played or no more plays are possible. Player with the highest score wins.

MEASURE MAGIC II (3, 6, 9, 12, 2, 3, 4, 2)

(8 8 8 8 4 4 4 2)

Objectives, Materials, Contents and Game Directions are the same as for MEASURE MAGIC I.

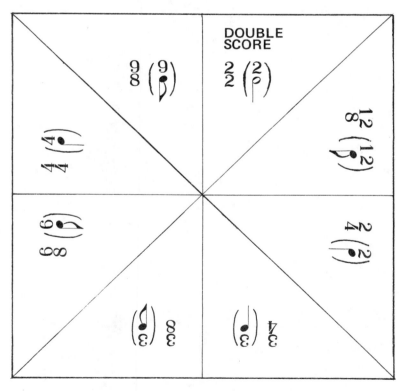

Game Board for Measure Magic II.

Note/Rest cards for Measure Magic II. (34 cards)

1. 𝅝

2. ▬ (whole rest)

3. 𝅗𝅥.

4. 𝅗𝅥 (2)

5. ▬ (half rest)

6. 𝅘𝅥 (5)

7. 𝄽 (4)

8. 𝅘𝅥.

9. 𝅘𝅥𝅮 (5)

10. 𝄾 (4)

11. 𝅘𝅥𝅮𝅘𝅥𝅮 (2)

12. 𝅘𝅥𝅮.

13. 𝅘𝅥𝅯 (4)

14. 𝄿

15. 𝅘𝅥𝅯𝅘𝅥𝅯𝅘𝅥𝅯𝅘𝅥𝅯

MEASURE MARBLES

Objectives:

1. To provide reinforcement of note/rest values, $\frac{2}{4}$, $\frac{3}{4}$, $\frac{4}{4}$, $\frac{5}{4}$.

2. To provide experiences with building measures in $\frac{2}{4}$, $\frac{3}{4}$, $\frac{4}{4}$, $\frac{5}{4}$.

Materials:

Shoe box, poster board, 3'' x 5'' index cards.

Contents:

"Measure Marbles" box, one marble, 10 card pockets, task cards.

Preparation:

Using the shoe box, make a "Measure Marbles" box as per diagram.

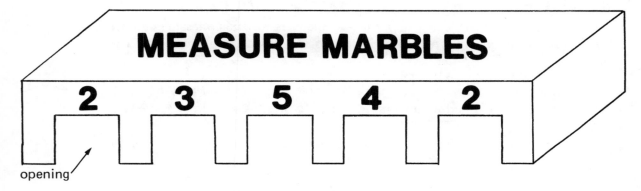

Cut card pockets from poster board, 8'' x 4-1/2''. Score at 4''. Cut V in front. Tape sides.

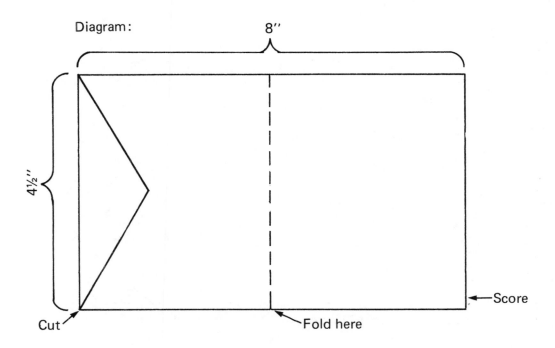

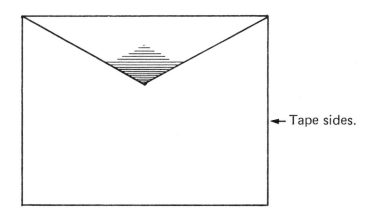

← Tape sides.

Game One: Make A Measure (2 to 4 Players)

Choose the level:

Player One rolls a marble. He then makes a measure which is the same number as his score, from the note/rest cards in the pocket. **For example:** He rolls a 5.

Measure ♩ ❘ ❘ ♪♪ ♩

If a marble doesn't go in an opening on the first roll, the player may try again to roll a number and build a measure. Player only gets his score if the measure he made is correct.

Player Two then takes his turn, and play continues until one player has 40 points.

Variation:

As the cards are played, they are taken out of the game. The game ends when the last player is able to match his roll with the number of beats left in the pocket. He adds 5 points to his score for "going out."

Cards for Level 1:

1. ❘ (10 cards)   3. ❀ (5 cards)

2. ⊓ (5 cards)   4. ♩ (5 cards)

Put in a pocket.
Label "Make a Measure, Level 1."

Cards for Level 2:

1. 𝅝 (2 cards)   5. ♩. (3 cards)

2. ▬ (2 cards)   6. ♩ (5 cards)   9. ♪♪♪ (1 card)

3. ♩ (5 cards)   7. ❀ (3 cards)   10. ♬♬ (3 cards)

4. ▬ (2 cards)   8. ♪♪ (5 cards)

Put in a pocket.
Label "Make a Measure, Level 2."

172

Game Two: Measure Marbles (2 to 4 Players)

Choose the level:

Level 1 (| ♫ 𝄽 𝅗𝅥)

Level 2 (𝅝 ▬ 𝅗𝅥 ▬ 𝅗𝅥. ♩ 𝄽 ♫ ♫ ♩ ♫♫♫)

Player One rolls a marble. He then takes a card from the pocket which has the same number as the score he rolled. He must correctly clap the measure which is on the card in order to get his score. **For example**: He rolls a 5 . . . 𝅗𝅥. 𝅗𝅥 (ta-a-a ta-a).

Answers are on the back of each card. As each card is played, it goes to the bottom of the pile in the pocket.

(*Note*: If the marble doesn't go in an opening on the first roll, the player may try again to get a number score.)

Player Two then rolls and play continues in this way until one player has 50 points.

Cards for Pocket 2, Level 1:

1. ♫ 𝄽

2. 𝄽 ♫

3. 𝄽 |

4. | 𝄽

5. ♫ |

6. | ♫

7. | |

8. 𝅗𝅥

Put rhythm sound answers on back of each card. Place in pocket and label

$\left\{ {2 \atop 4} \right\}^{2} \left\{ {2 \atop \bullet} \right\}$
Level 1

Cards for Pocket 3, Level 1:

1. ♫ | |

2. | ♫ |

3. ♫ ♫ ♫

4. | | |

5. 𝅗𝅥 𝄽

6. ♫ 𝅗𝅥

7. 𝅗𝅥 ♫

8. | 𝅗𝅥

9. 𝅗𝅥 |

10. ♫ 𝄽 |

11. | 𝄽 ♫

12. | ♫ 𝄽

13. 𝄽 ♫ |

14. ♫ | 𝄽

15. | | 𝄽

16. 𝄽 | |

17. | 𝄽 |

18. ♫ ♫ |

19. ♫ | ♫

20. | ♫ ♫

Put rhythm sound answers on back of each card. Place in pocket and label.

$\left\{ {3 \atop 4} \right\}^{3} \left\{ {3 \atop \bullet} \right\}$
Level 1

Cards for Pocket 4, Level 1:

1.
2.
3.
4.
5.
6.
7.
8.
9.
10.

11.
12.
13.
14.
15.
16.
17.
18.
19.
20.

Put rhythm sound answers on back of each card. Place in pocket and label

$\left\{\begin{matrix}4\\4\end{matrix}\right\}\left\{\begin{matrix}4\\♩\end{matrix}\right\}$
Level 1

Cards for Pocket 5, Level 1:

1.
2.
3.
4.
5.
6.
7.
8.
9.
10.

11.
12.
13.
14.
15.
16.
17.
18.
19.
20.

Put rhythm sound answers on back of each card. Place in pocket and label

$\left\{\begin{matrix}5\\5\end{matrix}\right\}\left\{\begin{matrix}5\\♩\end{matrix}\right\}$
Level 1

Cards for Pocket 2, Level 2:

1. 𝄽 ♫

2. ♫ 𝄽

3. ♫ ♩

4. ♩ 𝄽

5. 𝄽 ♩

6. ♩ ♫

7. ♩ ♩

8. 𝅗𝅥

Label

Cards for Pocket 3, Level 2:

1. 3:♫♫ 3:♫♫ ♩

2. ♫ 3:♫♫ ♩

3. ♩ ♩ ♫

4. ♩ ♫ ♩

5. ♫ ♫ ♫

6. ♫ ♩ ♩

7. 𝅗𝅥 𝄽

8. 𝄽 𝅗𝅥

9. 𝄽 ♩ ♩

10. ♩ 𝄽 ♩

11. ♩ ♩ ♩

12. ♬♬ 𝅗𝅥

13. 3:♬♬ 𝅗𝅥

14. ♫ 𝅗𝅥

15. 𝅗𝅥 ♫

16. ♩ 𝅗𝅥

17. 𝅗𝅥 ♩

18. 𝅗𝅥.

19. ♩ ♬♬ ♩

20. ♬♬ ♬♬ ♩

Cards for Pocket 4, Level 2:

1. ♬♬ ♩ ♬♬ ♩

2. 3:♬ ♫ 3:♬ ♫ ♩

3. ♬♬ ♫ ♫ 3:♫ ♩

4. ♫ ♫ ♩ ♬♬ ♩

175

5.

6.

7.

8.

9.

10.

11.

12.

13.

14.

15.

16.

17.

18.

19.

20.

Cards for Pocket 5, Level 2:

1.

2.

3.

4.

5.

6.

7.

8.

9.

10.

11.

12.

13.

14.

15.

16.

17.

18.

19.

20.

MEASURENOES

Objectives:

1. To reinforce concept of note values: $\frac{2}{4}, \frac{3}{4}, \frac{4}{4}, \frac{5}{4}$.
2. To provide experiences with time signatures: $\frac{2}{4}, \frac{3}{4}, \frac{4}{4}, \frac{5}{4}$.
3. To provide experiences with matching time signatures to measure sets.
4. To provide for incidental learning — conventional counting.
5. To provide extended learning in math (addition).

Materials:

Poster board.

Contents:

The measurenoes.

Preparation:

Cut 34 cards, 1″ x 2″ from poster board. Divide the cards in half with a line.

Draw on the cards as follows:

17. $\frac{2}{4}$ | $\frac{4}{4}$ (Make 2.)

18. $\frac{2}{4}$ | $\frac{3}{4}$ (Make 2.)

19. $\frac{3}{4}$ | $\frac{4}{4}$ (Make 2.)

20. $\frac{4}{4}$ | $\frac{5}{4}$ (Make 2.)

21. $\frac{4}{4}$ | $\frac{3}{4}$ (Make 2.)

22. $\frac{5}{4}$ | $\frac{2}{4}$

23. $\frac{5}{4}$ | $\frac{3}{4}$

24. $\frac{5}{4}$ | $\frac{4}{4}$ (Make 2.)

177

25. $\frac{4}{4}$ | $\frac{2}{4}$ 26. $\frac{2}{4}$ | $\frac{5}{4}$ 27. $\frac{3}{4}$ | $\frac{2}{4}$

Game Directions: (2, 3, or 4 Players)

Place cards face down in box. Each player chooses 3 MEASURENOES cards, sight unseen.

Player One puts one card in center of playing area, face up. He then takes another card from the box to replace this one.

Player Two must build on the card that Player One put down. If he can, he replaces the card he played. If not, he loses his turn.

(Note: If a player cannot build 2 turns in a row, he may put back one MEASURE-NOES card and take another one, playing it if he can.)

Play continues in this way until all MEASURENOES are used or no one can go. Player with the fewest cards left is the winner.

Special Instructions:

1. You may build in any direction, time signature to measure, measure to time signature.

2. You may use FREE boxes anywhere.

3. You may not build measure to measure, or time signature to time signature. Examples of possible plays.

MELODY DICE

Objectives:
1. To reinforce melodic reading skills.
2. To provide opportunities for notating melodies within the pentatonic scale.
3. To gain facility with hand signals.

Materials:
Poster board or heavy cardboard.

Contents:
Four syllable cubes and one cube with skill directions.

Preparation:
Prepare the cubes as in the general directions, same size or larger. Before taping, write on the squares as shown in the following example.:

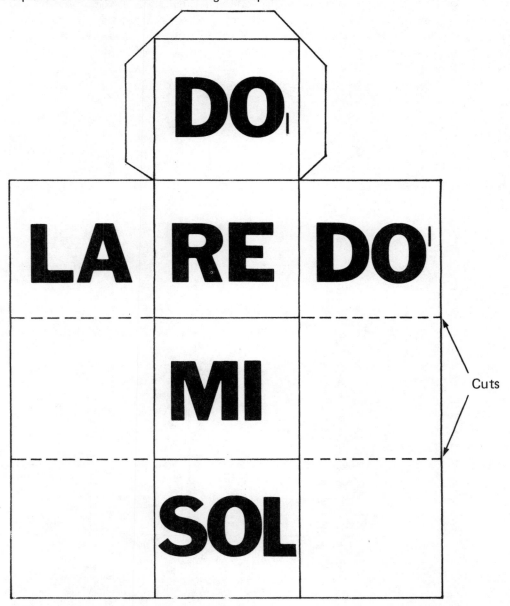

Make 4 of these melody dice. They may be color coded if so desired.

The fifth die will designate skills as follows:

    Side 1: Play on any bar instrument in the order of the roll. (1 Point)

    Side 2: Place on magnetic board, floor staff, or write it as you rolled it. (DO_1 is line 1.) (3 Points)

    Side 3: Sing as you rolled the pattern. (3 Points)

    Side 4: Place on magnetic board, floor staff, or write it as you rolled the pattern. (DO_1 is in Space 1.) (3 Points)

    Side 5: Step out pattern on floor staff in the order of the roll. (DO_1 is Line 1.) (3 Points)

    Side 6: Silent sing with hand signals as you rolled the pattern. (2 Points)

Game Directions: (2, 3, or 4 Players)

(Note: Use a soprano or alto bar instrument or keyboard instrument to give the starting pitch for singing. You may also check for accuracy on this instrument.)

Player One rolls all the dice upon which all the syllables have been written and places them in the order of the roll. He then rolls the die which tells what to do. If he performs the melody correctly, he scores the number of points as indicated.

The first player with 15 points is the winner.

MELODY HEARTS—DO IN A SPACE

Objectives:

1. To develop facility in melodic reading, do-re-mi-sol-la.
2. To provide experiences with applying the rules for placement of re, mi, sol, and la when do is in a space.

Materials:

Index cards.

Contents:

The playing cards.

Preparation:

Cut 36 cards from index cards, the size of regulation playing cards. Write on each card as follows:

On the back of each card, write as follows:

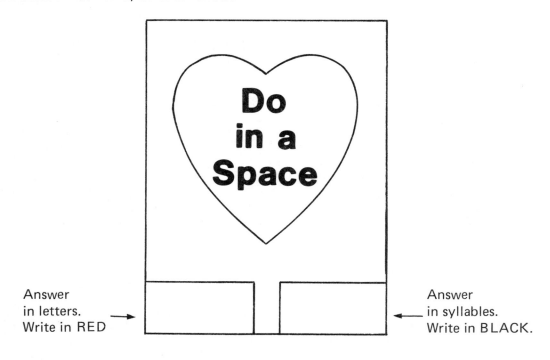

Answer in letters. Write in RED →

Do in a Space

← Answer in syllables. Write in BLACK.

Game Directions: 2, 3 or 4 Players)

Shuffle and deal out all cards to all players face up. (Answers are on the back of each card!) Each player arranges his cards in a pile in front of him, face up.

Player One looks at the melody pattern on his top card and calls out the syllable names of the notes. Then he checks his answer on back of the card. (Syllable answer is in *black.*) If correct, he puts the card in a discard pile in the center of the playing area.

Player Two follows the same procedure, adding his card to the discard pile if he is correct.

If any player makes a mistake in telling the syllables, he must pick up the *whole* discard pile. The game continues until one player is out of cards.

Variation: Instead of identifying notes by syllables, identify by letters. These answers are in *red.*

MELODY HEARTS—DO ON A LINE

Same Objectives, Materials, Contents, Preparation, and Game Directions, but DO is line 2.

MERRY MI

Objectives:
1. To provide experiences with perception of SOL-MI matches.
2. To provide experiences with facility in reading SOL-MI patterns.
3. To reinforce rule for placement of SOL-MI.

Materials:
   Index cards.

Contents:
   The playing cards.

Preparation:
   Cut 21 cards from index cards, the size of regulation playing cards. Make one of each of the following:

(**Note:** Note heads may be color coded — SOL-*red*, MI-*blue*. No key signatures are included at this beginning level of the melody sequence.)

21. Make one:

MERRY MI

Laminate all cards.

Game Directions: (2, 3 or 4 Players)
   Shuffle and deal out all cards. Each player arranges his cards in a hand. All players put down, in front of them, any pairs which they have in their hands.
   Player One then picks one card from Player Two, unseen. He puts this card in his hand and makes another pair if he can. Player Two then proceeds in the same way, picking from the next player and trying to make a pair.
   Play continues until all pairs have been made and one player is left with the "Merry Mi." He is the loser.
(Note: Matches are made SOL to MI.)

MISERABLE MICKEY

Objectives:
Perceptual recognition of like and unlike symbols.
(This game is designed for students who show symptoms of difficulty in the area of visual perception.)

Materials:
Poster board.

Contents:
The playing cards.

Preparation:
Cut 35 cards from poster board, the size of regulation playing cards.

Make 2 of each of the following:

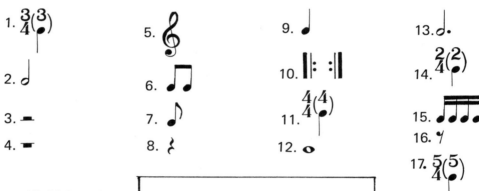

18. Make one :

Laminate all cards.

Game Directions: (2, 3, or 4 Players)

Shuffle and deal out all cards. Each player arranges his cards in a hand. All players put down, in front of them, any pairs which they have in their hands.

Player One then picks one card from Player Two, unseen. He puts this card in his hand and makes another pair if he can. Player Two then proceeds in the same way, picking from the next player and trying to make a pair.

Play continues until all pairs have been made and one player is left with the "Miserable Mickey." He is the loser.

THE MOVEMENT GAME

Objectives:
1. To explore a variety of body movements.
2. To provide opportunities for creativity in body movements through combinations of two or more possibilities.
3. To provide experiences in communicating through movement.

Materials:
Poster board, oak tag or index cards.

Contents:
51 cards cut to the size of a regulation playing card.

Preparation:
On the front of each card print one movement. On the back of each card, print, "The M Game."

Example:

Front   Back

Make 3 of each:

Skip	Hop	Bend
Pull	Bounce	Dodge
Gallop	Walk	Leap
Strike	Twist	Swing
Shake	Stretch	Run
Jump	Push	

Game Directions: (3, 4, 5, or 6 Players)

Shuffle and deal out all cards. (If 4, 5, or 6 people are playing, put the extra cards out of the game. All players should have the same number of cards.) Arrange the cards in your hand.

Player One chooses a card and performs the movement. The other players try to guess the movement. If they do, Player One melds the card (puts it down in front of him). If not, he keeps it.

Play continues in this way until one player has melded all his cards. He is the winner.

Note: Any player can use 2 or more cards at the same time, but must perform the movements at the same time.

Example: Walk and Swing. If successful, he melds both cards.

This game may also be played in teams as in CHARADES, with teammates having to guess the movement being performed by one of their members. A 60-second time limit is set for each guessing period. One point is scored for each correct solution.

MOVING THROUGH SPACE

Objectives:

1. To provide experiences with moving to a beat. (Movement may be to a basic beat, that is, a meter, or a rhythm pattern.)
2. To provide experiences with working in pairs.
3. To provide experiences with spatial relationships.
4. Estimating.
5. To reinforce math skills in measurement and making bar graphs.

Materials:

5'' x 8'' index cards, drum, yardstick, graph paper.

Contents:

The task card. Prepare the task card as follows:

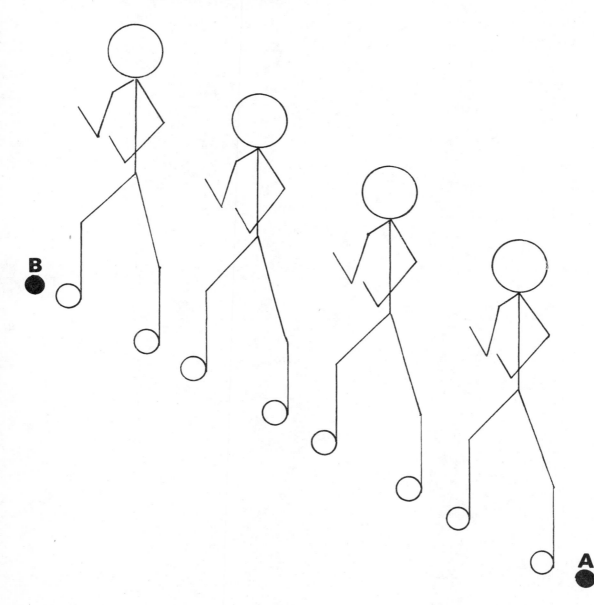

1. Work with a partner. One person will play the drum. He may play a basic beat or a rhythm pattern. Decide how long the pattern will be before beginning.

2. Starting from any point, A, one person will cover as much space as possible, moving with the beat or the rhythm being sounded on the drum! (**Note:** Player must be sure to move *with* the *beat* or *rhythm!*)

3. When the drum stops, the movement stops. Mark this point, B.

4. Measure the distance covered in movement.

5. Record the distance in inches, feet, and yards.

6. Now change places and repeat Steps 1, 2, 3, 4, and 5. (Second player must be sure to use the *same* beat set or rhythm pattern.)

7. Using graph paper, make a bar graph to show how far each person moved in the same amount of time.

MUSIC BY CHANCE

Objectives:
1. To provide experiences in the simultaneous reading of rhythm and melody.
2. To provide an environment for the simultaneous expression of rhythm and melody.
3. To reinforce skill of reading from left to right.

Materials:
Poster board in white, green, blue, red, and yellow or white board or cardboard that will be colored with permanent ink felt-tipped pens.

Contents:
Five cubes, one of each color, upon which have been drawn the rhythm symbols. (**Note:** The white cube will replace black as the DO_1 cube.)

Preparation:
Prepare the five cubes as in the general directions. Before taping, write on the squares as shown in the following example:

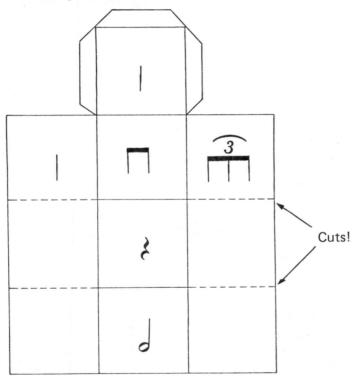

Cuts!

(**Note:** If color coding is not used, designate each cube as one note in the pentatonic scale and write its syllable on every side together with the rhythm symbols.)

Game Directions: (2, 3, or 4 Players)
(**Remember:** White will be DO_1, Green is RE, Blue is MI, Red is SOL, and Yellow is LA.)
Player One rolls the five cubes in any color order he chooses. He then places the cubes in the order of the roll, from left to right. He plays his melody on the keyboard, recorder or any bar instrument in the rhythm pattern as shown on the cubes. Example:

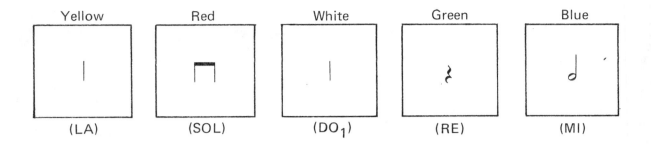

If played correctly, he scores 1 point. Play continues in this way until one player scores 10 points.

Variation:

Score 1 point for every cube in a round which is performed correctly rhythmically and melodically. The winning score will then be 20 points.

MUSIC LAND . . . GAME ONE

Objective:
To provide experiences with identifying notes and rests . . . reinforcement.

Materials:
Poster board.

Contents:
4 markers, playing board, one "die."

Preparation:
Make 4 markers, each about the size of a nickel, from scraps of poster board. Color each differently with permanent-inked markers.

Cut the playing board from poster board. The overall dimensions are 10" x 14". Each square on the game board should be 1" x 1" with a 1" border on all sides.

(Game board illustration appears on next page.)

Game Directions: (2, 3 or 4 Players)

1. Get one "die."

2. Player One puts his marker on START. He rolls the die and moves in the direction of the arrows for the total of the roll.

3. Player must correctly name the note or rest he lands on. If he cannot, he must return to the square he *came from,* not back to START each time.

4. If a player lands on FREE, he remains there without having to name anything.

5. Player must roll the exact number to enter the FINISH square.

6. The play continues in this way with each player moving in the direction of the arrows and identifying the notes/rests until one player enters the FINISH square and wins.

MUSIC LAND . . . . GAME TWO

Objective:
To provide experiences with drawing notes and rests.

All elements of the game are the same, but the notes and rests are replaced with the notes/rests names. Player must draw the note or rest designated in the square upon which he lands.

Example:

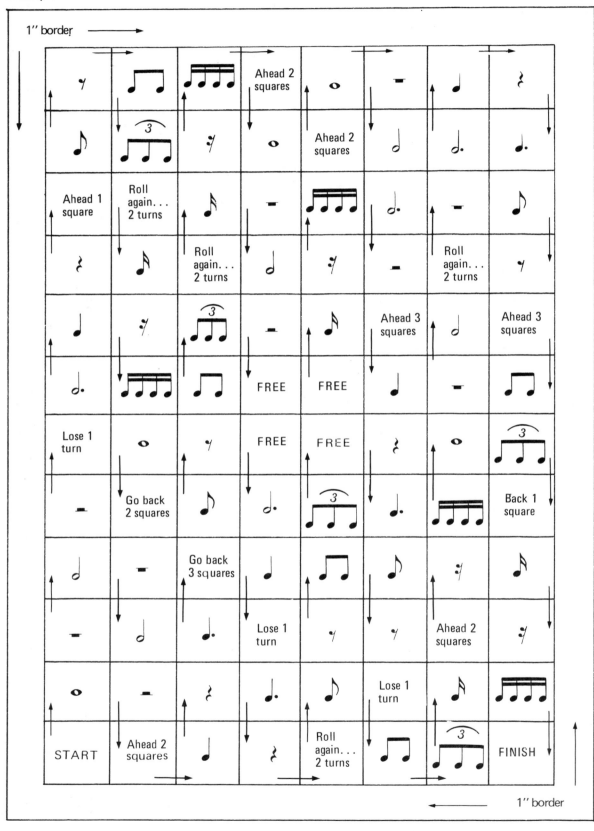

MUSICAL CHECKERS

Objectives:
1. To reinforce concept of note value relationships.
2. To provide opportunities for planning a strategy.

Materials:
A checker board and checkers, white poster board, Duco cement.

Contents:
Checker game board, note checkers and kings.

Preparation:
Cut 36 circles from poster board. Use a checker for pattern. Write on one set of circles with black ink marker, on one set with red ink marker. Each set should include:

2 whole note circles   𝅝   2 dotted half note circles   𝅗𝅥.

2 half note circles   𝅗𝅥•   2 dotted quarter note circles   ♩.

1 quarter note circle   ♩   1 dotted eighth note circle   ♪.

1 eighth note circle   ♪   1 sixteenth note circle   ♬

6 King circles (KING)

Laminate the circles. Glue circles written in black to black checkers, circles written in red to red checkers.

Game Directions: (2 Players)
One player takes the black note checkers and the red King checkers; the other player takes the red note checkers and the black King checkers. Each player arranges his note checkers as for regulation checkers, but in the note order of his choice.

Moves are made exactly as they are in regulation checkers, *but* jumps may only be made by a checker that is higher in value.

For example: Black ♩. can jump red ♪

Black ♪ cannot jump red 𝅗𝅥.

When a man is ready to be "kinged," use the King checkers. These Kings may move forward and backward and jump any of the opponent's checkers.

Game is over when one player has no more checkers or further progress is not possible.

MUSICAL FRACTIONS

Objectives:
1. To reinforce concept of equal values and the relationship of one note to another.
2. To provide extended learning in math (fractions).

Materials:
White and colored poster board.

Contents:
Game box, game boards, and fraction pieces.

Preparation:
Game cards are to be made from colored poster board. Cut four circles with a 10″ diameter. Write on each game board circle as follows:

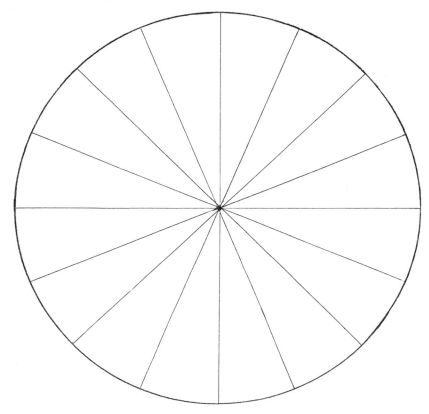

Using white poster board, make five circles 10″ in diameter. Prepare one as a whole note and cut the others as half, quarter, eighth and sixteenth notes. Draw the corresponding note on each piece.

Game Directions: (2, 3 or 4 Players)
Each player takes a game card and places it face up in front of him. All half note, quarter note, eighth note and sixteenth note pieces are kept in the open game box. (The whole note should not be included in the game.)

The Game:

Player One closes his eyes and takes a piece from the game box. He MUST take the FIRST piece he touches. He then places it on his game board, covering that part which is filled up by the piece he has picked. All other players do the same thing in turn as the game continues.

The OBJECT of the game is to be the first player to fill his game board. To WIN you must pick the exact note fraction to complete your covering of the game board. At any time a player may keep the piece he picked and return a piece from his game board to the game box if he thinks it will help him complete his game board.

By Yourself:

Using one game board, the whole note circle, and all the fraction pieces, write out and complete the following equations:

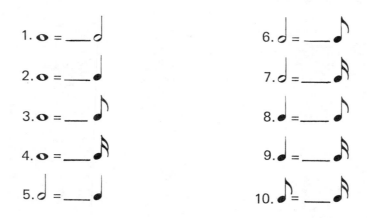

MUSICNOCHLE — $\frac{2}{4}$, $\frac{3}{4}$, $\frac{4}{4}$, $\frac{5}{4}$

Objectives:
1. To reinforce concept of note values.
2. To recognize rhythm pattern sets (measures).
3. To become conversant with a variety of rhythm patterns.
4. To provide extended learning in math (addition).

Materials:
White poster board, one 5'' x 8'' index card.

Contents:
52 playing cards, and an answer key.

Preparation:
Cut 52 playing cards from poster board.
Place one of the following rhythm patterns on the face of each card.

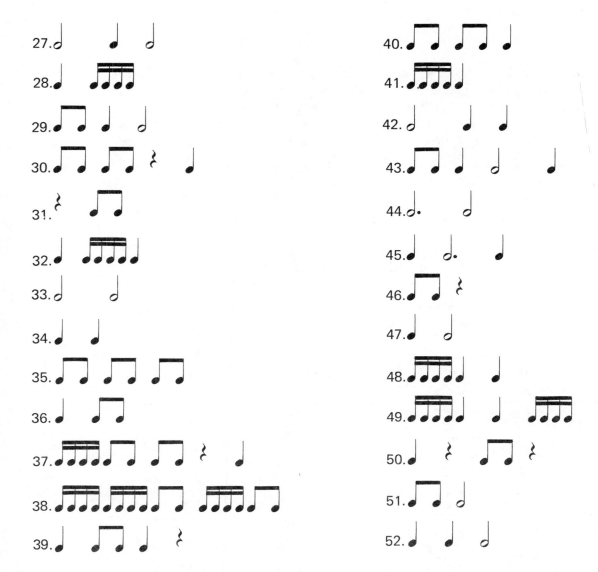

(Write game name on back of each card and prepare an answer key on the 5'' x 8'' index card stating the number of beats in each measure set.)

Game Directions: (For 2, 3, 4, 5, or 6 Players)
   There are 52 cards in the deck, divided into 4 sets — 13 measures are in 2, 4

13 measures are in 3, 13 measures are in 4, 13 measures are in 5.
            4   4   4

Object of the Game: To meld (put down in front of you) 4 or more measures in the same time signature.

Play of the Game:
   Shuffle and deal out 6 cards to each player. Put rest of deck in pile in center, face down.
   Player One draws a card from the deck and discards a card, face up, starting a discard pile. He then melds (puts down in front of him), face up, any grouping of 4 measures in the same time signature. For example, four measures in 4 4.

The next player follows the same procedure, melding if he can. Play continues in this way until one player has melded all his cards. If the pack of cards is used up before someone wins, the discard pile becomes the pack.

The player may meld more than 4 cards at one time. After melding, the player may add on to his set in the next round.

Keeping Score: Each player gets 5 points added to his score for every card he melded. Each player gets 5 points subtracted from his score for every card left in his hand.

To Win a Hand: The player must meld all his cards. Play as many "hands" (games) as desired. Player with highest score wins.

$$\text{MUSICNOCHLE} - \frac{3}{8}, \frac{6}{8}, \frac{9}{8}, \frac{12}{8}$$

All objectives are the same with the exception that the focus is on compound time. Materials and contents are the same.

Preparation:

Place one of the following rhythm patterns on the face of each card.

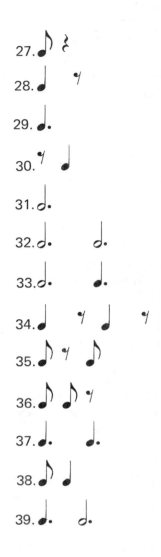

(Write game name on back of each card and prepare an answer key on the 5'' x 8'' index card stating the number of beats in each measure set.)

Game Directions: (For 2, 3, 4, 5, or 6 Players.)

There are 52 cards in the deck, divided into 4 sets — 13 measures are in $\frac{3}{8}$, 13 measures are in $\frac{6}{8}$, 13 measures are in $\frac{9}{8}$, 13 measures are in $\frac{12}{8}$.

Object of the Game: Same as preceding.

Play of the Game: Same, but example should now read: "For example, four measures in $\frac{6}{8}$".

OH, NUTS! ®

Objectives:
1. To reinforce the reading of simple rhythms.
2. To provide a remedial activity for the older child who has not achieved this skill.
3. To increase awareness of left to right and right to left movement.

Materials:

The "Oh, Nuts!" game from the Ideal Toy Manufacturing Company, unlined white cards.

Preparation:

Remove the marbles from inside each of the nuts. Cut white cards into pieces small enough to fit inside a nut, but large enough to write on. On each card write a simple rhythm pattern with notes and rests from the beginning of the rhythm sequence. Fold and place inside each nut.

Game Directions: (2 Players)

The first player picks a nut from the tree stump and opens it. He claps the rhythm he finds inside the nut. If correct, he scores 1 point. If he can also clap it backwards, he gets 2 more points for a total score of 3.

If he is not correct, he puts the rhythm card back inside the nut and puts the nut back into the tree stump. The next player follows the same procedure, and play continues until *all* the nuts have been played correctly. Player with the highest score wins.

(Note: The "eggs" from Legg's panty hose may be used in the same way as the nuts. They are the containers that hold the product and come in different colors. They may be placed in a basket and adapted in a similar way.)

This activity may be adapted for reading melodies, executing rhythms at more advanced levels within the sequence, or any identification skill.

® Registered trademark of the Ideal Toy Corporation.

OLD SOL

Objectives:

1. To provide experiences with perception of like placement of SOL-MI on the treble staff.
2. To provide instruction and remediation for older students who have not acquired this skill.

Materials:

Index cards.

Contents:

The playing cards.

Preparation:

Cut 21 cards from index cards, the size of regulation playing cards. Make 2 of each of the following:

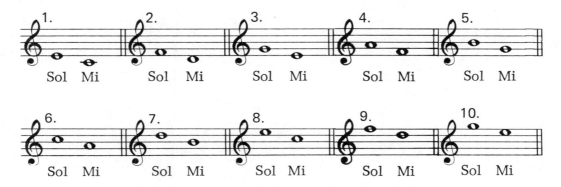

(**Note:** Note heads may be color coded — SOL-*red*, MI-*blue*.)
(No key signatures are included at this beginning level of the melodic sequence.)

Make one:

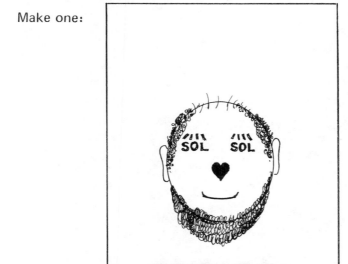

Laminate all cards.

203

Game Directions: (2, 3, or 4 Players)

Shuffle and deal out all cards. Each player arranges his cards in a hand. All players put down in front of them, any pairs which they have in their hands.

Player One then picks one card from Player Two, unseen. He puts this card in his hand and makes another pair if he can. Player Two then proceeds in the same way, picking from the next player and trying to make a pair.

Play continues until all pairs have been made and one player is left with the "Old Sol." He is the loser.

(**Note:** Matches are made between like SOL-MI placements.)

ONE ON ONE (BASKETBALL GAME)

Objectives:

1. To provide experiences with reading rhythm patterns in 2 3 4 and, 5
                                                4, 4, 4 and, 4.
2. To promote familiarity with many note/rest combinations which form 2, 3, 4 and 5 beat measures.
3. To reinforce knowledge of note values in 2 3 4 and, 5
                                             4, 4, 4 and, 4.
4. To provide opportunities for applying general music knowledge.
5. To provide extended learning in math (addition).

Materials:

100 3" x 5" index cards, white poster board.

Contents:

Game board, game cards, "block" cards, and two markers.

Preparation:

Prepare game board from poster board as follows:

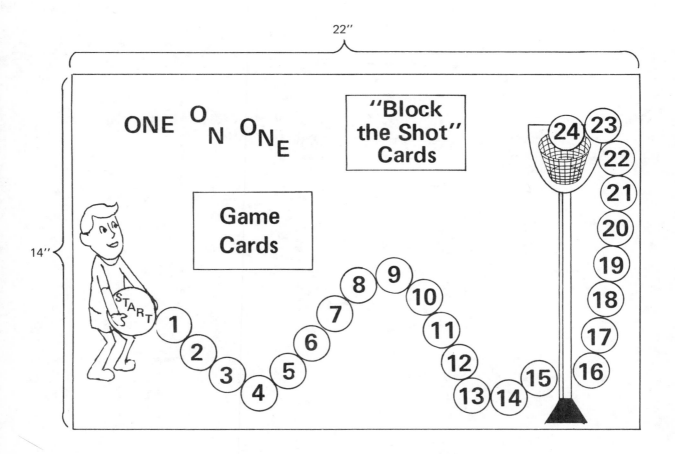

205

On the back of each of 50 index cards, write "Game Cards." Also write the answer, counts or rhythm sounds, and total value for each rhythm pattern on the back. Use light pencil so it will not show through. Prepare the front of each game card as follows:

On the back of each of 50 index cards, write "Block Cards." Also write the answer to the question or problem when necessary. Again, use light pencil. Prepare the front of each block card as follows:

1. If your opponent did not call out the correct number of beats on his game card, you may block by clapping the rhythm pattern correctly.
   (**Note:** Make ten of the above.)
2. Free "Block." Move your marker to START and begin your game.
   (**Note:** Make five of the above.)

Remaining cards contain questions or problems which require general music knowledge. Suggested questions are:

3. To Block: Name the lowest female singing voice.
4. To Block: What does this mean: *pp*
5. To Block: What does this mean? *mp*
6. To Block: What does this mean? *mf*
7. To Block: What does this mean? ⟩
8. To Block: What does this mean? ⟨
9. To Block: Name the missing syllables . . .
   DO — MI — SOL — TI DO
10. To Block: Name the missing syllables . . .
    DO RE — FA — LA — DO
11. To Block: What does this mean? *rit.*
12. To Block: Name the missing letters in the MUSIC
    alphabet . . . A — C — E — G
13. To Block: Name the missing letters in the MUSIC
    alphabet . . . AB — D — F —
14. To Block: Name the performing group which includes
    woodwinds, brass & percussion families.
15. To Block: Name the performing group which includes
    strings, woodwinds, brass & percussion families.
16. To Block: Name the highest female singing voice.
17. To Block: Name this sign . . . ♯
18. To Block: Name this sign . . . ♭
19. To Block: Name this sign . . . . . 𝄞
20. To Block: Name this sign . . . 𝄢
21. To Block: Name this sign . . ♮
22. To Block: What does this mean? *f*
23. To Block: What does this mean? *p*
24. To Block: What does this mean? *ff*
25. To Block: Name a single reed woodwind instrument.
26. To Block: Name a double reed woodwind instrument.
27. To Block: Name the drum which sounds actual pitches.
28. To Block: Name the percussion instrument whose bars are
    made of wood.
29. To Block: Name the percussion instrument which has
    different length tubes made of metal.
30. To Block: Name this sign . . . ‖: :‖
31. To Block: Name one woodwind instrument which has no
    reed.

32. To Block: Name the lowest voice brass instrument in the orchestra.
33. To Block: Name the string instrument with 47 strings & 7 pedals.
34. To Block: Name the highest voice brass instrument.
35. To Block: Name the brass instrument which was descended from the hunting horn.
36. To Block: Name the lowest voice instrument of the string family.
37. To Block: Name the string instrument with the highest voice (soprano).

Make 2 markers, the diameter of the circles on the game board.

Game Directions: (For 2 Players)

Shuffle & place Game Cards & Block Cards on the rectangles as marked on the playing board, face UP. (Answers are on the BACK of each card.)

(Note: All values are in 2, 3, 4, 5.)

4 4 4 4

Player One picks up TOP Game Card after placing his marker on START. He then adds up the number of beats in the rhythm pattern on his card & calls it out. Then, he checks the answer on the back. If correct, he moves the number of circles as there are beats in his pattern. (For Example: 3 beats — 3 circles.) Player One continues picking and calling out the number of beats in his patterns until he enters the basketball hoop & scores ONE point.

Note: If he is on CIRCLE 24, any pattern correctly called will get him through the hoop & he scores ONE point.

Player Two then picks up TOP Game Card after placing his marker on START. He continues in the same way as Player One.

If, at any point, a player DOES NOT correctly add up the number of beats in his rhythm pattern, his opponent BLOCKS the SHOT! The opponent picks up the TOP Block Card which is face UP and follows the directions.

There are 3 types of Block Cards.
1. "Blocker" must name or identify a musical object or answer a question. If correct, he moves HIS marker to the circle number where his opponent had been and he continues play with the Game Cards until he makes a basket. He still gets to start the NEXT ROUND.
2. "Blocker" gets a FREE BLOCK CARD and moves his marker to START. His opponent must remove his marker. This counts as the "Blocker's" round and, should he make a basket, his OPPONENT gets to start the next round.
3. "Blocker" gets a Clapping Card, and if he can clap his opponent's rhythm pattern correctly, he moves HIS marker to the circle number where his opponent had been and he continues play with game cards until he makes a basket. He still gets to start the next round.

The game continues until one player has 10 points, or if playing time runs out, player with highest score wins.

Note: Always place Game & Block cards on the bottom of each pile, FACE UP, after they have been played.

PALE PATTI

Objective:
To provide experiences with identification of notes and rests.

Materials:
Poster board.

Contents:
The playing cards and an answer key.

Preparation:
Cut 33 cards from poster board, the size of regulation playing cards. Write on each card as follows:

Note/Rest Card	The match	Note/Rest Card	The match
1. 𝅝	2. whole note	17. ♪	18. eighth rest
3. 𝅗𝅥	4. half note	19. ♪	20. sixteenth rest
5. ♩	6. quarter note	21. 𝅗𝅥.	22. dotted half note
7. ♪	8. eighth note	23. ♩.	24. dotted quarter note
9. ♬	10. sixteenth note	25. ♪.	26. dotted eighth note
11. ▬	12. whole rest	27. ♫	28. set of eighth notes
13. ▬	14. half rest	29. ♫♪ (3)	30. triplet
15. 𝄽	16. quarter rest	31. ♬♬	32. set of sixteenth notes

33. Make one:

Pale Patti

Prepare an answer key exactly like the above.
Laminate all cards.

Game Directions: (2, 3, or 4 Players)

Shuffle and deal out all cards. Each player arranges his cards in a hand. All players put down, in front of them, any pairs which they have in their hands.

Player One then picks one card from Player Two, unseen. He puts this card in his hand and makes another pair if he can. Player Two then proceeds in the same way, picking from the next player and trying to make a pair.

Play continues until all pairs have been made and one player is left with the "Pale Patti." He is the loser.

PENNY PITCH

Objectives:
(These will depend upon the purpose for which each set is designed. However, they may be generally stated.)
1. To provide experiences in identification and instant recall.
2. To provide opportunities for demonstration of a skill.
3. To provide experiences in visual perception.

Materials:
    Muffin tin (foil, plastic, or metal), cards cut to the size of each section, glue, or a sturdy, noncollapsible gift box, approximately 12" x 18", and a penny.

Contents:
    The game board and a penny.

Preparation:
    Example, the tin: (More than one tin may be required for a set.)

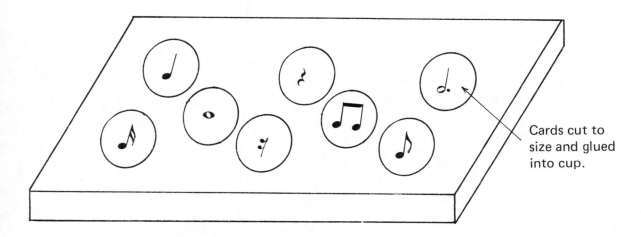

Cards cut to size and glued into cup.

Example, The box:

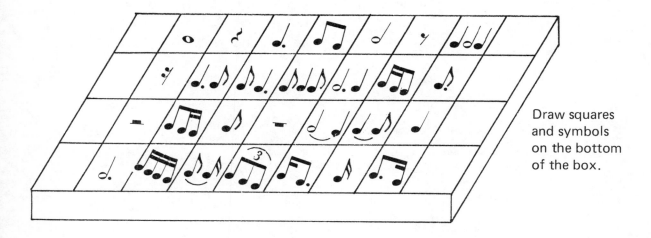

Draw squares and symbols on the bottom of the box.

Game Directions: (2, 3, or 4 Players)

Player One tosses the penny. He must identify the symbol upon which it lands. Score 1 point for each correct answer. Play continues in this way until one player reaches 20 points. He is the winner.

Suggestions for adaptation:

1. Identifying notes, singularly and in combination and rests.

(In each cup or square you may add the value for each note and rest, thereby teaching and/or reinforcing values. Scoring may be on the values.)

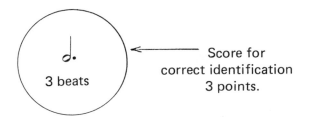

2. Letter names of notes.
   a. Draw the notes on staves in each square or cup.
   b. Designate the note to be written on a staff by the player.

3. Identifying intervals.

4. Identifying terms, signs, and symbols.

5. Identifying key signatures.

6. Identifying instruments of the orchestra from pictures.

7. Performing the rhythm upon which the penny lands. (May vary in levels of difficulty.)

8. Singing or playing a melody that is written on a staff.

PEOPLE IN HISTORY GAME

Objectives:
1. To provide experiences with identification, letter names (𝄞).
2. To provide Social Studies enrichment.

Materials:
3'' x 5'' lined index cards.

Contents:
Index cards on which names of important historical figures have been written in note heads and letters.

Preparation:
Prepare one card for each historical figure like the following example.

(Place answers on the back of each card.)

Game Directions:

Game One (Alone or 2 Players)
Challenge yourself or a friend. Each card has the name of an important person in our country's history written on it in note heads and letters. How many names can you say and spell in 3 minutes? Use the egg timer. Try again. Can you beat your own time?

Game Two (2, 3, or 4 Players)
Deal out all cards, face up. (Each player should have the same number of cards. Leave out any extras.) Each player places his cards in a pile in front of him as they are dealt, face up.

Player One calls out the name on his top card and spells it. If correct, he places it in the discard pile in the center of the table. If not, he puts the card on the bottom of his pile.

Play continues in this way until one player has no more cards. He is the winner. winner.

Game Three (2, 3, or 4 Players)

Shuffle cards and place in a pile in the center of the table, face up.

Player One takes the top card, calls out the name and spells it. If correct, he keeps the card. If not, it goes on the bottom of the pile in the center of the table.

Each player follows in turn. The player who has the most cards at the end of the game wins.

PHRASE PUZZLES
"America"
"America, the Beautiful"
"The Star-Spangled Banner"

Objectives:
1. To build and reinforce the song repertoire.
2. To provide language arts experiences (the phrase).
3. To provide Social Studies enrichment.

Materials:
4" x 6" lined index cards.

Contents:
A two-part puzzle for each phrase of each song.

Preparation:
On each card write out a phrase from the song being prepared. Laminate each card; then cut in 2 parts so that it is self-correcting.

(Note: Each cut within any given song must be different.)
Example:

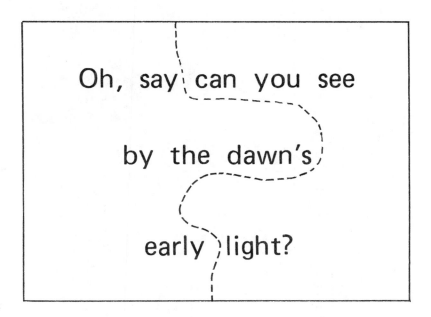

Directions:
Each phrase is in two parts. As you complete each phrase, write it on a sheet of paper. When you have finished matching and writing, number the phrases in the proper order. Then check the answer card to see if you are correct.

(Provide an answer card with the phrases numbered for each song.)

PICK-AND-PLAY

Objectives:
1. To provide experiences with identification of notes and rests.
2. To provide for reinforcement of note values, $\frac{2}{4}$, $\frac{3}{4}$, $\frac{4}{4}$, $\frac{5}{4}$ meters.
3. To provide for reinforcement of equal values concept.

Materials:
Large sheets of poster board, one "die."

Contents:
Game board, Notes, Rests, Values, Bonus, and Penalty Cards, 4 markers.

Preparation:
Cut cards from poster board, 2" x 2".

Notes Cards:
On back of each card, write NOTES and the name of the note drawn on the front.
Example:

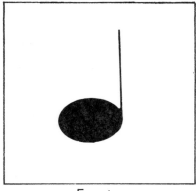

Front

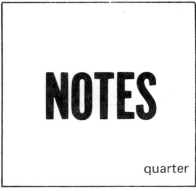

quarter

Back

Rest Cards:
Follow the same procedure.
Example:

Front

eighth

Back

216

Values Cards:

Follow the same procedure.

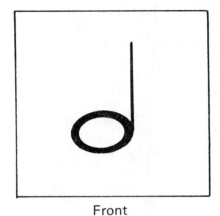

Front

2 beats

Back

Bonus Cards:

Follow the same procedure.

Note:
Make a
minimum
of 10
bonus cards.

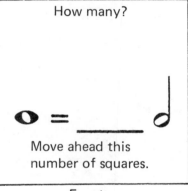

How many?

Move ahead this
number of squares.

Front

BONUS

2

Back

Penalty Cards:

Follow the same procedure.

Note:
Make a
minimum
of 10
penalty cards.

BOO HOO!

YOU MISSED
THE BONUS
SO LOSE 1 TURN.

Front

PENALTY

Back

Markers:

Make 4 markers from poster board, each one the size of a nickel. Using a permanent ink marker, color each one a different color.

The Board:

The size of the board may be left to the discretion of the teacher, but 2" squares are suggested. Double the dimensions of the sample board. Overall size should be 22" x 16". Cut from poster board.

(Game board illustration appears on next page.)

Game Directions: (2, 3, or 4 Players)

Place NOTES, RESTS, and VALUES cards in piles on the game board as indicated. Place BONUS cards on the BONUS square and PENALTY cards on the PENALTY square. Player picks from the BONUS pile whenever he answers a VALUES card correctly. Player takes a PENALTY card when he misses a BONUS answer.

Player One puts his marker on START. He rolls the "die" and moves this number of squares, following the directions on the board. Play continues in this way until one person wins. Player must roll the exact number to enter the WINNER square.

Setup piles (top):

- START
- NOTES PILE — Place face UP.
- RESTS PILE — Place Face UP.
- VALUES PILE — Place face UP.

Game board:

You're almost home! FREE SPOT.	Pick from the VALUES pile.	Don't move! You've lost a turn!	Pick from the RESTS pile.	Pick from the VALUES pile.	A mud puddle! Go back 2 spaces.	Go ahead 4 spaces.
Not again! Go back 2 spaces.	Pick from the RESTS pile.	Pick from the NOTES pile.	You deserve a rest! FREE SPOT!	Pick from the NOTES pile.	Pick from the RESTS pile.	Pick from the NOTES pile.
Pick from the NOTES pile.	Pick from the NOTES pile.	Pick from the RESTS pile.	Sorry, friend. Go back 2 spaces.	Pick from the NOTES pile.	Pick from the NOTES pile.	Pick from the RESTS pile.
You're getting closer, so lose 1 turn!	Nap Time! FREE SPOT.	Pick from the VALUES pile.	Take a deep breath! FREE SPOT!	Pick from the RESTS pile.	Have fun! Go ahead 5 spaces!	Oops! Go back 2 spaces.
Pick from the RESTS pile.	Pick from the VALUES pile.	Pick from the VALUES pile.	Pick from the VALUES pile.	Pick from the VALUES pile.	Pick from the VALUES pile.	Pick from the VALUES pile.
BELIEVE IT or NOT! FREE SPOT!	Pick from the RESTS pile.	Pick from the RESTS pile.	Pick from the RESTS pile.	Pick from the RESTS pile.	Oh, no! You lose 1 turn.	You're LUCKY! Go ahead 2 spaces.
Pick from the VALUES pile.	Pick from the NOTES pile.	Wow! Move ahead 3 spaces.	Thunder & lightning! Go back 2 spaces!	Pick from the NOTES pile.	SMILE! Go ahead 2 spaces.	Now you've done it! Go back 2 spaces.

Boxes (bottom):

- WINNER
- PENALTY PILE — Place face DOWN.
- BONUS PILE — Place face UP. If you miss the BONUS, take a PENALTY card.

POCKET RHYTHMS

Objectives:

1. To provide instruction in building measures in 2, 3, 4, 5.

                                                 4   4   4   4
2. To provide for experimentation with combinations of notes and rests in measure building.
3. To provide concrete experiences with note/rest values.
4. To introduce or reinforce the traditional system of counting.
5. To provide extended learning in math (addition).

Materials:

Poster board or heavy cardboard. Mystik tape, cloth or plastic.

Contents:

Pockets for 2, 3, 4, and 5 beat measures. Cards for notes and rests.

Pockets:

5 beat measure — Cut poster board or cardboard 6'' wide by 15'' long. Score 1-1/2'' from bottom along length of card. Fold to form pocket. Tape sides to length of card. Tape sides to close but clip in to open pocket. See diagrams.

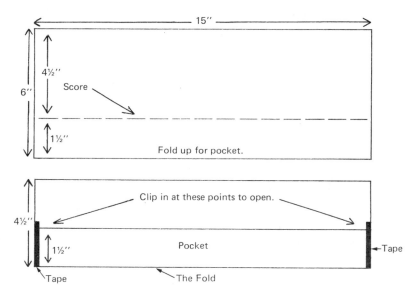

Divide into 5 measures, each 3'' wide by 4-1/2'' long. Mark each beat within the measure.

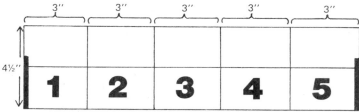

4 beat measure: Follow the same procedure, but cut card 12'' wide.

3 beat measure: Follow the same procedure, but cut card 9'' wide.

2 beat measure: Follow the same procedure, but cut card 6'' wide.

Cards:

From poster board cut 36 cards 3'' wide x 4-1/2'' long, 2 cards 4-1/2'' wide x 4-1/2'' long, 4 cards 1-1/2'' wide x 4-1/2'' long, 6 cards 6'' wide x 4-1/2'' long, 2 cards 9'' wide x 4-1/2'' long, 4 cards 12'' wide x 4-1/2'' long.;

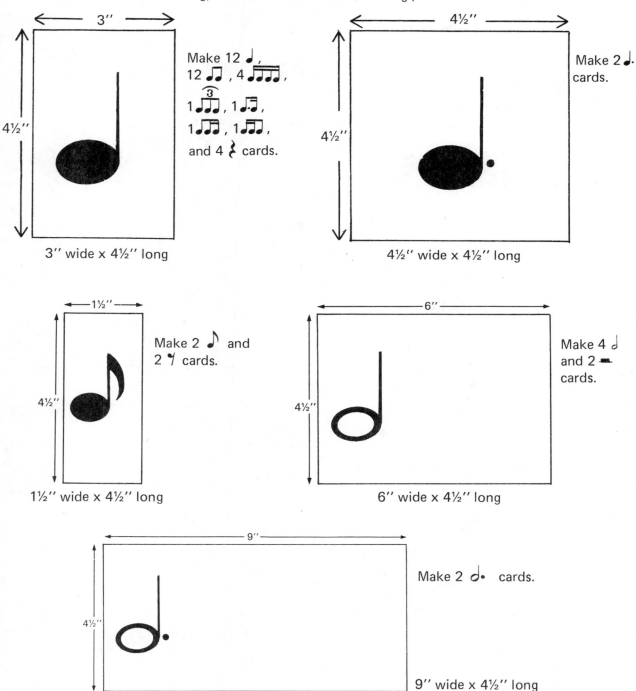

3'' wide x 4½'' long

4½'' wide x 4½'' long

1½'' wide x 4½'' long

6'' wide x 4½'' long

9'' wide x 4½'' long

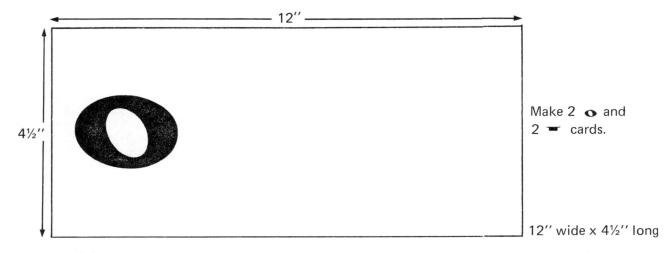

Make 2 𝐨 and 2 ⊐ cards.

12" wide x 4½" long

Directions for children:
"How to Use Pocket Rhythms"

A. 1. How many different 2 beat measures can you make? 3 beat measures? 4 beat measures? 5 beat measures?

   2. Make a list for each measure set on separate sheets of paper.

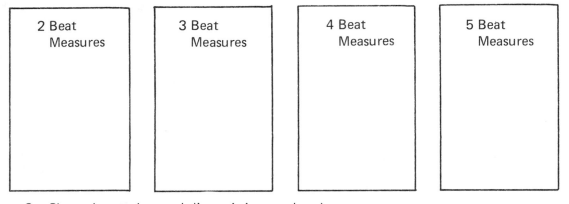

| 2 Beat Measures | 3 Beat Measures | 4 Beat Measures | 5 Beat Measures |

   3. Show the teacher each list as it is completed.

   4. Build rhythm patterns from your list. (4 measures in each pattern.)

   5. Join with one or two friends. Each person chooses a different non-pitched instrument and plays his 2 (2 beat measure) pattern. *When 2*
      4
      or more rhythms are sounded at the same time, they are called poly-rhythms.

   6. Do Steps 4 and 5 again with 3 beat, 4 beat, and 5 beat patterns.

B. 1. Play a game with a friend. Begin with the 2 beat pocket.

   2. Build your friend a 2 beat measure. He must clap it correctly. If he does, he scores 1 point.

   3. Now your friend builds a different 2 beat measure for you.

   4. Next round, use the 3 beat pocket, then 4 and 5. Play as many rounds as you choose.

   5. Player with highest score at the end of the game wins.

RECORDER 'ROUND AND 'ROUND

Objectives:
1. To motivate playing of soprano recorder.
2. To facilitate and reinforce melodic reading through the soprano recorder.

Materials:
Poster board.

Contents:
Game board, bonus cards, markers, two soprano recorders, and one die.

Preparation:
Make the playing board as per diagram, doubling the dimensions.

(See following page)

Make 15 bonus cards the dimensions of the Bonus Card rectangle. Each should be a short melody, simple rhythmically and melodically, to be played on the soprano recorder.

Make 4 penny-size game markers.

Game Directions: (2, 3 or 4 Players)

Each player needs a soprano recorder. You will also need one die.

Player One puts his marker on START and rolls the die. He moves the number of the roll in the direction of the arrows. If he lands on a "note" square, he plays this note on his recorder. If correct, he stays on this square. If not, he returns to START if this is on the first move. (At any other time, player returns to square from which he came if he plays his note incorrectly.)

Bonus Squares: Player takes a Bonus Card. He must play it correctly, rhythmically and melodically, to go ahead the number of squares written on the card. If incorrect, he goes back to the square from which he came but does not have to play the note again if there is one written on his square.

Penalty Squares: Player loses a turn or goes backwards as written on the square, but it then becomes a FREE spot — no notes to be played.

Player Two follows in turn and the play continues. First player to enter the FINISH wins.

(**Note:** You must roll the *exact* number to enter the FINISH square.)

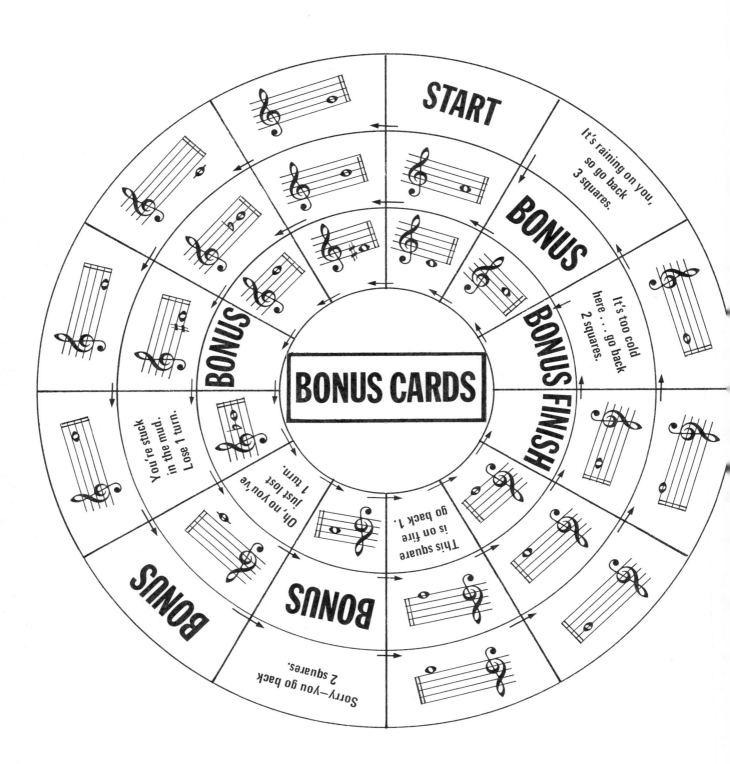

RHYTHM BASEBALL

Objectives:

1. To provide experiences with reading rhythm patterns of varying degrees of difficulty in $\frac{2}{4}$, $\frac{3}{4}$, $\frac{4}{4}$, and $\frac{5}{4}$.

2. To provide experiences with recognition of possible notes/rests combinations making 2, 3, 4, and 5 beat patterns.

Materials:

80 3" x 5" index cards, white or green poster board.

Contents:

Game board, game cube, game cards and markers.

Preparation:

Make the game board from poster board as follows:

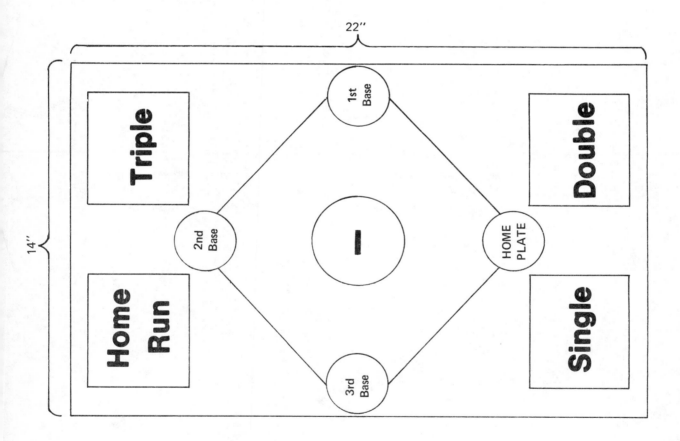

Make a game cube following the general directions for the cube. Each side should be 3″ x 3″. Write on the cube as follows:

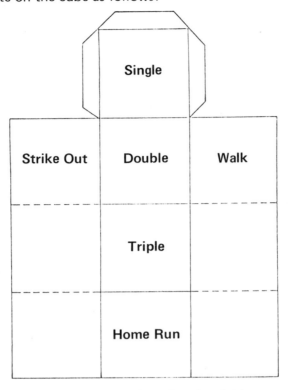

Make 9 game markers for each team, the size of a nickel. Use poster board.

On the back of 20 index cards write "Single." Also write the counts or rhythm sounds for each pattern on the back side. Write lightly in pencil so that it will not show through the card.

On the face of each card write as follows:

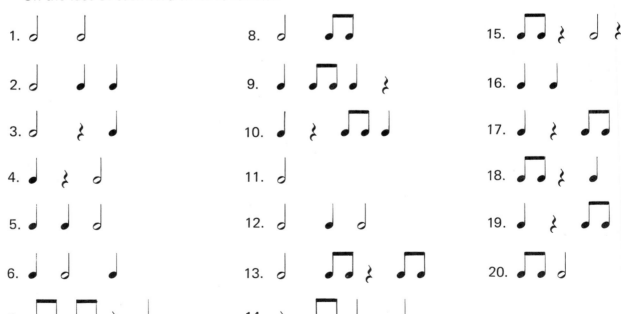

On the back of 20 index cards write "Double." Also write the counts or rhythm sounds for each pattern on the back side. Write lightly in pencil so that it will not show through the card.

On the face of each card write as follows:

1.

8. 𝅝

15.

2. ♩ —

9. ♫ ♩ ♩. 𝅘𝅥𝅮𝅘𝅥𝅮𝅘𝅥𝅮³

16. ♩.

3. ♩. ♩

10. ♫ 𝅘𝅥𝅮𝅘𝅥𝅮𝅘𝅥𝅮³ ♫ ♩

17. ♩ ♩.

4. ♩ 𝅘𝅥𝅮𝅘𝅥𝅮𝅘𝅥𝅮³ — ♩

11. ♩ 𝅝

18. ♩ ♩.

5. ♫ 𝅘𝅥𝅮𝅘𝅥𝅮𝅘𝅥𝅮³ ♩

12. 𝅝 ♩

19. ♩ 𝅘𝅥𝅮𝅘𝅥𝅮𝅘𝅥𝅮³

6. ♩ ♩. ♫

13. ♩ 𝅘𝅥𝅮𝅘𝅥𝅮𝅘𝅥𝅮³ ♩

20. 𝅘𝅥𝅮𝅘𝅥𝅮𝅘𝅥𝅮³ ♫

7. ⅃ ♩. ♩

14. ♩. ♩

On the back of 20 index cards write "Triple." Also write the counts or rhythm sounds for each pattern on the back side. Write lightly in pencil so that it will not show through the card.

On the face of each card write as follows:

1. ⅄ ♪ ⅄ ♪ ♩

8. ♪ ♩ ♪ ♩ ♩

15. ♪ ♩ ♪ ♩

2. ♩ ♩ 𝅘𝅥𝅯𝅘𝅥𝅯𝅘𝅥𝅯³ ♩

9. ♩ ♪ ♩ ♪ ♩

16. ♩. ♪ ♩.

3. 𝅘𝅥𝅯𝅘𝅥𝅯𝅘𝅥𝅯𝅘𝅥𝅯 𝅝

10. ♫ 𝅘𝅥𝅯𝅘𝅥𝅯𝅘𝅥𝅯𝅘𝅥𝅯 ♩. ♪

17. ♫ 𝅘𝅥𝅯𝅘𝅥𝅯𝅘𝅥𝅯𝅘𝅥𝅯

4. 𝅘𝅥𝅯𝅘𝅥𝅯𝅘𝅥𝅯𝅘𝅥𝅯 — ♩

11. ♩. ♪ 𝅘𝅥𝅯𝅘𝅥𝅯𝅘𝅥𝅯³ ♩

18. ♩. ♪ ♩

5. ♪ ♩ ♪

12. ♩. ♪ 𝅘𝅥𝅯𝅘𝅥𝅯𝅘𝅥𝅯𝅘𝅥𝅯 ♩

19. 𝅘𝅥𝅯𝅘𝅥𝅯𝅘𝅥𝅯𝅘𝅥𝅯 𝅘𝅥𝅯𝅘𝅥𝅯𝅘𝅥𝅯³

6. ♩ ⅃ 𝅘𝅥𝅯𝅘𝅥𝅯𝅘𝅥𝅯𝅘𝅥𝅯

13. ♩ ♩. ♪ ♩

20. 𝅘𝅥𝅯𝅘𝅥𝅯𝅘𝅥𝅯𝅘𝅥𝅯 ♩

7. ♩ 𝅘𝅥𝅯𝅘𝅥𝅯𝅘𝅥𝅯³ 𝅘𝅥𝅯𝅘𝅥𝅯𝅘𝅥𝅯𝅘𝅥𝅯

14. ♩ 𝅘𝅥𝅯𝅘𝅥𝅯𝅘𝅥𝅯𝅘𝅥𝅯 ♩

On the back of 20 index cards write "Home Run." Also write the counts or rhythm sounds for each pattern on the back side. Write lightly in pencil so that it will not show through the card.

On the face of each card write as follows:

Game Directions: (2 Players or 2 Teams of Players)
(When playing in teams, players take turns being "at bat.") Place all cards in marked rectangles on the playing board, FACE UP.

Player One (Team One) places his marker on home plate. He rolls the game cube and follows the directions:

Single   Take a card from the singles pack and clap the rhythm. If correct, go to First Base. Then send your next man to bat, using another marker and continue, first rolling the cube.

Double   Take a card from the doubles pack and clap the rhythm. If correct, go to Second Base. Then send your next man to bat, using another marker and continue, first rolling the cube.

Triple   Take a card from the triples pack and clap the rhythm. If correct, go to Third Base. Then send your next man to bat, using another marker and continue, first rolling the cube.

Home Run Take a card from the home run pack and clap the rhythm pattern. If correct, go around the bases. You have scored a run. Then send your next man to bat, using another marker and continue, first rolling the cube.

Strike Out You have rolled your man "OUT."

Walk   You move your marker to First Base without having to clap the rhythm pattern correctly. Then send your next man to bat, using another marker and continue, first rolling the cube.

Player One or Team One remains "at bat" until 3 outs are made. A player is out if he rolls a Strike Out or claps his rhythm incorrectly. When 3 outs have been made, Player Two or Team Two is "at bat" and play continues in the same way.

Scoring: A run is scored every time a man (marker) comes HOME, having gone around the bases. Player or Team with the most runs at the end of the game wins.
Note: An inning is only completed when BOTH teams have been "at bat." Play as many complete innings as time allows. Do NOT add in the score of any INCOMPLETE inning.

Stealing of bases is not allowed. A man (marker) is only moved to the next base when another marker is going to replace him.

Answers are on the BACK of each card so be sure to place them FACE UP on the rectangles.

RHYTHM DICE

Objectives:
1. To reinforce rhythmic reading skills.
2. To provide opportunities for creating word chains to given rhythm patterns.

Materials:
Poster board or heavy cardboard.

Contents:
Four note/rest cubes and one cube with skill directions.

Preparation:
Prepare the cubes as per general directions, same size or larger. Before taping, write on the squares as shown in the following example:

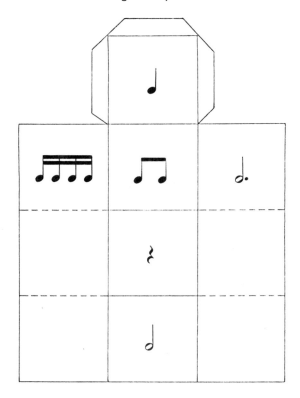

Notes/rests dice may each follow this pattern or may include any notes/rests of the reader's choice. Each die may be the same or each die may include a different set of notes/rests. The decision will be dependent upon the level to which the activity is directed. Make 4 of these dice.

The fifth die will designate skills as follows:

Side 1: Clap the rhythm and step the basic beat in the order of the roll. (4 Points)

Side 2: Clap in the order of the roll. (1 Point)

Side 3: Clap as you rolled it while you speak the rhythm sounds. (3 Points)

Side 4: Play as you rolled it on rhythm sticks. (1 Point)

Side 5: Make a chant or a word chain for your pattern. (10 Points)

Side 6: Free choice. (2 Points)

Game Directions: (2, 3, or 4 Players)

Player One rolls the dice with the notes/rests on them and places them in the order of the roll. He then rolls the die that tells what to do. If he performs the pattern correctly, he scores the number of points as indicated.

Special note:

Chant or word chain example.

Roll-y poll-y ted -dy bear.

Play continues in this way, each player scoring when correct. The first player with 25 points is the winner.

RHYTHM FOOTBALL
(Level 1, Intermediate; Level 2, Advanced)

Objectives:

1. To reinforce reading of rhythm patterns in $\frac{2}{4}$, $\frac{3}{4}$, $\frac{4}{4}$, $\frac{5}{4}$.

2. To review names of notes and rests.

Materials:

Green poster board, white poster board or oak tag.

Contents:

Game board, game cards, answer keys, extra point cards, and 2 markers.

Preparation:

Using green poster board, make a football field as follows:

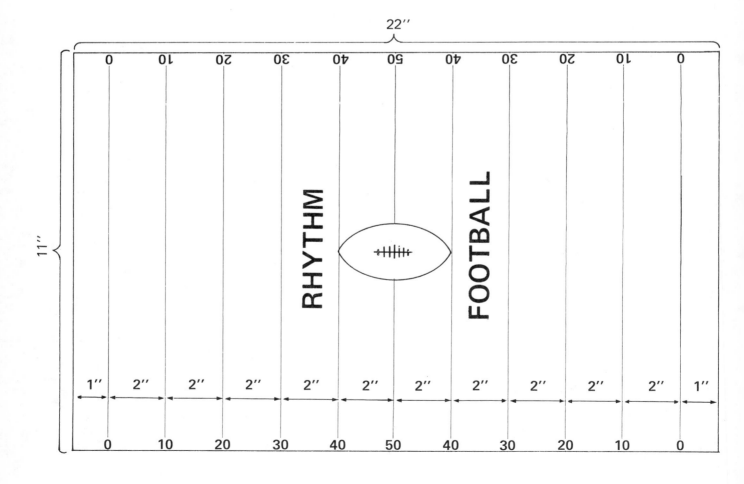

232

Cut 34 Rhythm Football cards from white poster board, 2-1/2'' x 3-1/2'' and write on as follows for Level 1:

29. 2/4 (rhythm notation)

30. 3/4 (rhythm notation)

31. Gain an extra 10 yards.
32. Gain an extra 20 yards.
33. Penalty — Lose 10 yards.
34. Penalty — Lose 20 yards.

(Make an answer key stating rhythm sounds or counting for each measure set.)
Cut 34 Rhythm Football cards from white poster board, 2-1/2'' x 3-1/2'' and write on as follows for Level 2:

1. 2/4 (rhythm notation)
2. 3/4 (rhythm notation)
3. 4/4 (rhythm notation)
4. 5/4 (rhythm notation)
5. 2/4 (rhythm notation)
6. 3/4 (rhythm notation)
7. 4/4 (rhythm notation)
8. 5/4 (rhythm notation)
9. 2/4 (rhythm notation)
10. 3/4 (rhythm notation)
11. 4/4 (rhythm notation)
12. 5/4 (rhythm notation)
13. 2/4 (rhythm notation)

14. 3/4 (rhythm notation)
15. 4/4 (rhythm notation)
16. 5/4 (rhythm notation)
17. 2/4 (rhythm notation)
18. 3/4 (rhythm notation)
19. 4/4 (rhythm notation)
20. 5/4 (rhythm notation)
21. 2/4 (rhythm notation)
22. 3/4 (rhythm notation)
23. 4/4 (rhythm notation)
24. 5/4 (rhythm notation)
25. 2/4 (rhythm notation)
26. 3/4 (rhythm notation)

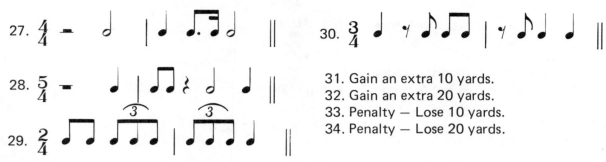

(Make an answer key stating rhythm sounds or counting for each measure set.)

Cut 16 Extra Point cards from white poster board, 2-1/2'' x 3-1/2'' and write on as follows (same for both levels):

1. 𝅝

2. 𝄻

3. 𝅗𝅥

4. 𝄼

5. 𝅗𝅥.

6. 𝅘𝅥

7. 𝄽

8. 𝅘𝅥.

9. 𝅘𝅥𝅮

10. 𝄾

11. 𝅘𝅥𝅮.

12. 𝅘𝅥𝅘𝅥

13. 𝅘𝅥𝅘𝅥𝅘𝅥 (3)

14. 𝅘𝅥𝅯

15. 𝄿

16. 𝅘𝅥𝅯𝅘𝅥𝅯𝅘𝅥𝅯𝅘𝅥𝅯

(Make an answer key naming each note, rest, and set of notes.)

Make 2 circular markers to represent each player.

Game Directions: (For 2 Players)

Each player places his marker on the 50 yard line and decides upon the direction he will go (the goal he is defending). The Rhythm Football cards and the Extra Point cards are shuffled and placed in piles, face down.

Player One turns up the first Rhythm Football card and claps and/or says the rhythm. If correct, he advances 10 yards in the direction of his goal. Then he continues turning up cards and sounding rhythms until he has made a touchdown.

If Player One sounds a rhythm incorrectly, he must remain where he is. Play is then given to Player Two. Player Two continues in the same way.

Should either player turn over an extra gain of yardage card, he follows the directions on the card. Then he continues turning up Rhythm Football cards and sounding the rhythm.

Should either player turn over a penalty card, he follows the directions on the card but MAY NOT continue. Play goes to his opponent. Play continues in this way until one player scores a touchdown . . . 6 points.

The player scoring a touchdown may try for the extra point. He turns up the top Extra Point card and must name the note or rest correctly. If so, he receives the extra point.

After each touchdown, both players return to the 50 yard line and begin again. Player with highest score at the end of the playing period wins.

Note: All Rhythm Football Cards and Extra Point Cards are placed on the bottom of the pile, face down, after they are used.

ROLL-A-RHYTHM

Objectives:
1. To reinforce rhythmic reading skills.
2. To reinforce skill of reading from left to right.

Materials:
Poster board or heavy cardboard.

Contents:
Four rhythm cubes (stick notation).

Preparation:
Prepare the cubes as per general directions, but double the size. (**Note:** For younger children at the beginning of the rhythm sequence, larger cubes with larger symbols are preferred.) Before taping, write on the squares as shown in the following example:

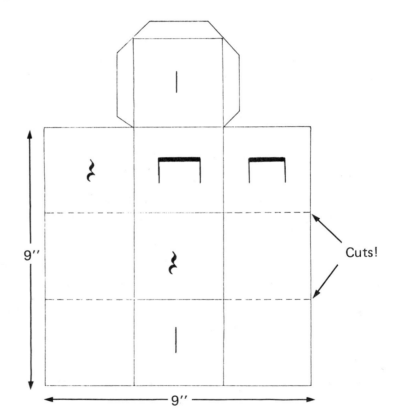

Game Directions:
If you are playing by yourself, roll the dice, one at a time. Place them in the order rolled, side by side, 1-2-3-4. Now, clap the rhythm!

When playing with a friend, take turns and check each other. Score 1 point for each pattern clapped correctly. 20 points wins the game!

RUMMY ONE

Objectives:
1. To provide experiences with reading rhythm patterns which include 𝄪 𝅗𝅥 and 𝄽.
2. To become familiar with 4 beat combinations.
3. To provide experiences with left to right progression.

Materials:
Oak tag or poster board.

Contents:
Playing cards and answer key.

Preparation:
Cut 34 cards of poster board or oak tag the size of regulation playing cards. Number each card in the right hand corner and prepare as follows:

1. | | | |
2. | ⊓ | |
3. | | ⊓ |
4. | | | ⊓
5. ⊓ | | |
6. ⊓ ⊓ | |
7. | ⊓ ⊓ |
8. | | ⊓ ⊓
9. | ⁊ | |
10. | | ⁊ |
11. | | | ⁊

12. | ⁊ | ⁊
13. | ⁊ ⁊ |
14. | ⊓ ⁊ |
15. | ⁊ ⊓ |
16. | | ⁊ ⊓
17. ⊓ ⁊ | |
18. ⊓ | ⁊ ⊓
19. ⊓ ⊓ ⁊ |
20. 𝅗𝅥 𝅗𝅥
21. 𝅗𝅥 | |
22. | | 𝅗𝅥

23. | 𝅗𝅥 |
24. 𝅗𝅥 ⊓ |
25. 𝅗𝅥 | ⊓
26. | ⊓ 𝅗𝅥
27. ⊓ | 𝅗𝅥
28. | 𝅗𝅥 ⊓
29. ⊓ 𝅗𝅥 |
30. | ⁊ 𝅗𝅥
31. ⊓ ⁊ 𝅗𝅥
32. 𝅗𝅥 ⁊ |
33. 𝅗𝅥 ⁊ ⊓
34. ⁊ 𝅗𝅥 ⁊

On back of each card write "Rummy One." Laminate all cards.

Prepare an answer key which corresponds to the number on each card and states the rhythm sound for each pattern. For example: 1. ta ta ta ta (| | | |)
(Note: Counting may be substituted for rhythm sounds. 1-2-3-4 [| | | |]).

Game Directions: (2, 3, or 4 Players)

Shuffle cards and place in a stack, face down, in center of the playing area.

Player One picks up the top card. He sounds the rhythm. If he is not correct, another player must hear the mistake and shout, "Rummy." The card goes to the player who was correct. (Check the Answer Key.)

Each player builds his own pile of cards. The winner is the player with the most cards at the end of the game.

RUMMY TWO

Objectives, Materials, and Contents are the same as for RUMMY ONE but patterns also include 𝄽 and 𝄾

Cards and answer key are prepared as follows:

1.
2.
3.
4.
5.
6.
7.
8.
9.
10.
11.

12.
13.
14.
15.
16.
17.
18.
19.
20.
21.
22.

23.
24.
25.
26.
27.
28.
29.
30.
31.
32.
33.

On back of each card write "RUMMY TWO." Laminate all cards.

34.

238

RUMMY THREE

Objectives:
1. To reinforce reading of advanced rhythm patterns.
2. To increase speed and facility in reading rhythms.
3. To expand the rhythm vocabulary.

Materials:
Oak tag or poster board.

Contents:
Playing cards and answer key.

Preparation:
Cut 34 cards of poster board, or oak tag, the size of regulation playing cards. Number each card in the right hand corner and prepare as follows:

On back of each card write "RUMMY THREE." Laminate all cards.

Prepare an answer key which corresponds to the number on each card and states the rhythm sound for each pattern.

Game Directions: (2, 3, or 4 Players)

Shuffle all cards and put stack in center of the playing area, face down.

Player One picks up top card, places it face up for all to see and claps the rhythm. If he is not correct, another player must hear the mistake and shout, "Rummy." The card goes to the player who was correct, the player who clapped the rhythm or the player who caught the error and shouted, "Rummy." (Check Answer Key if there is any question.)

Each player builds his own stack of cards. The winner is the player with the most cards at the end of the game.

SMD — DMS

Objectives:

Game 1, Level 1   To provide experiences with perception of like SOL-MI-DO patterns and like DO-MI-SOL patterns.

Game 2, Level 2   a. To provide opportunities for visual discrimination between ascending and descending patterns.

b. To reinforce rule for placement of SOL-MI-DO.

c. To provide experiences with matching ascending and descending patterns.

Materials:

Index cards.

Contents:

The playing cards.

Preparation:

Cut 33 cards from index cards, the size of regulation playing cards. Make 2 of each of the following:

Make one:

(**Note:** Note heads may be color coded—SOL-*red,* MI-*blue.* No key signatures are included at this beginning level of the melody sequence.)

Game Directions: (2, 3 or 4 Players)

Shuffle and deal out all cards. Each player arranges his cards in a hand. All players put down in front of them, any pairs which they have in their hands.

Player One then picks one card from Player Two, unseen. He puts this card in his hand and makes another pair if he can. Player Two then proceeds in the same way, picking from the next player and trying to make a pair.

Play continues until all pairs have been made and one player is left with the "SOL-MI-DO." He is the loser.

(**Note:** Game 1 matches are made between like SOL-MI-DO patterns and between like DO-MI-SOL patterns. Game 2 matches are made between ascending and descending patterns, DO-MI-SOL to SOL-MI-DO.)

SAD SAM

Objectives:

1. To reinforce note values concept (2, 3, 4, 5).
   (4 4 4 4)
2. To provide extended learning in math (addition of fractions).

Materials:

Poster board.

Contents:

The playing cards and an answer key.

Preparation:

Cut 37 cards from poster board, the size of regulation playing cards. Write on each card as follows:

Note/Rest Card	The match	Note/Rest Card	The match
1. 𝅝	2. 4 beats	19. 𝄽	20. 1 beat
3. ▬	4. 4 beats	21. 𝅘𝅥𝅮.	22. ¾ beat
5. 𝅘𝅥.	6. 3 beats	23. 𝅘𝅥𝅮 𝅘𝅥𝅮	24. ½ + ¼ = ¾ beat
7. 𝅗𝅥 𝅘𝅥	8. 2 + 1 = 3 beats	25. 𝅘𝅥𝅮	26. ½ beat
9. 𝅗𝅥	10. 2 beats	27. 𝄾	28. ½ beat
11. ▬	12. 2 beats	29. 𝅘𝅥 𝅘𝅥	30. ½ + ½ = 1 beat
13. 𝅘𝅥 𝅘𝅥𝅮	14. 1 + ½ = 1½ beats	31. 𝅘𝅥𝅮	32. ¼ beat
15. 𝅘𝅥.	16. 1½ beats	33. 𝄿	34. ¼ beat
17. 𝅘𝅥	18. 1 beat	35. 𝅘𝅥𝅯𝅘𝅥𝅯𝅘𝅥𝅯𝅘𝅥𝅯	36. ¼ + ¼ + ¼ + ¼ = 1 beat

Prepare an answer key exactly like the above.

37. Make one:

Sad Sam

Laminate all cards.

Game Directions: (2, 3, or 4 Players)

Shuffle and deal out all cards. Each player arranges his cards in a hand. All players put down, in front of them, any pairs which they have in their hands.

Player One then picks one card from Player Two, unseen. He puts this card in his hand and makes another pair if he can.

Player Two then proceeds in the same way, picking from the next player and trying to make a pair.

Play continues until all pairs have been made and one player is left with the "Sad Sam." He is the loser.

SELF-CORRECTING DEVICES

Objectives:
(These will depend upon the purpose for which each set is designed. However, they may be generally stated.)
1. To provide for experiences with identification; instruction and/or reinforcement.
2. To provide for remediation.

Materials:
5'' x 8'' index cards.

Contents:
The two-part puzzle sets.

Preparation:
(These devices are quickly constructed and give the student a means for checking answers immediately.)

1. Divide card in half with a light, penciled-in line.

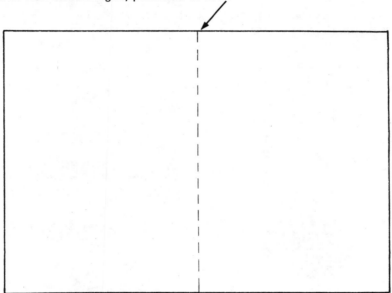

2. On one half, draw the item to be identified; on the other, its name.

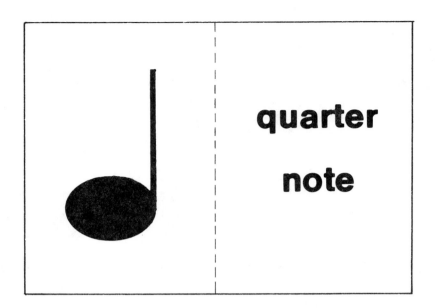

3. Laminate the card. Then cut it into two parts. Make each card within a given set a distinctively different cut.

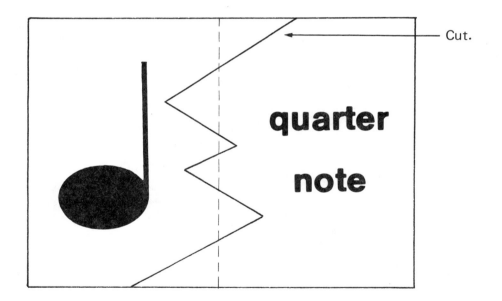

Cut.

Directions:
The child must match each one and write it on a sheet of paper as it is matched. (Provide staff paper when required.)

Possible Uses:
1. Identifying notes/rests.
2. Reading rhythms.*
3. Reviewing note/rest values.
4. Identifying key signatures.
5. Identifying intervals.
6. Identifying letter names of notes, 𝄞 and/or 𝄢
7. Spelling words in music notes.
8. Identifying signs and symbols.

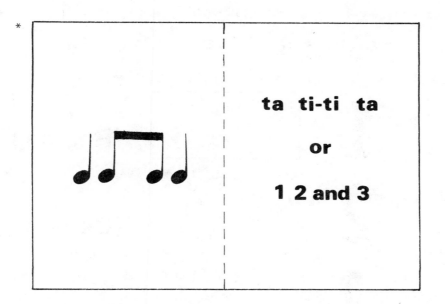

SHAPES, SHAPES, SHAPES!

Objectives:
1. To provide experiences in visual perception.
2. To motivate body movement activities.

Materials:
5'' x 8'' index card.

Contents:
The work card. Prepare the work card as follows:

SHAPES, SHAPES, SHAPES!

Using just **YOU**, how many different ways can you make these shapes?

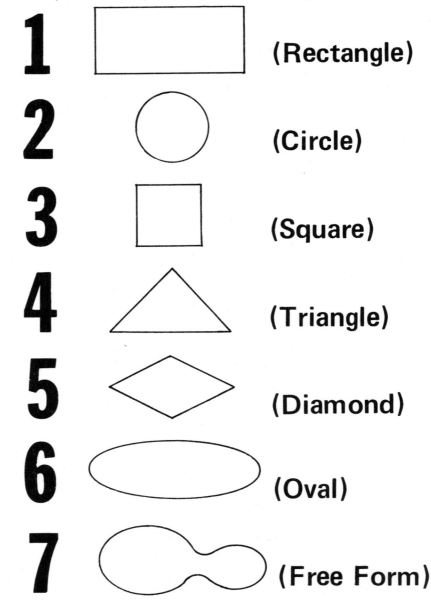

1 (Rectangle)

2 (Circle)

3 (Square)

4 (Triangle)

5 (Diamond)

6 (Oval)

7 (Free Form)

SOLVING A PROBLEM THROUGH MOVEMENT

Objectives:
1. To motivate body movement activities.
2. To provide opportunities for creativity through movement.
3. To provide experiences with moving to a beat set.
4. To provide experiences in solving problems of spatial relationships.
5. To provide for extended learnings in stating a problem in scientific terms.

Materials:

5'' x 8'' index cards.

Contents:

The task card. Prepare the task card as follows:

SOLVING A PROBLEM through
MOVEMENT . . .

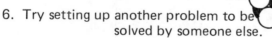

Ⓐ

1. You may work alone or with a partner.

2. Pick a starting point, (A). Set up the problem. To what point must you move? How many beats will you need to reach that point?

4. What movements will you use? Will you have things in your way... obstacles? What will they be?

3. If you are working alone, use the metrenome to sound the beats. You will have to count the beats as you move. If you are working with a partner, he will sound the beats on a drum.

5. Experiment with working out the problem, writing it as follows:
  a. Define the problem.
  b. Form a hypothesis (how you intend to solve the problem).
  c. Testing the hypothesis (the steps you followed).
  d. Your conclusion.

Ⓑ

6. Try setting up another problem to be solved by someone else.

SORTING ACTIVITIES/GAMES

General Objectives:
1. To provide for remediation and/or reinforcement of a concept or skill.
2. To refine the basic learning skills of visual perception and recall.

Materials:

Cardboard egg cartons, large and small boxes, aluminum muffin tins, and/or any divided container. Double-stick tape, transparent tape, index cards, oak tag, or poster board.

SORT-A-NOTE — LETTER NAMES ①

Specific Objectives:
1. To provide instruction in letter names (𝄞).
2. To reinforce note recognition skill.
3. To develop speed in note reading.
4. To remediate for the child who cognitively or perceptually is having a problem with this skill.

Contents:

Egg carton sorting box, game circles on which staves and note heads are placed with answers on the reverse side.

Preparation:

Make 72 circles from index cards, oak tag, or poster board. Use a quarter for pattern. On each of 12 circles, write as follows:

low C   low D   low E   low F   low G   A   B   high C

high D   high E   high F   high G

Be sure to include the 𝄞 on each circle as well as the letter name of the note.

Laminate each circle and place in random order in the cups of a cardboard egg carton with double-stick tape.

Prepare the remaining 60 circles as follows:

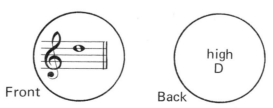

Front   Back

Make 5 of each of the 12 notes which have been placed in the egg carton. Laminate.

250

Directions for use:

A child may work alone or with a friend. The 60 circles are placed face up on work area. The child looks at each circle, calls the letter name, and places it in the proper cup. As he does this, an instant check is provided as the letter name is with the note in the cup. Should he be unable to name the note, he may turn over the circle to find out the letter name. Through repetition, he should gain in facility.

If two children are working together, it is suggested that they allow 15 seconds per turn. They may also keep score of correct placements.

Children working alone for speed may use egg timer to see how many circles they can place in 3 minutes.

SORT-A-NOTE — LETTER NAMES ②

Specific Objectives:

1. To refine note recognition skill ($\&$).
2. To develop speed and facility in note reading.

Contents:

Egg carton sorting box, game circles on which staves and note heads are placed with answers on the reverse side.

Preparation:

Same as Letter Names 1, but the 12 circles to be placed in each cup should only have the letter names written on them.

Example:

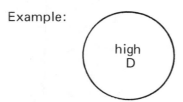

Directions for use:

Again, this activity may be engaged in by an individual child or 2 children as described in Letter Names 1, and the element of speed should be stressed.

Note: SORT-A-NOTE—LETTER NAMES 1 AND 2 may be adapted for reading ledger line notes, bass clef, or even alto clef notes for instrumentalists.

SORTING NOTES AND RESTS ①

Specific Objectives:
1. To instruct in kinds of notes and rests.
2. To reinforce this skill.
3. To develop speed in this skill.
4. To remediate for the child who cognitively or perceptually is having a problem with this skill.

Contents:

Egg carton sorting box, game circles on which are drawn a note, set of notes, or rests with answers on the reverse side.

Preparation:

Make 72 circles from index cards, oak tag, or poster board. Use a quarter for pattern. On each of 12 circles, write as follows:

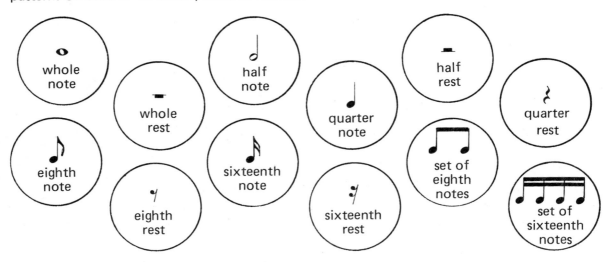

Laminate each circle and place in random order in the cups of a cardboard egg carton with double-stick tape.

Prepare the remaining 60 circles as follows:

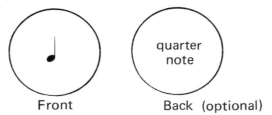

Front   Back (optional)

Make 5 of each of the 12 notes/rests which have been placed in the egg carton. Laminate.

Directions for use:

See SORT-A-NOTE—LETTER NAMES ①

SORTING NOTES AND RESTS ②

Specific Objectives:

1. To refine notes/rests recognition skill.
2. To develop speed and facility in recall.

Contents:

Egg carton sorting box, game circles on which are drawn a note, set of notes, or rests without answers on reverse side.

Preparation:

Make 72 circles from index cards, oak tag, or poster board. On each of 12 circles to be placed in cups, write as follows:

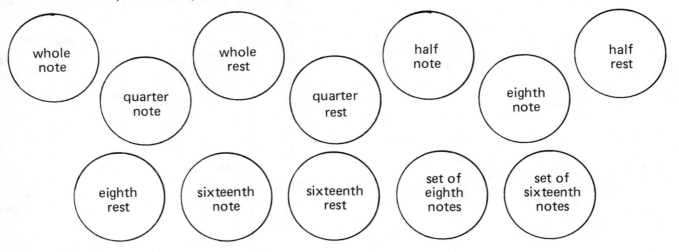

Prepare the remaining 60 circles as follows:

Example:
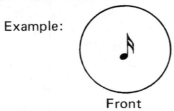

Front

Make 5 of each of the 12 notes/rests which have been placed in the egg carton. Laminate.

Directions for use:

See SORT-A-NOTE — LETTER NAMES ②

SORT-A-VALUE — 2, 3, 4, 5
4 4 4 4

Specific Objectives:

1. To reinforce recall skill of note/rest values in 2, 3, 4, 5
   4   4   4   4.
2. To develop speed and facility in working with note values.
3. To provide extended learning in math (addition).

Contents:

Egg carton sorting box, game circles on which are drawn a note, set of notes, or rests, answer key.

Preparation:

Make 34 circles from index cards, oak tag, or poster board. Use a quarter for pattern. On each of 8 circles, write as follows:

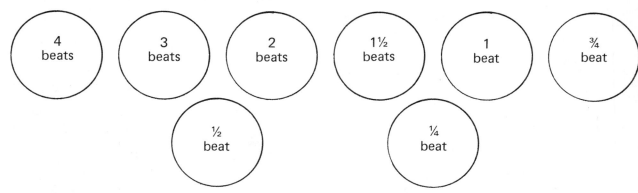

Laminate each circle and place in the cups of a cardboard egg carton with double-stick tape.

Prepare the remaining 26 circles as follows:

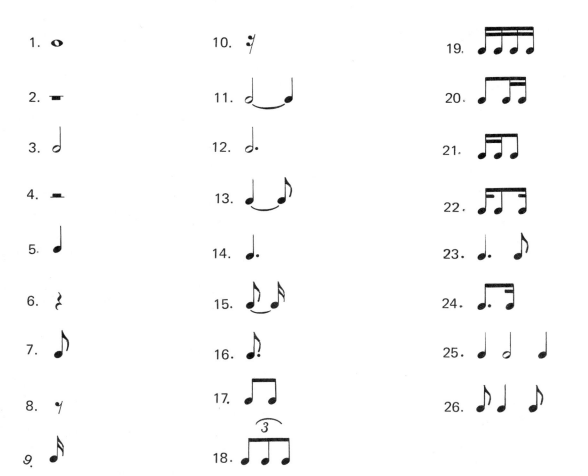

Laminate each circle. Make an answer key to be included with the activity.

Directions for use:

Working alone, the child will place each note/rest circle in the cup with the value he believes to be correct. Then, using the answer key, he will check his work, discover any errors, or report a perfect score to the teacher. It is suggested that direction and/or instruction should be given to correct errors in music math concepts and that the activity be repeated. For one or two children who have a firm foundation in the notes/rests values, the time factor challenge may be introduced.

$$\text{SORT-A-VALUE} - \frac{3, \ 6, \ 9, \ 12}{8 \ \ 8 \ \ 8 \ \ 8}$$

Specific Objectives:

1. To reinforce recall skill of note/rest values in $\frac{3, \ 6, \ 9, 12}{8 \ \ 8 \ \ 8 \ \ 8}$.

2. To develop speed and facility in working with note values in compound time.

3. To provide extended learning in math (addition).

Preparation:

Make 34 circles from index cards, oak tag, or poster board. Use a quarter for pattern. On each of 8 circles, write as follows:

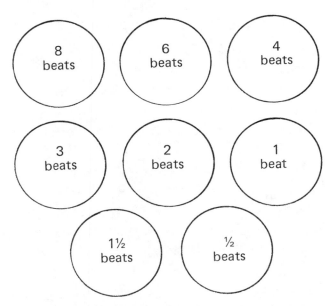

Laminate each circle and place in the cups of a cardboard egg carton with double-stick tape.

Prepare the remaining 26 circles as follows:

1. 𝅝   9. ♪   17. 𝅘𝅥𝅯𝅘𝅥𝅯𝅘𝅥𝅯

2. 𝄺   10. 𝄾   18. 𝅘𝅥 ♪

3. 𝅗𝅥   11. 𝅗𝅥 𝅘𝅥   19. ♪𝅘𝅥

4. 𝄼   12. 𝅗𝅥.   20. 𝅘𝅥. 𝅘𝅥𝅯

5. 𝅘𝅥   13. 𝅘𝅥 ♪   21. 𝅘𝅥𝅯𝅘𝅥𝅯𝅘𝅥𝅯𝅘𝅥𝅯

6. 𝄽   14. ♪.   22. 𝅘𝅥𝅮𝅘𝅥𝅯𝅘𝅥𝅯

7. ♪   15. ♪ 𝅘𝅥𝅯   23. 𝅘𝅥𝅮𝅘𝅥𝅮𝅘𝅥

8. 𝄿   16. ♪.   24. 𝅘𝅥𝅯𝅘𝅥𝅯𝅘𝅥𝅯𝅘𝅥𝅯𝅘𝅥𝅯𝅘𝅥𝅯

25. 𝅗𝅥 𝅘𝅥   26. 𝅘𝅥 𝅗𝅥

Laminate each circle. Make an answer key to be included with the activity.

Directions for use:
 See SORT-A-VALUE — 2, 3, 4, 5.
                            4 4 4 4

(**Note:** For all egg carton-sorting activities, transparent tape may be used to reinforce and secure the circle card within each cup.)

A SORTING ACTIVITY — INSTRUMENT FAMILIES

Specific Objectives:
 1. To become familiar with instrument names.
 2. To reinforce knowledge of instrument categories.

Contents:
 A sorting box, game cards on which have been written names of instruments, answer key.

Preparation:

(Note: I have included this activity and the following ones as examples of how you can use "junk" to create a game. A muffin tin, small boxes placed within a large box or any divided container may become your "sorting box.")

Attach a styrofoam divider to the bottom of a box the same size or larger as illustrated.

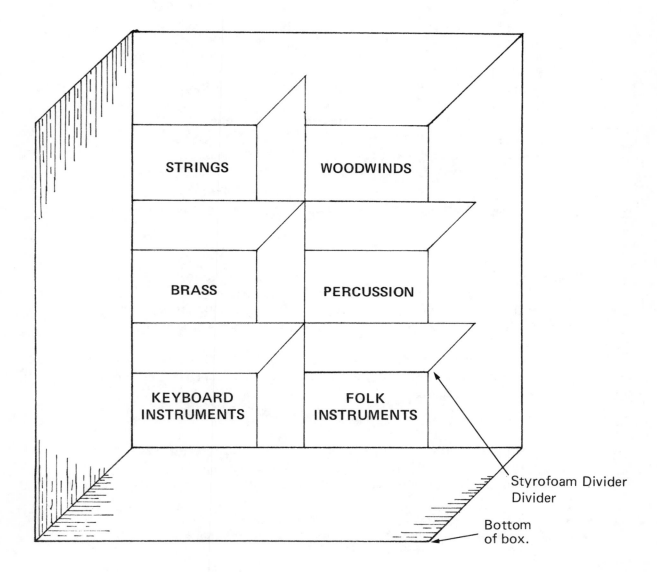

Use double-stick tape to attach divider, and write in each section as indicated.

Cut 46 cards the size of one part of the inner section of the divider. Write on each as follows:

1. violin	16. French horn	31. castanets
2. viola	17. trombone	32. triangle
3. cello	18. tuba	33. guiro
4. bass	19. sousaphone	34. bongos
5. harp	20. timpani	35. temple blocks
6. piccolo	21. snare drum	36. bells
7. flute	22. bass drum	37. piano
8. oboe	23. cymbals	38. organ
9. English horn	24. claves	39. harpsichord
10. clarinet	25. tambourine	40. clavichord
11. bass clarinet	26. gong	41. zither
12. saxophone	27. glockenspiel	42. guitar
13. bassoon	28. xylophone	43. harmonica
14. contra-bassoon	29. chimes	44. banjo
15. trumpet	30. maracas	45. ukulele
		46. tub bass

Laminate. Make an answer key which places the instruments in family groups.

Directions for use:

Alone, the child may be challenged as follows: "How quickly can you place each instrument in its proper family group? Time yourself. Try again. Can you beat your own time? Be sure to check your work with the answer key." Or, one child may challenge another.

As a game, directions may be as follows: For 2, 3, or 4 players. Shuffle and deal cards, face down. (For 2 players, use all cards; 3 players, leave out one card; 4 players, leave out 2 cards.)

Place sorting box in center of table. Each player places his cards in a pile, face down, in front of him.

Player One turns up his top card, reads aloud the instrument name, and places it in the proper section of the sorting box. Any other player may *challenge* if he thinks Player One has not placed his instrument card in the correct family group.

If Player One was correct, the player who *challenged* must put this card on the bottom of his pile. If Player One was *not* correct, he must take back his card and place it on the bottom of his pile.

Play continues in this way until one player has used all his cards. He is the winner.

SORT-A-MEASURE — 2, 3, 4, 5
4, 4, 4, 4

Specific Objectives:

1. To reinforce note value concept.
2. To increase awareness of the function of a time signature.
3. To increase awareness of possible note/rest combinations which make a measure in 2, 3, 4, and 5.
   4   4   4   4
4. To provide extended learning in math (addition).

Contents:

A sorting box, game cards on which have been drawn notes and rests in 2, 3, 4 and 5 beat combinations, answer key.

Preparation:

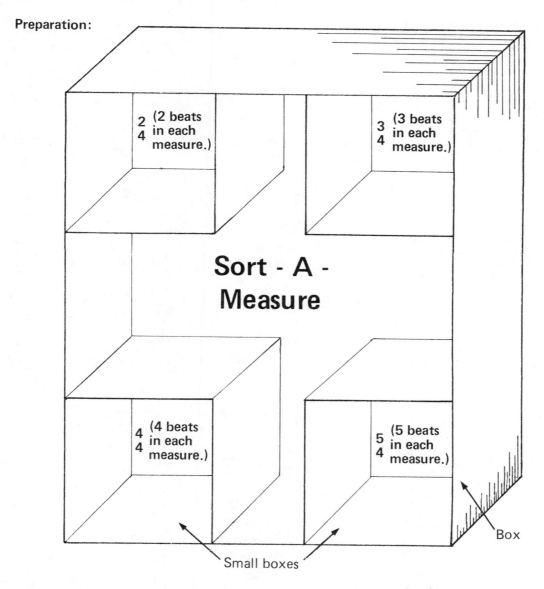

Sort - A - Measure

2/4 (2 beats in each measure.)

3/4 (3 beats in each measure.)

4/4 (4 beats in each measure.)

5/4 (5 beats in each measure.)

Box

Small boxes

One large box and 4 smaller ones provide the sorting board. Boxes are glued or attached with double-stick tape.

Cut 64 cards the size of the small boxes. (If boxes are not the same size, cut all cards to the smallest size.) Write on as follows:

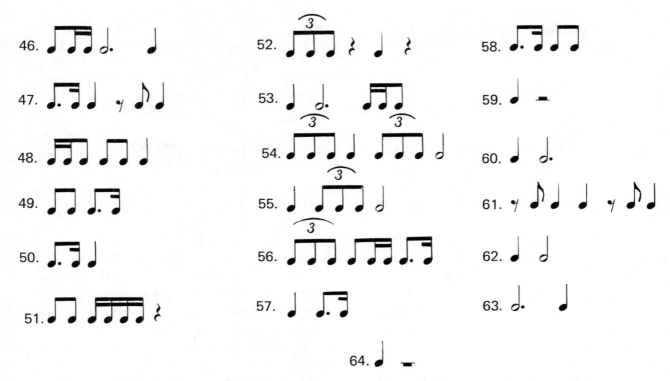

Laminate. Prepare an answer key which shows the measure groupings.

Directions for use: (For 3, 4, 5 or 6 Pláyers)

Shuffle and deal out all cards, face down. (For 3 players, leave out one card; 4 players, use all cards; 5 players, leave out four cards; 6 players, leave out four cards.) Place playing board in center of table. Each player places his cards in a pile, face down, in front of him.

Player One turns up his top card, counts up the number of beats in his measure and places the card in the correct "beat box." Any other player may *challenge* if he thinks Player One has not placed his measure card in the correct "beat box." If Player One was correct, the player who *challenged* must put this card on the bottom of his pile. If Player One was *not* correct, he must take back his measure card and place it on the bottom of his pile.

Play continues in this way until one player has used all his cards. He is the winner.

(Note: This game may be adapted for 3, 6, 9, 12
                                                8 8 8   8.)

KNOW YOUR INSTRUMENTS — A SORTING GAME

Specific Objectives:
1. To reinforce and/or instruct in instruments facts.
2. To increase ability to recall specific information.

Contents:
A sorting box with ten sections, each of which is a small box fitted within a larger box, game fact cards, answer key.

Preparation:

Prepare as for SORT-A-MEASURE, arranging and affixing boxes in an interesting pattern. Inside each box on your sorting board, write the name of one instrument you have chosen for this activity. Cut 70 cards, the dimensions of the smallest box for the fact cards. Write one fact on each card. Laminate.

Following are the instruments I chose for the activity, together with seven facts for each one:

VIOLIN — Has 4 strings — Played with a bow — Pizzicato — Soprano voice of string family — Viola belongs in same family — Cello belongs in same family — Has a bridge.

HARP — Has 47 strings — Has 7 pedals — Played with the fingers (plucked) — "Instrument of the angels" — Is a national symbol (Ireland) — Has been found in Egyptian tombs — Has red and blue strings.

FRENCH HORN — Its ancestor was the hunting horn — Can raise or lower pitches by putting hand in its bell — Originally made from the horn of an animal — Was used to call people together — The French greatly developed its use — Its shape is circular — Has been called the most difficult instrument to play.

TRUMPET — Highest voice of the brass instruments — Double and triple tonguing sound best on it — Was important to the military — There was once a competition in the playing of it at the Olympic Games — At first, it was a long, straight tube — It is mentioned in the Bible along with the harp — Louis Armstrong played it.

TROMBONE — Slide lengthens the tube — Some have valves and slides — Brass instrument which can play glissandos — Need good judgement and "ear" to play this brass — A brass which is not transposing — Tone is noble and deeper than trumpet — Like the trumpet and French horn, the lips in the mouthpiece act as a vibrating reed.

FLUTE — A woodwind that has no reed — Woodwind held to the side — Player blows across a mouth-hole — Tube that is stopped at one end — Piccolo is smaller and higher voiced "relative" — Once made of wood, it is now made of silver or nickel — Recorder is related to it.

CLARINET — A single-reed instrument — Pianissimo, crescendo and diminuendo most powerful in this woodwind — Woodwind with a high, middle and low voice — It is "the cat" in "Peter and the Wolf" — The saxophone mouthpiece is similar — It begins "The Rhapsody in Blue" — Most common is the B-flat kind.

OBOE — Double-reed woodwind — English horn is closely related — Its reed is very small — Has been called the most sensitive and expressive of the woodwinds — Plays "the duck" in "Peter and the Wolf" — The bassoon has a similar reed — Similar in appearance to clarinet except for mouthpiece.

TIMPANI — Also called "kettledrum" — Member of the percussion family — Is tuned by tightening and loosening the screws around its "head" — Played with sticks with soft heads — Can play a roll on it — Can sound like thunder — Drum that can play definite pitches.

PIANO (PIANOFORTE) — Its name means "soft-loud" — Keyboard instrument — Keys are black and white — Its ancestor is the harpsichord — Felt hammers hit the strings — Comes in different sizes and shapes — Has 2 or 3 pedals.

Make an answer key. Place fact cards in an envelope.

Directions for use:

(Alone) Take the cards from the envelope, one by one. Each card tells you something about just *one* of the instruments in the sorting board. Place each card in the instrument box in which you think it belongs. There are 7 facts for each instrument. Check all your answers with the answer key when you have finished. What is your score? A perfect score is 70. Write out each fact you missed, learn it, and show it to the teacher.

For 2, 3, or 4 Players. Player One takes one fact card from the envelope and places it in the instrument box on the sorting board in which he thinks it belongs. If there is *any question* as to whether he is correct or not, check with answer key immediately. Score 1 point for each correct answer.

Player with most points at end of game wins. (**Note:** Use all cards. Return any cards placed incorrectly to envelope and play them again.)

SPELL IT AND SING . . . NATIONAL SONGS
"America"
"America, the Beautiful"
"The Star-Spangled Banner"

Objectives:
1. To provide experiences with identification, letter names, 𝄞 .
2. To build and reinforce the song repertoire.
3. To provide language arts experiences (spelling skills).
4. To provide Social Studies enrichment.

Materials:
5'' x 8'' index cards.

Contents:
A set of cards for each song on which the words of each song have been written in note heads and letters.

Preparation:
Make each card into evenly spaced staves. Write one word per measure, using one color for all letters and another for note heads. Use as many cards as necessary to complete each set.

Example:

Directions:
Write out each word, filling in the missing letters which are written in note heads. Then chant the words in rhythm. Sing the song and tape your performance. Now listen to your performance. Check it with your written work.

SPRINKLE NOTES AND RESTS

Objective:

To provide for identification of notes and rests . . . reinforcement.

Materials:

Egg carton, oak tag.

Contents:

The notes/rests sprinkles and the egg carton.

Preparation:

Make 4 1/2" by 1/2" sprinkles of each note, rest, and note set. Here are some samples.

Laminate the sprinkles or cover with clear adhesive-backed paper.

The egg carton is used as is, but cover the lid and write on it the game name,

SPRINKLES

Game Directions: (2 Players)

Player One "sprinkles" the discs over all the cups. Then he picks a cup and names all the notes and rests discs he finds there. Any that he names incorrectly he puts back into the cup. Score 1 point for each correct answer. The "used" sprinkle discs are put back into the sprinkle envelope.

Player Two then picks a cup and play continues in this way until all the cups are empty.

Each player should have an equal number of chances. Player with the most points at the end of the game is the winner of that round.

Round 2, Player Two "sprinkles" and chooses first. Play as many rounds as time permits. Player with the most winning rounds wins "Sprinkles."

SUPER SHARP

Objectives:
1. To reinforce 1/2 step concept — sharps.
2. To provide experiences with perception of the natural with its corresponding sharp.

Materials:
Index cards.

Contents:
The playing cards.

Preparation:
Cut 25 cards from index cards, the size of regulation playing cards. Write on cards as follows:

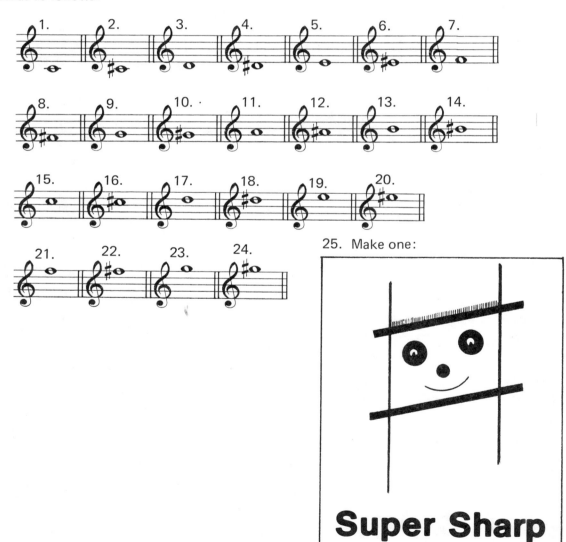

25. Make one:

Laminate all cards.

Game Directions: (2, 3, or 4 Players)

Shuffle and deal out all cards. Each player arranges his cards in a hand. All players put down, in front of them, any pairs which they have in their hands.

Player One then picks one card from Player Two, unseen. He then puts this card in his hand and makes another pair if he can. Player Two then proceeds in the same way, picking from the next player and trying to make a pair.

Play continues until all pairs have been made and one player is left with the "Super Sharp." He is the loser.

(Note: Matches are made between the natural and its sharp.)

FAT FLAT

Objectives, Materials, Contents, Preparation and Game Directions are the same as SUPER SHARP except that flats are substituted for sharps and Card 25 should be prepared as follows:

TRIPLE MATCH—NOTES, RESTS, NAMES

Objectives

To relate corresponding notes and rests.

Materials:

5" x 8" index cards.

Contents:

The "Triple Match" puzzle cards.

Preparation:

With a light pencil mark, divide cards into 3 parts, 2", 4" and 2". On left section draw a note, on right section draw the corresponding rest, and in the middle write the name. For example:

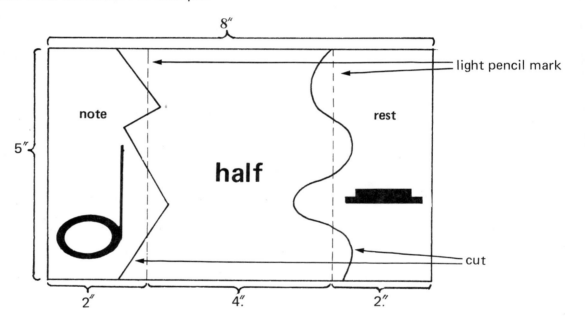

Laminate. Cut in 3 parts as a puzzle.

Directions for use:

Children will match notes and rests with names, then draw them in sets with corresponding names.

$$\frac{2}{4}, \frac{3}{4}, \frac{4}{4}, \frac{5}{4} \text{ WAR}$$

Objectives:
1. To reinforce note/rest value relationships.
2. To provide experiences with equal and comparative values of notes and rests.
3. To provide extended learning in math through music math.

Materials:
Poster board.

Contents:
The playing cards.

Preparation:
Cut 52 cards of poster board, the size of a regulation playing card. Write on each card as follows, making two of each:

Laminate each card.

Game Directions: (For 2 Players)

Shuffle and deal out all cards, face down. Each player arranges his cards in a pile in front of him. Then, each player turns up his top card. Player whose card is worth *more* in note or rest value "wins" both cards and adds these to the bottom of his pile.

If the turned-over cards are *equal* in value, WAR is declared. Each player counts out 3 cards, places them face down and then turns over the fourth card. The player whose top card is worth *more* wins all 8 cards and places them on the bottom of his pile.

The game continues in this way until one player is out of cards.

UPSIDE DOWN

Objectives:
1. To reinforce music reading skills.
   a. Melodic
   b. Rhythmic
   c. In combination
2. To provide additional reading experiences with a variety of time signatures (2, 3, 4, 5).
   (4 4 4 4)

Materials:
30 3'' x 5'' lined index cards.

Contents:
The ''Upside Down'' cards.

Preparation:
Write on each card as follows:

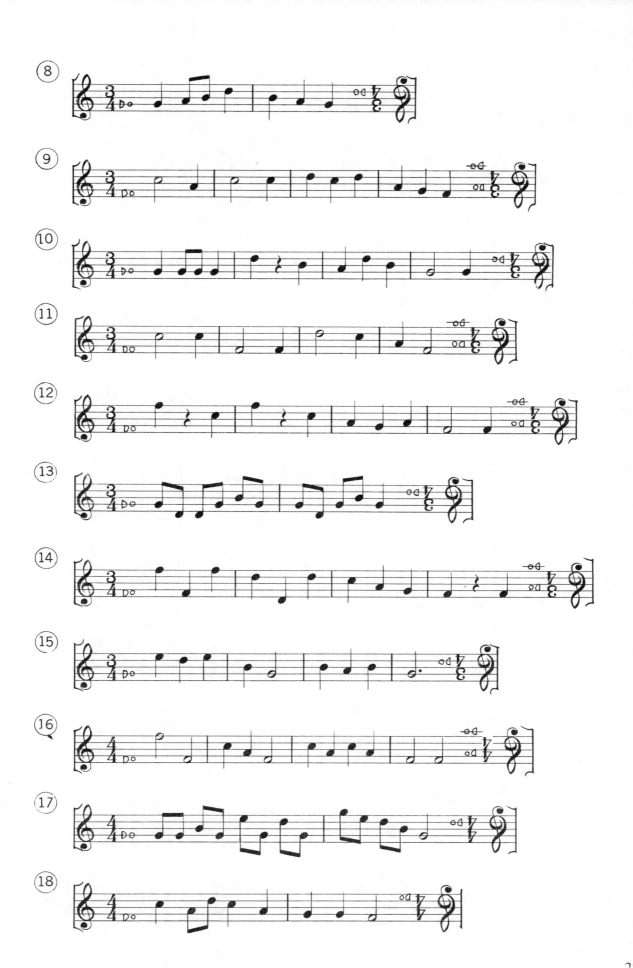

How to use "Upside Down":

1. Children may play melodies on any pitched instrument alone or with a partner.
2. "Upside Down" may be played as a small group game. Cards are placed face down. Child takes top card and plays it. He receives 1 point for EACH note in the melody he plays correct melodically and 1 extra point for performing the correct rhythm. Then he turns the card upside down and continues, receiving 2 points for EACH note in the melody he plays correct melodically and 2 extra points for performing the correct rhythm. Player to reach 100 points first wins.
3. "Upside Down" may be played as a "challenge." One child plays the melody and then challenges another child to play it "upside down." Then challenger and player change places with another melody.

Note: Children and teacher should discuss the "Upside Down" melodies and may be led as follows:
1. Which way did the melody sound best, right way up or upside down? Why?
2. When a melody is upside down do you sometimes sense a missing note at the end? Add the note you think is needed. What note did you add? Why did it make the melody sound better?

𝄞 and 𝄢 WAR

Objectives:

1. To reinforce reading of notes on both treble and bass staves.

2. To reinforce concept of higher and lower.

Materials:

Index cards. (These are preferable to poster board because you can ink in the already existing lines when making the staves.)

Contents:

The playing cards.

Preparation:

Cut 52 cards from index cards, regulation playing card size. Write on the cards as follows, making 2 of each:

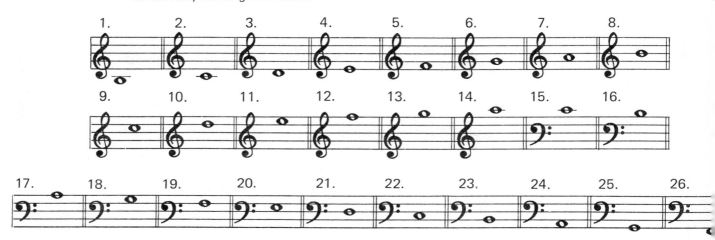

Laminate each card.

Game Directions: (2 Players)

Shuffle and deal out all cards. Each player arranges his cards in a pile in front of him, face down. Each player turns up the first card in his pack. The player whose card has the *highest* note wins the 2 cards and he places them on the bottom of his pile.

If both players turn up the *same note,* **WAR** is declared. Each player puts down his next 3 cards, face down, then turns over his fourth card. The player whose card has the highest note wins all 8 cards.

The game continues until one player is out of cards.

Careful: You are reading bass clef and treble clef.

Remember:

Both are middle C . . . the same note!

274

WEIGH-A-NOTE

Objectives:
1. To clarify concept of equal values.
2. To reinforce concept of note values.
3. To invite experimentation and exploration of note combinations for building measures.
4. To provide for extended learning in math (division).

Materials:
Balance scale, metal washers of varying sizes, index cards, heavy cardboard, masking tape.

Contents:
Balance scale, weights, and work cards.

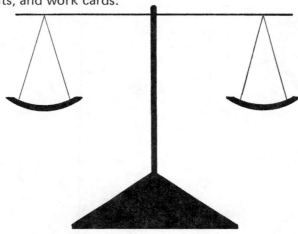

Preparation:
Make weight pockets from heavy cardboard, 1-1/2″ wide by 6″ long. Fold in thirds lengthwise and close with masking tape, leaving an opening at top for insertion of washers.

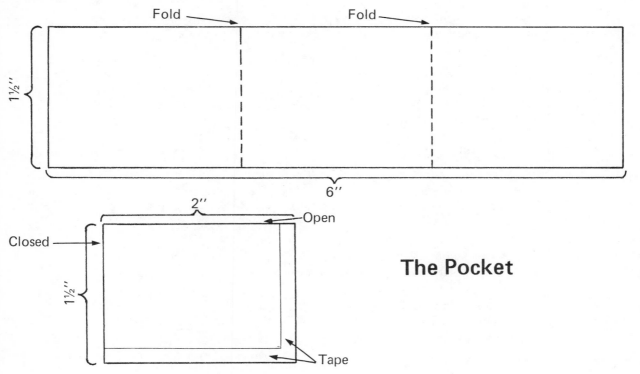

The Pocket

The Weights:

Using a scale that registers exact weights in ounces or grams, experiment with the metal washers until the weight for the whole note is the greatest, the half note is 1/2 the weight of the whole note, the dotted half note is 3/4 the weight of the whole note, the quarter note, eighth note triplet, eighth note set (♫), and sixteenth note set (♬♬) are each 1/4 the weight of the whole note, the dotted quarter note is 3/8 the weight of the whole note, and the single eighth note is 1/8 the weight of the whole note.

Place washers inside the pockets upon which the designated note(s) have been drawn.

Example: Amounts needed:

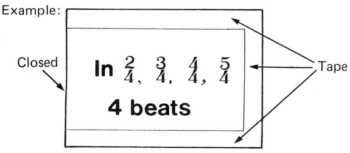 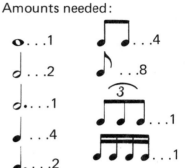

Using the same principle, make the following values for 2, 3, 4, 5 meters:
4 4 4 4

4 beats . . . . . . same weight as whole note.
3 beats . . . . . . same weight as dotted half note.
2 beats . . . . . . same weight as half note.
1-1/2 beats . . . same weight as dotted quarter note.
1 beat . . . . . . same weight as quarter note.
1/2 beat . . . . . same weight as eighth note.

Place in pockets as for notes, close with tape, and write values on front, together with the meters.

Example:

Closed   In $\frac{2}{4}$, $\frac{3}{4}$, $\frac{4}{4}$, $\frac{5}{4}$ ← Tape

4 beats

Using the same principle, make the following values for 3 6 9 12 meters:
8, 8, 8, 8

8 beats . . . same weight as whole note.
6 beats . . . same weight as dotted half note.
4 beats . . . same weight as half note.
3 beats . . . same weight as dotted quarter note.
2 beats . . . same weight as quarter note.
1 beat . . . same weight as eighth note.

Place in pockets as for notes, close with tape, and write values on front, together with the meters. (It is suggested that these "weight pockets" and their corresponding work cards be a different color from those for simple meters to avoid confusion.)

The Work Cards:
(Use index cards, the same color as those weights with which the student will be working.)

A. Using weights for 2,   3,   4,   5, find out how many beats each of the fol-
                              4   4   4   4

lowing is worth:

1. 𝅝 = _____ beats

2. 𝅗𝅥 = _____ beats

3. 𝅗𝅥. = _____ beats

4. ♩ = _____ beats

5. ♩. = _____ beats

6. ♫ = _____ beats

7. ♪ = _____ beats

8. (3) ♪♪♪ = _____ beats

9. ♬♬ = _____ beats

(Put answers on the back of the card.)

B. Using weights for 2,   3,   4,   5, how many different combinations can you
                              4 4 4 4

find to make a:
    2 beat measure
    3 beat measure
    4 beat measure
    5 beat measure
Write out each set of measures.

C. Complete these equations:

1. ♩ = _____ ♫ (set(s) of eighth notes)

2. ♩ = _____ ♪ (single eighth notes)

3. ♩ = _____ ♬♬ (set of sixteenth notes)

4. ♩ = _____ 𝅘𝅥𝅮𝅘𝅥𝅮𝅘𝅥𝅮 (3)

5. ♩. = _____ ♫ and _____ ♪

6. ♩. = _____ ♫ and _____ ♪

7. ♩. = _____ ♪

(Put answers on the back of the card.)

D. Complete these equations.

1. 𝅗𝅥 = _____ ♩

2. 𝅗𝅥 = _____ ♫ (set(s) of eighth notes)

3. 𝅗𝅥 = _____ ♪

4. 𝅗𝅥. = _____ 𝅗𝅥 and _____ ♩

5. 𝅗𝅥. = _____ ♩

6. 𝅗𝅥. = _____ ♫ (set(s) of eighth notes)

7. 𝅗𝅥. = _____ ♪

(Put answers on the back of the card.)

E. Complete these equations:

1. 𝅝 = _____ 𝅗𝅥

2. 𝅝 = _____ ♩

3. 𝅝 = _____ ♫ (set(s) of eighth notes)

4. 𝅝 = _____ ♪

(Put answers on the back of the card.)

F. Complete these equations:

1. ♪♪ = _____ ♪

2. ♪♪ = _____ ♪♪♪ (3)

3. ♪♪ = _____ ♪♪♪♪

(Put answers on the back of the card.)

G. Using weights for 3, 6, 9, 12, find out how many beats each of the fol-
                       8 8 8 8
   lowing is worth:

1. 𝅝   = _____ beats

2. 𝅗𝅥   = _____ beats

3. 𝅗𝅥.   = _____ beats

4. ♩   = _____ beats

5. ♩.   = _____ beats

6. ♪   = _____ beats

7. 𝅝 ♩ = _____ beats

8. 𝅗𝅥. 𝅗𝅥. = _____ beats

9. ♩ ♪ = _____ beats

10. ♪ ♩ = _____ beats

11. ♪ ♪ ♪ = _____ beats

(Put answers on the back of the cards.)

H. Using weights for 3   6   9   12   how many different combinations can
                     8, 8, 8, 8,
   you find to make a
      3 beat measure   9 beat measure
      6 beat measure   12 beat measure
   Write out each set of measures.

279

WHAT GOES UP ↑ OUGHT TO COME DOWN ↓ !
(A Music Reading Game with Sharps and Flats)

Objectives:
1. To reinforce half step concept.
2. To facilitate reading with ♯ and ♭
3. To provide extended learning in math (addition and subtraction).

Materials:
　Poster board.

Contents:
　Number and function cubes, game board, and four markers.

Preparation:
　Make two 2″ x 2″ cubes. Write on the cubes as follows:

	1	
5	2	6
	3	
	4	

	ADD +	
ADD +	SUB-TRACT −	SUB-TRACT −
	ADD +	
	SUB-TRACT −	

Make a game board as follows:

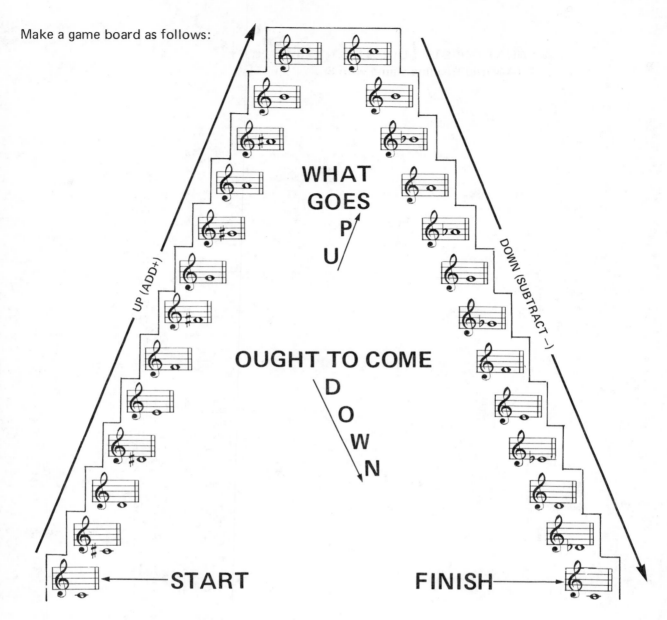

WHAT GOES UP OUGHT TO COME DOWN

UP (ADD+)
DOWN (SUBTRACT −)

START   FINISH

Make 4 markers, the size of a quarter.

Game Directions: (2, 3, or 4 Players)

Each player chooses a marker. Player One places his marker on the starting spot. He then rolls the number cube and the add/subtract cube. If he rolls an ADD (+), he moves *up* the number of half steps on the number cube. Then he tells the *Letter Name* of the note he lands on, being sure to include the ♯ or ♭ if it is written. If he is correct, he stays there. If not, he must *return to the spot he came from.* (He only returns to START at the beginning of the game.) If he rolls a SUBTRACT (−), he moves *down* the number of half steps on the number cube. (A SUBTRACT when he is on START means he cannot move.)

Player Two continues in the same way moving *up* with plus sign and *down* with minus sign.

When any player gets to the highest half step going *up*, he needs a + to cross over to the opposite half step. From then on, he needs − to move *down* to the FINISH spot. A player must roll the exact number to enter the FINISH spot, and he is the Winner.

CROSS INDEX

PAGE NUMBER →	DOTS AND TIES (119)	DOMINOTES (117)	DISCOVERING YOUR SPACE...THE SPACE AROUND YOU! (116)	DARTS (114)	DANCE - A - SHAPE (112)	CONTINENTS (111)	CONCENTRATION ♯ (110)	CONCENTRATION RESTS NAMES (109)	CONCENTRATION NOTES—RESTS MATCH (109)	CONCENTRATION NOTES—LETTER NAMES (108)	CONCENTRATION LETTER MATCH (108)	CONCENTRATION ♭ (110)	COMBO - CUBE (106)	CHALLENGES (104)	BINGO FIVE (103)	BINGO FOUR (103)	BINGO THREE (102)	BINGO TWO (101)	BINGO ONE (101)	BE A... (99)	ART AND MUSIC (97)	ANTS IN THE PANTS (96)	ALGEBRA MATHS (91)	ACTIVITIES FOR THE PENDULUM (89)	A SORTING ACTIVITY—INSTRUMENT FAMILIES (256)
ACCENTING																								●	
ALEATORIC MUSIC																									
ART ENRICHMENT																					●				
CHANTS																								●	
CHROMATICS				●																					
COLOR																					●				
COMPOSERS, CONDUCTORS				●																					
COMPOUND TIME	●																						●		
COUNTING, TRADITIONAL																									
CREATIVITY			●		●															●	●				
DIATONIC				●																					
DYNAMICS				●																	●				
EQUIVALENTS	●																								
FLATS				●								●													
FORM																					●				
GENERAL KNOWLEDGE				●																					
HALF-STEPS					●								●												
INSTRUMENTS, FACTS				●																				●	
INSTRUMENTS, IDENTIFYING													●				●							●	
INSTRUMENTS, PLAYING	●																				●				
INTERVALS																									
KEY SIGNATURE, IDENTIFYING				●																					
LANGUAGE ARTS, COMMUNICA						●															●				
LANGUAGE ARTS, SPELLING									●																
LANGUAGE ARTS, VOCABULAR																									
LETTER NAMES, 𝄞 and/or 𝄢				●						●	●	●	●		●										
LINE																					●				
MATH, ADDITION	●			●		●							●										●		
MATH, DIVISION																							●		
MATH, ESTIMATING/MEASURING			●																						
MATH, FRACTIONS																							●		
MATH, MULTIPLICATION																							●		
MATH, SUBTRACTION																									
MEASURE BUILDING	●			●									●												
MELODY				●																	●				
METER				●									●										●	●	
MOOD																									
MOVEMENT			●		●															●	●				
NOTES, DOTTED/TIED	●	●		●				●	●					●				●				●	●		
NOTES, IDENTIFYING		●		●				●	●					●				●				●			
PENTATONIC																									
PHRASING																					●				
POLYRHYTHMS	●																								
REPETITION/CONTRAST																					●				
RESTS, IDENTIFYING		●		●				●	●					●				●				●			
RHYTHM	●			●													●	●	●			●		●	
RHYTHMS, DOTTED/TIED	●			●													●								
SCIENCE ENRICHMENT																									
SELF-AWARENESS			●																						
SELF-EXPRESSION					●																●				
SHARPS				●			●																		
SIGNS		●		●										●			●								
SOCIAL STUDIES ENRICHMENT						●																			
SONG REPERTOIRE																									
SPATIAL RELATIONSHIPS																									
STAFF, PLACEMENT/PERCEPTIO																									
SYMBOLS		●		●										●				●							
TEMPO																								●	
TERMS				●														●							
TEXTURE																					●				
UNITY AND BALANCE																					●				
VALUES (NOTE/REST)	●			●									●											●	

CROSS INDEX

CROSS INDEX

Column games (left → right) with page numbers:

CONCEPT	RHYTHM BASEBALL (225)	RECORDER (223)	POCKET RHYTHMS (220)	PICK-AND-PLAY (216)	PHRASE PUZZLES (215)	PEOPLE IN HISTORY (213)	PENNY PITCH (211)	PALE PATTI (209)	ONE ON ONE (205)	OLD SOL (203)	OH, NUTS! (202)	MUSICNOCHLE 3,6,9,12 (200)	MUSICNOCHLE 2,3,4,5 (198)	MUSICAL FRACTIONS (196)	MUSICAL CHECKERS (195)	MUSIC LAND GAME TWO (193)	MUSIC LAND GAME ONE (193)	MUSIC BY CHANCE (191)	MOVING THROUGH SPACE (189)	MOVEMENT GAME (187)	MISERABLE MICKEY (186)	MERRY MI (184)	DO ON A LINE (183)	MELODY HEARTS (181)	DO IN A SPACE	MELODY HEARTS	MELODY DICE (179)	MEASURENOES (177)	MEASURE MARBLES (171)
ACCENTING																													
ALEATORIC MUSIC																		•											
ART ENRICHMENT																													
CHANTS																													
CHROMATICS																													
COLOR																													
COMPOSERS, CONDUCTORS																													
COMPOUND TIME																												•	
COUNTING, TRADITIONAL			•																										
CREATIVITY			•																	•									
DIATONIC		•																											
DYNAMICS																													
EQUIVALENTS				•										•	•														
FLATS		•																											
FORM																													
GENERAL KNOWLEDGE									•																				
HALF-STEPS																													
INSTRUMENTS, FACTS																													
INSTRUMENTS, IDENTIFYING																													
INSTRUMENTS, PLAYING		•	•															•									•		
INTERVALS							•																						
KEY SIGNATURE, IDENTIFYING							•																						
LANGUAGE ARTS, COMMUNICATING															•														
LANGUAGE ARTS, SPELLING																													
LANGUAGE ARTS, VOCABULARY																													
LETTER NAMES, 𝄞 and/or 𝄢		•				•	•															•	•						
LINE																													
MATH, ADDITION			•					•				•	•															•	•
MATH, DIVISION																													
MATH, ESTIMATING/MEASURING																			•										
MATH, FRACTIONS														•															
MATH, MULTIPLICATION																													
MATH, SUBTRACTION																													
MEASURE BUILDING		•																											•
MELODY		•					•	•										•			•	•	•	•			•		
METER																												•	•
MOOD																													
MOVEMENT																			•	•									
NOTES, DOTTED/TIED				•			•									•	•				•								
NOTES, IDENTIFYING				•			•	•								•	•				•								
PENTATONIC								•											•			•	•	•	•		•		
PHRASING					•																								
POLYRHYTHMS			•																										
REPETITION/CONTRAST					•		•	•								•	•	•											
RESTS, IDENTIFYING																													
RHYTHM	•	•					•	•	•		•	•	•					•										•	•
RHYTHMS, DOTTED/TIED	•	•						•	•			•	•															•	•
SCIENCE ENRICHMENT																													
SELF-AWARENESS																			•										
SELF-EXPRESSION																													
SHARPS		•																											
SIGNS							•														•								
SOCIAL STUDIES ENRICHMENT					•	•																							
SONG REPERTOIRE					•																								
SPATIAL RELATIONSHIPS																			•										
STAFF, PLACEMENT/PERCEPTION									•													•	•	•	•				
SYMBOLS							•														•								
TEMPO																													
TERMS							•																						
TEXTURE																													
UNITY AND BALANCE																													
VALUES (NOTE/REST)	•											•			•													•	•

CONCEPT	SPRINKLE NOTES AND RESTS (265)	NATIONAL SONGS (264)	SPELL IT AND SING... (264)	SORTING NOTES AND RESTS 2 (252)	SORTING NOTES AND RESTS 1 (251)	SORTING NOTES AND RESTS 3,6,9,12 8888 (255)	SORT-A-VALUE— 3,6,9,12 8888 (255)	SORT-A-VALUE— 2,3,4,5 444 (253)	SORT-A-NOTE—LETTER NAMES 2 (251)	SORT-A-NOTE—LETTER NAMES 1 (250)	SORT-A-MEASURE— 2,3,4,5 444 (259)	SOLVING A PROBLEM THROUGH MOVEMENT (249)	SHAPES, SHAPES, SHAPES! (248)	SELF-CORRECTING DEVICES (245)	SAD SAM (243)	SMD - DMS (241)	RUMMY THREE (239)	RUMMY TWO (238)	RUMMY ONE (237)	ROLL-A-RHYTHM (236)	RHYTHM FOOTBALL (232)	RHYTHM DICE (230)
ACCENTING																						
ALEATORIC MUSIC																						
ART ENRICHMENT																						
CHANTS																					●	
CHROMATICS																						
COLOR																						
COMPOSERS, CONDUCTORS																						
COMPOUND TIME							●															
COUNTING, TRADITIONAL																					●	
CREATIVITY													●									
DIATONIC																						
DYNAMICS																						
EQUIVALENTS																						
FLATS																						
FORM																						
GENERAL KNOWLEDGE																						
HALF-STEPS																						
INSTRUMENTS, FACTS																						
INSTRUMENTS, IDENTIFYING																						
INSTRUMENTS, PLAYING																						
INTERVALS														●								
KEY SIGNATURE, IDENTIFYING														●								
LANGUAGE ARTS, COMMUNICATING		●																				
LANGUAGE ARTS, SPELLING														●								
LANGUAGE ARTS, VOCABULARY																						
LETTER NAMES, 𝄞 and/or 𝄢		●								●	●			●								
LINE																						
MATH, ADDITION															●							
MATH, DIVISION																						
MATH, ESTIMATING/MEASURING																						
MATH, FRACTIONS																						
MATH, MULTIPLICATION																						
MATH, SUBTRACTION																						
MEASURE BUILDING																						
MELODY																●						
METER							●	●	●			●										●
MOOD																						
MOVEMENT												●	●									
NOTES, DOTTED/TIED	●			●	●									●							●	
NOTES, IDENTIFYING	●			●	●									●							●	
PENTATONIC																●						
PHRASING																						
POLYRHYTHMS																						
REPETITION/CONTRAST																						
RESTS, IDENTIFYING	●			●	●									●							●	
RHYTHM																●	●	●	●	●	●	●
RHYTHMS, DOTTED/TIED																	●	●		●		
SCIENCE ENRICHMENT												●										
SELF-AWARENESS																						
SELF-EXPRESSION													●									
SHARPS																						
SIGNS														●								
SOCIAL STUDIES ENRICHMENT		●																				
SONG REPERTOIRE		●																				
SPATIAL RELATIONSHIPS												●										
STAFF, PLACEMENT/PERCEPTION															●							
SYMBOLS														●								
TEMPO																						
TERMS																						
TEXTURE																						
UNITY AND BALANCE																						
VALUES (NOTE/REST)							●	●	●					●	●		●	●	●			

Nelson English

Language & Writing 9
Teacher's Guide

Authors
Don Aker
Dave Hodgkinson

Assessment
Connie Bray
David MacDonald
Michael Stubitsch
Brian Way

Nelson
Thomson Learning.

Australia • Canada • Denmark • Japan • Mexico • New Zealand • Philippines
Puerto Rico • Singapore • South Africa • Spain • United Kingdom • United States

1120 Birchmount Road
Scarborough, Ontario M1K 5G4
www.nelson.com
www.thomson.com

Canadian Cataloguing in Publication Data

Aker, Don, 1955–
    Language & writing 9. Teacher's guide

(Nelson English)
ISBN 0-17-618682-4

1. English language — Grammar — Study and teaching
(Secondary). 2. English language — Composition and
exercises — Study and teaching (Secondary). I. Hodgkinson,
Dave. II. Title. III. Title: Language and writing nine. Teacher's
guide. IV. Series.

PE1112.A39 1999 Suppl.   428.2   C99-932357-1

Director of Publishing: David Steele
Publisher: Carol Stokes
Executive Editor: Jessica Pegis
Project Editor: Laurel Bishop
Developmental Editor: Linda Sheppard
Production Co-ordinator: Renate McCloy
Composition: Carol Magee
Printer: Carswell

A special thanks to the teachers who attended the
Ontario Council of Teachers of English Conference
and numerous other focus groups for the
suggestions they provided to help shape Nelson
Thomson Learning's Grade 9 English literature and
language resources.

Printed and bound in Canada

TABLE OF CONTENTS

LANGUAGE & WRITING 9 AND THE ONTARIO GRADE 9 ENGLISH CURRICULUM

The Ontario curriculum lays out four strands to be developed in the English program: Literature Studies and Reading, Writing, Language, and Media Studies. The overall and specific expectations outlined for each of these strands have been incorporated into the *Language & Writing 9* student book and *Language & Writing 9 Teacher's Guide*. By using these resources, teachers can be assured that the knowledge and skills required for each of these strands will be addressed in their classrooms.

The methodology of the student book and *Teacher's Guide* is purposefully matched to prescribed curriculum expectations. The instruction in the *Teacher's Guide* is carefully designed to help teachers implement all the expectations. The writing models, activities, and exercises in both the student book and *Teacher's Guide* contribute to the acquisition of the knowledge and skills set forth in these expectations.

Language & Writing 9 uses an integrated approach to develop the knowledge and skills from each of the four strands. Each of the 12 units in the book begins with a model of the form of writing to be studied. This model provides a context for the development of knowledge and skills throughout the rest of the unit. Specific examples from the unit model are used throughout the unit to demonstrate the concepts and skills being developed.

The Ontario Curriculum Grades 9 and 10 for English states the following:
- In their English programs, teachers should introduce a rich variety of activities that integrate strands and provide for the explicit teaching of knowledge and skills. (page 4)
- It is important for students to have opportunities to develop their English skills and knowledge independently, in pairs, in small groups, and as a class. Students must be able to demonstrate that they have acquired the specified knowledge and skills. (page 4)

In *Language & Writing 9,* there is a balance of teacher-directed and independent activities. There are suggestions for activities and exercises to be done independently, in pairs and small groups, and as a whole class. In these activities and exercises, both deductive and inductive learning are fostered. Throughout the book, students are engaged in problem-solving activities that promote learning.

ACADEMIC AND APPLIED COURSES

Language & Writing 9 is designed to meet expectations for both the Applied and Academic Courses. The models provided include the genres and forms suggested in the curriculum for the two courses, including a range of literary and informational texts. The wide variety of models (e.g., stories, poems, Web pages, advertisements, and scripts) appeals to a range of student interests, reading abilities, and learning styles.

While the Ontario expectations for both courses are similar, *Language & Writing 9* differentiates the courses through the delivery. The Academic Course offers an in-depth and theoretical approach. The Applied Course offers more opportunities for modelling and practice, fewer extending opportunities, and more teacher support. The difference between the Academic and Applied Courses is primarily in the ways students construct knowledge: in Applied, they do so by moving from the concrete to the theoretical; in Academic, they move from the theoretical to the examples and beyond.

The *Teacher's Guide* provides specific instructional strategies for both the Academic and Applied Courses. The strategies and learning opportunities for the Academic

Course focus on theoretical and more abstract applications of the lesson concept, as well as more in-depth study and opportunities for extending the learning. The strategies for the Applied Course focus more on concrete applications.

PROGRAM DESIGN AND IMPLEMENTATION

Program Design

Research has shown that students' writing experiences should reflect their social and intellectual growth. Consequently, the presentation of writing forms in *Language & Writing 9,* like the treatment of language conventions, moves from simple to complex. Students begin the year with studies of familiar forms, drawing on real or imagined experiences (narration) to describe people, places, and things around them (description). Later sections have students organize and present factual information (exposition) and express opinions and convince others to think or act in a particular way (persuasion). This order enables students to move in their writing from the familiar to the unfamiliar, from the subjective to the objective, and from the personal to the practical.

In a school year comprising four terms, you may focus on one of these four types of writing each term. Each unit is designed to take approximately two weeks to complete, during which time you may integrate other aspects of your English program. For example, you may wish to incorporate Unit 4 (Poetry) with poetry study. In this way, students can apply to their reading ideas what they learn in Unit 4 about the unique characteristics of poetic forms.

Language & Writing 9 also presents grammar topics in simple-to-complex order, enabling you to begin the school year with a review of basic concepts before moving on to more complex topics. In much the same way, the Mechanics, Usage & Style, and Word Study & Spelling subsections first examine topics familiar to most students before covering more difficult concepts, as well as presentation issues. For example, in Unit 1, the Mechanics subsection focuses on rules for using commas. By the end of the book, in Unit 12, the Mechanics subsection is covering presentation matters such as letter formatting.

We highly recommend that the Writer's Workshop component be an ongoing part of each two-week unit and that related language activities be presented as mini-lessons during (rather than after) the Writer's Workshop. Although each unit offers direction in a particular form of writing, you might choose to have students publish only one or two pieces per section (there are three units in each section). In this way, students can write in all three forms of writing in a section and, at the end of the term, choose those they wish to publish. These published pieces, which will reflect a student's understanding of both the form and the language conventions studied during that unit, can then be one of several assessment components used in each section. Students can keep the draft pieces from the other units in their writing folders. They can be used as a source of information during writing conferences to help identify areas of growth and to establish future writing goals.

IMPLEMENTATION: USING NELSON ENGLISH LANGUAGE & WRITING 9 IN YOUR CLASSROOM

A Sample Unit Plan

Each unit should take approximately two weeks, based on 40 minutes per day. Additional time will be required at the beginning of each of the four sections in order to discuss the section's two introductory pages, and at the end of each section to review the writing forms covered in all the section units.

Your unit plan will also change depending on your timetable and the degree to which you integrate concepts in this text with the rest of your English program.

Outlined below is a possible two-week plan. Of course, topics can be rearranged or combined to reflect your teaching style, the need for variety, and the degree of emphasis you wish to place on each topic.

	Week One		**Week Two**
Day 1	Introduce the Unit Investigate the Form	Day 1	Writer's Workshop
Day 2	Writer's Workshop	Day 2	Usage & Style
Day 3	Writer's Workshop	Day 3	Word Study & Spelling
Day 4	Grammar	Day 4	Reflect and Build on Your Learning
Day 5	Mechanics	Day 5	Reflect and Build on Your Learning

THE CLASSROOM ENVIRONMENT

Research confirms what educators have always known: students perform better in an environment where they are valued as learners and as individuals. For this reason, we need to establish a respectful and supportive atmosphere where students feel safe to take risks in their learning. Numerous resources, many of them time-tested, outline methods that can help you to establish such an environment.

We need to remember that each student's language is a reflection of what she or he hears and speaks at home. Our goal must be to develop instructional materials and techniques that value all students' previous learning and help them to extend their knowledge of more formal forms of English, grammar, mechanics, usage, and spelling.

The following suggestions can help you meet the language-learning needs of individual students:

- Respond to the content of a piece before identifying errors in convention. The meaning of a piece should be the primary focus of any editor—teacher or peer. Focusing too quickly on convention can inhibit a student's development as a writer.
- Do not take ownership of a student's writing. Try to avoid handling a piece of writing until the student has completed his or her final draft. Instead, have the student read aloud to you or a peer those portions with which he or she requires assistance. Not only does this obligate the student to identify weaknesses that need attention, it lessens the time you have to spend correcting papers that students themselves should have revised and edited.
- Emphasize the positive. Regardless of the many writing problems present in a draft, comment on at least one language-related element the writer has done well.

- Model ways of responding to writing. Since the Writer's Workshop component emphasizes peer collaboration, ensure that students know how to talk meaningfully and supportively about one another's drafts. Role-play effective and ineffective peer conferences, and observe dialogue so you can praise—and share with the whole class—examples of successful conferences.
- Do not make students responsible for everything in a draft. Focus on aspects that reflect students' needs. Ensure that they are aware of concepts they must know, either by referring to the Learning Goals at the beginning of each unit or by keeping an individual skills list.
- Take part in Writer's Workshop activities and complete one piece of writing each term. Publishing a piece of your own writing, along with those of your students, emphasizes that you are all members of a community of writers.
- As much as possible, encourage students to write for real audiences. Provide opportunities for class publications and displays of writing.

WRITING IN THE CLASSROOM

The Writing Process

Few things are more intimidating than a blank sheet of paper. Few things are more frustrating than a page filled with words that don't say what we mean. These feelings of intimidation and frustration usually result when we think of writing as a kind of "silent dictation"—simply recording on paper ideas we already have in our heads. However, writing is not merely the act of recording what we know—it is a process that allows us to discover what we know, what we need to know, and how we can share our understanding with others.

Although few people write in exactly the same way, most completed pieces of writing have undergone similar processes, which are described on pages 10–15 of the student book, "The Writing Process: An Illustration." It is important that students view these pages on the writing process as a resource for them to use throughout the year.

While most students will already be familiar with the writing process, few will have seen the evolution of a piece from assigned task to final product, as depicted on pages 10–15. As they observe Gina, a high school writer, selecting and narrowing a topic, collecting and organizing information, drafting and revising a piece, and editing and proofreading the final copy, they will understand more clearly the strategies writers use and the questions they need to ask themselves as they prepare a piece for publication.

The following teaching suggestions are designed to introduce students to *Language & Writing 9*. As well, they can help you to address and prioritize issues associated with writing and establish a context for writing in the coming school year.

1. Have students form a large group, and ask them to list the stages in the writing process. Emphasize that writers seldom perform these activities in order from first to last. Often, a writer may begin drafting a piece of writing only to realize that she or he needs additional information and must therefore return to an earlier stage. In other words, the writing process is recursive, not simply linear.

2. Have students form groups that correspond to the four sections on pages 10–15—Prewriting, Drafting, Revising, and Editing and Proofreading. Have them jot down at least three ideas in their assigned section that they feel will be helpful to them as they undertake writing assignments in the coming year.

3. The following class, have students meet in groups according to their assigned section. (If groups are large, you might wish to divide each group into two

smaller groups to facilitate discussion.) Direct each group to select a recorder who will report the group's comments. When all groups have finished, have students reconvene as a class to share their ideas. Make sure that students have differentiated between the processes of revision and editing/proofreading.

4. As students discuss the four sections, many students will focus on the questions provided on pages 10–13. At this point, have students consider how writers use these questions, then have them suggest questions they can ask themselves when revising a piece of writing. Record these on the board. If necessary, you can share some or all of the following questions with students. They can choose and modify questions according to their needs.

Revision Questions
Title
- Is my title interesting? Does it reflect the topic of the piece?

Introduction
- Does my lead catch a reader's interest and identify (or hint at) the main, or controlling, idea of my piece?

Body
- Have I included enough information so my reader can understand the situation or problem?
- Have I included too much information? Are there parts I can leave out?
- Is the overall organizational pattern (e.g., chronological, spatial) and order of ideas and information appropriate to the topic and logical? Will any part confuse my reader?

Conclusion
- What do I want my reader to know, think, or feel at the end? Does my conclusion achieve what I want?

Although many students will be familiar with the physical processes of revising a piece of writing, demonstrations of deleting, cutting, and pasting in a word processing program should be supplemented with demonstrations of the same processes on paper. Students need to understand that writing is messy and they must feel free to manipulate a draft in a variety of ways.

As with the revision questions, you can share some or all of the following editing questions with students. They can choose, modify, or add to the questions according to their needs.

Editing Questions
1. Have I paragraphed my piece correctly (that is, grouped ideas that belong together)?

2. Have I used complete sentences? (Occasional sentence fragments are acceptable if they are intentional.)

3. Have I used a variety of sentence lengths and types (e.g., simple, compound, complex)?

4. Have I used nouns and verbs that create strong impressions?

5. Have I repeated words? Can I find other, more precise words to express the same ideas?

6. Do my pronouns agree with their antecedents in number and gender?

7. Do I use verb tenses consistently?

8. Have I used the passive voice too often?

9. Have I punctuated my piece correctly?

10. Have I spelled every word correctly?

ASSESSMENT

Forms of Assessment

Diagnostic, formative, and summative forms of assessment all play a part in any effective English program. Outlined below are the three forms of assessment, with key questions and examples of ways to determine student progress.

Type	Key Questions	Examples of How to Find Out
Diagnostic (before)	What knowledge and skills does a student possess prior to the study of a unit?	Information should be gathered by examining **previous writing** in the student's portfolio, by giving a **writing task** to the student, and/or by **assigning specific activities or exercises.**
Formative (during)	How do I know that the instructional strategies I use will result in the learning of knowledge and skills identified in each unit?	A student's **results on the activities and exercises** in both the Writer's Workshop and the conventions sections (Grammar, Mechanics, Usage & Style, and Word Study & Spelling) will provide you with this information. As well, **ongoing observation** of a student's writing and **interviews/conferences** provide valuable data.
Summative (after)	What knowledge and skills has a student learned during the study of this unit?	The **Assessment Tools** provided will enable you to rate a student's level of proficiency with the knowledge and skills identified at the beginning of each unit.

Participants in Assessment

Assessment of a student requires more than your input. A student, his or her peers, and parents or guardians also need to contribute to the assessment. The following chart outlines ways that each participant in the process can give information about a student's progress.

	Why Involved?	**How**
Self	Self-assessment, a valuable life skill, enables a student to take ownership of his or her learning.	Students can use the **Checkpoint** and **Looking Back sections** in each unit to question and consider their work. The **Student Self-Evaluation Checklists** can help them assess their work.
Peers	Peer evaluation enables students to understand and apply criteria to other students' work, providing them with opportunities to understand their own learning better.	Students can use the **Checkpoint** and **Looking Back** sections in each unit to assess one another's work.
Teacher	We are responsible for ongoing assessment, evaluation, and reporting in order to demonstrate growth and to be accountable to each student, his or her parents/guardians, and the school community.	**Writer's Workshop** activities, **Extra Practice,** and **Assessment Tools** provide us with information. As well, you may have access to exemplars that can be used to assess a student's level of development.
Parents/ Guardians	When parents/guardians become involved, they understand how their child is being evaluated, and better understand what she or he needs to know and be able to do.	Ask parents/guardians to **read the table of contents of the student book** in order to understand the program. They can also **examine their child's writing portfolio and the assessment tools.** If possible, provide parents/ guardians with **exemplars** that demonstrate what good writing looks like at this grade level.

An Overview of Nelson Language & Writing Assessment Instruments

Assessment is the process of collecting, analyzing, and recording information related to students' work. Sound assessment techniques that draw on a variety of samples can help us to identify strengths and weaknesses of each student, enabling us to tailor effective programs. The student book and this *Teacher's Guide* include a number of tools to help you assess students' progress:

In the student book
- Statements of learning goals
- Checkpoints
- Exercises and activities
- Looking Back
- Reflect and Build on Your Learning

In the Teacher's Guide
- Extra Practice pages
- Teacher Observation Checklists
- Student Self-Evaluation Checklists
- Assessment Rubrics

In the student book ...

Statements of Learning Goals

Students learn best when they understand the goals associated with a particular learning experience, which is why each of the four sections of the student book begins with an overview of the learning goals students are to achieve during the three section units that follow. Then, at the beginning of each of the 12 units, these goals are stated more specifically in the form of performance objectives. By communicating these goals in advance to students and parents, teachers establish specific expectations by which student performance will be assessed. Besides helping students take ownership of their learning, these goals enable peers to assess each other's performance during the units of study. As well, the goals communicate to parents and guardians the specific knowledge and skills students must acquire.

Checkpoints

Following each Investigating the Model feature, the Checkpoint encourages students to reflect on what they have learned about a specific model and then to apply this understanding to a genre as a whole. In this way, they are able to identify specific criteria they may use to assess the effectiveness of their own and other students' writing.

Exercises and Activities

These exercises offer teachers many mechanisms for formative assessment as well as summative evaluation. In particular, the Writer's Workshop in each unit offers students a process-based writing task with numerous opportunities for self- and peer-assessment.

Looking Back

This feature, at the end of each of the 12 units, invites students to focus on the conventions examined in the unit. It encourages students to reflect on their achievement of the learning goals and encourages them to make connections between the conventions of writing and the forms of writing in which they are used.

Reflect and Build on Your Learning

Found at the end of each of the four sections, this two-page feature encourages students to reflect on their learning in the section and to extend their learning by applying it to other forms of writing within a specific genre. This feature also provides numerous tasks that teachers can assign to assess student understanding of the various concepts examined during a major unit of study,

In the Teacher's Guide...

Extra Practice Pages

Extra Practice pages for each section can help you to identify areas in which students may require further practice. They should be administered at the end of each unit, but they might also be used as pretests at the beginning of each unit. Each page reflects the grammatical, mechanical, stylistic, and linguistic topics covered in the unit, and is accompanied by an answer key to facilitate assessment.

Assessment Rubrics

These enable you to assess accurately the extent to which students have achieved the learning goals outlined at the beginning of each unit. These rubrics (listed on page 299 pay special attention to understanding, thinking, communication, and application of learning. Specific criteria identify four levels of achievement as laid out in the Achievement Chart in *The Ontario Curriculum, Grades 9 and 10* for English. It is also recommended that these rubrics be used by students for self- and peer-assessment, thereby encouraging students to take control of their own learning and become independent learners.

TAKE A QUICK TOUR OF THE STUDENT BOOK

The student book is divided into three introductory parts and five main sections.
The three introductory parts are as follows.

Welcome
- Provides an inviting visual tour of a main section of the book through annotated reduced pages (pages 3–5)

Contents
- Provides the table of contents (pages 6–9)
- Contents are divided into clearly demarcated, colour-coded sections
- Each section is divided into units, twelve units in all for the book

The Writing Process: An Illustration
- Provides an overview of the writing process (pages 10–15)
- Includes practical suggestions to help students during the process
- Serves both as an introduction to the writing process and as a reference throughout the year

There are four main sections, colour-coded to the table of contents: narration, description, exposition, and persuasion.

Section Opener

- Describes the type of writing covered in the section
- Highlights features of the type of writing
- Highlights learning goals covered in the section

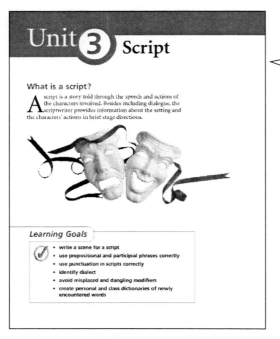

Unit **3** Script

What is a script?

A script is a story told through the speech and actions of the characters involved. Besides including dialogue, the scriptwriter provides information about the setting and the characters' actions in brief stage directions.

Learning Goals

- write a scene for a script
- use prepositional and participial phrases correctly
- use punctuation in scripts correctly
- identify dialect
- avoid misplaced and dangling modifiers
- create personal and class dictionaries of newly encountered words

Unit Introduction

- Describes the form of writing covered in the unit
- Highlights specific learning goals covered in the unit

In this scene from a stage play, Tim has been laid off from his factory job and is working for Mrs. Phipps, a retired mathematics professor. When Tim's wife, Ginny, is offered a job in another city, all three characters are thrown into conflict.

Odd Jobs

BY FRANK MOHER

MRS. PHIPPS's yard. It has snowed; there is a dull, grey light. Some green garbage bags sit to one side. TIM is out sweeping the walk. MRS. PHIPPS enters, wearing her sweater. She stands watching. TIM spots her.

MRS. PHIPPS: Your wife came to visit me yesterday.
TIM: Yeah, I, uh, heard about that.
MRS. PHIPPS: She told me you're not going to Regina.
TIM: That's right.
MRS. PHIPPS: That's true?
TIM: Uh-huh. That is to say I'm not goin' yet.
MRS. PHIPPS: I told her it was the silliest thing I'd ever heard.
TIM: Well, yer entitled to your opinion.
MRS. PHIPPS: She thinks so, too.
TIM: Uh-huh. Well, that's what makes this country great.
MRS. PHIPPS: Of course you're going to Regina. She's your wife. it's a good opportunity for her, you'll pack your tools and go.
TIM: You through dictatin' my life for me, Mrs. Phipps?
MRS. PHIPPS: Well, you're certainly not going to stay here!
TIM: Look, if Ginny wants to go to Regina, that's all right with me. Regina will still be there, y'know, whenever. As for me, I got things to do here. Now, you gonna move off the sidewalk so's I can sweep it?

Model

- Exemplifies the characteristics of the form of writing covered in the unit

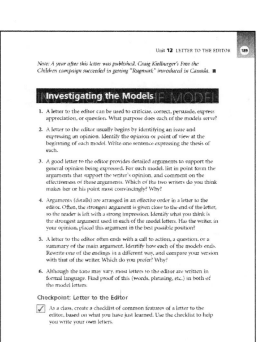

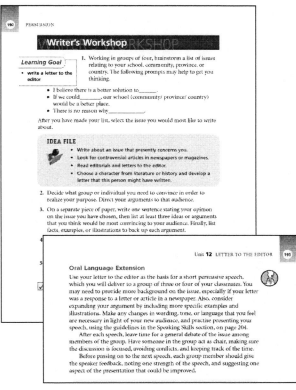

Investigating the Model

- Provides questions that encourage students to identify and discuss each of the characteristics of the form of writing
- Encourages students to develop a checklist of features for the form of writing (identified by a check mark logo)

Writer's Workshop

- Begins with a focus on students' own experiences as springboards for writing
- Uses the unit model as a reference point
- Activities guide students though all stages of the writing process
- Provides Oral Language Extension activities to address listening and speaking skills

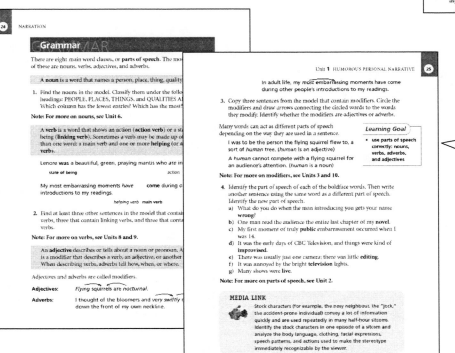

Conventions: Grammar, Mechanics, Usage & Style, Word Study & Spelling

- Provides four separate subsections for Grammar, Mechanics, Usage & Style, and Word Study & Spelling
- Each subsection covers related concepts as illustrated in the model
- Learning goals are reinforced in marginal boxes

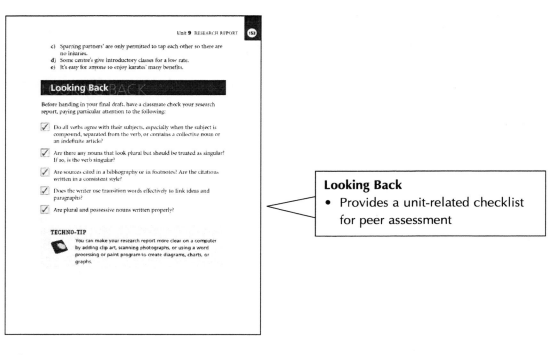

In addition in each unit ...

Media Link boxes with media-related activities that build on themes and writing forms in the unit

MEDIA LINK

Compare the front pages of three daily newspapers published on the same day. Analyze the layouts (colour, typeface, images, captions, headlines, amount of written copy and visual material), as well as the treatment of the lead story and the number and placement of other stories. Based on your analysis, identify the strengths and weaknesses of each front page, and describe the target reader for each newspaper. Summarize your findings in an oral report.

TECHNO-TIP

An excellent way to find nouns that are more specific is to use the thesaurus on your word processing program. Synonyms and antonyms are provided so that you can choose precise words. Be sure to check their meaning in a dictionary if you are unfamiliar with them.

Techno-Tip boxes to help students use technology effectively

Writing Tip boxes with suggestions to help students with their writing

WORD ORIGINS

and it was one of those epiphanies of childhood ...
—Leona Gom

Epiphany comes from the Greek words *epi*, meaning "to," and *phainein*, meaning "to show." Traditionally, Epiphany is a Christian religious festival celebrating Christ's appearance to the wise men. Irish author James Joyce introduced the term into literary usage in the novel *A Portrait of the Artist As a Young Man*. He used it to describe a sudden "revelation of the whatness of a thing," more commonly understood to be a recognition of its inner truth.

The prefix *epi-* can have other meanings. Find three other words in the dictionary that contain the prefix *epi-*, and record the meaning of the prefix and the words.

Word Origins give interesting background information on long-established and newer words

WRITING TIP

While sentence fragments are often used in everyday speech, they are seldom acceptable in writing. They may be used in writing to

- create effect in advertising, poetry, or fiction
- write dialogue, which is really conversation
- take notes
- record the answer to a question

IDEA FILE

To help you get started, think of the explanations that you have studied in various subjects in school over the past few years, including English; or develop some out-of-the-ordinary topics such as: How are potato chips made? or Why do black jeans go grey when you wash them?

Idea File boxes with tips and guidelines to help students successfully complete a particular activity

... all boxes are easily identifiable with unique logos.

Relect and Build on Your Learning

- Offers the opportunity at the end of each section to review, compare, and apply the writing forms covered in the three section units

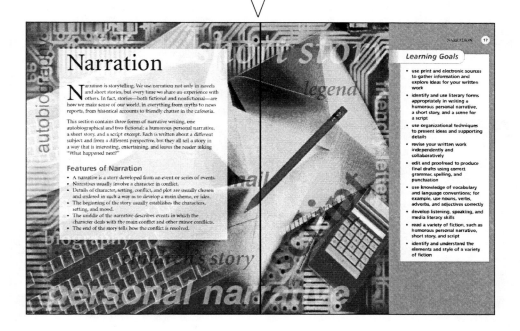

Narration

Narration is storytelling. We use narration not only in novels and short stories, but every time we share an experience with others. In fact, stories—both fictional and nonfictional—are how we make sense of our world, in everything from myths to news reports, from historical accounts to friendly chatter in the cafeteria.

This section contains three forms of narrative writing, one autobiographical and two fictional: a humorous personal narrative, a short story, and a script excerpt. Each is written about a different subject and from a different perspective, but they all tell a story in a way that is interesting, entertaining, and leaves the reader asking "What happened next?"

Features of Narration

- A narrative is a story developed from an event or series of events.
- Narratives usually involve a character in conflict.
- Details of character, setting, conflict, and plot are usually chosen and ordered in such a way as to develop a main theme, or idea.
- The beginning of the story usually establishes the characters, setting, and mood.
- The middle of the narrative describes events in which the character deals with the main conflict and other minor conflicts.
- The end of the story tells how the conflict is resolved.

NARRATION 17

Learning Goals

- use print and electronic sources to gather information and explore ideas for your written work
- identify and use literary forms appropriately in writing a humorous personal narrative, a short story, and a scene for a script
- use organizational techniques to present ideas and supporting details
- revise your written work independently and collaboratively
- edit and proofread to produce final drafts using correct grammar, spelling, and punctuation
- use knowledge of vocabulary and language conventions; for example, use nouns, verbs, adverbs, and adjectives correctly
- develop listening, speaking, and media literacy skills
- read a variety of fiction, such as humorous personal narrative, short story, and script
- identify and understand the elements and style of a variety of fiction

---

At the end of the book for ready reference

- Suggestions on how to improve speaking and listening skills
- Listing and discussion of transitional expressions
- Listing, with explanations, of key words used in assignments and tests
- Definitions and usage of commonly misspelled words
- Listing of common homophones. These pages are to be used by students as part of some activities and for reference.

TAKE A QUICK TOUR OF THE TEACHER'S GUIDE

The *Teacher's Guide* for *Language & Writing 9* contains four parts: Introduction, Instructional Strategies, Assessment Tools, and Curriculum Expectations Summaries for the Academic and Applied Courses.

INSTRUCTIONAL STRATEGIES

This section provides the following for each of the 12 units of the student book, one set for the Academic Course and one set for the Applied Course. Where suggestions are common for both courses, they are presented for the Academic Course, then cross-referenced in the Applied Course section. Some margin boxes are repeated in the Applied Course section.

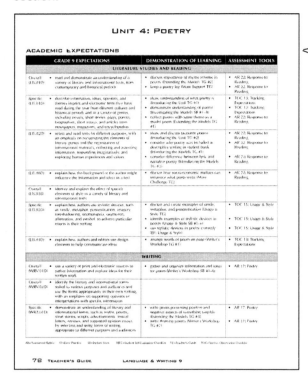

Expectations Chart
- Lists Grade 9 overall and specific expectations verbatim in left-hand column
- Shows in middle column where specifically in the student book and Teacher's Guide these expectations are met
- Lists related Assessment Tools

Planning Information
- Provides cross-references to other Nelson English Grade 9 resources—*Literature & Media 9* and *Write Source 2000*

Learning Goals
- Highlights specific learning goals covered in the unit

Introducing the Unit
- Offers suggestions for introducing the unit

Introducing the Model
- Offers suggestions for introducing the form of writing

Investigating the Model
- Provides suggestions for guiding students through this subsection, as well as answers or possible answers to the questions in the student book

Extending the Model
- Provides suggestions for extension activities based on the model

Writer's Workshop
- Provides suggestions for introducing and guiding each of the Writer's Workshop activities in the student book

Oral Language Extension
- Provides suggestions for guiding students through the Oral Language Extension subsection of the unit

Grammar, Mechanics, Usage & Style, Word Study & Spelling
- Provides discussion and suggestions for introducing skills in these areas within the context of the unit model
- Provides answers or possible answers to each of the questions in these subsections of the student book

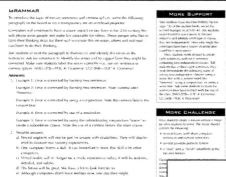

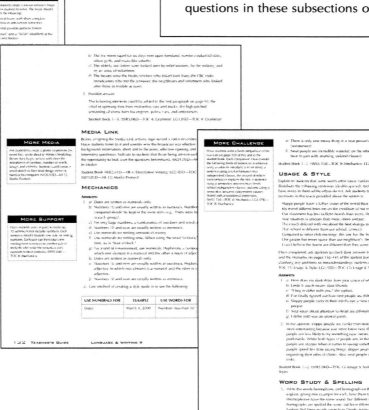

And more for each unit ...

More Support boxes with additional teaching tips for specific activities

More Challenge boxes suggesting more challenging projects

More Oral Language with additional oral language activities

More Media boxes with additional media activities

Extra Practice worksheets for Grammar, Mechanics, Usage & Style, and Word Study & Spelling (answers provided)

Assessment Tools

This section provides the following three types of assessment instruments. (For detailed discussion of the place of assessment in the program, see pages ix–xii.)

Teacher Observation Checklists
- Enable teachers to assess the extent to which students have achieved expectations

Student Self-Evaluation Checklists
- Allow students to assess their own and peers' achievement

Assessment Rubrics
- Provide specific criteria to identify the four levels of achievement outlined in the Achievement Chart for English in *The Ontario Curriculum Grades 9 and 10*
- Cover a variety of activities and forms such as conferencing, group presentation, responding to media, dramatization, comparison, newspaper article, and research report
- Can be used by both teachers and students

UNIT 1: HUMOROUS PERSONAL NARRATIVE

ACADEMIC EXPECTATIONS

	GRADE 9 EXPECTATIONS	DEMONSTRATION OF LEARNING	ASSESSMENT TOOLS
LITERATURE STUDIES AND READING			
Overall (LIV.01D)	• read and demonstrate an understanding of a variety of literary and informational texts, from contemporary and historical periods	• demonstrate understanding of humorous personal narrative (Investigating the Model SB #1–9) • share favourite passages from Atwood's works and explain why they are their favourite (Extending the Model TG #1) • consider how humorous stories evolve (Extending the Model TG #4)	• TOC 13: Tracking Expectations • AR 22: Response to Reading • TOC 13: Tracking Expectations
Specific (LI1.02D)	• select and read texts for different purposes, with an emphasis on recognizing the elements of literary genres and the organization of informational materials, collecting and assessing information, responding imaginatively, and exploring human experiences and values	• read biographies to identify subjects' embarrassing moments (Extending the Model TG #2)	• TOC 2: Conducting Research
(LI1.05D)	• analyze information, ideas, and elements in texts to make inferences about meaning	• identify types of humorous stories that present people in negative light (Extending the Model TG #5)	• AR 22: Response to Reading
(LI1.08D)	• explain how the background of the author might influence the information and ideas in a text	• discuss source material for writing (Investigating the Model TG #1) • discuss influence of childhood experiences on writing (Extending the Model TG #3)	• TOC 13: Tracking Expectations • TOC 13: Tracking Expectations
Overall (LIV.02D)	• demonstrate an understanding of the elements of a variety of literary and informational forms, with a focus on plays, short stories, and short essays	• identify similarities in humorous narratives (Introducing the Model TG #1) • demonstrate understanding of elements of humorous personal narrative (Investigating the Model SB #1–9) • identify differences between understatement and exaggeration in humorous stories (Writer's Workshop TG #5)	• AR 22: Response to Reading • TOC 13: Tracking Expectations • TOC 13: Tracking Expectations
Overall (LIV.03B)	• identify and explain the effect of specific elements of style in a variety of literary and informational texts	• discuss abrupt endings in humorous personal narratives (More Support TG)	• TOC 13: Tracking Expectations
WRITING			
Overall (WRV.01D)	• use a variety of print and electronic sources to gather information and explore ideas for their written work	• gather and organize information and ideas for humorous personal narrative (Writer's Workshop SB #1–4)	• AR 10: Humorous Personal Narrative
Specific (WR1.01D)	• investigate potential topics by formulating questions, identifying information needs, and developing research plans to gather data	• analyze the humour in experiences (Writer's Workshop TG #1) • share embarrassing experiences to help others generate topics (Writer's Workshop TG #2) • select subject for humorous personal narrative (Writer's Workshop TG #3)	• AR 10: Humorous Personal Narrative • AR 10: Humorous Personal Narrative • AR 10: Humorous Personal Narrative
(WR1.02D)	• locate and summarize information from print and electronic sources, including vertical files, periodicals, dictionaries, encyclopedias, electronic newsgroups, e-mail messages, and electronic databases	• take notes about their reminiscences (Introducing the Model TG #2)	• AR 10: Humorous Personal Narrative

AR=Assessment Rubric   EP=Extra Practice   SB=Student Book   SSEC=Student Self-Evaluation Checklist   TG=Teacher's Guide   TOC=Teacher Observation Checklist

GRADE 9 EXPECTATIONS		DEMONSTRATION OF LEARNING	ASSESSMENT TOOLS
WRITING (continued)			
Overall (WRV.02D)	• identify the literary and informational forms suited to various purposes and audiences and use the forms appropriately in their own writing, with an emphasis on supporting opinions or interpretations with specific information		
Specific (WR2.01D)	• demonstrate an understanding of literary and informational forms, such as myths, poems, short stories, scripts, advertisements, formal letters, reviews, and supported opinion essays, by selecting and using forms of writing appropriate to different purposes and audiences	• consider subtlety in writing humour (Writer's Workshop TG #4)	• AR 10: Humorous Personal Narrative
Overall (WRV.03D)	• use a variety of organizational techniques to present ideas and supporting details logically and coherently in written work	• write a draft of humorous personal narrative (Writer's Workshop SB #5)	• AR 10: Humorous Personal Narrative
Overall (WRV.04D)	• revise their written work, independently and collaboratively, with a focus on support for ideas and opinions, accuracy, clarity, and unity	• invent dialogue appropriate for context (Writer's Workshop TG #6) • revise humorous personal narrative (Writer's Workshop SB #6)	• AR 10: Humorous Personal Narrative • AR 10: Humorous Personal Narrative
Specific (WR4.01D)	• revise drafts to ensure that ideas are adequately developed with relevant supporting details and to achieve clarity and unity	• consider best place to begin and end story when revising (Writer's Workshop TG #7)	• AR 10: Humorous Personal Narrative
Overall (WRV.05D)	• edit and proofread to produce final drafts, using correct grammar, spelling, and punctuation, according to the conventions of standard Canadian English, with the support of print and electronic resources when appropriate	• edit and proofread humorous personal narrative (Writer's Workshop SB #6)	• AR 10: Humorous Personal Narrative
Specific (WR5.02B)	• select the publication method or vehicle most accessible or appealing to the intended audience	• publish a class collection of narratives (More Challenge TG)	• AR 12: Media Product
(WR5.03D)	• assess their facility with the writing process, documenting their use of different genres and forms in personal and assigned writing and identifying goals for writing improvement and growth	• include drafts and finished narrative in writing portfolio (More Challenge TG)	• TOC 3: Fiction Writing • TOC 9: Nonfiction Writing
(WR5.05D)	• use parts of speech correctly: nouns, pronouns, verbs, adverbs, adjectives, conjunctions, prepositions, and interjections	• examine usefulness of identifying parts of speech (Grammar TG #1) • identify common nouns and proper nouns (Grammar TG #2) • write sentences with only nouns, verbs, adjectives, and adverbs (Grammar TG #3) • use nouns, verbs, adverbs, and adjectives correctly (Grammar SB #1–4) • use nouns, verbs, adverbs, and adjectives correctly (EP: Grammar)	• TOC 4: Grammar • TOC 4: Grammar • TOC 4: Grammar • TOC 4: Grammar • TOC 4: Grammar
(WR5.10B)	• use consistent and appropriate verb tense and voice (i.e., active and passive) for clarity in narrative and expository writing	• discuss which verb tense generates more excitement (Usage & Style TG #1) • consider problems and value of writing in present tense (Usage & Style TG #2) • identify irregular verb tenses (Usage & Style TG #3) • write different forms of verb tense (Usage & Style TG #4) • use verb tense correctly (Usage & Style SB #1–3) • use correct verb tense (EP: Usage & Style)	• TOC 15: Usage & Style • TOC 15: Usage & Style • TOC 15: Usage & Style • TOC 15: Usage & Style • TOC 15: Usage & Style • TOC 15: Usage & Style
(WR5.15B)	• use punctuation correctly, including period, question mark, exclamation mark, comma, dash, apostrophe, colon, quotation marks, parentheses, and ellipses	• explain comma use (Mechanics TG) • use commas correctly (Mechanics SB #1–4) • eliminate unnecessary commas (EP: Mechanics)	• TOC 8: Mechanics • TOC 8: Mechanics • TOC 8: Mechanics

AR=Assessment Rubric   EP=Extra Practice   SB=Student Book   SSEC=Student Self-Evaluation Checklist   TG=Teacher's Guide   TOC=Teacher Observation Checklist

GRADE 9 EXPECTATIONS	DEMONSTRATION OF LEARNING	ASSESSMENT TOOLS
LANGUAGE		
Overall (LGV.01D)	• use knowledge of vocabulary and language conventions to speak, write, and read competently using a level of language appropriate to the purpose and audience		
Specific (LG1.03B)	• identify words borrowed from other languages and words and terms recently introduced to describe new ideas, inventions, and products, and explain their origins	• list words ending in *-ology* (Word Study & Spelling TG #1) • explain origin of modern words (Word Study & Spelling TG #2) • identify words borrowed from other languages (Word Study & Spelling SB #1–3) • identify how words and phrases came into use in English (EP: Word Study & Spelling)	• TOC 16: Word Study & Spelling • TOC 16: Word Study & Spelling • TOC 16: Word Study & Spelling • TOC 16: Word Study & Spelling
(LG1.05D)	• recognize, describe, and use correctly, in oral and written language, the language structures of standard Canadian English and its conventions of grammar and usage, including: – parts of speech: nouns, pronouns, verbs, adverbs, adjectives, conjunctions, prepositions, interjections – consistency of verb tense and voice	• examine usefulness of identifying parts of speech (Grammar TG #1) • identify common nouns and proper nouns (Grammar TG #2) • write sentences with only nouns, verbs, adjectives, and adverbs correctly (Grammar TG #3) • use nouns, verbs, adverbs, and adjectives correctly (Grammar SB #1–4) • use nouns, verbs, adverbs, and adjectives correctly (EP: Grammar) • discuss which verb tense generates more excitement (Usage & Style TG #1) • consider problems and value of writing in present tense (Usage & Style TG #2) • identify irregular verb tenses (Usage & Style TG #3) • write different forms of verb tense (Usage & Style TG #4) • use consistent and appropriate verb tense (Usage & Style SB #1–3) • use verb tense correctly (EP: Usage & Style)	• TOC 4: Grammar • TOC 4: Grammar • TOC 4: Grammar • TOC 4: Grammar • TOC 4: Grammar • TOC 15: Usage & Style • TOC 15: Usage & Style • TOC 15: Usage & Style • TOC 15: Usage & Style • TOC 15: Usage & Style • TOC 15: Usage & Style
(LG1.07B)	• recognize, describe, and use correctly, in oral and written language, the conventions of standard Canadian English for spelling, capitalization, and punctuation, including: – punctuation: period, question mark, exclamation mark, comma, dash, apostrophe, colon, quotation marks, parentheses, ellipses	• explain comma use (Mechanics TG) • use commas correctly (Mechanics SB #1–4) • use commas correctly (EP: Mechanics)	• TOC 8: Mechanics • TOC 8: Mechanics • TOC 8: Mechanics
Overall (LGV.02B)	• use listening techniques and oral communication skills to participate in classroom discussions and more formal activities, such as storytelling, role playing, and reporting/ presenting, for specific purposes and audiences	• discuss sense of humour (Introducing the Unit TG #1) • discuss what makes comedians funny (Introducing the Unit TG #2) • share funny stories and discuss their humour (Introducing the Unit TG #3)	• TOC 13: Tracking Expectations • TOC 13: Tracking Expectations • TOC 13: Tracking Expectations
Specific (LG2.03D)	• plan and make oral presentations to a small group or the class, selecting and using vocabulary and methods of delivery to suit audience and purpose	• make an oral presentation to the class (More Oral Language TG) • present humorous personal narrative as standup monologue (Oral Language Extension SB)	• SSEC 5: Oral Presentation • AR 15: Oral Language
(LG2.07D)	• analyze their own and others' oral presentations to identify strengths and weaknesses, and plan ways to improve their performance	• assess each other's oral presentations (More Oral Language TG)	• SSEC 5: Oral Presentation

AR=Assessment Rubric   EP=Extra Practice   SB=Student Book   SSEC=Student Self-Evaluation Checklist   TG=Teacher's Guide   TOC=Teacher Observation Checklist

GRADE 9 EXPECTATIONS	DEMONSTRATION OF LEARNING	ASSESSMENT TOOLS
MEDIA STUDIES		
Overall (MDV.01D) • use knowledge of elements, intended audiences, and production practices of a variety of media forms to analyze specific media works	• suggest examples of film and TV stereotypes (Investigating the Model TG #2)	• AR 21: Response to Media
Specific (MD1.01B) • demonstrate critical thinking skills by identifying the differences between explicit and implicit messages in media works	• explain why certain material is offensive (Oral Language Extension TG) • explore how stock characters in sitcoms can perpetuate harmful stereotypes (Media Link TG) • identify and analyze stock characters (Media Link SB)	• AR 21: Response to Media • AR 21: Response to Media • AR 21: Response to Media
(MD1.02D) • identify how elements of media forms are used in a variety of media works and explain the effects of different treatments	• discuss use of types of shots in filmmaking (More Media TG)	• AR 21: Response to Media

AR=Assessment Rubric   EP=Extra Practice   SB=Student Book   SSEC=Student Self-Evaluation Checklist   TG=Teacher's Guide   TOC=Teacher Observation Checklist

INSTRUCTIONAL STRATEGIES FOR THE ACADEMIC COURSE

PLANNING INFORMATION

Links to Other Nelson English 9 Resources

Literature & Media 9
Personal Narrative—See "The Goal Post" by Edward Smith, pp. 111–112 and "Early Days" by Maria Campbell, pp. 115–118.

Write Source 2000
Personal Narrative—"Autobiographical Writing," pp. 153–159; **Adjectives**—"Adjective," pp. 451–453; **Adverbs**—"Adverb," p. 454; **Commas**—"Comma," pp. 389–392; **Nouns**—"Noun," pp. 439–441; **Verbs**—"Verb," pp. 446–450

LEARNING GOALS

- write a humorous personal narrative
- use parts of speech correctly: nouns, verbs, adverbs, and adjectives
- use commas correctly
- use consistent and appropriate verb tense
- identify words borrowed from other languages

INTRODUCING THE UNIT

1. Ask students to respond to the adage "Laughter is the best medicine." Do they agree? Why or why not? How important do they feel it is to have a good sense of humour? Why? (LGV.02B—TOC 13: Tracking Expectations)

2. Ask students to identify people whom they find funny. These people might be professional comedians or local individuals (even classmates) that everyone would know. Ask them to suggest what makes these people funny—is it the individuals themselves, the stories they tell, or a combination of both? (LGV.02B—TOC 13: Tracking Expectations)

3. Ask students to share funny stories and/or jokes they have heard (that are suitable for the classroom), then have them identify what makes them funny. Are there common elements in these stories/jokes? Can they define humour? (LGV.02B—TOC 13: Tracking Expectations)

INTRODUCING THE MODEL

1. Before you begin the unit, mount photographs and articles of Margaret Atwood around the classroom for students to view. If possible, prepare a display of several writers—Canadian and international—noted for their humorous works. Humorous personal narratives abound in magazines such as *Reader's Digest*. Give students an opportunity to browse through these publications with the purpose of finding and sharing an especially humorous narrative with their classmates. Have one or more of your own favourites ready to share with students. Then have students identify similarities such as first-person point of view, brevity, and organization of details among these narratives. (LIV.02D—AR 22: Response to Reading)

2. Share James Thurber's definition of humour as "emotional chaos told about calmly and quietly in retrospect." Have students discuss Thurber's idea and determine what he is suggesting. Ask them to think about events in their own lives that were upsetting at the time but, in retrospect, seem humorous. They could take notes about their reminiscences, which could be used when they write their own humorous personal narratives. (WR1.02D—AR 10: Humorous Personal Narrative)

INVESTIGATING THE MODEL

1. Ask students if they were surprised that a world-renowned figure like Margaret Atwood would focus on an event from her childhood rather than an adult experience. Then share with them the following comment by Willa Cather: "Most of the basic material a writer works with is acquired before the age of fifteen." Students could discuss the implications of this statement with regard to their own writing. (LI1.08D—TOC 13: Tracking Expectations)

2. When discussing activity #3 about comic personae on page 21 of the student book, have students suggest characters in film and on television who fall into these categories. Students could then videotape from television examples of these three personae to share with the class. (MDV.01D—AR 21: Response to Media)

Answers:

1. Possible answer

   By setting the scene with the sentence "Much joy was contributed to the world, in those days, by the howlers, faux pas, bloopers, and pratfalls that were sent out, uncensored, over the airwaves," Atwood prepares the reader for an entertaining account of her public embarrassment.

2. Atwood establishes herself as a credible narrator by referring to her public readings (thereby confirming her success as a writer). At the same time, she reveals the humorous nature of her narrative by relating various ways she has been publicly humiliated during them. She clinches the reader's interest with the phrase "my first moment of truly public embarrassment."

3. Atwood portrays herself as a helpless victim of circumstances whose embarrassment results when she merely follows the instructions given her: "I was to be the person the flying squirrel flew to, a sort of human tree."

4. The main events of Atwood's narrative are arranged chronologically, but these are sandwiched between her memories of adult experiences. The initial adult experiences serve to establish Atwood as a fallible—and, therefore, sympathetic—individual, and the latter ones provide entertaining closure as they pale in comparison to the memory of her teenage experience.

5. Atwood's account of her first appearance on *Pet Corner* establishes for the reader the difference between Atwood the successful literary figure and Atwood the awkward teenager, who, "in lieu of cats," had an insect for a pet. Also, her wry observations (e.g., "I ... presumably electrified the audience with an account of what female praying mantises would eat") demonstrate her naiveté and prepare the reader for her ineffectual response to the frightened squirrel inside her clothing.

6. The first-person point of view is the most intimate because the reader hears the story directly from the person involved and, in this way, experiences the event through that person's perspective. However, this also requires the reader to consider what the narrator says because the author's voice is the only one heard. Since humorists often exaggerate details to heighten their impact, the reader must filter the information being received and determine whether the writer is being accurate or merely trying to evoke a particular reaction. Recounting the same experience in third-person point of view would lend more validity to Atwood's information but lessen the intimacy of her narrative.

7. Atwood could have included the woman's explanation of the habits of flying squirrels, but this would merely have delayed the more important account of the squirrel's disappearance inside Atwood's clothing. Atwood also could have included the woman's and the host's responses to Atwood's plight, but these responses would have shifted the focus from Atwood to the adults. By omitting their comments, Atwood allows the reader to concentrate on the hapless teenager and the extent of her humiliation.

8. Exaggeration is obvious in Atwood's description of live television ("Much joy was contributed to the world"), in her account of the audience's response to Lenore ("I ... presumably electrified the audience"), and in her brief reference to the incident with James Reaney (" ... I was choking to death.").

Sample criteria for a humorous personal narrative:

- entertains the reader
- has a beginning that establishes writer as credible narrator and identifies nature of event to be recounted
- often centres around typical character types
- has details that are often arranged in chronological order
- focuses on a single event
- is usually told from first-person point of view
- may include dialogue
- can be humorous through understatement and exaggeration
- often ends abruptly, forcing reader to imagine effect

9. Atwood's narrative might have ended immediately before the last paragraph. However, this paragraph provides entertaining closure as Atwood affirms that no adult experience "has been able to compete in embarrassment value" with the memory of her teenage experience.

Student Book 1.–9. (LIV.01D—TOC 13: Tracking Expectations; LIV.02D—TOC 13: Tracking Expectations)

EXTENDING THE MODEL

1. Direct students to other humorous works written by Atwood (not only articles and short stories but novels as well, such as *The Edible Woman* and *Lady Oracle*). Encourage students to read them and share favourite passages with the rest of the class, explaining why they are their favourite. (LIV.01D—AR 22: Response to Reading)

2. Ask students to research "most embarrassing" moments in the lives of noted past or contemporary figures. Encourage students to read biographies written about figures of interest to them. Have them compile and display a series of "most embarrassing moments" experienced by these figures. (LI1.02D—TOC 2: Conducting Research)

3. Have students investigate how childhood experiences might affect a writer's work besides being the focus of a personal narrative such as "A Flying Start." Students could read autobiographical and biographical information about an author of their choice and present what they have learned about the influence of childhood experiences on that author's later writing. (LI1.08D—TOC 13: Tracking Expectations)

4. Often, the most devastating catastrophes become the focus of humorous narratives. Have students consider the factors that influence the evolution and dissemination of humorous stories in our culture. Students might consider factors such as the news media, the Internet, and the entertainment industry. (LIV.01D—TOC 13: Tracking Expectations)

5. Ask students to identify the types of humorous stories that present individuals or groups in a negative light. Follow-up activities would have students prepare written or oral reports of the pernicious effects of such stories. (LI1.05D—AR 22: Response to Reading)

WRITER'S WORKSHOP

1. Have students respond to Will Rogers's comment in activity #1. Have them consider something they saw happen to another person that they found amusing, then consider why it probably was not amusing to that person. Further discussion could revisit James Thurber's definition of humour ("Humour is emotional chaos told about calmly and quietly in retrospect.") and emphasize that our most embarrassing experiences are often the best choices for humorous personal narratives. (WR1.01D—AR 10: Humorous Personal Narrative)

2. Have students return to the notes they jotted down about embarrassing experiences during the Introducing the Model activities. If possible, have some students briefly share their experiences. This will help others who are having difficulty recalling such experiences to generate some of their own. (WR1.01D—AR 10: Humorous Personal Narrative)

3. The more time that has elapsed since an embarrassing event occurred, the easier it will be to write about it effectively, so students might wish to avoid sharing experiences that happened within the past year. Once students have generated

In discussing activity #9 (page 21 of the student book), offer examples ("It was at that point I realized the back of my hospital gown had been wide open all along") to illustrate that abrupt endings emphasize the comic value of the event by forcing the reader to imagine its effects on the narrator. Have students find examples of such abrupt endings in magazines such as *Reader's Digest* and share with the class how such endings are superior to those that explain the humour of the event. (LIV.03B—TOC 13: Tracking Expectations)

To emphasize the importance of correctness in writing, you might have the class publish a collection of their narratives in a laminated volume to be placed in the classroom or school library. Other students in the school whose courses involve the skills necessary for the physical preparation of such a volume could assist in its preparation. A copy of a student's contribution to the volume—along with the various prewriting attempts and drafts—would also be included in a writing portfolio as documentation of the student's involvement in the writing process. (WR5.02B—AR 12: Media Product; WR5.03D—TOC 3: Fiction Writing; TOC 9: Nonfiction Writing)

An extension of the published classroom anthology would be to have students share their stories orally with the rest of the class. Referring to the "Oral Language Extension" on page 23 of the student book and to the "Speaking Skills" appendix on page 204 of the student book, the class will develop criteria for assessment of their performances and will assess their own and each other's oral stories.

Many students are gifted comedians but have no public forum for their talent. Have students participate in a joke-telling presentation, using the various techniques they identified in the Oral Language Extension activity on page 23 of the student book. This might be extended to comprise a portion of a school talent night or variety show. (LG2.03D—SSEC 5: Oral Presentation; LG2.07D—SSEC 5: Oral Presentation)

several embarrassing experiences, remind them to select the subject of their humorous personal narrative carefully—they should choose an experience that they are willing to share in writing, and it should be one that will not embarrass others who might have been involved. If necessary, students should request of others involved in the experience their permission to write about it. (This is especially important if students are writing about experiences involving family members.) (WR1.01D—AR 10: Humorous Personal Narrative)

4. As students begin drafting their narratives, have them consider the importance of subtlety in writing humour. Illustrate the difference between self-conscious humour that is embarrassing to observe (e.g., people who laugh at their own jokes and explain the punch line) and deadpan delivery that conveys wit with subtlety. Remind students to avoid explaining the humour in their narrative. (WR2.01D—AR 10: Humorous Personal Narrative)

5. Direct students to the examples of understatement and exaggeration on page 23 of the student book (Writing Tip). Read them aloud and have students identify the differences between these devices and the ways they generate humour. If possible, have them recall routines by standup comics who make use of either device, then encourage them to use one of these devices in their own narratives. (LIV.02D—TOC 13: Tracking Expectations)

6. Although Atwood does not include dialogue in her narrative, students should be aware that dialogue helps make writing vivid for a reader. Also, writers can use spoken language to heighten humour by incorporating funny expressions that capture a sense of the people involved. Because most people cannot remember the exact words spoken during a particular encounter, students should feel free to invent the dialogue that would be appropriate for that context. (WRV.04D—AR 10: Humorous Personal Narrative)

7. When students are ready to revise their narratives, remind them of the importance of timing when telling a joke and explain that the same is true of a humorous narrative. Therefore, they should look for the best place to begin and end their stories. Can they omit the first sentence or paragraph and still convey the necessary information? Can they omit the last sentence or paragraph and still achieve the desired effect? (WR4.01D—AR 10: Humorous Personal Narrative)

Student Book 1.–4. (WRV.01D—AR 10: Humorous Personal Narrative); 5. (WRV.03D—AR 10: Humorous Personal Narrative); 6. (WRV.04D—AR 10: Humorous Personal Narrative; WRV.05D—AR 10: Humorous Personal Narrative)

ORAL LANGUAGE EXTENSION

It is important that students choose standup routines that will not offend the teacher or members of the class. Teachers might wish to preview the videotaped routines or simply emphasize the need to select routines that can be enjoyed by all groups. To clarify this issue, teachers might have students generate a list of the sorts of material that would be offensive to certain groups.

With the prior knowledge and permission of the administrators and students' parents, teachers might wish to show a videotape of a standup routine that many find offensive for the purpose of helping students identify why such material is harmful. (MD1.01B—AR 21: Response to Media)

Student Book (LG2.03D—AR 15: Oral Language)

GRAMMAR

1. Many students see no value in being able to identify parts of speech. To illustrate the value of this understanding, ask them why doctors must learn the parts of the body or why mechanics must learn the parts of an automobile. Explain that

learning the parts of speech provides us with a vocabulary that we can use when talking about the technical elements of writing. (WR5.05D—TOC 4: Grammar; LG1.05D—TOC 4: Grammar)

2. When discussing nouns, point out the difference between **common nouns** (e.g., *camera, squirrel, uniform*) and **proper nouns** that name specific people, places, or things and are capitalized (e.g., *James Reaney*, Pet Corner, *CBC Television*). Ask students to identify at least three of each in the model. (WR5.05D—TOC 4: Grammar; LG1.05D—TOC 4: Grammar)

3. Nouns, verbs, adjectives, and adverbs are the most important parts of speech because we can write complete sentences using only these types of words. (See the example below.) Have students write three sentences of their own that include only nouns, verbs, adjectives, and adverbs. Ask them to read the sentences aloud and discuss what they notice about them. (They are repetitive and childlike, which explains the need for the other four parts of speech to be discussed in Unit 2.) (WR5.05D—TOC 4: Grammar; LG1.05D—TOC 4: Grammar)

Studios	**often**	**aired**	**uncensored**	**bloopers.**
noun	adverb	verb	adjective	noun

Answers:

1. Below are some of the nouns students may identify. Note that the PLACES column has no entries and the THINGS column has the most.

PEOPLE	PLACES	THINGS	QUALITIES AND IDEAS
audience		introductions	life
man		readings	joy
terrorist		chapter	embarrassment
sister-in-law		novel	paralysis
woman		name	cruelty
neighbour		shows	
James Reaney		camera	
		squirrel	
		airwaves	
		uniforms	

2. Possible answers

Sentences containing action verbs:
What do you **do** when the man introducing you **proposes** to read the audience the entire last chapter of your novel, **gets** your name wrong, or **characterizes** you as some kind of machine-gun-wielding radical terrorist?
At my school, we **wore** uniforms....
At last the owner of the flying squirrel **fished** the thing out via the back of my jumper.

Sentences containing linking verbs:

Many shows **were** live.

At that time, in lieu of cats, I **had** a beautiful, green, intelligent praying mantis....

Lenore **was** such a hit that *Pet Corner* decided to have me back.

Sentences containing helping (or auxiliary) verbs:

The woman who lived next door, and for whom I babysat, **had** somehow **become** the producer of a show called *Pet Corner*....

{This} was an old praying mantis, which **had** already **laid** its egg mass....

[I] electrified the audience with an account of what female praying mantises **would eat**....

3. Possible answers

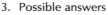

At that time, in lieu of cats, I had a beautiful, green, intelligent praying mantis called Lenore....

All modifiers are adjectives.

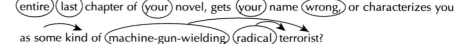

What do you do when the man introducing you proposes to read the audience the entire last chapter of your novel, gets your name wrong, or characterizes you as some kind of machine-gun-wielding radical terrorist?

All modifiers except for "wrong" are adjectives. "Wrong" is an adverb.

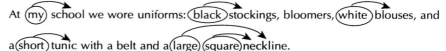

At my school we wore uniforms: black stockings, bloomers, white blouses, and a short tunic with a belt and a large square neckline.

All modifiers are adjectives.

4. a) adverb (Student sentence could use "wrong" as an adjective or verb.)
    b) noun (Student sentence could use "novel" as an adjective.)
    c) adjective (Student sentence could use "public" as a noun.)
    d) adjective (Student sentence could use "improvised" as a verb.)
    e) noun (Student sentence could use "editing" as a main verb or adjective.)
    f) adjective (Student sentence could use "television" as a noun.)
    g) adjective (Student sentence could use "live" as a verb.)

Student Book 1.–4. (WR5.05D—TOC 4: Grammar; LG1.05D—TOC 4: Grammar)

MEDIA LINK

Emphasize that sitcoms use stock characters for the sake of expediency (little screen time is needed to provide a backstory for these individuals). However, students might wish to explore how the use of stock characters can perpetuate harmful stereotypes (e.g., the impression that all athletes lack intelligence). (MD1.01B—AR 21: Response to Media)

Student Book (MD1.01B—AR 21: Response to Media)

MECHANICS

Although there are definite rules for comma use, it is also important to recognize the value of individual writer preference in punctuation. Put the following sentences (which do not adhere to the text rules for comma use) on the board and have students suggest why Atwood included commas where she did.

I thought of the bloomers, and swiftly reached down the front of my own neckline. Then I thought better of it, and began to lift the skirt.

MORE MEDIA

Note Atwood's use of filmmaking terminology ("close shot") in her narrative. Have students discuss the meaning of close shot and then have them identify other types of shots associated with filmmaking. Using cued videotapes of various films, students can illustrate each of the various types of shots and discuss their effects. Follow-up discussion could focus on the various types of shots that would be appropriate in a filmed version of their own humorous personal narratives. (MD1.02D—AR 21: Response to Media)

No rule requires the two verbs ("thought" and "reached") to be separated by a comma. If there were three verbs (e.g., I *thought* of the bloomers, *reached* down the front of my neckline, and *screamed*), the commas would be justified. In the sentences above, Atwood has inserted commas to create pauses for dramatic effect. (WR5.15B—TOC 8: Mechanics; LG1.07B—TOC 8: Mechanics)

Answers:

1. a) My next-door neighbour, the producer of *Pet Corner*, was impressed by Lenore. (separates an expression that refers to the same person)
   b) Other pets on the show included a talking parrot, a dancing dog, and a snake. (between items in a series)
   c) Near the end of the show, I pretended to be a tree for the squirrel to fly to. (after an introductory group of several words)
   d) Because the squirrel was a nocturnal animal, the lights bothered it. (separates a subordinate clause from the main clause that follows it)
   e) I was embarrassed as I tried to catch the frightened, wriggling, elusive animal. (replaces the word *and* between two or more adjectives)
   f) The audience, on the other hand, found the performance very entertaining. (sets off words that interrupt a flow of thought)
   g) The episode with the flying squirrel happened many years ago, but I still remember it clearly. (separates two complete sentences joined by *but*)

2. Possible answers
   Use commas to separate elements of an address. (Students should note that when an address appears within a sentence, a comma must follow the last element in the address.)
   Use a comma to separate the day from the year in a date. (Students should note that when a date appears within a sentence, a comma must follow the year.)
   Use a comma after the salutation in a friendly letter and after the closing in any letter.
   Use a comma after words like *yes, no, well* when they appear at the beginning of a sentence.
   Use a comma to separate dialogue from a speaker tag (unless the speaker tag follows dialogue ending with a question mark or exclamation point).
   Use commas to separate a person's name when the person is addressed directly in dialogue.

3. Most Canadians recognize Margaret Atwood as one of our country's finest novelists, but she is also an acclaimed short-story writer, essayist, and poet. Born in Ottawa, she began publishing her poems when she was 19. Her first book of poetry, *Double Persephone*, was published in 1961, and she won the Governor General's Award in 1966 for another volume of poetry (*The Circle Game*). She is the author of several critically acclaimed novels. One of her best-known novels, *The Handmaid's Tale*, earned her a second Governor General's Award in 1986. Both *The Handmaid's Tale* and an earlier novel, *Surfacing*, have been made into films.

4. Student work.

Student Book 1.–4. (WR5.15B—TOC 8: Mechanics; LG1.07B—TOC 8: Mechanics)

USAGE & STYLE

1. To illustrate the difference in effect between present tense and past tense, put the following sentences on the board and have students discuss which one generates more excitement. The present tense heightens the tension because it suggests the figure is still lurking there—as opposed to lurking there earlier and now absent. (LG1.05D—TOC 15: Usage & Style; WR5.10B—TOC 15: Usage & Style)

The hooded figure lurks in the shadows.

The hooded figure lurked in the shadows.

2. Have students locate novels written in the present tense and share a favourite passage with the class. Have them consider the problems inherent in writing a novel in the present tense and weigh these against the value of doing so. (LG1.05D—TOC 15: Usage & Style; WR5.10B—TOC 15: Usage & Style)

3. Students should consider the irregularities of verb tense. Write the following sentence from the model on the board and ask students to write the present-tense forms of the boldface verbs: *The woman who **lived** next door, and for whom I **babysat,** had somehow become the producer of a show called* Pet Corner. Ask students which verb is irregular in the past tense, and then have them identify at least five other verbs that have an irregular past-tense form. (LG1.05D—TOC 15: Usage & Style; WR5.05D—TOC 15: Usage & Style)

4. The second paragraph of "A Flying Start" contains one of the most irregular verbs in the English language. Have students identify this verb (was) and, working in pairs, write as many forms of this verb as they can, grouping them under the headings PRESENT TENSE and PAST TENSE. Then have them compare their work with that of another group. Did they forget any? (WR5.05D—TOC 15: Usage & Style)

Answers:
1. The following sentence contains both past- and present-tense verbs, but the author is justified in switching tenses because she is speaking directly to her readers (present tense) about an earlier event (past tense): "For those who may accuse me of cruelty to insects, let me point out that this was a) an old praying mantis, which had b) already laid its egg-mass, and which c) lived a good deal longer in my jar than it would have outside, as it was d) cold out there."

2. Last year, public-access cable television **provided** audiences with countless unplanned—yet highly entertaining—viewing experiences. On one show about unusual hobbies, a woman **brought** in three live bats to illustrate her involvement in ethology, the biological study of animal behaviour. She wanted to dispel several myths about bats, particularly the one that bats entangle themselves in women's long hair, and she removed one of the bats from its carrier and **placed** it on her head. Just at that moment, her folding chair collapsed and the bat **flew** off her head and landed on the long, bushy beard of the show's host. The show ended abruptly as the host leaped up and, flailing his arms in terror, **knocked** the television camera to the floor.

3. Student work.

Student Book 1.–3. (LG1.05D—TOC 15: Usage & Style; WR5.10B—TOC 15: Usage & Style)

WORD STUDY & SPELLING

1. Introduce this word study section by explaining that Margaret Atwood's interest in praying mantises probably arose from her father's work in entomology, which is the study of insects. The word "entomology" comes from the Greek words *entoma,* meaning "insects," and *logos,* meaning "discourse." In fact, all words that end in -*ology*—for example, *biology, psychology,* and *physiology*—refer to a particular body of knowledge. The study of the meaning and origin of words is another -*ology* word: "etymology." Students could make a list of other words ending in -*ology.* (LG1.03B—TOC 16: Word Study & Spelling)

2. When introducing activity #3 on page 31 of the student book, have students begin by considering words such as *electricity* and *computer,* which play such an important part in our lives, and then identifying their etymologies. *(Electricity* comes from the Greek *elektron,* meaning *amber,* which is the material in which electricity was first observed; *computer* comes from the Latin *com-,* meaning "together," and *putare,* meaning "to reckon.") Students should realize that even the names of modern devices often have their roots in words from the past. (LG1.03B—TOC 16: Word Study & Spelling)

Answers:

Possible answers

1. a) *entrée* (main dish served at dinner)
      C'est la vie. (That's life.)
      cavalier (nonchalant)
      roulette (game of chance)
      crepe (fabric with wrinkled surface)

   b) Aboriginal languages: igloo, wigwam, chinook, muskeg, caucus, toboggan
      Italian: crescendo, fresco, piano, piazza, pizza, bankrupt
      German: sauerkraut
      Spanish: breeze
      Philippine: boondocks
      Indian: shampoo

2. *Bloomers* comes from the name of Amelia Jenks Bloomer, an American reformer who campaigned against sexual discrimination and advocated temperance and women's suffrage. She appeared at lectures during the 1850s wearing full trousers, gathered at the ankle, under a short skirt. These later became known as bloomers. Other words in "A Flying Start" that were coined in various ways include *howlers* and *giggling* (which imitate sounds), *classmate* and *egg-mass* (formed by compounding), *CBC* (which is an acronym), and *bloopers* (which is an entirely invented word).

3. a) Possible answer
      television: Greek *tele,* meaning *at a distance,* and Latin *videre,* meaning *to see*
      microwave: Greek *mikros,* meaning *little,* and Old English *wafian,* meaning *to wave.*
      New inventions: *telewave* (a hand-held device that cooks food at a distance by sending a concentrated beam of electrical energy); *microvision* (an entertainment device worn on eyeglasses that projects a moving picture on the retina)

   b) Student work.

Student Book 1.–3. (LG1.03B—TOC 16: Word Study & Spelling)

ANSWERS TO EXTRA PRACTICE

Grammar

```
        N        Adv       V       Adj       N
1. a) Authors   often     give    spirited  readings.

        Adv       N         N       V       Adj       N
   b) Yesterday, Margaret  Atwood  gave    three    readings.

        Adj       N         V       Adv       Adv
   c) The     audience   arrived   very    early.

        Adj       N         V       Adv       Adv
   d) Her      last      novel    is       my      favourite.

        Adj       Adj       N      Adv      V     Adj      N
   e) A      gentle    breeze  slowly   fanned   the    pages.
```

2. a) adjective (Student sentence could use *green* as a noun.)
    b) verb (Student sentence could use *point* as a noun.)
    c) adjective (Student sentence could use *future* as a noun.)
    d) adverb (Student sentence could use *more* as an adjective.)
    e) noun (Student sentence could use *bulge* as a verb.)
(WR5.05D—TOC 4: Grammar; LG1.05D—TOC 4: Grammar)

Mechanics

As technology continues to grow, it is becoming more and more important for people to be able to communicate quickly and easily. Even very small businesses usually have more than one telephone line, at least one fax machine, and an Internet connection for e-mail. Many businesses even have their own Web sites that enable them to reach hundreds, even thousands, of prospective customers every month. However, successful business people understand that the most important aspect of communicating with customers is courtesy.
(WR5.15B—TOC 8: Mechanics; LG1.07B—TOC 8: Mechanics)

Usage & Style

Authors like Margaret Atwood are accustomed to giving readings but, as she says in the final paragraph of "A Flying Start," many things **can** and do go wrong during these events. People in charge of organizing author readings **need** to anticipate possible problems and eliminate these in advance. For example, successful organizers make sure that the facility where the author **appears** is suitable and available for the reading. As well, they place advertisements about upcoming readings in newspapers and on radio and television long before the event **takes** place. This ensures that the author **has** a large audience present for the reading. However, one of the most important details— the weather—is usually beyond their control.
(WR5.10B—TOC 15: Usage & Style; LG1.05D—TOC 15: Usage & Style)

Word Study & Spelling

1. jeans (from the name of the place where the heavy cloth was woven: Genoa, Italy)

2. maître d'hôtel (French for "steward of the house")

3. crash (from the sound)

4. UNICEF (acronym for the United Nations International Children's Emergency Fund)

5. moonwalk (compounding two existing words to form another word)

6. pro bono publico (Latin for "for the public good")

7. microscope (from the Greek *mikros,* meaning "small," and *skopium,* meaning "look at")

8. tangerine (from the name of one of the places where they are grown: Tangier, Morocco)

9. kaput (German for "destroyed")

10. cardigan (from the Earl of Cardigan, who always wore a jacket during his military campaigns)

11. NATO (acronym for the North Atlantic Treaty Organization)

12. transmit (from the Latin *trans,* meaning "across," and *mittere,* meaning "send")

13. modus operandi (Latin for "way of going about a job")

14. braille (from Louis Braille, the inventor)

15. frankfurter (from the German city of Frankfurt)

16. nudge (from the Norwegian *nugga*, meaning "to push")

17. newspaper (compounding two existing words to form another word)

18. zip (from the sound)

19. doily (from Doily, a famous haberdasher)

20. universe (from the Latin *unus,* meaning "one," and *versum,* meaning "to turn")

(LG1.03B—TOC 16: Word Study & Spelling)

GRADE 9 EXPECTATIONS	DEMONSTRATION OF LEARNING	ASSESSMENT TOOLS
LITERATURE STUDIES AND READING		
Overall (LIV.01P)	• read and demonstrate an understanding of a variety of literary and informational texts	• demonstrate understanding of humorous personal narrative (Investigating the Model SB #1–9) • share favourite passages from Atwood's works (Extending the Model TG #1)	• TOC 14: Tracking Expectations • AR 22: Response to Reading
Specific (LI1.05P)	• make inferences based on the information and ideas presented in texts	• identify types of humorous stories that present people in negative light (Extending the Model TG #2)	• AR 22: Response to Reading
Overall (LIV.02P)	• demonstrate an understanding of the elements of a variety of literary and informational forms, with a focus on plays, short stories, and newspaper and magazine articles	• read humorous narratives and identify similarities (Introducing the Model TG #1) • demonstrate understanding of humorous personal narrative (Investigating the Model SB #1–9)	• AR 22: Response to Reading • TOC 14: Tracking Expectations
Overall (LIV.03B)	• identify and explain the effect of specific elements of style in a variety of literary and informational texts	• discuss abrupt endings in humorous personal narratives (More Support TG)	• TOC 14: Tracking Expectations
WRITING		
Overall (WRV.01P)	• use print and electronic sources to gather information and explore ideas for their written work	• gather and organize information and ideas for humorous personal narrative (Writer's Workshop SB #1–4)	• AR 10: Humorous Personal Narrative
Specific (WR1.01P)	• investigate potential topics by asking questions, identifying informational needs, and developing research plans to gather data	• formulate questions to help generate details in narrative (Writer's Workshop TG #1–2)	• AR 10: Humorous Personal Narrative
(WR1.02P)	• locate and record information and ideas from print and electronic sources, including newspapers and magazines, dictionaries, encyclopedias, vertical files, and electronic databases	• make notes about reminiscences (Introducing the Model TG #2) • discuss ideas for humorous personal narrative (Writer's Workshop TG #3)	• AR 10: Humorous Personal Narrative • AR 10: Humorous Personal Narrative
Overall (WRV.03P)	• use a variety of forms of writing to express themselves, clarify their ideas, and engage the audience's attention, imagination, and interest	• write a draft of humorous personal narrative (Writer's Workshop SB #5)	• AR 10: Humorous Personal Narrative
Overall (WRV.04B)	• revise their written work, collaboratively and independently, with a focus on support for ideas, accuracy, clarity, and unity	• revise humorous personal narrative (Writer's Workshop SB #6)	• AR 10: Humorous Personal Narrative
Overall (WRV.05B)	• edit and proofread to produce final drafts, using correct grammar, spelling, and punctuation, according to the conventions of standard Canadian English specified for this course, with the support of print and electronic resources when appropriate	• edit and proofread humorous personal narrative (Writer's Workshop SB #6)	• AR 10: Humorous Personal Narrative
Specific (WR5.02B)	• select the publication method or vehicle most accessible or appealing to the intended audience	• publish a class collection of narratives (More Challenge TG)	• AR 12: Media Product
(WR5.03P)	• provide documentation showing their use of the writing process	• include drafts and finished narrative in writing portfolio (More Challenge TG)	• TOC 3: Fiction Writing • TOC 9: Nonfiction Writing

AR=Assessment Rubric   EP=Extra Practice   SB=Student Book   SSEC=Student Self-Evaluation Checklist   TG=Teacher's Guide   TOC=Teacher Observation Checklist

GRADE 9 EXPECTATIONS	DEMONSTRATION OF LEARNING	ASSESSMENT TOOLS
WRITING (continued)		
(WR5.05P) • identify and use parts of speech correctly: nouns, pronouns, verbs, adverbs, adjectives, conjunctions, prepositions, and interjections	• examine usefulness of identifying parts of speech (Grammar TG #1) • identify common nouns and proper nouns (Grammar TG #2) • write sentences with only nouns, verbs, adjectives, and adverbs (Grammar TG #3) • use nouns, verbs, adverbs, and adjectives correctly (Grammar SB #1–4) • use nouns, verbs, adverbs, and adjectives correctly (EP: Grammar)	• TOC 4: Grammar • TOC 4: Grammar • TOC 4: Grammar • TOC 4: Grammar • TOC 4: Grammar
(WR5.10B) • use consistent and appropriate verb tense and voice (i.e., active and passive) for clarity in narrative and expository writing	• identify difference between verb tenses (Usage & Style TG) • use verb tense correctly (Usage & Style SB #1–3) • use correct verb tense (EP: Usage & Style)	• TOC 15: Usage & Style • TOC 15: Usage & Style • TOC 15: Usage & Style
(WR5.15B) • use punctuation correctly, including period, question mark, exclamation mark, comma, dash, apostrophe, colon, quotation marks, parentheses, and ellipses	• explain comma use (Mechanics TG #1) • use commas correctly (Mechanics TG #2) • use commas correctly (Mechanics SB #1–4) • eliminate unnecessary commas (EP: Mechanics)	• TOC 8: Mechanics • TOC 8: Mechanics • TOC 8: Mechanics • TOC 8: Mechanics
LANGUAGE		
Overall (LGV.01P) • use knowledge of vocabulary and language conventions to speak, write, and read clearly and correctly		
Specific (LG1.03B) • identify words borrowed from other languages, and words and terms recently introduced to describe new ideas, inventions, and products, and explain their origins	• list words ending in -ology (Word Study & Spelling TG #1) • find words for modern devices with Greek or Latin roots (Word Study & Spelling TG #2) • identify words borrowed from other languages (Word Study & Spelling SB #1–3) • identify how words and phrases came into use in English (EP: Word Study & Spelling)	• TOC 16: Word Study & Spelling • TOC 16: Word Study & Spelling • TOC 16: Word Study & Spelling • TOC 16: Word Study & Spelling
(LG1.05P) • recognize, describe, and use correctly, in oral and written language, the language structures of standard Canadian English and its conventions of grammar and usage, including: – parts of speech: nouns, pronouns, verbs, adverbs, adjectives, conjunctions, prepositions, and interjections – consistency of verb tense and voice	• examine usefulness of identifying parts of speech (Grammar TG #1) • identify common nouns and proper nouns (Grammar TG #2) • write sentences with only nouns, verbs, adjectives, and adverbs (Grammar TG #3) • use nouns, verbs, adjectives, and adverbs correctly (Grammar SB #1–4) • use nouns, verbs, adjectives, and adverbs correctly (EP: Grammar) • identify difference between verb tenses (Usage & Style TG) • use verb tense correctly (Usage & Style SB #1–3) • use verb tense correctly (EP: Usage & Style)	• TOC 4: Grammar • TOC 4: Grammar • TOC 4: Grammar • TOC 4: Grammar • TOC 4: Grammar • TOC 15: Usage & Style • TOC 15: Usage & Style • TOC 15: Usage & Style

AR=Assessment Rubric   EP=Extra Practice   SB=Student Book   SSEC=Student Self-Evaluation Checklist   TG=Teacher's Guide   TOC=Teacher Observation Checklist

GRADE 9 EXPECTATIONS	DEMONSTRATION OF LEARNING	ASSESSMENT TOOLS
LANGUAGE (continued)		
(LG1.07B) • recognize, describe, and use correctly, in oral and written language, the conventions of standard Canadian English for spelling, capitalization, and punctuation, including: – punctuation: period, question mark, exclamation mark, comma, dash, apostrophe, colon, quotation marks, parentheses, ellipses	• explain comma use (Mechanics TG #1) • use commas correctly (Mechanics TG #2–3) • use commas correctly (Mechanics SB #1–4) • use commas correctly (EP: Mechanics)	• TOC 8: Mechanics • TOC 8: Mechanics • TOC 8: Mechanics • TOC 8: Mechanics
Overall (LGV.02B) • use listening techniques and oral communication skills to participate in classroom discussions and more formal activities, such as storytelling, role playing, and reporting/ presenting, for specific purposes and audiences	• explain importance of a sense of humour (Introducing the Unit TG #1) • suggest what makes people funny (Introducing the Unit TG #2) • role-play situations demonstrating harmful effects of showing people in negative light (Extending the Model TG #2) • tell jokes to the class (More Oral Language TG)	• TOC 14: Tracking Expectations • TOC 14: Tracking Expectations • AR 9: Group Presentation • TOC 11: Speaking
Specific (LG2.03P) • work with a partner to plan and make oral presentations to a small group, selecting and using vocabulary and methods of delivery to suit audience and purpose	• interview each other to generate details (Writer's Workshop TG #2) • present humorous personal narrative as standup monologue (Oral Language Extension SB)	• TOC 5: Group Work • AR 15: Oral Language
MEDIA STUDIES		
Overall (MDV.01P) • identify and describe the elements, intended audiences, and production practices of a variety of media forms	• suggest examples of film and TV stereotypes (Investigating the Model TG)	• AR 21: Response to Media
Specific (MD1.01B) • demonstrate critical thinking skills by identifying the differences between explicit and implicit messages in media works	• choose standup routines that are not offensive (Oral Language Extension TG) • identify and analyze stock characters (Media Link SB)	• AR 21: Response to Media • AR 21: Response to Media
(MD1.02P) • identify and describe the elements used to structure media works in a variety of forms	• prepare a visual dictionary of camera shots (More Media TG)	• AR 12: Media Product

AR=Assessment Rubric   EP=Extra Practice   SB=Student Book   SSEC=Student Self-Evaluation Checklist   TG=Teacher's Guide   TOC=Teacher Observation Checklist

INSTRUCTIONAL STRATEGIES FOR THE APPLIED COURSE

PLANNING INFORMATION

Links to Other Nelson English 9 Resources

Literature & Media 9
Personal Narrative—See "The Goal Post" by Edward Smith, pp. 111–112 and "Early Days" by Maria Campbell, pp. 115–118.

Write Source 2000
Personal Narrative—"Autobiographical Writing," pp. 153–159; **Adjectives**—"Adjective," pp. 451–453; **Adverbs**—"Adverb," p. 454; **Commas**—"Comma," pp. 389–392; **Nouns**—"Noun," pp. 439–441; **Verbs**—"Verb," pp. 446–450

INTRODUCING THE UNIT

1. Ask students to list the qualities they would most like a prospective friend to have. As most lists will likely include a sense of humour, have students explain why a sense of humour is important. What is there about a person that signifies the presence or absence of a good sense of humour? (LGV.02B—TOC 14: Tracking Expectations)

2. Ask students to identify people whom they find funny. These people might be professional comedians or local individuals (even classmates) whom everyone would know. Have them suggest what makes these people funny—is it the individuals themselves, the stories they tell, or a combination of both? (LGV.02B—TOC 14: Tracking Expectations)

INTRODUCING THE MODEL

1. Humorous personal narratives abound in magazines such as *Reader's Digest*. Give students an opportunity to browse through these publications with the purpose of finding and sharing an especially humorous narrative with their classmates. Have one or more of your own favourites ready to share with students. Then have students identify similarities such as first-person point of view, brevity, and organization of details among these narratives. (LIV.02P—AR 22: Response to Reading)

2. Activity #2 on page 5 from the Academic Course is appropriate for the Applied Course. (WR1.02P—AR 10: Humorous Personal Narrative)

INVESTIGATING THE MODEL

Activity #2 on page 5 from the Academic Course is appropriate for the Applied Course. (MDV.01P—AR 21: Response to Media)

Answers:
See the Academic Course on pages 6–7 for answers.
Student Book 1.–9. (LIV.01P—TOC 14: Tracking Expectations; LIV.02P—TOC 14: Tracking Expectations)

EXTENDING THE MODEL

1. Direct students to other humorous works written by Atwood (not only articles and short stories but novels as well, such as *The Edible Woman* and *Lady Oracle*). Encourage students to read them and share favourite passages with the rest of the class. (LIV.01P—AR 22: Response to Reading)

LEARNING GOALS

- write a humorous personal narrative
- use parts of speech correctly: nouns, verbs, adverbs, and adjectives
- use commas correctly
- use consistent and appropriate verb tense
- identify words borrowed from other languages

CHECKPOINT

Sample criteria for a humorous personal narrative:

- entertains the reader
- has a beginning that establishes writer as credible narrator and identifies nature of event to be recounted
- often centres around typical character types
- has details that are often arranged in chronological order
- focuses on a single event
- is usually told from first-person point of view
- may include dialogue
- can be humorous through understatement and exaggeration
- often ends abruptly, forcing reader to imagine effect

MORE SUPPORT

In discussing activity #9 (page 21 of the student book), offer examples ("It was at that point I realized the back of my hospital gown had been wide open all along") to illustrate that abrupt endings emphasize the comic value of the event by forcing the reader to imagine its effects on the narrator. Have students find examples of such abrupt endings in magazines such as *Reader's Digest* and share with the class how such endings are superior to those that explain the humour of the event. (LIV.03B—TOC 14: Tracking Expectations)

2. Many students see no harm in telling humorous stories that deride certain groups. Have students consider the types of humorous stories that present individuals or groups in a negative light. After discussion, assign students, working in groups of three or four, to role-play situations that demonstrate the harmful effects of such stories. (LI1.05P—AR 22: Response to Reading; LGV.02B—AR 9: Group Presentation)

WRITER'S WORKSHOP

1. Some students write more easily about an event when prompted by specific questions that help them focus on pertinent information. Have students consider the types of things another person might like to know about their embarrassing moment, and list their ideas or questions on the board. Students can then use these questions to help them generate the details they will include in their narratives. (WR1.01P—AR 10: Humorous Personal Narrative)

2. A variation of the above activity is to have students work in pairs to generate details orally, one person "interviewing" the other using the questions the class has listed (as well as any other questions that occur to the interviewer). When the writer has recorded all the details the interviewer has elicited, the two exchange roles and repeat the process. (WR1.01P—AR 10: Humorous Personal Narrative; LG2.03P—TOC 5: Group Work)

3. First drafts can be daunting for some students. Suggest that they talk through their humorous narratives with a partner before they begin writing their first drafts. (WR1.02P—AR 10: Humorous Personal Narrative)

Student Book 1.–4. (WRV.01P—AR 10: Humorous Personal Narrative); 5. (WRV.03P—AR 10: Humorous Personal Narrative); 6. (WRV.04B—AR 10: Humorous Personal Narrative; WRV.05B—AR 10: Humorous Personal Narrative)

ORAL LANGUAGE EXTENSION

It is important that students choose standup routines that will not offend the teacher or members of the class. Teachers might wish to preview the videotaped routines or simply emphasize the need to select routines that can be enjoyed by all groups. To clarify this issue, teachers might have students generate a list of the sorts of material that would be offensive to certain groups. (MD1.01B—AR 21: Response to Media)

Student Book (LG2.03P—AR 15: Oral Language)

GRAMMAR

The Grammar activities on pages 8–9 from the Academic Course are appropriate for the Applied Course.
1. (WR5.05P—TOC 4: Grammar; LG1.05P—TOC 4: Grammar)

2. (WR5.05P—TOC 4: Grammar; LG1.05P—TOC 4: Grammar)

3. (WR5.05P—TOC 4: Grammar; (LG1.05P—TOC 4: Grammar)

Answers:
See the Academic Course on pages 9–10 for answers.

Student Book 1.–4. (WR5.05P—TOC 4: Grammar; LG1.05P—TOC 4: Grammar)

MEDIA LINK

Student Book (MD1.01B—AR 21: Response to Media)

Mechanics

1. Students understand comma use better when they can *hear* a comma's function within a sentence. Without giving any information about comma use, orally dictate sentences requiring commas that indicate pauses, and have students share their dictations in pairs, discussing why they punctuated these sentences the way they did. Before proceeding with the Mechanics section of the unit, build on this discussion by having students suggest other uses of the comma. (WR5.15B—TOC 8: Mechanics; LG1.07B—TOC 8: Mechanics)

2. You might wish to have students master specific uses of the comma rather than all of those listed in the text. (WR5.15B—TOC 8: Mechanics; LG1.07B—TOC 8: Mechanics)

Answers:

See the Academic Course on page 11 for answers.

Student Book 1.–4. (WR5.15B—TOC 8: Mechanics; LG1.07B—TOC 8; Mechanics)

Usage & Style

Students often do not recognize tense inconsistency because of their own usage. For example, they may say, "Gerry **says** to me, 'I **saw** Phil in the cafeteria.'" Have students point out the difference between the two verb tenses using similar examples. Emphasize the difference between their informal usage (the switching of tenses in oral language is acceptable because the meaning is clear) and standard usage (the switching of tenses in writing can confuse the reader so verb tenses should be consistent). (WR5.10B—TOC 15: Usage & Style; LG1.05P—TOC 15: Usage & Style)

Answers:

See the Academic Course on page 12 for answers.

Student Book 1.–3. (WR5.10B—TOC 15: Usage & Style; LG1.05P—TOC 15: Usage & Style)

Word Study & Spelling

1. Activity #1 on page 12 from the Academic Course is appropriate for the Applied Course. (LG1.03B—TOC 16: Word Study & Spelling)

2. When introducing activity #3 on page 31 of the student book, have students begin by considering words such as *electricity* and *computer,* which play such an important part in our lives. (*Electricity* comes from the Greek *elektron,* meaning *amber,* which is the material in which electricity was first observed; *computer* comes from the Latin *com-,* meaning "together," and *putare,* meaning "to reckon.") Students should realize that even the names of modern devices often have their roots in words from the past. Scan the dictionary for words with Greek or Latin roots, then write some of these roots on the board. Students can make a list of words that come from them. (LG1.03B—TOC 16: Word Study & Spelling)

Answers:

See the Academic Course on page 13 for answers.

Student Book 1.–3. (LG1.03B—TOC 16: Word Study & Spelling)

Answers to Extra Practice

See the Academic Course on pages 13–15 for answers.

Grammar
(WR5.05P—TOC 4: Grammar; LG1.05P—TOC 4: Grammar)

Mechanics
(WR5.15B—TOC 8: Mechanics; LG1.07B—TOC 8: Mechanics)

Usage & Style
(WR5.10B—TOC 15: Usage & Style; LG1.05P—TOC 15: Usage & Style)

Word Study & Spelling
(LG1.03B—TOC 16: Word Study & Spelling)

GRAMMAR

NAME: _____ DATE: _____

1. Identify the part of speech of each word by writing N (noun), V (verb), Adj (adjective), or Adv (adverb) above it.

   a) Authors often give spirited readings.

   b) Yesterday, Margaret Atwood gave three readings.

   c) The audience arrived very early.

   d) Her last novel is my favourite.

   e) A gentle breeze slowly fanned the pages.

2. Identify the part of speech of each of the boldface words. Then write another sentence using the same word as a different part of speech. Identify the new part of speech.

   a) I had a beautiful, **green,** intelligent praying mantis called Lenore.

   _____

   b) The producer and Atwood **point** out that this was an old praying mantis.

   _____

   c) Lenore was not named after Atwood's **future** sister-in-law.

   _____

   d) But it was looking for something even **more** secluded.

   _____

   e) The squirrel could be seen as a travelling **bulge** moving around my waistline.

   _____

MECHANICS

NAME: _____ DATE: _____

Rewrite the following passage, eliminating unnecessary commas.

As technology continues to grow, it is becoming more, and more important for people to be able to communicate quickly, and easily. Even very small businesses, usually have more than one telephone line, at least one fax machine, and an Internet connection for e-mail. Many businesses even have their own Web sites that enable them to reach hundreds, even thousands, of prospective customers, every month. However, successful business people understand that the most important aspect of communicating, with customers is courtesy.

_____

_____

_____

_____

_____

_____

_____

_____

_____

_____

_____

_____

_____

_____

_____

_____

USAGE & STYLE

NAME: _____ DATE: _____

The following passage is supposed to be written in present tense, but it contains some past-tense verbs. Rewrite the passage using the correct tense throughout.

Authors like Margaret Atwood are accustomed to giving readings but, as she says in the final paragraph of "A Flying Start," many things could and do go wrong during these events. People in charge of organizing author readings needed to anticipate possible problems and eliminate these in advance. For example, successful organizers make sure that the facility where the author appeared is suitable and available for the reading. As well, they place advertisements about upcoming readings in newspapers and on radio and television long before the event took place. This ensures that the author had a large audience present for the reading. However, one of the most important details—the weather—is usually beyond their control.

_____

_____

_____

_____

_____

_____

_____

_____

_____

_____

_____

_____

_____

_____

_____

_____

_____

_____

WORD STUDY & SPELLING

NAME: _____ DATE: _____

Each of the following terms came into the English language in one of the following ways: some were borrowed from other languages; some were formed by arranging old words in new combinations; two existing words were combined to form a third word; some were formed by imitating sounds; some were formed from the first letters of a group of words (acronyms); some were named after people; some were named after places.

Using an etymological dictionary, identify how each of the following words and expressions came into use in the English language.

1. jeans _____

2. maître d'hôtel _____

3. crash _____

4. UNICEF _____

5. moonwalk _____

6. pro bono publico _____

7. microscope _____

8. tangerine _____

9. kaput _____

10. cardigan _____

11. NATO _____

12. transmit _____

13. modus operandi _____

14. braille _____

15. frankfurter _____

16. nudge _____

17. newspaper _____

18. zip _____

19. doily _____

20. universe _____

LANGUAGE & WRITING 9

Unit 2: Short Story

Academic Expectations

GRADE 9 EXPECTATIONS		DEMONSTRATION OF LEARNING	ASSESSMENT TOOLS
LITERATURE STUDIES AND READING			
Overall (LIV.01D)	• read and demonstrate an understanding of a variety of literary and informational texts, from contemporary and historical periods	• demonstrate understanding of short story (Investigating the Model SB #1–8)	• TOC 13: Tracking Expectations
Specific (LI1.01D)	• describe information, ideas, opinions, and themes in print and electronic texts they have read during the year from different cultures and historical periods and in a variety of genres, including novels, short stories, plays, poems, biographies, short essays, and articles from newspapers, magazines, and encyclopedias	• discuss differences in fictional and nonfictional short stories (Introducing the Unit TG #1)	• AR 22: Response to Reading
(LI1.02D)	• select and read texts for different purposes, with an emphasis on recognizing the elements of literary genres and the organization of informational materials, collecting and assessing information, responding imaginatively, and exploring human experiences and values	• discuss purposes of short stories (Introducing the Unit TG #1)	• AR 22: Response to Reading
(LI1.03B)	• describe a variety of reading strategies and select and use them effectively before, during, and after reading to understand texts	• predict story line using story vocabulary (Introducing the Model TG #3) • compare predictions with actual story line (Extending the Model TG #1–2)	• TOC 10: Reading Strategies • TOC 10: Reading Strategies
(LI1.07D)	• explain how readers' different backgrounds might influence the way they understand and interpret a text	• explain personal responses to short stories (Introducing the Unit TG #3) • examine personal attitudes in predicting conclusion (Extending the Model TG #2)	• AR 22: Response to Reading • AR 22: Response to Reading
Overall (LIV.02D)	• demonstrate an understanding of the elements of a variety of literary and informational forms, with a focus on plays, short stories, and short essays	• discuss definition of short story (Introducing the Unit TG #2)	• TOC 13: Tracking Expectations
Specific (LI2.02D)	• use knowledge of elements of the short story, such as plot, characterization, setting, conflict, theme, mood, and point of view, to understand and interpret examples of the genre	• demonstrate understanding of elements of short story (Investigating the Model SB #1–8) • imagine main character a year later (Extending the Model TG #4)	• TOC 13: Tracking Expectations • TOC 13: Tracking Expectations
Overall (LIV.03B)	• identify and explain the effect of specific elements of style in a variety of literary and informational texts		
Specific (LI3.02D)	• explain how authors use stylistic devices, such as simile, metaphor, personification, imagery, foreshadowing, onomatopoeia, oxymoron, alliteration, and symbol, to achieve particular effects in their writing	• describe stylistic devices in short story (Introducing the Unit TG #3) • discuss short story endings and foreshadowing (Usage & Style TG) • show how author has used foreshadowing in short story (Usage & Style SB #1–5)	• AR 22: Response to Reading • TOC 15: Usage & Style • TOC 15: Usage & Style
WRITING			
Overall (WRV.01D)	• use a variety of print and electronic sources to gather information and explore ideas for their written work	• gather and organize information and ideas for short story (Writer's Workshop SB #1–4)	• AR 24: Short Story
Specific (WR1.02D)	• locate and summarize information from print and electronic sources, including vertical files, periodicals, dictionaries, encyclopedias, electronic newsgroups, e-mail messages, and electronic databases	• write about personal experiences involving water (Introducing the Model TG #1) • recount kayaking or windsurfing experiences (Introducing the Model TG #2)	• AR 24: Short Story • TOC 13: Tracking Expectations

AR=Assessment Rubric   EP=Extra Practice   SB=Student Book   SSEC=Student Self-Evaluation Checklist   TG=Teacher's Guide   TOC=Teacher Observation Checklist

GRADE 9 EXPECTATIONS		DEMONSTRATION OF LEARNING	ASSESSMENT TOOLS
WRITING (continued)			
(WR1.03D)	• group and label information and ideas; evaluate the relevance, accuracy, and completeness of the information and ideas; and discard irrelevant material	• brainstorm changes main character might undergo (Writer's Workshop TG #1) • develop characterization and plot for short story (Writer's Workshop TG #2–3) • plot short story using flow chart (More Support TG)	• AR 24: Short Story • AR 24: Short Story • AR 24: Short Story
Overall (WRV.02D)	• identify the literary and informational forms suited to various purposes and audiences and use the forms appropriately in their own writing, with an emphasis on supporting opinions or interpretations with specific information		
Specific (WR2.01D)	• demonstrate an understanding of literary and informational forms, such as myths, poems, short stories, scripts, advertisements, formal letters, reviews, and supported opinion essays, by selecting and using forms of writing appropriate to different purposes and audiences	• write resolution to short story and provide justification (More Challenge TG #1)	• AR 24: Short Story
(WR2.02D)	• select first or third person and an appropriate level of language to suit the form, purpose, and audience of written work	• write part of short story in third-person point of view (More Challenge TG #2)	• AR 24: Short Story
Overall (WRV.03D)	• use a variety of organizational techniques to present ideas and supporting details logically and coherently in written work	• write out backstory (Writer's Workshop TG #4) • write a draft of short story (Writer's Workshop SB #5)	• AR 24: Short Story • AR 24: Short Story
Overall (WRV.04D)	• revise their written work, independently and collaboratively, with a focus on support for ideas and opinions, accuracy, clarity, and unity	• revise short story (Writer's Workshop SB #6)	• AR 24: Short Story
Specific (WR4.03D)	• make constructive suggestions to peers	• give constructive criticism to peers (More Oral Language TG)	• SSEC 6: Peer Assessment: Writing
Overall (WRV.05D)	• edit and proofread to produce final drafts, using correct grammar, spelling, and punctuation, according to the conventions of standard Canadian English, with the support of print and electronic resources when appropriate	• edit and proofread short story (Writer's Workshop SB #6)	• AR 24: Short Story
Specific (WR5.05D)	• use parts of speech correctly: nouns, pronouns, verbs, adverbs, adjectives, conjunctions, prepositions, and interjections	• rewrite passages without pronouns, prepositions, or conjunctions (Grammar TG) • use pronouns, prepositions, conjunctions, and interjections correctly (Grammar SB #1–3) • use pronouns, prepositions, conjunctions, and interjections correctly (EP: Grammar)	• TOC 4: Grammar • TOC 4: Grammar • TOC 4: Grammar
(WR5.16B)	• adapt punctuation and capitalization for the special requirements of direct quotations, scripts, dialogue, and poetry	• justify punctuation and capitalization of dialogue (Mechanics TG #1) • discuss speaker tags (Mechanics TG #2) • punctuate and capitalize dialogue correctly (Mechanics SB #1–3) • punctuate and capitalize dialogue correctly (EP: Mechanics)	• TOC 8: Mechanics • TOC 8: Mechanics • TOC 8: Mechanics • TOC 8: Mechanics

AR=Assessment Rubric   EP=Extra Practice   SB=Student Book   SSEC=Student Self-Evaluation Checklist   TG=Teacher's Guide   TOC=Teacher Observation Checklist

GRADE 9 EXPECTATIONS	DEMONSTRATION OF LEARNING	ASSESSMENT TOOLS
LANGUAGE		
Overall (LGV.01D) • use knowledge of vocabulary and language conventions to speak, write, and read competently using a level of language appropriate to the purpose and audience		
Specific (LG1.02B) • identify and explain examples of slang, jargon, dialect, and colloquialism, as well as of standard Canadian English, in literary texts and their own oral and written work	• discuss slang terms (Word Study & Spelling TG #1)	• TOC 16: Word Study & Spelling
(LG1.03B) • identify words borrowed from other languages and words and terms recently introduced to describe new ideas, inventions, and products, and explain their origins	• discuss how words change over time (Word Study & Spelling TG #2) • create class dictionary or posters of words that have changed over time (Word Study & Spelling TG #3) • identify how words change over time (Word Study & Spelling SB) • identify how words change over time (EP: Word Study & Spelling)	• TOC 16: Word Study & Spelling • TOC 16: Word Study & Spelling • TOC 16: Word Study & Spelling • TOC 16: Word Study & Spelling
(LG1.05D) • recognize, describe, and use correctly, in oral and written language, the language structures of standard Canadian English and its conventions of grammar and usage, including: – parts of speech: nouns, pronouns, verbs, adverbs, adjectives, conjunctions, prepositions, interjections	• rewrite passages without pronouns, prepositions, or conjunctions (Grammar TG) • use pronouns, prepositions, conjunctions, and interjections correctly (Grammar SB #1–3) • use pronouns, prepositions, conjunctions, and interjections correctly (EP: Grammar)	• TOC 4: Grammar • TOC 4: Grammar • TOC 4: Grammar
(LG1.07B) • recognize, describe, and use correctly, in oral and written language, the conventions of standard Canadian English for spelling, capitalization, and punctuation, including: – capitalization: of proper nouns and in direct quotations, scripts, dialogue, and poetry – punctuation: period, question mark, exclamation mark, comma, dash, apostrophe, colon, quotation marks, parentheses, ellipses	• justify punctuation and capitalization of dialogue (Mechanics TG #1) • discuss speaker tags (Mechanics TG #2) • punctuate and capitalize dialogue correctly (Mechanics SB #1–3) • punctuate and capitalize dialogue correctly (EP: Mechanics)	• TOC 8: Mechanics • TOC 8: Mechanics • TOC 8: Mechanics • TOC 8: Mechanics
Overall (LGV.02B) • use listening techniques and oral communication skills to participate in classroom discussions and more formal activities, such as storytelling, role playing, and reporting/ presenting, for specific purposes and audiences	• role-play author and editor discussing title of short story (Extending the Model TG #3)	• SSEC 5: Oral Presentation
Specific (LG2.01D) • communicate orally in group discussions for different purposes, with a focus on identifying key ideas and supporting details, distinguishing fact from opinion, asking clarifying questions, and following instructions	• share writing in writers' group (Oral Language Extension SB)	• TOC 5: Group Work
(LG2.02D) • communicate in group discussions by sharing the duties of the group, speaking in turn, listening actively, taking notes, paraphrasing key points made by others, exchanging and challenging ideas and information, asking appropriate questions, reconsidering their own ideas and opinions, managing conflict, and respecting the opinions of others	• develop code of conduct for working in a group (More Oral Language TG)	• TOC 5: Group Work

AR=Assessment Rubric   EP=Extra Practice   SB=Student Book   SSEC=Student Self-Evaluation Checklist   TG=Teacher's Guide   TOC=Teacher Observation Checklist

GRADE 9 EXPECTATIONS		DEMONSTRATION OF LEARNING	ASSESSMENT TOOLS
MEDIA STUDIES			
Overall (MDV.01D)	• use knowledge of the elements, intended audiences, and production practices of a variety of media forms to analyze specific media works	• identify reasons for TV program successes (Media Link TG) • analyze film adaptations of literary works (More Media TG)	• AR 21: Response to Media • AR 21: Response to Media
Overall (MDV.02D)	• use knowledge of a variety of media forms, purposes, and audiences to create media works and describe their intended effect		
Specific (MD2.01D)	• adapt a work of literature to another media form and determine what aspects have been strengthened and/or weakened by the adaptation	• plan TV dramatization of "The Kayak" (Media Link SB)	• AR 12: Media Product
(MD2.02D)	• create media works for different purposes and explain how each has been designed to achieve its particular purpose	• create print advertisement for TV drama (Media Link SB)	• AR 12: Media Product

AR=Assessment Rubric   EP=Extra Practice   SB=Student Book   SSEC=Student Self-Evaluation Checklist   TG=Teacher's Guide   TOC=Teacher Observation Checklist

INSTRUCTIONAL STRATEGIES FOR THE ACADEMIC COURSE

PLANNING INFORMATION

Links to Other Nelson English 9 Resources

Literature & Media 9
Short Fiction—See the Short Fiction unit for 17 short fiction selections, pp. 1–108.

Write Source 2000
Short Fiction—"Writing Stories," pp. 183–192; **Conjunctions**—"Conjunction," p. 456; **Interjections**—"Interjection," pp. 390, 398; **Prepositions**—"Preposition," p. 455; **Pronouns**—"Pronoun," pp. 441–445; **Rules for Writing Dialogue**—"Writing/Revising/Editing," pp. 190–191, "To Set Off Dialogue," p. 390, "Quotation Marks," p. 399

INTRODUCING THE UNIT

1. Storytelling is important in all cultures. Ask students why people tell stories. Have them consider the difference between stories about real events and stories about fictional events and characters. What is the purpose of a fictional story? What is the purpose of a story about a real event? How are these differences reflected in their literary elements? (LI1.01D—AR 22: Response to Reading; LI1.02D—AR 22: Response to Reading)

2. Ask students to define a short story in their own words. Then ask them to read and comment on the explanation provided in the student book on page 32. How did their ideas mirror this definition? How did their ideas differ from this definition? Can they provide a better, more comprehensive, definition of a short story? (LIV.02D—TOC 13: Tracking Expectations)

3. Ask students to identify two or three short stories they find memorable. Have them jot down the titles, along with a few comments about what made these stories so striking. How have their personal experiences shaped their interpretation of these stories? Can they remember any stylistic devices, e.g., striking imagery, that made the writing effective? (LI1.07D—AR 22: Response to Reading; LI3.02D—AR 22: Response to Reading)

INTRODUCING THE MODEL

1. Before you ask students to read the story, mount photographs and posters of water sports around your classroom. Encourage students to reflect on—and write about—their own personal experiences involving the water. (WR1.02D—AR 24: Short Story)

2. Ask students if any of them have ever kayaked or windsurfed. Those who have might recount experiences that will help build a context for reading "The Kayak." (WR1.02D—TOC 13: Tracking Expectations)

3. Write each of the following words on individual pieces of paper and place them in an envelope: Teresa, Jamie, kayak, windsurfer, campfire, waves, parents, legs, rescue, rocks, current, awkwardness, wheelchair, marshmallows, storm. (Make several similar envelopes, one for each group of three or four students.) Before students read the story, ask each group to examine the words and predict what the story will be about. Encourage the groups to arrange and rearrange the words as several different lists. What story line is suggested by each list? Ask students to share their favourite story line with the rest of the class. (LI1.03B—TOC 10: Reading Strategies)

INVESTIGATING THE MODEL

Answers:

1. The lead uses action (kayaking through swirling waters) to catch the reader's attention. The lead also introduces the main character (a young, female paddler), and establishes the setting (a windy day on Georgian Bay) and the point of view (first-person). The action immediately suggests the story conflict (a struggle with the elements). The italicized phrase (*"It's more difficult now"*) suggests an internal conflict that will remain a mystery—for now. The narrator's struggle to accept her disability is not revealed until much later in the story.

2. The narrator feels trapped by her disability and the overprotectiveness of her parents. She yearns to be independent, but she thinks she cannot be, and her inner turmoil is mirrored by the storm on the bay. Because this inner struggle has no immediate resolution, it is viewed as more significant than the storm that ends as the narrator reaches shore.

3. Possible answers

   "This is my special place. Out here, I feel safe and secure.... The blue boat is an extension of my legs. I can do anything: I can go anywhere. Totally independent."

   "I stay in my kayak. Half the kayak is on land. The rest is in the water. I feel trapped, like a beached whale."

   "A fat bullfrog croaks and jumps into the water. I want to jump in after him and swim away somewhere safe."

   "The silence drags on. A mosquito buzzes around my head. So annoying. Why can't they both leave?"

   "He doesn't say anything. I wish he would leave. The air feels heavy and suffocating."

4. An author's choice of viewpoint shapes his or her entire story because it controls the information the reader will receive. The first-person point of view is the most intimate because the reader hears the story directly from the person involved; it also requires the reader to weigh what the narrator says because it is the only voice heard. (When writing in the third person, the author can insert his or her own views more freely.) The first-person viewpoint is limiting to some degree because only those details that are known and understood by the character can be included. By choosing the first-person point of view, Debbie Spring lets her readers view events directly through the eyes of the main character. And, because Teresa does not reveal her disability until the end of the story, we can share Jamie's surprise at this revelation.

5. Possible answers

   "I stop stroking with my double-bladed paddle and push my bangs from my face." (This detail arises naturally from the action of paddling.)

   "The windsurfer looks around 18. I take a quick glance at his tanned muscles and sandy, blond hair. He seems vulnerable and afraid." (Jamie's apparent physical strength contrasts with his vulnerability, which draws the reader into the story's external conflict.)

   "His teeth chatter. The water churns around his board. He is soaked. I don't like the blue colour of his lips." (This detail arises directly from the action taking place—teeth chattering, water churning.)

CHECKPOINT

Sample criteria for a short story:

- has lead that catches reader's attention, identifies main character, introduces conflict, defines setting, and establishes point of view
- has plot that revolves around conflict, either external or internal
- often uses details of setting to reflect or help the reader empathize with main character's state of mind
- is usually written from first-person or third-person point of view
- often includes physical details about characters
- often spans relatively brief time period
- reveals character using dialogue, reactions of other characters, physical description, and actions
- has a theme that is closely tied to change occurring in story

6. The most important example of background detail appears in the following passage. Here, the author skillfully conveys events of several months in a few brief thoughts:

"I've seen it all before. Awkwardness. Forced conversation. A feeble excuse and a fast getaway. My closer friends tried a little harder. They lasted two or three visits. Then, they stopped coming around."

7.

Technique	Example
dialogue	"'I don't need pity,' I retort. Jamie smiles. 'Actually, I need a date. Everybody is a couple, except me.'"
reactions of other characters	"I motion for my parents to leave me alone. Surprised, they move away, but stay close by."
	"'Teresa,' he clears his throat. 'I didn't know.' I watch his discomfort."
physical description	"I stop stroking with my double-bladed paddle and push my bangs from my face."
the character's own words and actions	"My hands turn white as I clutch the armrests of my wheelchair. 'What you really want to know is how long I've been crippled.'"

8. Our view of Teresa changes abruptly as she moves from being a confident lifesaver to someone who is dependent on others. Our surprise forces us to rethink our own impressions of a person in a wheelchair. Equally important is the change Teresa experiences when Jamie refuses to be put off by her defensiveness. In responding to his invitation to go to the campfire, she realizes that she can cope on land as easily as she does in the water, a realization that is reflected in her comment, "... I see two images of me: the helpless child on land and the independent woman on water. I blink and the land and water merge. I become one."

Student Book 1.–8. (LIV.01D—TOC 13: Tracking Expectations; LI2.02D—TOC 13: Tracking Expectations)

Extending the Model

1. After students have read and investigated the model, ask them to review the story lines they predicted during Introducing the Model, activity #3, and compare them with the actual story line. Which words in the activity were helpful? Which were misleading? Have them create their own list of words that would be appropriate for this activity. (LI1.03B—TOC 10: Reading Strategies)

2. Encourage students to consider why they made the predictions they did. For example, if they predicted that the female character would be rescued as opposed to being the rescuer, ask them to think about how their own attitudes may have influenced this conclusion. (LI1.03B—TOC 10: Reading Strategies; LI1.07D— AR 22: Response to Reading)

3. Have students role-play the author whose editor has asked her to change the title of the story. Half the class working in small groups could justify leaving the title as it is. The other half (also working in small groups) could create a title they feel is more appropriate for the story, focusing on issues of content and theme. (LGV.02B—SSEC 5: Oral Presentation)

4. Have students imagine Teresa in the same kayak a year later, reflecting on the past 12 months. What have been the high points during that year? What have been the low points? Has she coped with the moments of disappointment? How have these events—positive and negative—affected her? (LI2.02D—TOC 13: Tracking Expectations)

MORE CHALLENGE

1. Give students copies of another story, omitting its resolution (usually the last three or four paragraphs). Have them write a resolution to the story (give them a maximum word length). They must not only resolve the conflict responsibility (i.e., their resolution must grow out of events and details included in the original) but they should also try to imitate the author's style of writing. An appropriate extension of this activity requires students to write a one-page essay justifying their ending, using details from the original story to support the choices they have made. Another extension would be to copy on a handout several of students' brief endings along with the actual ending. Students could then try to identify the real ending (either in small-group discussion or in writing). The emphasis of this activity is not to guess the "real" ending but to focus on issues such as purpose and style. (Often, a class will find a fellow student's ending superior to the author's.) (WR2.01D—AR 24: Short Story)

2. Students could experiment with author viewpoint by writing a portion of the story in one (or all three) of the third-person points of view: omniscient (narrator is all-knowing, able to convey information about the actions, thoughts, and feelings of all people involved), limited omniscient (narrator conveys the thoughts and feelings of only one person involved), and objective (narrator conveys only those things that he or she can see or hear). Review the definitions of each viewpoint before students begin this activity. Follow-up discussion could focus on which viewpoints were most effective in relation to the author's purpose. (WR2.02D—AR 24: Short Story)

Some students might find it easier to plot their stories using a graphic organizer in the form of a flow chart. Illustrate for students how to use an organizer by having them suggest a character to include in a box at the top of a sample flow chart. Once they have decided what the conflict of this example story will be, have them suggest a series of possible events that will take place, writing their suggestions on a flow chart. Encourage them to offer whatever comes to mind because even the most ridiculous suggestions can sometimes result in wonderful story ideas—the importance of this exercise is to encourage the flow of creative thought. Once students have exhausted their ideas, have them choose the most interesting and plausible story line from the suggestions given. Then have them complete their own flow charts based on the characters they have created in the Writer's Workshop activities. (WR1.03D—AR 24: Short Story)

Provide opportunities early in the year for students to practise responding to writing that is not written by fellow classmates. Model effective (and ineffective) responses to writing, having students refer to the suggestions in the Idea File on page 40 of the student book. Once they are accustomed to response protocols, have students share pieces of their own writing.

It can be extremely helpful at the beginning of the year to have each class generate its own code of conduct that identifies five or six helpful behaviours for the classroom. (Have students meet in pairs, then combine to form larger groups of four, then eight, and so on, to discuss this.) More than just a classroom management technique, this process and resulting code of conduct should enable every student to feel valued and to participate without fear of ridicule. (WR4.03D—SSEC 0: Peer Assessment; LG2.02D—TOC 5: Group Work)

WRITER'S WORKSHOP

1. Ask students to identify a film they have seen recently that intrigued them. Next, ask them to identify the main character and, in 25 words or less, explain what happens to that person in the film. Have students share their summaries with a partner and discuss what the summaries have in common. Most students will recognize that the character experiences a change of some sort, either in situation or in attitude. Once students recognize that change is an integral component of all stories, have them brainstorm some changes that a character in their own short story might undergo. (WR1.03D—AR 24: Short Story)

2. Help students recognize the difference between round characters (those that have depth and complexity and are filled with conflicts and surprises) and flat characters (those that exhibit a single dominant trait) by having them list all the characters in "The Kayak" and identify what they learned about each of them. They will quickly see that Teresa's parents are flat characters (exhibiting only concern for their daughter) while Teresa is round (exhibiting a number of feelings and doubts). Each student should strive to create a round main character. (WR1.03D—AR 24: Short Story)

3. To help students recognize that writing is a process of making choices, have them create a flow chart of "The Kayak" (or another story), indicating the main events of the plot in separate blocks using blue ink. Using ink of a different colour, students can branch out from each of these events, identifying other possible plot developments. Encourage them to attach more sheets of paper as branches grow in various ways and to follow all new plots (however ridiculous) to completion. When they have finished this task, have them share their most interesting—and realistic—plots with the class. Discussion could focus not only on the importance of making realistic plot choices in their own writing, but in assessing the effectiveness of the author's choices in the original story. (WR1.03D—AR 24: Short Story)

4. The "necessary information" mentioned in activity #5 in the student book is often referred to as "backstory," the part of a story that drives what happens later. (For example, in "The Kayak," Teresa's backstory is the accident that paralysed her and now keeps her from having a close relationship with other people her own age, which is what she wants most.) Encourage students to develop a clear sense of their own main character's backstory. It is often helpful for some students to write out this backstory. Although much of this will never appear in their story, this writing will give them a stronger sense of who their character is. Once they have recorded the backstory on paper, they can then select the most relevant details and consider how best to include them in the body of their story. (WRV.03D—AR 24: Short Story)

Student Book 1.–4. (WRV.01D—AR 24: Short Story); 5. (WRV.03D—AR 24: Short Story); 6. (WRV.04D—AR 24: Short Story; WRV.05D—AR 24: Short Story)

ORAL LANGUAGE EXTENSION

Teachers wishing to learn more about guiding cooperative learning/writing groups should refer to the following sources:

Hill, Susan, and Tim Hill (1990). *The Collaborative Classroom: A Guide to Cooperative Learning.* Portsmouth, NH: Heinemann.

Spear, Karen (1988). *Sharing Writing: Peer Response Groups in English Classes.* Portsmouth, NH: Heinemann.

Spear, Karen, et al (1993). *Peer Response Groups in Action: Writing Together in Secondary Schools.* Portsmouth, NH: Heinemann.

Student Book (LG2.01D—TOC 5: Group Work)

GRAMMAR

Although this section will serve as a review for most students, they should recognize the value of the four function words in adding variety to writing. Have them rewrite the excerpt that begins on page 34 of the student book "I toss the rope ..." without using any pronouns. Then have them read both versions aloud and comment on the effectiveness of the example over their rewrite. You could further emphasize the importance of the function words by asking them to write a short passage that does not contain prepositions or conjunctions, then read it aloud to confirm the repetitive quality of the writing. (WR5.05D—TOC 4: Grammar; LG1.05D—TOC 4: Grammar)

Answers:

1. a) "where" — relative pronoun that takes the place of "Cousin Island"
        "around" — preposition showing a relationship between "steer" and "rocks"
    b) "that" — pronoun that takes the place of Jamie's comment
        "in" — preposition showing a relationship between "shout" and "water skiing"
        "when" — subordinating conjunction joining two thoughts
    c) "it" — pronoun that takes the place of the phrase "returning to shore"
        "because" — subordinating conjunction joining two thoughts
        "against" — preposition showing a relationship between "going" and "current"
    d) "at" — preposition showing a relationship between "good" and "sports"
        "but" — coordinating conjunction joining two independent clauses
        "them" — pronoun that takes the place of "sports"
    e) "Wow" — interjection that reveals strong feeling

2. a) "after" — subordinating conjunction joining two thoughts
    b) "after" — preposition showing a relationship between "went" and "storm"
    c) "until" — preposition showing a relationship between "asked" and "day"
    d) "until" — subordinating conjunction joining two thoughts

3.

Pronouns	Prepositions	Conjunction	Interjection
I	in	and	huh
my	of		
it	into		
where	on		
this	with		
one	from		
anything	out		
where	to		
	around		
	between		
	toward		

Student Book (WR5.05D—TOC 4: Grammar; LG1.05D—TOC 4: Grammar)

MEDIA LINK

Have students examine publicity campaigns used to promote new fall television programs, identifying the various reasons a program is successful (time slot being one of the most important). Ask students why programs that receive high praise from critics do not always find an audience. (MDV.01D—AR 21: Response to Media)

Student Book (MD2.01D—AR 12: Media Product; MD2.02D—AR 12: Media Product)

MECHANICS

1. Sometimes students are unsure whether conversations in their stories are actual dialogue (quoted speech) or indirect quotation (summarized talk). Put the following sentences (which lack capital letters and punctuation) on an overhead and have them determine which is indirect quotation. Have students rewrite the

---

MORE MEDIA

Much can be learned about a literary work by assessing the effectiveness of a film adaptation of it. In preparation for the Media Link activity, have students read short stories that have been produced as short films, then view the films and comment on the decisions made by the screenwriter and director in their adaptation. (If possible, have students work in groups reading/viewing different stories/adaptations, then presenting their findings to the class as a whole.) Students can then apply what they have learned about film adaptations to the planning of their television dramatization of "The Kayak." (MDV.01D—AR 21: Response to Media)

other one, and then have them justify their punctuation/capitalization, thereby establishing a context from which students can examine the rules for writing dialogue. (WR5.16B—TOC 8: Mechanics; LG1.07B—TOC 8: Mechanics)

   a) teresa said that she took kayaking lessons the summer after her accident

   b) teresa said i took kayaking lessons the summer after my accident

2. Each of the sentences in activity #2 in the student book contains a tag that identifies who is speaking. Often, however, speaker tags are not necessary. Have students copy a passage of dialogue from "The Kayak" that does not include a speaker tag and explain why it was not necessary for the author to include one. Ask students to suggest why writers should avoid using speaker tags for every exchange of dialogue. (WR5.16B—TOC 8: Mechanics; LG1.07B—TOC 8: Mechanics)

Answers:

1. a) A question mark—rather than a comma—separates this speaker tag from the dialogue.
   RULE: When the spoken words form a question, include a question mark inside the quotation marks.

   b) The question mark does not appear inside the quotation marks because "Hit it" is not a question.
   RULE: Include end punctuation inside the quotation marks that reflects the intent of the spoken passage.

   c) The word "is" is not capitalized because it is not the beginning of the dialogue.
   RULE: When a speaker tag interrupts a sentence of dialogue, do not capitalize the remaining part of the sentence.

   d) An exclamation point—rather than a comma—separates this speaker tag from the dialogue.
   RULE: Include end punctuation inside the quotation marks that reflects the intent or emotion of the spoken passage.

   e) The exclamation point does not appear inside the quotation marks because the emphasis is delivered by the main speaker, not the speaker being quoted.
   RULE: Use end punctuation that reflects the intent or emotion of the person being quoted.

2. a) "There looks to be a storm coming up," said Teresa's father.
   b) "I'll be careful on the lake," she assured him.
   c) He asked, "Do you want me to go out with you?"
   d) "Dad," Teresa said, "you know I've kayaked in the rain before."
   e) "I know you have," he said. "It's just that the forecast is calling for wind."
   f) "I'm sixteen years old!" Teresa shouted. "I'm not a baby anymore!"

3. Student work.

Student Book 1.–3. (WR5.16B—TOC 8: Mechanics; LG1.07B—TOC 8: Mechanics)

USAGE & STYLE

Ask students if they have ever been disappointed by a story that ended with a sentence like "It was all a dream." Explain how readers who invest time in reading a story and getting to know the characters feel cheated when they discover that none of the story occurred in the first place. Ask why younger writers are more prone to writing such endings (e.g., they grow tired of writing their story and merely want to end it, or they are unsure how to end it). (LI3.02D—TOC 15: Usage & Style)

Answers:

1. The line "I feel wild and free" contrasts dramatically with Teresa's view of her life in her wheelchair, and foreshadows the revelation that she feels trapped on land.

The italicized line *"It's more difficult now"* suggests that Teresa found kayaking easier during an earlier time, foreshadowing the revelation that her accident has altered the experience of kayaking.

2. Possible answer

    Four passages are given below:

    "The blue boat is an extension of my legs. I can do anything: I can go anywhere. Totally independent." (This foreshadows the eventual contrast between the freedom of the kayak and Teresa's view of her wheelchair as a prison.)

    "Nobody lets me grow up. My parents treat me like a baby. I'm 16, too old to be pampered." (This foreshadows the attention displayed by Teresa's parents at the end of the story.)

    "'You don't know what it's like being so helpless,' Jamie says. I bite my lip." (This underscores the irony that is implicit when Teresa listens to Jamie's comment, and foreshadows the revelation of her physical helplessness.)

    "I've never had a boyfriend. Who would be interested in me?" (This foreshadows the closing scene when Jamie expresses interest in Teresa and she is initially unable to respond to his overture.)

3. Teresa's anxious reaction to the loon's disappearance under the water foreshadows her terror at seeing Jamie trapped under the sail of the windsurfer.

4. The title "The Kayak" focuses on the one thing in Teresa's life that still offers her freedom and independence. In this way, the story's ending, in which Teresa is freed from the bonds of her own bitterness, is foreshadowed by the story's title. The kayak is also important because Teresa's legs are no longer useless when she is in the kayak. Therefore, the use of this object in the title underscores the need to view Teresa—and others like her—as a whole human being rather than as the prisoner of a wheelchair.

5. Student work.

Student book 1.–5. (LI3.02D—TOC 15: Usage & Style)

WORD STUDY & SPELLING

1. Ask students if they can think of any words that have changed in meaning in recent years. Encourage them to consider common slang terms as well as words older family members may use in different contexts. (LG1.02B—TOC 16: Word Study & Spelling)

2. Have students reread the passage on page 36 of the student book where Teresa slaps at a mosquito, and ask them to list all the words we might use when referring to this insect. When they have shared them, explain that "bug" has referred to insects since the 1600s but in the 1500s, it meant "a conceited person," and in the 1300s it meant "an object of terror." Then ask students what modern meaning we now associate with this word (a problem with a computer program). Use this discussion to introduce the idea that words often change in meaning. (LG1.03B—TOC 16: Word Study & Spelling)

3. Ask students to describe the process that occurs as words change meaning over time. How does it start? How does the new meaning become entrenched? Can the old meaning ever be resurrected? Why or why not? Have students create a class dictionary or series of posters depicting common words that have undergone changes in their original meaning. (LG1.03B—TOC 16: Word Study & Spelling)

Answers:
1. a) specialization
   b) degradation
   c) degradation
   d) generalization
   e) degradation
   f) generalization
   g) elevation

Student Book (LG1.03B—TOC 16: Word Study & Spelling)

ANSWERS TO EXTRA PRACTICE

Grammar
1. he — pronoun
   underneath — preposition

2. of — preposition
   and — coordinating conjunction
   me — pronoun

3. as — subordinating conjunction

4. Ouch — interjection
   on — preposition

5. but — coordinating conjunction
   from — preposition

(WR5.05D—TOC 4: Grammar; LG1.05D—TOC 4: Grammar)

Mechanics
1. Wanda glanced at the clock above the teacher's head and whispered, "Only five more minutes until the weekend."

2. Turning slightly, her friend Laura asked, "Are you going to Ryan's party tonight?"

3. Wanda told her she was not sure yet.

4. "Do you still have to work this evening?" asked Laura.

5. "Until nine," Wanda groaned, "but I think my boss will let me go early if I ask her."

(WR5.16B—TOC 8: Mechanics; LG1.07B—TOC 8: Mechanics)

Usage & Style
No extra practice applicable for foreshadowing.

Word Study & Spelling
1. elevation

2. degradation

3. generalization

4. specialization

5. generalization

(LG1.03B—TOC 16: Word Study & Spelling)

GRADE 9 EXPECTATIONS		DEMONSTRATION OF LEARNING	ASSESSMENT TOOLS
LITERATURE STUDIES AND READING			
Overall (LIV.01P)	• read and demonstrate an understanding of a variety of literary and informational texts	• demonstrate understanding of short story (Investigating the Model SB #1–8)	• TOC 14: Tracking Expectations
Specific (LI1.01P)	• describe information, ideas, opinions, and themes in texts they have read during the year from a variety of print and electronic sources, including biographies, short stories, poems, plays, novels, brochures, and articles from newspapers, magazines, and encyclopedias	• discuss differences in fictional and nonfictional short stories (Introducing the Unit TG #1)	• AR 22: Response to Reading
(LI1.02P)	• select and read texts for a variety of purposes, with an emphasis on recognizing the elements of literary genres and the organization of informational materials, collecting and using information, extending personal knowledge, and responding imaginatively	• discuss purposes of short stories (Introducing the Unit TG #1)	• AR 22: Response to Reading
(LI1.03B)	• describe a variety of reading strategies and select and use them effectively before, during, and after reading to understand texts	• predict story line using story vocabulary (Introducing the Model TG #3)	• TOC 10: Reading Strategies
(LI1.07P)	• identify how readers' different backgrounds might influence the way they understand and interpret a text	• explain personal responses to short stories (Introducing the Unit TG #3)	• AR 22: Response to Reading
Overall (LIV.02P)	• demonstrate an understanding of the elements of a variety of literary and informational forms, with a focus on plays, short stories, and newspaper and magazine articles	• discuss definition of short story (Introducing the Unit TG #2)	• TOC 14: Tracking Expectations
Specific (LI2.02P)	• use knowledge of elements of the short story, such as plot, character, setting, conflict, theme, and atmosphere, to understand and interpret texts in the genre	• demonstrate understanding of elements of short story (Investigating the Model SB #1–8) • describe Teresa's character (Extending the Model TG #1) • suggest alternative conflicts to follow original story (Extending the Model TG #2) • identify original ending of short story and discuss purpose and style (More Challenge TG)	• TOC 14: Tracking Expectations • TOC 14: Tracking Expectations • TOC 14: Tracking Expectations • AR 22: Response to Reading
Overall (LIV.03B)	• identify and explain the effect of specific elements of style in a variety of literary and informational texts		
Specific (LI3.01P)	• explain how authors use stylistic devices, such as simile, metaphor, personification, imagery, and foreshadowing, to achieve intended effects	• describe stylistic devices in short story (Introducing the Unit TG #3) • discuss short story endings and foreshadowing (Usage & Style TG) • show how author has used foreshadowing in short story (Usage & Style SB #1–5)	• AR 22: Response to Reading • TOC 15: Usage & Style • TOC 15: Usage & Style
WRITING			
Overall (WRV.01P)	• use print and electronic sources to gather information and explore ideas for their written work	• gather and organize information and ideas for short story (Writer's Workshop SB #1–4)	• AR 24: Short Story
Specific (WR1.01P)	• investigate potential topics by asking questions, identifying information needs, and developing research plans to gather data	• use graphic organizer to record details of main characters (Writer's Workshop TG #1)	• AR 24: Short Story

AR=Assessment Rubric   EP=Extra Practice   SB=Student Book   SSEC=Student Self-Evaluation Checklist   TG=Teacher's Guide   TOC=Teacher Observation Checklist

WRITING (continued)		
(WR1.02P) • locate and record information and ideas from print and electronic sources, including newspapers and magazines, dictionaries, encyclopedias, vertical files, and electronic databases	• write about personal experiences involving water (Introducing the Model TG #1) • recount kayaking or windsurfing experiences (Introducing the Model TG #2)	• AR 24: Short Story • AR 24: Short Story
(WR1.03P) • sort and group information and ideas, assess their relevance and accuracy, and discard irrelevant material	• use picture drawn of main character to develop ideas (Writer's Workshop TG #2) • plot short story using flow chart (More Support TG)	• AR 24: Short Story • AR 24: Short Story
Overall (WRV.03P) • use a variety of forms of writing to express themselves, clarify their ideas, and engage the audience's attention, imagination, and interest	• write a draft of short story (Writer's Workshop SB #5)	• AR 24: Short Story
Specific (WR3.04P) • use changes in time, place, or speaker to structure narrative paragraphs	• write short story (Writer's Workshop SB #5)	• AR 24: Short Story
Overall (WRV.04B) • revise their written work, collaboratively and independently, with a focus on support for ideas, accuracy, clarity, and unity	• revise short story (Writer's Workshop SB #6)	• AR 24: Short Story
Specific (WR4.03P) • make constructive suggestions to peers, using prompts, checklists, open-ended statements, and questions	• give constructive criticism to peers (More Oral Language TG)	• SSEC 6: Peer Assessment: Writing
Overall (WRV.05B) • edit and proofread to produce final drafts, using correct grammar, spelling, and punctuation, according to the conventions of standard Canadian English specified for this course, with the support of print and electronic resources when appropriate	• edit and proofread short story (Writer's Workshop SB #6)	• AR 24: Short Story
Specific (WR5.05P) • identify and use parts of speech correctly: nouns, pronouns, verbs, adverbs, adjectives, conjunctions, prepositions, and interjections	• rewrite passage without pronouns, prepositions, or conjunctions (Grammar TG) • use pronouns, prepositions, conjunctions, and interjections correctly (Grammar SB #1–3) • use pronouns, prepositions, conjunctions, and interjections correctly (EP: Grammar)	• TOC 4: Grammar • TOC 4: Grammar • TOC 4: Grammar
WR5.16B • adapt punctuation and capitalization for the special requirements of direct quotations, scripts, dialogue, and poetry	• punctuate and capitalize dialogue correctly (Mechanics TG) • punctuate and capitalize dialogue correctly (Mechanics SB #1–3) • punctuate and capitalize dialogue correctly (EP: Mechanics)	• TOC 8: Mechanics • TOC 8: Mechanics • TOC 8: Mechanics
LANGUAGE		
Overall (LGV.01P) • use knowledge of vocabulary and language conventions to speak, write, and read clearly and correctly		
Specific (LG1.02B) • identify and explain examples of slang, jargon, dialect, and colloquialism, as well as of standard Canadian English, in literary texts and their own oral and written work	• discuss slang terms (Word Study & Spelling TG #1)	• TOC 16: Word Study & Spelling

AR=Assessment Rubric   EP=Extra Practice   SB=Student Book   SSEC=Student Self-Evaluation Checklist   TG=Teacher's Guide   TOC=Teacher Observation Checklist

LANGUAGE (continued)		
(LG1.03B) • identify words borrowed from other languages, and words and terms recently introduced to describe new ideas, inventions, and products, and explain their origins	• discuss how words change over time (Word Study & Spelling TG #2) • create class dictionary or posters of words that have changed over time (Word Study & Spelling TG #3) • identify how words change over time (Word Study & Spelling SB) • identify how words change over time (EP: Word Study & Spelling	• TOC 16: Word Study & Spelling • TOC 16: Word Study & Spelling • TOC 16: Word Study & Spelling • TOC 16: Word Study & Spelling
(LG1.05P) • recognize, describe, and use correctly, in oral and written language, the language structures of standard Canadian English and its conventions of grammar and usage, including: – parts of speech: nouns, pronouns, verbs, adverbs, adjectives, conjunctions, prepositions, and interjections	• rewrite passages without pronouns, prepositions, or conjunctions (Grammar TG) • use pronouns, prepositions, conjunctions, and interjections correctly (Grammar SB #1–3) • use pronouns, prepositions, conjunctions, and interjections correctly (EP: Grammar)	• TOC 4: Grammar • TOC 4: Grammar • TOC 4: Grammar
(LG1.07B) • recognize, describe, and use correctly, in oral and written language, the conventions of standard Canadian English for spelling, capitalization, and punctuation, including: – capitalization: of proper nouns and in direct quotations, scripts, dialogue, and poetry – punctuation: period, question mark, exclamation mark, comma, dash, apostrophe, colon, quotation marks, parentheses, ellipses	• punctuate and capitalize dialogue correctly (Mechanics TG) • punctuate and capitalize dialogue correctly (Mechanics SB #1–3) • punctuate and capitalize dialogue correctly (EP: Mechanics)	• TOC 8: Mechanics • TOC 8: Mechanics • TOC 8: Mechanics
Overall (LGV.02B) • use listening techniques and oral communication skills to participate in classroom discussions and more formal activities, such as storytelling, role playing, and reporting/presenting, for specific purposes and audiences		
Specific (LG2.01P) • use listening techniques and oral communication skills to participate in group discussions	• develop code of conduct for working in a group (More Oral Language TG) • share writing in writers' group (Oral Language Extension SB)	• TOC 5: Group Work • TOC 5: Group Work
MEDIA STUDIES		
Overall (MDV.01P) • identify and describe the elements, intended audiences, and production practices of a variety of media forms	• identify reasons for TV program successes (Media Link TG)	• AR 21: Response to Media
Specific (MD1.03P) • compare the reactions of different people or groups to a variety of media works	• predict TV hits and record results (More Media TG)	• AR 21: Response to Media
Overall (MDV.02P) • use knowledge of a variety of media forms, purposes, and audiences to create media works		
Specific (MD2.01P) • adapt a work of literature for presentation in another media form	• write story in storybook form (Writer's Workshop TG #4) • plan TV dramatization of "The Kayak" (Media Link SB)	• AR 12: Media Product • AR 12: Media Product
(MD2.02P) • create media works for different purposes	• create print advertisement for TV drama (Media Link SB)	• AR 12: Media Product

AR=Assessment Rubric   EP=Extra Practice   SB=Student Book   SSEC=Student Self-Evaluation Checklist   TG=Teacher's Guide   TOC=Teacher Observation Checklist

INSTRUCTIONAL STRATEGIES FOR THE APPLIED COURSE

PLANNING INFORMATION

Links to Other Nelson English 9 Resources

Literature & Media 9
Short Fiction—See the Short Fiction unit for 17 short fiction selections, pp. 1–108.

Write Source 2000
Short Fiction—"Writing Stories," pp. 183–192; **Conjunctions**—"Conjunction," p. 456; **Interjections**—"Interjection," pp. 390, 398; **Prepositions**—"Preposition," p. 455; **Pronouns**—"Pronoun," pp. 441–445; **Rules for Writing Dialogue**—"Writing/Revising/Editing," pp. 190–191, "To Set Off Dialogue," p. 390, "Quotation Marks," p. 399

INTRODUCING THE UNIT

The activities on page 31 from the Academic Course are appropriate for the Applied Course.

1. (LI1.01P—AR 22: Response to Reading; LI1.02P—AR 22: Response to Reading)

2. (LIV.02P—TOC 14: Tracking Expectations)

3. (LI1.07P—AR 22: Response to Reading; LI3.01P—AR 22: Response to Reading)

INTRODUCING THE MODEL

The activities on page 31 from the Academic Course are appropriate for the Applied Course.

1. (WR1.02P—AR 24: Short Story)

2. (WR1.02P—AR 24: Short Story)

3. (LI1.03B—TOC 10: Reading Strategies)

INVESTIGATING THE MODEL

See the Academic Course on pages 32–33 for answers.
Student Book (LIV.01P—TOC 14: Tracking Expectations; LI2.02P—TOC 14: Tracking Expectations)

EXTENDING THE MODEL

1. Have students cast the part of Teresa for an upcoming film adaptation (selecting from either real actors or local individuals familiar to everyone) and defend their selections. In advance of casting, they should create a word list to describe Teresa's character. Reassure students that some of the words will contradict each other, e.g., "determined" and "scared," but that contradictions are implicit in human character. Ask them to explain how the actor to be cast in the role of Teresa would be able to display the qualities on the list. (In the case of real actors, for example, students could refer to another character they have played.) (LI2.02P—TOC 14: Tracking Expectations)

2. Have students extend their understanding of the main character by inventing a different situation or conflict following the ending of the original story. Ask them to respond to the demands of this new situation. Discussion should focus on the reasons behind their responses. (LI2.02P—TOC 14: Tracking Expectations)

LEARNING GOALS

- write a short story
- use parts of speech correctly: pronouns, prepositions, conjunctions, and interjections
- punctuate and capitalize dialogue correctly
- identify elements of foreshadowing in short stories
- identify how words change over time

CHECKPOINT

Sample criteria for a short story:

- has lead that catches reader's attention, identifies main character, introduces conflict, defines setting, and establishes point of view
- has plot that revolves around conflict, either external or internal
- often uses details of setting to reflect or empathize with main character's state of mind
- is usually written from first-person or third-person point of view
- often includes physical details about characters
- often spans relatively brief time period
- reveals character using dialogue, reactions of other characters, physical description, and actions
- has a theme that is closely tied to change occurring in story

---

Writer's Workshop

1. Some students find it easier to brainstorm using a graphic organizer. Design one (or suggest that students invent their own) that will encourage them to think about and record multiple details about their main character. For example, an outline of a person's head and torso with lines drawn to the head (things they think about), heart (things they care about), and hands (things they like to do) can often elicit more ideas than a blank page. (WR1.01P—AR 24: Short Story)

2. Encourage students to draw a picture of their main character and to share what they know about him or her with a partner. As they share their ideas, the partner can write down the details that will be incorporated in the story. (WR1.03P—AR 24: Short Story)

3. If the task of writing an entire story seems daunting, ask students to write an ending only. Read "The Kayak" (or another story) aloud, stopping at a point prior to the resolution of the conflict (usually before the last three or four paragraphs). They must resolve the conflict responsibly (i.e., their resolution must grow out of events and details included in the original). The purpose of this activity is to involve students in the same decisions all writers make when they choose an ending for their story. Discussion can focus on the reasons behind their choices. (WRV.03P—AR 24: Short Story)

4. Students can plan and write a short story in storybook form for very young readers, looking at techniques for sketching rudimentary figures, creating a storyboard, and so forth. (These activities might be integrated with their work in art and media studies.) Students could read the final draft of their storybooks to young readers at a nearby elementary school. This would heighten the oral language component of the project. (MD2.01P—AR 12: Media Product)

Student Book 1.–4. (WRV.01P—AR 24: Short Story); 5. (WRV.03P—AR 24: Short Story; WR3.04P—AR 24: Short Story); 6. (WRV.04B—AR 24: Short Story; WRV.05B—AR 24: Short Story)

Oral Language Extension

Teachers wishing to learn more about guiding cooperative learning/writing groups should refer to the following sources:

Hill, Susan, and Tim Hill (1990). *The Collaborative Classroom: A Guide to Cooperative Learning.* Portsmouth, NH: Heinemann.

Spear, Karen (1988). *Sharing Writing: Peer Response Groups in English Classes.* Portsmouth, NH: Heinemann.

Spear, Karen, et al (1993). *Peer Response Groups in Action: Writing Together in Secondary Schools.* Portsmouth, NH: Heinemann.

Student Book (LG2.01P—TOC 5: Group Work)

Grammar

The Grammar activity on page 35 from the Academic Course is appropriate for the Applied Course.
(WR5.05P—TOC 4: Grammar; LG1.05P—TOC 4: Grammar)

Answers:
See the Academic Course on page 35 for answers.
Student Book (WR5.05P—TOC 4: Grammar; LG1.05P—TOC 4: Grammar)

MORE CHALLENGE

Copy students' endings from activity #3 for Writer's Workshop in the *Teacher's Guide* along with the author's and have students attempt (either in small-group discussion or in writing) to identify the original ending. The emphasis of this activity is not selecting the "real" ending but, instead, encouraging discussion that focuses on such issues as purpose and style. (Often, a class will find a fellow student's ending superior to the author's.) (LI2.02P—AR 22: Response to Reading)

MORE SUPPORT

Some students might find it easier to plot their stories using a graphic organizer in the form of a flow chart. Illustrate for students how to use the organizer by having them suggest a character to include in a box at the top of a sample flow chart. Once they have decided what the conflict of this example story will be, have them suggest a series of possible events that will take place, writing their suggestions on a flow chart. Encourage them to offer whatever comes to mind because even the most ridiculous suggestions can sometimes result in wonderful story ideas—the importance of this exercise is to encourage the flow of creative thought. Once students have exhausted their ideas, have them choose the most interesting and plausible story line from the suggestions given. Then have them complete their own flow charts based on the characters they have created in the Writer's Workshop activities. (WR1.03P—AR 24: Short Story)

MORE ORAL LANGUAGE

Provide opportunities early in the year for students to practise responding to writing that is not written by fellow classmates. Model effective (and ineffective) responses to writing, having students refer to the suggestions in the Idea File on page 40 of the student book. Once they are accustomed to response protocols, have students share pieces of their own writing.

It can be extremely helpful at the beginning of the year to have each class generate its own code of conduct that identifies five or six helpful behaviours for the classroom. (Have students meet in pairs, then combine to form larger groups of four, then eight, and so on, to discuss this.) More than just a classroom management technique, this process and resulting code of conduct should enable every student to feel valued and to participate without fear of ridicule. (WR4.03P—SSEC 6: Peer Assessment: Writing; LG2.01P—TOC 5: Group Work)

MEDIA LINK

The activity on page 35 from the Academic Course is appropriate for the Applied Course.
(MDV.01P—AR 21: Response to Media)
Student Book (MD2.01P—AR 12: Media Product; MD2.02P—AR 12: Media Product)

MECHANICS

Provide copies of a passage from a high-interest story that contains both dialogue and indirect quotation, but no identifying punctuation marks. Have students read the passage aloud at least twice, the first time to familiarize themselves with the content, and the second time to listen for dialogue. In small groups, students should underline the dialogue, and suggest ways to punctuate and capitalize the dialogue. As follow-up, have them compare their work with the original passage containing appropriate punctuation and capitalization related to dialogue. On a separate sheet of paper, ask them to rewrite one or two of their sentences that contained an error. Beside each sentence, they should write down at least one rule they need to observe when writing dialogue. (WR5.16B—TOC 8: Mechanics; LG1.07B—TOC 8: Mechanics)

Answers:
See the Academic Course on page 36 for answers.
Student Book 1.–3. (WR5.16B—TOC 8: Mechanics; LG1.07B—TOC 8: Mechanics)

USAGE & STYLE

Choose a short, high-interest story and read it aloud to the class, stopping at a crucial moment just prior to the story's resolution and continuing instead with "Suddenly Doofus could hear a buzzing sound and he/she turned to see his/her clock radio flash 7:00 a.m. in red numerals. He/she was lying in his/her bed. It had all been a dream." Be prepared for a negative reaction from the class, and have students discuss why the ending was so disappointing. Encourage students to see that writers need to prepare their readers for their endings—nowhere in the story did the writer prepare them to accept that the action took place in a dream. Then ask them to suggest how the story might have ended based on what came before. Finally, share the original ending and ask students if they think the writer adequately prepared them for it. (LI3.01P—TOC 15: Usage & Style)

Answers:
See the Academic Course on pages 36–37 for answers.
Student Book 1.–5. (LI3.01P—TOC 15: Usage & Style)

WORD STUDY & SPELLING

The Word Study & Spelling activities on page 37 from the Academic Course are appropriate for the Applied Course.

1. (LG1.02B—TOC 16: Word Study & Spelling)

2. (LG1.03B—TOC 16: Word Study & Spelling)

3. (LG1.03B—TOC 16: Word Study & Spelling)

Answers:
See the Academic Course on page 38 for answers.
Student Book (LG1.03B—TOC 16: Word Study & Spelling)

ANSWERS TO EXTRA PRACTICE

See the Academic Course on page 38 for answers.

Grammar

(WR5.05P—TOC 4: Grammar; LG1.05P—TOC 4: Grammar)

Mechanics

(WR5.16B—TOC 8: Mechanics; LG1.07B—TOC 8: Mechanics)

Usage & Style

No extra practice applicable for foreshadowing.

Word Study & Spelling

(LG1.03B—TOC 16: Word Study & Spelling

GRAMMAR

NAME: _____ DATE: _____

Identify the part of speech of each boldface word.

1. **He** is trapped **underneath** the sail.

2. Powerful swirls **of** wind **and** current toss **me** about.

3. The waves peak wildly **as** the storm picks up.

4. **"Ouch!"** Jamie shouts as the windsurfer's sail crashes down **on** him.

5. The rain stops, **but** the storm is far **from** over.

MECHANICS

NAME: _____ DATE: _____

Rewrite the following sentences inserting necessary capital letters and punctuation.

1. wanda glanced at the clock above the teacher's head and whispered only five more minutes until the weekend

_____

_____

2. turning slightly, her friend laura asked are you going to ryan's party tonight

_____

_____

3. wanda told her she was not sure yet

_____

_____

4. do you still have to work this evening asked laura

_____

_____

5. until eight replied wanda but i think my boss will let me go early if i ask her

_____

_____

WORD STUDY & SPELLING

NAME: _____ DATE: _____

Identify whether the meaning of each of the following words has been generalized, specialized, elevated, or degraded. The original meaning of the word is given in parentheses.

1. glorious (boastful)_____

2. gossip (friend) _____

3. butcher (a person who killed and sold goats)_____

4. deer (any wild animal)_____

5. picture (a painting)_____

LANGUAGE & WRITING 9

UNIT 3: SCRIPT

ACADEMIC EXPECTATIONS

GRADE 9 EXPECTATIONS		DEMONSTRATION OF LEARNING	ASSESSMENT TOOLS
LITERATURE STUDIES AND READING			
Overall (LIV.01D)	• read and demonstrate an understanding of a variety of literary and informational texts, from contemporary and historical periods	• demonstrate understanding of forms of narration (Reflecting on Narrative Writing Forms SB #1–2)	• TOC 13: Tracking Expectations
Specific (LI1.02D)	• select and read texts for different purposes, with an emphasis on recognizing the elements of literary genres and the organization of informational materials, collecting and assessing information, responding imaginatively, and exploring human experiences and values	• investigate functions of drama (Introducing the Unit TG #2) • discuss how families are affected by employment changes (Introducing the Model TG #1)	• TOC 13: Tracking Expectations • TOC 13: Tracking Expectations
(LI1.05D)	• analyze information, ideas, and elements in texts to make inferences about meaning	• discuss importance of characters in model (Extending the Model TG #1) • speculate on what happens before and after model (Extending the Model TG #3)	• TOC 13: Tracking Expectations • AR 23: Script
(LI1.06D)	• use specific evidence from a text to support opinions and judgments	• consider audition advice and conduct mock auditions (Extending the Model TG #2) • speculate on scenes before and after model (More Support TG)	• TOC 13: Tracking Expectations • TOC 13: Tracking Expectations
Overall (LIV.02D)	• demonstrate an understanding of the elements of a variety of literary and informational forms, with a focus on plays, short stories, and short essays	• compare four forms of narrative writing (Looking Over Narrative Writing Forms SB #1)	• TOC 13: Tracking Expectations
Specific (LI2.01D)	• use knowledge of elements of drama, such as plot and subplot, character portrayal, conflict, dramatic structure, dramatic purpose, dramatic irony, dialogue, and stage directions, to understand and interpret examples of the genre	• attend performance of local theatre group and question actors and director (Introducing the Unit TG #4) • question local playwright about crafting a play (Introducing the Unit TG #5) • understand and interpret short story (Investigating the Model SB #1–8) • read portions of model aloud (Writer's Workshop TG #3)	• TOC 13: Tracking Expectations • TOC 13: Tracking Expectations • TOC 13: Tracking Expectations • TOC 13: Tracking Expectations
(L12.03D)	• use knowledge of elements of short essays, such as introductions, thesis statements, topic sentences, supporting details, connecting words, and conclusions, to understand and interpret examples of the genre	• read essay to note content and elements (Using the Narrative Writing Forms SB #3)	• TOC 13: Tracking Expectations
Overall (LIV.03B)	• identify and explain the effect of specific elements of style in a variety of literary and informational texts		
Specific (LI3.03D)	• explain how authors and editors use design elements to help communicate ideas	• identify script forms and discuss format (Introducing the Unit TG #3)	• TOC 13: Tracking Expectations
WRITING			
Overall (WRV.01D)	• use a variety of print and electronic sources to gather information and explore ideas for their written work	• gather and organize information and ideas for script (Writer's Workshop SB #1–6)	• AR 23: Script
Specific (WR1.01D)	• investigate potential topics by formulating questions, identifying information needs, and developing research plans to gather data	• brainstorm elements of backstory (Writer's Workshop TG #1) • suggest possible settings with partners (Writer's Workshop TG #2) • generate and clarify details for humorous personal narrative (Using the Narrative Writing Forms TG #1)	• AR 23: Script • AR 23: Script • AR 10: Humorous Personal Narrative

AR=Assessment Rubric   EP=Extra Practice   SB=Student Book   SSEC=Student Self-Evaluation Checklist   TG=Teacher's Guide   TOC=Teacher Observation Checklist

GRADE 9 EXPECTATIONS	DEMONSTRATION OF LEARNING	ASSESSMENT TOOLS
WRITING (continued)		
(WR1.02D) • locate and summarize information from print and electronic sources, including vertical files, periodicals, dictionaries, encyclopedias, electronic newsgroups, e-mail messages, and electronic databases	• write about role-playing experiences from childhood and analyze their appeal (Introducing the Unit TG #1)	• TOC 13: Tracking Expectations
(WR1.04D) • use the information and ideas generated by research to develop the content of written work	• develop ways to make subtext obvious (Writer's Workshop TG #4)	• AR 23: Script
Overall (WRV.02D) • identify the literary and informational forms suited to various purposes and audiences and use the forms appropriately in their own writing, with an emphasis on supporting opinions or interpretations with specific information		
Specific (WR2.01D) • demonstrate an understanding of literary and informational forms, such as myths, poems, short stories, scripts, advertisements, formal letters, reviews, and supported opinion essays, by selecting and using forms of writing appropriate to different purposes and audiences	• write a script about two historical figures (More Challenge TG)	• AR 23: Script
Overall (WRV.03D) • use a variety of organizational techniques to present ideas and supporting details logically and coherently in written work	• write a single scene (Writer's Workshop TG #5) • write a draft of script (Writer's Workshop SB #7) • write a humorous personal narrative (Using the Narrative Writing Forms SB #1) • write a script about two imaginary beings (Using the Narrative Writing Forms SB #2) • write an essay on an element of a short story (Using the Narrative Writing Forms SB #3)	• AR 23: Script • AR 23: Script • AR 10: Humorous Personal Narrative • AR 23: Script • AR 8: Expository Writing
Specific (WR3.05D) • structure expository paragraphs using a topic sentence, supporting sentences to develop the topic, connecting words to link the sentences, and a concluding sentence	• write an essay on an element of a short story (Using the Narrative Writing Forms SB #3)	• AR 8: Expository Writing
Overall (WRV.04D) • revise their written work, independently and collaboratively, with a focus on support for ideas and opinions, accuracy, clarity, and unity	• revise script (Writer's Workshop SB #8) • revise humorous personal narrative (Using the Narrative Writing Forms SB #1) • revise script about two imaginary beings (Using the Narrative Writing Forms SB #2) • revise essay on an element of a short story (Using the Narrative Writing Forms SB #3)	• AR 23: Script • AR 10: Humorous Personal Narrative • AR 23: Script • AR 8: Expository Writing
Specific (WR4.03D) • make constructive suggestions to peers	• list criteria to assess effectiveness of scenes (Oral Language Extension TG)	• AR 5: Dramatization
(WR4.04B) • consider reactions from teachers, peers, and others in revising and editing written work	• workshop scripts (Oral Language Extension SB)	• AR 23: Script
Overall (WRV.05D) • edit and proofread to produce final drafts, using correct grammar, spelling, and punctuation, according to the conventions of standard Canadian English, with the support of print and electronic resources when appropriate	• edit and proofread script (Writer's Workshop SB #8) • edit and proofread personal narrative (Using the Narrative Writing Forms SB #1) • edit and proofread script about two imaginary beings (Using the Narrative Writing Forms SB #2) • edit and proofread essay on an element of a short story (Using the Narrative Writing Forms SB #3)	• AR 23: Script • AR 10: Humorous Personal Narrative • AR 23: Script • AR 8: Expository Writing

AR=Assessment Rubric   EP=Extra Practice   SB=Student Book   SSEC=Student Self-Evaluation Checklist   TG=Teacher's Guide   TOC=Teacher Observation Checklist

WRITING (continued)			
Specific (WR5.06D)	• construct complete and correct compound and complex sentences, using the following sentence components as required: subject, predicate, object, subject complement; main and subordinate clauses; prepositional and participial phrases	• identify phrases used in script dialogue (Grammar TG #1) • identify phrases (Grammar TG #2) • identify prepositional and participial phrases (Grammar SB #1–3) • avoid misplaced and dangling modifiers (Usage & Style TG #1–2) • avoid misplaced and dangling modifiers (Usage & Style SB #1–2) • identify prepositional and participial phrases (EP: Grammar) • eliminate misplaced and dangling modifiers (EP: Usage & Style)	• TOC 4: Grammar • TOC 4: Grammar • TOC 4: Grammar • TOC 15: Usage & Style • TOC 15: Usage & Style • TOC 4: Grammar • TOC 15: Usage & Style
(WR5.11B)	• use knowledge of a wide range of spelling patterns and rules to identify, analyze, and correct spelling errors	• use mnemonic devices for difficult words (Word Study & Spelling TG #1) • use mnemonic devices to learn spelling (Word Study & Spelling SB #1) • create personal and class dictionaries of difficult words (Word Study & Spelling SB #2)	• TOC 16: Word Study & Spelling • TOC 16: Word Study & Spelling • TOC 16: Word Study & Spelling
(WR5.16B)	• adapt punctuation and capitalization for the special requirements of direct quotations, scripts, dialogue, and poetry	• identify and use adaptations of punctuation and capitalization in dialogue (Mechanics SB #2–4) • identify mechanical devices used for dialogue (EP: Mechanics)	• TOC 8: Mechanics • TOC 8: Mechanics
LANGUAGE			
Overall (LGV.01D)	• use knowledge of vocabulary and language conventions to speak, write, and read competently using a level of language appropriate to the purpose and audience		
Specific (LG1.02B)	• identify and explain examples of slang, jargon, dialect, and colloquialism, as well as of standard Canadian English, in literary texts and their own oral and written work	• identify examples of slang in transcripts of conversations (Mechanics TG) • identify examples of slang and dialect (Using the Narrative Writing Forms SB #4)	• TOC 8: Mechanics • TOC 16: Word Study & Spelling
(LG1.03B)	• identify words borrowed from other languages and words and terms recently introduced to describe new ideas, inventions, and products, and explain their origins	• find word roots (Word Study & Spelling TG #2) • find word origins in Shakespearean plays (Word Origins SB) • find English words matching Latin roots (EP: Word Study & Spelling) • identify invented words and acronyms (Using the Narrative Writing Forms SB #4)	• TOC 16: Word Study & Spelling • TOC 16: Word Study & Spelling • TOC 16: Word Study & Spelling • TOC 16: Word Study & Spelling
(LG1.04B)	• select words and phrases appropriate to informal and formal styles, to suit the purpose and intended audience of oral and written work	• identify passages that show informal speech (Mechanics SB #1, 5)	• TOC 8: Mechanics
(LG1.05D)	• recognize, describe, and use correctly, in oral and written language, the language structures of standard Canadian English and its conventions of grammar and usage, including: – components of sentences: subject, predicate, object, subject complement, prepositional and participial phrases, main and subordinate clauses	• identify phrases used in script dialogue (Grammar TG #1) • identify phrases (Grammar TG #2) • identify use of prepositional and participial phrases (Grammar SB #1–3) • avoid misplaced and dangling modifiers (Usage & Style TG #1–2) • correct modifier problems (Usage & Style SB #1–2) • identify prepositional and participial phrases (EP: Grammar) • eliminate misplaced and dangling modifiers (EP: Usage & Style)	• TOC 4: Grammar • TOC 4: Grammar • TOC 4: Grammar • TOC 15: Usage & Style • TOC 15: Usage & Style • TOC 4: Grammar • TOC 15: Usage & Style

AR=Assessment Rubric   EP=Extra Practice   SB=Student Book   SSEC=Student Self-Evaluation Checklist   TG=Teacher's Guide   TOC=Teacher Observation Checklist

GRADE 9 EXPECTATIONS	DEMONSTRATION OF LEARNING	ASSESSMENT TOOLS
LANGUAGE (continued)		
Overall (LGV.02B) • use listening techniques and oral communication skills to participate in classroom discussions and more formal activities, such as storytelling, role playing, and reporting/ presenting, for specific purposes and audiences		
Specific (LG2.01D) • communicate orally in group discussions for different purposes, with a focus on identifying key ideas and supporting details, distinguishing fact from opinion, asking clarifying questions, and following instructions	• discuss the value of work (Introducing the Model TG #2) • share ideas on family relocation (Introducing the Model TG #3) • work in a group to plan and write an essay (Using the Narrative Writing Forms TG #3)	• TOC 11: Speaking • TOC 11: Speaking • TOC 5: Group Work
(LG2.03D) • plan and make oral presentations to a small group or the class, selecting and using vocabulary and methods of delivery to suit audience and purpose	• prepare a taped performance of a play (Using the Narrative Writing Forms TG #2)	• AR 5: Dramatization
(LG2.05D) • practise with cue cards and relaxation exercises (and with visual aids and technology, if used) to ensure confident delivery in oral presentations	• use tongue-twisters as performance warm-up (More Oral Language TG)	• TOC 11: Speaking
MEDIA STUDIES		
Overall (MDV.01D) • use knowledge of the elements, intended audiences, and production practices of a variety of media forms to analyze specific media works	• compare film versions of Shakespearean scene (Using the Narrative Writing Forms TG #5) • compare film version of Shakespearean scene with original version (Using the Narrative Writing Forms SB #5)	• AR 21: Response to Media • AR 21: Response to Media
Specific (MD1.02D) • identify how elements of media forms are used in a variety of media works and explain the effects of different treatments)	• examine differences between stage plays and screenplays (More Media TG)	• AR 21: Response to Media
Overall (MDV.02D) • use knowledge of a variety of media forms, purposes, and audiences to create media works and describe their intended effect		
Specific (MD2.01D) • adapt a work of literature to another media form and determine what aspects have been strengthened and/or weakened by the adaptation	• practise art exercises before creating storyboard (Media Link TG) • create storyboard for script (Media Link SB)	• AR 12: Media Product • AR 12: Media Product

AR=Assessment Rubric   EP=Extra Practice   SB=Student Book   SSEC=Student Self-Evaluation Checklist   TG=Teacher's Guide   TOC=Teacher Observation Checklist

INSTRUCTIONAL STRATEGIES FOR THE ACADEMIC COURSE

PLANNING INFORMATION

Links to Other Nelson English 9 Resources

Literature & Media 9
Drama—See the Drama unit for five script selections, pp. 204–282.

Write Source 2000
Misplaced Modifiers—"Misplaced Modifiers," p. 91; **Prepositional Phrases**—"Prepositional Phrase," p. 455

LEARNING GOALS

- write a scene for a script
- use prepositional and participial phrases correctly
- use punctuation in scripts correctly
- identify dialect
- avoid misplaced and dangling modifiers
- create personal and class dictionaries of newly encountered words

INTRODUCING THE UNIT

1. Introduce the unit by asking students to list some of the role-playing games young children enjoy (e.g., "cops and robbers," "playing house"). Ask students to write in their journals for a few moments about a role-playing experience from their childhood. Then, ask them to consider why this activity is so appealing to young children. What role-playing experiences appeal to people in their current age group? Why? (WR1.02D—TOC 13: Tracking Expectations)

2. Explain that many of us view dramatic performance as mere entertainment, but throughout history it has served other roles. Have students investigate (or simply discuss as a class) the various functions dramatic performance has had (e.g., providing instruction, celebrating a society's culture, sharing information, providing entertainment). What do they feel is the most important function served by dramatic performance in today's society? Why? (LI1.02D—TOC 13: Tracking Expectations)

3. Have students identify the various forms of scripts (e.g., stage scripts, television scripts, screenplays, radio plays) and share what they know about each format. (LI3.03D—TOC 13: Tracking Expectations)

4. If possible, take students to see a performance by a local theatre group, and arrange for a question-and-answer period with the actors and director following the performance. If this is not possible, plan to begin this unit when a school drama group is ready to perform a play, and arrange for the group to speak to the students about presenting a play. (LI2.01D—TOC 13: Tracking Expectations)

5. If possible, invite a local playwright to speak to the class about crafting a play. Allow time for students to ask questions. (LI2.01D—TOC 13: Tracking Expectations)

INTRODUCING THE MODEL

1. Share with students news or feature articles on the changing face of employment, and invite discussion of how families are affected by such trends as downsizing and cutbacks. (LI1.02D—TOC 13: Tracking Expectations)

2. Ask students to consider the value of work. Although many people long for instant lottery wealth, even the richest people may have jobs. Besides earning money to pay for basic needs, why do people work? Have students consider the emotional impact of losing one's job. (LG2.01D—TOC 11: Speaking)

3. Students can share their ideas regarding the impact on the family when one member is offered a job in another part of the country. (LG2.01D—TOC 11: Speaking)

Answers:

1. Two conflicts are established in this scene. The first is the external conflict between Tim and Mrs. Phipps, who is trying to encourage Tim to go to Regina with his wife despite Tim's refusal. The second conflict, an internal one, is suggested rather than developed in this scene and involves Tim's decision to remain behind while his wife moves to Regina.

2. The choice of Mrs. Phipps's yard as the setting of the scene helps establish the relationship between the two characters. The fact that the younger man is sweeping the walk for the older woman suggests he is either a son or someone hired to work for her. (This is clarified in the scene's opening dialogue.) Also, the choice of late fall (indicated by the light snowfall and the characters' preparation for winter) is significant because the physical cold and the death and decay in nature (indicating the end of a life cycle) suggest that something else may be coming to an end (in this case, the characters' relationships).

3. The playwright included directions regarding the characters' actions on stage, but he omitted directions about how the actors should deliver their lines. Decisions regarding delivery ultimately belong to the director and actors who interpret the script, but an effective script will convey through the context and words of a scene the emotion that is intended. A writer will, however, include stage directions for delivery if a passage is to be spoken differently (e.g., ironically, sarcastically) than the context might suggest.

4.

Dialogue	What is revealed
I told her it was the silliest thing I'd ever heard.	Mrs. Phipps's curt comment reveals her no-nonsense manner.
As for me, I got things to do here. Now, you gonna move off the sidewalk so's I can sweep it?	Tim's abrupt change of topic reflects his avoidance of the issue of his wife's moving. It offers justification for his refusal to move to Regina ("I got things to do here"). Also, his nonstandard language usage ("gonna," "so's") emphasizes the difference in education between the two characters.
I'LL SPREAD THE LEAVES, ALL RIGHT MRS. PHIPPS? HERE, I'M SPREADIN' THE LEAVES. HOW'S THAT? HUH? I'M SPREADIN' THE LEAVES! MORE LEAVES! WHOOPEE! LET'S SPREAD THEM LEAVES! HOWZAT? HUH? YOU THINK THAT'S ENOUGH?	Tim's outburst reveals his frustration at not being able to make Mrs. Phipps understand how he feels. It also suggests he may be frustrated by the contrast between his wife's success (job opportunity) and his own failure (having been laid off from the factory).
Yes. I think that will do.	Mrs. Phipps's simple statement reveals she has goaded Tim into reacting in such a way that she can now fire him, thereby eliminating his reason for not accompanying his wife to Regina.

5. In the following exchange, neither Tim nor Mrs. Phipps states she is trying to force him to accompany his wife to Regina, but we understand that this is clearly her intention, which makes the actual statement of her intention unnecessary.

CHECKPOINT

Sample criteria for a script:

- presents characters in conflict

- has a setting that meets requirements of plot, sets mood, or conveys information about characters and/or theme

- includes ways to enhance dramatic value through dialogue, action, and presentation

- has dialogue or actions that convey strong impression of characters

- may convey meaning through absence of words

- uses scenes to serve a particular purpose

TIM:	Mrs. Phipps, I know why you're doing this.
MRS. PHIPPS:	Do you?
TIM:	Yes.
MRS. PHIPPS:	Well then?
TIM:	The answer is no.

6. When Mrs. Phipps refuses to move off the sidewalk to allow Tim to sweep, she demonstrates both her determination and the fact that she cares about what happens to Tim and his wife. When Tim tears open the bags and flings the leaves about, he reveals his frustration at not being able to make Mrs. Phipps understand how he feels. It also suggests he may be frustrated by the contrast between his wife's success (job opportunity) and his own failure (having been laid off from the factory).

7. This scene reveals that Mrs. Phipps cares about what happens between Tim and his wife, to the extent that she is willing to fire him to ensure that he and Ginny remain together. It also reveals the inner turmoil that Tim is experiencing in light of his wife's job offer and his own lack of employment.

Student Book 1.–7. (LI2.01D—TOC 13: Tracking Expectations)

EXTENDING THE MODEL

1. Sometimes, a character in a script may not appear on stage but still plays an important part in the action that occurs. Have students consider how this is true of Tim's wife, Ginny, in the model. (LI1.05D—TOC 13: Tracking Expectations)

2. Unlike a short story, a script is meant to be read aloud. Have students consider what advice they would give to actors planning to audition for the roles of Tim and Mrs. Phipps. This advice could be translated into the criteria a director might use when selecting actors for these roles. If possible, have students conduct mock auditions and then choose the two actors based on their criteria. (LI1.06D—TOC 13: Tracking Expectations)

3. Because the model is only an excerpt, students may wish to speculate on what happens in the play prior to the scene in the text and what happens afterward. Have them write about and/or discuss their ideas, offering reasons for their speculation. (LI1.05D—AR 23: Script)

WRITER'S WORKSHOP

1. In completing activity #2, students are creating a "backstory" for their characters, past experiences that drive what will happen in their scene. Once they have identified details about their characters that are significant to their scene, have them consider how these details might be revealed quickly to their audience. Have students brainstorm such things as actions, reactions, and dialogue that could be used to convey elements of backstory. (WR1.01D—AR 23: Script)

2. Students should understand that the setting of a play conveys an enormous amount of information to an audience in a very short time. They might consider, for example, the very different impressions that would be conveyed of a young male leaning against the wall of a darkened alley and that same young male leaning against the wall of a hospital waiting room. Working in small groups, students can share with partners what they want their audience to know about their characters. Partners can then suggest various settings they feel would convey the information most effectively. (WR1.01D—AR 23: Script)

3. Real conversations—whether at home, in the school cafeteria, at the mall, or on the telephone—may last a long time, but seldom does a person speak at great length uninterrupted. Instead, individual comments are usually brief as the

conversation moves back and forth. Students can recognize this by reading portions of the model aloud. (LI2.01D—TOC 13: Tracking Expectations)

4. The **text** of a script refers to the actual words that are spoken, while the **subtext** is the meaning that these words have for other characters or for the audience. Because plays are mostly dialogue, it is important for students to recognize the difference between text and subtext, and use this distinction in their own writing. Illustrate with simple passages such as the following comment overheard in a school cafeteria: "Wonderful! Tuna Surprise *again!*" Students can interpret the difference between the text and subtext, and then suggest ways a scriptwriter could make the subtext obvious to the audience (e.g., through a character's actions). (WR1.04D—AR 23: Script)

5. Emphasize through activity #4 that students will be writing a single scene rather than an entire script. Although they need not resolve the conflict between their characters, they need to find an appropriate place to end their scene. (WRV.03D—AR 23: Script)

Student Book 1.–6. (WRV.01D—AR 23: Script); 7. (WRV.03D—AR 23: Script); 8. (WRV.04D—AR 23: Script; WRV.05D—AR 23: Script)

ORAL LANGUAGE EXTENSION

If possible, ask a director of a local theatre group—or a drama teacher—to speak to the class regarding the criteria used to assess the effectiveness of a scene. Students could use these comments to create a list of criteria the class will use to assess the completed projects. (WR4.03D—AR 5: Dramatization)

Student Book (WR4.04B—AR 23: Script)

GRAMMAR

1. Much dialogue consists of phrases rather than complete sentences. For example, a character's reply to the question "Do you drink coffee?" might be "All the time," which is a phrase. Have students share some of their script dialogue orally and listen for phrases they have used. Record these on the board and have students identify what they have in common (they lack both a subject and a verb). Identify these structures as phrases, and have students refer to the grammar section for a more complete description. (WR5.06D—TOC 4: Grammar; LG1.05D—TOC 4: Grammar)

2. Emphasize that, although they often consist of more than one word, phrases function as a single unit within a sentence. Put the following sentences on the board and have students copy them and identify the type of phrase underlined in each. (WR5.06D—TOC 4: Grammar; LG1.05D—TOC 4: Grammar)

> Your wife came to visit me yesterday. (noun phrase)
>
> Of course you are going to Regina. (verb phrase)
>
> Look, if Ginny wants to go to Regina, that's all right. (adjective phrase)
>
> Well, you're certainly not going to stay here! (adverb phrase)

Answers:

1. Possible answers
   sweeping the walk
   wearing a sweater
   starting toward the bags
   jumping on the pile of bags
   ripping one open

2. a) to Regina — prepositional phrase acting as an adverb
   b) to your opinion — prepositional phrase acting as an adverb
   c) for her — prepositional phrase acting as an adjective
   d) in the lawn — prepositional phrase acting as an adverb

3. Possible answer

   Now you gonna move <u>off the sidewalk</u> so's I can sweep it? — prepositional
   phrase acting as an adverb

Student Book 1.–3. (WR5.06D—TOC 4: Grammar; LG1.05D—TOC 4: Grammar)

MEDIA LINK

While some students enjoy drawing, others find the exercise difficult and the results
embarrassing. Students could be grouped so that each group includes at least one
artistically inclined member. If possible, arrange for an art teacher to provide students
with instruction and exercises in simple forms and perspective. This guidance will
render storyboard creation less intimidating and more meaningful.
(MD2.01D—AR 12: Media Product)

Student Book (MD2.01D—AR 12: Media Product)

MECHANICS

Assign students to record (with permission) part of a conversation with their friends
outside of class. Students can choose 30 seconds of the conversation suitable for
classroom discussion to share with the class. (Suggest they cue the tape in advance.)
Most informal conversations such as these will contain slang, contractions, and
interruptions. Have students write a transcript of the recorded conversation, keeping in
mind the need to reflect the casual style of the language. (LG1.02B—TOC 8:
Mechanics)

Answers:

1. Possible answers

   TIM: *Uh-huh.* That is not to say *I'm* not *goin'* yet.
   TIM: Well, *yer* entitled to your opinion.
   TIM: *You through dictatin'* my life for me, Mrs. Phipps?
   TIM: *Just leave it go,* Mrs. Phipps, would you just leave it go? *I got this walk to
          clean. I got weatherstrippin' to do.* And that garage is a rat's nest. I haven't
          even begun *to get 'er cleaned out.*

2. **Capital letters** are used to indicate characters' names, both at the beginning of
   dialogue and within stage directions. (As well, a passage written entirely in capital
   letters indicates the passage is delivered forcefully.) A **colon** usually follows the
   characters' names, separating the names from the dialogue. **Square brackets** are
   used to separate stage directions from spoken dialogue, and these stage directions
   are usually written in *italics*. The **long dash** indicates that dialogue has ended
   abruptly (usually because of an interruption), while **ellipsis** dots indicate the
   trailing off of a character's words.

3.–5. Student work.

Student Book 1., 5. (LG1.04B—TOC 8: Mechanics); 2.–4. (WR5.16B—TOC 8:
Mechanics)

USAGE & STYLE

1. Explain that writers recognize the value of modifiers because they add depth to
   writing; however, writers must be careful to place modifiers in their sentences so

they refer directly to the appropriate words. Introduce the problem of misplaced and dangling modifiers by providing the following examples on the board and having students identify what makes each of them humorous. (WR5.06D—TOC 15: Usage & Style; LG1.05D—TOC 15: Usage & Style)

a) Laughing, the dog leaped into Doug's lap and licked his face.

b) I once saw a loon paddling a canoe across the lake.

c) Lying by the side of the road, the ambulance came upon the accident victim.

2. Have students compete with each other to create the funniest dangling and/or misplaced modifier. Each pair of students could prepare the erroneous sentence on a poster that includes a graphic identifying the error and a correct version of the same sentence. (WR5.06D—TOC 15: Usage & Style; LG1.05D—TOC 15: Usage & Style)

Answers:

1. a) Working near the shed, Tim notices a broom with a long handle.

   b) Tim starts to carry downstairs several cartons filled with math books.

   c) While Mrs. Phipps is working on several math equations in her office, the wind suddenly blows her papers out the window.

   d) Wearing her sweater, Mrs. Phipps is greeted in the yard by Tim.

   e) With an angry look, Tim sweeps the leaves to one side.

2. Student work.

Student Book 1.–2. (WR5.06D—TOC 15: Usage & Style; LG1.05D—TOC 15: Usage & Style)

WORD STUDY & SPELLING

1. Ask students to generate a list of words they typically have trouble spelling. Record the words on the board and have students share ways they remember the spellings of these words. Make a note of these and then draw their attention to the Word Study & Spelling section of this unit. (WR5.11B—TOC 16: Word Study & Spelling)

2. When introducing word origins, share with students a brief history of the English language. Explain that, although the English language began to develop in what is now Great Britain, it evolved from a number of different sources, among them Celtic languages, German dialects, Latin, and Norman French, which contained many Greek and Latin words. For example, the boldface word in the following stage direction has its roots in several different languages:

> MRS. PHIPPS'S *yard. It has snowed; there is a dull, grey light.*

> *yard:*   from the Old English *geard,* the German *garten,* the Latin *hortus,* and the Greek *chortos*

In the script, Mrs. Phipps tells Tim, "Seeing as it's October—" The word *October* comes from the Latin word *octo,* meaning *eight,* and refers to the early Roman calendar in which October was the eighth month. Have students find the roots of the other eleven months of the year. (LG1.03B—TOC 16: Word Study & Spelling)

Answers:

1. Possible answers

   a) forty — "I bought 40 ties *for Ty.*" (mnemonic)

   b) weather — "*We* want *wet we*ather." (mnemonic)

   c) certainly — "It is cer*tainly plain* to see." (mnemonic)

   d) spread — bread, thread (similar patterns)

   e) through — "The golf ball rolled th*rough* the *rough.*" (mnemonic)

   f) opportunity — opportunity, community (similar patterns)

2. Student work.

Student Book 1.–2. (WR5.11B—TOC 16: Word Study & Spelling)

WORD ORIGINS

Answers:
brave new world:
"O brave new world, / That has such people in't!" *The Tempest,* Act V, sc. i, line 183.

a sea change:
"Full fathom five thy father lies; / Of his bones are coral made; / Those are pearls that were his eyes: Nothing of him that doth fade / But doth suffer a sea-change / Into something rich and strange." *The Tempest,* Act I, sc. ii, line 401.

all that glisters (glitters) is not gold:
"All that glisters is not gold — / Often have you heard that told." *Merchant of Venice,* Act II, sc. vii, line 65. This line originally came from the parable "Do not hold as gold all that shines as gold," attributed to Alain de Lille.

the course of true love never did run smooth:
"For aught that I could ever read, / Could ever hear by tale or history, / The course of true love never did run smooth." *A Midsummer Night's Dream,* Act I, sc. i, line 132)

What's in a name?
"What's in a name? That which we call a rose / By any other name would smell as sweet." *Romeo and Juliet,* Act II, sc. ii, line 43.

Student Book (LG1.03B—TOC 16: Word Study & Spelling)

ANSWERS TO EXTRA PRACTICE

Grammar
1. a) adjective phrase
   b) not a phrase — clause
   c) adjective phrase
   d) verb phrase
   e) noun phrase
   f) adverb phrase
   g) not a phrase — clause
   h) noun phrase

2. a) Covered in cobwebs, the interior of the garage was not a comfortable place to work.

   b) The leaves packed in the plastic bags would protect the flower beds from cold temperatures.

   c) None.

   d) The job waiting in Regina was the new beginning that Ginny wanted.

   e) Mrs. Phipps was unprepared for Tim's reaction.

   f) Staring in disbelief, Tim watched as Mrs. Phipps walked away.

   g) Mrs. Phipps looked at the bags piled by the walkway.

   h) Starting toward the bags, Mrs. Phipps said, "I'll just have to spread them myself."

3. Possible answers
   a) Hoping Regina would be a fresh start, Ginny looked forward to moving.
   b) Afraid of starting over again, Tim was willing to lose his wife.
   c) Understanding the fear Tim felt, Mrs. Phipps wanted him to confront it.

4. a) acting as an adverb
   b) acting as an adjective
   c) acting as an adverb
   d) acting as an adverb
   e) acting as an adjective

(WR5.06D—TOC 4: Grammar; LG1.05D—TOC 4: Grammar)

Mechanics

1. Nonstandard spelling helps convey the sound of slang, e.g., Whaddya wanna know for?

2. Contractions help convey the sound of informal speech, e.g., C'mon, buddy. What're friends for?

3. Ellipsis dots convey the sense of the voice trailing off, e.g., Well, if it's not too much trouble ...

4. The long dash conveys the sound of a person's speech being interrupted, e.g., Now, you coulda come, too, if you'd—

5. Block letters convey the sound of emphasized words, e.g., Now what's THAT supposed to mean?

6. Stage directions in italics tell how the line should be spoken aloud, e.g., [*sarcastically*]

(WR5.16B—TOC 8: Mechanics)

Usage & Style:

1. a) Tim found several cans of paint stacked by the garage.
   b) Exhausted, Mrs. Phipps finally found the lawn spreader in the garage.
   c) Tim cleaned up the fallen leaves lying in the gutter.
   d) Correct.
   e) Insecticide was applied by a pest-control expert to the brown patch on the lawn.
   f) Bent nearly double, the broken rake was taken away by the garbage truck.

(WR5.06D—TOC 15: Usage & Style; LG1.05—TOC 15: Usage & Style)

Word Study & Spelling:

1. a) contra: Latin meaning *opposite* (country)
   b) lassus: Latin *lassus* meaning *tired* (later)
   c) intitulare: Latin *in*, meaning *in*, and *titulus*, meaning *title* (entitled)
   d) opinio: Latin *opinio* (opinion)
   e) basis: Latin *basis* and Greek *bainein* meaning *to go* (basement)
   f) certus: Latin meaning *to decide* (certainly)
   g) opportunus: Latin *ob*, meaning *before*, and *portu*s, meaning *a harbour* (opportunity)
   h) dictare: Latin meaning *to say* (dictate)
   i) visitare: Latin meaning *to go see* (visit)
   j) nidus: Latin (nest)

(LG1.03B—TOC 16: Word Study & Spelling)

REFLECT AND BUILD ON YOUR LEARNING

REFLECTING ON NARRATIVE WRITING FORMS

1. Student work.

2. Possible answer

   Other narrative forms include anecdote, autobiography, biography, chronicle, confession, dialogue, diary, documentary, fable, fairy tale, fantasy, folktale, historical narrative, legend, memoir, monologue, myth, novel, parable, screenplay, and urban tale.

   Example: Legends are stories that are often based on some kernel of truth—the hero or heroine may have been a real person, or the event in the legend really may have happened. However, as legends are passed down, storytellers exaggerate aspects of the story, so legends often end up to be more fiction than fact.

Student Book 1.–2. (LIV.01D—TOC 13: Tracking Expectations)

LOOKING OVER NARRATIVE WRITING FORMS

1. Possible answer

CRITERIA	PERSONAL NARRATIVE	SHORT STORY	SCRIPT	LEGEND
Dialogue	usually limited use; establishes context	moderate to extensive use; reveals character and advances the plot	used extensively to reveal character and define the action	usually limited use; reveals the character of the hero/heroine
Character	characters are usually "flat"	main characters are "round" while secondary characters are "flat"	main characters are "round" while secondary characters are "flat"	characters are usually "flat," revealing a single, dominant trait
Conflict	usually external	may be internal or external or a combination of both	may be internal or external or a combination of both	usually external
Setting	provides a physical context for the conflict	provides a physical context for the conflict and often helps convey an understanding of the main character	provides a physical context for the conflict and helps convey an understanding of character	usually plays a major role in establishing the conflict and functions as a backdrop for the hero/heroine to demonstrate his/her particular heroic quality
Resolution	focuses on the impact the event/incident has on the narrator	embodies a change in character or situation that reveals an understanding about life and living	embodies a change in character or situation that reveals an understanding about life and living	emphasizes a particular attribute of the hero/heroine

Student Book 1. (LIV.02D—TOC 13: Tracking Expectations)

USING THE NARRATIVE WRITING FORMS

1. Encourage students to tell their event to a partner as a means of generating/clarifying details. Caution students about presenting former teachers and/or classmates in a negative light. If they must do so, suggest they change the names of people involved and make sure that those written about are unidentifiable. (WR1.01D—AR 10: Humorous Personal Narrative)

Student Book 1. (WRV.03D—AR 10: Humorous Personal Narrative; WRV.04D—AR 10: Humorous Personal Narrative; WRV.05D—AR 10: Humorous Personal Narrative)

2. An excellent one-act radio play called "Epilogue: The Weans," by Robert Nathan (CBS Radio Workshop Play, 1960), presents future humans excavating the ruins of several twentieth-century American cities and reporting incorrect (and humorous) interpretations of cultural icons (e.g., rock-and-roll music, Academy Awards). Besides an effective model for students to follow when writing their own scripts, it offers a valuable opportunity for oral language development as students can work in groups to prepare a taped performance of the play. (An alternative approach is to enlist the aid of a senior drama instructor whose older students could prepare a recording of the radio play for presentation to the class before students work on their own scripts.) (LG2.03D—AR 5: Dramatization)

Student Book 2. (WRV.03D—AR 23: Script; WRV.04D—AR 23: Script; WRV.05D—AR 23: Script)

3. Since this section focuses on narrative writing and this task requires students to write exposition, it is worthwhile to have them review the elements of the expository essay before they begin. Refer students to the essay on pages 14–15 of the student book, and ask them to read it twice, first for content, then again to identify particular characteristics of essay form (components such as introduction, body, and conclusion; organization of main ideas in single paragraphs; development of supporting details; use of transitional expressions).

   Before students attempt their individual essays, have them write a group essay analyzing a particular element of "The Kayak." For example, students might focus on the role that setting plays in the development of the story's theme. Through whole-class discussion, students could identify three to four ideas that might be included in the essay, after which each group would write a paragraph on one of these ideas (for comparison purposes, two groups could work on the same idea). Subsequent whole-class sharing and discussion of work (presented on the overhead projector) can identify strengths of each paragraph as well as address weaknesses and strategies for improvement. Finally, students can identify the most effective order for their paragraphs as well as a variety of ways to introduce and conclude the essay. The value of this approach is that, besides offering students a model to follow when writing their own essays, the group format makes the process nonthreatening and supportive (the class can comment on a group's paragraph rather than an individual's paragraph). (LG2.01D—TOC 5: Group Work)

Student Book 3. (LI2.03D—TOC 13: Tracking Expectations; WRV.03D—AR 8: Expository Writing; WR3.05D—AR 8: Expository Writing; WRV.04D—AR 8: Expository Writing; WRV.05D—AR 8: Expository Writing)

4. Possible answers

BORROWED	SLANG/ INVENTED	DIALECT	ACRONYMS
chiffon (French) chimpanzee (West African) chocolate (Spanish) khaki (Hindustani) nouveau riche (French) debonair (French) bodega (Spanish) bravo (Italian) briquette (French)	oly (snapping one end of a skateboard to get off the ground) buff (muscular) hoopdee (junky car) illed on (cursed out) peeps (group of friends) phat (sweet, nice) skeev (nasty—East Boston only) 'rents (parents) 24/7 (all the time)	spigot (tap) glowworm (firefly) chesterfield (sofa) bugaboo (object of terror) parlour (living room) pram (baby carriage) autoroute (highway) lift (elevator) flat (apartment)	AWOL (absent without official leave) ARROW (antiresonant reflecting optical waveguide) ASCII (American standard code for information interchange) DRAM (dynamic random access memory) DVD (digital versatile disc) HTML (hypertext markup language) HTTP (hypertext transport protocol) IRC (internet relay chat)

Student Book 4. (LG1.02B—TOC 16: Word Study & Spelling; LG1.03B—TOC 16: Word Study & Spelling)

5. An interesting extension of this activity is to have students compare various film versions of the same Shakespearean scene. For example, students might view the balcony scene in *Romeo & Juliet* as presented in George Cukor's 1936 film, Franco Zeffirelli's 1968 film, and Baz Luhrmann's 1996 film, examining not only the differences in cinematic techniques but also the influence of the culture of the time period in which each film was made. (MDV.01D—AR 21: Response to Media)

Student Book 5. (MDV.01D—AR 21: Response to Media)

GRADE 9 EXPECTATIONS		DEMONSTRATION OF LEARNING	ASSESSMENT TOOLS
LITERATURE STUDIES AND READING			
Overall (LIV.01P)	• read and demonstrate an understanding of a variety of literary and informational texts	• demonstrate understanding of forms of narration (Reflecting on Narrative Writing Forms SB #1–2)	• TOC 14: Tracking Expectations
Specific (LI1.02P)	• select and read texts for a variety of purposes, with an emphasis on recognizing the elements of literary genres and the organization of informational materials, collecting and using information, extending personal knowledge, and responding imaginatively	• investigate functions of drama (Introducing the Unit TG #2) • discuss how families are affected by employment changes (Introducing the Model TG #1)	• TOC 14: Tracking Expectations • TOC 14: Tracking Expectations
(LI1.05P)	• make inferences based on the information and ideas presented in texts	• speculate on what happens before and after model (Extending the Model TG #2)	• AR 23: Script
(LI1.06B)	• use specific references from a text to support opinions and judgments	• consider audition advice and conduct mock auditions (Extending the Model TG #1)	• TOC 14: Tracking Expectations
Overall (LIV.02P)	• demonstrate an understanding of the elements of a variety of literary and informational forms, with a focus on plays, short stories, and newspaper and magazine articles	• compare four forms of narrative writing (Looking Over Narrative Writing Forms SB #1)	• TOC 14: Tracking Expectations
Specific (LI2.01P)	• use knowledge of elements of drama, such as plot and subplot, character development and revelation, conflict, dialogue, and stage directions, to understand and interpret texts in the genre	• attend performance of local theatre group and question actors and director (Introducing the Unit TG #4) • question local playwright about crafting a play (Introducing the Unit TG #5) • understand and interpret short story (Investigating the Model SB #1–8)	• TOC 14: Tracking Expectations • TOC 14: Tracking Expectations • TOC 14: Tracking Expectations
Overall (LIV.03B)	• identify and explain the effect of specific elements of style in a variety of literary and informational texts		
Specific (LI3.03P)	• explain how authors and editors use design elements to help convey meaning	• identify script forms and discuss format (Introducing the Unit TG #3)	• TOC 14: Tracking Expectations
WRITING			
Overall (WRV.01P)	• use print and electronic sources to gather information and explore ideas for their written work	• gather and organize information and ideas for script (Writer's Workshop SB #1–6)	• AR 23: Script
Specific (WR1.01P)	• investigate potential topics by asking questions, identifying information needs, and developing research plans to gather data	• generate and clarify details for humorous personal narrative (Using the Narrative Writing Forms TG #1)	• AR 10: Humorous Personal Narrative
(WR1.02P)	• locate and record information and ideas from print and electronic sources, including newspapers and magazines, dictionaries, encyclopedias, vertical files, and electronic databases	• write about role-playing experiences from childhood and analyze their appeal (Introducing the Unit TG #1)	• TOC 14: Tracking Expectations
Overall (WRV.02P)	• identify the literary and informational forms suited to specific purposes and audiences and use the forms appropriately in their own writing, with an emphasis on communicating information accurately		

AR=Assessment Rubric   EP=Extra Practice   SB=Student Book   SSEC=Student Self-Evaluation Checklist   TG=Teacher's Guide   TOC=Teacher Observation Checklist

GRADE 9 EXPECTATIONS	DEMONSTRATION OF LEARNING	ASSESSMENT TOOLS
WRITING (continued)		
Specific (WR2.03P) • demonstrate an understanding of literary and informational forms of writing, such as letters, personal narratives, short stories, answers to homework questions, summaries, and reports on research topics, by selecting a form appropriate to the specific purpose and audience for each piece of writing	• write simple dialogue using script template (Writer's Workshop TG #1) • work in groups to record dialogue on template (Writer's Workshop TG #2) • write a script of a scene from favourite short story or novel (More Challenge TG) • write a humorous personal narrative (Using the Narrative Writing Forms SB #1) • write a script about two imaginary beings (Using the Narrative Writing Forms SB #2) • write essay on element of short story (Using the Narrative Writing Forms SB #3)	• AR 23: Script • AR 23: Script • AR 23: Script • AR 10: Humorous Personal Narrative • AR 23: Script • AR 8: Expository Writing
Overall (WRV.03P) • use a variety of forms of writing to express themselves, clarify their ideas, and engage the audience's attention, imagination, and interest	• work in groups to write a script (Writer's Workshop TG #3) • write draft of script (Writer's Workshop SB #7) • write a humorous personal narrative (Using the Narrative Writing Forms SB #1) • write a script about two imaginary beings (Using the Narrative Writing Forms SB #2) • write an essay on an element of a short story (Using the Narrative Writing Forms SB #3)	• AR 23: Script • AR 23: Script • AR 10: Humorous Personal Narrative • AR 23: Script • AR 8: Expository Writing
Specific (WR3.02P) • structure expository paragraphs using a topic sentence, supporting sentences to develop the topic, connecting words to link the sentences, and a concluding sentence	• write an essay on an element of a short story (Using the Narrative Writing Forms SB #3)	• AR 8: Expository Writing
Overall (WRV.04B) • revise their written work, collaboratively and independently, with a focus on support for ideas, accuracy, clarity, and unity	• revise script (Writer's Workshop SB #8) • revise humorous personal narrative (Using the Narrative Writing Forms SB #1) • revise script about two imaginary beings (Using the Narrative Writing Forms SB #2) • revise essay on an element of a short story (Using the Narrative Writing Forms SB #3)	• AR 23: Script • AR 10: Humorous Personal Narrative • AR 23: Script • AR 8: Expository Writing
Specific (WR4.03P) • make constructive suggestions to peers, using prompts, checklists, open-ended statements, and questions	• list criteria to assess effectiveness of scenes (Oral Language Extension TG #1)	• AR 5: Dramatization
(WR4.04B) • consider reactions from teachers, peers, and others in revising and editing written work	• workshop scripts (Oral Language Extension SB)	• AR 23: Script
Overall (WRV.05B) • edit and proofread to produce final drafts, using correct grammar, spelling, and punctuation, according to the conventions of standard Canadian English specified for this course, with the support of print and electronic resources when appropriate	• edit and proofread script (Writer's Workshop SB #8) • edit and proofread personal narrative (Using the Narrative Writing Forms SB #1) • edit and proofread script about two imaginary beings (Using the Narrative Writing Forms SB #2) • edit and proofread essay on an element of a short story (Using the Narrative Writing Forms SB #3)	• AR 23: Script • AR 10: Humorous Personal Narrative • AR 23: Script • AR 8: Expository Writing
Specific (WR5.06P) • construct complete and correct compound and complex sentences, using the following sentence components as required: subject, predicate, object, subject complement; main and subordinate clauses; prepositional phrases	• identify phrases used in script dialogue (Grammar TG #1) • identify phrases (Grammar TG #2) • identify prepositional and participial phrases (Grammar SB #1–3) • avoid misplaced and dangling modifiers (Usage & Style TG #1–2) • avoid misplaced and dangling modifiers (Usage & Style SB #1–2) • identify prepositional and participial phrases (EP: Grammar) • eliminate misplaced and dangling modifiers (EP: Usage & Style)	• TOC 4: Grammar • TOC 4: Grammar • TOC 4: Grammar • TOC 15: Usage & Style • TOC 15: Usage & Style • TOC 4: Grammar • TOC 15: Usage & Style

AR=Assessment Rubric   EP=Extra Practice   SB=Student Book   SSEC=Student Self-Evaluation Checklist   TG=Teacher's Guide   TOC=Teacher Observation Checklist

GRADE 9 EXPECTATIONS	DEMONSTRATION OF LEARNING	ASSESSMENT TOOLS
WRITING (continued)		
(WR5.11B) • use knowledge of a wide range of spelling patterns and rules to identify, analyze, and correct spelling errors	• use mnemonic devices for difficult words (Word Study & Spelling TG #1–2)	• TOC 16: Word Study & Spelling
(WR5.16B) • adapt punctuation and capitalization for the special requirements of direct quotations, scripts, dialogue, and poetry	• identify and use adaptations of punctuation and capitalization in dialogue (Mechanics SB #2–4) • identify mechanical devices used for dialogue (EP: Mechanics)	• TOC 8: Mechanics • TOC 8: Mechanics
LANGUAGE		
Overall (LGV.01P) • use knowledge of vocabulary and language conventions to speak, write, and read clearly and correctly		
Specific (LG1.02B) • identify and explain examples of slang, jargon, dialect, and colloquialism, as well as of standard Canadian English, in literary texts and their own oral and written work	• identify examples of slang in transcripts of conversation (Mechanics TG) • identify examples of slang and dialect (Using the Narrative Writing Forms SB #4)	• TOC 8: Mechanics • TOC 16: Word Study & Spelling
(LG1.03B) • identify words borrowed from other languages, and words and terms recently introduced to describe new ideas, inventions, and products, and explain their origins	• find word roots (Word Study & Spelling TG #2) • find word origins in Shakespearean plays (Word Origins SB) • find English words matching Latin roots (EP: Word Study & Spelling) • identify invented words and acronyms (Using the Narrative Writing Forms SB #4)	• TOC 16: Word Study & Spelling • TOC 16: Word Study & Spelling • TOC 16: Word Study & Spelling • TOC 16: Word Study & Spelling
(LG1.04B) • select words and phrases appropriate to informal and formal styles, to suit the purpose and intended audience of oral and written work	• identify passages that show informal speech (Mechanics SB #1, 5)	• TOC 8: Mechanics
(LG1.05P) • recognize, describe, and use correctly, in oral and written language, the language structures of standard Canadian English and its conventions of grammar and usage, including: – components of sentences: subject, predicate, object, subject complement, prepositional phrases, main and subordinate clauses	• identify phrases used in script dialogue (Grammar TG #1) • identify phrases (Grammar TG #2) • identify prepositional and participial phrases (Grammar SB #1–3) • avoid misplaced and dangling modifiers (Usage & Style TG #1–2) • avoid misplaced and dangling modifiers (Usage & Style TG #1–2) • identify prepositional and participial phrases (EP: Grammar) • eliminate misplaced and dangling modifiers (EP: Usage & Style)	• TOC 4: Grammar • TOC 4: Grammar • TOC 4: Grammar • TOC 15: Usage & Style • TOC 15: Usage & Style • TOC 4: Grammar • TOC 15: Usage & Style
Overall (LGV.02B) • use listening techniques and oral communication skills to participate in classroom discussions and more formal activities, such as storytelling, role playing, and reporting/presenting, for specific purposes and audiences	• read lines in workshopping scripts with classmates (Oral Language Extension TG #2) • present reader's theatre performance of scenes before and after model (More Support TG) • prepare a taped performance of a play (Using the Narrative Writing Forms TG #2)	• SSEC 5: Oral Presentation • AR 9: Group Presentation • AR 5: Dramatization
Specific (LG2.01P) • use listening techniques and oral communication skills to participate in group discussions	• discuss the value of work (Introducing the Model TG #2) • share ideas on family relocation (Introducing the Model TG #3) • identify ways to demonstrate group accountability (Writer's Workshop TG #3) • work in a group to plan and write an essay (Using the Narrative Writing Forms TG #3)	• TOC 11: Speaking • TOC 11: Speaking • SSEC 2: Group Work • TOC 5: Group Work

AR=Assessment Rubric   EP=Extra Practice   SB=Student Book   SSEC=Student Self-Evaluation Checklist   TG=Teacher's Guide   TOC=Teacher Observation Checklist

GRADE 9 EXPECTATIONS	DEMONSTRATION OF LEARNING	ASSESSMENT TOOLS
LANGUAGE (continued)		
(LG2.05P) • practise with cue cards, use breathing exercises, and rehearse with peers (and with visual aids and technology, if used), to ensure confident delivery in oral presentations	• use tongue-twisters as performance warm-up (More Oral Language TG)	• TOC 11: Speaking
MEDIA STUDIES		
Overall (MDV.01P) • identify and describe the elements, intended audiences, and production practices of a variety of media forms	• compare film versions of Shakespearean scene (Using the Narrative Writing Forms TG #5) • compare film version of Shakespearean scene with original version (Using the Narrative Writing Forms SB #5)	• AR 21: Response to Media • AR 21: Response to Media
Specific (MD1.02P) • identify and describe the elements used to structure media works in a variety of forms	• examine differences between stage plays and screenplays (More Media TG)	• AR 21: Response to Media
Overall (MDV.02P) • use knowledge of a variety of media forms, purposes, and audiences to create media works		
Specific (MD2.01P) • adapt a work of literature for presentation in another media form	• practise art exercises before creating storyboard (Media Link TG)	• AR 12: Media Product

AR=Assessment Rubric   EP=Extra Practice   SB=Student Book   SSEC=Student Self-Evaluation Checklist   TG=Teacher's Guide   TOC=Teacher Observation Checklist

INSTRUCTIONAL STRATEGIES FOR THE APPLIED COURSE

LEARNING GOALS

- write a scene for a script
- use prepositional and participial phrases correctly
- use punctuation in scripts correctly
- identify dialect
- avoid misplaced and dangling modifiers
- create personal and class dictionaries of newly encountered words

CHECKPOINT

Sample criteria for a script:

- presents characters in conflict
- has a setting that meets requirements of plot, sets mood, or conveys information about characters and/or theme
- includes ways to enhance dramatic value through dialogue, action, and presentation
- has dialogue or actions that convey strong impression of characters
- may convey meaning through absence of words
- uses scenes to serve a particular purpose

PLANNING INFORMATION

Links to Other Nelson English 9 Resources

Literature & Media 9
Drama—See the Drama unit for five script selections, pp. 204–282.

Write Source 2000
Misplaced Modifiers—"Misplaced Modifiers," p. 91; **Prepositional Phrases**—"Prepositional Phrase," p. 455

INTRODUCING THE UNIT

The activities on page 53 from the Academic Course are appropriate for the Applied Course.

1. (WR1.02P—TOC 14: Tracking Expectations)
2. (LI1.02P—TOC 14: Tracking Expectations)
3. (LI3.03P—TOC 14: Tracking Expectations)
4. (LI2.01P—TOC 14: Tracking Expectations)
5. (LI2.01P—TOC 14: Tracking Expectations)

INTRODUCING THE MODEL

The activities on page 53 from the Academic Course are appropriate for the Applied Course.

1. (LI1.02P—TOC 14: Tracking Expectations)
2. (LG2.01P—TOC 11: Speaking)
3. (LG2.01P—TOC 11: Speaking)

INVESTIGATING THE MODEL

Answers:
See the Academic Course on pages 54–55 for answers.
Student Book (LI2.01P—TOC 14: Tracking Expectations)

EXTENDING THE MODEL

Activities #2–3 on page 55 from the Academic Course are appropriate for the Applied Course.

1. (LI1.06B—TOC 14: Tracking Expectations)
2. (LI1.05P—AR 23: Script)

WRITER'S WORKSHOP

1. Because scripts are an unfamiliar writing form to many students, script templates are helpful in allowing students to focus on the content rather than the form of their scripts. Prepare a script template with blocks down the left margin (for characters' names) and two to three lines to the right of each block (for dialogue). Rather than overwhelming them with the task of writing an entire scene, begin by having students write a simple dialogue using the template to familiarize them with the script form. (WR2.03P—AR 23: Script)

2. To support the above activity, have students form groups of four. In each group, one pair will carry on a brief conversation following a simple prompt (e.g., an incident at the last dance, plans for an upcoming concert) while the other pair will record the substance of their dialogue on the template. At the end of the conversation, they compare notes and fill in any gaps in their script. Then the speakers assume the role of recorders as the others engage in a brief conversation. Following this activity, groups share with the class not only their scripts but also what they have learned about writing dialogue. (WR2.03P—AR 23: Script)

3. Consider having students work in groups of two or three to draft, polish, and submit a final script. Working in a group will enable students to brainstorm orally a variety of characters and dramatic situations, and generate and test the realism of dialogue. Ensure that students recognize the criteria that will determine the successful completion of any task representing a portion of the assessment. Students should identify ways they can demonstrate their accountability (e.g., include an opportunity for self- and/or group-assessment, require the completion of a work log outlining tasks performed). (WRV.03P—AR 23: Script; LG2.01P—TOC 5: Group Work)

Student Book 1.–6. (WRV.01P—AR 23: Script); 7. (WRV.03P—AR 23: Script); 8. (WRV.04B—AR 23: Script; WRV.05B—AR 23: Script)

ORAL LANGUAGE EXTENSION

1. The activity on page 56 from the Academic Course is appropriate for the Applied Course. (WR4.03P—AR 5: Dramatization)

2. Rather than having students memorize the lines of the scenes they will enact in the Oral Language Extension, teachers may prefer to have students read the lines, focusing on oral delivery, use of gesture, placement on stage, and movement. (LGV.02B—SSEC 5: Oral Presentation)

Student Book (WR4.04B—AR 23: Script)

GRAMMAR

The Grammar activities on page 56 from the Academic Course are appropriate for the Applied Course.
   1. (WR5.06P—TOC 4: Grammar; LG1.05P—TOC 4: Grammar)

   2. (WR5.06P—TOC 4: Grammar; LG1.05P—TOC 4: Grammar)

Answers:

See the Academic Course on pages 56–57 for answers.
   1. (WR5.06P—TOC 4: Grammar; LG1.05P—TOC 4: Grammar)

   2. (WR5.06P—TOC 4: Grammar; LG1.05P—TOC 4: Grammar)

   3. (WR5.06P—TOC 4: Grammar; LG1.05P—TOC 4: Grammar)

Student Book 1.–3. (WR5.06P—TOC 4: Grammar; LG1.05P—TOC 4: Grammar)

MEDIA LINK

The activity on page 57 from the Academic Course is appropriate for the Applied Course. (MD2.01D—AR 12: Media Product)

Student Book (MD2.01D—AR 12: Media Product)

MORE CHALLENGE

Have students choose a pivotal scene from a favourite short story or novel and rewrite it in script form. The script should reveal not only the conflict between the people involved but also a sense of their characters. (WR2.03P—AR 23: Script)

MORE SUPPORT

Obtain copies of Frank Moher's *Odd Jobs*, published by Blizzard Publishing/International Reading Theatre. Students could present a reader's theatre performance of selected scenes occuring before and after the model. (LGV.02B—AR 9: Group Presentation)

MORE ORAL LANGUAGE

Students nervous about performing before their class can be put at ease through the use of warm-up activities. One of the least threatening is the oral presentation of tongue-twisters. Assign a different tongue-twister to each student. Students then work in pairs to practise their delivery keeping in mind appropriate tone, inflection, and physical gestures. Pairs perform before the class by repeating their tongue-twisters at least five times, speaking to each other as if in conversation. The short length of the tongue-twisters means that students need not memorize lengthy lines—instead, they focus on the physical and oral delivery. Since most people make mistakes when repeating tongue-twisters, the humorous results can relieve performance anxiety. (LG2.05P—TOC 11: Speaking)

MORE MEDIA

Students could examine the differences between stage plays and screenplays. For example, stage plays are driven primarily by dialogue while screenplays are a much more visual medium. To illustrate the difference, have students view the under-credit (opening) sequences of several films and identify all the information a viewer receives about a film (e.g., setting, tone, information about main character) before the main action begins. Have them suggest an under-credit sequence for a film version of "Odd Jobs." (MD1.02P—AR 21: Response to Media)

MECHANICS

The Mechanics activity on page 57 from the Academic Course is appropriate for the Applied Course. (LG1.02B—TOC 8: Mechanics)

Answers:

See the Academic Course on page 57 for answers.

1. (LG1.04B—TOC 8: Mechanics)

2. (WR5.16B—TOC 8: Mechanics; LG1.07B—TOC 8: Mechanics)

3.–5. (LGV.01P—TOC 8: Mechanics)

Student Book 1., 5. (LG1.04B—TOC 8: Mechanics); 2.–4. (WR5.16B—TOC 8: Mechanics)

USAGE & STYLE

The Usage & Style activities on pages 57–58 from the Academic Course are appropriate for the Applied Course.

1. (WR5.06P—TOC 15: Usage & Style; LG1.05P—TOC 15: Usage & Style)

2. (WR5.06P—TOC 15: Usage & Style; LG1.05P—TOC 15: Usage & Style)

Answers:

See the Academic Course on page 58 for answers.

Student Book 1.–2. (WR5.06P—TOC 15: Usage & Style; LG1.05P—TOC 15: Usage & Style)

WORD STUDY & SPELLING

The Word Study & Spelling activities on page 58 from the Academic Course are appropriate for the Applied Course.

1. (WR5.11B—TOC 16: Word Study & Spelling)

2. (LG1.03B—TOC 16: Word Study & Spelling)

Answers:

See the Academic Course on pages 58–59 for answers.

Student Book 1.–2. (WR5.11B—TOC 16: Word Study & Spelling)

WORD ORIGINS

Answers:

See the Academic Course on page 59 for answers.

Student Book (LG1.03B—TOC 16: Word Study & Spelling)

ANSWERS TO EXTRA PRACTICE

See the Academic Course on pages 59–60 for answers.

Grammar

(WR5.06P—TOC 4: Grammar; LG1.05P—TOC 4: Grammar)

Mechanics

(WR5.16B—TOC 8: Mechanics)

Usage & Style

(WR5.06P—TOC 15: Usage & Style; LG1.05P—TOC 15: Usage & Style)

Word Study & Spelling

(LG1.03B—TOC 16: Word Study & Spelling)

Reflect and Build on Your Learning

Reflecting on Narrative Writing Forms

Answers:

1. Student work.

2. Possible answer

Other narrative forms include anecdote, autobiography, biography, chronicle, confession, dialogue, diary, documentary, fable, fairy tale, fantasy, folktale, historical narrative, legend, memoir, monologue, myth, novel, parable, screenplay, and urban tale.

Example: Legends are stories that are often based on some kernel of truth—the hero or heroine may have been a real person, or the event in the legend really may have happened. However, as legends are passed down, storytellers exaggerate aspects of the story, so legends often end up to be more fiction than fact.

Student Book 1.–2. (LIV.01P—TOC 13: Tracking Expectations)

Looking Over Narrative Writing Forms

Answers:

1. Possible answer

CRITERIA	PERSONAL NARRATIVE	SHORT STORY	SCRIPT	LEGEND
Dialogue	usually limited use; establishes context	moderate to extensive use; reveals character and advances the plot	used extensively to reveal character and define the action	usually limited use; reveals the character of the hero/heroine
Character	characters are usually "flat"	main characters are "round" while secondary characters are "flat"	main characters are "round" while secondary characters are "flat"	characters are usually "flat," revealing a single, dominant trait
Conflict	usually external	may be internal or external or a combination of both	may be internal or external or a combination of both	usually external
Setting	provides a physical context for the conflict	provides a physical context for the conflict and often helps convey an understanding of the main character	provides a physical context for the conflict and helps convey an understanding of character	usually plays a major role in establishing the conflict and functions as a backdrop for the hero/heroine to demonstrate his/her particular heroic quality
Resolution	focuses on the impact the event/incident has on the narrator	embodies a change in character or situation that reveals an understanding about life and living	embodies a change in character or situation that reveals an understanding about life and living	emphasizes a particular attribute of the hero/heroine

Student Book 1. (LIV.02P—TOC 13: Tracking Expectations)

USING THE NARRATIVE WRITING FORMS

1. Encourage students to tell their event to a partner as a means of generating/clarifying details. Caution students about presenting former teachers and/or classmates in a negative light. If they must do so, suggest they change the names of people involved and make sure that those written about are unidentifiable. (WR1.01P—AR 10: Humorous Personal Narrative)

Student Book 1. (WRV.03P—AR 10: Humorous Personal Narrative; WRV.04B—AR 10: Humorous Personal Narrative; WRV.05B—AR 10: Humorous Personal Narrative)

2. An excellent one-act radio play called "Epilogue: The Weans," by Robert Nathan (CBS Radio Workshop Play, 1960), presents future humans excavating the ruins of several twentieth-century American cities and reporting incorrect (and humorous) interpretations of cultural icons (e.g., rock-and-roll music, Academy Awards). Besides an effective model for students to follow when writing their own scripts, it offers a valuable opportunity for oral language development as students can work in groups to prepare a taped performance of the play. (An alternative approach is to enlist the aid of a senior drama instructor whose older students could prepare a recording of the radio play for presentation to the class before students work on their own scripts.) (LGV.02B—AR 5: Dramatization)

Student Book 2. (WRV.03P—AR 23: Script; WRV.04B—AR 23: Script; WRV.05B—AR 23: Script)

3. Since this section focuses on narrative writing and this task requires students to write exposition, it is worthwhile to have them review the elements of the expository essay before they begin. Refer students to the essay on pages 14–15 of the student book, and ask them to read it twice, first for content, then again to identify particular characteristics of essay form (components such as introduction, body, and conclusion; organization of main ideas in single paragraphs; development of supporting details; use of transitional expressions).

Before students attempt their individual essays, have them write a group essay analyzing a particular element of "The Kayak." For example, students might focus on the role that setting plays in the development of the story's theme. Through whole-class discussion, students could identify three to four ideas that might be included in the essay, after which each group would write a paragraph on one of these ideas (for comparison purposes, two groups could work on the same idea). Subsequent whole-class sharing and discussion of work (presented on the overhead projector) can identify strengths of each paragraph as well as address weaknesses and strategies for improvement. Finally, students can identify the most effective order for their paragraphs as well as a variety of ways to introduce and conclude the essay. The value of this approach is that, besides offering students a model to follow when writing their own essays, the group format makes the process nonthreatening and supportive (the class can comment on a group's paragraph rather than an individual's paragraph). (LG2.01P—TOC 5: Group Work)

Student Book 3. (WRV.03P—AR 8: Expository Writing; WR3.02P—AR 8: Expository Writing; WRV.04B—AR 8: Expository Writing; WRV.05B—AR 8: Expository Writing)

4. Possible answers

BORROWED	SLANG/INVENTED	DIALECT	ACRONYMS
chiffon (French) chimpanzee (West African) chocolate (Spanish) khaki (Hindustani) nouveau riche (French) debonair (French) bodega (Spanish) bravo (Italian) briquette (French)	oly (snapping one end of a skateboard to get off the ground) buff (muscular) hoopdee (junky car) illed on (cursed out) peeps (group of friends) phat (sweet, nice) skeev (nasty—East Boston only) 'rents (parents) 24/7 (all the time)	spigot (tap) glowworm (firefly) chesterfield (sofa) bugaboo (object of terror) parlour (living room) pram (baby carriage) autoroute (highway) lift (elevator) flat (apartment)	AWOL (absent without official leave) ARROW (antiresonant reflecting optical waveguide) ASCII (American standard code for information interchange) DRAM (dynamic random access memory) DVD (digital versatile disc) HTML (hypertext markup language) HTTP (hypertext transport protocol) IRC (internet relay chat)

Student Book 4. (LG1.02B—TOC 16: Word Study & Spelling; LG1.03B—TOC 16: Word Study & Spelling)

5. An interesting extension of this activity is to have students compare various film versions of the same Shakespearean scene. For example, students might view the balcony scene in *Romeo & Juliet* as presented in George Cukor's 1936 film, Franco Zeffirelli's 1968 film, and Baz Luhrmann's 1996 film, examining not only the differences in cinematic techniques but also the influence of the culture of the time period in which each film was made. (MDV.01P—AR 21: Response to Media)

Student Book 5. (MDV.01P—AR 21: Response to Media)

GRAMMAR

NAME: _____ DATE: _____

1. Tell whether each of the italicized word groups below is a phrase. If it is a phrase, tell what kind.

   a) I told her it was *the silliest* thing I'd ever heard. _____

   b) I think *that will do.* _____

   c) Well, you're entitled to *your own* opinion. _____

   d) Ginny *was going* to Regina to work. _____

   e) Mrs. Phipps's garage was *a rat's nest.* _____

   f) I will *most certainly* finish spreading the leaves. _____

   g) Well, *I have* all winter, don't I? _____

   h) Tim planned to finish *the painting* in the basement. _____

2. Underline any participial phrases you find in the following sentences and draw an arrow to the noun each phrase is modifying. If there is no participial phrase, write *None.*

   a) Covered in cobwebs, the interior of the garage was not a comfortable place to work.

   b) The leaves packed in the plastic bags would protect the flower beds from cold temperatures.

   c) Tim jumped all over the bags of leaves.

   d) The job waiting in Regina was the new beginning that Ginny wanted.

   e) Mrs. Phipps was unprepared for Tim's reaction.

   f) Staring in disbelief, Tim watched as Mrs. Phipps walked away.

   g) Mrs. Phipps looked at the bags piled by the walkway.

   h) Starting toward the bags, Mrs. Phipps said, "I'll just have to spread them myself."

3. Combine the following sentences by making one a participial phrase and inserting it into the other.

   a) Ginny hoped Regina would be a fresh start. She looked forward to moving. _____

   b) Tim was afraid of starting over again. He was willing to lose his wife. _____

   c) Mrs. Phipps understood the fear Tim felt. She wanted him to confront it. _____

4. Tell whether each of the italicized prepositional phrases below is acting as an adjective or an adverb.

   a) Ginny went *to Regina* at the end of the week. _____

   b) The brown spots *in the lawn* were fertilizer burns. _____

   c) Mrs. Phipps glances *at the bags.* _____

   d) She found the rake *in the garage.* _____

   e) The piece of paper *on the table* was Tim's last cheque. _____

MECHANICS

NAME: _____ DATE: _____

Explain at least five mechanical devices used in the following script to help readers know how the dialogue should sound. Give an example of each device.

JERRY: Finished yer homework yet, Tom?

TOM: S'far's I know, I done it all. [*suspiciously*] Whaddya wanna know for?

JERRY: Well, ah ... you see ... ah ... I kinda didn't have time to get all mine done ...

TOM: And you wanna copy mine, right?

JERRY: Well, if it's not too much trouble ...

TOM: Nah, no trouble at all. [*sarcastically*] I don't mind that I spent almost two hours on it last night while you and Jake went to the movies.

JERRY: Now, you coulda come, too, if you'd—

TOM: But I didn't. I did my homework instead. Like YOU were supposed to do.

JERRY: C'mon, buddy. What're friends for?

TOM: Friends don't use other friends.

JERRY: Now what's THAT supposed to mean?

_____

_____

_____

_____

_____

_____

_____

_____

_____

_____

USAGE & STYLE

NAME: _____ DATE: _____

1. Rewrite the following sentences, making changes that will correct any modifier problems. If a sentence contains no modifier problem, write *Correct.*

    a) Stacked by the garage, Tim found several cans of old paint.

    _____

    _____

    b) Mrs. Phipps finally found the lawn spreader exhausted in the garage.

    _____

    _____

    c) Lying in the gutter, Tim cleaned up the fallen leaves.

    _____

    _____

    d) Startled by a knock on the door, Mrs. Phipps found Tim's wife, Ginny, waiting on the step.

    _____

    _____

    e) Insecticide was applied to the brown patch by a pest-control expert on the lawn.

    _____

    _____

    f) Bent nearly double, the garbage truck took the broken rake away.

    _____

    _____

WORD STUDY & SPELLING

NAME: _____   DATE: _____

1. Below is a list of Latin roots of English words that appear in the script *Odd Jobs.* Find the English word that matches each root. Check an etymological dictionary to see if you are right.

    a) contra _____

    b) lassus _____

    c) intitulare_____

    d) opinio_____

    e) basis _____

    f) certus _____

    g) opportunus_____

    h) dictare _____

    i) visitare _____

    j) nidus _____

UNIT 4: POETRY

ACADEMIC EXPECTATIONS

GRADE 9 EXPECTATIONS		DEMONSTRATION OF LEARNING	ASSESSMENT TOOLS
LITERATURE STUDIES AND READING			
Overall (LIV.01D)	• read and demonstrate an understanding of a variety of literary and informational texts, from contemporary and historical periods	• discuss importance of rhyme scheme in poetry (Extending the Models TG #2) • keep a poetry log (More Support TG)	• AR 22: Response to Reading • AR 22: Response to Reading
Specific (LI1.01D)	• describe information, ideas, opinions, and themes in print and electronic texts they have read during the year from different cultures and historical periods and in a variety of genres, including novels, short stories, plays, poems, biographies, short essays, and articles from newspapers, magazines, and encyclopedias	• share understanding of what poetry is (Introducing the Unit TG #1) • demonstrate understanding of poems (Investigating the Models SB #1–8) • collect poems with same theme as a model poem (Extending the Models TG #1)	• TOC 13: Tracking Expectations • TOC 13: Tracking Expectations • AR 22: Response to Reading
(LI1.02D)	• select and read texts for different purposes, with an emphasis on recognizing the elements of literary genres and the organization of informational materials, collecting and assessing information, responding imaginatively, and exploring human experiences and values	• share and discuss favourite poems (Introducing the Unit TG #2) • consider why poetry was included in descriptive writing in student book (Introducing the Models TG #1) • consider difference between lyric and narrative poetry (Introducing the Models TG #2)	• AR 22: Response to Reading • AR 22: Response to Reading • AR 22: Response to Reading
(LI1.08D)	• explain how the background of the author might influence the information and ideas in a text	• discuss how socio-economic realities can influence what poets write (More Challenge TG)	• AR 22: Response to Reading
Overall (LIV.03B)	• identify and explain the effect of specific elements of style in a variety of literary and informational texts		
Specific (LI3.02D)	• explain how authors use stylistic devices, such as simile, metaphor, personification, imagery, foreshadowing, onomatopoeia, oxymoron, alliteration, and symbol, to achieve particular effects in their writing	• discuss and create examples of simile, metaphor, and personification (Usage & Style TG) • identify examples of stylistic devices in poetry (Usage & Style SB #1–6) • use stylistic devices in poetry correctly (EP: Usage & Style)	• TOC 15: Usage & Style • TOC 15: Usage & Style • TOC 15: Usage & Style
(LI3.03D)	• explain how authors and editors use design elements to help communicate ideas	• arrange words of poem on page (Writer's Workshop TG #1)	• TOC 13: Tracking Expectations
WRITING			
Overall (WRV.01D)	• use a variety of print and electronic sources to gather information and explore ideas for their written work	• gather and organize information and ideas for poem (Writer's Workshop SB #1–6)	• AR 17: Poetry
Overall (WRV.02D)	• identify the literary and informational forms suited to various purposes and audiences and use the forms appropriately in their own writing, with an emphasis on supporting opinions or interpretations with specific information		
Specific (WR2.01D)	• demonstrate an understanding of literary and informational forms, such as myths, poems, short stories, scripts, advertisements, formal letters, reviews, and supported opinion essays, by selecting and using forms of writing appropriate to different purposes and audiences	• write poem presenting positive and negative aspects of something tangible (Extending the Models TG #3) • write rhyming poems (Writer's Workshop TG #2)	• AR 17: Poetry • AR 17: Poetry

AR=Assessment Rubric   EP=Extra Practice   SB=Student Book   SSEC=Student Self-Evaluation Checklist   TG=Teacher's Guide   TOC=Teacher Observation Checklist

GRADE 9 EXPECTATIONS		DEMONSTRATION OF LEARNING	ASSESSMENT TOOLS
WRITING (continued)			
Overall (WRV.03D)	• use a variety of organizational techniques to present ideas and supporting details logically and coherently in written work	• arrange phrases and sentences for poem on page (Writer's Workshop SB #7)	• AR 17: Poetry
Overall (WRV.04D)	• revise their written work, independently and collaboratively, with a focus on support for ideas and opinions, accuracy, clarity, and unity	• revise poem (Writer's Workshop SB #8)	• AR 17: Poetry
Overall (WRV.05D)	• edit and proofread to produce final drafts, using correct grammar, spelling, and punctuation, according to the conventions of standard Canadian English, with the support of print and electronic resources when appropriate	• edit and proofread poem (Writer's Workshop SB #8)	• AR 17: Poetry
Specific (WR5.06D)	• construct complete and correct compound and complex sentences, using the following sentence components as required: subject, predicate, object, subject complement; main and subordinate clauses; prepositional and participial phrases	• identify simple subject and simple predicate (Grammar TG #1) • create and identify simple subject and simple predicate in long, convoluted sentences (Grammar TG #2) • determine main and subordinate clauses (Grammar TG #3) • write two versions of sentences—with main action in main clause and main action in subordinate clause (Grammar TG #4) • use subjects and predicates, main and subordinate clauses correctly (Grammar SB #1–6) • use subjects and predicates, main and subordinate clauses correctly (EP: Grammar)	• TOC 4: Grammar • TOC 4: Grammar • TOC 4: Grammar • TOC 4: Grammar • TOC 4: Grammar • TOC 4: Grammar
(WR5.16B)	• adapt punctuation and capitalization for the special requirements of direct quotations, scripts, dialogue, and poetry	• discuss use of punctuation in poem (Mechanics TG) • analyze use of punctuation in model poems (Mechanics SB #1–5) • use punctuation correctly in poetry (EP: Mechanics)	• TOC 8: Mechanics • TOC 8: Mechanics • TOC 8: Mechanics
LANGUAGE			
Overall (LGV.01D)	• use knowledge of vocabulary and language conventions to speak, write, and read competently using a level of language appropriate to the purpose and audience		
Specific (LG1.01B)	• describe strategies used to expand vocabulary and provide evidence of other vocabulary-building activities	• determine meaning of prefixes (Word Study & Spelling TG) • find and explain meaning of words with prefix -epi (Word Origins SB) • find and use words with prefixes (Word Study & Spelling TG #1–6) • identify and use words with prefixes (EP: Word Study & Spelling)	• TOC 16: Word Study & Spelling • TOC 16: Word Study & Spelling • TOC 16: Word Study & Spelling • TOC 16: Word Study & Spelling

AR=Assessment Rubric   EP=Extra Practice   SB=Student Book   SSEC=Student Self-Evaluation Checklist   TG=Teacher's Guide   TOC=Teacher Observation Checklist

GRADE 9 EXPECTATIONS	DEMONSTRATION OF LEARNING	ASSESSMENT TOOLS
LANGUAGE (continued)		
(LG1.05D) • recognize, describe, and use correctly, in oral and written language, the language structures of standard Canadian English and its conventions of grammar and usage, including: – components of sentences: subject, predicate, object, subject complement, prepositional and participial phrases, main and subordinate clauses	• identify simple subject and simple predicate (Grammar TG #1) • create and identify simple subject and simple predicate in long, convoluted sentences (Grammar TG #2) • determine main and subordinate clauses (Grammar TG #3) • write two versions of sentences—with main action in main clause and main action in subordinate clause (Grammar TG #4) • use subjects and predicates, main and subordinate clauses correctly (Grammar SB #1–6) • use subjects and predicates, main and subordinate clauses correctly (EP: Grammar)	• TOC 4: Grammar • TOC 4: Grammar • TOC 4: Grammar • TOC 4: Grammar • TOC 4: Grammar • TOC 4: Grammar
Overall (LGV.02B) • use listening techniques and oral communication skills to participate in classroom discussions and more formal activities, such as storytelling, role playing, and reporting/ presenting, for specific purposes and audiences		
Specific (LG2.03D) • plan and make oral presentations to a small group or the class, selecting and using vocabulary and methods of delivery to suit audience and purpose	• present collection of poems as oral reading (Extending the Models TG #1) • give reader's theatre presentation of poem (Oral Language Extension SB) • present choral reading of poem (More Oral Language TG)	• AR 9: Group Presentation • SSEC 5: Oral Presentation • AR 9: Group Presentation
(LG2.04D) • use specific examples, facial expressions, gestures, intonation, humour, and visual aids and technology, as appropriate, to engage the audience's interest during oral presentations	• present oral delivery of poem including sound effects (Oral Language Extension SB)	• TOC 11: Speaking
MEDIA STUDIES		
Overall (MDV.01D) • use knowledge of the elements, intended audiences, and production practices of a variety of media forms to analyze specific media works	• interpret a music video (Media Link SB)	• AR 21: Response to Media
Overall (MDV.02D) • use knowledge of a variety of media forms, purposes, and audiences to create media works and describe their intended effect		
Specific (MD2.01D) • adapt a work of literature to another media form and determine what aspects have been strengthened and/or weakened by the adaptation	• plan filming of poem as video, using storyboard form (More Media TG)	• AR 12: Media Product

AR=Assessment Rubric   EP=Extra Practice   SB=Student Book   SSEC=Student Self-Evaluation Checklist   TG=Teacher's Guide   TOC=Teacher Observation Checklist

INSTRUCTIONAL STRATEGIES FOR THE ACADEMIC COURSE

PLANNING INFORMATION

Links to Other Nelson English 9 Resources

Literature & Media 9
Poetry—See the Poetry unit for 22 poetry selections, pp. 176–202.

Write Source 2000
Poetry—"Writing Poetry," pp. 193–207; **Main and Subordinate Clauses**—"Clauses,"
p. 436; **Prefixes**—"Prefixes," pp. 329–330; **Stylistic Devices**—"Writing Techniques,"
pp. 138–140, "Traditional Techniques of Poetry," pp. 202–203; **Subjects and
Predicates**—"Parts of a Sentence," pp. 434–435

LEARNING GOALS

- write a poem to explore your feelings
- use subjects and predicates correctly
- use main and subordinate clauses correctly
- adapt punctuation for poetry
- understand how authors use stylistic devices to achieve particular effects
- explore how prefixes affect the spelling of a word

INTRODUCING THE UNIT

1. Have students write about and then share with the class their understanding of what poetry is. Refer them to the explanation in the student book on page 66. Do they agree with either Coleridge's definition of poetry or the one offered in the text? Why or why not? (LI1.01D—TOC 13: Tracking Expectations)

2. Many students have difficulty reading poetry for understanding, often finding it difficult to reconcile the difference between the **text** (the actual words) of a poem and its **subtext** (the ideas and emotions that the poem evokes). To illustrate this difference, share one or two favourite poems of your own, reading them aloud and explaining why they appeal to you. Invite students to bring in their own favourite poems to share with the class. If time permits, set aside a few minutes each lesson during the unit for students to share and discuss favourite poems. (LI1.02D—AR 22: Response to Reading)

INTRODUCING THE MODELS

1. Ask students why they think poetry was included in the descriptive writing section of the student book. They might consider the use of figurative language to convey vivid impressions. Tell them that, as they read the three poems, they should focus not only on their content but also on the ideas and impressions that they evoke. (LI1.02D—AR 22: Response to Reading)

2. Students should be aware of the difference between lyric poetry (which presents a personal, often intense display of emotions) and narrative poetry (which tells a story). Explain that, as they read the three poems in the student book, they might consider what makes each one lyric rather than narrative in genre. (LI1.02D— AR 22: Response to Reading)

INVESTIGATING THE MODELS

Answers:

1. "Neither Out Far Nor In Deep"—People on a shoreline stand mesmerized watching a ship pass.
   "Energy"—A woman recalls a childhood memory of her father showing her that just as cold can be stored in an icehouse, heat can be stored in a woodpile.
   "Fingerprints"—Annoyed by a child's continual insolence, the narrator notices bruises on the child's arms and face.

2. Possible answer
   The image of the bruises in "Fingerprints" evokes a strong emotional response in many readers who react sympathetically to the battered child.

3. Possible questions posed about "Neither Out Far Nor In Deep": Why have the people gone to the beach in the first place? Why do you say they cannot look out far since nothing is blocking their view? What "watch" are the people keeping?

4. Possible answers
"Neither Out Far Nor In Deep"—"The wetter ground like glass / Reflects a standing gull." This image of life on land being reflected by water conveys the strong connection felt by people for the sea.
"Energy"—"And then, that miraculous discovery / in burning July," This image of burning heat is repeated in the reference to the woodpile, which in turn will be burned.
"Fingerprints"—"you sit with thin arms / crossed defiantly ... Your arms are thin, / aren't they?" The repetition of the image of thin arms, first as a statement and then as a question, emphasizes the change in the narrator's perspective toward the child.

5. The rhythmical pattern of the poem suggests the rhythmical motion of waves (or the ebb and flow of the tides—and life).

6. The free verse conveys the impression of a person speaking, sharing something of importance with the reader.

7. The repetitive quality of this rhyming pattern suggests a cycle that is repeated over and over, like the swing of a pendulum (the passage of time), which emphasizes the poet's assertion that "The people along the sand / ... look at the sea all day."

8. The line breaks in Frost's poem emphasize the rhyme scheme, and the space after every fourth line focuses attention on the content of each stanza (the people on the land, the ship on the sea, the contrast between the land and the sea, and the question the poet raises about the connection between the people and the sea).

In free verse, line breaks lend importance to words and phrases by isolating them, such as Gom's line "epiphanies of childhood," and Johnson's "Insolent child." and "Poor child." The short lines in both poems suggest a halting account of the experiences shared by the narrators, and the space in Johnson's poem emphasizes a difference between the first and second parts of the poem (i.e., a change in attitude toward the subject).

Student Book 1.–8. (LI1.01D—TOC 13: Tracking Expectations)

EXTENDING THE MODELS

1. Have students, working in groups of two to three, choose one of the student book poems as a central theme and then search for and compile a collection of five to seven other poems written about the same theme (e.g., students choosing "Neither Out Far Nor In Deep" might look for poems about the relationship between human beings and the sea). They might present their collection as an oral reading accompanied by a discussion of the way in which the various poets have presented the theme in their writing. (LI1.01D—AR 22: Response to Reading; LG2.03D—AR 9: Group Presentation)

2 Robert Frost once commented that writing poetry without rhyme is like playing tennis without a net. Have students discuss the validity of this comment, especially in light of the fact that Frost, too, wrote unrhymed poetry. Is rhyme more for the poet or for the reader? (LIV.01D—AR 22: Response to Reading)

3. Kim Johnson wrote "Fingerprints" using as a model the poem "Arctic Willow," in which the narrator at first disparages the tree, then sees beyond his superficial examination and recognizes the marvel of its survival in such a harsh environment. Encourage students to select something tangible toward which they

feel negatively. Then have them try to see it through more positive or sympathetic eyes, and present their dual observations in poem form. (WR2.01D—AR 17: Poetry)

Writer's Workshop

1. When poets write poems, they must not only consider the words they choose but how they will arrange these words on the page. The division of a poem into "lines" and their arrangement and spacing on the page influence the meaning a reader gets from a poem. The following are just a few of the reasons poets break and skip lines where they do: for a poem that rhymes, a line will end with a rhyming word so that the reader can easily *see* and *hear* the rhyme; for an important idea that needs to stand out or for the beginning of a new thought, a word or phrase will be written on a line by itself; and for showing a change in feeling, a line may be skipped. Choose a poem and present it to the class rewritten in paragraph form. Have students in groups of two or three read it carefully at least twice and decide where lines should end and, if they think it is necessary, where lines should be skipped. Once they are satisfied with the way the poem should look, have them copy it on a large sheet of chart paper. Mount the versions around the room and have the groups give reasons for their arrangement. (LI3.03D—TOC 13: Tracking Expectations)

2. Suggest that students find rhyming poems they like and read some to the rest of the class. One poet who often took rhyme to excess with comic results was Ogden Nash. An example of this is shown in his couplet "Poets aren't very useful, / Because they aren't consumeful or over produceful." Have students write rhyming poems using the strategy of generating a number of rhyming words and then choosing the most appropriate ones. (WR2.01D—AR 17: Poetry)

Student Book 1.–6. (WRV.01D—AR 17: Poetry); 7. (WRV.03D—AR 17: Poetry); 8. (WRV.04D—AR 17: Poetry; WRV.05D—AR 17: Poetry)

Oral Language Extension

Student Book (LG2.03D—SSEC 5: Oral Presentation; LG2.04D—TOC 11: Speaking)

Grammar

1. Emphasize that knowing the simple subject and simple predicate is the key to understanding the construction of a sentence—all other elements are added to one or other of these building blocks. Some students may need practice in identifying the simple subject and simple predicate, especially when other verb forms are present. Two rules for the simple predicate are: (1) **A verb ending in *-ing* cannot be the main verb unless a helping verb precedes it.** (2) **The simple predicate typically follows the simple subject in a sentence.** Give students the following pair of sentences and ask them to use the above rules to identify the simple subject and simple predicate in each. Help them recognize that *waiting* and *tugging* are not verbs but modifiers that provide information about the subject (*Tracey*). (WR5.06D—TOC 4: Grammar; LG1.05D—TOC 4: Grammar)

> Waiting in the doorway, Tracey nervously tugged at the sleeve of her sweater. (*Tracey/tugged*)

> Tracey waited in the doorway, nervously tugging at the sleeve of her sweater. (*Tracey/waited*)

2. Have students work in teams of three or four to invent long, convoluted (yet correctly constructed) sentences and, on a separate piece of paper, identify the simple subject and simple predicate in each. Then have students exchange their

More Oral Language

Introduce the concept of reader's theatre through choral reading. Because choral reading involves reading aloud, shy students are less intimidated by the prospect of performing as a group. As well, choral reading is an effective means of having students appreciate the power of oral interpretation because the large number of voices lends drama and importance to the written words. Select a poem that includes several words and expressions that appeal particularly to sounds (e.g., onomatopoeia, alliteration) and have the class practise reading it chorally, making sure they respond to punctuation, line breaks, and spaces. (LG2.03D—AR 9: Group Presentation)

sentences with opposing teams who must identify the simple subject and simple predicate in each. (WR5.06D—TOC 4: Grammar; LG1.05D—TOC 4: Grammar)

3. Some students have difficulty distinguishing between clauses and phrases. Write the following sentence on the board: *When writing poetry, some authors begin with lists of impressions.* Have students identify the grammatical structure of the first part (an adjective phrase modifying "authors") and the second part (a clause because it contains both a verb and its subject). Then write the following on the board: *When they write poetry, some authors begin with lists of impressions.* Ask students to determine if the first underlined structure is still a phrase (no, because it now contains both a verb and its subject). Once they have identified it as a clause, have them consider the difference between the first clause and the second clause (the first is a **subordinate**—or dependent—clause because it does not make a complete thought; the second is a **main**—or independent—clause because it makes a complete thought and can stand alone as a sentence). Ask students if they can suggest another order for this sentence (i.e., *Some authors begin with lists of impressions when they write poetry.*). When the sentence is written in this order, students can more easily recognize that *when* is a subordinating conjunction joining two structures. (WR5.06D—TOC 4: Grammar; LG1.05D—TOC 4: Grammar)

4. Have students refer to the Writing Tip on page 74 of the student book that discusses the difference between main action and qualifying information. Have students invent several sentences that include main and subordinate clauses, and have them write two versions of each: one that places the main action in the main clause and one that places it in the subordinate clause. Have them share these with partners who must identify which construction is better. (WR5.06D—TOC 4: Grammar; LG1.05D—TOC 4: Grammar)

Answers:

1. simple subject = *water*; simple predicate = *comes*

   simple subject = *arms*; simple predicate = *are*

2.

	Complete Subject	Complete Predicate	Type
a)	The people along the sand	turn and look one way.	shows action
b)	They	turn their back on the land.	shows action
c)	They	look at the sea all day.	shows action
d)	One of the jobs	was putting up ice in winter.	explains condition
e)	It	was one of those epiphanies of childhood.	explains condition

3. simple subject = *ground*; simple predicate = *reflects*

   The wetter ground reflects a standing gull like glass. This structure lacks the rhythm of the original and does not adhere to the rhyme scheme in the poem.

4.

	Subject	Predicate
a)	Your defiance at home	has caused them to pick you up.
b)	You	have fallen off your bicycle.

5. Student work.

6. a) phrase (lacks a verb)
   b) main clause (contains both a subject and verb and makes a complete thought)
   c) subordinate clause (contains both a subject and verb but does not make a complete thought)
   d) main clause (contains both a subject and verb and makes a complete thought)
   e) subordinate clause (contains both a subject and verb but does not make a complete thought)
   f) phrase (lacks both a subject and a verb)
   g) phrase (lacks both a subject and a verb)
   h) main clause (contains both a subject and verb and makes a complete thought)
   i) main clause (contains both a subject and verb and makes a complete thought)
   j) phrase (lacks a verb)

Student Book 1.–6. (WR5.06D—TOC 4: Grammar; LG1.05D—TOC 4: Grammar)

Media Link

Student Book (MDV.01D—AR 21: Response to Media)

Mechanics

Often, students mistakenly assume that poets break all the rules of convention that prose writers follow. While this is true in some cases, students need to recognize that punctuation is an important tool for conveying meaning in poetry. Select a poem that students are not likely to have read before and that contains several forms of punctuation. Present the poem without punctuation to students and have two or three of them read it aloud. Have classmates comment on the readings, making suggestions for other oral interpretations. Then display the original poem and have the same students read it aloud. Follow-up discussion will focus on the impact the punctuation had on their ability to read the poem for meaning. (WR5.16B—TOC 8: Mechanics)

Answers:

1. The extended pause in the second passage emphasizes the contrast in direction between the movement of the water (toward the land) and the gaze of the people (toward the sea).

2. The first two lines of the first stanza end with a period while the same lines of the second stanza end with a semicolon. The period suggests the end of one thought (the introduction of the people) and the beginning of another (their connection to the sea). The semicolon indicates a connection between two thoughts (the contrast between the movement of the ship and the stillness of the gull).

3. The dash indicates an abrupt halt, as though the poet waits for a moment, considering what the truth might be. Frost might have used a comma here, but it would not have given the same dramatic emphasis to the pause.

4. As in Frost's poem, the dash in "Fingerprints" indicates an abrupt halt. Unlike Frost, however, Johnson uses the dash to signify a complete change in focus (from the severity of the bruises to a superficial explanation of their cause).

5. Gom uses commas more than any other form of punctuation.

Student Book 1.–5. (WR5.16B—TOC 8: Mechanics)

Usage & Style

Assist students in differentiating among simile, metaphor, and personification. All are figurative comparisons because they compare things that are unlike in nature (e.g., hair and silk) but have similar qualities (e.g., softness). Metaphors can be especially vivid because they require readers to participate in making the comparison by mentally

> ### MORE MEDIA
>
> Have students select a poem and plan the filming of it as a video. This will consist of a voice-over reading of the poem accompanied by visuals (still photography or action or a combination of both). Students can plan their poetry video in storyboard form. If possible, have students film the videos and show them to the class. An extension of this activity would be to compare the end result with the storyboard plan, identifying where and why any changes were made. (MD2.01D—AR 12: Media Product)

associating one image with another. Writers create metaphors in many ways: they may state that one thing *is* another (*Fred is a bear in the morning.*); they may use a *specific verb* to create a metaphor (*The teacher flew down the hall.*—The teacher is being compared to a bird or a plane to emphasize how quickly he moved.); they may use a *specific noun* to create a metaphor (*The sliver of moonlight lit up her face.*—the noun *sliver*, which is a long, narrow piece of something, makes us see that it was a very narrow beam of light.). Personification can be subtle, drawing a comparison using a single word. For example, in the sentence *The storm raged all night*, the writer gives the storm the human emotion of anger using the single verb *raged*. A single adjective can also reveal personification; for example, *majesty* is a term usually associated with kings and queens, so the phrase *majestic forest* emphasizes the grandeur of the wooded area being described. Have students generate their own figurative comparisons. (LI3.02D—TOC 15: Usage & Style)

Answers:

1. "The wetter ground like glass / Reflects a standing gull." This is an effective comparison because flat, wet sand acts as a mirror reflecting anything above it (in this case, the gull).

2. Possible answer
   "... one of life's great harmonies ..." Gom compares the understanding she achieves to a harmony, which is the fitting together of parts to form a connected whole.

3. Possible answer
   Words/phrases often associated by some readers with the sea include *vast, empty, unforgiving,* and *cruel,* while others often think of the sea as *the cradle of life, gently rocking,* and *soothing,* and still others think of it as *mysterious, a great adventure,* and *a beckoning challenge.* Frost's poem seems to suggest the third perception, so for these readers the sea might symbolize the yearning experienced by people who "cannot look out far ... [and] cannot look in deep" (in other words, people whose day-to-day lives are mundane and unfulfilled).

4. Possible answer
   Alfred, Lord Tennyson's poem "The Eagle" begins with a well-known example of personification: "He clasps the crag with crooked hands ..."

5. a) Student work.
   b) Possible answers
   "Neither Out Far Nor In Deep" — screech (gull), crash (waves)
   "Energy" — scrape (ice), thunk (wood)
   "Fingerprints" — slap (hand), bang (body)

6. Student work.

Student Book 1.–6. (LI3.02D—TOC 15: Usage & Style)

WORD STUDY & SPELLING

Have students work with a partner to list several common prefixes. Then have them add these prefixes to root words and suggest what effect each prefix has on the meaning of the root word. In this way, they will be determining the meaning of prefixes. (LG1.01B—TOC 16: Word Study & Spelling)

WORD ORIGINS

Possible answers
epicentre *(epi* meaning *upon, kentron* meaning *point),* epidermis *(epi* meaning *upon, derma* meaning *skin),* epilogue *(epi* meaning *upon, legein* meaning *to speak),* epilepsy

(*epi* meaning *upon*, *lambanein* meaning *to seize*), epigram (*epi* meaning *upon*, *graphein* meaning *to write*) (LG1.01B—TOC 16: Word Study & Spelling)

Answers:

1. Possible answers
   reflects (rewrite, retell), **a**shore (aside, ascribe), **dis**obedient (disenchant, disadvantage), **in**solent (insecure, insincere), **de**fiance (deprived, detach). *Re* adds the meaning "to do again." *A* adds the meaning "on." *Dis, in,* and *de* usually suggest the opposite meaning of the root word.

2. **Dis**covery and **dis**obedient. In both cases, the prefix suggested the opposite meaning of the root word. Other examples: discharge, disband, disappear.

3. Possible answer
   Words with *in-* prefixes: inability, inaccurate, inactive, inadequate, incapable, indefensible, indefinite, inedible, inexcusable, infamous, inharmonious, insecure, insoluble, intolerable
   Words with *im-* prefixes: immaterial, immature, immobile, immortal, immutable, impatient, impenetrable, imperceptible, imperfect, impersonal, impolite, impossible, impractical, impure
   Words with *il-* prefixes: illegal, illegible, illimitable, illiterate, illogical, etc.
   Rule: Use *im-* when the root word begins with *m* or *p*, and use *il-* when the root word begins with *l*.

4. Possible answers
   illusion, image, instep, instinct

5. a) incur   b) embassy
   c) impact   d) empire
   e) embody   f) implant
   g) embroider   h) indulge
   i) install   j) embarrass
   k) important   l) impulse
   m) embankment   n) impaired
   o) imposter   p) employ
   q) imply   r) imperial

6. Possible answers
   pre-/per- words (Correct forms are in italics.)
   a) *persevere*, presevere
   b) perscribe, *prescribe*
   c) presist, *persist*
   d) *permit*, premit
   e) *prefer*, perfer
   f) *perform*, preform
   g) pretain, *pertain*
   h) pervail, *prevail*
   i) *prevent*, pervent
   j) perpare, *prepare*
   k) *prerogative*, perrogative
   l) percede, *precede*
   m) *persuade*, presuade

Student Book 1.–6. (LG1.01B—TOC 16: Word Study & Spelling)

Answers to Extra Practice

Grammar

1.

Simple Subject	Simple Predicate
a) Monday	is
b) You	run
c) sister	worked
d) child	wept
e) family	likes

2. a) phrase
   b) main clause
   c) subordinate clause
   d) phrase
   e) subordinate clause

(WR5.06D—TOC 4: Grammar; LG1.05D—TOC 4: Grammar)

Mechanics

Bad Dream (original)

A few minutes ago
you called out my name
and I found you sitting in the middle of your bed
in the dark
trembling.

What had stepped out of your dreams and chased
you
this time?

"JustapretendbearDaddy?"

I stroke your hair, damp with sweat, and
in a moment, you're asleep.

I dread the time that's coming —
the time when your tears can't be kissed away
by me.

Don Aker

NOTE TO TEACHERS: The purpose of this extra practice activity is *not* to have students arrive at the original arrangement shown above—which is unlikely—but, instead, to have students consider the choices a poet makes when physically arranging a poem on the page. Rather than assessing their arrangements, assess the *reasons* they have provided for their arrangements.

(WR5.16B—TOC 8: Mechanics)

Usage & Style
1. metaphor

2. personification

3. onomatopoeia

4. metaphor

5. simile

6. onomatopoeia

7. alliteration

8. simile

9. metaphor

10. alliteration

11. oxymoron

12. personification

(LI3.02D—TOC 15: Usage & Style)

Word Study & Spelling
1. dissatisfied

2. illegal

3. improper

4. enthralled

5. entwine

6. perspire

7. intoxicate

8. extraordinary

9. anticlimax

10. intramurals

(LG1.01B—TOC 16: Word Study & Spelling)

GRADE 9 EXPECTATIONS	DEMONSTRATION OF LEARNING	ASSESSMENT TOOLS
LITERATURE STUDIES AND READING		
Overall (LIV.01P) • read and demonstrate an understanding of a variety of literary and informational texts	• discuss how socio-economic realities can influence what poets write (More Challenge TG) • keep a poetry log (More Support TG)	• AR 22: Response to Reading • AR 22: Response to Reading
Specific (LI1.01P) • describe information, ideas, opinions, and themes in texts they have read during the year from a variety of print and electronic sources, including biographies, short stories, poems, plays, novels, brochures, and articles from newspapers, magazines, and encyclopedias	• share understanding of what poetry is (Introducing the Unit TG #1) • demonstrate understanding of poems (Investigating the Models SB #1–8)	• TOC 14: Tracking Expectations • TOC 14: Tracking Expectations
(LI1.02P) • select and read texts for a variety of purposes, with an emphasis on recognizing the elements of literary genres and the organization of informational materials, collecting and using information, extending personal knowledge, and responding imaginatively	• share and discuss favourite poems (Introducing the Unit TG #2) • share knowledge of poets and predict what 16-year-old poet might write about (Introducing the Models TG #1)	• AR 22: Response to Reading • TOC 14: Tracking Expectations
(LI1.03B) • describe a variety of reading strategies and select and use them effectively before, during, and after reading to understand texts	• free-write impressions of titles and first lines of poems (Introducing the Models TG #2)	• TOC 10: Reading Strategies
(LI1.06B) • use specific references from a text to support opinions and judgments	• choose photographs for model poems and justify choice (Extending the Models TG #1)	• AR 22: Response to Reading
Overall (LIV.03B) • identify and explain the effect of specific elements of style in a variety of literary and informational texts		
Specific (LI3.02P) • explain how authors choose words and phrases to achieve intended effects	• brainstorm verbs for use in metaphors (Usage & Style TG) • identify examples of stylistic devices in poetry (Usage & Style SB #1–6) • use stylistic devices in poetry correctly (EP: Usage & Style)	• TOC 15: Usage & Style • TOC 15: Usage & Style • TOC 15: Usage & Style
(LI3.03P) • explain how authors and editors use design elements to help convey meaning	• arrange words of poem on page (Writer's Workshop TG #1)	• TOC 14: Tracking Expectations
WRITING		
Overall (WRV.01P) • use print and electronic sources to gather information and explore ideas for their written work	• gather and organize information and ideas for poem (Writer's Workshop SB #1–6)	• AR 17: Poetry
Overall (WRV.02P) • identify the literary and informational forms suited to specific purposes and audiences and use the forms appropriately in their own writing, with an emphasis on communicating information accurately		
Specific (WR2.03P) • demonstrate an understanding of literary and informational forms of writing, such as letters, personal narratives, short stories, answers to homework questions, summaries, and reports on research topics, by selecting a form appropriate to the specific purpose and audience for each piece of writing	• write poem presenting positive and negative aspects of something tangible (Extending the Models TG #2) • write rhyming poems (Writer's Workshop TG #2) • arrange sentences as found poems (Writer's Workshop TG #3)	• AR 17: Poetry • AR 17: Poetry • AR 17: Poetry

AR=Assessment Rubric   EP=Extra Practice   SB=Student Book   SSEC=Student Self-Evaluation Checklist   TG=Teacher's Guide   TOC=Teacher Observation Checklist

GRADE 9 EXPECTATIONS	DEMONSTRATION OF LEARNING	ASSESSMENT TOOLS
WRITING (continued)		
Overall (WRV.03P) • use a variety of forms of writing to express themselves, clarify their ideas, and engage the audience's attention, imagination, and interest	• arrange phrases and sentences for poem on page (Writer's Workshop SB #7)	• AR 17: Poetry
Overall (WRV.04B) • revise their written work, collaboratively and independently, with a focus on support for ideas, accuracy, clarity, and unity	• revise poem (Writer's Workshop SB #8)	• AR 17: Poetry
Overall (WRV.05B) • edit and proofread to produce final drafts, using correct grammar, spelling, and punctuation, according to the conventions of standard Canadian English specified for this course, with the support of print and electronic resources when appropriate	• edit and proofread poem (Writer's Workshop SB #8)	• AR 17: Poetry
Specific (WR5.06P) • construct complete and correct compound and complex sentences, using the following sentence components as required: subject, predicate, object, subject complement; main and subordinate clauses; prepositional phrases	• use web to identify simple subject and simple predicate in sentences (Grammar TG #1) • create and identify simple subject and simple predicate in long, convoluted sentences (Grammar TG #2) • determine main and subordinate clauses (Grammar TG #3) • write two versions of sentences—with main action in main clause and main action in subordinate clause (Grammar TG #4) • use subjects and predicates, main and subordinate clauses correctly (Grammar SB #1–6) • use subjects and predicates, main and subordinate clauses correctly (EP: Grammar)	• TOC 4: Grammar • TOC 4: Grammar • TOC 4: Grammar • TOC 4: Grammar • TOC 4: Grammar • TOC 4: Grammar
(WR5.16B) • adapt punctuation and capitalization for the special requirements of direct quotations, scripts, dialogue, and poetry	• discuss use of punctuation in poems (Mechanics TG) • analyze use of punctuation in model poems (Mechanics SB #1–5) • use punctuation correctly in poetry (EP: Mechanics)	• TOC 8: Mechanics • TOC 8: Mechanics • TOC 8: Mechanics
LANGUAGE		
Overall (LGV.01P) • use knowledge of vocabulary and language conventions to speak, write, and read clearly and correctly		
Specific (LG1.01B) • describe strategies used to expand vocabulary and provide evidence of other vocabulary-building activities	• discuss prefixes and their effect on meaning (Word Study & Spelling TG #1) • use pronunciation as guide to correct spelling of words with prefixes (Word Study & Spelling TG #2) • find and explain meaning of words with prefix -epi (Word Origins SB) • find and use words with prefixes (Word Study & Spelling SB #1–6) • identify and use words with prefixes (EP: Word Study & Spelling)	• TOC 16: Word Study & Spelling • TOC 16: Word Study & Spelling • TOC 16: Word Study & Spelling • TOC 16: Word Study & Spelling • TOC 16: Word Study & Spelling

AR=Assessment Rubric   EP=Extra Practice   SB=Student Book   SSEC=Student Self-Evaluation Checklist   TG=Teacher's Guide   TOC=Teacher Observation Checklist

GRADE 9 EXPECTATIONS	DEMONSTRATION OF LEARNING	ASSESSMENT TOOLS
LANGUAGE (continued)		
(LG1.05P) • recognize, describe, and use correctly, in oral and written language, the language structures of standard Canadian English and its conventions of grammar and usage, including: – components of sentences: subject, predicate, object, subject complement, prepositional phrases, main and subordinate clauses	• use web to identify simple subject and simple predicate in sentences (Grammar TG #1) • create and identify simple subject and simple predicate in long, convoluted sentences (Grammar TG #2) • determine main and subordinate clauses (Grammar TG #3) • write two versions of sentences—with main action in main clause and main action in subordinate clause (Grammar TG #4) • use subjects and predicates, main and subordinate clauses correctly (Grammar SB #1–6) • use subjects and predicates, main and subordinate clauses correctly (EP: Grammar)	• TOC 4: Grammar • TOC 4: Grammar • TOC 4: Grammar • TOC 4: Grammar • TOC 4: Grammar • TOC 4: Grammar
Overall (LGV.02B) • use listening techniques and oral communication skills to participate in classroom discussions and more formal activities, such as storytelling, role playing, and reporting/presenting, for specific purposes and audiences	• present choral reading of poem (More Oral Language TG)	• AR 9: Group Presentation
Specific (LG2.03P) • work with a partner to plan and make oral presentations to a small group, selecting and using vocabulary and methods of delivery to suit audience and purpose	• give reader's theatre presentation of poem (Oral Language Extension SB)	• SSEC 5: Oral Presentation
MEDIA STUDIES		
Overall (MDV.01P) • identify and describe the elements, intended audiences, and production practices of a variety of media forms	• interpret a music video (Media Link SB)	• AR 21: Response to Media
Overall (MDV.02P) • use knowledge of a variety of media forms, purposes, and audiences to create media works		
Specific (MD2.01P) • adapt a work of literature for presentation in another media form	• plan filming of poem as video, using storyboard form (More Media TG)	• AR 12: Media Product
(MD2.02P) • create media works for different purposes	• create poster demonstrating metaphors (Usage & Style TG)	• AR 12: Media Product

AR=Assessment Rubric   EP=Extra Practice   SB=Student Book   SSEC=Student Self-Evaluation Checklist   TG=Teacher's Guide   TOC=Teacher Observation Checklist

INSTRUCTIONAL STRATEGIES FOR THE APPLIED COURSE

PLANNING INFORMATION

Links to Other Nelson English 9 Resources

Literature & Media 9
Poetry—See the Poetry unit for 22 poetry selections, pp. 176–202.

Write Source 2000
Poetry—"Writing Poetry," pp. 193–207; **Main and Subordinate Clauses**—"Clauses," p. 436; **Prefixes**—"Prefixes," pp. 329–330; **Stylistic Devices**—"Writing Techniques," pp. 138–140, "Traditional Techniques of Poetry," pp. 202–203; **Subjects and Predicates**—"Parts of a Sentence," pp. 434–435

INTRODUCING THE UNIT

The activities on page 81 from the Academic Course are appropriate for the Applied Course.

1. (LI1.01P—TOC 14: Tracking Expectations)

2. (LI1.02P—AR 22: Response to Reading)

INTRODUCING THE MODELS

1. List the authors of the first two poems from the student book on the board and ask students if they are familiar with either of them. Have them share any previous knowledge they may have about these poets. Write Kim Johnson's name on the board and indicate that she was a 16-year-old student at the time she wrote "Fingerprints." Have them predict the sorts of things someone of that age might choose to write about in a poem. (LI1.02P—TOC 14: Tracking Expectations)

2. Have students write the titles of each of the poems from the student book on separate sheets of paper. Then beneath each title have them free-write their impressions of what the titles suggest. Give students the opportunity to share their impressions. Students could do the same free-writing activity using the first line of each poem. When they have read the poems, have them return to their initial impressions and answer the question: Did these impressions help or hinder them in determining the focus of each poem? (LI1.03B—TOC 10: Reading Strategies)

INVESTIGATING THE MODELS

See the Academic Course on pages 81–82 for answers.

Student Book 1.–9. (LI1.01P—TOC 14: Tracking Expectations)

EXTENDING THE MODELS

1. Have students comment on the illustrations chosen for each of the poems in the student book and explain whether they think they were suitable choices. Would they have photographed other subjects? Have students locate photographs in newspapers, magazines, or the Web that they feel are equally or more appropriate for use with each poem. Students should support their choices with specific references to each poem, relating the contents and mood of the photograph to details in the poems. (LI1.06B—AR 22: Response to Reading)

2. Activity #3 on pages 82–83 from the Academic Course is appropriate for the Applied Course. (WR2.03P—AR 17: Poetry)

LEARNING GOALS

- write a poem to explore your feelings
- use subjects and predicates correctly
- use main and subordinate clauses correctly
- adapt punctuation for poetry
- understand how authors use stylistic devices to achieve particular effects
- explore how prefixes affect the spelling of a word

CHECKPOINT

Sample criteria for a poem:

- often focuses on a single moment
- evokes a strong emotional response
- has sensory details that convey a particular understanding or impression
- may follow rhythmical pattern or may imitate flow of natural speech (free verse)
- has line breaks, spaces, and punctuation that contribute to overall theme
- may or may not follow definite rhyming pattern

MORE CHALLENGE

Have students debate the impact that socio-economic realities have had on poets, drawing on perceptions of writers such as the following:

"Women have always been poor, not for two hundred years merely, but from the beginning of time.... Women, then, have not had a dog's chance of writing poetry. That is why I have laid so much stress on money and a room of one's own." (Virginia Woolf)

"Respect the children of the poor—from them come most poets." (Mendele Mocher Sforim)

(LIV.01P—AR 22: Response to Reading)

WRITER'S WORKSHOP

Activities #1–2 on page 83 from the Academic Course are appropriate for the Applied Course.

1. (LI3.03P—TOC 14: Tracking Expectations)

2. (WR2.03P—AR 17: Poetry)

3. Found poetry is prose that is rewritten in poem form. Have students choose two or three sentences from a book, newspaper, or magazine and rearrange them in the form of a poem. Then have them rearrange the sentences in two more ways. After choosing the one arrangement they think is most effective and giving it a title, students should write a paragraph justifying their choice. All three arrangements and the source used are included in the assignment. (WR2.03P—AR 17: Poetry)

Student Book 1.–6. (WRV.01P—AR 17: Poetry); 7. (WRV.03P—AR 17: Poetry); 8. (WRV.04B—AR 17: Poetry; WRV.05B—AR 17: Poetry)

ORAL LANGUAGE EXTENSION

Students could work in pairs and give their reader's theatre presentation to a small group.

Student Book (LG2.03P—SSEC 5: Oral Presentation)

GRAMMAR

1. To assist students in identifying the simple subject and simple predicate of a sentence, write a sentence in the form of a web. Draw a circle around the main noun and another circle around the main verb. Then cluster the other words in the sentence around whichever word they seem to modify or explain. Have students work with partners to draw webs of other sentences, moving from very short, simple sentences to longer, more complex ones. This work will also assist them in identifying phrases that act as modifiers. Emphasize that knowing the simple subject and simple predicate is the key to understanding the construction of a sentence. All other elements in the sentence are added to one or the other of these building blocks. (WR5.06P—TOC 4: Grammar; LG1.05P—TOC 4: Grammar)

Activities #2–4 on pages 83–84 from the Academic Course are appropriate for the Applied Course. (WR5.06P—TOC 4: Grammar; LG1.05P—TOC 4: Grammar)

Answers:
See the Academic Course on pages 84–85 for answers.

Student Book 1.–6. (WR5.06P—TOC 4: Grammar; LG1.05P—TOC 4: Grammar)

MEDIA LINK

Student Book (MDV.01P—AR 21: Response to Media)

MECHANICS

One student described poetry as "skinny writing" because lines seldom go all the way to the margins. To help understand why writers punctuate and "break" lines of unrhymed poems where they do, read "Energy" and "Fingerprints" aloud at least twice, pausing briefly at the ends of lines, longer at commas and dashes, and even longer at periods. Then, have students suggest reasons why the authors punctuated and broke their lines where they did. Whatever reasons students offer, they should reflect that punctuation and line breaks are not arbitrary but, instead, they help readers interpret a poem orally and convey images/ideas that are at the heart of a poem.

(WR5.16B—TOC 8: Mechanics)

MORE SUPPORT

Encourage students to read and respond to a variety of poems of their own choosing. Have them keep a poetry log. They could record the name of the poem, the book it comes from, the page number, and a short response to the poem telling what they liked about it. (LIV.01P—AR 22: Response to Reading)

MORE ORAL LANGUAGE

Introduce the concept of reader's theatre through choral reading. Because choral reading involves reading aloud, shy students are less intimidated by the prospect of performing as a group. As well, choral reading is an effective means of having students appreciate the power of oral interpretation because the large number of voices lends drama and importance to the written words. Select a poem that includes several words and expressions that appeal particularly to sounds (e.g., onomatopoeia, alliteration) and have the class practise reading it chorally, making sure they respond to punctuation, line breaks, and spaces. (LGV.02B—AR 9: Group Presentation)

MORE MEDIA

Have students select a poem and plan the filming of it as a video. This will consist of a voice-over reading of the poem accompanied by visuals (still photography or action or a combination of both). Students can plan their poetry video in storyboard form. If possible, have students film the videos and show them to the class. An extension of this activity would be to compare the end result with the storyboard plan, identifying where and why any changes were made. (MD2.01P—AR 12: Media Product)

Answers:

See the Academic Course on page 85 for answers.

Student Book 1.–5. (WR5.16B—TOC 8: Mechanics)

Usage & Style

Many students think of metaphor simply as a comparison that does not use *like* or *as* (e.g., *Life is a highway*). Referring to the example in the student book, emphasize the importance of verbs in the creation of vivid metaphors. Have students brainstorm several verbs which, when used in a sentence, suggest a metaphor (e.g., *flew*; *The teacher flew down the hall.*). Once they have generated this list, students then create posters that visually demonstrate the metaphor created in each sentence. (LI3.02P—TOC 15: Usage & Style; MD2.02P—AR 12: Media Product)

Answers:

See the Academic Course on page 86 for answers.

Student Book 1.–6. (LI3.02P—TOC 15: Usage & Style)

Word Study & Spelling

1. List several root words on the board or overhead (e.g., appear, happy) and then ask students to add one or more letters to each word to change its meaning. Students should have little difficulty adding prefixes like *dis-* (disappear), *un-* (unhappy). Follow-up discussion can focus on what prefixes are and the effects they have on meaning, as well as the fact that adding prefixes does not change the spelling of a word. (LG1.01B—TOC 16: Word Study & Spelling)

2. Emphasize the importance of pronunciation in spelling words correctly. To introduce activity #5 in the student book, write the word *personal* on the board and ask students to suggest a prefix that will give it the opposite meaning. If students suggest both *im-* and *in-*, ask them to enunciate the word, listening for sounds that will suggest the correct choice. Suggest that students use this strategy to spell words correctly before checking their answers in a dictionary. (LG1.01B—TOC 16: Word Study & Spelling)

Word Origins

See the Academic Course on pages 86–87 00 for answers.

Student Book (LG1.01B—TOC 16: Word Study & Spelling)

Answers:

See the Academic Course on pages 86–87 for answers.

Student Book 1.–6. (LG1.01B—TOC 16: Word Study & Spelling)

Answers to Extra Practice

See the Academic Course on page 88 for answers.

Grammar
(WR5.06P—TOC 4: Grammar; LG1.05P—TOC 4: Grammar)

Mechanics
(WR5.16B—TOC 8: Mechanics)

Usage & Style
(LI3.02P—TOC 15: Usage & Style)

Word Study & Spelling
(LG1.01B—TOC 16: Word Study & Spelling)

GRAMMAR

NAME: _____ DATE: _____

1. Underline the simple subject and circle the simple predicate in each of the following sentences:

   a) Luckily, next Monday is a holiday.

   b) You run to the office for help!

   c) Rayeanne's older sister worked as a computer programmer in Regina.

   d) Wandering among the trees in the park, the lost child wept softly for her mother.

   e) During the fall, my family likes to go camping.

2. Indicate whether each of the following is a phrase, a main clause, or a subordinate clause.

   a) slipping into the icy water under the grey November sky

   _____

   b) every person took the first-aid course

   _____

   c) since the store opened in February last year

   _____

   d) each of the six towering figures

   _____

   e) when the clock in the hallway struck four

   _____

MECHANICS

NAME: _____ **DATE:** _____

The following paragraph is actually a poem rewritten in paragraph form. Read it carefully at least twice and decide where lines should end and, if you think it is necessary, where lines should be skipped. Write out your arrangement and then read it aloud to see if this arrangement contributes to the overall effect of the poem. Make any changes you feel are necessary and then make a good copy. On a separate sheet of paper that you will attach to your poem, write a detailed paragraph explaining your reasons for this arrangement.

Bad Dream

A few minutes ago you called out my name and I found you sitting in the middle of your bed in the dark trembling. What had stepped out of your dreams and chased you this time? "Just a pretend bear, Daddy?" I stroke your hair, damp with sweat, and in a moment, you're asleep. I dread the time that's coming—the time when your tears can't be kissed away by me.

Don Aker

USAGE & STYLE

NAME: _____ DATE: _____

Each of the following sentences makes use of figurative language to convey sensory impressions. Beside each, tell which figurative device is being used: simile, metaphor, personification, oxymoron, alliteration, or onomatopoeia.

1. The road was a silver ribbon of moonlight through the forest.

   _____

2. The waves reached up and swept the child off the rock.

   _____

3. Grey dishwater splashed onto the floor.

   _____

4. The excited students burst through the doorway.

   _____

5. Like an orange ball, the sun rolled over the horizon.

   _____

6. The policeman snapped his fingers and his dog returned to his side.

   _____

7. Sheryl sat silently in her seat.

   _____

8. His smile was as hard as nails.

   _____

9. Moonlight seeped between the curtains into Barbara's eyes.

   _____

10. The butler picked up pieces of the porcelain vase.

    _____

11. Before Romeo left Juliet, he described their parting as sweet sorrow.

    _____

12. Storm clouds in the distant sky threatened to ruin the campers' weekend.

    _____

WORD STUDY & SPELLING

NAME: _____ DATE: _____

Look carefully at the following pairs of words and choose the correct spelling in each.

1. disatisfied, dissatisfied

   _____

2. illegal, ilegal

   _____

3. emproper, improper

   _____

4. inthralled, enthralled

   _____

5. intwine, entwine

   _____

6. perspire, prespire

   _____

7. entoxicate, intoxicate

   _____

8. extraordinary, extrordinary

   _____

9. anticlimax, anteclimax

   _____

10. intramurals, entramurals

    _____

UNIT 5: PROFILE

ACADEMIC EXPECTATIONS

GRADE 9 EXPECTATIONS		DEMONSTRATION OF LEARNING	ASSESSMENT TOOLS
LITERATURE STUDIES AND READING			
Overall (LIV.01D)	• read and demonstrate an understanding of a variety of literary and informational texts, from contemporary and historical periods		
Specific (LI1.01D)	• describe information, ideas, opinions, and themes in print and electronic texts they have read during the year from different cultures and historical periods and in a variety of genres, including novels, short stories, plays, poems, biographies, short essays, and articles from newspapers, magazines, and encyclopedias	• demonstrate understanding of profile (Investigating the Model SB #1–6)	• TOC 13: Tracking Expectations
Overall (LIV.02D)	• demonstrate an understanding of the elements of a variety of literary and informational forms, with a focus on plays, short stories, and short essays	• compare profile with biography (Extending the Model TG #2) • analyze profiles to see if they adhere to Checkpoint criteria (More Challenge TG, page 104)	• TOC 13: Tracking Expectations • AR 22: Response to Reading
WRITING			
Overall (WRV.01D)	• use a variety of print and electronic sources to gather information and explore ideas for their written work	• choose subject and gather information (Writer's Workshop SB #1–4)	• AR 19: Profile
Specific (WR1.01D)	• investigate potential topics by formulating questions, identifying information needs, and developing research plans to gather data	• brainstorm interesting subjects for profiles (Writer's Workshop TG #1)	• AR 19: Profile
(WR1.02D)	• locate and summarize information from print and electronic sources, including vertical files, periodicals, dictionaries, encyclopedias, electronic newsgroups, e-mail messages, and electronic databases	• write a statement of purpose for profile (Writer's Workshop TG #2) • brainstorm actions, comments, and details of profile subject as well as setting (Writer's Workshop TG #3)	• AR 19: Profile • AR 19: Profile
(WR1.03D)	• group and label information and ideas; evaluate the relevance, accuracy, and completeness of the information and ideas; and discard irrelevant material	• organize details of profile (Writer's Workshop TG #4)	• AR 0: Profile
Overall (WRV.02D)	• identify the literary and informational forms suited to various purposes and audiences and use the forms appropriately in their own writing, with an emphasis on supporting opinions or interpretations with specific information		
Specific (WR2.01D)	• demonstrate an understanding of literary and informational forms, such as myths, poems, short stories, scripts, advertisements, formal letters, reviews, and supported opinion essays, by selecting and using forms of writing appropriate to different purposes and audiences	• invent comments by possible interviewees in profile (Extending the Model TG #1)	• TOC 13: Tracking Expectations
Overall (WRV.03D)	• use a variety of organizational techniques to present ideas and supporting details logically and coherently in written work	• write draft of profile (Writer's Workshop SB #5) • write profile of themselves from someone else's point of view (More Challenge TG page 105)	• AR 19: Profile • AR 19: Profile

AR=Assessment Rubric   EP=Extra Practice   SB=Student Book   SSEC=Student Self-Evaluation Checklist   TG=Teacher's Guide   TOC=Teacher Observation Checklist

GRADE 9 EXPECTATIONS	DEMONSTRATION OF LEARNING	ASSESSMENT TOOLS
WRITING (continued)		
Specific (WR3.02D) • use changes in time, place, speaker, or point of view to structure narrative paragraphs	• write same scene in first-person point of view and three third-person points of view (Usage & Style TG) • use first- and third-person points of view (EP: Usage & Style)	• TOC 15: Usage & Style • TOC 15: Usage & Style
Overall (WRV.04D) • revise their written work, independently and collaboratively, with a focus on support for ideas and opinions, accuracy, clarity, and unity	• use revision questions to revise profile (Writer's Workshop TG #6) • revise profile (Writer's Workshop SB #6)	• AR 19: Profile • AR 19: Profile
Specific (WR4.02B) • revise drafts to ensure consistency in use of first or third person and use of an appropriate level of language	• write and correct passages for appropriate point of view (Usage & Style SB #1–3)	• TOC 15: Usage & Style
Overall (WRV.05D) • edit and proofread to produce final drafts, using correct grammar, spelling, and punctuation, according to the conventions of standard Canadian English, with the support of print and electronic resources when appropriate	• use editing questions to edit and proofread profile (Writer's Workshop TG #6) • edit and proofead profile (Writer's Workshop SB #6)	• AR 19: Profile • AR 19: Profile
Specific (WR5.03D) • assess their facility with the writing process, documenting their use of different genres and forms in personal and assigned writing and identifying goals for writing improvement and growth	• record writing process for profile, assess success, and set goals for future projects (Writer's Workshop TG #5)	• AR 3: Conferencing
(WR5.06D) • construct complete and correct compound and complex sentences, using the following sentence components as required: subject, predicate, object, subject complement; main and subordinate clauses; prepositional and participial phrases	• write passages including simple sentences to emphasize a point (Grammar TG #1) • discuss compound and complex sentences (Grammar TG #2) • write compound-complex sentences (More Challenge TG page 107) • write simple sentences (More Support TG) • write simple, compound, and complex sentences (Grammar SB #1–6) • write simple, compound, and complex sentences (EP: Grammar)	• TOC 4: Grammar • TOC 4: Grammar • TOC 4: Grammar • TOC 4: Grammar • TOC 4: Grammar • TOC 4: Grammar
(WR5.16B) • adapt punctuation and capitalization for the special requirements of direct quotations, scripts, dialogue, and poetry	• discuss value of including spoken words in profile (Mechanics TG #1) • identify and explain quoted comments in model profile (Mechanics TG #2) • rewrite quoted passages (Mechanics SB #1–4) • use punctuation in quotations correctly (EP: Mechanics)	• TOC 8: Mechanics • TOC 8: Mechanics • TOC 8: Mechanics • TOC 8: Mechanics
LANGUAGE		
Overall (LGV.01D) • use knowledge of vocabulary and language conventions to speak, write, and read competently using a level of language appropriate to the purpose and audience		
Specific (LG1.01B) • describe strategies used to expand vocabulary and provide evidence of other vocabulary-building activities	• understand rules for spelling words with suffixes (Word Study & Spelling TG #1) • list words with suffixes that are frequently misspelled (Word Study & Spelling TG #2) • use words with suffixes correctly (Word Study & Spelling SB #1–4) • use words with suffixes correctly (EP: Word Study & Spelling)	• TOC 16: Word Study & Spelling • TOC 16: Word Study & Spelling • TOC 16: Word Study & Spelling • TOC 16: Word Study & Spelling

AR=Assessment Rubric   EP=Extra Practice   SB=Student Book   SSEC=Student Self-Evaluation Checklist   TG=Teacher's Guide   TOC=Teacher Observation Checklist

GRADE 9 EXPECTATIONS	DEMONSTRATION OF LEARNING	ASSESSMENT TOOLS
LANGUAGE (continued)		
(LG1.03B) • identify words borrowed from other languages and words and terms recently introduced to describe new ideas, inventions, and products, and explain their origins	• find word origins for sports terms (Word Origins SB) • research origins of sports words (More Support TG, page 112)	• TOC 16: Word Study & Spelling • TOC 16: Word Study & Spelling
(LG1.05D) • recognize, describe, and use correctly, in oral and written language, the language structures of standard Canadian English and its conventions of grammar and usage, including: – simple, compound, and complex sentences	• write passages including simple sentences to emphasize a point (Grammar TG #1) • discuss compound and complex sentences (Grammar TG #2) • write compound-complex sentences (More Challenge TG, page 107) • write simple sentences (More Support TG, page 107) • write simple, compound, and complex sentences (Grammar TG #1–6) • write simple, compound, and complex sentences (EP: Grammar)	• TOC 4: Grammar • TOC 4: Grammar • TOC 4: Grammar • TOC 4: Grammar • TOC 4: Grammar • TOC 4: Grammar
Overall (LGV.02B) • use listening techniques and oral communication skills to participate in classroom discussions and more formal activities, such as storytelling, role playing, and reporting/presenting, for specific purposes and audiences	• share in-line skating experiences (Introducing the Unit TG #1) • describe in-line skating equipment (Introducing the Unit TG #2) • discuss focus of profile as quality, skill, or experience of person (Introducing the Model TG #1) • practise identifying particular quality, skill, or experience of individuals (Introducing the Model TG #2)	• TOC 13: Tracking Expectations • TOC 13: Tracking Expectations • TOC 13: Tracking Expectations • TOC 13: Tracking Expectations
Specific (LG2.03D) • plan and make oral presentations to a small group or the class, selecting and using vocabulary and methods of delivery to suit audience and purpose	• re-enact *Front Page Challenge* to practise focusing on an individual (Oral Language Extension SB)	• AR 15: Oral Language
(LG2.06D) • explain how oral communication skills can contribute to success in all curriculum areas and the world outside the school	• conduct a survey to determine importance of oral communication skills (More Oral Language TG)	• TOC 2: Conducting Research
MEDIA STUDIES		
Overall (MDV.01D) • use knowledge of the elements, intended audiences, and production practices of a variety of media forms to analyze specific media works	• discuss personal qualities most recognized by media (Extending the Model TG #3) • compare recorded radio broadcast of model profile with written form (More Media TG)	• AR 21: Response to Media • AR 21: Response to Media
Specific (MD1.02D) • identify how elements of media forms are used in a variety of media works and explain the effects of different treatments	• assess effectiveness of methods used in two film versions of same event (Media Link TG) • analyze use of visual techniques in videoclip of sporting event (Media Link SB)	• AR 21: Response to Media • AR 21: Response to Media
Overall (MDV.02D) • use knowledge of a variety of media forms, purposes, and audiences to create media works and describe their intended effect	• record model profile as radio broadcast and compare with written form (More Media TG)	• AR 12: Media Product
Specific (MD2.02D) • create media works for different purposes and explain how each has been designed to achieve its particular purpose	• create two versions of same school event and discuss effects used (Media Link TG)	• AR 12: Media Product

AR=Assessment Rubric   EP=Extra Practice   SB=Student Book   SSEC=Student Self-Evaluation Checklist   TG=Teacher's Guide   TOC=Teacher Observation Checklist

INSTRUCTIONAL STRATEGIES FOR THE ACADEMIC COURSE

PLANNING INFORMATION

Links to Other Nelson English 9 Resources

Literature & Media 9
Magazine Profile—See "Tom Longboat" by Jack Granatstein, pp. 121–122.

Write Source 2000
Ellipsis—"Ellipsis," p. 388; **Point of View**—"Point of View," p. 344; **Simple, Compound, and Complex Sentences**—"Kinds of Sentences," pp. 437–438; **Suffixes**—"Suffixes," p. 331

INTRODUCING THE UNIT

1. Create a display of photographs of in-line skaters and/or videotape an in-line skating competition and share it with students, who can then share their own experiences or those of other people they know. (LGV.02B—TOC 13: Tracking Expectations)

2. Bring in (or invite students to bring in) in-line skating equipment. Most school populations include students who are proficient in-line skaters. Arrange to have a student describe the equipment and its uses and, if possible (with appropriate permission and safety precautions), demonstrate its use. (LGV.02B—TOC 13: Tracking Expectations)

INTRODUCING THE MODEL

1. Collect pictures of well-known international and/or local individuals and prepare simple line-drawing profiles of these individuals on white paper. Have students try to identify the subjects of these profiles (or, if necessary, provide the photographs and have students match profiles with photographs). Students could then point out the particular physical features that enabled them to identify each individual. Use this to introduce the idea that written profiles focus on a particular quality or skill or experience of a person, rather than on a visible feature. (LGV.02B—TOC 13: Tracking Expectations)

2. Post photographs of various public figures (e.g., athletes or actors who appeal to students) around the classroom and invite students to do the same. In subsequent discussion, students can identify a particular quality or skill or experience that makes each individual worthy of public recognition. (LGV.02B—TOC 13: Tracking Expectations)

INVESTIGATING THE MODEL

Answers:

1. The author immediately establishes Sean Knight's identity by stating his name and age and then conveys his uniqueness by describing him performing an in-line skating move—sliding several metres on a metal hand railing—and identifying him as ranking 12th among aggressive skaters in Canada.

2. The article focuses entirely on Knight's involvement in in-line skating, beginning with a description of his entrance into the sport and continuing with his current success and future goals. Even the discussion of in-line skating equipment and moves and comments by family members are included to provide the reader with a better understanding of Knight and his involvement in the sport.

3. With the exception of the opening paragraph, which describes Knight's current position in Canadian in-line skating, the profile is arranged in chronological order, beginning with a description of how he entered the sport, continuing with his current success, and ending with a look toward the future. This method of organization is appropriate not only because it is a logical means of providing information about a person but also because it provides much-needed background for a reader who may have no knowledge of the sport of in-line skating.

Hill might also have focused on Knight's schooling and personal relationships and the impact his commitment to in-line skating has had on both.

4. The author's use of descriptors such as "lanky," "athletic," and "champion" conveys his physical prowess while phrases like "highly personable youth" give readers a sense of his character.

5. Sean's comments reveal his youthfulness ("She freaked out"), his love for the sport ("You see something and if you have the guts, you try it"), his admiration for its champions ("We got to talk to them"), and his appreciation for his parents ("they support me big time").

Other people whom Hill might have interviewed were his teachers (especially physical education teachers and coaches), classmates, and other members of the 519 Crew.

6. Possible answer
The model's conclusion—which reveals Hill's confidence in Knight's future success—affirms that he is a worthy subject for a profile.

Student Book 1.–6. (LI1.01D—TOC 13: Tracking Expectations)

EXTENDING THE MODEL

1. Have students invent comments by people listed in Investigating the Model activity #5 (those whom Hill might have interviewed for the Sean Knight profile, but didn't). (WR2.01D—TOC 13: Tracking Expectations)

2. Have students compare a profile with a biography, discussing not only the obvious difference in length but also the difference in focus (the biography attempts to recount the experiences of a person's lifetime while a profile describes that person at a particular point in time). (LIV.02D—TOC 13: Tracking Expectations)

3. Assign students to collect at least three profiles found in various teen, sports, or news magazines. Have students read them and then share briefly with the class what they learned about the individuals profiled. Subsequent class discussion could identify the qualities most recognized and applauded by the media. Ask students whether these are qualities they admire, or if there are other qualities they feel are more worthy of recognition. (MDV.01D—AR 21: Response to Media)

WRITER'S WORKSHOP

1. Most students can list at least a few famous people (e.g., actors and musicians) whose profiles might interest them. Many, however, will have difficulty identifying people in their communities who would make interesting subjects for profiles. Students need to be reminded that all people—especially those who have lived a long time—have experienced things that are worth documenting. Try asking students "Do you know ..." questions such as the following: Do you know someone who has lived in other parts of the country or the world? Do you know someone who has an unusual job? Do you know someone who can speak more than one language?

NOTE: You might wish to caution students against identifying people who might be embarrassed by their distinction, such as people who have been the perpetrators or victims of crimes. (WR1.01D—AR 19: Profile)

2. It is crucial that students narrow the focus of their profiles. Help them to do so by explaining that their task is to identify exactly what they would like others to know about their subject. Provide an opportunity for students to discuss this with a partner before writing a statement of purpose. Partners can ask clarifying questions like "What do you mean by...." and rephrase what they have heard. Model this focusing activity by identifying a subject, and explaining and jotting down the reasons for your choice. You could ask the class to choose one reason for the focus of your profile. (WR1.02D)—AR 19: Profile)

3. Readers appreciate being shown rather than told, so details like action, dialogue, and setting are as important in descriptive writing as they are in narrative writing. Have students brainstorm actions and comments that are characteristic of the person they are profiling, Have them identify a particular setting for their subject. This will further convey a sense of what the person is like. Have students consider a description of the subject's clothing as well. The more details students gather before writing a draft, the easier it will be for them. (WR1.02D—AR 19: Profile)

4. Discuss with students the importance of anticipating the reader's needs. They will be presenting their information to readers who have no prior knowledge of the subject. You might model the process by organizing details of your own profile, illustrating on the board or on an overhead projector details you will include and their order. Provide students with an opportunity to discuss their own information and its arrangement in small groups. (WR1.03D—AR 19: Profile)

5. Have students record their writing process including brainstorming, exploratory drafts, notes about peer/teacher writing conferences, and revisions. Students should be encouraged to assess their success with the writing process and to set goals for future projects. (WR5.03D—AR 3: Conferencing)

6. Offer students guidelines in the form of questions they may use when revising and editing their profiles. (WRV.04D—AR 19: Profile; WRV.05D—AR 19: Profile)

MORE CHALLENGE

Ask students to write a profile of themselves, but from someone else's point of view. Students might choose the point of view of a fellow student, teacher, coach, or employer. (WRV.03D—AR 19: Profile)

Revision Questions	
Title	• Is my title interesting? Does it reflect the topic of the piece?
Beginning Questions	• Does my lead catch a reader's interest and identify (or hint at) the main idea of my piece?
Middle Questions	• Have I included enough information so my reader can understand the situation or problem? • Have I shown (using actions/thoughts/feelings/ dialogue/examples) or told my reader what is happening? • Have I included too much information? Are there parts I can leave out? • Is the order correct (the piece flows easily)? Will any part confuse my reader?
End Questions	• What do I want my reader to think/feel/know at the end? Does my ending do this?

Editing Questions

- Have I paragraphed my piece correctly (grouped ideas that belong together)?
- Have I used complete sentences? (Sentence fragments are acceptable as long as they are intentional.)
- Have I used a variety of sentences (e.g., type, length)?
- Have I used the same point of view throughout my piece?
- Are my verbs mainly present-tense or past-tense? Do I need to change them?
- Have I used nouns and verbs that create strong impressions?
- Have I repeated words unnecessarily? Can I find other words that will express the same ideas?
- Have I punctuated my piece correctly?
- Have I used any words incorrectly?
- Have I spelled every word correctly?

Student Book 1.–4. (WRV.01D—AR 19: Profile); 5. (WRV.03D—AR 19: Profile); 6. (WRV.04D—AR 19: Profile; WRV.05D—AR 19: Profile)

MORE ORAL LANGUAGE

Bring to students' attention the fact that television personalities have mastered oral communication skills that enable them to speak and listen effectively on camera. Have students survey a variety of adults in their community to determine the importance of oral communication skills beyond school and television. Students could first develop the survey they will use to collect their data and then identify a means of selecting a random sampling of the community's adult population. (The statistical aspects of this project could be integrated with a unit in mathematics that examines these topics.) (LG2.06D—TOC 2: Conducting Research)

ORAL LANGUAGE EXTENSION

Many students will be unfamiliar with the TV program *Front Page Challenge*. If possible, obtain videotapes of one or more installments so students will understand how the game is played. Prepare in advance some *Front Page Challenge* examples of well-known local and international figures for students who might find the task difficult. Re-enacting *Front Page Challenge* is an excellent activity for cross-curricular involvement and can be incorporated with other disciplines such as social studies and science to meet a variety of curricular expectations.

Student Book (LG2.03D—AR 15: Oral Language)

GRAMMAR

1. Often, students mistakenly believe that strong writing consists of long, very complex sentences, but professional writers understand the importance of being able to state an idea clearly using as few words as possible. To emphasize this, share with students two very different passages written about the same subject, one of them straightforward and the other convoluted. It is also important for students to recognize that too many simple sentences will make writing sound repetitive and stilted, but a short, simple sentence is often an effective way of emphasizing a point. Have students practise writing passages that reflect this use (e.g., *Weaving unsteadily, Brian tossed the empty beer bottle into the bushes and he told Sheryl to give him the keys to the car. She refused*). (WR5.06D—TOC 4: Grammar; LG1.05D—TOC 4: Grammar)

2. Students should recognize that the difference between compound and complex sentences involves more than the type of conjunction used to join thoughts together. When the action in one sentence depends on the action in another sentence, it is more appropriate to subordinate one of the sentences. Put the following simple sentences on the board: *I overslept. I was able to arrive at the meeting on time.* Have students combine them using *although* to form a complex sentence. Most students will write: *Although I overslept, I was able to arrive at the meeting on time.* Have them suggest why this sentence is more appropriate than the following: *I overslept although I was able to arrive at the meeting on time.* Discuss the importance of putting the main action in the main clause. (WR5.06D—TOC 4: Grammar; LG1.05D—TOC 4: Grammar)

Answers:

1.

	Simple Subject	Simple Predicate
a)	Sean Knight	tends
b)	teen	is
c)	Knight	turned

2. These grammatical constructions are phrases that modify (add information about) the subject or the verb.

3. Possible answers

   They offer us drinks and stuff. simple subject — *they*, simple predicate — *offer*
   One of Knight's favourite moves involves rolling up a "launch" ramp backward, completing two spins in mid air, then landing, preferably upright.
   simple subject — *one*, simple predicate — *involves*

4. a) simple sentence: simple subject — *step*, simple predicate — *was*
   b) complex sentence: subordinate clause followed by main clause
   c) compound sentence: two main clauses joined by *and*
   d) complex sentence: main clause followed by subordinate clause
   e) simple sentence: simple subject — *Neighbours*, simple predicate — *view*
   f) simple sentence: simple subject — *wheels*, simple predicate — *wear ... and get*
   g) complex sentence: subordinate clause followed by main clause

5. a) compound: *They come out to watch us, and they offer us drinks and stuff.*
      complex: *When they come out to watch us, they offer us drinks and stuff.* The complex sentence is superior because the action in the main clause happens as a result of the action in the subordinate clause.

   b) compound: *Sean watched the pros through the critical eye of a learner, and he was deeply impressed by their abilities.*
      complex: *As Sean watched the pros through the critical eye of a learner, he was deeply impressed by their abilities.* The complex sentence is superior because the action in the main clause happens as a result of the action in the subordinate clause.

   c) compound: *Sean realizes the amount of work necessary to reach each higher level, but he has also learned about the importance of quality skates.*
      complex: *When Sean realizes the amount of work necessary to reach each higher level, he has also learned about the importance of quality skates.* The compound sentence is superior because neither action is more important than the other (one cannot be subordinated).

   d) compound: *This summer, the Canadian Nationals came to Toronto, and Sean was able to place in the top five during a qualifier on the previous weekend.*
      complex: *When the Canadian Nationals came to Toronto this summer, Sean was able to place in the top five during a qualifier on the previous weekend.* The complex sentence is superior because the action in the main clause happens as a result of the action in the subordinate clause.

6. Student work.

Student Book 1.–6. (WR5.06D—TOC 4: Grammar; LG1.05D—TOC 4: Grammar)

MORE CHALLENGE

A fourth type of sentence structure is the compound-complex sentence, which contains two or more independent clauses and one or more subordinate clauses. For example,

subordinate clause   independent clause

<u>If Sean Knight continues to improve,</u> *he may switch from amateur to professional status,* **and this will affect his current standing in the sport.**

   independent clause

Introduce students to this structure and have them identify examples of it in their reading. Then have them write compound-complex sentences on their own. (WR5.06D—TOC 4: Grammar; LG1.05D—TOC 4: Grammar)

MORE SUPPORT

Show students that simple sentences can create a sense of movement in a piece of writing, drawing the reader toward a conclusion, as in the following passage: *Our class spent months raising money for our year-end trip. We had bake sales. We held car washes. We painted fences. We raked yards. By mid-May, though, we were still two hundred dollars short.* Have students write similar passages.

Some students might mistakenly think the following sentence has two subjects and predicates because there are two verbs: *By entering the marathon, Celine* **demonstrated** *her determination to win and* **inspired** *the rest of us with her positive outlook.* However, show students that there is only one subject for both verbs—*Celine.* Then show students how to make this sentence a compound sentence by adding another subject (e.g., *she*): *By entering the marathon,* **Celine demonstrated** *her determination to win and* **she inspired** *the rest of us with her positive outlook.* (WR5.06D—TOC 4: Grammar; LG1.05D—TOC 4: Grammar)

MEDIA LINK

Have students suggest ordinary events that happen daily around the school (e.g., delivery of cafeteria food, courier service, dismissal) and then have them select one that can be videotaped easily during class time. Working in groups of three or four and using at least two video cameras per group, students could videotape the event and then prepare two 90-second films. (Use of more than one video camera allows them to dub together portions of different tapes.) The two films must convey very different impressions of the same event by means of visual techniques and sound effects. Groups could present their films and discuss the desired and achieved effects. Students then assess the effectiveness of the methods employed. (MD2.02D—AR 12: Media Product; MD1.02D—AR 21: Response to Media)

Student Book (MD1.02D—AR 21: Response to Media)

MECHANICS

1. Before you begin the unit, choose passages of dialogue spoken by well-known figures that convey a sense of who they are—newspapers and magazines often present weekly "memorable quotes" that are suitable for this purpose. (An alternative approach is to draw from literature dialogue of memorable characters that reveals something about their personalities and goals.) Share these passages with students and have them discuss what the passages reveal about these people/characters. Discuss with students the value of including a person's actual spoken words in their profile. (WR5.16B—TOC 8: Mechanics)

2. Ellipsis points have more than one function. Remind students of their work with ellipses in Unit 3 of the *Teacher's Guide* during which they made dialogue sound realistic by indicating where a comment trails off unfinished. Many students do not distinguish between parentheses and square brackets, often referring to both as brackets. However, as students incorporate their subject's comments into their profiles, a knowledge of the function of square brackets will enable them to insert clarifying information. They can use square brackets in other forms of academic writing, particularly critical essays that draw on a number of sources for supporting commentary. Students should learn to integrate quoted material smoothly into their writing. Have them identify quoted comments in the model profile and explain how the author integrates this material. (WR5.16B—TOC 8: Mechanics)

Answers:

1. The author may have left out details about other skaters who placed in those standings. Information about other skaters is not relevant—only Knight's standing is of importance to the reader.

2. Student work.

3. Student work.

4. a) Valerie Hill describes in-line skates as being "shaped similar to a downhill ski boot but ... with shocks in the heel area."
   b) "[The skates] can easily run up to $400, [and] ... wheels ... cost about $80 per set."
   c) "Judges," according to Hill, "are looking ... above all [for] level of difficulty, particularly ... the height gained during a jump."
   d) Hill concludes by announcing Sean's plans for the future: "Next summer, Knight plans on attending Camp Woodward, [which] ... recruits the best in the sport ... in in-line skating."
   Student Book 1.–4. (WR5.16B—TOC 8: Mechanics)

USAGE & STYLE

One of the most important decisions a writer must make when writing a piece is the choice of **point of view** because it shapes what the writer will share in that piece as well as how the reader will respond to it. There are two main points of view: **first person**, in which the writer is a *participant* in the events being narrated, and **third person**, in which the writer reports the events that *others* are participating in.

There are, however, varying degrees of third-person point of view in narrative writing, especially fiction. For example, in the **omniscient** point of view, the narrator is all-knowing, able to convey information about the actions, thoughts, and feelings of all people involved. In the **limited omniscient** point of view, the narrator is able to convey the thoughts and feelings of only one person involved. Writing from the **objective** point of view, the narrator conveys only those things that he or she can see or hear. Have students write a brief scene in which the narrator comes into conflict with another person using the first-person point of view. Then have them write this same scene three more times, using each of the three third-person points of view. (WR3.02D—TOC 15: Usage & Style)

Answers:

1. Possible answer

   At 16 years of age, the lanky and athletic Sean Knight, in my opinion, tends to attract a lot of attention, particularly after leaping onto a narrow metal hand railing on his in-line skates and sliding several metres before making a perfect landing. I learned that the Guelph teen is a champion "aggressive skater," a term describing the high level of skill necessary to perform numerous mind-boggling tricks while spinning along on eight little plastic wheels. I discovered that he currently holds a 12th-place ranking in Canada—not bad for a kid who started skating less than three years ago.

   The advantage of the first-person point of view is that its intimacy heightens the author's credibility (the writer is speaking from experience and relaying this directly to the reader). There are, however, disadvantages: the narrator gets in the way of the piece, being on equal footing with the subject (causing the piece to be longer), therefore detracting the reader from the focus of the profile; also, this point of view is laden with personal impressions that may not be correct, so the profile becomes much more subjective (and, consequently, less reliable).

2. a) *lanky, athletic, perfect*
   b) *not bad for a kid who ...*
   c) *promising, just might make it to the top*

3. Student work.

Student Book 1.–3. (WR4.02B—TOC 15: Usage & Style)

WORD STUDY & SPELLING

1. Many people are unsure whether the spelling of a root word changes when a suffix is added to it. Have students recall (or discover) some of the rules involving the spelling of words with suffixes. They may need to refer to a dictionary to be sure of their spelling in some cases.

   a) Add the following suffixes to the following words:
      move + ment
      replace + ment
      hope + ful
      care + ful
      What happened to each root word when you added these suffixes?

b) Add the following suffixes to the words below:

    manage + er

    love + able

    believe + able

What happened to each root word when you added these suffixes?

c) Explain a rule that determines when a suffix will change the spelling of the root word.

d) Add the following suffixes to the words below:

    change + able

    manage + able

    replace + able

    trace + able

Write a rule that explains the difference between these words and those in b).
(LG1.01B—TOC 16: Word Study & Spelling)

2. Some students will need further work in doubling the final letter of the root word when adding a suffix. Dictate the following words, and have students share their spellings of them and their reasons for spelling them as they did:

    commitment

    flowing

    dreaming

    profiting

    singing

    swimming

    fitted

Help students recognize the rules for doubling below:

1. If the word ends in a consonant, do NOT double the final consonant if:
   a) the suffix begins with a consonant (*commitment*)
   b) the final consonant is not pronounced (*flowing*)
   c) the final consonant is preceded by more than one vowel (*dreaming*)
   d) the final consonant ends in a syllable that is not stressed (*profiting*)
   e) the last two letters are both consonants (*singing*)

2. Double the final consonant in most other cases (*swimming, fitted*).

Have students generate a list of words with suffixes that are frequently misspelled.
(LG1.01B—TOC 16: Word Study & Spelling)

Answers:

1. a) All three words have the same root word (*compete*).

Word	Part of Speech
competition	noun
competitive	adjective
competed	verb

b) *reaction:* Her *reaction* was a surprised yelp.

participation: The fund-raising campaign requires everyone's *participation.*

argumentative: Kelly became *argumentative* during the debate.

aggressive: The dog revealed *aggressive* behaviour.

deleted: Hank *deleted* his document from my disk.

regretted: We *regretted* Darren's decision to leave the group.

Yes, these words function as the same parts of speech as the words *competition, competitive,* and *competed.*

2. Possible answers
   b) **-ed**   **push + ed = pushed**
   c) **-ing**   **flash + ing = flashing**
   d) **-er**   **small + er = smaller**
   e) **-est**   **fast + est = fastest**
   f) **-ly**   **slow + ly = slowly**
   g) **-en**   **thick + en = thicken**

3.

GENERALIZATION	EXPLANATION
1. consonant + consonant = no change	When adding a suffix beginning with a consonant to a word that ends in a vowel or a consonant, make no change to the root (e.g., *movement, fearful*).
2. consonant + vowel = no change	When adding a suffix beginning with a vowel to a word that ends in a consonant, make no change (e.g., *landing*).
3. vowel + vowel = drop final vowel on root	When adding a suffix beginning with a vowel to a word that ends in a vowel, usually drop the final vowel of the root word (e.g., *merged, typing*). However, if dropping the final vowel changes the pronunciation of the word, the vowel generally stays (e.g., *manageable, traceable, being, seeing*).
4. -y + suffix = -y changes to -i	Words that end in -y change the -y to -i before most suffixes (e.g., *plentiful, carried*), **except** -ing (e.g., *carrying*).
5. -ie + -ing = -ie changes to -y	Words that end in -ie change to -y before adding the suffix -ing (e.g., *tying*).

MORE SUPPORT

Have students recognize the influence of the French language in several North American sports by having them investigate the origins of tennis (from the French *tenez*, imperative form of *tenir*, meaning *to take, receive*), hockey (from the Old French *hoquet*, meaning *a crook*), and lacrosse (which originated in contests among various North American Aboriginals and received its modern name from French Canadians who thought the shaft of the stick resembled a bishop's *crosier*, or *crosse*). Have groups of students research the origin of other sports with respect to the influence of language on names. For example, the game of badminton is believed to have been invented in India, where British army officers learned the game about 1870. In 1873 the Duke of Beaufort introduced the sport at his country estate, Badminton, from which the game takes its name. (LG1.03B—TOC 16: Word Study & Spelling)

4. a) *athlete* — generalization #3   d) *wonder* — generalization #1
   b) *temporary* — generalization #4   e) *entertain* — generalization #1
   c) *aggress* — generalization #2

Student Book 1. –4. (LG1.01B—TOC 16: Word Study & Spelling)

WORD ORIGINS

Answers:
ski — from the Norwegian language
golf — from the Dutch *kolf*, meaning a club
marathon — the name of the town about 32 km from Athens, Greece (In 490 B.C.E., a soldier ran this distance without stopping, bringing news of a Greek victory over the Persians.)
soccer: an abbreviation of the last word in *Football Association*

Student Book (LG1.03B—TOC 16: Word Study & Spelling)

Answers to Extra Practice

Grammar

1. complex   2. simple   3. simple
4. complex   5. compound

(WR5.06D—TOC 4: Grammar; LG1.05D—TOC 4: Grammar)

Mechanics

1. Officer Medynski describes Ben as "a very gentle animal ... [that is] accustomed to the various noises and problems associated with ... an urban area like Bishopville."

2. The police officer remembers "many ... traffic jams that blocked [his] vehicle and delayed [him] from performing [his] duties."

3. According to Officer Medynski, "[Youths] often ... take to Ben right away, patting him and offering him treats."

(WR5.16B—TOC 8: Mechanics)

Usage & Style

1. "Although some citizens may have concerns about the large size of the imposing animal ..." The use of the adjective *imposing* conveys the writer's sense of being dwarfed by the horse. This is appropriate since the word contributes to the reader's understanding of the horse's size without influencing the reader's opinion of the subject of the article.

2. "In fact, Medynski, who is a handsome, 10-year veteran of the police force ..." The use of the adjective *handsome* conveys the physical attraction the writer feels for the officer, and this is not appropriate since it has nothing to do with the subject of the article, nor with how well the police officer is able to perform his duties.

3. "Besides his claim that horses are 'a more convenient form of transportation,' Medynski enthusiastically maintains that ..." The use of the adverb *enthusiastically* conveys the writer's admiration for the officer's spirited approach to his job. Some students may find this subjectivity inappropriate since it is a personal opinion of the officer's manner, while others may feel the word only contributes to the overall intent of the article, which is to convey the benefit of the mounted police brigade to the city.

(WR3.02D—TOC 15: Usage & Style)

Word Study & Spelling

1. Root: power
   Generalization: When adding a suffix beginning with a consonant to a word that ends in a vowel or a consonant, make no change to the root.

2. Root: imagine
   Generalization: When adding a suffix beginning with a vowel to a word that ends in a vowel, usually drop the final vowel of the root word.

3. Root: hero
   Generalization: When adding a suffix beginning with a vowel to a word that ends in a vowel, usually drop the final vowel of the root word; *however*, if dropping the final vowel changes the pronunciation of the word, as it does in this case, the vowel generally stays.

4. Root: exhibit
   Generalization: When adding a suffix beginning with a vowel to a word that ends in a consonant, make no change.

5. Root: plenty
   Generalization: Words that end in -*y* change the -*y* to -*i* before most suffixes (except -*ing*).

(LG1.01B—TOC 16: Word Study & Spelling)

	GRADE 9 EXPECTATIONS	DEMONSTRATION OF LEARNING	ASSESSMENT TOOLS
LITERATURE STUDIES AND READING			
Overall (LIV.01P)	• read and demonstrate an understanding of a variety of literary and informational texts		
Specific (LI1.01P)	• describe information, ideas, opinions, and themes in texts they have read during the year from a variety of print and electronic sources, including biographies, short stories, poems, plays, novels, brochures, and articles from newspapers, magazines, and encyclopedias	• demonstrate understanding of profile (Investigating the Model SB #1–6)	• TOC 14: Tracking Expectations
Overall (LIV.02P)	• demonstrate an understanding of the elements of a variety of literary and informational forms, with a focus on plays, short stories, and newspaper and magazine articles	• analyze profiles to see if they adhere to Checkpoint criteria (More Challenge TG, page 116)	• AR 22: Response to Reading
WRITING			
Overall (WRV.01P)	• use print and electronic sources to gather information and explore ideas for their written work	• choose subject and gather information (Writer's Workshop SB #1–4)	• AR 19: Profile
Specific (WR1.01P)	• investigate potential topics by asking questions, identifying information needs, and developing research plans to gather data	• brainstorm interesting subjects for profiles (Writer's Workshop TG #1) • use graphic organizer to generate information about subject for profile (More Support TG, page 117)	• AR 19: Profile • AR 19: Profile
(WR1.02P)	• locate and record information and ideas from print and electronic sources, including newspapers and magazines, dictionaries, encyclopedias, vertical files, and electronic databases	• write a statement of purpose for profile (Writer's Workshop TG #2) • brainstorm actions, comments, and details of profile subject as well as setting (Writer's Workshop TG #3)	• AR 19: Profile • AR 19: Profile
(WR1.03P)	• sort and group information and ideas, assess their relevance and accuracy, and discard irrelevant material	• organize details of profile (Writer's Workshop TG #4)	• AR 19: Profile
(WR1.04P)	• use the information and ideas generated by research to explore topics for written work	• role-play various points of view (Usage & Style TG)	• TOC 15: Usage & Style
Overall (WRV.02P)	• identify the literary and informational forms suited to specific purposes and audiences and use the forms appropriately in their own writing, with an emphasis on communicating information accurately		
Specific (WR2.03P)	• demonstrate an understanding of literary and informational forms of writing, such as letters, personal narratives, short stories, answers to homework questions, summaries, and reports on research topics, by selecting a form appropriate to the specific purpose and audience for each piece of writing	• write a dialogue between Sean Knight and a fellow in-line skater (Extending the Model TG #1)	• AR 19: Profile
Overall (WRV.03P)	• use a variety of forms of writing to express themselves, clarify their ideas, and engage the audience's attention, imagination, and interest	• write draft of profile (Writer's Workshop SB #5) • write profile of themselves from someone else's point of view (More Challenge TG, page 117)	• AR 19: Profile • AR 19: Profile

AR=Assessment Rubric   EP=Extra Practice   SB=Student Book   SSEC=Student Self-Evaluation Checklist   TG=Teacher's Guide   TOC=Teacher Observation Checklist

	GRADE 9 EXPECTATIONS	DEMONSTRATION OF LEARNING	ASSESSMENT TOOLS
	WRITING (continued)		
Overall (WRV.04B)	• revise their written work, collaboratively and independently, with a focus on support for ideas, accuracy, clarity, and unity	• use revision questions to revise profile (Writer's Workshop TG #6)	• AR 19: Profile
Specific (WR4.02B)	• revise drafts to ensure consistency in use of first or third person and use of an appropriate level of language	• write and correct passages for appropriate point of view (Usage & Style SB #1–3) • use first- and third-person points of view (EP: Usage & Style)	• TOC 15: Usage & Style • TOC 15: Usage & Style
Overall (WRV.05B)	• edit and proofread to produce final drafts, using correct grammar, spelling, and punctuation, according to the conventions of standard Canadian English specified for this course, with the support of print and electronic resources when appropriate	• use editing questions to edit and proofread profile (Writer's Workshop TG #6) • edit and proofread profile (Writer's Workshop SB #6)	• AR 19: Profile • AR 19: Profile
Specific (WR5.03P)	• provide documentation showing their use of the writing process	• record writing process for profile, assess success, and set goals for future projects (Writer's Workshop TG #5)	• AR 3: Conferencing
(WR5.06P)	• construct complete and correct compound and complex sentences, using the following sentence components as required: subject, predicate, object, subject complement; main and subordinate clauses; prepositional phrases	• add to simple subject and predicate to build more detailed sentences (Grammar TG #1) • write passages including simple sentences to emphasize a point (Grammar TG #2) • write simple sentences (Grammar TG #3) • understand construction of compound sentence (Grammar TG #4) • discuss compound and complex sentences (Grammar TG #5) • write simple, compound, and complex sentences (Grammar SB #1–6) • write simple, compound, and complex sentences (EP: Grammar)	• TOC 4: Grammar • TOC 4: Grammar • TOC 4: Grammar • TOC 4: Grammar • TOC 4: Grammar • TOC 4: Grammar • TOC 4: Grammar
(WR5.16B)	• adapt punctuation and capitalization for the special requirements of direct quotations, scripts, dialogue, and poetry	• discuss value of including spoken words in profile (Mechanics TG #1) • identify and explain quoted comments in model profile (Mechanics TG #2) • rewrite quoted passages (Mechanics SB #1–4) • use punctuation in quotations correctly (EP: Mechanics)	• TOC 8: Mechanics • TOC 8: Mechanics • TOC 8: Mechanics • TOC 8: Mechanics
	LANGUAGE		
Overall (LGV.01P)	• use knowledge of vocabulary and language conventions to speak, write, and read clearly and correctly		
Specific (LG1.01B)	• describe strategies used to expand vocabulary	• understand rules for spelling words with suffixes (Word Study & Spelling TG #1) • list words with suffixes that are frequently misspelled (Word Study & Spelling TG #2) • use words with suffixes correctly (Word Study & Spelling SB #1–4) • use words with suffixes correctly (EP: Word Study & Spelling)	• TOC 16: Word Study & Spelling • TOC 16: Word Study & Spelling • TOC 16: Word Study & Spelling • TOC 16: Word Study & Spelling
(LG1.03B)	• identify words borrowed from other languages, and words and terms recently introduced to describe new ideas, inventions, and products, and explain their origins	• find word origins for sports terms (Word Origins SB) • research origins of sports words (More Support TG, page 118)	• TOC 16: Word Study & Spelling • TOC 16: Word Study & Spelling

AR=Assessment Rubric   EP=Extra Practice   SB=Student Book   SSEC=Student Self-Evaluation Checklist   TG=Teacher's Guide   TOC=Teacher Observation Checklist

GRADE 9 EXPECTATIONS	DEMONSTRATION OF LEARNING	ASSESSMENT TOOLS
LANGUAGE (continued)		
(LG1.05P) • recognize, describe, and use correctly, in oral and written language, the language structures of standard Canadian English and its conventions of grammar and usage, including: – simple, compound, and complex sentences	• add to simple subject and predicate to build more detailed sentences (Grammar TG #1) • write passages including simple sentences to emphasize a point (Grammar TG #2) • write simple sentences (Grammar TG #3) • understand construction of compound sentence (Grammar TG #4) • discuss compound and complex sentences (Grammar TG #5) • write simple, compound, and complex sentences (Grammar SB #1–6) • write simple, compound, and complex sentences (EP: Grammar)	• TOC 4: Grammar • TOC 4: Grammar • TOC 4: Grammar • TOC 4: Grammar • TOC 4: Grammar • TOC 4: Grammar • TOC 4: Grammar
Overall (LGV.02B) • use listening techniques and oral communication skills to participate in classroom discussions and more formal activities, such as storytelling, role playing, and reporting/presenting, for specific purposes and audiences	• share in-line skating experiences (Introducing the Unit TG #1) • describe in-line skating equipment (Introducing the Unit TG #2) • discuss focus of profile as quality, skill, or experience of person (Introducing the Model TG #1) • practise identifying particular quality, skill, or experience of individuals (Introducing the Model TG #2) • re-enact *Front Page Challenge* to practise focusing on an individual (Oral Language Extension SB)	• TOC 14: Tracking Expectations • TOC 14: Tracking Expectations • TOC 14: Tracking Expectations • TOC 14: Tracking Expectations • AR 15: Oral Language
Specific (LG2.04P) • use eye contact, specific examples, humour, and visual aids and technology, as appropriate, to engage the audience's interest during oral presentations	• interview partners and present introductory speech (More Oral Language TG)	• TOC 1: Conducting an Interview
MEDIA STUDIES		
Overall (MDV.01P) • identify and describe the elements, intended audiences, and production practices of a variety of media forms	• discuss personal qualities most recognized by media (Extending the Model TG #2) • compare recorded radio broadcast of model profile with written form (More Media TG)	• AR 21: Response to Media • AR 21: Response to Media
Specific (MD1.02P) • identify and describe the elements used to structure media works in a variety of forms	• analyze use of visual techniques in videoclip of sporting event (Media Link SB)	• AR 21: Response to Media
Overall (MDV.02P) • use knowledge of a variety of media forms, purposes, and audiences to create media works	• record model profile as radio broadcast and compare with written form (More Media TG)	• AR 12: Media Product

AR=Assessment Rubric   EP=Extra Practice   SB=Student Book   SSEC=Student Self-Evaluation Checklist   TG=Teacher's Guide   TOC=Teacher Observation Checklist

Instructional Strategies for the Applied Course

Learning Goals

- write a profile
- construct simple, compound, and complex sentences
- use ellipses and square brackets in direct quotations
- select first or third person to suit the form, purpose, and audience
- expand vocabulary by using suffixes

Planning Information

Links to Other Nelson English 9 Resources

Literature & Media 9
Magazine Profile—See "Tom Longboat" by Jack Granatstein, pp. 121–122.

Write Source 2000
Ellipsis—"Ellipsis," p. 388; **Point of View**—"Point of View," p. 344; **Simple, Compound, and Complex Sentences**—"Kinds of Sentences," pp. 437–438; **Suffixes**—"Suffixes," p. 331

Introducing the Unit

The activities on page 103 from the Academic Course are appropriate for the Applied Course.

1. (LGV.02B—TOC 14: Tracking Expectations)

2. (LGV.02B—TOC 14: Tracking Expectations)

Introducing the Model

1. Students, working in pairs, draw each other's profiles on unlined paper. (If students wish, the paper can be taped to a vertical surface and the subject can stand sideways close to the paper to make it easier for the partner to trace a profile.) The subject's name is written on the back of the paper with a number on the front and all are shuffled, then displayed around the room. Without discussion, each student individually tries to match the profiles with their subjects. Subsequent discussion will introduce the idea that *written* profiles focus on a particular feature (i.e., quality or skill or experience) of an individual. (LGV.02B—TOC 14: Tracking Expectations)

NOTE: Before their discussion, students should be cautioned against making comments about physical features that might embarrass the subjects of the drawings.

2. Activity #2 on page 103 from the Academic Course is appropriate for the Applied Course. (LGV.02B—TOC 14: Tracking Expectations)

Checkpoint

Sample criteria for a profile:

- often begins with scene or action that establishes identity and uniqueness of subject
- usually focuses on a single experience or quality that makes subject unique or intriguing
- may be arranged in a number of ways, e.g., chronological or each section focusing on a new idea
- may include comments by subject or by others about subject
- often ends with personal reflection by writer about subject

Investigating the Model

Answers:
See the Academic Course on pages 103–104 for answers.

Student Book 1.–6. (LI1.01P—TOC 14: Tracking Expectations)

Extending the Model

1. Have students identify the in-line skating terms included in the profile, adding any they might know themselves. Ask them what effect this terminology has on readers (conveys a sense of the sport through the language associated with it). As a follow-up to this discussion of the importance of word choice, have students write a dialogue between Sean Knight and a fellow member of the 519 Crew, describing his feelings before an upcoming competition. This dialogue should include some of the skater terminology included in the profile as well as any other terms students might feel appropriate to the context. (WR2.03P—AR 19: Profile)

More Challenge

As an extension of Extending the Model activity #2, students could write a brief essay analyzing whether the profiles they found adhere to the criteria identified in Checkpoint or whether they reveal other characteristics. (LIV.02P—AR 22: Response to Reading)

2. Activity #3 on page 104 from the Academic Course is appropriate for the Applied Course. (MDV.01P—AR 21: Response to Media)

WRITER'S WORKSHOP

The activities on pages 104–106 from the Academic Course are appropriate for the Applied Course.

1. (WR1.01P—AR 22: Response to Reading)

2. (WR1.02P—AR 19: Profile)

3. (WR1.02P—AR 19: Profile)

4. (WR1.03P—AR 19: Profile)

5. (WR5.03P—AR 3: Conferencing)

6. (WRV.04B—AR 19: Profile; WRV.05B—AR 19: Profile)

Student Book 1.–4. (WRV.01P—AR 19: Profile); 5. (WRV.03P—AR 19: Profile); 6. (WRV.04B—AR 19: Profile; WRV.05B—AR 19: Profile)

ORAL LANGUAGE EXTENSION

The activity on page 106 from the Academic Course is appropriate for the Applied Course.

Student Book (LGV.02B—AR 15: Oral Language)

GRAMMAR

1. Record on the board a simple subject and predicate suggested by a student. Have the class invent more information about that subject and predicate to be inserted as modifying phrases, making the sentence longer and more detailed. At this point, emphasize that at the heart of this sentence remains the foundation—a single subject and predicate. Then, have students, working in pairs, suggest their own simple subject and predicate and build longer, more detailed sentences while maintaining the foundation of simple sentences. (WR5.06P—TOC 4: Grammar; LG1.05P—TOC 4: Grammar)

2. It is important for students to recognize that too many simple sentences will make writing sound repetitive and stilted, but a short, simple sentence is often an effective way of emphasizing a point. Have students practise writing passages that reflect this use (e.g., *Having stayed up half the night watching videos, Brian was unprepared to give his presentation in class the next morning, and he was hoping Mr. Redding would give him an extension. He was wrong.*)
(WR5.06P—TOC 4: Grammar; LG1.05P—TOC 4: Grammar)

3. Show students that simple sentences can create a sense of movement in a piece of writing, drawing the reader toward a conclusion, as in the following passage: *Our class spent months raising money for our year-end trip. We had bake sales. We held car washes. We painted fences. We raked yards. By mid-May, though, we were still two hundred dollars short.* Have students write similar passages.
(WR5.06P—TOC 4: Grammar; LG1.05P—TOC 4: Grammar)

4. Some students might mistakenly think the following sentence has two subjects and predicates because there are two verbs: *By entering the marathon, Celine **demonstrated** her determination to win and **inspired** the rest of us with her positive outlook.* However, show students that there is only one subject for both verbs—*Celine.* Then show students how to make this sentence a compound sentence by adding another subject (e.g., *she*): *By entering the marathon, **Celine demonstrated** her determination to win and **she inspired** the rest of us with her positive outlook.* (WR5.06P—TOC 4: Grammar; LG1.05P—TOC 4: Grammar)

MORE CHALLENGE

Ask students to write a profile of themselves, but from someone else's point of view. Students might choose the point of view of a fellow student, teacher, coach, or employer. (WRV.03P—AR 19: Profile)

MORE SUPPORT

Some students may find a graphic organizer useful in helping them generate information about the person they are profiling. Students could use the following prompts to gather details about their subject:

- name/age of subject
- focus (what do I want people to know/understand/appreciate most about this person?)
- personal history
- physical description
- typical clothing
- place usually found
- typical actions
- typical comments
- comments made by others

(WR1.01P—AR 19: Profile)

MORE ORAL LANGUAGE

Have each student interview someone in the classroom whom they do not know well and prepare a brief speech of introduction to share with the class. Before pairing up, students should brainstorm the kinds of questions they might like to ask concerning family members, places lived before, hobbies, and future plans. Give students 15 minutes to interview their partners, after which the partners exchange roles and repeat the process. Finally, assign students to prepare a brief introductory speech they will deliver to the class following the suggestions listed in the Speaking Skills appendix on page 204 of the student book. (LG2.04P—TOC 1: Conducting an Interview)

5. Activity #2 on pages 106–107 from the Academic Course is appropriate for the Applied Course. (WR5.06P—TOC 4: Grammar; LG1.05P—TOC 4: Grammar)

Answers:

See the Academic Course on pages 107–108 for answers.

Student Book 1.–6. (WR5.06P—TOC 4: Grammar; LG1.06P—TOC 4: Grammar)

MEDIA LINK

Teachers may wish to have students focus on a limited number of visual techniques and sound effects when analyzing the videoclip of a sporting event. Suggest that students create a separate section in their binder or folder for their findings, to be added to as the year progresses. (MD1.02P—AR 21: Response to Media)

MECHANICS

The activities on page 108 from the Academic Course are appropriate for the Applied Course.

1. (WR5.16B—TOC 8: Mechanics)

2. (WR5.16B—TOC 8: Mechanics)

Answers:

See the Academic Course on pages 108–109 for answers.

Student Book 1.–4. (WR5.16B—TOC 8: Mechanics)

USAGE & STYLE

An effective means of helping students recognize the impact of point of view in a piece of writing is to have students consider the witness statements given at a scene by an individual involved and by a bystander. Role-playing various points of view would illustrate the difference between the information provided by someone emotionally involved and the information given by a person who was not a participant. (WR1.04P—TOC 15: Usage & Style)

Answers:

See the Academic Course on page 109 for answers.

Student Book 1.–3. (WR4.02B—TOC 15: Usage & Style)

WORD STUDY & SPELLING

The activities on pages 109–110 from the Academic Course are appropriate for the Applied Course.

1. (LG1.01B—TOC 16: Word Study & Spelling)

2. (LG1.01B—TOC 16: Word Study & Spelling)

Answers:

See the Academic Course on pages 110–111 for answers.

Student Book 1.–4. (LG1.01B—TOC 16: Word Study & Spelling)

WORD ORIGINS

See the Academic Course on page 111 for answers.

Student Book (LG1.03B—TOC 16: Word Study & Spelling)

ANSWERS TO EXTRA PRACTICE

See the Academic Course on page 112 for answers.

Grammar

(WR5.06P—TOC 4: Grammar; LG1.05P—TOC 4: Grammar)

Mechanics

(WR5.16B—TOC 8: Mechanics)

Usage & Style

(WR4.02B—TOC 15: Usage & Style)

Word Study & Spelling

(LG1.01B—TOC 16: Word Study & Spelling)

GRAMMAR

NAME: _____ DATE: _____

Tell whether each of the following sentences is simple, compound, or complex in structure.

1. Every one of the people sitting on the bus gasped in surprise as the car ahead of them overturned.

_____

2. The sound of sirens wailing in the distance grew increasingly louder.

_____

3. Even bystanders and people in surrounding buildings rushed to help.

_____

4. When the police arrived, the crowd moved back to give them room to assist the victims.

_____

5. We waited, but we could do nothing.

_____

LANGUAGE & WRITING 9

MECHANICS

NAME: _____ DATE: _____

Big Ben

Constable Rick Medynski, a member of Bishopville's mounted police brigade, has patrolled the city on his horse, Ben, for four years. Although some citizens may have concerns about the large size of the imposing animal, Medynski assures listeners that the horse is a wonderful asset to the city's police force. "Ben," says Medynski, "is a very gentle animal. He's smart, too, and well-trained so he's accustomed to the various noises and problems associated with large numbers of people moving about in an urban area like Bishopville." In fact, Medynski, who is a handsome, 10-year veteran of the police force, says that the mounted police brigade is uniquely suited to patrolling the city because horses are able to take police officers places where cars cannot go, such as down narrow alleys and past snarled traffic tie-ups. "I was assigned to highway patrol duty for five years before being reassigned to the mounted police division. I remember being frustrated many times by traffic jams that blocked my vehicle and delayed me from performing my duties." Besides his claim that horses are "a more convenient form of transportation," Medynski enthusiastically maintains that Ben is also a great help bridging barriers between troubled youths and the police department. "Young people often don't feel comfortable talking to a police officer in a cruiser, but most of them take to Ben right away, patting him and offering him treats."

Check the following passages against the words in the passage above and rewrite them, adding quotation marks, ellipsis points, and square brackets where they are needed.

1. Officer Medynski describes Ben as a very gentle animal that is accustomed to the various noises and problems associated with an urban area like Bishopville.

   _____

   _____

2. The police officer remembers many traffic jams that blocked his vehicle and delayed him from performing his duties.

   _____

   _____

3. According to Officer Medynski, youths often take to Ben right away, patting him and offering him treats.

   _____

   _____

USAGE & STYLE

NAME: _____ DATE: _____

Although the third-person point of view is used in the following article, the author manages to interject a personal opinion in various places. Find three passages that convey the author's own impressions and tell whether they are appropriate for the piece, giving reasons for your ideas.

Big Ben

Constable Rick Medynski, a member of Bishopville's mounted police brigade, has patrolled the city on his horse, Ben, for four years. Although some citizens may have concerns about the large size of the imposing animal, Medynski assures listeners that the horse is a wonderful asset to the city's police force. "Ben," says Medynski, "is a very gentle animal. He's smart, too, and well-trained so he's accustomed to the various noises and problems associated with large numbers of people moving about in an urban area like Bishopville." In fact, Medynski, who is a handsome, 10-year veteran of the police force, says that the mounted police brigade is uniquely suited to patrolling the city because horses are able to take police officers places where cars cannot go, such as down narrow alleys and past snarled traffic tie-ups. "I was assigned to highway patrol duty for five years before being reassigned to the mounted police division. I remember being frustrated many times by traffic jams that blocked my vehicle and delayed me from performing my duties." Besides his claim that horses are "a more convenient form of transportation," Medynski enthusiastically maintains that Ben is also a great help bridging barriers between troubled youths and the police department. "Young people often don't feel comfortable talking to a police officer in a cruiser, but most of them take to Ben right away, patting him and offering him treats."

_____

_____

_____

_____

_____

_____

_____

_____

_____

_____

WORD STUDY & SPELLING

NAME: _____ DATE: _____

_____

Below are words that have suffixes. For each word, write its root and then summarize the generalization that governs the spelling of the word.

1. powerful

_____

_____

_____

2. imaginary

_____

_____

_____

3. heroism

_____

_____

_____

4. exhibition

_____

_____

_____

5. plentiful

_____

_____

UNIT 6: EVENT DESCRIPTION

ACADEMIC EXPECTATIONS

GRADE 9 EXPECTATIONS		DEMONSTRATION OF LEARNING	ASSESSMENT TOOLS
LITERATURE STUDIES AND READING			
Overall (LIV.01D)	• read and demonstrate an understanding of a variety of literary and informational texts, from contemporary and historical periods	• demonstrate understanding of forms of description (Reflecting on Descriptive Writing Forms SB #1–2)	• TOC 13: Tracking Expectations
Specific (LI1.01D)	• describe information, ideas, opinions, and themes in print and electronic texts they have read during the year from different cultures and historical periods and in a variety of genres, including novels, short stories, plays, poems, biographies, short essays, and articles from newspapers, magazines, and encyclopedias	• judge accuracy of news report of event (Introducing the Unit TG #3) • compare language and amount of detail in newspaper or magazine article with model (Extending the Model TG #1)	• TOC 13: Tracking Expectations • AR 22: Response to Reading
(LI1.02D)	• select and read texts for different purposes, with an emphasis on recognizing the elements of literary genres and the organization of informational materials, collecting and assessing information, responding imaginatively, and exploring human experiences and values	• discuss effectiveness of model (Investigating the Model TG #1)	• AR 22: Response to Reading
(LI1.03B)	• describe a variety of reading strategies and select and use them effectively before, during, and after reading to understand texts	• list predictions about model based on title, photographs, and prior knowledge of power failures (Introducing the Model TG #1) • note which predictions were included in model (Introducing the Model TG #2)	• TOC 10: Reading Strategies • TOC 10: Reading Strategies
(LI1.04D)	• locate explicit information and ideas in texts to use in developing opinions and interpretations	• locate information and ideas in model to support opinions (Investigating the Model SB #1–7)	• AR 22: Response to Reading
(LI1.06D)	• use specific evidence from a text to support opinions and judgments	• use evidence to compare model with television report (Extending the Model TG #2)	• AR 22: Response to Reading
Overall (LIV.02D)	• demonstrate an understanding of the elements of a variety of literary and informational forms, with a focus on plays, short stories, and short essays	• suggest details relating to sound, feel, taste, and smell for event description (Introducing the Unit TG #2) • compare four forms of descriptive writing (Looking Over Descriptive Writing Forms SB #1)	• TOC 13: Tracking Expectations • TOC 13: Tracking Expectations
Overall (LIV.03B)	• identify and explain the effect of specific elements of style in a variety of literary and informational texts		
Specific (LI3.01D)	• explain how authors use diction and phrasing to achieve particular effects in their writing	• speculate on why author used parallel structure (Grammar TG #1) • complete series of parallel descriptive phrases (Grammar TG #2) • discuss ways to create vivid description (Usage & Style TG #1)	• TOC 4: Grammar • TOC 4: Grammar • TOC 15: Usage & Style
WRITING			
Overall (WRV.01D)	• use a variety of print and electronic sources to gather information and explore ideas for their written work	• gather and organize information for event description (Writer's Workshop SB #1–5)	• AR 6: Event Description

AR=Assessment Rubric   EP=Extra Practice   SB=Student Book   SSEC=Student Self-Evaluation Checklist   TG=Teacher's Guide   TOC=Teacher Observation Checklist

WRITING (continued)		
Specific (WR1.01D) • investigate potential topics by formulating questions, identifying information needs, and developing research plans to gather data	• list details contributing to main impression of memorable event (Introducing the Unit TG #1) • brainstorm list of topics for event description (Writer's Workshop TG #1) • question each other to generate details (Writer's Workshop TG #2)	• AR 6: Event Description • AR 6: Event Description • AR 6: Event Description
(WR1.03D) • group and label information and ideas; evaluate the relevance, accuracy, and completeness of the information and ideas; and discard irrelevant material	• categorize participants of event description (Writer's Workshop TG #3) • plan organizational pattern for event description (Writer's Workshop TG #4)	• AR 6: Event Description • AR 6: Event Description
Overall (WRV.02D) • identify the literary and informational forms suited to various purposes and audiences and use the forms appropriately in their own writing, with an emphasis on supporting opinions or interpretations with specific information		
Specific (WR2.01D) • demonstrate an understanding of literary and informational forms, such as myths, poems, short stories, scripts, advertisements, formal letters, reviews, and supported opinion essays, by selecting and using forms of writing appropriate to different purposes and audiences	• write up event for school newspaper (Media Link SB)	• AR 4: Descriptive Writing
Overall (WRV.03D) • use a variety of organizational techniques to present ideas and supporting details logically and coherently in written work	• write draft of event description (Writer's Workshop SB #6–7) • write profile of historical figure (Using the Descriptive Writing Forms SB #1) • write descriptive poem of a familiar place (Using the Descriptive Writing Forms SB #2) • write essay on newspaper description of an event (Using the Descriptive Writing Forms SB #4)	• AR 6: Event Description • AR 19: Profile • AR 17: Poetry • AR 8: Expository Writing
Specific (WR3.01D) • use a unifying image, mood, or voice to structure descriptive paragraphs or poems	• write about an imaginary experience as hero, villain, or victim of the ice storm (Extending the Model TG #3) • write descriptive setting that represents a state of mind (More Challenge TG, page 130)	• AR 6: Event Description • AR 6: Event Description
Overall (WRV.04D) • revise their written work, independently and collaboratively, with a focus on support for ideas and opinions, accuracy, clarity, and unity	• revise event description (Writer's Workshop SB #8) • revise profile of historical figure (Using the Descriptive Writing Forms SB #1) • revise descriptive poem (Using the Descriptive Writing Forms SB #2) • revise essay on newspaper description of event (Using the Descriptive Writing Forms SB #4)	• AR 6: Event Description • AR 19: Profile • AR 17: Poetry • AR 8: Expository Writing
Overall (WRV.05D) • edit and proofread to produce final drafts, using correct grammar, spelling, and punctuation, according to the conventions of standard Canadian English, with the support of print and electronic resources when appropriate	• edit and proofread event description (Writer's Workshop SB #8) • edit and proofread profile of historical figure (Using the Descriptive Writing Forms SB #1) • edit and proofread descriptive poem (Using the Descriptive Writing Forms SB #2) • edit and proofread essay on newspaper description of event (Using the Descriptive Writing Forms SB #4)	• AR 6: Event Description • AR 19: Profile • AR 17: Poetry • AR 8: Expository Writing

AR=Assessment Rubric   EP=Extra Practice   SB=Student Book   SSEC=Student Self-Evaluation Checklist   TG=Teacher's Guide   TOC=Teacher Observation Checklist

GRADE 9 EXPECTATIONS	DEMONSTRATION OF LEARNING	ASSESSMENT TOOLS
WRITING (continued)		
Specific (WR5.04B) • edit and proofread their own and others' writing, identifying and correcting errors according to the requirements for grammar, usage, spelling, and punctuation	• present numerical information correctly (Mechanics SB #1–3) • write numbers correctly (More Support TG) • correct sentences with errors in numerical information (EP: Mechanics)	• TOC 8: Mechanics • TOC 8: Mechanics • TOC 8: Mechanics
(WR5.06D) • construct complete and correct compound and complex sentences, using the following sentence components as required: subject, predicate, object, subject complement; main and subordinate clauses; prepositional and participial phrases	• identify parallel structure in sentences (Grammar TG #2) • construct complete sentences that include parallel structure (Grammar SB #1–3) • write a paragraph including parallel sentences (More Challenge TG, page 131) • correct sentences with parallel structure (EP: Grammar)	• TOC 4: Grammar • TOC 4: Grammar • TOC 4: Grammar • TOC 4: Grammar
(WR5.11B) • use knowledge of a wide range of spelling patterns and rules to identify, analyze, and correct spelling errors	• give examples for spelling strategies (Word Study & Spelling TG #1) • suggest spelling strategies for listed words (EP: Word Study & Spelling) • give examples for spelling strategies (Word Study & Spelling TG #1)	• TOC 16: Word Study & Spelling • TOC 16: Word Study & Spelling • TOC 16: Word Study & Spelling
LANGUAGE		
Overall (LGV.01D) • use knowledge of vocabulary and language conventions to speak, write, and read competently using a level of language appropriate to the purpose and audience		
Specific (LG1.01B) • describe strategies used to expand vocabulary and provide evidence of other vocabulary-building activities	• define meaning of words using context (Word Study & Spelling TG #2)	• TOC 16: Word Study & Spelling
(LG1.03B) • identify words borrowed from other languages and words and terms recently introduced to describe new ideas, inventions, and products, and explain their origins	• give meaning of words (Word Study & Spelling TG #2) • give meaning and origins of words (Word Origins SB)	• TOC 16: Word Study & Spelling • TOC 16: Word Study & Spelling
(LG1.04B) • select words and phrases appropriate to informal and formal styles, to suit the purpose and intended audience of oral and written work	• choose precise words (Usage & Style TG #2) • use precise words correctly (Usage & Style SB #1–3) • rewrite sentences using precise nouns, vivid verbs, and effective modifiers (EP: Usage & Style)	• TOC 15: Usage & Style • TOC 15: Usage & Style • TOC 15: Usage & Style
(LG1.05D) • recognize, describe, and use correctly, in oral and written language, the language structures of standard Canadian English and its conventions of grammar and usage, including: – components of sentences: subject, predicate, object, subject complement, prepositional and participial phrases, main and subordinate clauses	• construct complete sentences that include parallel structure (Grammar SB #1–3) • write a paragraph including parallel sentences (More Challenge TG, page 131)	• TOC 4: Grammar • TOC 4: Grammar
Overall (LGV.02B) • use listening techniques and oral communication skills to participate in classroom discussions and more formal activities, such as storytelling, role playing, and reporting/presenting, for specific purposes and audiences	• present profile of historical figure as an interview (Using the Descriptive Writing Forms SB #1)	• TOC 1: Conducting an Interview

AR=Assessment Rubric   EP=Extra Practice   SB=Student Book   SSEC=Student Self-Evaluation Checklist   TG=Teacher's Guide   TOC=Teacher Observation Checklist

GRADE 9 EXPECTATIONS	DEMONSTRATION OF LEARNING	ASSESSMENT TOOLS
LANGUAGE (continued)		
Specific (LG2.01D) • communicate orally in group discussions for different purposes, with a focus on identifying key ideas and supporting details, distinguishing fact from opinion, asking clarifying questions, and following instructions	• understand how to develop effective questions (Oral Language Extension TG #2)	• TOC 13: Tracking Expectations
(LG2.02D) • communicate in group discussions by sharing the duties of the group, speaking in turn, listening actively, taking notes, paraphrasing key points made by others, exchanging and challenging ideas and information, asking appropriate questions, reconsidering their own ideas and opinions, managing conflict, and respecting the opinions of others	• discuss roles in group work and appoint members as leader, clarifier, encourager, and checker (Oral Language Extension TG #1)	• SSEC 2: Group Work
(LG2.03D) • plan and make oral presentations to a small group or the class, selecting and using vocabulary and methods of delivery to suit audience and purpose	• present a radio news report on the ice storm (More Oral Language TG)	• AR 15: Oral Language
(LG2.05D) • practise with cue cards and relaxation exercises (and with visual aids and technology, if used) to ensure confident delivery in oral presentations	• practise speaking with confidence and expression (Media Link SB)	• TOC 11: Speaking
MEDIA STUDIES		
Overall (MDV.01D) • use knowledge of the elements, intended audiences, and production practices of a variety of media forms to analyze specific media works	• compare model with television report (Extending the Model TG #2)	• AR 21: Response to Media
Specific (MD1.02D) • identify how elements of media forms are used in a variety of media works and explain the effects of different treatments	• give reasons for choosing other photographs for model (Investigating the Model TG #2) • identify why a radio broadcast is effective (Media Link TG)	• AR 21: Response to Media • AR 21: Response to Media
Overall (MDV.02D) • use knowledge of a variety of media forms, purposes, and audiences to create media works and describe their intended effect	• tape radio news item about an event (Media Link SB) • rewrite event for school newspaper (Using the Descriptive Writing Forms SB #3)	• AR 12: Media Product • AR 12: Media Product
Specific (MD2.02D) • create media works for different purposes and explain how each has been designed to achieve its particular purpose	• create a poster to promote event they wrote about (More Media TG)	• AR 12: Media Product

AR=Assessment Rubric   EP=Extra Practice   SB=Student Book   SSEC=Student Self-Evaluation Checklist   TG=Teacher's Guide   TOC=Teacher Observation Checklist

PLANNING INFORMATION

Links to Other Nelson English 9 Resources

Literature & Media 9
Event Description—See "Anna Lang" by John Melady, pp. 123–129.

Write Source 2000
Descriptive Writing—"Descriptive Paragraph," p. 100, "Writing About an Event," p. 126; **Numerical Information**—"Numbers," p. 410; **Parallel Structure**—"Parallelism," p. 140; **Precise and Interesting Nouns, Verbs, and Modifiers**—"Using Strong, Colourful Words," pp. 135–136; **Spelling Strategies**—"Improved Spelling," pp. 411–418

INTRODUCING THE UNIT

1. While some descriptions focus only on a person, place, thing, feeling, or idea, an event description integrates all of these to create an overall impression. Ask students to identify events they have found memorable in their lives. Have them write in a single statement the main impression each of these events created. Then ask students to list specific details about these events that they feel contributed to their main impression. (WR1.01D—AR 6: Event Description)

2. Ask students to examine the photograph at the beginning of the unit on page 96 to identify the kind of event being portrayed. Discuss with them the effectiveness of the picture alone (sight) in creating an impression of the event. Ask them what other details would need to be added to a written event description. Students should suggest those relating to sound, feel, taste, and smell. (LIV.02D—TOC 13: Tracking Expectations)

3. Ask students if they have ever attended an event that was later written up in a local newspaper or in their school newsletter. Have students comment on whether they felt the written report gave a true picture of the event. Why or why not? (LI1.01D—TOC 13: Tracking Expectations)

INTRODUCING THE MODEL

1. Ask students to read the title of the model and examine the photographs on pages 97 and 98 of the student book to predict what this article is about. Then, using their own experiences during power failures, have them predict some of the details they might expect to read about in the event description. Make a list of these predictions on the board. (LI1.03B—TOC 10: Reading Strategies)

2. After students have read the model, have them note which predicted details Eric Harris included in "Struck Powerless." Indicate to students that predicting what is in a story before they read it, and then reading the story to find out which of their predictions are included is an excellent reading strategy enabling them to remember more of the details in a piece of writing. (LI1.03B—TOC 10: Reading Strategies)

INVESTIGATING THE MODEL

1. Ask students to discuss the overall effectiveness of "Struck Powerless" in capturing the essence of the storm and its results. (LI1.02D—AR 22: Response to Reading)

2. If possible, borrow a copy of the book *The Ice Storm: An Historic Record in Photographs of January, 1998* by Mark Abley for students to look through to find two photographs they would have chosen to include with the model instead of

the photographs in the student book. Ask students to give reasons for their choice.
(MD1.02D—AR 21: Response to Media)

Answers:

1. The second sentence of the event description establishes the serious mood ("The Storm of the Millennium") and the subject (the ice storm that hit parts of Quebec and Ontario in January of 1998).

2. This event description which appeared in *Canadian Geographic* was intended for an adult audience with a high level of reading ability. The language and details (e.g., prerogative, stalemate, Zamboni, strata, liberation forces) require readers with a broad background of knowledge.

3. The writer uses a chronological order in his event description. The piece begins with the coming of the rain, moves to the forming of the ice and its effects, and ends with a reflection on the overall impact of the storm.

4. Possible answer

   Ten facts presented in the model are: the ice storm lasted six days; the ice storm took place in January, 1998; more than 80 millimetres of ice rain fell in six days; transmission towers near Saint-Hyacinthe, Que., and Cornwall, Ont. fell; broadcasters on CBC Radio gave reports on the damage, repairs, relief, and the weather; Roland Parent died of carbon monoxide poisoning; Margaret Heath died of hypothermia; the hydro pole outside the author's window leaned at a 70-degree angle; a 12-metre green ash stood in the author's front yard before the storm; and the author and his wife moved to Mountain Township, Ont., in 1987.

   The writer makes the facts relevant and interesting by using numerous specific examples and figurative language. Illustrations include metaphors (e.g., an atmospheric Zamboni), similes (e.g., transmission towers crumpled like exhausted marathon runners), oxymorons (e.g., ice rain), and onomatopoeia (e.g., rumble, snapped, cracked).

5. Possible answers

   Ten examples where the author presents his own opinion or subjective impressions are: "spectacle of Nature's prerogative"; "an atmospheric Zamboni"; "like exhausted marathon runners"; "The heroes"; "The victims"; "The single-minded *Financial Post*"; "Everyone had defining moments to recall, heart-rendering and humanitarian"; "icon of the rural disaster zone"; "Our 12-day trial by firelight was not life-threatening"; and "We will be more sociable with neighbours and strangers."

6. Possible answers

   Five examples where the author appeals to the reader's senses are: "splintered violently under loads 30 times their own weight"; "the utter darkness"; "frigid residences"; "fed and comforted the homeless thousands"; and "the glassy crashing of ice."

   Student work.

7. Possible answer

   In the second paragraph, the first two sentences explain the "meteorological forces" mentioned in the introductory paragraph and the last two sentences describe the "extraordinary burden of ice on a landscape accustomed to icy burdens" also mentioned in the introductory paragraph. The third paragraph supports the "spectacle of Nature's prerogative" found in the first sentence of the article. The eighth paragraph on page 98, beginning with "The toll was

---

CHECKPOINT

Sample criteria for an event description:

- often contains a topic sentence that names subject and establishes tone

- contains level of language and choice of detail to suit interests and understanding of reader

- usually follows organizational pattern that is chronological, spatial, or that presents overall impression of event down to specific details

- must convey information accurately

- is usually written from narrator's point of view

- often contains details that appeal to five senses of sight, hearing, smell, taste, and touch

- contains paragraphs that relate back to introductory paragraph

---

immeasurable," supports the idea that "It was, indisputably, the storm of the century" in the first paragraph.

Student Book 1.–7. (LI1.04D—AR 22: Response to Reading)

EXTENDING THE MODEL

1. Ask students to find one other newspaper or magazine article written on the ice storm and to compare the language and amount of detail provided with that in "Struck Powerless." (LI1.01D—AR 22: Response to Reading)

2. If possible, contact a television station to find out if they have any reports on the ice storm available for loan. Have students view the report and compare the effectiveness of the television report with that of the model. What was the model able to do that the television report could not (level of language, use of imagery, amount of detail)? What was the television report able to do that the model could not (footage showing damage done by the storm, interviews with people)? (LI1.06D—AR 22: Response to Reading; MDV.01D—AR 21: Response to Media)

3. Have students take on the role of a hero, a villain, or a victim of the ice storm and write about an experience they might have had from one of these perspectives. Remind them to first establish the overall impression they want to give. Students who lived through the ice storm of 1998 could write about an imaginary experience. (WR3.01D—AR 6: Event Description)

WRITER'S WORKSHOP

1. To supplement the number of topics in the student book, have students brainstorm a further list, keeping in mind that they should be ones they have experienced themselves rather than fictional events. If students have photographs or videos of the events they are going to describe, suggest that they use these to help relive the experience. (WR1.01D—AR 6: Event Description)

2. Some students write more easily about an event when prompted by specific questions. Have students consider the kinds of details another person might like to know about the event which will help make the event real. Students could list their ideas or questions on the board for use in generating details or they could work in pairs to generate details orally, one person interviewing the other using the questions the class has listed. (WR1.01D—AR 6: Event Description)

3. Students may wish to provide information using a similar method as that on page 98 of the student book where the topic is presented (the heroes, the villains, the victims) followed by examples. Suggest that they categorize the people who are part of their event description first (e.g., winners, losers, spectators, performers) before detailing their actions. (WR1.03D—AR 6: Event Description)

4. Discuss with students the fact that they will be presenting their information to readers who may have no prior knowledge of the event. Once they have decided which organizational pattern to follow (spatial, chronological, overall impression moving to specific details), you might model one of these patterns by organizing details of an event you have experienced. Illustrate on the board or on an overhead projector the details you will include and their order. Provide students with an opportunity to discuss their own information and its arrangement in small groups. (WR1.03D—AR 6: Event Description)

Student Book 1.–5. (WRV.01D—AR 6: Event Description); 6.–7. (WRV.03D—AR 6: Event Description); 8. (WRV.04D—AR 6: Event Description; WRV.05D—AR 6: Event Description)

MORE CHALLENGE

Have students work in pairs to list words to describe a state of mind (for example, loneliness, joy, peace). Students could then choose one of the states and write a descriptive setting that represents it (for example, peace: walking on the beach in the early morning). (WR3.01D—AR 6: Event Description)

ORAL LANGUAGE EXTENSION

1. Have students read and discuss the roles explained in the Idea File on page 102 of the student book before assigning the activities for the Oral Language Extension. Direct students to appoint members of their groups to each of the four roles: leader, clarifier, encourager, and checker. Have students use the Student Self-Evaluation Checklist: Group Work to assess how well they worked together. (LG2.02D—SSEC 2: Group Work)

2. The activities in the Oral Language Extension provide students with the opportunity to develop effective questions for an interview and to anticipate questions that might be asked of them. You may wish to conduct a mini-lesson on developing effective questions before students begin. Ask them to provide the characteristics of a good question. Then list these points on the board or on a large sheet of paper which can be hung in the classroom. Some of the characteristics of good questions are the following:
   - open-ended, for example, "What do you think about ...?"
   - interesting for both interviewer and the person interviewed
   - short, clear, and direct

   Students should avoid the use of questions that can be answered only by "yes" or "no." They should always remember to allow themselves time to listen carefully to the answers.

   (LG2.01D—TOC 13: Tracking Expectations)

GRAMMAR

1. To assist students in understanding the concept of parallel structure, write the following sentence from the model on the board or on a transparency for the overhead projector:

   > Unfamiliar sounds and sights occurred each day: the glassy crashing of ice falling from trees distant and near; the unceasing rumble of generators reverberating across the countryside; the convoys of hydro, military, and phone crews on roadsides like liberation forces; the utter darkness.

   Ask students to read the sentence and to speculate on why the author used this type of structure to present his information (a lot of parallel ideas can be presented in one sentence). (LI3.01D—TOC 4: Grammar)

2. Before assigning the Grammar activities in the student book, discuss the Writing Tip on page 103 where the common elements of a sentence are identified. Ask students to develop two more sentences in a similar format. For example,

The hydro workers	arose	early in the morning
	toiled	through the day
	collapsed	late at night

(WR5.06D—TOC 4: Grammar)

Answers:

1. The subject of the first sentence contains three nouns, each preceded by a single adjective. The second sentence contains a phrase with two nouns, each preceded by an adjective and followed by an adverb. The third sentence contains three phrases, each beginning with the pronoun "of."

2. Possible answers
   a) The ice storm provoked a range of reactions, created dangerous situations, and produced heroes.

MORE ORAL LANGUAGE

Have students use the information in "Struck Powerless" to write and present a brief news report (no more than one minute) about the storm that might have been given on the radio. Remind them that a good news report answers the questions of who, what, where, why, when, and how. They will need to simplify some of the language for the general public. Students could rehearse their reports, paying particular attention to the pace at which they present their material. Have some students present their news reports to the class. (LG2.03D—AR 15: Oral Language)

MORE CHALLENGE

Using the following example from the model, discuss the use of parallel sentences.

> Like many, we vowed we will consume less energy and be less reliant on one source. We will be more sociable with neighbours and strangers. And we will be acutely aware that we are as susceptible as the people of the Saguenay, the Red River, or anywhere else to the destructive power of nature.

Ask students to write a paragraph with a minimum of three parallel sentences that could be used in an event description. Have them explain the parallel structure in their paragraphs to the class. (WR5.06D—TOC 4: Grammar; LG1.05D—TOC 4: Grammar)

---

b) The ice storm raged for six days over open farmland, conifer-cloaked hillsides, urban grids, and maze-like suburbs.
c) The elderly and infirm were looked after by relief workers, by the military, and by an army of volunteers.
d) The heroes were the Hydro workers who risked their lives; the CBC radio broadcasters who fed the airwaves; the neighbours and volunteers who looked after those in trouble or need.

3. Possible answer

The following elements could be added to the first paragraph on page 98: the whirl of spinning tires from motionless cars and trucks; the high-pitched screaming of sirens from fire engines, police cars, and ambulances.

Student Book 1.–3. (WR5.06D—TOC 4: Grammar; LG1.05D—TOC 4: Grammar)

MEDIA LINK

Before assigning the Media Link activity, tape record a radio description of an event. Have students listen to it and identify why the broadcast was effective (good background information, short and to the point, effective opening and closing, interesting questions). Indicate to students that those being interviewed should have the opportunity to look over the questions beforehand. (MD1.02D—AR 21: Response to Media)

Student Book (WR2.01D—AR 4: Descriptive Writing; LG2.05D—TOC 11: Speaking; MDV.02D—AR 12: Media Product)

MECHANICS

Answers:
1. a) Dates are written as numerals only.
   b) Numbers 10 and over are usually written as numerals. Numbers being compared should be kept in the same style (e.g., There were between 8 and 10 in each group.).
   c) For very large numbers, a combination of numbers and words can be used.
   d) Numbers 10 and over are usually written as numerals.
   e) Use numerals for writing amounts of money.
   f) Use numerals for writing time. When using the word "o'clock," spell out the time, as in "four o'clock."
   g) For a unit of measurement, use numerals. Hyphenate a compound adjective in which one element is a numeral and the other a noun or adjective.
   h) Dates are written as numerals only.
   i) Numbers 10 and over are usually written as numerals. Hyphenate a compound adjective in which one element is a numeral and the other is a noun or adjective.
   j) Numbers 10 and over are usually written as numerals.

2. One method of creating a style guide is to use the following:

USE NUMERALS FOR	EXAMPLE	USE WORDS FOR	EXAMPLE
Dates	March 4, 2000	Numbers less than 10	five

MORE MEDIA

Ask students to create a poster to promote the event they wrote about in Writer's Workshop. Before they begin, review with them the importance of typeface, number of words, image, and visibility. Students could create a small sketch of their final design either by hand or by computer. (MD2.02D—AR 12: Media Product)

MORE SUPPORT

Have students work in pairs to make up 10 sentences that include numbers. Each sentence should illustrate one rule for writing numbers. Each pair can then take turns reading their sentences to another pair of students who write the sentences with numbers written correctly. (WR5.04B—TOC 8: Mechanics)

a) percentages — numerals (6 percent)

b) temperatures — numerals with abbreviations and symbols (15°C)

c) numbers that appear as the first word in a sentence — words (fifteen)

d) page numbers — numerals (pages 10–16)

e) addresses — numerals (14 Victoria Road)

f) decimals — numerals (3.7692)

g) telephone numbers — numerals (291-4763)

h) postal codes — numerals (N2M 5R8)

i) a number that comes before a compound modifier that includes another number — (The package contained forty-eight 15-centimetre toys.)

3. Student work.

Student Book (WR5.04B—TOC 8: Mechanics)

USAGE & STYLE

1. Write the following two sentences on the board:

   Ice covered the trees.

   Ice rain encased every limb and crevice of the bent trees.

   Ask students which of these two sentences provides a clearer picture in the reader's mind. How did the author of the second sentence create a vivid description (specific nouns and verbs)? Indicate to students that descriptive writing, to be effective, must contain precise nouns, vivid verbs, and effective modifiers that show rather than tell what the person, place, or thing was like. (LI3.01D—TOC 15: Usage & Style)

2. Ask students to suggest how each of the following sentences could be revised to provide a clearer picture for the reader. (LG1.04B—TOC 15: Usage & Style)

   a) The wires dangled from the poles.

   b) The people who helped others worked hard.

Answers:

1. Possible answer

   Five verbs are splintered, crumpled, hauled, swirled, and dangled.

   Three nouns are spectacle, burden, and stalemate.

   Three modifiers are glassy, unhaltingly, and waist-thick.

2. Possible answers

   a) The entire landscape was encased in tough, hard-shelled ice.

   b) The catastrophe punctuated our slave-like dependency on the juice flowing through the hydro lines.

   c) Elderly citizens shivered in the iceboxes they once called homes.

   d) Ontario-Quebec linemen toiled in exhaustion trying to rekindle warmth and reestablish normal vision.

   e) People were stuffed and cramped into less-than-adequate numbers of shelters.

3. Student work.

Student Book 1.–3. (LG1.04B—TOC 15: Usage & Style)

WORD STUDY & SPELLING

1. Ask students to add an additional example for each of the sounding, visual, and tactile strategies listed on pages 107–108 of the student book. (WR5.11B— TOC 16: Word Study & Spelling)

2. Eric Harris uses rich vocabulary to enhance his event description "Struck Powerless." Ask students to find each of the following sentence segments from the model and read the entire sentence in which it is located. Then have them define the meaning of the underlined word. (LG1.03B—TOC 16: Word Study & Spelling)

Example: <u>Persisting</u> for six days
persisting — refusing to stop or change

a) that <u>periodic</u> disruption of Pacific Ocean currents
periodic — happening or appearing at regular intervals
b) A <u>stalemate</u> ensued
stalemate — situation in which further action is blocked; a deadlock
c) An atmospheric <u>Zamboni</u>
Zamboni — trademark for a machine that resurfaces an ice rink by scraping and removing old ice and laying down a new coating
d) the unceasing rumble of generators <u>reverberating</u>
reverberating — to resound in or as if in a succession of echoes
e) owners struggled to <u>quantify</u> their losses
quantify — to determine or express the quantity of
f) lay <u>cloven</u> down the trunk
cloven — split; divided
g) fragility of our <u>nordic</u> existence
of, relating to, or characteristic of Scandinavia
h) we are as <u>susceptible</u> as the people of the Saguenay
susceptible — easily affected

Answers:
1. Student work.

2. Possible answer

actually — may forget to double the "l"; remember the word "ally"

friend — the "i" is silent; remember "I am your friend"

something — may forget the silent "e"; remember that it is a compound word made up of "some" and "thing"

accident —may forget the double "c"; pronounce the word correctly and use the following visual reminder: ac cident

government — may forget the "n"; pronounce the word correctly and use the following sentence: Vern is running for government.

Student Book 1.–2. (WR5.11B—TOC 16: Word Study & Spelling)

WORD ORIGINS

Answers:
poutine — French-fried potatoes topped with cheese curds and covered with a sauce, usually brown gravy (French Canadian)

muskeg — swamp or bog formed by accumulation of sphagnum moss, leaves, and decayed matter resembling peat (Cree)

tourtiere — pie made of ground meat or poultry, often pork, with onions, herbs, and spices (French Canadian)

allophone — person whose principal language or mother tongue is neither English nor French (Canadian)

muskie — short form of muskellunge, a large food and game fish of the pike family found in lakes and rivers of North America (French Canadian; Cree) *chinook* — warm, dry westerly wind that blows down from the Rocky Mountains into Alberta and sometimes Saskatchewan, causing a dramatic temperature rise in winter (Chehalis)

Student Book (LG1.03B—TOC 16: Word Study & Spelling)

ANSWERS TO EXTRA PRACTICE

Grammar

1. The storm created new heroes, caused some persons to become villains, and produced victims.

2. In the future we will consume less energy, appreciate mother nature's power, and socialize more with our neighbours.

3. Death was caused by carbon monoxide poisoning, by fires, and by hypothermia.

4. Everyone had to survive without electricity, to care for their neighbours, and to keep clear of dangling wires and falling branches.

5. The victim was tall, had black hair and eyes, and was known for his strength.

6. The limb, which filled the doorway, and which six men could hardly lift, was moved to a safer location.

7. The experience taught me two lessons: not to be without candles at all times and not to be without plenty of firewood for the fireplace.

8. Three qualities of the heroes were kindness, bravery, and caring.

9. Ice overpowered everything, bringing down lines, coating buildings, and bending trees to the breaking point.

10. Birches and cedars doubled over, brittle poplars split and snapped, and maples lost large limbs.

(WR5.06D—TOC 4: Grammar)

Mechanics

1. Forty-five thousand

2. 6 p.m.

3. 30

4. $20 thousand

5. 4

6. three; 2-metre trees

7. 0°C

8. 50 percent

9. 8

10. 30; 50

(WR5.04B—TOC 8: Mechanics)

Usage & Style
Possible answers
1. Many urban residents of Montreal received broken bones from falling on ice, during and after the storm.

2. The immeasurable destruction caused major concern for apple growers and sugarbush owners.

3. Farmers with fruit trees will discover the amount of damage to their produce in the early spring. It is expected that some 20 to 25 percent of apple trees sustained some measure of structural damage.

4. Other severe but less damaging ice storms hit Ontario and Quebec in 1942, 1961, and 1986.

5. The mayor of Ottawa predicted that it will cost $100 million to repair hydro lines, to fix buildings damaged by falling trees and water, and to pay city crews to clean up the fallen debris.

(LG1.04B—TOC 15: Usage & Style)

Word Study & Spelling
Possible answers

1. unseasonably — sounding (sound the word out in your head)

2. periodic — visual (highlight the letter "i")

3. reverberating — sounding (sound the word out in your head one syllable at a time)

4. weight — sounding (think of another word with the same pattern (for example, wealth)

5. generators — sounding (using correct pronunciation)

6. price-gougers — visual (highlight the difficult letters "ou")

7. immeasurable — sounding (using correct pronunciation)

8. manpower — visual (break the compound word into two words)

9. addiction — sounding (using correct pronunciation)

10. susceptible — tactile (write the word)

(WR5.11B—TOC 16: Word Study & Spelling)

Reflect and Build on Your Learning

Reflecting on Descriptive Writing Forms

1. Student work.

2. Possible answer

   Other descriptive forms include advertisement, brochure, catalogue, character sketch, epitaph, eulogy, feature article, haiku, journal, lyric, ode, poster, requiem, travelogue, soliloquy, and sonnet.

   Example: A travelogue is a description of a journey or trip. Its purpose may be to convince readers to take the trip themselves or simply to describe vividly what the writer experienced while travelling.

   Student Book. 1.–2. (LIV.01D—TOC 13: Tracking Expectations)

Looking Over Descriptive Writing Forms

1. Possible answer

CRITERIA	POETRY	PROFILE	EVENT DESCRIPTION	TRAVELOGUE
Sensory details	used extensively	often focuses on visual and auditory details, but appeals to other senses where possible	used extensively	used extensively
Figurative language	used extensively, especially comparisons and language that appeals to sound	moderate to extensive use	used extensively	used extensively
Focus	everything contributes to evoking a specific emotional response	focuses on a particular quality, skill, or experience of the subject	conveys a single overall impression of the event	conveys a single overall impression of the place or trip
Organization	myriad forms possible, each of which suggests its own organizational pattern	usually arranged chronologically or from overall impression to specific details	spatial, chronological, or from overall impression to specific details	usually from overall impression to specific details but may follow a chronological order as well
Point of view	may be written in first or third person	usually written in third person	usually written in third person	may be written in first or third person

Student Book. 1. (LIV.02D—TOC 13: Tracking Expectations)

USING THE DESCRIPTIVE WRITING FORMS

1. Since this task requires students to conduct research about a historical figure, it is worthwhile to refer them to pages 145–146 of the student book before they begin the task. Although students are writing a profile rather than a full research report, some may benefit from reviewing the process of first consulting general resources to form an overall impression of their subject and then referring to more specialized sources for specific information regarding a particular quality, skill, or experience that will become the focus of their profile. Also, you might at this time distinguish between primary and secondary resources (page 144), and suggest that students interview someone who has information to share about the subject of the profile. (For example, if the profile were about former prime minister Lester B. Pearson, the student could interview local political figures who recall Mr. Pearson's years in office; if the profile were about someone who lived much earlier, the student could interview a teacher or museum historian who has particular knowledge about that person.)

   This assignment offers excellent opportunities for cross-curricular collaboration and could be given in conjunction with work students are doing in other classes. Before you begin this unit, you might meet with the social studies teacher to discuss ways this assignment could reflect expectations of both curricula, as well as the logistics of teaching and assessing its various components as a team.

   Presenting the profile in the form of an imagined interview offers students an opportunity to work in pairs and offers teachers an opportunity to incorporate drama and oral language components within the unit. Assessment could then include—besides the information researched and its organization—the extent to which students dress for the part, give a well-rehearsed performance, and utilize public-speaking techniques.

   Student Book 1. (WRV.03D—AR 19: Profile; WRV.04D—AR 19: Profile; WRV.05D—AR 19: Profile; LGV.02B—TOC 1: Conducting an Interview)

2. One approach to this task that often yields excellent results is to have students follow Kim Johnson's model of seeing a subject twice—first superficially and then, upon further investigation, more clearly (either sympathetically or critically). This requires students to examine their subject on more than one level, which is the key to strong poetic writing.

   To introduce this task, have students first write poems about their school. Have them brainstorm numerous places within the school where students commonly meet and have pairs of students each choose one place. With permission from the school's administrators, give the pairs one entire class period to go to their assigned location and record as many sensory details about it as possible, their purpose being to present a vivid impression of that place in poem form. (These poems could be presented later in poster form and displayed at these particular locations for others to read.) Once students have written poems about locations within the school, they can then proceed with the text assignment of writing poems about places in their community.

   Student Book. 2. (WRV.03D—AR 17: Poetry; WRV.04D—AR 17: Poetry; WRV.05D—AR 17: Poetry; MDV.02D—AR 12: Media Product)

3. Review with students the most common organizational patterns followed in event descriptions: spatial (moving from one location to another), chronological (time), or from an overall impression of the event to specific details that describe it. Have them list in the order they appear the main ideas/details of their event description to help them determine the pattern they follow. Then have them rearrange the same details in other orders to help them identify which of the other patterns lends itself better to their particular event description. Computer word-processing

would facilitate this activity by enabling students to arrange their details quickly and easily in a variety of orders.

Student Book. 3. (WRV.03D—AR 6: Event Description; WRV.04D—AR 6: Event Description; WRV.05D—AR 6: Event Description)

4. It will be useful to assign students well in advance of this unit to begin collecting newspaper accounts of events they have witnessed themselves (for example, concerts, festivals, and sporting events). In doing so, students will have a variety of writing models to refer to when writing their own event descriptions and, equally important, they will be able to move immediately from writing their own descriptions to a critical examination of professionally written pieces.

   Because the emotional viewpoint of a newspaper writer may differ considerably from that of students who have witnessed—even participated in—the event, this activity offers a valuable opportunity to extend discussion of the concept of point of view introduced in Unit 5.

Student Book. 4. (WRV.03D—AR 8: Expository Writing; WRV.04D—AR 8: Expository Writing; WRV.05D—AR 8: Expository Writing)

	GRADE 9 EXPECTATIONS	DEMONSTRATION OF LEARNING	ASSESSMENT TOOLS
LITERATURE STUDIES AND READING			
Overall (LIV.01P)	• read and demonstrate an understanding of a variety of literary and informational texts	• demonstrate understanding of forms of description (Reflecting on Descriptive Writing Forms SB #1–2)	• TOC 14: Tracking Expectations
Specific (LI1.01P)	• describe information, ideas, opinions, and themes in texts they have read during the year from a variety of print and electronic sources, including biographies, short stories, poems, plays, novels, brochures, and articles from newspapers, magazines, and encyclopedias	• judge accuracy of news report of event (Introducing the Unit TG #3) • compare language and amount of detail in newspaper or magazine article with model (Extending the Model TG #1)	• TOC 14: Tracking Expectations
(LI1.02P)	• select and read texts for a variety of purposes, with an emphasis on recognizing the elements of literary genres and the organization of informational materials, collecting and using information, extending personal knowledge, and responding imaginatively	• discuss effectiveness of model (Investigating the Model TG #1)	• AR 22: Response to Reading
(LI1.03B)	• describe a variety of reading strategies and select and use them effectively before, during, and after reading to understand texts	• list predictions about model based on title, photographs, and prior knowledge of power failures (Introducing the Model TG #1) • note which predictions were included in model (Introducing the Model TG #2)	• TOC 10: Reading Strategies • TOC 10: Reading Strategies
(LI1.04P)	• locate and use explicit information and ideas from texts in forming opinions and developing generalizations	• locate information and ideas in model to support opinions (Investigating the Model SB #1–7)	• AR 22: Response to Reading
(LI1.06B)	• use specific references from a text to support opinions and judgments	• use evidence to compare model with television report (Extending the Model TG #2)	• AR 22: Response to Reading
Overall (LIV.02P)	• demonstrate an understanding of the elements of a variety of literary and informational forms, with a focus on plays, short stories, and newspaper and magazine articles	• suggest details relating to sound, feel, taste, and smell for event description (Introducing the Unit TG #2) • compare four forms of descriptive writing (Looking Over Descriptive Writing Forms SB #1)	• TOC 14: Tracking Expectations • TOC 14: Tracking Expectations
Overall (LIV.03B)	• identify and explain the effect of specific elements of style in a variety of literary and informational texts		
Specific (LI3.02P)	• explain how authors choose words and phrases to achieve intended effects	• speculate on why author used parallel structure (Grammar TG #1) • complete series of parallel descriptive phrases (Grammar TG #2) • discuss ways to create vivid description (Usage & Style TG #1)	• TOC 4: Grammar • TOC 4: Grammar • TOC 15: Usage & Style
WRITING			
Overall (WRV.01P)	• use print and electronic sources to gather information and explore ideas for their written work	• gather and organize information for event description (Writer's Workshop SB #1–5)	• AR 6: Event Description
Specific (WR1.01P)	• investigate potential topics by asking questions, identifying information needs, and developing research plans to gather data	• list details contributing to main impression of memorable event (Introducing the Unit TG #1) • brainstorm list of topics for event description (Writer's Workshop TG #1) • question each other to generate details (Writer's Workshop TG #2)	• AR 6: Event Description • AR 6: Event Description • AR 6: Event Description

AR=Assessment Rubric   EP=Extra Practice   SB=Student Book   SSEC=Student Self-Evaluation Checklist   TG=Teacher's Guide   TOC=Teacher Observation Checklist

GRADE 9 EXPECTATIONS	DEMONSTRATION OF LEARNING	ASSESSMENT TOOLS
WRITING (continued)		
(WR1.03P) • sort and group information and ideas, assess their relevance and accuracy, and discard irrelevant material	• categorize participants of event description (Writer's Workshop TG #3) • plan organizational pattern for event description (Writer's Workshop TG #4)	• AR 6: Event Description • AR 6: Event Description
Overall (WRV.02P) • identify the literary and informational forms suited to specific purposes and audiences and use the forms appropriately in their own writing, with an emphasis on communicating information accurately		
Specific (WR2.03P) • demonstrate an understanding of literary and informational forms of writing, such as letters, personal narratives, short stories, answers to homework questions, summaries, and reports on research topics, by selecting a form appropriate to the specific purpose and audience for each piece of writing	• write up event for school newspaper (Media Link SB)	• AR 4: Descriptive Writing
Overall (WRV.03P) • use a variety of forms of writing to express themselves, clarify their ideas, and engage the audience's attention, imagination, and interest	• write draft of event description (Writer's Workshop SB #6–7) • write profile of historical figure (Using the Descriptive Writing Forms SB #1) • write descriptive poem of a familiar place (Using the Descriptive Writing Forms SB #2) • write essay on newspaper description of an event (Using the Descriptive Writing Forms SB #4)	• AR 6: Event Description • AR 19: Profile • AR 17: Poetry • AR 8: Expository Writing
Specific (WR3.03P) • use a unifying image, emotion, or sensation to structure descriptive paragraphs or poems	• write about an imaginary experience as hero, villain, or victim of the ice storm (Extending the Model TG #3) • write descriptive setting that represents a state of mind (More Challenge TG, page 145)	• AR 6: Event Description • AR 6: Event Description
Overall (WRV.04B) • revise their written work, collaboratively and independently, with a focus on support for ideas, accuracy, clarity, and unity	• revise event description (Writer's Workshop SB #8) • revise profile of historical figure (Using the Descriptive Writing Forms SB #1) • revise descriptive poem (Using the Descriptive Writing Forms SB #2) • revise essay on newspaper description of event (Using the Descriptive Writing Forms SB #4)	• AR 6: Event Description • AR 19: Profile • AR 17: Poetry • AR 8: Expository Writing
Specific (WR4.01P) • revise drafts to ensure that ideas are adequately developed with supporting details, and to achieve clarity and unity	• revise draft of essay for clarity and supporting details	• AR 8: Expository Writing
Overall (WRV.05B) • edit and proofread to produce final drafts, using correct grammar, spelling, and punctuation, according to the conventions of standard Canadian English specified for this course, with the support of print and electronic resources when appropriate	• edit and proofread event description (Writer's Workshop SB #8) • edit and proofread profile of historical figure (Using the Descriptive Writing Forms SB #1) • edit and proofread descriptive poem (Using the Descriptive Writing Forms SB #2) • edit and proofread essay on newspaper description of event (Using the Descriptive Writing Forms SB #4)	• AR 6: Event Description • AR 19: Profile • AR 17: Poetry • AR 8: Expository Writing

AR=Assessment Rubric   EP=Extra Practice   SB=Student Book   SSEC=Student Self-Evaluation Checklist   TG=Teacher's Guide   TOC=Teacher Observation Checklist

GRADE 9 EXPECTATIONS		DEMONSTRATION OF LEARNING	ASSESSMENT TOOLS
		WRITING (continued)	
Specific (WR5.04B)	• edit and proofread their own and others' writing, identifying and correcting errors according to the requirements for grammar, usage, spelling, and punctuation	• present numerical information correctly (Mechanics SB #1–3) • write numbers correctly (More Support TG, page 146) • correct sentences with errors in numerical information (EP: Mechanics)	• TOC 8: Mechanics • TOC 8: Mechanics • TOC 8: Mechanics
(WR5.06P)	• construct complete and correct compound and complex sentences, using the following sentence components as required: subject, predicate, object, subject complement; main and subordinate clauses; prepositional phrases	• identify parallel structure in sentences (Grammar TG #2) • construct complete sentences that include parallel structure (Grammar SB #1–3) • correct sentences with parallel structure (EP: Grammar)	• TOC 4: Grammar • TOC 4: Grammar • TOC 4: Grammar
(WR5.11B)	• use knowledge of a wide range of spelling patterns and rules to identify, analyze, and correct spelling errors	• give examples for spelling strategies (Word Study & Spelling TG #1) • suggest spelling strategies for listed words (EP: Word Study & Spelling) • give examples for spelling strategies (Word Study & Spelling TG #1)	• TOC 16: Word Study & Spelling • TOC 16: Word Study & Spelling • TOC 16: Word Study & Spelling
		LANGUAGE	
Overall (LGV.01P)	• use knowledge of vocabulary and language conventions to speak, write, and read clearly and correctly		
Specific (LG1.01B)	• describe strategies used to expand vocabulary and provide evidence of other vocabulary-building activities	• define meaning of words using context (Word Study & Spelling TG #2)	• TOC 16: Word Study & Spelling
Specific (LG1.03B)	• identify words borrowed from other languages, and words and terms recently introduced to describe new ideas, inventions, and products, and explain their origins	• give meaning of words (Word Study & Spelling TG #2) • give meaning and origins of words (Word Origins SB)	• TOC 16: Word Study & Spelling • TOC 16: Word Study & Spelling
(LG1.04B)	• select words and phrases appropriate to informal and formal styles, to suit the purpose and intended audience of oral and written work	• choose precise words (Usage & Style TG #2) • use precise words correctly (Usage & Style SB #1–3) • compose sentences using vivid verbs (More Support TG, page 146) • rewrite sentences using precise nouns, vivid verbs, and effective modifiers (EP: Usage & Style)	• TOC 15: Usage & Style • TOC 15: Usage & Style • TOC 15: Usage & Style • TOC 15: Usage & Style
(LG1.05P)	• recognize, describe, and use correctly, in oral and written language, the language structures of standard Canadian English and its conventions of grammar and usage, including: – components of sentences: subject, predicate, object, subject complement, prepositional phrases, main and subordinate clauses	• construct complete sentences that include parallel structure (Grammar SB #1–3)	• TOC 4: Grammar
Overall (LGV.02B)	• use listening techniques and oral communication skills to participate in classroom discussions and more formal activities, such as storytelling, role playing, and reporting/presenting, for specific purposes and audiences	• present profile of historical figure as an interview (Using the Descriptive Writing Forms SB #1)	• TOC 1: Conducting an Interview

AR=Assessment Rubric   EP=Extra Practice   SB=Student Book   SSEC=Student Self-Evaluation Checklist   TG=Teacher's Guide   TOC=Teacher Observation Checklist

GRADE 9 EXPECTATIONS	DEMONSTRATION OF LEARNING	ASSESSMENT TOOLS
LANGUAGE (continued)		
Specific (LG2.01P) • use listening techniques and oral communication skills to participate in group discussions	• discuss roles in group work and appoint members as leader, clarifier, encourager, and checker (Oral Language Extension TG #1) • understand how to develop effective questions (Oral Language Extension TG #2)	• SSEC 2: Group Work • TOC 14: Tracking Expectations
(LG2.03P) • work with a partner to plan and make oral presentations to a small group, selecting and using vocabulary and methods of delivery to suit audience and purpose	• present a radio news report on the ice storm (More Oral Language TG)	• AR 15: Oral Language
(LG2.05P) • practise with cue cards, use breathing exercises, and rehearse with peers, to ensure confident delivery in oral presentations	• practise speaking with confidence and expression (Media Link SB)	• TOC 11: Speaking
MEDIA STUDIES		
Overall (MDV.01P) • identify and describe the elements, intended audiences, and production practices of a variety of media forms	• compare model with television report (Extending the Model TG #2)	• AR 21: Response to Media
Specific (MD1.02P) • identify and describe the elements used to structure media works in a variety of forms	• give reasons for choosing other photographs for model (Investigating the Model TG #2) • identify why a radio broadcast is effective (Media Link TG)	• AR 21: Reponse to Media • AR 21: Response to Media
Overall (MDV.02P) • use knowledge of a variety of media forms, purposes, and audiences to create media works	• tape radio news item about an event (Media Link SB) • rewrite event for school newspaper (Using the Descriptive Writing Forms SB #3)	• AR 12: Media Product • AR 12: Media Product
Specific (MD2.02P) • create media works for different purposes	• create a poster to promote event they wrote about (More Media TG)	• AR 12: Media Product

AR=Assessment Rubric   EP=Extra Practice   SB=Student Book   SSEC=Student Self-Evaluation Checklist   TG=Teacher's Guide   TOC=Teacher Observation Checklist

INSTRUCTIONAL STRATEGIES FOR THE APPLIED COURSE

PLANNING INFORMATION

Links to Other Nelson English 9 Resources

Literature & Media 9
Event Description—See "Anna Lang" by John Melady, pp. 123–129.

Write Source 2000
Descriptive Writing—"Descriptive Paragraph," p. 100, "Writing About an Event," p. 126; **Numerical Information**—"Numbers," p. 410; **Parallel Structure**—"Parallelism," p. 140; **Precise and Interesting Nouns, Verbs, and Modifiers**—"Using Strong, Colourful Words," pp. 135–136; **Spelling Strategies**—"Improved Spelling," pp. 411–418

INTRODUCING THE UNIT

The activities on page 128 from the Academic Course are appropriate for the Applied Course.

1. (WR1.01P—AR 6: Event Description)

2. (LIV.02P—TOC 14: Tracking Expectations)

3. (LI1.01P—TOC 14: Tracking Expectations)

INTRODUCING THE MODEL

The activities on page 128 from the Academic Course are appropriate for the Applied Course.

1. (LI1.03B—TOC 10: Reading Strategies)

2. (LI1.03B—TOC 10: Reading Strategies)

INVESTIGATING THE MODEL

The activities on pages 128–129 from the Academic Course are appropriate for the Applied Course.

1. (LI1.02P—AR 22: Response to Reading)

2. (MD1.02P—AR 21: Response to Media)

Answers:
See the Academic Course on pages 129–130 for answers.

Student Book 1.–7. (LI1.04P—AR 22: Response to Reading)

EXTENDING THE MODEL

The activities on page 130 from the Academic Course are appropriate for the Applied Course.

1. (LI1.01P—AR 22: Response to Reading)

2. (LI1.06B—AR 22: Response to Reading; MDV.01P—AR 21: Response to Media)

3. (WR3.03P—AR 6: Event Description)

Writer's Workshop

The activities on page 130 from the Academic Course are appropriate for the Applied Course.

1. (WR1.01P—AR 6: Event Description)

2. (WR1.01P—AR 6: Event Description)

3. (WR1.03P—AR 6: Event Description)

4. (WR1.03P—AR 6: Event Description)

The scope of the assignment could be limited to describing a setting before, during, and after an event (for example, the cafeteria before, during, and after lunch). This will help students in organizing their writing.

Student Book 1.–5. (WRV.01P—AR 6: Event Description); 6.–7. (WRV.03P—AR 6: Event Description); 8. (WRV.04B—AR 6: Event Description; WRV.05B—AR 6: Event Description)

Oral Language Extension

The activities on page 131 from the Academic Course are appropriate for the Applied Course.

1. (LG2.01P—SSEC 2: Group Work)

2. (LG2.01P—TOC 14: Tracking Expectations)

Grammar

The activities on page 131 from the Academic Course are appropriate for the Applied Course.

1. (LI3.02P—TOC 4: Grammar)

2. (WR5.06P—TOC 4: Grammar)

Answers:

See the Academic Course on pages 131–132 for answers.

Student Book 1.–3. (WR5.06P—TOC 4: Grammar; LG1.05P—TOC 4: Grammar)

Media Link

Before assigning the Media Link activity, tape record a radio description of an event. Have students listen to it and identify why the broadcast was effective (good background information, short and to the point, effective opening and closing, interesting questions). Indicate to students that those being interviewed should have the opportunity to look over the questions beforehand. (MD1.02P—AR 21: Response to Media)

Student Book (WR2.03P—AR 4: Descriptive Writing; LG2.05P—TOC 11: Speaking; MDV.02P—AR 12: Media Product)

Mechanics

One option for activity #2 in the student book is to provide students with a list of rules for writing numbers and then have them find examples of these rules in some of their school textbooks.

Answers:

See the Academic Course on pages 132–133 for answers.

Student Book 1.–3. (WR5.04B—TOC 8: Mechanics)

MORE CHALLENGE

Have students work in pairs to list words to describe a state of mind (for example, loneliness, joy, peace). Students could then choose one of the states and write a descriptive setting that represents it (for example, peace: walking on the beach in the early morning). (WR3.03P—AR 6: Event Description)

MORE ORAL LANGUAGE

Have students use the information in "Struck Powerless" to write and present a brief news report (no more than one minute) about the storm that might have been given on the radio. Remind them that a good news report answers the questions of who, what, where, why, when, and how. They will need to simplify some of the language for the general public. Students could rehearse their reports, paying particular attention to the pace at which they present their material. Students could work in pairs and present their news reports to small groups. (LG2.03P—AR 15: Oral Language)

MORE MEDIA

Ask students to create a poster to promote the event they wrote about in Writer's Workshop. Before they begin, review with them the importance of typeface, number of words, image, and visibility. Students could create a small sketch of their final design either by hand or by computer. (MD2.02P—AR 12: Media Product)

USAGE & STYLE

The activities on page 133 from the Academic Course are appropriate for the Applied Course.

1. (LI3.02P—TOC 15: Usage & Style)

2. (LG1.04B—TOC 15: Usage & Style)

Answers:

See the Academic Course on page 133 for answers.

Student Book 1.–3. (LG1.04B—TOC 15: Usage & Style)

WORD STUDY & SPELLING

The activities on pages 133–134 from the Academic Course are appropriate for the Applied Course.

1. (WR5.11B—TOC 16: Word Study & Spelling)

2. (LG1.01B—TOC 16: Word Study & Spelling)

Answers:

See the Academic Course on page 134 for answers.

Student Book 1.–2. (WR5.11B—TOC 16: Word Study & Spelling)

WORD ORIGINS

See the Academic Course on pages 134–135 for answers.

Student Book (LG1.03B—TOC 16: Word Study & Spelling)

ANSWERS TO EXTRA PRACTICE

See the Academic Course on pages 135–136 for answers.

Grammar
(WR5.06P—TOC 4: Grammar)

Mechanics
(WR5.04B—TOC 8: Mechanics)

Usage & Style
(LG1.04B—TOC 15: Usage & Style)

Word Study & Spelling
(WR5.11B—TOC 16: Word Study & Spelling)

REFLECT AND BUILD ON YOUR LEARNING

REFLECTING ON DESCRIPTIVE WRITING FORMS

1. Student work.

2. Possible answer

   Other descriptive forms include advertisement, brochure, catalogue, character sketch, epitaph, eulogy, feature article, haiku, journal, lyric, ode, poster, requiem, travelogue, soliloquy, and sonnet.

   Example: A travelogue is a description of a journey or trip. Its purpose may be to convince readers to take the trip themselves or simply to describe vividly what the writer experienced while travelling.

   Student Book. 1.–2. (LIV.01P—TOC 14: Tracking Expectations)

LOOKING OVER DESCRIPTIVE WRITING FORMS

1. Possible answer

CRITERIA	POETRY	PROFILE	EVENT DESCRIPTION	TRAVELOGUE
Sensory details	used extensively	often focuses on visual and auditory details, but appeals to other senses where possible	used extensively	used extensively
Figurative language	used extensively, especially comparisons and language that appeals to sound	moderate to extensive use	used extensively	used extensively
Focus	everything contributes to evoking a specific emotional response	focuses on a particular quality, skill, or experience of the subject	conveys a single overall impression of the event	conveys a single overall impression of the place or trip
Organization	myriad forms possible, each of which suggests its own organizational pattern	usually arranged chronologically or from overall impression to specific details	spatial, chronological, or from overall impression to specific details	usually from overall impression to specific details but may follow a chronological order as well
Point of view	may be written in first or third person	usually written in third person	usually written in third person	may be written in first or third person

Student Book. 1. (LIV.02P—TOC 14: Tracking Expectations)

Using the Descriptive Writing Forms

1. Since this task requires students to conduct research about a historical figure, it is worthwhile to refer them to pages 145–146 of the student book before they begin the task. Although students are writing a profile rather than a full research report, some may benefit from reviewing the process of first consulting general resources to form an overall impression of their subject and then referring to more specialized sources for specific information regarding a particular quality, skill, or experience that will become the focus of their profile. Also, you might at this time distinguish between primary and secondary resources (page 144), and suggest that students interview someone who has information to share about the subject of the profile. (For example, if the profile were about former prime minister Lester B. Pearson, the student could interview local political figures who recall Mr. Pearson's years in office; if the profile were about someone who lived much earlier, the student could interview a teacher or museum historian who has particular knowledge about that person.)

    This assignment offers excellent opportunities for cross-curricular collaboration and could be given in conjunction with work students are doing in other classes. Before you begin this unit, you might meet with the social studies teacher to discuss ways this assignment could reflect expectations of both curricula, as well as the logistics of teaching and assessing its various components as a team.

    Presenting the profile in the form of an imagined interview offers students an opportunity to work in pairs and offers teachers an opportunity to incorporate drama and oral language components within the unit. Assessment could then include—besides the information researched and its organization—the extent to which students dress for the part, give a well-rehearsed performance, and utilize public-speaking techniques.

    Student Book 1. (WRV.03P—AR 19: Profile; WRV.04B—AR 19: Profile; WRV.05B—AR 19: Profile; LGV.02B—TOC 1: Conducting an Interview)

2. One approach to this task that often yields excellent results is to have students follow Kim Johnson's model of seeing a subject twice—first superficially and then, upon further investigation, more clearly (either sympathetically or critically). This requires students to examine their subject on more than one level, which is the key to strong poetic writing.

    To introduce this task, have students first write poems about their school. Have them brainstorm numerous places within the school where students commonly meet and have pairs of students each choose one place. With permission from the school's administrators, give the pairs one entire class period to go to their assigned location and record as many sensory details about it as possible, their purpose being to present a vivid impression of that place in poem form. (These poems could be presented later in poster form and displayed at these particular locations for others to read.) Once students have written poems about locations within the school, they can then proceed with the text assignment of writing poems about places in their community.

    Student Book. 2. (WRV.03P—AR 17: Poetry; WRV.04B—AR 17: Poetry; WRV.05B—AR 17: Poetry; MDV.02P—AR 12: Media Product)

3. Review with students the most common organizational patterns followed in event descriptions: spatial (moving from one location to another), chronological (time), or from an overall impression of the event to specific details that describe it. Have them list in the order they appear the main ideas/details of their event description to help them determine the pattern they follow. Then have them rearrange the same details in other orders to help them identify which of the other patterns lends itself better to their particular event description. Computer word-processing

would facilitate this activity by enabling students to arrange their details quickly and easily in a variety of orders.

Student Book. 3. (WRV.03P—AR 6: Event Description; WRV.04B—AR 6: Event Description; WRV.05B—AR 6: Event Description)

4. It will be useful to assign students well in advance of this unit to begin collecting newspaper accounts of events they have witnessed themselves (for example, concerts, festivals, and sporting events). In doing so, students will have a variety of writing models to refer to when writing their own event descriptions and, equally important, they will be able to move immediately from writing their own descriptions to a critical examination of professionally written pieces.

Because the emotional viewpoint of a newspaper writer may differ considerably from that of students who have witnessed—even participated in—the event, this activity offers a valuable opportunity to extend discussion of the concept of point of view introduced in Unit 5.

Student Book. 4. (WRV.03P—AR 8: Expository Writing; WRV.04B—AR 8: Expository Writing; WR4.01P—AR 8: Expository Writing; WRV.05B—AR 8: Expository Writing)

GRAMMAR

NAME: _____ **DATE:** _____

Each of the following passages contains a mistake in parallel structure. Find the common elements and parallel structures of each sentence. Isolate the error, and suggest a way to correct it.

1. The storm created new heroes, caused some persons to become villains, and other people were victims.

   _____

2. In the future we will consume less energy, appreciate what the power of mother nature is like, and socialize more with our neighbours.

   _____

3. Death was caused by carbon monoxide poisoning, by fires, and hypothermia.

   _____

4. Everyone had to survive without electricity, to care for their neighbours, and keep clear of dangling wires and falling branches.

   _____

5. The victim was tall, black hair and eyes, and was known for his strength.

   _____

6. The limb, filling the doorway, and which six men could hardly lift, was moved to a safer location.

   _____

7. The experience taught me two lessons: not to be without candles at all times and I shall not again be without plenty of firewood for the fireplace.

   _____

8. Three qualities of the heroes were kindness, bravery, and they were caring.

   _____

9. Ice overpowered everything, bringing down lines, coating buildings, and trees were bent to the breaking point.

   _____

10. Birches and cedars doubled over, brittle poplars split and snapped, and it caused many maples to lose large limbs.

   _____

MECHANICS

NAME: _____ DATE: _____

Correct any errors in the numbers in the following sentences.

1. 45 000 people were still without power in Quebec on January the twentieth.

   _____

2. People dreaded the darkness which began each evening about six p.m.

   _____

3. It will take 15 to thirty years before some farms fully recuperate.

   _____

4. The damage to our house alone was estimated at twenty thousand dollars.

   _____

5. Each year on January fourth, I will remember the storm of 1998.

   _____

6. We planted 3 new two metre trees in our front yard.

   _____

7. I now get nervous when the temperature hovers around zero degrees Celsius during the winter.

   _____

8. About 50% of the city was without power.

   _____

9. Over eight mm of freezing rain accumulated January four to 10.

   _____

10. The weight on each limb increased by an estimated thirty to fifty times.

   _____

USAGE & STYLE

NAME: _____   DATE: _____

Rewrite the following sentences to make each one more interesting by using precise nouns, vivid verbs, and more effective modifiers.

1. Some people were hurt during the storm.

   _____

   _____

2. The damage created concern for people who depend on trees for their living.

   _____

   _____

3. Growers will find out about the extent of the damage in the spring.

   _____

   _____

4. This is not the first storm to hit this part of the country.

   _____

   _____

5. The head of the city predicted it will cost a lot of money to repair the damage.

   _____

   _____

WORD STUDY & SPELLING

NAME: _____ DATE: _____

Suggest one sounding, visual, or tactile strategy that would be suitable for learning to spell each of the following words.

1. unseasonably

   _____

2. periodic

   _____

3. reverberating

   _____

4. weight

   _____

5. generators

   _____

6. price-gougers

   _____

7. immeasurable

   _____

8. manpower

   _____

9. addiction

   _____

10. susceptible

   _____

UNIT 7: EXPLANATION

ACADEMIC EXPECTATIONS

GRADE 9 EXPECTATIONS		DEMONSTRATION OF LEARNING	ASSESSMENT TOOLS
LITERATURE STUDIES AND READING			
Overall (LIV.01D)	• read and demonstrate an understanding of a variety of literary and informational texts, from contemporary and historical periods		
Specific (LI1.01D)	• describe information, ideas, opinions, and themes in print and electronic texts they have read during the year from different cultures and historical periods and in a variety of genres, including novels, short stories, plays, poems, biographies, short essays, and articles from newspapers, magazines, and encyclopedias	• give explanations of rainbows to the class (Extending the Model TG #1)	• TOC 11: Speaking
(LI1.03B)	• describe a variety of reading strategies and select and use them effectively before, during, and after reading to understand texts	• speculate on answer to question in title "Why Must Rainbows Be Curved?" using illustrations (Introducing the Model TG #1) • check to see if speculations on model were correct (Introducing the Model TG #2)	• TOC 10: Reading Strategies • TOC 10: Reading Strategies
(LI1.04D)	• locate explicit information and ideas in texts to use in developing opinions and interpretations	• give interpretations of model using examples from student book (Investigating the Model SB #1–5)	• AR 22: Response to Reading
(LI1.06D)	• use specific evidence from a text to support opinions and judgments	• comment on effectiveness of model in giving explanation (Introducing the Model TG #3)	• TOC 13: Tracking Expectations
Overall (LIV.02D)	• demonstrate an understanding of the elements of a variety of literary and informational forms, with a focus on plays, short stories, and short essays	• share explanations and categorize them as to "how" and "why" (Introducing the Unit TG #1) • discuss as a class examples of explanations (Introducing the Unit TG #2)	• TOC 13: Tracking Expectations • TOC 13: Tracking Expectations
WRITING			
Overall (WRV.01D)	• use a variety of print and electronic sources to gather information and explore ideas for their written work	• collect examples of explanations for class display (Extending the Model TG #2) • gather and organize information for explanation (Writer's Workshop SB #1–4)	• AR 7: Explanation • AR 7: Explanation
Specific (WR1.01D)	• investigate potential topics by formulating questions, identifying information needs, and developing research plans to gather data	• share with class questions younger family members would like answered (Writer's Workshop TG #1) • skim science and technology and social studies curricula and how-to books for topics (Writer's Workshop TG #2)	• AR 7: Explanation • AR 7: Explanation
(WR1.03D)	• group and label information and ideas, evaluate the relevance, accuracy, and completeness of the information and ideas; and discard irrelevant material	• discuss which concepts in explanation need illustrative material (Writer's Workshop TG #3)	• AR 7: Explanation
Overall (WRV.03D)	• use a variety of organizational techniques to present ideas and supporting details logically and coherently in written work	• write draft of explanation (Writer's Workshop SB #5–6)	• AR 7: Explanation
Overall (WRV.04D)	• revise their written work, independently and collaboratively, with a focus on support for ideas and opinions, accuracy, clarity, and unity	• revise explanation (Writer's Workshop SB #7)	• AR 7: Explanation

AR=Assessment Rubric   EP=Extra Practice   SB=Student Book   SSEC=Student Self-Evaluation Checklist   TG=Teacher's Guide   TOC=Teacher Observation Checklist

GRADE 9 EXPECTATIONS		DEMONSTRATION OF LEARNING	ASSESSMENT TOOLS
WRITING (continued)			
Overall (WRV.05D)	• edit and proofread to produce final drafts, using correct grammar, spelling, and punctuation, according to the conventions of standard Canadian English, with the support of print and electronic resources when appropriate	• edit and proofread explanation (Writer's Workshop SB #7)	• AR 7: Explanation
Specific (WR5.02B)	• select the publication method or vehicle most accessible or appealing to the intended audience	• create a "Book of Explanations" for school library (Extending the Model TG #3)	• AR 12: Media Product
(WR5.06D)	• construct complete and correct compound and complex sentences, using the following sentence components as required: subject, predicate, object, subject complement; main and subordinate clauses; prepositional and participial phrases	• explain difference between direct and indirect object (Grammar TG #1) • explain difference between transitive and intransitive verbs (Grammar TG #2) • explain subject complement (Grammar TG #3) • identify and use direct and indirect objects (Grammar SB #1–2) • identify and use transitive and intransitive verbs (Grammar SB #3–4) • identify subject complement (Grammar SB #5) • discuss direct and indirect objects, transitive and intransitive verbs, and subject complements (Grammar SB #6–7) • write complete sentences as required (More Challenge TG, page 160) • identify sentence components (EP: Grammar)	• TOC 4: Grammar • TOC 4: Grammar • TOC 4: Grammar • TOC 4: Grammar • TOC 4: Grammar • TOC 4: Grammar • TOC 4: Grammar • TOC 4: Grammar • TOC 4: Grammar
(WR5.10B)	• use consistent and appropriate verb tense and voice (i.e., active and passive) for clarity in narrative and expository writing	• discuss use of active and passive voice (Usage & Style TG) • use active and passive voice correctly (Usage & Style SB #1–3) • turn passive constructions into active ones (More Support TG) • use active and passive voice correctly (EP: Usage & Style)	• TOC 15: Usage & Style • TOC 15: Usage & Style • TOC 15: Usage & Style • TOC 15: Usage & Style
(WR5.15B)	• use punctuation correctly, including period, question mark, exclamation mark, comma, dash, apostrophe, colon, quotation marks, parentheses, and ellipses	• use punctuation correctly in definitions (Mechanics SB #1–3) • insert definitions in sentences using correct punctuation (EP: Mechanics)	• TOC 8: Mechanics • TOC 8: Mechanics
LANGUAGE			
Overall (LGV.01D)	• use knowledge of vocabulary and language conventions to speak, write, and read competently using a level of language appropriate to the purpose and audience		
Specific (LG1.01B)	• describe strategies used to expand vocabulary and provide evidence of other vocabulary-building activities	• discuss using roots to find meaning of words (Word Study & Spelling TG #1) • research etymological information (Word Study & Spelling TG #2)	• TOC 16: Word Study & Spelling • TOC 16: Word Study & Spelling
(LG1.03B)	• identify words borrowed from other languages and words and terms recently introduced to describe new ideas, inventions, and products, and explain their origins	• find words with Greek and Latin roots (Word Study & Spelling SB #1–2) • find words that come from a variety of languages (More Challenge TG, page 162) • identify roots as Latin or Greek (EP: Word Study & Spelling)	• TOC 16: Word Study & Spelling • TOC 16: Word Study & Spelling • TOC 16: Word Study & Spelling

AR=Assessment Rubric   EP=Extra Practice   SB=Student Book   SSEC=Student Self-Evaluation Checklist   TG=Teacher's Guide   TOC=Teacher Observation Checklist

GRADE 9 EXPECTATIONS	DEMONSTRATION OF LEARNING	ASSESSMENT TOOLS
LANGUAGE (continued)		
(LG1.05D) • recognize, describe, and use correctly, in oral and written language, the language structures of standard Canadian English and its conventions of grammar and usage, including: – components of sentences: subject, predicate, object, subject complement, prepositional and participial phrases, main and subordinate clauses – consistency of verb tense and voice	• explain difference between direct and indirect object (Grammar TG #1) • explain difference between transitive and intransitive verbs (Grammar TG #2) • explain subject complement (Grammar TG #3) • identify and use direct and indirect objects (Grammar SB #1–2) • identify and use transitive and intransitive verbs (Grammar SB #3–4) • identify subject complement (Grammar SB #5) • discuss direct and indirect objects, transitive and intransitive verbs, and subject complements (Grammar SB #6–7) • write complete sentences as required (More Challenge TG, page 160) • identify sentence components (EP: Grammar) • discuss use of active and passive voice (Usage & Style TG) • use active and passive voice correctly (Usage & Style SB #1–3) • turn passive constructions into active ones (More Support TG) • use active and passive voice correctly (EP: Usage & Style	• TOC 4: Grammar • TOC 4: Grammar • TOC 4: Grammar • TOC 4: Grammar • TOC 4: Grammar • TOC 4: Grammar • TOC 4: Grammar • TOC 4: Grammar • TOC 4: Grammar • TOC 15: Usage & Style • TOC 15: Usage & Style • TOC 15: Usage & Style • TOC 15: Usage & Style
(LG1.07B) • recognize, describe, and use correctly, in oral and written language, the conventions of standard Canadian English for spelling, capitalization, and punctuation, including: – punctuation: period, question mark, exclamation mark, comma, dash, apostrophe, colon, quotation marks, parentheses, ellipses	• use punctuation correctly in definitions (Mechanics SB #1–3) • insert definitions in sentences using correct punctuation (EP: Mechanics)	• TOC 8: Mechanics • TOC 8: Mechanics
Overall (LGV.02B) • use listening techniques and oral communication skills to participate in classroom discussions and more formal activities, such as storytelling, role playing, and reporting/presenting, for specific purposes and audiences		
Specific (LG2.03D) • plan and make oral presentations to a small group or the class, selecting and using vocabulary and methods of delivery to suit audience and purpose; gather ideas and information; plan, create, rehearse, revise, and assess presentations such as dramatizations, reports, and speeches	• prepare and present demonstration of a process (Oral Language Extension SB) • develop and present how-to speeches, getting feedback from audience (More Oral Language TG)	• AR 15: Oral Language • SSEC 5: Oral Presentation
(LG2.04D) • use specific examples, facial expressions, gestures, intonation, humour, and visual aids and technology, as appropriate, to engage the audience's interest during oral presentations	• present demonstration of a process (Oral Language Extension SB)	• TOC 11: Speaking
MEDIA STUDIES		
Overall (MDV.01D) • use knowledge of the elements, intended audiences, and production practices of a variety of media forms to analyze specific media works	• critique how-to video (More Media TG)	• AR 21: Response to Media
Specific (MD1.02D) • identify how elements of media forms are used in a variety of media works and explain the effects of different treatments	• explain how special effects are used in analytical videos (Media Link SB)	• AR 21: Response to Media

AR=Assessment Rubric   EP=Extra Practice   SB=Student Book   SSEC=Student Self-Evaluation Checklist   TG=Teacher's Guide   TOC=Teacher Observation Checklist

INSTRUCTIONAL STRATEGIES FOR THE ACADEMIC COURSE

PLANNING INFORMATION

Links to Other Nelson English 9 Resources

Literature & Media 9

Explanation—See "Some How-to's of Making Videos" by Todd Mercer, pp. 311–316 and "Interactive Writer's Handbook, Q & A" by Darryl Wimberley and Jon Samsel, pp. 326–332.

Write Source 2000

Explanation—"Writing an Explanation," p. 127; **Active and Passive Voice**—"Voice of Verbs," p. 447; **Direct and Indirect Objects**—"Direct Object," p. 435; "Indirect Object," p. 436; **Punctuation for Definitions**—"Writing a Definition," p. 125; "Colon for Emphasis," p. 394, "Dash for Emphasis," p. 395, "Parentheses to Add Information," p. 395; **Subject Complement**—"Predicate Adjective," p. 452; **Transitive and Intransitive Verbs**—"Use of Action Verbs," p. 450

INTRODUCING THE UNIT

1. To introduce this unit, have students read the paragraph on page 114 of the student book entitled "What is an explanation?" Ask them to share some examples of explanations they have heard, read, or given, either in school or with friends and family. List their examples on the board and then ask them to categorize their explanations into two groups: explanations that tell *why* something happens and explanations that tell *how* something happens. (LIV.02D—TOC 13: Tracking Expectations)

2. Have students find examples of explanations in their copies of *Language & Writing 9* to contribute to a short class discussion. (The writing process section, section openers, the introductory question and answers at the beginning of each unit, and some pages in the appendix all contain examples of explanations.) (LIV.02D—TOC 13: Tracking Expectations)

INTRODUCING THE MODEL

1. Divide students into groups of four and ask them to speculate on the answer to the question in the title of the model: Why Must Rainbows Be Curved? Suggest that they use the two illustrations to assist them in their discussions. Write some of their explanations on the board. Ask the class to discuss which explanation gives the best answer to the question. (LI1.03B—TOC 10: Reading Strategies)

2. Students could then read the model to find out how Ira Flatow explains why rainbows must be curved. Have them compare the explanation in the model with their explanations on the board, placing a checkmark beside those that were correct or partially correct. (LI1.03B—TOC 10: Reading Strategies)

3. Ask students to comment on the overall effectiveness of the model. Did the author answer the question asked in the title? Was the explanation easy to understand? (LI1.06D—TOC 13: Tracking Expectations)

INVESTIGATING THE MODEL

Answers:

1. The question, which is presented in the first paragraph of the model, is why rainbows are curved. The opening paragraph also provides background information explaining how the author became interested in answering this question.

2. The model includes several step-by-step explanations. One example is the formation of a rainbow: sunlight enters the front of a raindrop; gets bent; is separated into its constituent colours; the colours bounce off the back of the raindrop and are bent again, exiting through the front. Another pattern in this model shows a move from the effect (curved rainbow) to the cause (angle of deflection).

Possible answer

3. An illustration of a hand painting the band in the sky would have been helpful in understanding the explanation given for the curve in the rainbow.

4. Two examples of analogies are first, a movie theatre with the sun acting as film projector and the dark storm clouds serving as the screen and second, painting a band in the sky with a paintbrush and canvas, or paper and pencil.

5. The language in this piece suggests that it was written for a person who knows very little about rainbows. This is evident from the nontechnical language, the visual support, and the analogies used to explain the process.

Student Book 1.–5. (LI1.04D—AR 22: Response to Reading)

EXTENDING THE MODEL

1. Ask for student volunteers to explain to the class (without looking at the model) either what rainbows are and how they are formed or why rainbows are curved. Using the explanation checklist, have students evaluate the explanations. (LI1.01D—TOC 11: Speaking)

2. Have students bring to class examples of explanations that answer why or how questions. These may be from textbooks, "how-to" books, manuals, instructions, or directions given out as part of a course. Students can also check with the teacher-librarian and other teachers in the school for additional resources containing explanations including Web sites, videos, and CD-ROMs. Have students set up a display of these resources in the classroom for everyone to browse through. Such a collection will illustrate the range and scope of explanations in use in everyday life both inside and outside school. These resources may also provide students with ideas for writing their own explanations as suggested in Writer's Workshop. (WRV.01D—AR 7: Explanation)

3. As a follow-up to this unit, have some students compile a "Book of Explanations," using the writing produced by their classmates. The student editors will have to add a title page, copyright page, table of contents (including titles and authors' names), and front and back covers. The book could then be displayed in the school library or in a feeder-school library for other students to read. (WR5.02B—AR 12: Media Product)

WRITER'S WORKSHOP

1. In addition to brainstorming a list of possible topics for their written explanations as suggested in the first activity in the student book, students could ask younger family members for a list of questions that they would like explained. Ask students to bring these questions to class to share with other classmates. (WR1.01D—AR 7: Explanation)

2. For more topic ideas, provide students with a list of items covered in the science and technology and social studies curricula for grades two to four; or suggest that they skim through "how-to" books available in the school's resource centre or public library. (WR1.01D—AR 7: Explanation)

3. Remind students that diagrams or illustrations may need to be included with their explanations. To find out what would be most useful, have them share their explanations with a small group of classmates and then discuss with them which concepts or ideas would benefit from illustrative material. Younger family members could also make suggestions for diagrams or illustrations. (WR1.03D—AR 7: Explanation)

Student Book 1.–4. (WRV.01D—AR 7: Explanation); 5.–6. (WRV.03D—AR 7: Explanation); 7. (WRV.04D—AR 7: Explanation; WRV.05D—AR 7: Explanation)

ORAL LANGUAGE EXTENSION

If students decide to use their written explanations as the basis for their oral presentations, they may have to modify the content somewhat as a result of their answers to the questions on student book page 119.

Student Book (LG2.03D—AR 15: Oral Language; LG2.04D—TOC 11: Speaking)

GRAMMAR

1. Students should already be familiar with the terminology—direct and indirect objects, transitive and intransitive verbs, and subject complements—used in this unit. If not, it will be necessary for you to work through the examples given in the text; as well, you may want to use the sentences below to give students more practice with the concepts. Ask students to use the following sentence pairs to explain the difference between a direct and indirect object. (WR5.06D—TOC 4: Grammar; LG1.05D—TOC 4: Grammar)

> The student gave an effective explanation.
> The student gave the teacher an effective explanation.

2. Use the following sentences to explain the difference between transitive and intransitive verbs. Emphasize that the word *transitive* means "to carry across." (WR5.06D—TOC 4: Grammar; LG1.05D—TOC 4: Grammar)

> The rainbow coloured the sky.
> The rainbow faded after the storm.

3. Use the following sentences to explain subject complement. (WR5.06D—TOC 4: Grammar; LG1.05D—TOC 4: Grammar)

> The thunder was loud.
> Your position is important.
> The rainbow is a spectrum of colours.

Answers:

1. a) Try an experiment. (experiment — direct object)
   b) My travelling companion asked me a question. (me — indirect object; question — direct object)
   c) I gave my companion an explanation. (companion — indirect object; explanation — direct object)
   d) The light enters the drop in a straight line. (drop — direct object)
   e) Mother nature provides the raindrop with sunlight. (raindrop — direct object)
   f) We noticed them in the distance. (them — direct object)

2. Possible answers

   The teacher gave us three assignments for next week. (us — indirect object; assignments — direct object)
   My parents provided food for the refugees. (food — direct object; refugees — indirect object)

Student Book 1.–2. (WR5.06D—TOC 4: Grammar; LG1.05D—TOC 4: Grammar)

Students could develop short "how-to" speeches based on a task they perform well at home, at work, or at school. For their explanations, they should rely mainly on their own expertise. Suggest that they bring in visual aids to support their speeches if they think this would be helpful. Remind students that a good introduction and conclusion are always necessary for an effective oral presentation.

Divide the class into small groups for the speech presentations. At the end of each speech, have the other students in the group provide feedback to the speaker by telling what they have learned. Members of the group may wish to ask questions to find out more about some of the points made in the speaker's explanation. (LG2.03D—SSEC 5: Oral Presentation)

MORE CHALLENGE

Write the following common sentence patterns and examples on the board, or provide them on a worksheet. Ask students to write one sentence for each sentence pattern; then to rewrite each one to include modifiers.

Example: Our allies destroyed the ship. During the fierce battle, our allies destroyed the ship from the air.

Sentence Patterns

subject — action verb (Sudbury produces.)
subject — action verb — direct object (Sudbury produces nickel.)
subject — action verb — indirect object — direct object (Sudbury gives visitors tours.)
subject — linking verb — subject complement (Sudbury is industrious.)
(WR5.06D—TOC 4: Grammar; LG1.05D—TOC 4: Grammar)

MORE MEDIA

How-to videos are now available in some hardware stores and building centres to explain how to build decks, patios, and other items. Also, some television shows specialize in explaining how to build additions or do renovations. Show one of these videos or a taped TV show and have students critique it for its content and clarity. Ask students to identify what other kinds of information would be required to complete the project shown in the video (for example, a list of equipment necessary, a list of building supplies needed, blueprints, drawings, and sketches). (MDV.01D—AR 21: Response to Media)

3. a) The angle of deflection for each colour varies. (varies — intransitive)
    b) The colours meet your eyes at a 42-degree angle. (meet — transitive)
    c) Rainbows emerge only during or right after the storm. (emerge — intransitive)
    d) The drops of water deflect the sunlight. (deflect — transitive)

4. Possible answers

    The basketball team won the game last Friday. (won — transitive)

    The band played some new music at the last dance. (played — transitive)

    The wind blew very hard all night. (blew — intransitive)

    The band played until about 4 a.m. (played — intransitive)

Student Book 3.–4. (WR5.06D—TOC 4: Grammar; LG1.05D—TOC 4: Grammar)

5. a) The rainbow was captivating. (captivating — describes the subject)
    b) A prism is a solid glass object. (object — renames the subject)
    c) The raindrops are little prisms. (prisms — renames the subject)
    d) Rainbow "circles" are quite common. (common — describes the subject)
    e) The rainbow seems faded. (faded — describes the subject)

Student Book 5. (WR5.06D—TOC 4: Grammar; LG1.05D—TOC 4: Grammar)

6.–7. Student work.

Student Book 6.–7. (WR5.06D—TOC 4: Grammar; LG1.05D—TOC 4: Grammar)

MEDIA LINK

The use of this activity will depend on the amount of equipment available in your school. It might also be linked to a project students are already working on in their media studies or to the Oral Language Extension activity on pages 118–119 of the student book. Students could prepare a video of their demonstrations to use with a younger audience. (MD1.02D—AR 21: Response to Media)

MECHANICS

Answers:

1. The example using the dashes emphasizes the definition to a greater extent. The example using parentheses de-emphasizes the definition.

2. Possible answers

    a) You can break sunlight into a rainbow by passing it through a *prism* (a transparent piece of glass with triangular ends).
    b) The angle of bending or turning aside varies with each colour. This is known as *deflection.*
    c) Isaac Newton pointed out that sunlight streaming through a prism will be broken up or distributed into several colours—a *spectrum*—ranging from red to violet.

Two other ways of explaining terms are to provide information about the term immediately after it has been used (for example, *Some people worry about radiation, a term used to describe rays of tiny high-speed particles that shoot out from many different sources, both natural and artificial.*) or to provide a dictionary-type definition (for example, *We are studying how to write an explanation: a method of telling how something is, was, or should be done.*).

3. Student work.

Student Book 1.–3. (WR5.15B—TOC 8: Mechanics; LG1.07B—TOC 8: Mechanics)

USAGE & STYLE

This section focuses on the use of active and passive voice. Explain to students that a passive verb is usually not as strong as an active one. Therefore, most writers prefer to use active verbs whenever possible to make their writing more interesting and lively. Active verbs generally are simpler and more direct. However, the passive voice has its uses too. It is useful if you do not know who did the action, if the actor is unimportant, or if you want to emphasize who or what was the receiver of the action rather than who or what performed it. Write the following sets of sentences on the board.

> Juri explained the process.
> The process was explained by Juri.
>
> Marissa lost the instructions.
> The instructions were lost by Marissa.
>
> The student made a clear explanation.
> A clear explanation was made by the student.

Through questioning, establish that in the first sentence of each pair, the subject is the doer or actor in the sentence: What is the subject of the first sentence? (Juri) What does the subject do in the sentence? (explain) Indicate that a verb is active when its subject performs the action of the verb. (Juri explained)

Through questioning, establish that in the second sentence of each pair, the subject is acted upon, or has something done to it. For example, in the first pair: What is the subject of the second sentence? (process) What does the verb in the second sentence do? (explain) Which word names the receiver of the action or has something done to it? (process) Indicate that a verb is passive when the subject is the receiver of the action: that is, has something done to it. Have students note that the direct objects of the first sentences in each pair have become the subjects in the second sentences. Also note that helping verbs in the passive voice use forms of the verb "to be" (am, is, be, are, was, were, been). (WR5.10B—TOC 15: Usage & Style; LG1.05D—TOC 15: Usage & Style)

Answers:

1. As you know, sunlight is composed of all the colours of the rainbow. As you know, all the colours of the rainbow compose sunlight.

   Isaac Newton pointed out that sunlight streaming through a prism will be broken up into a spectrum of colours ranging from red to violet.

   Isaac Newton pointed out that a prism will break up sunlight streaming through it into a spectrum of colours ranging from red to violet.

2.–3. Student work.

Student Book 1.–3. (WR5.10B—TOC 15: Usage & Style; LG1.05D—TOC 15: Usage & Style)

WORD STUDY & SPELLING

1. Review the different ways that words came into being in the English language. Point out to students that many English words are derived from other languages. Latin, in particular (about one-fourth to one-half of English vocabulary comes from Latin), has had a major influence on the English language. Greek has also had a strong influence, particularly in the field of science. Explain to students that in many words, they should be able to identify a root or core that comes from a Latin or Greek word. In English, the root will often have different prefixes or

---

MORE SUPPORT

Point out that sometimes passive constructions are used to avoid naming the real performer of an action. Have students turn the following passive sentences into active ones by supplying a subject for the verb. (WR5.10B—TOC 15: Usage & Style; LG1.05D—TOC 15: Usage & Style)

a) A rainbow was seen last night.

b) The colours could be seen in the distance.

c) The prism was broken accidentally.

d) Several rainbows have been seen recently.

e) An explanation was given in science class.

suffixes added to it to make up the word. Students will then discover that this root or core is found in many words with related meanings.

Use the Latin examples below to explain to students that roots give words their meanings. Words are formed by combining roots, prefixes, and suffixes. We use the term "root" when the root is recognizable as an English word or part of a word. (LG1.01B—TOC 16: Word Study & Spelling)

Root	Meaning	English Word
dens (Latin)	tooth	dental, dentist, trident
turba (Latin)	confusion	disturb, perturb, turbulent

2. Review with students the meaning of etymology (the study of the sources and development of words) and what the etymology of a word often looks like in a dictionary. Divide students into groups and have them look for good sources of etymological information for words and report back to the class. One group could look at print dictionaries, one group at online sources, and one at dictionaries available on CD-ROM. (LG1.01B—TOC 16: Word Study & Spelling)

Answers:
Possible answers:

1. a) producing — Latin root is *produc* from *producere* (to extend, bring forth)
      product or producer (and several others)

   b) spectrum — Latin root is *spect* from *spectare* (to observe) and *specere* (to look at)
      spectacle

   c) refracted — Latin root is *refract* and comes from *refractus* (broken up)
      refraction

   d) deflection — Latin root is *flect* from *flectere* (to bend)
      deflect

   e) directions — Latin root is *direct* from *directus* and from *dirigere* (to guide)
      direct (and several others)

   f) degree — Latin root is *deg* from *de + gradus* (step or grade); also old French *degre*
      degrade

   g) gradations — Latin root is *grad* from *gradus* (step)
      grade (and several others)

   h) difference — Latin root is *differ* from *differre* (literally, to bear off in different directions, hence scatter, put off, be different)
      differ (and several others)

   i) position — Latin root is *positio* from *positio* (a positioning, affirmation, and from *ponere* (to place, lay down)
      positive — from *ponere* only

2. Possible answers
   a) biology, biography, biopsy, biochemist
   b) microbe, microchip, microcosm, microfiche
   c) macroeconomics, macroscopic, macrocosm
   d) kilogram, kilometre, kilowatt
   e) geography, geology, geometry, geophysics
   f) ecology, economic, economy
   h) zoological, zoology, zoophyte

MORE CHALLENGE

Have students work in small groups to find two words that come from each of the languages given below. For sources, students can use their own knowledge, students from other countries, dictionaries, language teachers, or other resources in the resource centre. Two examples for each language are provided below. (LG1.03B—TOC 16: Word Study & Spelling)

Arabic — sugar, cotton

Dutch — splice, pack

Spain — canyon, mosquito

Chinese — tea, pekoe

German — Fahrenheit, diesel

India — chutney, curry

Italian — sonnet, piano

French —matinee, garage

i) bilingual, bicycle, bisect, bipartisan

j) biology, ecology, astrology, technology

k) philosophy, theosophy

l) autograph, telegraph, photograph, graphic

Student Book 1.–2. (LG1.03B—TOC 16: Word Study & Spelling)

ANSWERS TO EXTRA PRACTICE

Grammar

      LV   SC

1. She seems studious.

                     TV   DO

2. During the evening, the workers completed the addition.

          LV   SC

3. Our neighbours are very friendly.

      TV   IO   DO

4. Sarah handed Kyle her ticket before the game.

         TV IO   DO

5. Our English teacher taught us how to write explanations.

        IV

6. They sit quietly.

       LV SC

7. This apple tastes sour.

     LV   SC

8. Carl is an excellent student.

    TV   IO   DO

9. We left the waitress a generous tip.

      TV   IO   DO

10. Our class gave the young students a presentation on writing explanations.

(WR5.06D—TOC 4: Grammar; LG1.05D—TOC 4: Grammar)

Mechanics

Possible answers

1. The *microscope* (an instrument with a lens for making small things look bigger) is useful in the study of biology.

2. An *aqueduct*—a structure that supports a channel or large pipe to bring water from a distance—was used to get water to the remote village.

3. The space craft was on a perfect *trajectory*: the curved path of something moving through space.

4. That type of problem can usually be corrected by an *ophthalmologist*: a physician who specializes in the branch of medicine that deals with the structure, function, and diseases of the eye.

5. The light is the result of using a *filament*—the wire that gives off light in an electric light bulb.

6. Most engines lose some of their compression (the reduction in volume of gas by the application of pressure) over time.

(WR5.15B—TOC 8: Mechanics; LG1.07B—TOC 8: Mechanics)

Usage & Style

1. a) A
   b) P
   c) P
   d) A
   e) A
   f) P
   g) A
   h) P

2. Possible answers
   a) The puck hit the referee.
   b) The students completed the work during their spare.
   c) The students washed cars to raise money.
   d) The referee removed our best player for the last five minutes.
   e) The police had informed the gang of the consequences.

3. Possible answers
   a) My e-mail is always answered on the day I receive it.
   b) Basketball was invented by a Canadian.
   c) Many buildings on the river basin were damaged by the spring floods.
   d) The gate was shut by the security officer.
   e) The puzzle was quickly solved by you.

(WR5.10B—TOC 15: Usage & Style; LG1.05D—TOC 15: Usage & Style)

Word Study & Spelling

1. a) form — from Latin *forma* (shape)
   b) astro — from Greek *astron* (star)
   c) port — from Latin *portare* (to carry)
   d) turb — from Latin *turba* (confusion)
   e) hydr — from Greek *hudor* (water)
   f) stru — from Latin *struere* (to build)
   g) phys — from Greek *phusis* (nature)

2. a) uniform, transform
   b) astronomy, asterisk
   c) transport, porter
   d) disturb, turbine
   e) hydrant, hydroelectric
   f) destructive, instruct
   g) physicist, physician

(LG1.03B—TOC 16: Word Study & Spelling)

	GRADE 9 EXPECTATIONS	DEMONSTRATION OF LEARNING	ASSESSMENT TOOLS
LITERATURE STUDIES AND READING			
Overall (LIV.01P)	• read and demonstrate an understanding of a variety of literary and informational texts		
Specific (LI1.01P)	• describe information, ideas, opinions, and themes in texts they have read during the year from a variety of print and electronic sources, including biographies, short stories, poems, plays, novels, brochures, and articles from newspapers, magazines, and encyclopedias	• give explanations of rainbows to the class (Extending the Model TG #2)	• TOC 11: Speaking
(LI1.03B)	• describe a variety of reading strategies and select and use them effectively before, during, and after reading to understand texts	• speculate on answer to question in title "Why Must Rainbows Be Curved?" using illustrations (Introducing the Model TG #2) • check to see if speculations on model were correct (Introducing the Model TG #3)	• TOC 10: Reading Strategies • TOC 10: Reading Strategies
(LI1.04P)	• locate and use explicit information and ideas from texts in forming opinions and developing generalizations	• give interpretations of model using examples from student book (Investigating the Model SB #1–5)	• AR 22: Response to Reading
(LI1.06B)	• use specific references from a text to support opinions and judgments	• comment on effectiveness of model in giving explanation (Introducing the Model TG #4)	• TOC 14: Tracking Expectations
Overall (LIV.02P)	• demonstrate an understanding of the elements of a variety of literary and informational forms, with a focus on plays, short stories, and newspaper and magazine articles	• share explanations and categorize them as to "how" and "why" (Introducing the Unit TG #1) • discuss as a class examples of explanations (Introducing the Unit TG #2) • analyze explanations as to why they were difficult to understand (Introducing the Model TG #1) • discuss appropriate length for explanation (Extending the Model TG #1)	• TOC 14: Tracking Expectations • TOC 14: Tracking Expectations • TOC 14: Tracking Expectations • TOC 14: Tracking Expectations
WRITING			
Overall (WRV.01P)	• use print and electronic sources to gather information and explore ideas for their written work	• collect examples of explanations for class display (Extending the Model TG #3) • gather and organize information for explanation (Writer's Workshop SB #1–4)	• AR 7: Explanation • AR 7: Explanation
Specific (WR1.01P)	• investigate potential topics by asking questions, identifying information needs, and developing research plans to gather data	• share with class questions younger family members would like answered (Writer's Workshop TG #1) • skim science and technology and social studies curricula and how-to books for topics (Writer's Workshop TG #2)	• AR 7: Explanation • AR 7: Explanation
(WR1.03P)	• sort and group information and ideas, assess their relevance and accuracy, and discard irrelevant material	• discuss which concepts in explanation need illustrative material (Writer's Workshop TG #3)	• AR 7: Explanation
Overall (WRV.02P)	• identify the literary and informational forms suited to specific purposes and audiences and use the forms appropriately in their own writing, with an emphasis on communicating information accurately	• collect examples of explanations for ideas for their own writing (Extending the Model TG #3)	• AR 7: Explanation
Overall (WRV.03P)	• use a variety of forms of writing to express themselves, clarify their ideas, and engage the audience's attention, imagination, and interest	• write draft of explanation (Writer's Workshop SB #5–6)	• AR 7: Explanation
Overall (WRV.04B)	• revise their written work, collaboratively and independently, with a focus on support for ideas, accuracy, clarity, and unity	• revise explanation (Writer's Workshop SB #7)	• AR 7: Explanation

AR=Assessment Rubric   EP=Extra Practice   SB=Student Book   SSEC=Student Self-Evaluation Checklist   TG=Teacher's Guide   TOC=Teacher Observation Checklist

GRADE 9 EXPECTATIONS	DEMONSTRATION OF LEARNING	ASSESSMENT TOOLS
WRITING (continued)		
Overall (WRV.05B) • edit and proofread to produce final drafts, using correct grammar, spelling, and punctuation, according to the conventions of standard Canadian English specified for this course, with the support of print and electronic resources when appropriate	• edit and proofread explanation (Writer's Workshop SB #7)	• AR 7: Explanation
Specific (WR5.02B) • select the publication method or vehicle most accessible or appealing to the intended audience	• create a "Book of Explanations" for school library (Extending the Model TG #4)	• AR 12: Media Product
(WR5.06P) • construct complete and correct compound and complex sentences, using the following sentence components as required: subject, predicate, object, subject complement; main and subordinate clauses; prepositional phrases	• explain difference between direct and indirect object (Grammar TG #1) • explain difference between transitive and intransitive verbs (Grammar TG #2) • explain subject complement (Grammar TG #3) • identify and use direct and indirect objects (Grammar SB #1–2) • identify and use transitive and intransitive verbs (Grammar SB #3–4) • identify subject complement (Grammar SB #5) • discuss direct and indirect objects, transitive and intransitive verbs, and subject complements (Grammar SB #6–7) • use direct objects and subject complements in sentences (More Support TG, page 169) • write descriptive sentences using subject complements (More Challenge TG) • identify sentence components (EP: Grammar)	• TOC 4: Grammar • TOC 4: Grammar • TOC 4: Grammar • TOC 4: Grammar • TOC 4: Grammar • TOC 4: Grammar • TOC 4: Grammar • TOC 4: Grammar • TOC 4: Grammar • TOC 4: Grammar
(WR5.10B) • use consistent and appropriate verb tense and voice (i.e., active and passive) for clarity in narrative and expository writing	• discuss use of active and passive voice (Usage & Style TG) • use active and passive voice correctly (Usage & Style SB #1–3) • turn passive constructions into active ones (More Support TG, page 170) • use active and passive voice correctly (EP: Usage & Style)	• TOC 15: Usage & Style • TOC 15: Usage & Style • TOC 15: Usage & Style • TOC 15: Usage & Style
(WR5.15B) • use punctuation correctly, including period, question mark, exclamation mark, comma, dash, apostrophe, colon, quotation marks, parentheses, and ellipses	• check that correct punctuation has been used in definitions (Mechanics TG) • use punctuation correctly in definitions (Mechanics SB #1–3) • rewrite definitions using correct punctuation (More Support TG, page 170) • insert definitions in sentences using correct punctuation (EP: Mechanics)	• TOC 8: Mechanics • TOC 8: Mechanics • TOC 8: Mechanics • TOC 8: Mechanics
LANGUAGE		
Overall (LGV.01P) • use knowledge of vocabulary and language conventions to speak, write, and read clearly and correctly		
Specific (LG1.01B) • describe strategies used to expand vocabulary and provide evidence of other vocabulary-building activities	• discuss using roots to find meaning of words (Word Study & Spelling TG #1) • research etymological information (Word Study & Spelling TG #2)	• TOC 16: Word Study & Spelling • TOC 16: Word Study & Spelling

AR=Assessment Rubric   EP=Extra Practice   SB=Student Book   SSEC=Student Self-Evaluation Checklist   TG=Teacher's Guide   TOC=Teacher Observation Checklist

GRADE 9 EXPECTATIONS	DEMONSTRATION OF LEARNING	ASSESSMENT TOOLS
LANGUAGE (continued)		
(LG1.03B) • identify words borrowed from other languages, and words and terms recently introduced to describe new ideas, inventions, and products, and explain their origins	• find words with Greek and Latin roots (Word Study & Spelling SB #1–2) • identify roots as Latin or Greek (EP: Word Study & Spelling)	• TOC 16: Word Study & Spelling • TOC 16: Word Study & Spelling
(LG1.05P) • recognize, describe, and use correctly, in oral and written language, the language structures of standard Canadian English and its conventions of grammar and usage, including: – components of sentences: subject, predicate, object, subject complement, prepositional phrases, main and subordinate clauses – consistency of verb tense and voice	• explain difference between direct and indirect object (Grammar TG #1) • explain difference between transitive and intransitive verbs (Grammar TG #2) • explain subject complement (Grammar TG #3) • identify and use direct and indirect objects (Grammar SB #1–2) • identify and use transitive and intransitive verbs (Grammar SB #3–4) • identify subject complement (Grammar SB #5) • discuss direct and indirect objects, transitive and intransitive verbs, and subject complements (Grammar SB #6–7) • use direct objects and subject complements in sentences (More Support TG, page 169) • write descriptive sentences using subject complements (More Challenge TG) • identify sentence components (EP: Grammar) • discuss use of active and passive voice (Usage & Style TG) • use active and passive voice correctly (Usage & Style SB #1–3) • turn passive constructions into active ones (More Support TG, page 170) • use active and passive voice correctly (EP: Usage & Style)	• TOC 4: Grammar • TOC 4: Grammar • TOC 4: Grammar • TOC 4: Grammar • TOC 4: Grammar • TOC 4: Grammar • TOC 4: Grammar • TOC 4: Grammar • TOC 4: Grammar • TOC 4: Grammar • TOC 15: Usage & Style • TOC 15: Usage & Style • TOC 15: Usage & Style • TOC 15: Usage & Style
(LG1.07B) • recognize, describe, and use correctly, in oral and written language, the conventions of standard Canadian English for spelling, capitalization, and punctuation, including: – punctuation: period, question mark, exclamation mark, comma, dash, apostrophe, colon, quotation marks, parentheses, ellipses	• use punctuation correctly in definitions (Mechanics SB #1–3) • rewrite definitions using correct punctuation (More Support TG, page 170) • insert definitions in sentences using correct punctuation (EP: Mechanics)	• TOC 8: Mechanics • TOC 8: Mechanics • TOC 8: Mechanics
Overall (LGV.02B) • use listening techniques and oral communication skills to participate in classroom discussions and more formal activities, such as storytelling, role playing, and reporting/ presenting, for specific purposes and audiences		
Specific (LG2.03P) • work with a partner to plan and make oral presentations to a small group, selecting and using vocabulary and methods of delivery to suit audience and purpose	• prepare and present demonstration of a process (Oral Language Extension SB) • develop and present how-to speeches, getting feedback from audience (More Oral Language TG)	• AR 15: Oral Language • SSEC 5: Oral Presentation
MEDIA STUDIES		
Overall (MDV.01P) • identify and describe the elements, intended audiences, and production practices of a variety of media forms	• critique how-to video (More Media TG)	• AR 21: Response to Media
Specific (MD1.02P) • identify and describe the elements used to structure media works in a variety of forms	• explain how special effects are used in analytical videos (Media Link SB)	• AR 21: Response to Media

AR=Assessment Rubric   EP=Extra Practice   SB=Student Book   SSEC=Student Self-Evaluation Checklist   TG=Teacher's Guide   TOC=Teacher Observation Checklist

Instructional Strategies for the Applied Course

Planning Information

Links to Other Nelson English 9 Resources

Literature & Media 9

Explanation—See "Some How-to's of Making Videos" by Todd Mercer, pp. 311–316 and "Interactive Writer's Handbook, Q & A" by Darryl Wimberley and Jon Samsel, pp. 326–332.

Write Source 2000

Explanation—"Writing an Explanation," p. 127; **Active and Passive Voice**—"Voice of Verbs," p. 447; **Direct and Indirect Objects**—"Direct Object," p. 435, "Indirect Object," p. 436; **Punctuation for Definitions**—"Writing a Definition," p. 125, "Colon for Emphasis," p. 394, "Dash for Emphasis," p. 395, "Parentheses to Add Information," p. 395; **Subject Complement**—"Predicate Adjective," p. 452; **Transitive and Intransitive Verbs**—"Use of Action Verbs," p. 450

Introducing the Unit

The activities on page 157 from the Academic Course are appropriate for the Applied Course.
1. (LIV.02P—TOC 14: Tracking Expectations)

2. (LIV.02P—TOC 14: Tracking Expectations)

Introducing the Model

1. Ask students to share experiences of times when they were given explanations that were difficult to follow. Have students analyze what made the explanations difficult. Using Checkpoint on page 168 of this guide, work with students to compile a list of items that contribute to a good explanation. (LIV.02P—TOC 14: Tracking Expectations)

Activities #1–3 on page 157 from the Academic Course are appropriate for the Applied Course.

2. (LI1.03B—TOC 10: Reading Strategies)

3. (LI1.03B—TOC 10: Reading Strategies)

4. (LI1.06B—TOC 14: Tracking Expectations)

Investigating the Model

See the Academic Course on pages 157–158 for the answers.

Student Book 1.–5. (LI1.04P—AR 22: Response to Reading)

Extending the Model

1. Ask students to comment on the length of the model explanation. Did they find it too long, too short, or just about the right length? Students should give reasons for their answers. What should determine the appropriate length of an explanation? (It should be long enough to provide an adequate explanation, but should not be so long that it includes unnecessary information.) (LIV.02P—TOC 14: Tracking Expectations)

Learning Goals

- write an explanation
- use direct and indirect objects, transitive and intransitive verbs, and subject complements
- learn proper punctuation for definitions
- explain the use of active and passive voice in explanations
- recognize Greek and Latin roots

Checkpoint

Sample criteria for an explanation:

- often begins with questions or statement and then provides answer or supplies details to back up assertion
- usually proceeds step by step, and moves from cause to effect (or effect to cause)
- is often supported by visual aids, such as diagrams and illustrations
- often uses analogies to assist nonspecialist
- has language, amount of detail, and use of technical terms that depend on expertise of audience

The activities on page 158 from the Academic Course are appropriate for the Applied Course.

2. (LI1.01P—TOC 11: Speaking)

3. (WRV.01P—AR 7: Explanation; WRV.02P—AR 7: Explanation)

4. (WR5.02B—AR 12: Media Product)

WRITER'S WORKSHOP

The activities on pages 158–159 from the Academic Course are appropriate for the Applied Course.

1. (WR1.01P—AR 7: Explanation)

2. (WR1.01P—AR 7: Explanation)

3. (WR1.03P—AR 7: Explanation)

Student Book 1.–4. (WRV.01P—AR 7: Explanation); 5.–6. (WRV.03P—AR 7: Explanation); 7. (WRV.04B—AR 7: Explanation; WRV.05B—AR 7: Explanation)

ORAL LANGUAGE EXTENSION

If students decide to use their written explanations as the basis for their oral presentations, they may have to modify the content somewhat as a result of their answers to the questions on student book page 119.

Student Book (LG2.03P—AR 15: Oral Language)

GRAMMAR

The activities on page 159 from the Academic Course are appropriate for the Applied Course.

1. (WR5.06P—TOC 4: Grammar; LG1.05P—TOC 4: Grammar)

2. (WR5.06P—TOC 4: Grammar; LG1.05P—TOC 4: Grammar)

3. (WR5.06P—TOC 4: Grammar; LG1.05P—TOC 4: Grammar)

Answers:

See the Academic Course on pages 159–160 for answers.

Student Book 1.–2. (WR5.06P—TOC 4: Grammar; LG1.05P—TOC 4: Grammar) 3.–4. (WR5.06P—TOC 4: Grammar; LG1.05P—TOC 4: Grammar) 5. (WR.5.06P—TOC 4: Grammar; LG1.05P—TOC 4: Grammar) 6.–7. (WR5.06P—TOC 4: Grammar; LG1.05P—TOC 4: Grammar)

MEDIA LINK

The use of this activity will depend on the amount of equipment available in your school. It might also be linked to a project students are already working on in their media studies or to the Oral Language Extension activity on pages 118–119 of the student book. Students could prepare a video of their demonstrations to use with a younger audience. (MD1.02P—AR 21: Response to Media)

MORE ORAL LANGUAGE

Students could develop short "how-to" speeches based on a task they perform well at home, at work, or at school. For their explanations, they should rely mainly on their own expertise. Suggest that they bring in visual aids to support their speeches if they think this would be helpful. Remind students that a good introduction and conclusion are always necessary for an effective oral presentation.

Divide the class into small groups for the speech presentations. At the end of each speech, have the other students in the group provide feedback to the speaker by telling what they have learned. Members of the group may wish to ask questions to find out more about some of the points made in the speaker's explanation. (LG2.03P—SSEC 5: Oral Presentation)

MORE SUPPORT

The following activity can be used to further clarify the use of direct objects and subject complements. Place the following groups of sentences in three columns on the board. Underline each of the verbs.

I laid my book on the desk.	I lay down yesterday.	She is correct.
You raise the ladder.	We rise at eight.	The players were tired.
He set the alarm clock.	They sit quietly.	They became famous.

Ask students to identify the group of sentences that include the following to complete the thought:

- action verbs requiring objects (column 2)
- action verbs not requiring objects (column 1)
- subject complements (column 3)

Have students work in pairs to create two short sentences to add to each of the columns of sentences. (WR5.06P—TOC 4: Grammar; LG1.05P—TOC 4: Grammar)

MORE CHALLENGE

Ask students to cut a picture out of a magazine or newspaper, or use a picture in a textbook. Have them write five descriptive sentences about the picture using linking verbs and subject complements. (WR5.06P—TOC 4: Grammar; LG1.05P—TOC 4: Grammar)

Example: The car in the picture appears damaged.

MECHANICS

In writing explanations, students must often include definitions of new terms they are introducing to the reader. Sometimes students write definitions that are too narrow or seem incomplete (for example, "A pear is an odd-shaped fruit, bigger at one end than another."). A better way to word this would be: "A pear is a sweet, juicy, edible fruit rounded at one end and smaller toward the stem end." After using this example, have students write on the board some of the definitions they have written in their explanations. Ask the class to assess the completeness of these definitions and whether or not correct punctuation has been used. (WR5.15B—TOC 8: Mechanics; LG1.07B—TOC 8: Mechanics)

See the Academic Course on pages 160–161 for answers.

Student Book 1.–3. (WR5.15B—TOC 8: Mechanics; LG1.07B—TOC 8: Mechanics)

USAGE & STYLE

The activity on page 161 from the Academic Course is appropriate for the Applied Course. (WR5.10B—TOC 15: Usage & Style; LG1.05P—TOC 15: Usage & Style)

See the Academic Course on page 161 for answers.

Student Book 1.–3. (WR5.10B—TOC 15: Usage & Style; LG1.05P—TOC 15: Usage & Style)

WORD STUDY & SPELLING

The activities on pages 161–162 from the Academic Course are appropriate for the Applied Course.

1. (LG1.01B—TOC 16: Word Study & Spelling)

2. (LG1.01B—TOC 16: Word Study & Spelling)

Answers:

See the Academic Course on pages 162–163 for answers.

Student Book 1.–2. (LG1.03B—TOC 16: Word Study & Spelling)

ANSWERS TO EXTRA PRACTICE

See the Academic Course on pages 163–164 for answers.

Grammar

(WR5.06P—TOC 4: Grammar; LG1.05P—TOC 4: Grammar)

Mechanics

(WR5.15B—TOC 8: Mechanics; LG1.07B—TOC 8: Mechanics)

Usage & Style

(WR5.10B—TOC 15: Usage & Style; LG1.05P—TOC 15: Usage & Style)

Word Study & Spelling

(LG1.03B—TOC 16: Word Study & Spelling)

GRAMMAR

NAME: _____ **DATE:** _____

Identify the transitive verbs (TV), intransitive verbs (IV), linking verbs (LV), direct objects (DO), indirect objects (IO), and subject complements (SC) in each of the following sentences. Write your answers directly above the words or phrases in the sentences.

1. She seems studious.

2. During the evening, the workers completed the addition.

3. Our neighbours are very friendly.

4. Sarah handed Kyle her ticket before the game.

5. Our English teacher taught us how to write explanations.

6. They sit quietly.

7. This apple tastes sour.

8. Carl is an excellent student.

9. We left the waitress a generous tip.

10. Our class gave the young students a presentation on writing explanations.

MECHANICS

NAME: _____ DATE: _____

Rewrite each of the following sentences, inserting a simple definition of the italicized word. Use each of the methods (parentheses, dashes, and a colon) studied in this unit two times. Use your dictionary to help you find suitable definitions.

1. The *microscope* is useful in the study of biology.

   _____

   _____

2. An *aqueduct* was used to get water to the remote village.

   _____

   _____

3. The *trajectory* of the space craft was perfect.

   _____

   _____

4. An *ophthalmologist* can usually correct the problem.

   _____

   _____

5. The light is the result of using a *filament*.

   _____

   _____

6. Most engines lose some of their *compression* over time.

   _____

   _____

USAGE & STYLE

NAME: _____ DATE: _____

1. Identify the following sentences as active (A) or passive (P).

   a) The class planned the excursion for next Thursday.

   b) The door was shut by the custodian.

   c) During the scuffle, the man was injured by the thief.

   d) We were planning the party for Saturday night.

   e) The manager gave the job to Samantha.

   f) Our flight to Vancouver on Monday has been cancelled.

   g) Martha completed her report last night.

   h) The furniture you were expecting was delivered by the store today.

2. Rewrite each of the following sentences in the active voice.

   a) The referee was hit by the puck.

   _____

   b) The work was completed by the students during their spare.

   _____

   c) The cars were washed by the students to raise money.

   _____

   d) Our best player was removed by the referee for the last five minutes.

   _____

   e) The gang had been informed of the consequences by the police.

   _____

3. Rewrite each of the following sentences in the passive voice.

   a) I always answer an e-mail on the day it is received.

   _____

   b) A Canadian invented basketball.

   _____

   c) The early spring floods damaged many buildings on the river basin.

   _____

   d) The security officer shut the gate.

   _____

   e) You solved the puzzle quickly.

   _____

WORD STUDY & SPELLING

NAME: _____ DATE: _____

1. The following words contain a root from either Latin or Greek. Identify the root in each word and indicate whether it is Latin or Greek.

   a) formation

   _____

   b) astronaut

   _____

   c) portable

   _____

   d) turbulent

   _____

   e) dehydrate

   _____

   f) structure

   _____

   g) physical

   _____

2. For each of the roots identified in the first activity, identify two other words with the same root.

   a) _____

   b) _____

   c) _____

   d) _____

   e) _____

   f) _____

   g) _____

ACADEMIC EXPECTATIONS

GRADE 9 EXPECTATIONS		DEMONSTRATION OF LEARNING	ASSESSMENT TOOLS
LITERATURE STUDIES AND READING			
Overall (LIV.01D)	• read and demonstrate an understanding of a variety of literary and informational texts, from contemporary and historical periods		
Specific (LI1.02D)	• select and read texts for different purposes, with an emphasis on recognizing the elements of literary genres and the organization of informational materials, collecting and assessing information, responding imaginatively, and exploring human experiences and values	• discuss reaction to model (Introducing the Model TG #3) • discuss importance of abstracts to business people (Extending the Model TG #3)	• AR 22: Response to Reading • AR 22: Response to Reading
(LI1.03B)	• describe a variety of reading strategies and select and use them effectively before, during, and after reading to understand texts	• speculate on questions title raises in reader's mind; read to discover which questions were answered (Introducing the Model TG #2) • summarize science fiction book or film for discussion (Extending the Model TG #4)	• TOC 10: Reading Strategies • TOC 10: Reading Strategies
(LI1.04D)	• locate explicit information and ideas in texts to use in developing opinions and interpretations	• give examples from model for use in interpretation (Investigating the Model SB #1–5)	• AR 22: Response to Reading
(LI1.05D)	• analyze information, ideas, and elements in texts to make inferences about meaning	• identify paragraph giving essence of précis (Extending the Model TG #1)	• AR 22: Response to Reading
Overall (LIV.02D)	• demonstrate an understanding of the elements of a variety of literary and informational forms, with a focus on plays, short stories, and short essays	• identify situations where they have had to summarize material (Introducing the Unit TG #1) • define "summary" (Introducing the Unit TG #2) • compare a précis with original article (Investigating the Model TG)	• TOC 13: Tracking Expectations • TOC 13: Tracking Expectations • TOC 13: Tracking Expectations
Specific (LI2.02D)	• use knowledge of elements of the short story, such as plot, characterization, setting, conflict, theme, mood, and point of view, to understand and interpret examples of the genre	• review features of short stories (Media Link TG)	• AR 22: Response to Reading
Overall (LIV.03B)	• identify and explain the effect of specific elements of style in a variety of literary and informational texts		
Specific (LI3.03D)	• explain how authors and editors use design elements to help communicate ideas	• explain whether illustration represents précis (Introducing the Unit TG #3)	• TOC 13: Tracking Expectations
WRITING			
Overall (WRV.01D)	• use a variety of print and electronic sources to gather information and explore ideas for their written work	• research articles on role of computers in the future (Extending the Model TG #2) • gather and organize ideas for précis (Writer's Workshop SB #1–4)	• AR 18: Précis • AR 18: Précis
Overall (WRV.03D)	• use a variety of organizational techniques to present ideas and supporting details logically and coherently in written work	• write a précis of an article on computers (Extending the Model TG #2) • work through writing process of précis as a class (Writer's Workshop TG) • write a précis (Writer's Workshop SB #5–6)	• AR 18: Précis • AR 18: Précis • AR 18: Précis
Overall (WRV.04D)	• revise their written work, independently and collaboratively, with a focus on support for ideas and opinions, accuracy, clarity, and unity	• revise précis (Writer's Workshop SB #7)	• AR 18: Précis

AR=Assessment Rubric   EP=Extra Practice   SB=Student Book   SSEC=Student Self-Evaluation Checklist   TG=Teacher's Guide   TOC=Teacher Observation Checklist

GRADE 9 EXPECTATIONS	DEMONSTRATION OF LEARNING	ASSESSMENT TOOLS
WRITING (continued)		
Overall (WRV.05D)	• edit and proofread to produce final drafts, using correct grammar, spelling, and punctuation, according to the conventions of standard Canadian English, with the support of print and electronic resources when appropriate	• edit and proofread précis (Writer's Workshop SB #7)	• AR 18: Précis
Specific (WR5.06D)	• construct complete and correct compound and complex sentences, using the following sentence components as required: subject, predicate, object, subject complement; main and subordinate clauses; prepositional and participial phrases	• use and punctuate essential and nonessential clauses correctly (Mechanics TG) • explain and use essential and nonessential clauses correctly (Mechanics SB #1–3) • correct and punctuate essential and nonessential clauses correctly (EP: Mechanics)	• TOC 8: Mechanics • TOC 8: Mechanics • TOC 8: Mechanics
(WR5.07B)	• identify and correct sentence fragments, run-on sentences, and comma splices	• correct run-on sentences and comma splices (Grammar TG) • correct run-on sentences and comma splices (Grammar SB #1–3) • avoid run-on sentences (More Support TG, page 181) • solve run-on sentence maze (More Challenge TG, page 181) • correct run-on sentences and comma splices (EP: Grammar)	• TOC 4: Grammar • TOC 4: Grammar • TOC 4: Grammar • TOC 4: Grammar • TOC 4: Grammar
LANGUAGE		
Overall (LGV.01D)	• use knowledge of vocabulary and language conventions to speak, write, and read competently using a level of language appropriate to the purpose and audience	• suggest alternative wording for gobbledygook in sentences (Usage & Style TG #3) • eliminate wordiness in sentences (Usage & Style SB #1, page 137) • eliminate gobbledygook in sentences (EP: Usage & Style)	• TOC 15: Usage & Style • TOC 15: Usage & Style • TOC 15: Usage & Style
Specific (LG1.01B)	• describe strategies used to expand vocabulary and provide evidence of other vocabulary-building activities	• list uses of dictionaries and thesauri (Word Study & Spelling TG) • use dictionaries and thesauri to find word replacements (Word Study & Spelling SB #1–3) • compare three dictionaries or three thesauri (More Support TG, page 184) • use thesaurus to find alternative words (EP: Word Study & Spelling)	• TOC 16: Word Study & Spelling • TOC 16: Word Study & Spelling • TOC 16: Word Study & Spelling • TOC 16: Word Study & Spelling
(LG1.02B)	• identify and explain examples of slang, jargon, dialect, and colloquialism, as well as of standard Canadian English, in literary texts and their own oral and written work	• develop lists of jargon used by particular groups (Usage & Style TG #1) • explain what to do when jargon is inappropriate (Usage & Style TG #2) • give examples of jargon (Usage & Style SB #1–2, page 136) • eliminate jargon from sentences (EP: Usage & Style)	• TOC 15: Usage & Style • TOC 15: Usage & Style • TOC 15: Usage & Style • TOC 15: Usage & Style
(LG1.03B)	• identify words borrowed from other languages and words and terms recently introduced to describe new ideas, inventions, and products, and explain their origins	• explain Latin root in given words (Word Origins SB)	• TOC 16: Word Study & Spelling
(LG1.05D)	• recognize, describe, and use correctly, in oral and written language, the language structures of standard Canadian English and its conventions of grammar and usage, including: – components of sentences: subject, predicate, object, subject complement, prepositional and participial phrases, main and subordinate clauses	• use and punctuate essential and nonessential clauses correctly (Mechanics TG) • explain and use essential and nonessential clauses correctly (Mechanics SB #1–3) • correct and punctuate essential and nonessential clauses (EP: Mechanics)	• TOC 8: Mechanics • TOC 8: Mechanics • TOC 8: Mechanics

AR=Assessment Rubric   EP=Extra Practice   SB=Student Book   SSEC=Student Self-Evaluation Checklist   TG=Teacher's Guide   TOC=Teacher Observation Checklist

GRADE 9 EXPECTATIONS	DEMONSTRATION OF LEARNING	ASSESSMENT TOOLS
LANGUAGE (continued)		
(LG1.06B) • recognize, describe, and correct sentence errors in oral and written language	• correct run-on sentences and comma splices (Grammar TG)	• TOC 4: Grammar
	• correct run-on sentences and comma splices (Grammar SB #1–3)	• TOC 4: Grammar
	• avoid run-on sentences (More Support TG, page 181)	• TOC 4: Grammar
	• solve run-on sentence maze (More Challenge TG, page 181)	• TOC 4: Grammar
	• correct run-on sentences and comma splices (EP: Grammar)	• TOC 4: Grammar
Overall (LGV.02B) • use listening techniques and oral communication skills to participate in classroom discussions and more formal activities, such as storytelling, role playing, and reporting/ presenting, for specific purposes and audiences	• discuss topic of précis "When Machines Think" (Introducing the Model TG #1)	• TOC 13: Tracking Expectations
Specific (LG2.02D) • communicate in group discussions by sharing the duties of the group, speaking in turn, listening actively, taking notes, paraphrasing key points made by others, exchanging and challenging ideas and information, asking appropriate questions, reconsidering their own ideas and opinions, managing conflict, and respecting the opinions of others	• take notes as partner reads article (Oral Language Extension SB)	• TOC 7: Listening
(LG2.03D) • plan and make oral presentations to a small group or the class, selecting and using vocabulary and methods of delivery to suit audience and purpose; gather ideas and information; plan, create, rehearse, revise, and assess presentations such as dramatizations, reports, and speeches	• present summary of group discussion to classmates (Extending the Model TG #4) • conduct informal debate (More Oral Language TG)	• TOC 5: Group Work • TOC 11: Speaking
(LG2.07D) • analyze their own and others' oral presentations to identify strengths and weaknesses, and plan ways to improve their performance	• evaluate oral summaries and compare with classmate's précis (Oral Language Extension TG) • evaluate performance of debaters (More Oral Language TG)	• TOC 7: Listening • SSEC 5: Oral Presentation
MEDIA STUDIES		
Overall (MDV.02D) • use knowledge of a variety of media forms, purposes, and audiences to create media works and describe their intended effect	• create plot summary for movie that spoofs sci-fi films (Media Link SB)	• AR 12: Media Product
Specific (MD2.02D) • create media works for different purposes and explain how each has been designed to achieve its particular purpose	• write brief news report for newspaper based on full-length article (More Media TG)	• AR 12: Media Product

AR=Assessment Rubric   EP=Extra Practice   SB=Student Book   SSEC=Student Self-Evaluation Checklist   TG=Teacher's Guide   TOC=Teacher Observation Checklist

INSTRUCTIONAL STRATEGIES FOR THE ACADEMIC COURSE

LEARNING GOALS

- write a précis
- recognize and correct run-on sentences and comma splices
- punctuate essential and nonessential clauses correctly
- identify and explain examples of jargon
- use a dictionary and thesaurus for finding word replacements

PLANNING INFORMATION

Links to Other Nelson English 9 Resources

Write Source 2000

Comma Splices—"Comma Splice," p. 86; **Dictionary**—"Checking a Dictionary," pp. 326–327; **Punctuation for Essential and Nonessential Clauses**—"Comma to Set Off Phrases and Clauses," p. 392; **Run-on Sentences**—"Run-on Sentence," p. 87; **Thesaurus**—"Referring to a Thesaurus," p. 325

INTRODUCING THE UNIT

1. Writing effective summaries is an important life skill which students will use many times during their school and working lives. To introduce this unit, ask students to identify situations, both in and out of school, where they have had to summarize something, either for themselves or for someone else. Record their responses on the board. Their responses might include taking notes, summarizing a chapter of a book, writing a book report, writing a speech, telling about a place they visited, giving a summary of a performance, or relating their opinions about an issue. (LIV.02D—TOC 13: Tracking Expectations)

2. Have students write their own definitions of the term "summary." Ask them to share their definitions with the rest of the class. (LIV.02D—TOC 13: Tracking Expectations)

3. Point out to students that while most summaries share similar characteristics, they can differ in length, style, and content. In this unit, they will be learning about one particular type of summary called a précis. Ask students to read the written explanation of a précis on page 126 of the student book. Do they find the illustration accompanying the explanation an effective way to represent the topic? Why or why not? (LI3.03D—TOC 13: Tracking Expectations)

INTRODUCING THE MODEL

1. The student book contains both a précis and the article on which the précis is based. The title of both texts is "When Machines Think." Point out to students that one dictionary definition of thinking is: a way of reasoning; judgment. With the definition in front of them on the board, have students discuss the following question: Given this definition, do machines currently think or are they merely processors of information? (LGV.02B—TOC 13: Tracking Expectations)

2. Ask students to read the title of the précis. Have them suggest a list of questions this title could raise in a reader's mind. (Examples might be: Will machines help us to think? Will a machine's thinking be superior to human thought?) Write the questions on the board. Then have students read both the précis and the original article to find out which of their questions were answered. (LI1.03B—TOC 10: Reading Strategies)

3. Ask students if they were surprised by any of the information provided in the précis and the original text. Find out how the information made them feel. Do they think life will be better when machines are able to think? (LI1.02D—AR 22: Response to Reading)

INVESTIGATING THE MODEL

Ask students what the main difference is between the précis and the original article (amount of information). Ask them when they think that a person would prefer to read a précis instead of the original article. (Possible answers are when you need only the main points or when you need to acquire information quickly.) (LIV.02D—TOC 13: Tracking Expectations)

Answers:

1. The précis has eliminated nonessential details, multiple examples, illustration of ideas, and secondary ideas. The précis contains only the most important ideas, combined into clear, concise sentences.

2. Possible answers

   Five examples of details that have been omitted:

   "If I learn French, or read *War and Peace,* I can't readily download that learning to you."

   "We have cochlear implants that restore hearing to deaf individuals."

   "Recently, scientists from Emory University in Atlanta placed a chip in the brain of a paralyzed stroke victim who can now begin to communicate and control his environment directly from his brain."

   "These implants will also plug us in directly to the World Wide Web."

   "So instead of just phoning a friend, you can meet in a virtual French café in Paris, or stroll down a virtual Champs Elysées, and it will seem very real."

   Two examples of details that have been included:

   "By 2019, a $1000 computer will match the processing power of the human brain, and by 2029, it will be equivalent to 1000 human brains."

   "We already have neural implants to treat Parkinson's disease and other conditions."

   The first detail is used to establish when particular events will occur, and to make readers aware of the cost of these future machines. The second detail provides one example of a neural implant.

3. Possible answers

   "Under development is a retina implant that will perform a similar function for blind people, basically replacing the visual processing circuits of the brain." (multiple example)

   "In the 2020s, neural implants will not be just for people with disabilities. There will be ubiquitous use of neural implants to improve our sensory experiences, perception, memory, and logical thinking." (illustration of an idea)

   "And virtual reality will not be the crude experience that you may have experienced today in arcade games." (unimportant idea)

4. The following are examples of text that have been condensed or reworded to make them more efficient:

   "By 2019, a $1000 computer will match the processing power of the human brain, and by 2029, it will be equivalent to 1000 human brains."

   "Computers can easily share their knowledge with billions of other computers."

   "More are under development."

   "By 2030, it will take a village of human brains to match a $1000 computer; by around 2055, a $1000 computer will equal the processing power of all human brains."

> ## CHECKPOINT
>
> Sample criteria for a précis:
>
> - is about one-third the length of the original
> - presents only main ideas and omits nonessential details
> - eliminates unimportant ideas, repetition, multiple examples, illustrations of ideas, and figurative language
> - may contain phrases or sentences from original document
> - has ideas that are condensed or reworded more efficiently from original
> - usually copies level of formality and tone of original

"Brain-scanning technologies are rapidly increasing their ability to solve problems."

"Consciousness will be a critical issue."

5. The original article is serious in tone, and is written at a semi-formal level. The author of the précis has imitated this style very effectively.

Student Book 1.–5. (LI1.04D—AR 22: Response to Reading)

Extending the Model

1. Ask students to identify the paragraph which captures the essence of the précis (last paragraph). (LI1.05D—AR 22: Response to Reading)

2. Have students who are interested in computers research other articles about the role computers will play in the future. Ask them to write a précis of one of these articles. Students could then consider whether another person reading the précis would understand the main idea of the original article. As a check, suggest that students give their précis to another member of the class to write down the main idea of the original article. Writers will then see how successful they have been in writing their précis. (WRV.01D—AR 18: Précis; WRV.03D—AR 18: Précis)

3. Obtain an abstract of a business report from the Business Department in your school. Provide it to students to read and discuss with them why summaries of this type are important to people in business. (LI1.02D—AR 22: Response to Reading)

4. Ask students to summarize any science fiction books or films that they have read or seen in which machines think. This could be done in point form and then used for small group discussions. In light of the article "When Machines Think," one question they might consider is: Did this ability of machines to think result in a positive or negative environment for humans? You may want to ask the small groups to appoint one member to summarize the group's discussion for the rest of the class. (LI1.03B—TOC 10: Reading Strategies; LG2.03D—TOC 5: Group Work)

Writer's Workshop

Before students begin their précis, you may want to work through the writing process as a class. Choose a short article of no more than one page, and make a transparency of it for the overhead projector. Then have the class work through steps #2–4 of the Writer's Workshop on student book page 131. Read what is left of the text. Ask students to suggest which sentences need to be reworked or reworded for a rough draft. Remind them that a précis should contain only important ideas expressed in clear sentences. (WRV.03D—AR 18: Précis)

Student Book 1.–4. (WRV.01D—AR 18: Précis); 5.–6. (WRV.03D—AR 18: Précis); 7. (WRV.04D—AR 18: Précis; WRV.05D—AR 18: Précis)

Oral Language Extension

This activity emphasizes the importance of good listening skills for notetaking and for preparing summaries. The listener must select the main ideas given by the speaker. Emphasize that the reader should read slowly enough for the listener to absorb the ideas and to write appropriate notes. After students have completed the activity in the student book, ask them to compare the skills of notetaking with that of writing a précis. What aspect of the exercise did they find most difficult? Was the content of their oral summary close to the précis written by the other student? What suggestions do they have for someone who might have difficulty with this type of task? (LG2.07D—TOC 7: Listening)

Student Book (LG2.02D—TOC 7: Listening)

More Oral Language

Working in groups of four (two students "for" and two students "against"), have students conduct an informal debate on the following statement: Life will be better when machines are more intelligent than humans. Provide students with some simple guidelines for conducting a debate and give them some time to prepare their arguments. Then, have two groups team up, one acting as the audience and the other conducting the debate. The group acting as audience can evaluate the performance of the debaters. (LG2.03D—TOC 11: Speaking; LG2.07D—SSEC 5: Oral Presentation)

GRAMMAR

To introduce the topic of run-on sentences and comma splices, write the following paragraph on the board or on a transparency for an overhead projector:

Computers will continue to have a major impact on our lives in the 21st century this will please some people and make life miserable for others. Those people who like to have their thinking done for them will welcome this intrusion, others will not trust machines to do their thinking.

Ask students to read the paragraph to themselves and identify the errors in the sentences. Ask for volunteers to identify the errors and to suggest how they might be corrected. Make sure students label the errors correctly (i.e., run-on sentence or comma splice). (WR5.07B—TOC 4: Grammar; LG1.06B—TOC 4: Grammar)

Answers:

1. Example 1: Error is corrected by forming two sentences.

   Example 2: Error is corrected by forming two sentences. Note comma after "however."

   Example 3: Error is corrected by using a conjunction. Note the comma before the conjunction.

   Example 4: Error is corrected by use of a semicolon.

   Example 5: Error is corrected by using the subordinating conjunction "since" to create a subordinate clause. Note the use of a comma before the main clause.

2. Possible answers
   a) Neural implants will not be just for people with disabilities. They will also be used to improve our sensory experiences.
   b) One computer learns a skill. It can immediately share that skill with other computers.
   c) Virtual reality will no longer be a crude experience; rather, it will be realistic, detailed, and subtle.
   d) The future will be great. We have a lot to look forward to.
   e) Although computers don't have feelings now, one day they might.

3. Student work.

Student Book 1.–3. (WR5.07B—TOC 4: Grammar; LG1.06B—TOC 4: Grammar)

MEDIA LINK

Before students begin the Media Link activity, you may want to review with them the major features of short stories including plot, characters, setting, and theme. These are outlined in Unit 2 on student book pages 37 and 39. If you think students will have difficulty identifying character types, recurring themes, and plot conventions, you could do this part of the assignment as a whole-class activity instead of using small groups. In this way, you can support the students' observations and stimulate further discussion and understanding of the concepts. (LI2.02D—AR 22: Response to Reading)

Student Book (MDV.02D—AR 12: Media Product)

MECHANICS

To assist students in understanding the concept of essential and nonessential clauses, use the two sets of sentences on the following page to explain the idea that some clauses in a sentence are essential to the basic meaning of a sentence, while other clauses are not essential—that is, the sentence would not lose its meaning if they were taken out. Point out that a clause considered essential is not set off with commas while a clause considered nonessential is set off with commas.

MORE SUPPORT

After students have read the Writing Tip on page 133 of the student book, revisit the second example in activity #1. Ask students to point out the two clauses in the first sentence and identify what type of clause they are (independent). How else might the correction have been made? (A semicolon could have been used.)

Have students work in pairs to create eight sentences, with each sentence containing two independent clauses. Tell students that in their eight sentences, they must demonstrate the following ways of joining two independent clauses: using a semicolon with a joining word like "however"; using a conjunction; or using a semicolon. Ask some students to share the sentences they have written with the rest of the class. (WR5.07B—TOC 4: Grammar; LG1.06B—TOC 4: Grammar)

MORE CHALLENGE

Have students create a run-on sentence maze for other students to solve. The maze should contain the following:

- several boxes with short complete sentences and run-on sentences
- several possible paths to follow
- a "start" and a "finish" identified at the top and bottom

There should be only *one* path containing complete sentences which solves the puzzle. Before assigning the activity, show students an example of a maze to ensure they understand how mazes work. (WR5.07B—TOC 4: Grammar; LG1.06B—TOC 4: Grammar)

MORE MEDIA

Newspapers often have précis-like reports, sometimes called "In Brief," that are usually found in a narrow column at the side of a page. These reports include only the highlights of a news event. Provide some examples of these reports for students to read. Then note on the board what they see as the main features of this type of writing. Ask students to write a short news report based on a longer newspaper article of their choice. (MD2.02D—AR 12: Media Product)

Neural implants that are being developed will improve our memories.
Neural implants, which are being developed, will improve our memories.

In the first example above, the clause beginning with "that" is not set off with commas because the information is necessary to identify which neural implants are being referred to—that is, those that are being developed (not just any neural implants). In the second sentence, the fact that the implants are being developed is incidental to the fact that neural implants will improve our memories—so, commas are used around the "which" clause.

The girl who is standing next to the office door is my best friend.
Charlene, who is standing next to the office door, is my best friend.

In the first sentence above, the clause beginning with "who" is not set off with commas because the information is necessary to identify which girl it is who is the best friend of the speaker. In the second sentence, the fact that Charlene is standing by the office door is incidental to the main idea—that is, that Charlene is the best friend of the speaker—so, the "who" clause has commas around it. In other words, if the "who" clause was taken out, it wouldn't affect the meaning of the sentence.

Point out that in the sentences without commas, the information in the subordinate clause is necessary to identify both the "neural implants" in the first example and the "girl" in the second example. (WR5.06D—TOC 8: Mechanics; LG1.05D—TOC 8: Mechanics)

Answers:

1. a) The human brain, which has 100 trillion neural connections, is a very complex organism.
    b) Computer consciousness, which is not an issue yet, will become critically important in the future.
    c) The scanners that we use in medicine today will be far surpassed by the new generation of scanners.
    d) Should computers that are capable of feeling pain and pleasure be treated as living things?

2. a) The first sentence indicates that the future, which Kurzweil just happens to foresee, is full of amazing technological advances. The second sentence refers specifically to the future that Kurzweil foresees as being the one that is full of amazing technological advances.
    b) The first sentence indicates that a special class of computers—those modelled on the human brain—will want the same rights and privileges as people. The second sentence says that all computers will want the same rights and privileges as people. The fact that they are modelled on the human brain is incidental (that is, nonessential) so the information is put in a clause with commas.
    c) In the first sentence, the books referred to are only those that a human being would have read from cover to cover. In the second sentence, all books are referred to. The fact that a human being would have read them from cover to cover is incidental.
    d) The first sentence refers only to the quality of virtual reality that we are familiar with today as the one that will be improved. In the second sentence, any virtual reality, whether we are familiar with it or not, will be much improved in the future.

3. Student work.

Student Book 1.–3. (WR5.06D—TOC 8: Mechanics; LG1.05D—TOC 8: Mechanics)

USAGE & STYLE

1. Have students read the definition of jargon in the student book and the paragraph that follows on page 136. Point out that many occupations have a language of their own which workers use to communicate among themselves on a daily basis. Divide the class into groups of five and ask each group to develop a list of 10 words of jargon for an occupation of their choice. Have each group share its results with the class. (LG1.02B—TOC 15: Usage & Style)

2. Ask students to identify when the use of jargon is appropriate and when it is inappropriate. (It is appropriate when the audience will understand it and inappropriate when the audience will have difficulty understanding it.) What should writers do when jargon is inappropriate? (They can change the terminology or provide definitions of the terms which may cause difficulty). (LG1.02B— TOC 15: Usage & Style)

3. Write the following sentence on the board:

   > The storage room for the Physical Education Department contains many items that have become disarranged and entangled because those responsible for the administration of the room have failed to carry out their duties judiciously.

   Ask students to comment on the effectiveness of this sentence, and then have them suggest alternative wordings to make it more effective. (Example: The storage room for the Physical Education Department is a mess because those responsible for keeping it clean have not done so.) Tell students that the original convoluted sentence is an example of a type of writing called gobbledygook. Ask students why someone might use gobbledygook. (Possible reasons: to make the topic sound more technical or scientific; to soften the message.) (LGV.01D— TOC 15: Usage & Style)

Answers (page 136):

1. Possible answer

   Three examples of jargon are: neural implants; integrated circuits; neurotransmitter.

2. Possible answer
   Two examples from the various subject areas are:
   Science: mitosis, density
   Geography: forest harvesting, urban renewal
   Physical Education: heart-rate monitor, warm-up and cool-down exercises
   Mathematics: integers, polynomials
   English: précis, expository

Answers (page 137):
Possible answers:
1. a) Scientists think we will eventually accept new technology.
   b) In this millennium we will invent computers that will not only reduce work, but also make it easier to do.
   c) One approach to designing intelligent computers will be to copy the human brain so that computers will begin to act like humans.
Student Book, page 136 1.–2. (LG1.02B—TOC 15: Usage & Style);
page 137 1. (LGV.01D)—TOC 15: Usage & Style)

WORD STUDY & SPELLING

This section will serve mainly as a review for students, but it will also emphasize that a dictionary has several uses beyond finding the meaning of a word. If you presently do not have a wide collection of dictionaries and thesauri in your classroom, try to get extra copies for the work in this section.

Working in pairs, have students create a chart with two headings "Dictionary" and "Thesaurus." Ask students to list their uses. Make sure they do this without looking at either type of publication. Ask students to share their results, and list the various uses on the board. For dictionaries, they can compare their list with that in activity #3 on page 138 of the student book to see if any uses have been missed. Point out that the features of dictionaries and thesauri are often listed at the front of these tools. (LG1.01B—TOC 16: Word Study & Spelling)

Answers:
Possible answers
1. a) method
    b) implied
    c) critical
    d) prophecy
    e) accelerating

2. Possible answers

    a) We can already make a computer similar to a human brain. (11 words)
    b) Once computers can think like humans, they will soon be quicker than we are at compiling information. (17 words)
    c) Who is to say that we won't have to relinquish the planet to computers one day? (16 words)
    d) The combining of people and machines is inevitable. (8 words)

3. Other information in a dictionary might include syllabification, variant spellings, and pictures or drawings.

Student Book 1.–3. (LG1.01B—TOC 16: Word Study & Spelling)

WORD ORIGINS

Answers:
scissors: used to cut
precise: cut to include only the exact amount
incisor: a tooth for cutting or gnawing
decision: other options are cut

Student Book (LG1.03B—TOC 16: Word Study & Spelling)

ANSWERS TO EXTRA PRACTICE

Grammar
Possible answers
1. This précis is difficult to understand. For instance, I do not understand some of the technical words.

2. That movie was excellent. The film techniques were superior to anything I have seen.

3. There is one minute left; Vancouver has a man advantage.

4. I like science fiction series. *Star Trek: The Next Generation* is my favourite.

5. Sit in the gold section. You'll see best there.

6. First, the cars are painted, and then a clear coat is applied.

7. The car crashed, but the driver escaped unharmed.

8. My friends will be going. As well, some of my boyfriend's friends will attend.

9. What do you think of our school swim team? It hasn't lost a meet yet.

10. I have several friends coming to my party; among them are Todd and Mike.

11. Since I do not have a ride, I will not be able to attend.

12. The amusement park had many good rides. For example, there was a water slide and a roller coaster.

13. Your theory is interesting; however, I must disagree with it.

14. The lake was frozen, and the fields were covered with snow.

(WR5.07B—TOC 4: Grammar; LG1.06B—TOC 4: Grammar)

Mechanics

1. NE

2. NE

3. E

4. E

5. E

Possible answers

6. Windows, which are often dirty, should be washed frequently.

7. The jacket that is in poor condition belongs to Suzanne.

8. New cars that did not have rust protection deteriorated quickly in the 1980s.

9. Next year, the finals, which will be in Toronto, will be well attended.

10. The textbook, which has been here for some time, will be turned in to the office.

(WR5.06D—TOC 8: Mechanics; LG1.06B—TOC 8: Mechanics)

Usage & Style
Possible answers

1. When the case was brought to court, the person on trial did not appear.

2. The air force was successful in winning the battle.

3. The child seems to be suffering only scrapes and bruises to the outer layer of skin near the nose.

4. Both parties agreed to a mutually beneficial agreement.

5. Since money is in short supply, we will need to use our savings.

6. The person who hesitates is lost.

7. The speaker was known for his use of unnecessary words and indirect language.

8. Honesty is the best policy.

9. Is there not a better way to solve the problem?

10. Please provide clear directions.

(LGV.01D—TOC 15: Usage & Style; LG1.02B—TOC 15: Usage & Style)

Word Study & Spelling

Possible answers

1. worked: toiled, sweated, laboured

2. messy: unkempt, untidy, dishevelled

3. idyllic: heavenly, pastoral, peaceful

4. impure: contaminated, filthy, tainted

5. inlet: bay, cove, passage

(LG1.01B—TOC 16: Word Study & Spelling)

GRADE 9 EXPECTATIONS		DEMONSTRATION OF LEARNING	ASSESSMENT TOOLS
LITERATURE STUDIES AND READING			
Overall (LIV.01P)	• read and demonstrate an understanding of a variety of literary and informational texts		
Specific (LI1.02P)	• select and read texts for a variety of purposes, with an emphasis on recognizing the elements of literary genres and the organization of informational materials, collecting and using information, extending personal knowledge, and responding imaginatively	• discuss reaction to model (Introducing the Model TG #2) • discuss importance of abstracts to business people (Extending the Model TG #3)	• AR 22: Response to Reading • AR 22: Response to Reading
(LI1.03B)	• describe a variety of reading strategies and select and use them effectively before, during, and after reading to understand texts	• speculate on questions title raises in reader's mind; read to discover which questions were answered (Introducing the Model TG #1)	• TOC 10: Reading Strategies
(LI1.04P)	• locate and use explicit information and ideas from texts in forming opinions and developing generalizations	• give examples from model for use in interpretation (Investigating the Model SB #1–5)	• AR 22: Response to Reading
(LI1.05P)	• make inferences based on the information and ideas presented in texts	• identify paragraph giving essence of précis (Extending the Model TG #1)	• AR 22: Response to Reading
Overall (LIV.02P)	• demonstrate an understanding of the elements of a variety of literary and informational forms, with a focus on plays, short stories, and short essays, and newspaper and magazine articles	• identify situations where they have had to summarize material (Introducing the Unit TG #1) • define "summary" (Introducing the Unit TG #2) • compare a précis with original article (Investigating the Model TG)	• TOC 14: Tracking Expectations • TOC 14: Tracking Expectations • TOC 14: Tracking Expectations
Specific (LI2.02P)	• use knowledge of elements of the short story, such as plot, character, setting, conflict, theme, and atmosphere to understand and interpret texts in the genre	• review features of short stories (Media Link TG)	• AR 22: Response to Reading
Overall (LIV.03B)	• identify and explain the effect of specific elements of style in a variety of literary and informational texts		
Specific (LI3.03P)	• explain how authors and editors use design elements to help convey meaning	• explain whether illustration represents précis (Introducing the Unit TG #3)	• TOC 14: Tracking Expectations
WRITING			
Overall (WRV.01P)	• use print and electronic sources to gather information and explore ideas for their written work	• research articles on role of computers in the future (Extending the Model TG #2) • gather and organize ideas for précis (Writer's Workshop SB #1–4)	• AR 18: Précis • AR 18: Précis
Overall (WRV.02P)	• identify the literary and informational forms suited to specific purposes and audiences and use the forms appropriately in their own writing, with an emphasis on communicating information accurately		
Specific (WR2.04P)	• use the third-person singular and an appropriate level of language in expository forms requiring objectivity	• write précis on article about future of computers (Extending the Model TG #2)	• AR 18: Précis
Overall (WRV.03P)	• use a variety of forms of writing to express themselves, clarify their ideas, and engage the audience's attention, imagination, and interest	• write a précis of an article on computers (Extending the Model TG #2) • work through writing process of précis as a class (Writer's Workshop TG) • write a précis (Writer's Workshop SB #5–6)	• AR 18: Précis • AR 18: Précis • AR 18: Précis
Overall (WRV.04B)	• revise their written work, collaboratively, and independently, with a focus on support for ideas, accuracy, clarity, and unity	• revise précis (Writer's Workshop SB #7)	• AR 18: Précis

AR=Assessment Rubric   EP=Extra Practice   SB=Student Book   SSEC=Student Self-Evaluation Checklist   TG=Teacher's Guide   TOC=Teacher Observation Checklist

GRADE 9 EXPECTATIONS	DEMONSTRATION OF LEARNING	ASSESSMENT TOOLS
WRITING (continued)		
Overall (WRV.05B) • edit and proofread to produce final drafts, using correct grammar, spelling, and punctuation, according to the conventions of standard Canadian English, specified for this course, with the support of print and electronic resources when appropriate	• edit and proofread précis (Writer's Workshop SB #7)	• AR 18: Précis
Specific (WR5.06P) • construct complete and correct compound and complex sentences, using the following sentence components as required: subject, predicate, object, subject complement; main and subordinate clauses; prepositional phrases	• use and punctuate essential and nonessential clauses correctly (Mechanics TG) • explain and use essential and nonessential clauses correctly (Mechanics SB #1–3) • correct and punctuate essential and nonessential clauses correctly (EP: Mechanics)	• TOC 8: Mechanics • TOC 8: Mechanics • TOC 8: Mechanics
(WR5.07B) • identify and correct sentence fragments, run-on sentences, and comma splices	• correct run-on sentences and comma splices (Grammar TG) • identify examples of two sentences combined into one (More Support TG) • correct run-on sentences and comma splices (Grammar SB #1–3) • correct run-on sentences and comma splices (EP: Grammar)	• TOC 4: Grammar • TOC 4: Grammar • TOC 4: Grammar • TOC 4: Grammar
LANGUAGE		
Overall (LGV.01P) • use knowledge of vocabulary and language conventions to speak, write, and read clearly and correctly	• suggest alternative wording for gobbledygook in sentences (Usage & Style TG #3) • give original proverbs for wordy sentences (Usage & Style TG #4) • eliminate wordiness in sentences (Usage & Style SB #1, page 137) • devise wordy sentences for proverbs (More Challenge TG) • eliminate gobbledygook in sentences (EP: Usage & Style)	• TOC 15: Usage & Style • TOC 15: Usage & Style • TOC 15: Usage & Style • TOC 15: Usage & Style • TOC 15: Usage & Style
Specific (LG1.01B) • describe strategies used to expand vocabulary and provide evidence of other vocabulary-building activities	• list uses of dictionaries and thesauri (Word Study & Spelling TG) • use dictionaries and thesauri to find word replacements (Word Study & Spelling SB #1–3) • use thesaurus to find alternative words (EP: Word Study & Spelling)	• TOC 16: Word Study & Spelling • TOC 16: Word Study & Spelling • TOC 16: Word Study & Spelling
(LG1.02B) • identify and explain examples of slang, jargon, dialect, and colloquialism, as well as of standard Canadian English, in literary texts and their own oral and written work	• develop lists of jargon used by particular groups (Usage & Style TG #1) • explain what to do when jargon is inappropriate (Usage & Style TG #2) • give examples of jargon (Usage & Style SB #1–2, page 136) • eliminate jargon from sentences (EP: Usage & Style)	• TOC 15: Usage & Style • TOC 15: Usage & Style • TOC 15: Usage & Style • TOC 15: Usage & Style
(LG1.03B) • identify words borrowed from other languages and words and terms recently introduced to describe new ideas, inventions, and products, and explain their origins	• explain Latin root in given words (Word Origins SB)	• TOC 16: Word Study & Spelling
(LG1.05P) • recognize, describe, and use correctly, in oral and written language, the language structures of standard Canadian English and its conventions of grammar and usage, including: – components of sentences: subject, predicate, object, subject complement, prepositional and participial phrases, main and subordinate clauses	• use and punctuate essential and nonessential clauses correctly (Mechanics TG) • explain and use essential and nonessential clauses correctly (Mechanics SB #1–3) • correct and punctuate essential and nonessential clauses (EP: Mechanics)	• TOC 8: Mechanics • TOC 8: Mechanics • TOC 8: Mechanics

AR=Assessment Rubric   EP=Extra Practice   SB=Student Book   SSEC=Student Self-Evaluation Checklist   TG=Teacher's Guide   TOC=Teacher Observation Checklist

GRADE 9 EXPECTATIONS	DEMONSTRATION OF LEARNING	ASSESSMENT TOOLS
LANGUAGE (continued)		
(LG1.06B) • recognize, describe, and correct sentence errors in oral and written language	• correct run-on sentences and comma splices (Grammar TG) • identify example of two sentences combined into one (More Support TG) • correct run-on sentences and comma splices (Grammar SB #1–3) • correct run-on sentences and comma splices (EP: Grammar)	• TOC 4: Grammar • TOC 4: Grammar • TOC 4: Grammar • TOC 4: Grammar
Overall (LGV.02B) • use listening techniques and oral communication skills to participate in classroom discussions and more formal activities, such as storytelling, role playing, and reporting/presenting, for specific purposes and audiences		
Specific (LG2.02P) • use techniques of effective listening and demonstrate an understanding of oral presentations by restating the main ideas presented and identifying the strengths and weaknesses of presentations	• take notes as teacher reads article to class (Oral Language Extension TG) • takes notes as partner reads article (Oral Language Extension SB)	• TOC 7: Listening • TOC 7: Listening
(LG2.03P) • work with a partner to plan and make oral presentations to a small group, selecting and using vocabulary and methods of delivery to suit audience and purpose	• conduct informal debate (More Oral Language TG)	• TOC 11: Speaking
(LG2.07P) • analyze their own and others' oral communication skills, identifying strengths and weaknesses and suggesting ways to improve	• evaluate performance of debaters (More Oral Language TG)	• SSEC 5: Oral Presentation
MEDIA STUDIES		
Overall (MDV.02P) • use knowledge of a variety of media forms, purposes, and audiences to create media works	• create plot summary for movie that spoofs sci-fi films (Media Link SB)	• AR 12: Media Product
Specific (MD2.02P) • create media works for different purposes	• write brief news report for newspaper based on full-length article (More Media TG)	• AR 12: Media Product

AR=Assessment Rubric   EP=Extra Practice   SB=Student Book   SSEC=Student Self-Evaluation Checklist   TG=Teacher's Guide   TOC=Teacher Observation Checklist

INSTRUCTIONAL STRATEGIES FOR THE APPLIED COURSE

LEARNING GOALS

- write a précis
- recognize and correct run-on sentences and comma splices
- punctuate essential and nonessential clauses correctly
- identify and explain examples of jargon
- use a dictionary and thesaurus for finding word replacements

PLANNING INFORMATION

Links to Other Nelson English 9 Resources

Write Source 2000
Comma Splices—"Comma Splice," p. 86; **Dictionary**—"Checking a Dictionary," pp. 326–327; **Punctuation for Essential and Nonessential Clauses**—"Comma to Set Off Phrases and Clauses," p. 392; **Run-on Sentences**—"Run-on Sentence," p. 87; **Thesaurus**—"Referring to a Thesaurus," p. 325

INTRODUCING THE UNIT

The activities on page 178 from the Academic Course are appropriate for the Applied Course.

1. (LIV.02P—TOC 14: Tracking Expectations)

2. (LIV.02P—TOC 14: Tracking Expectations)

3. (LI3.03P—TOC 14: Tracking Expectations)

INTRODUCING THE MODEL

Activity #2 on page 178 from the Academic Course is appropriate for the Applied Course.

1. (LI1.03B—TOC 10: Reading Strategies)

Activity #3 on page 178 from the Academic Course is appropriate for the Applied Course. Point out to students that both the précis and the original article contain some difficult vocabulary. As they read both items for this activity, ask them to note any words or phrases which they have difficulty understanding. Discuss these words or phrases with them following their reading of the two texts.

2. (LI1.02P—AR 22: Response to Reading)

CHECKPOINT

Sample criteria for a précis:

- is about one-third the length of the original
- presents only main ideas and omits nonessential details
- eliminates unimportant ideas, repetition, multiple examples, illustrations of ideas, and figurative language
- may contain phrases or sentences from original document
- has ideas that are condensed or reworded more efficiently from original
- usually copies level of formality and tone of original

INVESTIGATING THE MODEL

The activity on pages 178–179 from the Academic Course is appropriate for the Applied Course. (LIV.02P—TOC 14: Tracking Expectations)

Due to the reading level of the original article, and the demands of some of the activities in this section, you may wish to give students the option of completing the activities in the student book by working together in pairs or in groups of three or four.

Answers:

See the Academic Course on pages 179–180 for the answers.

Student Book 1.–5. (LI1.04P—AR 22: Response to Reading)

EXTENDING THE MODEL

Activities #1–3 on page 180 from the Academic Course are appropriate for the Applied Course.

1. (LI1.05P—AR 22: Response to Reading)

2. (WRV.01P—AR 18: Précis; WR2.04P—AR 18: Précis; WRV.03P—AR 18: Précis)

3. (LI1.02P—AR 22: Response to Reading)

WRITER'S WORKSHOP

The activity on page 180 from the Academic Course is appropriate for the Applied Course.
(WRV.03P—AR 18: Précis)

Student Book 1.–4. (WRV.01P—AR 18: Précis); 5.–6. (WRV.03P—AR 18: Précis)
7. (WRV.04B—AR 18: Précis; WRV.05B—AR 18: Précis)

ORAL LANGUAGE EXTENSION

Before assigning this activity, clarify for students what they are to do. As a warm-up activity, read an article to the class and ask students to take notes and write a brief summary in their notebooks. Choose an article that is not too long and that will be of interest. Have one or two students read their summaries to the class and discuss whether all the main points in the article were covered in the summaries.
(LG2.02P—TOC 7: Listening)

Student Book (LG2.02P—TOC 7: Listening)

GRAMMAR

Introduce the topic of run-on sentences and comma splices using the following examples:

> Some people like computers other people do not trust the machines.
> Thinking computers will be here soon, they will change our lives.
> Last summer I attended a computer camp they discussed the future of computers.
> Our new computer is complex, it will take some time to learn to use it.

As a group, discuss, label, and correct the sentences. (WR5.07B—TOC 4: Grammar; LG1.06B—TOC 4: Grammar)

Answers:
See the Academic Course on page 181 for answers.

Student Book 1.–3. (WR5.07B—TOC 4: Grammar; LG1.06B—TOC 4: Grammar)

MEDIA LINK

The activity on page 181 from the Academic Course is appropriate for the Applied Course. (LI2.02P—AR 22: Response to Reading)

Student Book (MDV.02P—AR 12: Media Product)

MECHANICS

The activity on pages 181–182 from the Academic Course is appropriate for the Applied Course. (WR5.06P—TOC 8: Mechanics; LG1.05P—TOC 8: Mechanics)

Answers:
See the Academic Course on page 182 for answers.

Student Book 1.–3. (WR5.06P—TOC 8: Mechanics; LG1.05P—TOC 8: Mechanics)

USAGE & STYLE

Activities #1–3 on page 183 from the Academic Course are appropriate for the Applied Course.

1. (LG1.02B—TOC 15: Usage & Style)

2. (LG1.02B—TOC 15: Usage & Style)

3. (LGV.01P—TOC 15: Usage & Style)

MORE ORAL LANGUAGE

Working in groups of four (two students "for" and two students "against"), have students conduct an informal debate on the following statement: Life will be better when machines are more intelligent than humans. Provide students with some simple guidelines for conducting a debate and give them some time to prepare their arguments. Then, have two groups team up, one acting as the audience and the other conducting the debate. The group acting as audience can evaluate the performance of the debaters. (LG2.03P—TOC 11: Speaking; LG2.07P—SSEC 5: Oral Presentation)

MORE SUPPORT

Ask students to find five examples of two sentences combined into one from texts used in their courses. You may wish to write examples on the board (one for each method shown in the student book on pages 132 and 133) to use for discussion and support before students begin this activity. Have each student share the sentences found with another student in the class. (WR5.07B—TOC 4: Grammar; LG1.06B—TOC 4: Grammar)

MORE MEDIA

Newspapers often have précis-like reports, sometimes called "In Brief," that are usually found in a narrow column at the side of a page. These reports include only the highlights of a news event. Provide some examples of these reports for students to read. Then note on the board what they see as the main features of this type of writing. Ask students to write a short news report based on a longer newspaper article of their choice. (MD2.02P—AR 12: Media Product)

4. Give students the following sentences. Ask them what familiar proverb is concealed in each one. After students have identified the proverb, discuss with them why they think the original proverb is preferable to the reworded version. (LGV.01P—TOC 15: Usage & Style)

   a) When you look at that picture, you can see many interesting, beautiful things that would take a thousand words to describe. (A picture is worth a thousand words.)

   b) After all is said and done, one's own home is a grand place where you can do all the things that you enjoy doing without anyone bothering you. (There is no place like home.)

   c) It is not at all possible, or indeed feasible, to criticize the contents of a great novel by examining its outside cover alone. (Don't judge a book by its cover.)

   d) If you have a problem, it is often advisable and sometimes good practice to involve another person in the solution to the problem. (Two heads are better than one.)

   e) It is advisable to always try to anticipate what is going to happen before you proceed in doing what may cause you injury or mental stress. (Think before you leap.)

Answers:

See the Academic Course on page 183 for answers.

Student Book, page 136 1.–2. (LG1.02B—TOC 15: Usage & Style);
page 137 1. (LGV.01P—TOC 15: Usage & Style)

WORD STUDY & SPELLING

The activity on pages 183–184 from the Academic Course is appropriate for the Applied Course. (LG1.01B—TOC 16: Word Study & Spelling)

Answers:
See the Academic Course on page 184 for answers.

Student Book 1.–3. (LG1.01B—TOC 16: Word Study & Spelling)

WORD ORIGINS

Answers:
See the Academic Course on page 184 for answers.

Student Book (LG1.03B—TOC 16: Word Study & Spelling)

ANSWERS TO EXTRA PRACTICE

See the Academic Course on pages 184–186 for answers.

Grammar
(WR5.07B—TOC 4: Grammar; LG1.06B—TOC 4: Grammar)

Mechanics
(WR5.06P—TOC 8: Mechanics; LG1.05P—TOC 8: Mechanics)

Usage & Style
(LGV.01P—TOC 15: Usage & Style; LG1.02B—TOC 15: Usage & Style)

Word Study & Spelling
(LG1.01B—TOC 16: Word Study & Spelling)

murd

GRAMMAR

NAME: _____ DATE: _____

Rewrite the following run-on sentences correctly.

1. This précis is difficult to understand, for instance, I do not understand some of the technical words.

   _____

2. That movie was excellent the film techniques were superior to anything I have seen.

   _____

3. There is one minute left, Vancouver has a man advantage.

   _____

4. I like science fiction series *Star Trek: The Next Generation* is my favourite.

   _____

5. Sit in the gold section you'll see best there.

   _____

6. First the cars are painted then a clear coat is applied.

   _____

7. The car crashed the driver escaped unharmed.

   _____

8. My friends will be going as well some of my boyfriend's friends will attend.

   _____

9. What do you think of our school swim team it hasn't lost a meet yet.

   _____

10. I have several friends coming to my party among them are Todd and Mike

    _____

11. Since I do not have a ride I will not be able to attend.

    _____

12. The amusement park had many good rides, for example, there was a water slide and a roller coaster.

    _____

13. Your theory is interesting however I must disagree with it.

    _____

14. The lake was frozen the fields were covered with snow.

    _____

MECHANICS

NAME: _____ DATE: _____

Identify whether the italicized clauses in the following sentences are essential (E) or nonessential (NE).

1. Computers, *which are increasing in power every six months,* will soon copy our thinking processes.

   _____

2. The trip, *which we are taking on Tuesday,* should be a great deal of fun.

   _____

3. Pop cans *that are left in the parking lot* must be recycled.

   _____

4. Cars *that run on electric power* are becoming more popular.

   _____

5. Should houses *that contain dangerous materials* have people living in them?

   _____

Rewrite the following sentences, inserting the information in parentheses as an essential (that) or nonessential (which) clause. Remember to punctuate correctly.

6. Windows (are often dirty) should be washed frequently.

   _____

7. The jacket (is in poor condition) belongs to Suzanne.

   _____

8. New cars (did not have rust protection) deteriorated quickly in the 1980s.

   _____

9. Next year the finals (will be in Toronto) will be well attended.

   _____

10. The textbook (has been here for some time) will be turned in to the office.

    _____

USAGE & STYLE

NAME: _____ DATE: _____

Rewrite the following sentences containing jargon/gobbledygook to make them more understandable to the average person.

1. When the court case was brought to court, the defendant did not appear.

   _____

2. The air force was successful in defusing the aggressive behaviour of its opposition.

   _____

3. The child seems to be suffering only abrasions and contusions to the epidermal layer near the nasal passages.

   _____

4. Both parties decided that their diverse positions would be better met if they came together in one harmonious relationship, which would be beneficial to both of them.

   _____

5. Since our financial assets are in short supply, we will need to call on our reserves.

   _____

6. The person who fails to make a quick decision will find herself in a situation that is quite unfavourable.

   _____

7. The speaker was known for his circumlocution.

   _____

8. You will only gain the trust of people when you are straightforward with them and avoid trying to lead them in the wrong direction.

   _____

9. Is there not a better way to decide on an answer that will better represent the intended purpose?

   _____

10. Please provide us with an explicit explanation which will give us the best possible directions.

   _____

WORD STUDY & SPELLING

NAME: _____   DATE: _____

Use a thesaurus to find three alternative words for each of the italicized words in the sentences below.

1. The labourers *worked* tirelessly under the hot sun.

   _____

2. Her hair was very *messy*.

   _____

3. We longed to be back in that *idyllic* setting.

   _____

4. The water is *impure*.

   _____

5. We anchored our boat in the *inlet* overnight.

   _____

ACADEMIC EXPECTATIONS

GRADE 9 EXPECTATIONS		DEMONSTRATION OF LEARNING	ASSESSMENT TOOLS
LITERATURE STUDIES AND READING			
Overall (LIV.01D)	• read and demonstrate an understanding of a variety of literary and informational texts, from contemporary and historical periods	• demonstrate understanding of forms of exposition (Reflecting on Expository Writing Forms SB #1–2)	• TOC 13: Tracking Expectations
Specific (LI1.02D)	• select and read texts for different purposes, with an emphasis on recognizing the elements of literary genres and the organization of informational materials, collecting and assessing information, responding imaginatively, and exploring human experiences and values	• read newspaper report to find characteristics of research report (Extending the Model TG #3)	• TOC 13: Tracking Expectations
(LI1.03B)	• describe a variety of reading strategies and select and use them effectively before, during, and after reading to understand texts	• speculate on reason for title of research report (Introducing the Model TG #2)	• TOC 10: Reading Strategies
(LI1.04D)	• locate explicit information and ideas in texts to use in developing opinions and interpretations	• give interpretations of model using examples from student book (Investigating the Model SB #1–6) • select key statements from model to feature in boldface (Extending the Model TG #4) • comment on effectiveness of conclusion of model (Introducing the Model TG #4)	• AR 22: Response to Reading • TOC 13: Tracking Expectations • TOC 13: Tracking Expectations
(LI1.06D)	• use specific evidence from a text to support opinions and judgments	• discuss effectiveness of conclusion (Extending the Model TG #2)	• TOC 13: Tracking Expectations
Overall (LIV.02D)	• demonstrate an understanding of the elements of a variety of literary and informational forms, with a focus on plays, short stories, and short essays	• discuss purpose and importance of research reports (Introducing the Unit TG #1) • discuss research students have done in the past (Introducing the Unit TG #2) • analyze research reports (Extending the Model TG #1) • discuss results of analysis of research reports (Extending the Model TG #2) • give how-to presentations on aspects of writing research reports (More Challenge TG, page 203) • compare four forms of expository writing (Looking Over Expository Writing Forms SB #1) • explain usefulness of knowledge of expository writing forms (Using the Expository Writing Forms SB #1)	• TOC 13: Tracking Expectations • TOC 13: Tracking Expectations • TOC 13: Tracking Expectations • TOC 13: Tracking Expectations • TOC 13: Tracking Expectations • TOC 13: Tracking Expectations • TOC 13: Tracking Expectations
Overall (LIV.03B)	• identify and explain the effect of specific elements of style in a variety of literary and informational texts		
Specific (LI3.03D)	• explain how authors and editors use design elements to help communicate ideas	• assess visual support for model and their own research reports (More Media TG)	• TOC 13: Tracking Expectations
WRITING			
Overall (WRV.01D)	• use a variety of print and electronic sources to gather information and explore ideas for their written work	• create chart giving steps and time required to write a research report (Writer's Workshop TG) • gather and organize information for research report (Writer's Workshop SB #1–7)	• AR 20: Research Report • AR 20: Research Report

AR=Assessment Rubric   EP=Extra Practice   SB=Student Book   SSEC=Student Self-Evaluation Checklist   TG=Teacher's Guide   TOC=Teacher Observation Checklist

GRADE 9 EXPECTATIONS		DEMONSTRATION OF LEARNING	ASSESSMENT TOOLS
WRITING (continued)			
Specific (WR1.01D)	• investigate potential topics by formulating questions, identifying information needs, and developing research plans to gather data	• draw up list of questions and conduct interview of karate expert (Introducing the Model TG #3)	• AR 20: Research Report
Overall (WRV.02D)	• identify the literary and informational forms suited to various purposes and audiences and use the forms appropriately in their own writing, with an emphasis on supporting opinions or interpretations with specific information	• use model research report in writing (More Support TG, page 203)	• AR 20: Research Report
Overall (WRV.03D)	• use a variety of organizational techniques to present ideas and supporting details logically and coherently in written work	• write a research report (Writer's Workshop SB #8) • write instructions on how to use a Web search engine to find information (Using the Expository Writing Forms SB #2) • write an essay on accuracy and significance of an explanation (Using the Expository Writing Forms SB #3) • write a research report on jargon or origin of English words (Using the Expository Writing Forms SB #4) • write a précis (Using the Expository Writing Forms SB #5)	• AR 20: Research Report • AR 7: Explanation • AR 8: Expository Writing • AR 20: Research Report • AR 18: Précis
Specific (WR3.03D)	• use a single controlling idea and connecting words to structure a series of paragraphs	• discuss use of transitions to achieve coherence (Usage & Style TG) • rewrite paragraphs using transitions (EP: Usage & Style)	• TOC 15: Usage & Style • TOC 15: Usage & Style
(WR3.04D)	• use key words from questions or prompts to organize ideas, information, and evidence in homework answers	• answer questions on expository forms (Using the Expository Writing Forms SB #1)	• TOC 13: Tracking Expectations
(WR5.05D)	• structure expository paragraphs using a topic sentence, supporting sentences to develop the topic, connecting words to link the sentences, and a concluding sentence	• write a short essay on explanation (Using the Expository Writing Forms SB #3)	• AR 8: Expository Writing
Overall (WRV.04D)	• revise their written work, independently and collaboratively, with a focus on support for ideas and opinions, accuracy, clarity, and unity	• revise research report (Writer's Workshop SB #9) • revise instructions on Web search engine (Using the Expository Writing Forms SB #2) • revise essay on explanation (Using the Expository Writing Forms SB #3) • revise research report (Using the Expository Writing Forms SB #4) • revise précis (Using the Expository Writing Forms SB #5)	• AR 20: Research Report • AR 7: Explanation • AR 8: Expository Writing • AR 20: Research Report • AR 18: Précis
Overall (WRV.05D)	• edit and proofread to produce final drafts, using correct grammar, spelling, and punctuation, according to the conventions of standard Canadian English, with the support of print and electronic resources when appropriate	• edit and proofread research report (Writer's Workshop SB #9) • edit and proofread instructions on Web search engine (Using the Expository Writing Forms SB #2) • edit and proofread essay on explanation (Using the Expository Writing Forms SB #3) • edit and proofread research report (Using the Expository Writing Forms SB #4) • edit and proofread précis (Using the Expository Writing Forms SB #5)	• AR 20: Research Report • AR 7: Explanation • AR 8: Expository Writing • AR 20: Research Report • AR 18: Précis
Specific (WR5.01D)	• identify sources of ideas, information, and quotations in writing and independent research projects	• explain how bibliography is created (Mechanics TG) • create bibliographic entries (Mechanics SB #1–3) • compare APA and MLA style of bibliography (More Challenge TG, page 205) • write correct form of bibliography, in-text citation, and footnote (EP: Mechanics)	• TOC 8: Mechanics • TOC 8: Mechanics • TOC 8: Mechanics • TOC 8: Mechanics

AR=Assessment Rubric   EP=Extra Practice   SB=Student Book   SSEC=Student Self-Evaluation Checklist   TG=Teacher's Guide   TOC=Teacher Observation Checklist

	GRADE 9 EXPECTATIONS	DEMONSTRATION OF LEARNING	ASSESSMENT TOOLS
WRITING (continued)			
(WR5.05D)	• use parts of speech correctly: nouns, pronouns, verbs, adverbs, adjectives, conjunctions, prepositions, and interjections	• use correlative conjunctions correctly (More Challenge TG, page 205)	• TOC 15: Usage & Style
(WR5.08B)	• make compound subjects agree with verbs in simple and compound sentences	• give correct form of verb (Grammar TG #1) • rewrite sentences using indefinite pronouns (Grammar TG #2) • correct sentences for subject-verb agreement (Grammar SB #1–2) • write sentences using pronouns: all, any, none, some, most (More Challenge TG, page 204) • correct sentences so verb agrees with subject (EP: Grammar)	• TOC 4: Grammar • TOC 4: Grammar • TOC 4: Grammar • TOC 4: Grammar • TOC 4: Grammar
(WR5.13B)	• use the apostrophe correctly when spelling contractions and possessives	• identify and use singular and plural possessives (Word Study & Spelling TG) • punctuate plurals and possessives correctly (Word Study & Spelling SB #1–3) • correct errors in plurals and plural possessives (EP: Word Study & Spelling)	• TOC 16: Word Study & Spelling • TOC 16: Word Study & Spelling • TOC 16: Word Study & Spelling
LANGUAGE			
Overall (LGV.01D)	• use knowledge of vocabulary and language conventions to speak, write, and read competently using a level of language appropriate to the purpose and audience		
Specific (LG1.03B)	• identify words borrowed from other languages and words and terms recently introduced to describe new ideas, inventions, and products, and explain their origins	• give meaning and origin of words borrowed from Japanese (Word Origins TG) • give plural or singular forms of words borrowed from other languages (More Challenge TG, page 206)	• TOC 16: Word Study & Spelling • TOC 16: Word Study & Spelling
(LG1.05D)	• recognize, describe, and use correctly, in oral and written language, the language structures of standard Canadian English and its conventions of grammar and usage, including: – parts of speech: nouns, pronouns, verbs, adverbs, adjectives, conjunctions, prepositions, interjections – agreement between subject and verb, and between pronoun and antecedent	• give correct form of verb (Grammar TG #1) • rewrite sentences using indefinite pronouns (Grammar TG #2) • correct sentences for subject-verb agreement (Grammar SB #1–2) • write sentences using pronouns: all, any, none, some, most (More Challenge TG, page 204) • use transitions correctly (Usage & Style SB #1–3) • use correlative conjunctions correctly (More Challenge TG, page 205) • correct sentences so verb agrees with subject (EP: Grammar)	• TOC 4: Grammar • TOC 4: Grammar • TOC 4: Grammar • TOC 4: Grammar • TOC 15: Usage & Style • TOC 15: Usage & Style • TOC 15: Usage & Style
(LG1.07B)	• recognize, describe, and use correctly, in oral and written language, the conventions of standard Canadian English for spelling, capitalization, and punctuation, including: – punctuation: period, question mark, exclamation mark, comma, dash, apostrophe, colon, quotation marks, parentheses, ellipses	• identify and use singular and plural possessives (Word Study & Spelling TG) • punctuate plurals and possessives correctly (Word Study & Spelling SB #1–3)	• TOC 16: Word Study & Spelling • TOC 16: Word Study & Spelling
Overall (LGV.02B)	• use listening techniques and oral communication skills to participate in classroom discussions and more formal activities, such as storytelling, role playing, and reporting/presenting, for specific purposes and audiences		

AR=Assessment Rubric   EP=Extra Practice   SB=Student Book   SSEC=Student Self-Evaluation Checklist   TG=Teacher's Guide   TOC=Teacher Observation Checklist

GRADE 9 EXPECTATIONS	DEMONSTRATION OF LEARNING	ASSESSMENT TOOLS
LANGUAGE (continued)		
Specific (LG2.01D) • communicate orally in group discussions for different purposes, with a focus on identifying key ideas and supporting details, distinguishing fact from opinion, asking clarifying questions, and following instructions	• share knowledge of karate and martial arts (Introducing the Model TG #1)	• TOC 13: Tracking Expectations
(LG2.03D) • plan and make oral presentations to a small group or the class, selecting and using vocabulary and methods of delivery to suit audience and purpose; gather ideas and information; plan, create, rehearse, revise, and assess presentations such as dramatizations, reports, and speeches	• give a one- to three-minute talk on an aspect of writing their research report (More Oral Language TG) • give oral presentation of research report (Media Link SB)	• TOC 11: Speaking • SSEC 5: Oral Presentation
(LG2.05D) • practise with cue cards and relaxation exercises (and with visual aids and technology, if used) to ensure confident delivery in oral presentations	• rehearse oral presentation several times (Media Link SB)	• TOC 11: Speaking
MEDIA STUDIES		
Overall (MDV.01D) • use knowledge of the elements, intended audiences, and production practices of a variety of media forms to analyze specific media works		
Specific (MD1.02D) • identify how elements of media forms are used in a variety of media works and explain the effects of different treatments	• watch multimedia presentations examining information provided and medium used (Oral Language Extension TG)	• AR 21: Response to Media
Overall (MDV.02D) • use knowledge of a variety of media forms, purposes, and audiences to create media works and describe their intended effect		
Specific (MD2.01D) • adapt a work of literature to another media form and determine what aspects have been strengthened and/or weakened by the adaptation	• present a research report as a multimedia presentation (Oral Language Extension SB)	• AR 12: Media Product

AR=Assessment Rubric   EP=Extra Practice   SB=Student Book   SSEC=Student Self-Evaluation Checklist   TG=Teacher's Guide   TOC=Teacher Observation Checklist

INSTRUCTIONAL STRATEGIES FOR THE ACADEMIC COURSE

PLANNING INFORMATION

Links to Other Nelson English 9 Resources

Write Source 2000

Research Report—"Writing Research Papers," pp. 223–235; **Apostrophe**—"Apostrophe," p. 403; **Bibliography**—"Adding a Works-Cited Page," p. 230, "Sample Works—Cited Entries," p. 231–232, "Sample Internet Entries," p. 232; **Subject-Verb Agreement**—"Write Agreeable Sentences," pp. 88–89; **Transition Words**—"Transitions or Linking Words," p. 106

INTRODUCING THE UNIT

1. To introduce this unit, ask students the following questions:

   - What is a research report? (a report based on information from outside sources such as encyclopedias, articles, books, or the World Wide Web)
   - Why is it important to learn to write a research report? (Research reports are required in secondary and post-secondary courses and in some occupations; and they may be useful for personal projects.)
   - What occupations would require you to know how to write and read a research report? (most professions, e.g., engineering, science, university teaching, law, business)
   - Where would you find research reports for many occupations? (in professional journals, e.g., *Journal of Medicine*)
   - How would doing research to buy a new CD player be similar to doing a research report in one of your courses in school? (You use a similar process: searching resources, summarizing findings, reaching a conclusion.)

   Conclude the discussion by emphasizing that knowing how to write a research report is an important life skill that students will use many times during their educational and professional lives. (LIV.02D—TOC 13: Tracking Expectations)

2. Have students read "What is a research report?" on page 140 of the student book and then hold an informal discussion about research that students have done for various projects either in or outside of school. (LIV.02D—TOC 13: Tracking Expectations)

INTRODUCING THE MODEL

1. Ask students if any of them have ever taken karate lessons. Those who have might recount their experiences as a way to build a context for reading the research report model "The Way of the Empty Hand." If no students have taken karate lessons, have students share what they know about karate and the other martial arts. (LG2.01D—TOC 13: Tracking Expectations)

2. Ask students to speculate on why "The Way of the Empty Hand" was chosen as a title for the model. Have students read the model to find out the answer. Students may be interested to know that the author, Jill Peacock, was 16 years old when she wrote the report. At the time she had her purple belt in karate. (LI1.03B—TOC 10: Reading Strategies)

3. Invite an instructor from a karate school or a student in your school who takes karate to come to your class to be interviewed about their work. Ask for two student volunteers to act as the interviewers and have them draw up a list of questions to ask the guest. The students should form their questions as if they were part of their primary research for a research report. After the interview, have students discuss what they learned from the interview and how they think

information from interviews can contribute to a research report. (WR1.01D—AR 20: Research Report)

4. The conclusion of a report usually summarizes the main point, and refers back to the introduction. Ask students to comment on the effectiveness of the conclusion of the model. (LI1.06D—TOC 13: Tracking Expectations)

INVESTIGATING THE MODEL

Answers:

1. Possible answers
   The founding father of modern karate is considered to be Gichin Funakoshi.
   Karate originated on the Japanese island of Okinawa.
   A series of nine coloured belts shows the student's rank.
   The traditional uniform made of heavy cotton is known as the gi.
   One significant part of grading is the kata.

2. The introduction effectively identifies the topic and catches the reader's interest through the use of a clear visual image of karate students beginning a class. The article was written for teenagers or adults interested in knowing more about karate. The language, while quite simple, has several technical terms in it.

3. The main headings the author might have used include: Introduction, Benefits of Karate, History of Karate, Levels and Grading, Sparring, Weapons, Types of Karate, Conclusion.

4. Exceptions to the general rules:

   - use of second person instead of third person: "It can help you become a calmer person, improve your self-esteem, and get you into shape (Brimner 14)." Reason: direct quote from another source.
   - Use of past tense instead of present in description: "In 1903, Funakoshi demonstrated karate to the commissioner of an Okinawan school and it became ... " Reason: description of something that happened in the past.
   - Change in logical order. In "The Way of the Empty Hand," the types of karate are described at the end of the report when the writer is inviting the reader to start karate. Normally, the types of karate would appear near the beginning of the report. Logical order may change depending on the needs of the writer.

5. Compare: use examples to show how two things are similar and different
   Example: "Many participants find the kata fascinating because it looks similar to a dance but also has a practical aspect to it." (page 142)
   Contrast: use examples to show how two things are different
   Example: "Judo comes from Japan and features many throwing techniques. Kung fu originated in China and includes movements based on the differing nature of particular animals." (page 143)
   Define: give the meaning of a word or subject, the group or class to which it belongs, its function, and how it is different from the others in that group
   Example: "One significant part of the grading is the kata. This is a series of self-defence movements put together to create an artistic demonstration of the technique." (page 142)
   Classify: separate ideas or items into groups with similar characteristics
   Example: "As karate students progress, they can begin to use weapons. These include tonfas, which are wooden and similar to a police officer's nightstick, seis (pronounced "sighs"), which look like a pair of miniature pitchforks because of their three prongs, and bows. Bows are long wooden staffs that have the thickness of a pool cue." (page 143)

CHECKPOINT

Sample criteria for a research report:

- presents or summarizes factual information in clear, concise, and accurate form
- has interesting introduction that explains topic
- describes key information arranged into subtopics in body of report
- is written in third person, present tense, and in logical order
- compares, contrasts, defines, or classifies
- acknowledges primary and secondary resources

---

6. Primary sources include interviews with Kimberley Young-Yow and Michael Walsh. The use of primary resources adds authenticity to the report.

Student Book 1.–6. (LI1.04D—AR 22: Response to Reading)

EXTENDING THE MODEL

1. For this activity, ask colleagues to lend you some research reports done by grade 9 students in their subject areas and add these to research reports you have collected previously. Make two copies of each one and distribute these in class, so that each pair of students has the same report to work with.

   Working in pairs, students should answer the following questions about the research report you have given them. In each pair, one student should be responsible for taking notes.
   - What is the purpose of the report? (to inform readers about a certain subject)
   - How does the report accomplish this purpose? (provides important factual information from both primary and secondary sources)
   - Who is the audience for the report? (answers will vary)
   - What are some important skills necessary for writing a research report? (developing an action plan, developing a focus for the topic, selecting suitable resources, skimming and scanning sources for information, interviewing skills, summarizing, writing skills, evaluating and revising work)
   - How was computer technology used in preparing the report? (searches, typing the report, checking spelling) (LIV.02D—TOC 13: Tracking Expectations)

2. Write the following headings on the board or overhead transparency: Purpose, Audience, Skills, Computer Technology. Ask students to share their findings from the activity above. Summarize their responses under the headings and discuss the results in each category. (LIV.02D—TOC 13: Tracking Expectations)

3. Point out to students that many newspaper reports are very similar to research reports. Ask students to find one newspaper report containing all the characteristics of a research report as outlined in their class checklist. Have students exchange newspaper reports, and check to see if all characteristics are present. (LI1.02D—TOC 13: Tracking Expectations)

4. Sometimes editors of newspaper reports choose a short sentence or quotation from a piece and repeat it in larger print. These are sometimes referred to as "pull quotes" since they are short quotes pulled from the main article. This is done to create interest in the article, and to highlight key statements. Choose a few articles which use this technique, and show them to the class. Ask students to select three key statements or phrases from the model which might have been used for this purpose. (LI1.04D—TOC 13: Tracking Expectations)

MORE CHALLENGE

Using the jigsaw method of instruction, ask groups of students to prepare brief, how-to presentations for the class on some or all of the following subjects. (LIV.02D—TOC 13: Tracking Expectations)

- Narrow a Topic
- Write a Focus (Thesis) Statement
- Use Search Engines to Find Information
- Distinguish Between Fact and Opinion
- Write Point-Form Notes
- Develop File Cards
- Write a Bibliography

WRITER'S WORKSHOP

Ask students how the following statement might apply to the writing of a research report: "The secret of handling any big job is to break it down into a number of smaller jobs which you can handle one at a time." Organize students into groups of four and ask them to develop a chart outlining the various steps necessary to develop a research report. They should draw up their final version on a large piece of paper or on an overhead transparency that can be shared with the rest of the class. Tell them to include beside each step the approximate percentage of time they would spend on that step. (WRV.01D—AR 20: Research Report)

MORE SUPPORT

Some students may need the use of model research reports to assist them in working through the various stages of the process. Provide copies of model grade 9 research reports that can be signed out by students for their use at school or at home. (WRV.02D—AR 20: Research Report)

Student Book 1.–7. (WRV.01D—AR 20: Research Report); 8. (WRV.03D—AR 20: Research Report); 9. (WRV.04D—AR 20: Research Report; WRV.05D—AR 20: Research Report)

ORAL LANGUAGE EXTENSION

Since this activity is multidimensional, the groups should comprise students who exhibit a range of ability and a variety of strengths (e.g., computer, presentation, and videotaping skills). You will need to limit the scope of the documentary presentations to the amount of time available for their development and presentation. Ask other teachers in your school if they have examples of student-prepared multimedia presentations for the class to view, or obtain a segment of a current documentary from your board resources or from television. Ask students to examine the amount and kinds of information presented, and the medium (oral, visual) used. (MD1.02D—AR 21: Response to Media)

Student Book (MD2.01D—AR 12: Media Product)

GRAMMAR

1. Indicate to students that subject-verb agreement is one of the most common errors in grammar. To help them understand why this is the case, slowly read the following sentences to students. Have them write down the correct form of the verb in their notebooks. Then have them use the rules for subject-verb agreement in the student book to check their answers. The correct choices are underlined below. (WR5.08B—TOC 4: Grammar; LG1.05D—TOC 4: Grammar)

   a) Jill and Kimberley (<u>provide</u>, provides) assistance to the instructor with most classes.
   b) Neither the instructor nor the students (knows, <u>knew</u>) the reason for the delay.
   c) The group of students (<u>is</u> are) ready to do karate.
   d) The belts on the display (is, <u>are</u>) mine.
   e) Everybody (<u>is</u>, are) to receive his or her belt today.
   f) Few of the students (is, <u>are</u>) receiving their black belts this year.
   g) Most of the students (travels, <u>travel</u>) to competitions with their families.
   h) News about the new technique (<u>is</u>, are) spreading quickly.

2. Have students rewrite the following sentences, replacing the noun subjects with indefinite pronouns. For assistance, they can refer to the list of indefinite pronouns on page 41 of the student book. (WR5.08B—TOC 4: Grammar; LG1.05D—TOC 4: Grammar)

   a) Jill and Kimberley like karate.
   b) One hundred percent of the students moved on to the next level.
   c) At least 300 people attended the competition.
   d) About half of the people who attended the meet were parents.
   e) The mind and body are stronger as a result of taking karate.

Answers:

1. a) benefits — benefit   b) have — has
   c) correct   d) have — has
   e) correct   f) correct
   g) have — has

2. Student work.

Student Book 1.–2. (WR5.08B—TOC 4: Grammar; LG1.05D—TOC 4: Grammar)

MEDIA LINK

Check with a guidance counsellor to see what resources (e.g., books, pamphlets, video series) are available to support this activity. Students may be able to find appropriate Web sites on the Internet. Due to time constraints, you may wish to have students make their presentations to small groups.

Student Book (LG2.03D—SSEC 5: Oral Presentation; LG2.05D—TOC 11: Speaking)

MORE ORAL LANGUAGE

Ask students to prepare a one- to three-minute talk on their written report. They should choose one of the following options:

- Explain why your report should be included in a capsule to be dug up in 100 years.
- Deliver a sales talk for your report.
- Explain what you got out of writing your report.
- Defend the statement: This report should be read by everyone in this class.
- Explain the most difficult obstacle you had in writing your report and how you overcame it.

(LG2.03D—TOC 11: Speaking)

MORE CHALLENGE

Have students write two sentences for each of the following pronouns: all, any, none, some, most. The first sentence should contain a plural subject. The second sentence should include a singular subject. (WR5.08B—TOC 4: Grammar; LG1.05D—TOC 4: Grammar)

MORE MEDIA

Ask students to assess the effectiveness of the title of the model and the photographs which accompany it. If they had written the model, would they have chosen the same title, and the same photographs? Why or why not? Discuss with students what makes an effective title and what kinds of items make good visual support. Ask them to assess these features in their own research reports. (LI3.03D—TOC 13: Tracking Expectations)

MECHANICS

Working in groups of four, and using the model bibliography on page 143 of the student book and the examples of entries on pages 212–213, ask students to answer the following questions. (WR5.01D—TOC 8: Mechanics)

- What two main purposes does a bibliography serve? (tells reader where writer obtained information; provides sources should reader want more information)
- Besides books, what other sources of information might be contained in a bibliography? (pamphlets, newspaper or magazine articles, CD-ROMs, Web sites, television or radio shows, films, videos, interviews)
- Are all entries in a bibliography written exactly the same? What differences are there? (amount and kind of information, recognition of authorship/creators, punctuation)
- What order is used to list sources? (alphabetical)
- What spacing is used between entries? (double space)

Answers:

1. Aker, Don, and David Hodgkinson. <u>Language & Writing 9</u>. Toronto: Nelson Thomson Learning, 1999.

   ——[1] Don Aker and David Hodgkinson, *Language & Writing 9* (Toronto: Nelson Thomson Learning,1999) 151.

2.–3. Student work.

Student Book 1.–3. (WR5.01D—TOC 8: Mechanics)

USAGE & STYLE

Discuss with students the importance of coherence—that is, the proper arrangement of ideas, and bridging the gap between sentences—in paragraphs and in a complete piece of writing. Point out to them that one way of achieving coherence in writing is through the use of transitional devices. (WR3.03D—TOC 15: Usage & Style)

Answers:

1. Possible answers
   "Although it originated on the Japanese island of ... " (joins ideas in a paragraph)
   "Various kicking techniques may have come from Thailand, *whereas* the open-handed ... " (connects ideas in a paragraph)
   "Today, there are many different forms of karate." (joins ideas in paragraphs)
   "Another Japanese martial art is kendo." (connects ideas between paragraphs)

2.–3. Student work.

Student Book 1.–3. (LG1.05D—TOC 15: Usage & Style)

WORD ORIGINS

Answers:

karaoke — a form of entertainment in which an amateur sings accompanied by a specially prepared recording without the usual lead vocal part (from Japanese *kara* meaning *empty* and *oke* meaning *orchestra*)

tsunami — a very large ocean wave caused by an underwater earthquake or volcanic eruption (from Japanese *tsu* meaning *port* and *nami* meaning *wave*)

sushi — small cakes of cold, cooked rice wrapped in seaweed, dressed with vinegar, and topped or wrapped with slices of raw or cooked fish, eggs, or vegetables (Japanese)

sayonara — goodbye (Japanese)

MORE CHALLENGE

Obtain guidelines for writing bibliographies in the style used by the American Psychological Association. Provide students with a sample bibliography using this style. Ask them to compare the entries of the sample bibliography with the entries as given on pages 212–213 of the student book (Modern Language Association). Ask students to explain which style they prefer and why. (WR5.01D—TOC 8: Mechanics)

MORE CHALLENGE

Another way of joining two ideas together in a sentence is to use correlative conjunctions (coordinate conjunctions used in pairs). Use the following example to explain the concept of the correlative conjunction:

Neither the expense of the lessons, nor the commitment of time was going to prevent me from taking karate lessons.

Ask students, working in pairs, to review coordinating conjunctions on page 42 of the student book, and then to use each of the following correlative conjunctions in a sentence:

either, or; not only, but also; both, and; whether, or; just, as; just, so; as, so.

(WR5.05D—TOC 15: Usage & Style; LG1.05D—TOC 15: Usage & Style) kamikaze — Japanese pilot in World War II trained to make a suicidal crash attack especially upon a ship (from Japanese *kami* meaning *divine* and *kaze* meaning *wind*)

tofu — protein-rich food made from soybean extract (from Japanese *tofu* — originally from China: *doufu* — *dou* meaning *bean* and *fu* meaning curdled)

(LG1.03B—TOC 16: Word Study & Spelling)

WORD STUDY & SPELLING

Have students identify the nouns below as singular, singular possessive, plural, or plural possessive. Have them make a chart with those headings and insert the nouns in the appropriate columns. Then ask students to complete all of the columns for each noun. You could ask volunteers to provide sentences using one of the nouns to demonstrate correct use. (WR5.13B—TOC 16: Word Study & Spelling; LG1.07B—TOC 16: Word Study & Spelling)

Mondays	women's	Mike's	Millers'	Manitoba's
glove	soprano's	heroes'	feet	knives

Answers:

1. a) student's — singular possessive   b) Students — plural
    c) Students' — plural possessive

2. Possible answers

    To form the plural of most nouns, add "s." Examples: pencils, circles, holidays

    To form a plural when a singular noun ends in "s, sh, ch, x, or z," add "es." Examples: passes, pushes, porches, taxes, buzzes

    To form the possessive of a plural noun that ends in "s," add an apostrophe. Examples: sisters', artists', students'

    To form the possessive of a plural noun that does not end in "s," add an apostrophe and "s." Examples: people's, women's

3. a) Kimberley's   b) students'
    c) partners   d) centres
    e) karate's

Student Book 1.–3. (WR5.13B—TOC 16: Word Study & Spelling; LG1.07B—TOC 16: Word Study & Spelling)

ANSWERS TO EXTRA PRACTICE

Grammar

1. were	2. saw	3. is	4. was
5. are	6. has	7. doesn't	8. were
9. plans	10. were	11. is	12. is
13. want	14. causes	15. live	

(WR5.08B—TOC 4: Grammar; LG1.05D—TOC 4: Grammar)

Mechanics
BIBLIOGRAPHY

Blinck, Tina P. "Puppy Love." <u>The Modern Dog Encyclopedia</u>. 5th ed. 1991.
Coleman, Jack, and Mary Wilson. <u>Going to the Dogs</u>. Vancouver: Canine, 1999.
Dogcatcher, Michael. Personal interview. 17 Apr. 1999.
<u>Dog Facts</u>. CD-ROM. Texas: Doggone, 1996.
"Dog Tales." <u>Pets Corner</u>. Host William Greyhound. DOG Television. 18 Jan. 1998.
Hugh Robertson, "Humans: A Dog's Best Friend." <u>The Globe and Mail</u> 7 Oct. 1998: D19.
Turabian, Susan. <u>Dog Tired</u>. Charlottetown: Kennel Publishing, 1993.

IN-TEXT CITATION

Training your dog can be a wonderful experience (Turabian, 22).
Every dog has a personality of its own (Robertson, 16).

FOOTNOTE

—
[1] Jane Dogged and Linda Mann, *We Live in a Doggie Bag World* (Hamilton: Dogmatic Press, 1995) 89.
(WR5.01D—TOC 8: Mechanics)

Usage & Style

Possible answer:

This year I decided to take karate. Although I didn't know much about the sport, I had seen it in movies and on television, and I thought I might enjoy it. So, I asked a friend of mine who was already taking karate if there was space available at his school. He said there was, and soon I was attending my first class. First, I was invited to watch the class so I would see what happened during a typical lesson. I was thoroughly impressed. Furthermore, I knew that I had made the right decision.

Soon I became good at karate and I began entering competitions. Although I did not win anything in my first competition, I did place third in my second competition and second in my most recent one.

I am improving. As a result, I am hoping to do even better in the future.
(WR3.03D—TOC 15: Usage & Style)

Word Study & Spelling

1. a) copies   b) wishes   c) hooves
    d) geese   e) spies   f) moose
    g) windows   h) tomatoes   i) leaves
    j) years   k) coaches   l) teeth
    m) knives   n) radios   o) bunches
    p) echoes   q) foxes   r) salmon
    s) men   t) photos   u) waitresses

2. a) workers'   b) families'   c) doctors'
    d) people's   e) experts'   f) sheep's
    g) women's   h) teachers'   i) friends'
    j) Elliotts'   k) mice's   l) Oilers'
    m) men's   n) guests'   o) racers'

3. a) I attended the Don Mills school to take karate.
    b) The schools' mottoes were displayed in the corridors.
    c) The doctors measured the pulses of the students giving blood.
    d) The heroes were recognized for their deeds of bravery.
    e) Our team's defeat was hard to take, but our coaches' attitudes remained positive.
    f) My friends' karate club will meet on Saturdays.
    g) The painter's (or painters') and the sculptor's (or sculptors') supplies arrived early for the workshop.
    h) The two girls carried their friends' books to their lockers.
    i) The trout were biting on the three fishermen's fishing lines at the same time.

(WR5.13B—TOC 16: Word Study & Spelling)

Reflect and Build on Your Learning

Reflecting on Expository Writing Forms

1. Student work.

2. Possible answer

   Other expository forms include factual account, procedures, instructions, cause and effect, process analysis, comparison, definition, hard news story, giving directions, memo, business letter, guide, announcement, lab report, summary, problem-solution essay, and message.

   Example: A factual account is the retelling of an event. It focuses on presenting the facts in the order in which they happened. It would be used to recount an experience or an event in history—to report on an event if you were asked only to recount the facts.

   Student Book 1.–2. (LIV.01D—TOC 13: Tracking Expectations)

Looking Over Expository Writing Forms

1. Possible answer

CRITERIA	EXPLANATION	PRÉCIS	RESEARCH REPORT	FACTUAL ACCOUNT
Purpose	explains how or why something happens or happened	presents a summary of a written passage	presents or summarizes factual information based on research	recounts an event by presenting the facts
Organization	begins with a question; then proceeds step by step	same information and organization as original	usually arranged by subtopics	arranged in the order in which it happened
Details	step-by-step details	eliminates unnecessary details	provides important facts	often answers five W questions
Tense	present or past	same as original	usually present	usually past
Visuals	usually present	not usually used	may or may not be used	usually not present

Student Book 1. (LIV.02D—TOC 13: Tracking Expectations)

Using the Expository Writing Forms

1. Possible answers

   A knowledge of the features of these forms helps make you a better reader because you can predict the organization of pieces of writing before you begin to read them. It will help make you a better writer because you will be able to include the features required in a particular form of writing.

   Student Book 1. (LIV.02D—TOC 13: Tracking Expectations; WR3.04D—TOC 13: Tracking Expectations)

2. Organize the groups in your classroom so that each group has at least two people in it who have a thorough understanding of search engines and how they operate. Topics of interest to ten- or eleven-year-olds may be obtained from younger brothers or sisters, or obtained from curriculum guidelines available for this age

group (grades 5–6). You may find such guidelines in your resource centre, or you may be able to borrow copies from a teacher in one of your feeder schools.

To become familiar with the level of language necessary for students at this age level, ask members of your class to bring in novels or informational books from their brothers or sisters, or ask them to check reading materials available for this age group in the public library.

Student Book 2. (WRV.03D—AR 7: Explanation; WRV.04D—AR 7: Explanation; WRV.05D—AR 7: Explanation)

3. By this time of the year students should be familiar with the term "essay." Emphasize that an essay is any short piece of writing that analyzes or interprets something in a personal way. Support could be provided to students by working through an example of an explanation from a short story, novel, or play studied in class. By doing this, you can make sure that students understand what the essay should be about (the accuracy and significance of the explanation), and emphasize that their answers should focus on the questions in the text. As well, you might want to review the characteristics of the essay form.

Student Book 3. (WRV.03D—AR 8: Expository Writing; WR3.05D—AR 8: Expository Writing; WRV.04D—AR 8: Expository Writing; WRV.05D—AR 8: Expository Writing)

4. The research report does not have to be limited to the two topics identified in the student book. If they wish, students could investigate the jargon used by teenagers or by people in a particular occupation. If these topics do not appeal to you or your students, or if you think insufficient resources are available to research these topics, provide students with a list of other topics related in some way to the English curriculum.

Student Book 4. (WRV.03D—AR 20: Research Report; WRV.04D—AR 20: Research Report; WRV.05D—AR 20: Research Report)

5. This activity should be straightforward for students. Remind them that the research reports or essays required for this activity may come from any subject area studied during the year.

Student Book 5. (WRV.03D—AR 18: Précis; WRV.04D—AR 18: Précis; WRV.05D—AR 18: Précis)

GRADE 9 EXPECTATIONS	DEMONSTRATION OF LEARNING	ASSESSMENT TOOLS
LITERATURE STUDIES AND READING		
Overall (LIV.01P)	• read and demonstrate an understanding of a variety of literary and informational texts	• demonstrate understanding of forms of exposition (Reflecting on Expository Writing Forms SB #1–2)	• TOC 14: Tracking Expectations
Specific (LI1.02P)	• select and read texts for a variety of purposes, with an emphasis on recognizing the elements of literary genres and the organization of informational materials, collecting and using information, extending personal knowledge, and responding imaginatively	• compare newspaper report with model research report (Extending the Model TG #3)	• TOC 14: Tracking Expectations
(LI1.03B)	• describe a variety of reading strategies and select and use them effectively before, during, and after reading to understand texts	• predict content of model using title, bibliography, and photographs (Introducing the Model TG #1) • speculate on reason for title of research report (Introducing the Model TG #3)	• TOC 10: Reading Strategies • TOC 10: Reading Strategies
(LI1.04P)	• locate and use explicit information and ideas from texts in forming opinions and developing generalizations	• give interpretation of model using examples from student book (Investigating the Model SB #1–6)	• AR 22: Response to Reading
Overall (LIV.02P)	• demonstrate an understanding of the elements of a variety of literary and informational forms, with a focus on plays, short stories, and newspaper and magazine articles	• discuss purpose and importance of research reports (Introducing the Unit TG) • analyze research reports (Extending the Model TG #1) • discuss results of analysis of research reports (Extending the Model #2) • compare four forms of expository writing (Looking Over Expository Writing Forms SB #1) • explain usefulness of knowledge of expository writing forms (Using the Expository Writing Forms SB #1)	• TOC 14: Tracking Expectations • TOC 14: Tracking Expectations • TOC 14: Tracking Expectations • TOC 14: Tracking Expectations • TOC 14: Tracking Expectations
(LIV.03B)	• identify and explain the effect of specific elements of style in a variety of literary and informational texts		
Specific (LI3.03P)	• explain how authors and editors use design elements to help convey meaning	• assess visual support for model and their own research reports (More Media TG)	• TOC 14: Tracking Expectations
WRITING		
Overall (WRV.01P)	• use print and electronic sources to gather information and explore ideas for their written work	• create chart giving steps and time required to write a research report (Writer's Workshop TG) • gather and organize information for research report (Writer's Workshop SB #1–7)	• AR 20: Research Report • AR 20: Research Report
Overall (WRV.03P)	• use a variety of forms of writing to express themselves, clarify their ideas, and engage the audience's attention, imagination, and interest	• write a research report (Writer's Workshop SB #8) • write instructions on how to use a Web search engine to find information (Using the Expository Writing Forms SB #2) • write an essay on accuracy and significance of an explanation (Using the Expository Writing Forms SB #3) • write a research report on jargon or origin of English words (Using the Expository Writing Forms SB #4) • write a précis (Using the Expository Writing Forms SB #5)	• AR 20: Research Report • AR 7: Explanation • AR 8: Expository Writing • AR 20: Research Report • AR 18: Précis
Specific (WR3.01P)	• use key words in questions or prompts to organize information and ideas in homework answers	• answer questions on expository forms (Using the Expository Writing Forms SB #1)	• TOC 14: Tracking Expectations

AR=Assessment Rubric   EP=Extra Practice   SB=Student Book   SSEC=Student Self-Evaluation Checklist   TG=Teacher's Guide   TOC=Teacher Observation Checklist

GRADE 9 EXPECTATIONS	DEMONSTRATION OF LEARNING	ASSESSMENT TOOLS
WRITING (continued)		
(WR3.02P) • structure expository paragraphs using a topic sentence, supporting sentences to develop the topic, connecting words to link the sentences, and a concluding sentence	• write a short essay on explanation (Using the Expository Writing Forms SB #3)	• AR 8: Expository Writing
(WR3.07P) • present directions, instructions, and reports of investigations in a logical order, using an organizational pattern such as examples, chronological order, or comparison	• write instructions on Web search engine (Using the Expository Writing Forms SB #2)	• AR 7: Explanation
Specific (WR3.05P) • use a single controlling idea to structure a series of paragraphs	• discuss use of transitions to achieve coherence (Usage & Style TG) • rewrite paragraphs using transitions (EP: Usage & Style)	• TOC 15: Usage & Style • TOC 15: Usage & Style
Overall (WRV.04B) • revise their written work, collaboratively and independently, with a focus on support for ideas, accuracy, clarity, and unity	• revise research report (Writer's Workshop SB #9) • revise instructions on Web search engine (Using the Expository Writing Forms SB #2) • revise essay on explanation (Using the Expository Writing Forms SB #3) • revise research report (Using the Expository Writing Forms SB #4) • revise précis (Using the Expository Writing Forms SB #5)	• AR 20: Research Report • AR 7: Explanation • AR 8: Expository Writing • AR 20: Research Report • AR 18: Précis
Overall (WRV.05B) • edit and proofread to produce final drafts, using correct grammar, spelling, and punctuation, according to the conventions of standard Canadian English specified for this course, with the support of print and electronic resources when appropriate	• edit and proofread research report (Writer's Workshop SB #9) • edit and proofread instructions on Web engine (Using the Expository Writing Forms SB #2) • edit and proofread essay on explanation (Using the Expository Writing Forms SB #3) • edit and proofread research report (Using the Expository Writing Forms SB #4) • edit and proofread précis (Using the Expository Writing Forms SB #5)	• AR 20: Research Report • AR 8: Expository Writing • AR 20: Research Report • AR 20: Research Report • AR 18: Précis
Specific (WR5.01P) • identify sources of ideas, information, and quotations in written work	• explain how bibliography is created (Mechanics TG) • correct errors in bibliography (More Challenge TG, page 216) • create bibliographic entries (Mechanics SB #1–3) • write correct form of bibliography, in-text citation, and footnote (EP: Mechanics)	• TOC 8: Mechanics • TOC 8: Mechanics • TOC 8: Mechanics • TOC 8: Mechanics
(WR5.06P) • construct complete and correct compound and complex sentences, using the following sentence components as required: subject, predicate, object, subject complement; main and subordinate clauses; prepositional phrases	• identify subject and prepositional phrase (More Support TG, page 215)	• TOC 4: Grammar
(WR5.08B) • make compound subjects agree with verbs in simple and compound sentences	• give correct form of verb (Grammar TG #1) • rewrite sentences using indefinite pronouns (Grammar TG #2) • correct sentences for subject-verb agreement (Grammar SB #1–2) • write sentences to demonstrate rules for subject-verb agreement (More Challenge TG, page 215) • correct sentences so verb agrees with subject (EP: Grammar)	• TOC 4: Grammar • TOC 4: Grammar • TOC 4: Grammar • TOC 4: Grammar • TOC 4: Grammar

AR=Assessment Rubric   EP=Extra Practice   SB=Student Book   SSEC=Student Self-Evaluation Checklist   TG=Teacher's Guide   TOC=Teacher Observation Checklist

GRADE 9 EXPECTATIONS		DEMONSTRATION OF LEARNING	ASSESSMENT TOOLS
WRITING (continued)			
(WR5.13B)	• use the apostrophe correctly when spelling contractions and possessives	• identify and use singular and plural possessives (Word Study & Spelling TG) • punctuate plurals and possessives correctly (Word Study & Spelling SB #1–3) • correct errors in plurals and plural possessives (EP: Word Study & Spelling)	• TOC 16: Word Study & Spelling • TOC 16: Word Study & Spelling • TOC 16: Word Study & Spelling
LANGUAGE			
(LGV.01P)	• use knowledge of vocabulary and language conventions to speak, write, and read clearly and correctly		
Specific (LG1.03B)	• identify words borrowed from other languages, and words and terms recently introduced to describe new ideas, inventions, and products, and explain their origins	• give meaning and origin of words borrowed from Japanese (Word Origins SB)	• TOC 16: Word Study & Spelling
(LG1.05P)	• recognize, describe, and use correctly, in oral and written language, the language structures of standard Canadian English and its conventions of grammar and usage, including: – parts of speech: nouns, pronouns, verbs, adverbs, adjectives, conjunctions, prepositions, and interjections – agreement between subject and verb, and between pronoun and antecedent	• give correct form of verb (Grammar TG #1) • rewrite sentences using indefinite pronouns (Grammar TG #2) • correct sentences for subject-verb agreement (Grammar SB #1–2) • identify subject and prepositional phrase (More Support TG, page 215) • write sentences to demonstrate rules for subject-verb agreement (More Challenge TG, page 215) • use transitions correctly (Usage & Style SB #1–3) • find transition words in newspaper reports (More Challenge TG, page 216) • correct sentences so verb agrees with subject (EP: Grammar)	• TOC 4: Grammar • TOC 4: Grammar • TOC 4: Grammar • TOC 4: Grammar • TOC 4: Grammar • TOC 15: Usage & Style • TOC 15: Usage & Style • TOC 4: Grammar
(LG1.07B)	• recognize, describe, and use correctly, in oral and written language, the conventions of standard Canadian English for spelling, capitalization, and punctuation, including: – punctuation: period, question mark, exclamation mark, comma, dash, apostrophe, colon, quotation marks, parentheses, ellipses	• identify and use singular and plural possessives (Word Study & Spelling TG) • punctuate plurals and possessives correctly (Word Study & Spelling SB #1–3) • correct errors in plurals and plural possessives (EP: Word Study & Spelling)	• TOC 16: Word Study & Spelling • TOC 16: Word Study & Spelling • TOC 16: Word Study & Spelling
Overall (LGV.02B)	• use listening techniques and oral communication skills to participate in classroom discussions and more formal activities, such as storytelling, role playing, and reporting/presenting, for specific purposes and audiences		
Specific (LG2.01P)	• use listening techniques and oral communication skills to participate in group discussions	• share knowledge of karate and martial arts (Introducing the Model TG #2)	• TOC 14: Tracking Expectations
(LG2.03P)	• work with a partner to plan and make oral presentations to a small group, selecting and using vocabulary and methods of delivery to suit audience and purpose	• give a one- to three-minute talk on an aspect of writing their research report (More Oral Language TG) • give oral presentation of research report (Media Link SB)	• TOC 11: Speaking • SSEC 5: Oral Presentation
(LG2.05P)	• practise with cue cards, use breathing exercises, and rehearse with peers (and with visual aids and technology, if used), to ensure confident delivery in oral presentations	• rehearse oral presentation several times (Media Link SB)	• TOC 11: Speaking

AR=Assessment Rubric   EP=Extra Practice   SB=Student Book   SSEC=Student Self-Evaluation Checklist   TG=Teacher's Guide   TOC=Teacher Observation Checklist

GRADE 9 EXPECTATIONS	DEMONSTRATION OF LEARNING	ASSESSMENT TOOLS
MEDIA STUDIES		
Overall (MDV.01P) • identify and describe the elements, intended audiences, and production practices of a variety of media forms		
Specific (MD1.02P) • identify and describe the elements used to structure media works in a variety of forms	• watch multimedia presentations examining information provided and medium used (Oral Language Extension TG)	• AR 21: Response to Media
Overall (MDV.02P) • use knowledge of a variety of media forms, purposes, and audiences to create media works		
Specific (MD2.01P) • adapt a work of literature for presentation in another media form	• present a research report as a multimedia presentation (Oral Language SB)	• AR 12: Media Product

AR=Assessment Rubric   EP=Extra Practice   SB=Student Book   SSEC=Student Self-Evaluation Checklist   TG=Teacher's Guide   TOC=Teacher Observation Checklist

INSTRUCTIONAL STRATEGIES FOR THE APPLIED COURSE

LEARNING GOALS

- write a research report
- use subject-verb agreement correctly
- create a bibliography
- use transitions to connect ideas
- use apostrophes for possessives correctly

PLANNING INFORMATION

Links to Other Nelson English 9 Resources

Write Source 2000

Research Report—"Writing Research Papers," pp. 223–235; **Apostrophe**—"Apostrophe," p. 403; **Bibliography**—"Adding a Works-Cited Page," p. 230, "Sample Works—Cited Entries," pp. 231–232, "Sample Internet Entries," p. 232; **Subject-Verb Agreement**—"Write Agreeable Sentences," pp. 88–89; **Transition Words**—"Transitions or Linking Words," p. 106

INTRODUCING THE UNIT

Introduce the topic of research reports by posing the following situation to students: Sometimes you or your family buy things that cost a great deal of money (e.g., television, car, computer, CD player). To get the best value for your money, you often do some investigative work before making the purchase. You might check out a report in a consumer magazine or on a Web site. You might do some comparative shopping in several stores and discuss the item with different salespeople. You might ask friends who have bought the same item whether they are pleased with their purchase. Ask students the following questions:

- What name can be given to this kind of investigative work? (research)
- What name do we use for reports that provide information based on research? (research reports)
- How would research to buy something be similar to research you might have to do for one of your courses? (look at a variety of different sources for factual information)
- What occupations would require you to know how to write a research report? (most professions: business, law, science)

Conclude the discussion by emphasizing that knowing how to write a research report is an important life skill that students will use many times during their educational and professional lives. (LIV.02P—TOC 14: Tracking Expectations)

INTRODUCING THE MODEL

1. Have students read the title and the bibliography of the model, and look at the photographs. Ask them what these items tell the reader about the contents of the model. (LI1.03B—TOC 10: Reading Strategies)

Activities #1–2 on page 201 from the Academic Course are appropriate for the Applied Course.

2. (LG2.01P—TOC 14: Tracking Expectations)

3. (LI1.03B—TOC 10: Reading Strategies)

INVESTIGATING THE MODEL

See the Academic Course on pages 202–203 for answers. Student Book 1.–6. (LI1.04P—AR 22: Response to Reading)

EXTENDING THE MODEL

Activities #1–2 on page 203 from the Academic Course are appropriate for the Applied Course.

1. (LIV.02P—TOC 14: Tracking Expectations)

CHECKPOINT

Sample criteria for a research report:

- presents or summarizes factual information in clear, concise, and accurate form
- has interesting introduction that explains topic
- describes key information arranged into subtopics in body of report
- is written in third person, present tense, and in logical order
- compares, contrasts, defines, or classifies
- acknowledges primary and secondary resources

2. (LIV.02P—TOC 14: Tracking Expectations)

3. Provide students with a copy of a newspaper report that is somewhat factual. Have students work in groups of four and ask them to compare the newspaper report with the model, pointing out similarities and differences. Suggest that they use the checklist of common features of research reports that the class created in Checkpoint as the basis for their comparison. Have them first make a list of all the similarities and then a list of all the differences. (LI1.02P—TOC 14: Tracking Expectations)

WRITER'S WORKSHOP

The activity on page 203 from the Academic Course is appropriate for the Applied Course.

(WRV.01P—AR 20: Research Report)

Student Book 1.–7. (WRV.01P—AR 20: Research Report); 8. WRV.03P—AR 20: Research Report); 9. (WRV.04B—AR 20: Research Report; WRV.05B—AR 20: Research Report)

ORAL LANGUAGE EXTENSION

The activity on page 204 from the Academic Course is appropriate for the Applied Course. (MD1.02P—AR 21: Response to Media)

Student Book (MD2.01P—AR 12: Media Product)

GRAMMAR

The activities on page 204 from the Academic Course are appropriate for the Applied Course.
1. (WR5.08B—TOC 4: Grammar; LG1.05P—TOC 4: Grammar)

2. (WR5.08B—TOC 4: Grammar; LG1.05P—TOC 4: Grammar)

Answers:
See the Academic Course on page 204 for answers.

Student Book 1.–2. (WR5.08B—TOC 4: Grammar; LG1.05P—TOC 4: Grammar)

MEDIA LINK

Check with a guidance counsellor to see what resources (e.g., books, pamphlets, video series) are available to support this activity. Students may be able to find appropriate Web sites on the Internet. Due to time constraints, you may wish to have students make their presentations to small groups.

Student Book (LG2.03P—SSEC 5: Oral Presentation; LG2.05P—TOC 11: Speaking)

MECHANICS

The activity on page 205 from the Academic Course is appropriate for the Applied Course. (WR5.01P—TOC 8: Mechanics)

Answers:
See the Academic Course on page 205 for answers.

Student Book 1.–3. (WR5.01P—TOC 8: Mechanics)

MORE ORAL LANGUAGE

Ask students to prepare a one- to three-minute talk on their written report. They should choose one of the following options:

- Explain why your report should be included in a capsule to be dug up in 100 years.
- Deliver a sales talk for your report.
- Explain what you got out of writing your report.
- Defend the statement: This report should be read by everyone in this class.
- Explain the most difficult obstacle you had in writing your report and how you overcame it.

(LG2.03P—TOC 11: Speaking)

MORE SUPPORT

Use the following sentences to emphasize that the subject of the verb is never found in a prepositional phrase. Ask students to identify the subject and the prepositional phrase in each sentence. Clarify where there is any confusion. Simple subjects are underlined. (WR5.06B—TOC 4: Grammar; LG1.05P—TOC 4: Grammar)

- Those <u>books</u> on karate are mine.
- <u>One</u> of the students was late for class.
- Many <u>students</u> in the class come from my neighbourhood.
- The <u>sensei</u>, in addition to the students, have gone.
- My <u>jacket</u>, as well as my gym bag, was left at my class.

MORE CHALLENGE

Have students work in pairs and ask them to write one sentence to demonstrate the application of the rules on pages 148–149 of the student book. Remind them that they can use the sentence examples as a guide in creating their own examples. (WR5.08P—TOC 4: Grammar; LG1.05P—TOC 4: Grammar)

MORE MEDIA

Ask students to assess the effectiveness of the title of the model and the photographs which accompany it. If they had written the model, would they have chosen the same title, and the same photographs? Why or why not? Discuss with students what makes an effective title and what kinds of items make good visual support. Ask them to assess these features in their own research report. (LI3.03P—TOC 14: Tracking Expectations)

USAGE & STYLE

The activity on page 205 from the Academic Course is appropriate for the Applied Course.

(WR3.05P—TOC 15: Usage & Style)

Answers:

See the Academic Course on page 205 for answers.

Student Book 1.–3. (LG1.05P—TOC 15: Usage & Style)

WORD ORIGINS

Answers:

See the Academic Course on page 206 for answers.

(LG1.03B—TOC 16: Word Study & Spelling)

WORD STUDY & SPELLING

The activity on page 206 from the Academic Course is appropriate for the Applied Course.

(WR5.13B—TOC 16: Word Study & Spelling; LG1.07B—TOC 16: Word Study & Spelling)

Answers:

See the Academic Course on page 206 for answers.

Student Book 1.–3. (WR5.13B—TOC 16: Word Study & Spelling; LG1.07B—TOC 16: Word Study & Spelling)

ANSWERS TO EXTRA PRACTICE

See the Academic Course on pages 207–208 for answers.

Grammar
(WR5.08B—TOC 4: Grammar; LG1.05P—TOC 4: Grammar)

Mechanics
(WR5.01P—TOC 8: Mechanics)

Usage & Style
(WR3.05P—TOC 15: Usage & Style)

Word Study & Spelling
(WR5.13B—TOC 16: Word Study & Spelling)

REFLECT AND BUILD ON YOUR LEARNING

REFLECTING ON EXPOSITORY WRITING FORMS

1. Student work.

2. Possible answer

   Other expository forms include factual account, procedures, instructions, cause and effect, process analysis, comparison, definition, hard news story, giving directions, memo, business letter, guide, announcement, lab report, summary, problem-solution essay, and message.

   Example: A factual account is the retelling of an event. It focuses on presenting the facts in the order in which they happened. It would be used to recount an experience or an event in history—to report on an event if you were asked only to recount the facts.

Student Book 1.–2. (LIV.01P—TOC 14: Tracking Expectations)

LOOKING OVER EXPOSITORY WRITING FORMS

1. Possible answer

CRITERIA	EXPLANATION	PRÉCIS	RESEARCH REPORT	FACTUAL ACCOUNT
Purpose	explains how or why something happens or happened	presents a summary of a written passage	presents or summarizes factual information based on research	recounts an event by presenting the facts
Organization	begins with a question; then proceeds step by step	same information and organization as original	usually arranged by subtopics	arranged in the order in which it happened
Details	step-by-step details	eliminates unnecessary details	provides important facts	often answers five W questions
Tense	present or past	same as original	usually present	usually past
Visuals	usually present	not usually used	may or may not be used	usually not present

Student Book 1. (LIV.02P—TOC 14: Tracking Expectations)

USING THE EXPOSITORY WRITING FORMS

1. Possible answers

   A knowledge of the features of these forms helps make you a better reader because you can predict the organization of pieces of writing before you begin to read them. It will help make you a better writer because you will be able to include the features required in a particular form of writing.

Student Book 1. (LIV.02P—TOC 14: Tracking Expectations; WR3.01P—TOC 14: Tracking Expectations)

2. Organize the groups in your classroom so that each group has at least two people in it who have a thorough understanding of search engines and how they operate. Topics of interest to ten- or eleven-year-olds may be obtained from younger

brothers or sisters, or obtained from curriculum guidelines available for this age group (grades 5–6). You may find such guidelines in your resource centre, or you may be able to borrow copies from a teacher in one of your feeder schools.

To become familiar with the level of language necessary for students at this age level, ask members of your class to bring in novels or informational books from their brothers or sisters, or ask them to check reading materials available for this age group in the public library.

Student Book 2. (WRV.03P—AR 7: Explanation; WR3.07P—AR 7: Explanation; WRV.04B—AR 7: Explanation; WRV.05B—AR 7: Explanation)

3. By this time of the year students should be familiar with the term "essay." Emphasize that an essay is any short piece of writing that analyzes or interprets something in a personal way. Support could be provided to students by working through an example of an explanation from a short story, novel, or play studied in class. By doing this, you can make sure that students understand what the essay should be about (the accuracy and significance of the explanation), and emphasize that their answers should focus on the questions in the text. As well, you might want to review the characteristics of the essay form.

Student Book 3. (WRV.03P—AR 8: Expository Writing; WR3.02P—AR 8: Expository Wrtiting; WRV.04B—AR 8: Expository Writing; WRV.05B—AR 8: Expository Writing)

4. The research report does not have to be limited to the two topics identified in the student book. If they wish, students could investigate the jargon used by teenagers or by people in a particular occupation. If these topics do not appeal to you or your students, or if you think insufficient resources are available to research these topics, provide students with a list of other topics related in some way to the English curriculum.

Student Book 4. (WRV.03P—AR 20: Research Report; WRV.04B—AR 20: Research Report; WRV.05B—AR 20: Research Report)

5. This activity should be straightforward for students. Remind them that the research reports or essays required for this activity may come from any subject area studied during the year.

Student Book 5. (WRV.03P—AR 18: Précis; WRV.04B—AR 18: Précis; WRV.05B—AR 18: Précis)

GRAMMAR

NAME: _____ DATE: _____

Underline the form of the verb that agrees with the subject in each of the following sentences.

1. Many of the stars (was, were) seen through the telescope.

2. Neither the players nor their coach (saw, seen) the hidden ball.

3. Physics (is, are) a necessary subject for future engineers.

4. The crowd (was, were) beginning to get angry.

5. Canada and the United States (is, are) major trading partners.

6. Everybody in the room (has, have) heard that story before.

7. It (doesn't, don't) matter to me.

8. There (was, were) few people in the stands for the game.

9. The family (plan, plans) to have a reunion this summer.

10. Many of Jim's friends (was, were) at his birthday party.

11. Either Sonya or her sister (is, are) staying home with the sick dog.

12. The choice of the judges (is, are) final.

13. You, like many other students in this room, (want, wants) to get an English credit.

14. Almost every year, drought or heavy rain (cause, causes) damage to crops.

15. Cinda and her family (lives, live) in Kitchener.

MECHANICS

NAME: _____ DATE: _____

Correct any errors made in the following fictitious bibliography, in-text citations, and footnote.

BIBLIOGRAPHY

Jack Coleman, and Mary Wilson. Going to the Dogs. Vancouver: Canine, 1999

Robertson, Hugh Humans: A Dog's Best Friend. The Globe and Mail, October 7, 1998, page D 19

Dog Faxs. CD Rom. Doggone; Texas: 1996.

Dog Tales. Pets Corner. Host: William Greyhound DOG Television. Jan.18. 1998.

Michael Dogcatcher. Personal Interview, 17 Apr 1999

Turabian Susan. Dog Tired Charlottetown Kennel Publishing 1993

Blincq, Tina p. "Puppy Love. The Modern Dog Encyclopaedia. Edition 5, 1991.

IN-TEXT CITATION

Training your dog can be a wonderful experience Turbian, Pg.22

Every dog has a personality of its own (Hugh, 16)

FOOTNOTE

_____

1. Dogged, Jane and Mann, Linda. We Live in a Doggie Bag World (Hamilton, 1997): Dogmatic Press), 89.

USAGE & STYLE

NAME: _____   DATE: _____

Rewrite the following paragraphs by adding transitional devices to connect one idea to another. You will have to decide where adding these transitions will improve the piece of writing. Space has been left after each paragraph for your rewritten text. You may use the back of the page to complete the exercise.

This year I decided to take karate. I didn't know much about the sport. I had seen it in movies and on television. I thought I might enjoy it. I asked a friend of mine who was already taking karate if there was space available at his school. He said there was. I attended my first class. I was invited to watch the class. The purpose was to see what happened during a typical lesson. I was thoroughly impressed. I knew that I had made the right decision.

_____

_____

_____

_____

_____

_____

_____

I became good at karate. I began entering competitions. I did not win anything in my first competition. I placed third in my second competition and second in my most recent competition.

_____

_____

_____

I am improving. In my next competition, I am hoping to do even better.

_____

_____

_____

WORD STUDY & SPELLING

NAME: _____ DATE: _____

On the line provided, write the plural form of each of the following words.

1. a) copy_____
   b) wish_____
   c) hoof_____

   d) goose_____
   e) spy_____
   f) moose_____

   g) window_____
   h) tomato_____
   i) leaf_____

   j) year_____
   k) coach_____
   l) tooth_____

   m) knife_____
   n) radio_____
   o) bunch_____

   p) echo_____
   q) fox_____
   r) salmon_____

   s) man_____
   t) photo_____
   u) waitress_____

On the line provided, write the possessive form of each of the following plural nouns.

2. a) workers_____
   b) families_____
   c) doctors_____

   d) people_____
   e) experts_____
   f) sheep_____

   g) women_____
   h) teachers_____
   i) friends_____

   j) Elliotts_____
   k) mice_____
   l) Oilers_____

   m) mens_____
   n) guests_____
   o) racers_____

Correct any errors in the plurals or possessive plurals in the following sentences.

3. a) I attended the Don Mills' school to take karate. _____

   b) The schools mottoes were displayed in the corridors. _____

   c) The doctors' measured the pulses of the student's giving blood. _____

   d) The heroes were recognized for their deeds' of bravery. _____

   e) Our teams defeat was hard to take, but our coaches attitudes remained positive._____

   _____

   f) My friends's karate club will meet on Saturdays'. _____

   g) The painters and the sculptors supplies arrived early for the workshop. _____

   _____

   h) The two girl's carried their friend's books to their lockers'. _____

   i) The trouts were biting on the three fishermans fishing lines at the same time. _____

   _____

Unit 10: Comparison

Academic Expectations

GRADE 9 EXPECTATIONS		DEMONSTRATION OF LEARNING	ASSESSMENT TOOLS
LITERATURE STUDIES AND READING			
Overall (LIV.01D)	• read and demonstrate an understanding of a variety of literary and informational texts, from contemporary and historical periods		
Specific (LI1.02D)	• select and read texts for different purposes, with an emphasis on recognizing the elements of literary genres and the organization of informational materials, collecting and assessing information, responding imaginatively, and exploring human experiences and values	• speculate on motivation for writing model comparison and discuss what subject matter is easiest to write about (Extending the Model TG #2) • find humorous comparisons for class folder (Extending the Model TG #3)	• TOC 13: Tracking Expectations • TOC 13: Tracking Expectations
(LI1.03B)	• describe a variety of reading strategies and select and use them effectively before, during, and after reading to understand texts	• take a survey of class to create class profile of neat vs. sloppy people (Introducing the Model TG #1)	• TOC 13: Tracking Expectations
(LI1.04D)	• locate explicit information and ideas in texts to use in developing opinions and interpretations	• consider categories for comparison (Introducing the Unit TG #2) • give examples from model for use in interpretation (Investigating the Model SB #1–6) • make a group decision as to the three best examples of humour in model comparison (Oral Language Extension TG)	• TOC 13: Tracking Expectations • AR 22: Response to Reading • TOC 13: Tracking Expectations
(LI1.05D)	• analyze information, ideas, and elements in texts to make inferences about meaning	• support or reject author's judgments about human behaviour (Investigating the Model TG #2)	• TOC 13: Tracking Expectations
(LI1.06D)	• use specific evidence from a text to support opinions and judgments	• give reasons for author's position and purpose in using comparison form (Introducing the Model TG #2) • tell whether author has influenced their neat-vs.-sloppy behaviour (Investigating the Model TG #1)	• AR 22: Response to Reading • AR 22: Response to Reading
(LI1.07D)	• explain how readers' different backgrounds might influence the way they understand and interpret a text	• explain how readers respond differently to humour (Investigating the Model TG #3)	• TOC 13: Tracking Expectations
Overall (LIV.02D)	• demonstrate an understanding of the elements of a variety of literary and informational forms, with a focus on plays, short stories, and short essays	• work through as a class how to write a comparison (Introducing the Unit TG #1)	• TOC 13: Tracking Expectations
WRITING			
Overall (WRV.01D)	• use a variety of print and electronic sources to gather information and explore ideas for their written work	• gather and organize ideas for comparison (Writer's Workshop SB #1–6)	• AR 2: Comparison
Specific (WR1.01D)	• investigate potential topics by formulating questions, identifying information needs, and developing research plans to gather data	• consider methods of obtaining information when choosing topic for comparison (Writer's Workshop TG #1) • write five possible topic sentences for comparison (Writer's Workshop TG #2)	• AR 2: Comparison • AR 2: Comparison
(WR1.03D)	• group and label information and ideas, evaluate the relevance, accuracy, and completeness of the information and ideas; and discard irrelevant material	• use charts to compare information (More Support TG, page 229)	• AR 2: Comparison

AR=Assessment Rubric   EP=Extra Practice   SB=Student Book   SSEC=Student Self-Evaluation Checklist   TG=Teacher's Guide   TOC=Teacher Observation Checklist

WRITING (continued)		
Overall (WRV.03D) • use a variety of organizational techniques to present ideas and supporting details logically and coherently in written work	• write a comparison of two feelings (More Challenge TG, page 229) • write a comparison (Writer's Workshop SB #7)	• AR 2: Comparison • AR 2: Comparison
Overall (WRV.04D) • revise their written work, independently and collaboratively, with a focus on support for ideas and opinions, accuracy, clarity, and unity	• revise comparison (Writer's Workshop SB #8)	• AR 2: Comparison
Overall (WRV.05D) • edit and proofread to produce final drafts, using correct grammar, spelling, and punctuation, according to the conventions of standard Canadian English, with the support of print and electronic resources when appropriate	• edit and proofread comparison (Writer's Workshop SB #8)	• AR 2: Comparison
Specific (WR5.05D) • use parts of speech correctly: nouns, pronouns, verbs, adverbs, adjectives, conjunctions, prepositions, and interjections	• identify positive, comparative, and superlative forms of adjectives and adverbs (Grammar TG) • use comparative and superlative forms of adjectives and adverbs correctly (Grammar SB #1–2) • provide comparative or superlative form of adjectives or adverbs in cloze activity (More Support TG, page 231) • explain reasoning for decision to use comparative or superlative form of adjectives or adverbs (More Challenge TG, page 231) • use comparative or superlative form of adjectives or adverbs (EP: Grammar)	• TOC 4: Grammar • TOC 4: Grammar • TOC 4: Grammar • TOC 4: Grammar • TOC 4: Grammar
(WR5.06D) • construct complete and correct compound and complex sentences, using the following sentence components as required: subject, predicate, object, subject complement; main and subordinate clauses; prepositional and participial phrases	• correct errors in comparison sentences (Usage & Style TG) • correct errors in comparison sentences (Usage & Style SB #1–2) • correct errors in comparison sentences (EP: Usage & Style)	• TOC 15: Usage & Style • TOC 15: Usage & Style
(WR5.12B) • use and spell homophones correctly	• in pairs, list 10 homophones and 10 homographs (Word Study & Spelling TG #1) • learn strategy for spelling homophones (Word Study & Spelling TG #2) • use and spell homophones correctly (Word Study & Spelling SB #1–2) • use homophones correctly (EP: Word Study & Spelling)	• TOC 16: Word Study & Spelling • TOC 16: Word Study & Spelling • TOC 16: Word Study & Spelling • TOC 16: Word Study & Spelling
(WR5.15B) • use punctuation correctly, including period, question mark, exclamation mark, comma, dash, apostrophe, colon, quotation marks, parentheses, and ellipses	• use colons, semicolons, and dashes correctly (Mechanics TG) • use colons and semicolons correctly (Mechanics SB #1–2) • write a brief comparison of two cats using colons and semicolons (More Challenge TG, page 232) • use colons and semicolons correctly in comparison sentences (EP: Mechanics)	• TOC 8: Mechanics • TOC 8: Mechanics • TOC 8: Mechanics • TOC 8: Mechanics
LANGUAGE		
Overall (LGV.01D) • use knowledge of vocabulary and language conventions to speak, write, and read competently using a level of language appropriate to the purpose and audience		

AR=Assessment Rubric   EP=Extra Practice   SB=Student Book   SSEC=Student Self-Evaluation Checklist   TG=Teacher's Guide   TOC=Teacher Observation Checklist

	GRADE 9 EXPECTATIONS	DEMONSTRATION OF LEARNING	ASSESSMENT TOOLS
	LANGUAGE (continued)		
Specific (LG1.03B)	• identify words borrowed from other languages and words and terms recently introduced to describe new ideas, inventions, and products, and explain their origins	• find Arabic roots of words (Word Origins SB)	• TOC 16: Word Study & Spelling
Specific (LG1.05D)	• recognize, describe, and use correctly, in oral and written language, the language structures of standard Canadian English and its conventions of grammar and usage, including: – parts of speech: nouns, pronouns, verbs, adverbs, adjectives, conjunctions, prepositions, interjections – components of sentences: subject, predicate, object, subject complement, prepositional and participial phrases, main and subordinate clauses	• identify positive, comparative, and superlative forms of adjectives and adverbs (Grammar TG) • use comparative and superlative forms of adjectives and adverbs correctly (Grammar SB #1–2) • provide comparative or superlative form of adjectives or adverbs in cloze activity (More Support TG, page 231) • explain reasoning for decision to use comparative or superlative form of adjectives or adverbs (More Challenge TG, page 231) • correct errors in comparison sentences (Usage & Style TG) • correct errors in comparison sentences (Usage & Style SB #1–2) • use comparative or superlative form of adjectives or adverbs (EP: Grammar) • correct errors in comparison sentences (EP: Usage & Style)	• TOC 4: Grammar • TOC 4: Grammar • TOC 4: Grammar • TOC 4: Grammar • TOC 15: Usage & Style • TOC 15: Usage & Style • TOC 4: Grammar • TOC 15: Usage & Style
(LG1.07B)	• recognize, describe, and use correctly, in oral and written language, the conventions of standard Canadian English for spelling, capitalization, and punctuation, including: – spelling: homophones and possessive pronouns and adjectives – punctuation: period, question mark, exclamation mark, comma, dash, apostrophe, colon, quotation marks, parentheses, ellipses	• use colons, semicolons, and dashes correctly (Mechanics TG) • use colons and semicolons correctly (Mechanics SB #1–2) • write a brief comparison of two cats using colons and semicolons (More Challenge TG, page 232) • in pairs, list 10 homophones and 10 homographs (Word Study & Spelling TG #1) • learn strategy for spelling homophones (Word Study & Spelling TG #2) • use and spell homophones correctly (Word Study & Spelling SB #1–2) • use colons and semicolons correctly in comparison sentences (EP: Mechanics) • use homophones correctly (EP: Word Study & Spelling)	• TOC 8: Mechanics • TOC 8: Mechanics • TOC 8: Mechanics • TOC 16: Word Study & Spelling • TOC 16: Word Study & Spelling • TOC 16: Word Study & Spelling • TOC 8: Mechanics • TOC 16: Word Study & Spelling
Overall (LGV.02B)	• use listening techniques and oral communication skills to participate in classroom discussions and more formal activities, such as storytelling, role playing, and reporting/presenting, for specific purposes and audiences	• role-play argument between neat people and sloppy people (Extending the Model TG #1)	• SSEC 5: Oral Presentation
Specific (LG2.01D)	• communicate orally in group discussions for different purposes, with a focus on identifying key ideas and supporting details, distinguishing fact from opinion, asking clarifying questions, and following instructions	• listen critically to partner's comparison and take notes (More Oral Language TG)	• TOC 7: Listening
(LG2.07D)	• analyze their own and others' oral presentations to identify strengths and weaknesses, and plan ways to improve their performance	• present role-play on group behaviour for class to identify problems and suggest solutions (Oral Language Extension SB)	• SSEC 2: Group Work

AR=Assessment Rubric   EP=Extra Practice   SB=Student Book   SSEC=Student Self-Evaluation Checklist   TG=Teacher's Guide   TOC=Teacher Observation Checklist

GRADE 9 EXPECTATIONS		DEMONSTRATION OF LEARNING	ASSESSMENT TOOLS
MEDIA STUDIES			
Overall (MDV.01D)	• use knowledge of the elements, intended audiences, and production practices of a variety of media forms to analyze specific media works	• discuss best method of writing comparison for newspaper (Media Link TG)	• AR 21: Response to Media
Specific (MD1.02D)	• identify how elements of media forms are used in a variety of media works and explain the effects of different treatments	• compare front pages of three daily newspapers (Media Link SB)	• AR 21: Response to Media
(MD1.03D)	• compare and explain their own and their peers' reactions to a variety of media works	• compare reactions to three newspapers as regards types of news and their appeal (More Media TG)	• AR 21: Response to Media

AR=Assessment Rubric   EP=Extra Practice   SB=Student Book   SSEC=Student Self-Evaluation Checklist   TG=Teacher's Guide   TOC=Teacher Observation Checklist

PLANNING INFORMATION

Links to Other Nelson English 9 Resources

Literature & Media 9
See "Mr. Preston (and Mr. Rawat) Go to New Delhi" by John Stackhouse, pp. 152–154 and "Dogs and Books" by Christie Blatchford, pp. 168–170.

Write Source 2000
Comparison—"Comparison/Contrast," p. 312; **Colons**—"Colon," p. 394; **Comparative and Superlative**—"Forms of Adjectives," p. 453; "Adverb," p. 454; **Dashes**—"Dash," p. 395; **Homophones**—"Using the Right Word," pp. 419–433; **Semicolons**—"Semicolon," p. 393

LEARNING GOALS

- write a comparison
- use comparative and superlative forms of adjectives and adverbs correctly
- use colons, semicolons, and dashes correctly
- recognize and correct errors in comparison sentences
- learn to use homophones correctly

INTRODUCING THE UNIT

1. In this unit, comparisons are studied as a writing technique for examining the similarities *and* differences of two or more subjects or for identifying the similarities *or* differences of two or more subjects exclusively. Begin by asking students to think about situations where they use comparisons in everyday life. List examples on the board and point out how they use comparisons for different purposes: for example, to persuade a friend to do one thing rather than another; to explain how two technologies differ—a mountain bike versus a racing bicycle; or to describe two different items—perhaps two different travel destinations.

   Put three headings—Persuasion, Exposition, and Description—on the board and discuss with students how to categorize their examples under the different headings. Then take one of the examples and work through with the class how to go about writing a comparison. Encourage students to suggest how the two things being compared are similar and how they are different. (LIV.02D—TOC 13: Tracking Expectations)

2. Have students read the opening paragraph of the unit and then discuss briefly what categories they would use to compare the two cats in the illustration: perhaps, physical description, role, habitat, and food. (LI1.04D—TOC 13: Tracking Expectations)

INTRODUCING THE MODEL

1. Put the following line graph on the board.

   Very Neat   Neat Most of the Time   Sloppy Most of the Time   Very Sloppy

   Ask students to copy the graph in their notebooks and put a check mark somewhere on the line to describe the usual condition of their bedrooms. Take a survey of the class for each of the categories to create a class profile, noting the numbers for each category on the graph. Ask those students who made a check mark on the left side of the line to give reasons why it is important for them to keep their bedrooms neat. Record, in point form, some of their answers under the left side of the chart. Repeat the process with those students who made a check mark on the right side of the line, recording their answers under the right side of the chart. (LI1.03B—TOC 13: Tracking Expectations)

2. Ask students to read the model to determine which of the positions (neat or sloppy) the author favours, and the reasons for her position. Discuss their answers briefly and then ask them to suggest what the author's purpose was in using comparison for this piece. (LI1.06D—AR 22: Response to Reading)

INVESTIGATING THE MODEL

1. After students have read the model, ask if any of them who said that their rooms were "neat" or "neat most of the time" have changed their minds about keeping their bedrooms neat. Why or why not? What do they think about the way Suzanne Britt has characterized neat people? (LI1.06D—AR 22: Response to Reading)

2. The author states that the distinction between neat people and sloppy people is moral. What does she mean by this? (moral: of or concerned with the judgment of the goodness or badness of human action and character). Which of her judgments about human action or behaviour do you think are valid? Which do you think are invalid? (LI1.05D—AR 22: Response to Reading)

3. Humour is often difficult to write. Ask students if they agree with this statement and if so, to suggest some reasons for it. Then ask them to comment on Suzanne Britt's use of humour. (Humour is difficult to write because not all people find humour in the same things, often because of differences in culture, gender, religion, or experiences. One reason why Britt's humour may work is because she uses exaggeration based on examples which most people can relate to from their everyday lives.) (LI1.07D—TOC 13: Tracking Expectations)

Answers:

1. Possible answers
   Britt's purpose affects her presentation in the following ways:
   Word Choice (examples: "lazier and meaner"; "a heavenly vision"; "Never-Never Land"; "noble reasons"; "loving attention"; "excavation"; "bums and clods"; "sentimental salvaging")
   Organization: She writes about sloppy people first because she believes their position is the better one.
   Content: The following examples show how Britt chooses to write very positively about sloppy people and very negatively about neat people.
   "Sloppy people, you see, are not really sloppy."
   "They aim too high and wide."
   "They give loving attention to every detail."
   "Sloppy people carry in their mind's eye a heavenly vision, a precise plan, that is so perfect, it can't be achieved in this world or the next."
   "Neat people are bums and clods at heart."
   "Everything is just another dust catcher to them."
   "Neat people are especially vicious with mail."
   "A neat person would just bulldoze the desk."

2. The author bases her points for comparison on observation and analysis. It is valid because most of her argument is based on her own opinions rather than on facts. If this article were based on research, it would present only facts, not opinions. The humour of the model would be lost.

3. Thesis: Neat people are lazier and meaner than sloppy people. Four possible paragraphs that relate to the thesis:
   The third paragraph on page 159 tries to show how diligently sloppy people work to carry out their precise plan.
   The second paragraph on page 160 demonstrates how neat people are mean: "Neat people will toy with the idea of throwing the children out of the house just to cut down on the clutter."
   Again, the fifth paragraph on page 160 shows how "mean" neat people can be: "No sentimental salvaging of birthday cards or the last letter a dying relative ever wrote. Into the trash it goes."

CHECKPOINT

Sample criteria for a comparison:

- is used in descriptive, expository, or persuasive writing to examine two or more subjects

- uses points for comparison based on direct observation, analysis, or research

- contains a thesis sentence that limits scope and reveals purpose

- is usually organized by block method (arranged by subject) or by point-by-point method (arranged by characteristics)

- may include both common elements of topics and distinctions between or among topics

The last paragraph on page 160 shows how neat people are lazy: "I knew a neat person once who threw away a perfectly good dish drainer because it had mold on it. The drainer was too much trouble to wash."

4. Britt uses the Block Method. In the first half of her comparison, she emphasizes how superior sloppy people are and in the second half, she criticizes neat people. This organization allows her to: provide stronger arguments than if she used the Point-by-Point Method; use different criteria for describing the traits of sloppy people (e.g., "Sloppy people ... are not really sloppy.") and neat people (e.g., "Neat people place neatness above everything, even economics."); avoid having to describe the same characteristic for both sloppy people and neat people.

5. Suzanne Britt focuses on differences. This allows her to cite many humorous examples to show how sloppy people are superior to neat people and allows her to avoid weakening the effect of her writing by admitting any similarities between the two.

6. In the model, the comparison simply stops at the end of the section describing neat people. The piece might have ended with a conclusion or summary relating back to the thesis in the opening paragraph. However, with a piece of writing meant to entertain as opposed to inform, the exaggeration of the last statement is probably a more effective way to maintain the humour of the piece rather than trying to sum up the argument.

Student Book 1.–6. (LI1.04D—AR 22: Response to Reading)

EXTENDING THE MODEL

1. In groups of four, have students role-play neat people and sloppy people. Two of the students will be neat people, and two students, sloppy people. Provide the following situation: The four of you are spending a week together camping. You are all sleeping in one tent. After three days, you are beginning to argue among yourselves about the state of your campsite and the interior of the tent. Ask students to role-play the argument which takes place and to bring the role-play to a satisfactory conclusion. (LGV.02B—SSEC 5: Oral Presentation)

2. Have students speculate on Suzanne Britt's motivation for writing about neat people and sloppy people. Why is it easier to write about things you have experienced yourself? (LI1.02D—TOC 13: Tracking Expectations)

3. Ask students to search out other humorous comparisons to bring to class. Place them in a folder entitled "Humorous Comparisons" and circulate for all to read. These comparisons could also be used for ideas for the Writer's Workshop. (LI1.02D—TOC 13: Tracking Expectations)

WRITER'S WORKSHOP

1. When considering their topics, ask students to consider the three methods of obtaining information for their comparisons: direct observation, analysis, and research. Their choice of method may influence their choice of topic. Since the research report in Unit 9 emphasized the use of research, you may wish to limit students to the use of direct observation and analysis for this assignment. If so, they would need to limit their topics to those which require this type of information-gathering. (WR1.01D—AR 2: Comparison)

2. Ask students to use the chart on the following page to write five possible topic sentences. One example is provided. (WR1.01D—AR 2: Comparison)

Key Point	Topic Sentence
cost	A trip to Florida will cost you less than a cruise.

Student Book 1.–6. (WRV.01D—AR 2: Comparison); 7. (WRV.03D—AR 2: Comparison); 8. (WRV.04D—AR 2: Comparison; WRV.05D—AR 2: Comparison)

MORE ORAL LANGUAGE

Point out to students that every day people appeal to them to accept particular points of view. These appeals come from print, television, and from family and friends. In order to make decisions about things they hear, they must be good critical listeners. Have students work with a partner in the following activity: students take turns reading their comparisons to each other; as one person reads, the other listens carefully for the following: introduction, thesis, topic sentences and examples, and summary or conclusion; each student writes a few notes while listening and afterward completes the notes by filling in important details; students tell each other why they agree or disagree with the thesis and then critique the examples used. (LG2.01D—TOC 7: Listening)

MORE CHALLENGE

Sometimes it is difficult to know when to use an adjective and when to use an adverb. Ask students which of the following sentences they think is correct.

Trash grows *quick* in a sloppy person's room.

Trash grows *quickly* in a sloppy person's room.

Explain to students that they can ask two questions to determine whether an adjective or adverb is required:

- What kind of word does the modifier describe? (If the word is a noun or pronoun, use an adjective. If the word is an action verb, adjective, or adverb, use an adverb.)
- Does the modifier tell how, when, where, or to what extent? (If so, the modifier should probably be an adverb.)

Have students work in small groups to develop examples demonstrating the difficulty of deciding whether to use an adjective or an adverb. Each group could put an example on the board and ask the class which sentence is correct and whether the modifier is an adjective or an adverb, giving their reasoning for the choice using the two questions suggested above. (WR5.05D—TOC 4: Grammar; LG1.05D—TOC 4: Grammar)

ORAL LANGUAGE EXTENSION

You may wish to assign a topic for the role-play suggested in the student book to illustrate a poorly functioning group. One possibility is to have students reread the model on their own and pick out three examples of humour that they liked the best. Then have them discuss their individual choices in their groups and role-play coming to a group decision on the three best examples. (LI1.04D—TOC 13: Tracking Expectations)

Student Book (LG2.07D—SSEC 2: Group Work)

GRAMMAR

Point out to students that we use the term "comparison" to refer to adjectives and adverbs that show varying degrees of intensity. Ask students for the formal names given to these three degrees of intensity (positive, comparative, and superlative), and when each form should be used. (Use comparative when comparing two things; use superlative when comparing more than two things.) Write the sets of sentences below on the board. Ask students to identify the part of speech of the underlined words in each of the sentence groups (first and fourth groups: adjectives; second and third groups: adverbs). Then have students name which form of adjective or adverb is in each sentence. (The first sentence in each group contains the positive, the second sentence, the comparative, and the third sentence, the superlative.)

His comparison was <u>clear</u>.
His comparison was <u>clearer</u> than mine.
His comparison was the <u>clearest</u> in the class.

She finished writing her comparison <u>early</u>.
She finished writing her comparison <u>earlier</u> than me.
She finished writing her comparison <u>earliest</u> of all.

My comparison was <u>tightly</u> structured.
My comparison was <u>more tightly</u> structured.
My comparison was <u>the most tightly</u> structured.

Their comparison provided <u>little</u> information.
Their comparison provided <u>less</u> information than ours.
Their comparison provided <u>the least</u> information of all.

Ask students why "less" is used instead of "littler" in the second last sentence, and "least" instead of "littlest" in the last sentence. (Some comparatives and superlatives are formed in irregular ways.) (WR5.05D—TOC 4: Grammar; LG1.05D—TOC 4: Grammar)

Answers:

1. Most people think that being neat is better than being messy, but Suzanne Britt has a different idea. She believes that neat people are the meaner of the two personality types, and that the sloppier you are, the better you are. Britt may be better informed than I, but in my experience we neat people are more likely to have time to be nice. Unlike sloppy people, we get the more boring work out of the way so we can concentrate on helping others. Besides, neat people are the

least likely of all people to "watch the rasslin' on TV" because we could never stand to see all those bodies littering the ring!

2. Possible answers

Of the two types of people, sloppy people seem the happier.

Sam is sloppy; Terry is sloppier.

Sloppy people have better stories to tell than neat people.

Neat people answer their mail sooner than sloppy people.

Neat people empty the trash more often than sloppy people.

Student Book 1.–2. (WR5.05D—TOC 4: Grammar; LG1.05D—TOC 4: Grammar)

MEDIA LINK

Discuss with students the way newspaper articles are written in inverted pyramid style (most important to least important). Why does a newspaper usually structure its facts this way? (Editors can cut the length of the story and it will still appear as a whole piece.) Given that newspaper articles are organized this way, which method (Block or Point-by-Point) would you be most likely to use if you were writing a comparison for a newspaper? (Point-by-Point) (MDV.01D—AR 21: Response to Media)

If you are not able to obtain sufficient newspapers for each student, have students do the activity in small groups.

Student Book (MD1.02D—AR 21: Response to Media)

MECHANICS

Divide the class into six groups. Using the jigsaw method—two groups of experts for each of the colon, the semicolon, and the dash—have students list all of the rules they know for using these punctuation marks. Students may refer to a handbook for the rules, but only after they have tried to list all of them on their own. When students return to their home groups, they must give a brief review of the use of their assigned punctuation marks using examples. In particular, their review should refer to the use of punctuation marks as outlined in the student book, including the information highlighted in purple, and the two Writing Tip boxes. (WR5.15B—TOC 8: Mechanics; LG1.07B—TOC 8: Mechanics)

Answers:

1. Possible answers

Looking at a sloppy person's room, you might observe some of the following: books spilling onto the floor, clothes piling up in the hamper and the closet, family mementos accumulating in every drawer, the desk buried under mounds of paper, and unread magazines threatening to reach the ceiling.

A neat person files the following items of mail in the trash can: ads, catalogues, pleas for charitable contributions, church bulletins, and money-saving coupons.

A neat person would not consider any of the following: clipping a coupon, saving a leftover, reusing plastic nondairy whipped cream containers, or rinsing off tin foil and draping it over the unmoldy dish drainer.

2. a) Neat people are worse than sloppy people in two ways: they are lazier and meaner. (restatement or description)
   b) A neat person uses a three-step process for everything: he will look at it, try to decide if it has immediate use, and, finding none, throw it in the trash. (list)
   c) A common theme runs through all these examples: it is better to be too sloppy than too neat. (description of common theme)
   d) Neat people don't care about process; however, they like results. (related clauses)

The following is an oral cloze activity. Ask students to listen to the sentences you are about to read. Tell them that in each sentence they will hear you say the word "blank," and then, at the end of the sentence, the positive form of the word. They are to fill in the blank with the comparative or superlative form. Ask students to write their answers in their notebooks. (WR5.05D—TOC 4: Grammar; LG1.05D—TOC 4: Grammar)

a) The temperature is _____ today than it was yesterday. (warm)

b) I will need to be _____ in following the directions next time. (careful)

c) Of all the televisions available, this one performs the _____. (good)

d) I finished writing my comparison_____ than Laura. (fast)

e) She is the _____ musician in the orchestra. (bad)

f) I found this trip to be _____ than our last one. (enjoyable)

Have students work in small groups for the following activity. Examine the front pages of the three newspapers and classify them according to the following categories: good news, bad news, and neutral news. Collect the results from each group and compare them, paper to paper. Then have students rank the items on the front page of each newspaper according to the following: the most important news; the most interesting news; the items that most people would read first; the items that would appeal to older readers; the items that would appeal to younger readers. Have students share their results, and discuss the implications (the most important news is not always the most interesting; newspapers must try to appeal to a variety of readers; newspapers are mostly designed for older readers). (MD1.03D—AR 21: Response to Media)

e) There is only one messy thing in a neat person's house: the trash can. (restatement)

f) Neat people are incredibly wasteful; on the other hand, messy people can't bear to part with anything. (related clauses)

Student Book 1.–2. (WR5.15B—TOC 8: Mechanics; LG1.07B—TOC 8: Mechanics)

USAGE & STYLE

Explain to students that some words often cause confusion when used in comparisons. Distribute the following sentences (double-spaced). Indicate that some of the sentences have errors in them while others do not. Ask students to make any corrections necessary in the space provided above the sentence.

Sloppy people have a loftier vision of the world then neat people. (than)

My friend differed from me on the condition of our room. (differed with)

Our classroom has less bulletin boards than yours. (fewer)

Your situation is uniquer than mine. (more unique)

The coach differed with me about the best strategy to use. (correct)

That school is different from our school. (correct)

Compared to other club meetings, this one has the least members. (fewest)

Our garage has fewer space than our neighbour's. (less)

I can't believe the teams are different than they were before. (correct)

Once completed, ask students to check their answers for errors using the purple boxes and the examples on pages 168–169 of the student book. Take up the correct answers, clarifying any problems or misunderstandings students may have. (WR5.06D—TOC 15: Usage & Style; LG1.05D—TOC 15: Usage & Style)

Answers:

1. a) How does my desk differ *from* your vision of what a desk should look like?
   b) Linda is much neater *than* Rhonda.
   c) "I beg to differ *with* you," she replied.
   d) I've finally figured out how neat people are different *from* sloppy people.
   e) Sloppy people carry in their mind's eye a view that is different from *that of* neat people.
   f) Your ideas about attention to detail are different *from* mine.
   g) I differ *with* you on several points.

2. In my opinion, sloppy people are *cooler* than neat people. For one thing, they are *more* entertaining because you never know how they will manage things. Neat people are less *likely* to try something new; rather, their approach to life is more predictable. While both types of people are, in their own way, *different*, sloppy people are *sharper* when it comes to saving something valuable. While neat people spend *less* time saving things, sloppy people savour the time spent organizing their piles of clutter. Also, neat people spend *fewer* hours at important tasks.

Student Book 1.–2. (WR5.06D—TOC 15: Usage & Style; LG1.05D—TOC 15: Usage & Style)

WORD STUDY & SPELLING

1. Write the words homophone and homograph on the board. Ask students to explain, giving one example for each, how these types of words are different. (Homophones have the same sound, but different meanings and spellings; homographs are spelled the same, but have different meanings and origins.) Explain that these words come from Greek: *homo* meaning *same*; *phone* meaning *sound*; *graph* meaning *writing*. Add more examples if necessary.

Examples: Homophones: where, wear; road, rowed, rode
           Homographs: palm meaning palm of your hand and palm referring to
           a tree; nag meaning an old horse and nag meaning "to annoy"

Working in pairs, ask students to make a list of 10 homophones and
10 homographs. Ask for student volunteers to compile a class list of these word
pairs and triplets. Post the list in the class. (WR5.12B—TOC 16: Word Study &
Spelling; LG1.07B—TOC 16: Word Study & Spelling)

2. Place the following sets of words on the board.

sail: sailor, sailboard, sailboat   sale: saleable, salesperson, sales tax

Point out to students that one way to differentiate homophones is to associate
each word with other words that they know with similar meanings and/or spelling
patterns. Ask students how the words following each of the homophones on the
board would help them to differentiate the spelling of the homophones. Compile
a class list of words for each homophone from the list in activity #1 above.
(WR5.12B—TOC 16: Word Study & Spelling; LG1.07B—TOC 16: Word Study &
Spelling)

Answers:

1. a) two, too   b) sea   c) witch
   d) male   e) threw   f) there, they're
   g) by, bye   h) new, gnu   i) hole

Possible sentences for a) and b):
a) I wore two different coloured socks to school by mistake and in addition, I got
   there too late for my first class.
b) You could see the sea from the top window of the old mansion.

2. Possible answers
   b) see: seem, seen, seek   sea: seal, seabed, seacoast
   f) their: theirs   there: therefore, thereabouts, thereafter
                                      they're: they'll, they'd, they've
   g) buy: buyer, buy time, buy out by: bypass, bygone, bylaw, byproduct
                                      bye: bye-bye, good bye
   h) knew: know, knowledge   new: newborn, news, Newfoundland
   i) whole: wholesome,   hole: hole-in-one, in the hole
      wholehearted, wholeness

Student Book 1.–2. (WR5.12B—TOC 16: Word Study & Spelling; LG1.07B—TOC 16:
Word Study & Spelling)

WORD ORIGINS

Answers:

zero: originally from the Arabic word *sifr* meaning *nothing* or *cipher*;
one of the meanings of *cipher* in the dictionary is "the
mathematical symbol (0) denoting absence of quantity: zero"

algebra: originally from the Arabic words *al-jabr* meaning *the (science of) reuniting*:
al, the + *jabr*, reunification or bonesetting

checkmate: originally from the Arabic words *shah mat* meaning *the king is dead; shah*
is from Persian and means *king*

safari: from the Arabic word *safari* meaning *journey*

Student Book (LG1.03B—TOC 16: Word Study & Spelling)

ANSWERS TO EXTRA PRACTICE

Grammar

1. Of the four comparisons, this one is the most interesting.

2. Knowledge about writing forms has become more important to high school students.

3. These exercises were completed the fastest.

4. Who scored more baskets during the first half of the game, Leah or Samantha?

5. This type of shoe is the best of all.

6. Raymond is working more slowly than Jeff.

7. All of the comparisons were good, but Noah's was best.

8. Which of these exercises is the most difficult?

9. Of the six cars tested, this one used the least gas.

10. The friendliest person in our group is Mara.

(WR5.05D—TOC 4: Grammar; LG1.05D—TOC 4: Grammar)

Mechanics

1. In our dance competition, the first place winner gets gold; second place, silver; and third place, bronze.

2. Following are the medals which will be awarded at the dance competition: gold, silver, and bronze.

3. There will be pizza available after the dance; however, it will cost $2.00 per slice.

4. The star player scored three goals; the fans went wild.

5. The following foods are needed for the Food Bank: soup, peanut butter, and cereal.

6. The following cities are experiencing tremendous growth: Vancouver, British Columbia; Calgary, Alberta; Waterloo, Ontario; and Halifax, Nova Scotia.

7. Not a sound was to be heard; not a breath was to be taken.

8. I found a knapsack containing the following: two textbooks, a lunch bag, and a pencil case.

9. I do not plan on attending the practice; moreover, I am writing a letter to the coach.

10. The problem looks very easy; in fact, it is quite difficult.

(WR5.15B—TOC 8: Mechanics; LG1.07B—TOC 8: Mechanics)

Usage & Style

1. He is much neater than his friends.

2. I think I am very different from you.

3. Their approach to the problem is unique.

4. Your locker has less clutter than mine.

5. My teacher differed with me on the solution to the problem.

6. Tell me that your manners and conduct are different from what they were last week.

7. There were fewer peanuts in the jar following the movie.

8. We cleaned up the mess, put the furniture back in place, then turned down the music.

9. The colour of her jacket is different from yours.

10. I differ with Tara's idea about the best use of the funds.

(WR5.06D—TOC 15: Usage & Style; LG1.05D—TOC 15: Usage & Style)

Word Study & Spelling

1. The sale at the store included some two-for-one items.

2. I sent the principal a copy of the minutes from our student council meeting.

3. Do you think we should paint the ceiling white or blue?

4. You're not going to bleach your hair red, are you?

5. The weather is going to be foul tomorrow. Plan to wear something warm.

6. Did you buy some cereal at the grocery store when you were there?

7. They hoped for peace after the reign of the dictator ended.

8. Will you please buy me something for my weak condition?

9. We heard that the creek will have its course changed. Do you know why this is so?

10. The lead pail was too heavy to lift. A wooden one would have been more practical.

(WR5.12B—TOC 16: Word Study & Spelling; LG1.07B—TOC 16: Word Study & Spelling)

GRADE 9 EXPECTATIONS	DEMONSTRATION OF LEARNING	ASSESSMENT TOOLS
LITERATURE STUDIES AND READING		
Overall (LIV.01P)	• read and demonstrate an understanding of a variety of literary and informational texts		
Specific (LI1.02P)	• select and read texts for a variety of purposes, with an emphasis on recognizing the elements of literary genres and the organization of informational materials, collecting and using information, extending personal knowledge, and responding imaginatively	• discover whether author compares similarities, differences, or both (Introducing the Model TG #1) • speculate on motivation for writing model comparison and discuss what subject matter is easiest to write about (Extending the Model TG #2)	• AR 22: Response to Reading • TOC 14: Tracking Expectations
(LI1.03B)	• describe a variety of reading strategies and select and use them effectively before, during, and after reading to understand texts	• share experiences when comparisons were made (Introducing the Unit TG) • take a survey of class to create class profile of neat vs. sloppy people (Introducing the Model TG #2)	• TOC 14: Tracking Expectations • TOC 14: Tracking Expectations
(LI1.04P)	• locate and use explicit information and ideas from texts in forming opinions and developing generalizations	• create lists to clarify author's position and identify main arguments (Investigating the Model TG #2) • give examples from model for use in interpretation (Investigating the Model SB #1–6) • choose three topic sentences from model and explain effectiveness (Extending the Model TG #3) • make a group decision as to the three best examples of humour in model comparison (Oral Language Extension TG)	• TOC 14: Tracking Expectations • AR 22: Response to Reading • AR 22: Response to Reading • TOC 14: Tracking Expectations
(LI1.06B)	• use specific references from a text to support opinions and judgments	• tell whether author has influenced their neat-vs.-sloppy behaviour (Investigating the Model TG #2)	• AR 22: Response to Reading
Overall (L1V.02P)	• demonstrate an understanding of the elements of a variety of literary and informational forms, with a focus on plays, short stories, and newspaper and magazine articles		
Specific (L12.03P)	• use knowledge of elements of newspaper and magazine articles, such as headlines, leads, the five W's (who, what, where, when, and why), titles, subtitles, and photographs, to understand and interpret texts in the genre	• examine and compare newspapers (More Media TG)	• TOC 14: Tracking Expectations
WRITING		
Overall (WRV.01P)	• use print and electronic sources to gather information and explore ideas for their written work	• gather and organize ideas for comparison (Writer's Workshop SB #1–6)	• AR 2: Comparison
Specific (WR1.01P)	• investigate potential topics by asking questions, identifying information needs, and developing research plans to gather data	• write five possible topic sentences for comparison (Writer's Workshop TG #2)	• AR 2: Comparison
Overall (WRV.03P)	• use a variety of forms of writing to express themselves, clarify their ideas, and engage the audience's attention, imagination, and interest	• rewrite model comparison from opposite point of view (Writer's Workshop TG #1) • write a comparison (Writer's Workshop SB #7)	• AR 2: Comparison • AR 2: Comparison
Overall (WRV.04B)	• revise their written work, collaboratively and independently, with a focus on support for ideas, accuracy, clarity, and unity	• revise comparison (Writer's Workshop SB #8)	• AR 2: Comparison
Overall (WRV.05B)	• edit and proofread to produce final drafts, using correct grammar, spelling, and punctuation, according to the conventions of standard Canadian English specified for this course, with the support of print and electronic resources when appropriate	• edit and proofread comparison (Writer's Workshop SB #8)	• AR 2: Comparison

AR=Assessment Rubric   EP=Extra Practice   SB=Student Book   SSEC=Student Self-Evaluation Checklist   TG=Teacher's Guide   TOC=Teacher Observation Checklist

WRITING (continued)		
Specific (WR5.05P) • identify and use parts of speech correctly: nouns, pronouns, verbs, adverbs, adjectives, conjunctions, prepositions, and interjections	• identify positive, comparative, and superlative forms of adjectives and adverbs (Grammar TG) • use comparative and superlative forms of adjectives and adverbs correctly (Grammar SB #1–2) • correct sentences with comparative or superlative forms of adjectives or adverbs (More Challenge TG, page 241) • use comparative or superlative forms of adjectives or adverbs (EP: Grammar)	• TOC 4: Grammar • TOC 4: Grammar • TOC 4: Grammar • TOC 4: Grammar
(WR5.06P) • construct complete and correct compound and complex sentences, using the following sentence components as required: subject, predicate, object, subject complement; main and subordinate clauses; prepositional phrases	• correct errors in comparison sentences (Usage & Style TG) • correct errors in comparison sentences (Usage & Style SB #1–2) • correct errors in comparison sentences (EP: Usage & Style)	• TOC 15: Usage & Style • TOC 15: Usage & Style • TOC 15: Usage & Style
(WR5.12B) • use and spell homophones correctly	• identify homophones in sentences (Word Study & Spelling TG) • use and spell homophones correctly (Word Study & Spelling SB #1–2) • write homophones (More Support TG, page 242) • use homophones correctly (EP: Word Study & Spelling)	• TOC 16: Word Study & Spelling • TOC 16: Word Study & Spelling • TOC 16: Word Study & Spelling • TOC 16: Word Study & Spelling
(WR5.15B) • use punctuation correctly, including period, question mark, exclamation mark, comma, dash, apostrophe, colon, quotation marks, parentheses, and ellipses	• scan through newspapers and magazines to find examples of sentences that illustrate rules for colons, semicolons, and dashes (Mechanics TG #1) • insert correct punctuation in sentences and justify (Mechanics TG #2) • explain reasons for punctuation (More Challenge TG, page 242) • use colons and semicolons correctly in comparison sentences (EP: Mechanics)	• TOC 8: Mechanics • TOC 8: Mechanics • TOC 8: Mechanics • TOC 8: Mechanics
LANGUAGE		
Overall (LGV.01P) • use knowledge of vocabulary and language conventions to speak, write, and read clearly and correctly		
Specific (LG1.03B) • identify words borrowed from other languages, and words and terms recently introduced to describe new ideas, inventions, and products, and explain their origins	• find Arabic roots of words (Word Origins SB)	• TOC 16: Word Study & Spelling
(LG1.05P) • recognize, describe, and use correctly, in oral and written language, the language structures of standard Canadian English and its conventions of grammar and usage, including: – parts of speech: nouns, pronouns, verbs, adverbs, adjectives, conjunctions, prepositions, and interjections – components of sentences: subject, predicate, object, subject complement, prepositional phrases, main and subordinate clauses	• identify positive, comparative, and superlative forms of adjectives and adverbs (Grammar TG) • use comparative and superlative forms of adjectives and adverbs (Grammar SB #1–2) • correct sentences with comparative or superlative forms of adjectives or adverbs (More Challenge TG, page 241) • correct errors in comparison sentences (Usage & Style TG) • correct errors in comparison sentences (Usage & Style SB #1–2) • use comparative or superlative form of adjectives or adverbs (EP: Grammar) • correct errors in comparison sentences (EP: Usage & Style	• TOC 4: Grammar • TOC 4: Grammar • TOC 4: Grammar • TOC 15: Usage & Style • TOC 15: Usage & Style • TOC 4: Grammar • TOC 15: Usage & Style

AR=Assessment Rubric   EP=Extra Practice   SB=Student Book   SSEC=Student Self-Evaluation Checklist   TG=Teacher's Guide   TOC=Teacher Observation Checklist

GRADE 9 EXPECTATIONS	DEMONSTRATION OF LEARNING	ASSESSMENT TOOLS
LANGUAGE (continued)		
(LG1.07B) • recognize, describe, and use correctly, in oral and written language, the conventions of standard Canadian English for spelling, capitalization, and punctuation, including: – spelling: homophones and possessive pronouns and adjectives – punctuation: period, question mark, exclamation mark, comma, dash, apostrophe, colon, quotation marks, parentheses, ellipses	• scan through newspapers and magazines to find examples of sentences that illustrate rules for colons, semicolons, and dashes (Mechanics TG #1) • insert correct punctuation in sentences and justify (Mechanics #2) • explain reasons for punctuation (More Challenge TG, page 242) • identify homophones in sentences (Word Study & Spelling TG) • identify homophones in sentences (Word Study & Spelling SB #1–2) • write homophones (More Support TG, page 242) • use colons and semicolons correctly in comparison sentences (EP: Mechanics) • use homophones correctly (EP: Word Study & Spelling)	• TOC 8: Mechanics • TOC 8: Mechanics • TOC 8: Mechanics • TOC 16: Word Study & Spelling • TOC 16: Word Study & Spelling • TOC 16: Word Study & Spelling • TOC 8: Mechanics • TOC 16: Word Study & Spelling
Overall (LGV.02B) • use listening techniques and oral communication skills to participate in classroom discussions and more formal activities, such as storytelling, role playing, and reporting/ presenting, for specific purposes and audiences	• role-play argument between neat people and sloppy people (Extending the Model TG #1)	• SSEC 5: Oral Presentation
Specific (LG2.03P) • work with a partner to plan and make oral presentations to a small group, selecting and using vocabulary and methods of delivery to suit audience and purpose	• listen critically to partner's comparison and take notes (More Oral Language TG)	• TOC 7: Listening
(LG2.07P) • analyze their own and others' oral communication skills, identifying strengths and weaknesses and suggesting ways to improve	• present role-play on group behaviour for class to identify problems and suggest solutions (Oral Language Extension SB)	• SSEC 2: Group Work
MEDIA STUDIES		
Overall (MDV.01P) • identify and describe the elements, intended audiences, and production practices of a variety of media forms	• discuss best method of writing comparison for newspaper (Media Link TG)	• AR 21: Response to Media
Specific (MD1.02P) • identify and describe the elements used to structure media works in a variety of forms	• compare front pages of three daily newspapers (Media Link SB)	• AR 21: Response to Media
(MD1.03P) • compare the reactions of different people or groups to a variety of media works	• compare reactions to three newspapers as regards types of news and their appeal (More Media TG)	• AR 21: Respnse to Media

AR=Assessment Rubric   EP=Extra Practice   SB=Student Book   SSEC=Student Self-Evaluation Checklist   TG=Teacher's Guide   TOC=Teacher Observation Checklist

LEARNING GOALS

- write a comparison
- use comparative and superlative forms of adjectives and adverbs correctly
- use colons, semicolons, and dashes correctly
- recognize and correct errors in comparison sentences
- learn to use homophones correctly

PLANNING INFORMATION

Links to Other Nelson English 9 Resources

Literature & Media 9

See "Mr. Preston (and Mr. Rawat) Go to New Delhi" by John Stackhouse, pp. 152–154 and "Dogs and Books" by Christie Blatchford, pp. 168–170.

Write Source 2000

Comparison—"Comparison/Contrast," p. 312; **Colons**—"Colon," p. 394; **Comparative and Superlative**—"Forms of Adjectives," p. 453; "Adverb," p. 454; **Dashes**—"Dash," p. 395; **Homophones**—"Using the Right Word," pp. 419–433; **Semicolons**—"Semicolon," p. 393

INTRODUCING THE UNIT

Point out to students that people are constantly comparing things in everyday life like clothes and friends. Have students work in pairs and ask them to list five other things that they might compare (e.g., music, feelings, classrooms, moods, jobs). Suggest they think back over the past week for situations where they have made comparisons. Then ask them to share some of these situations including a brief description of when or where the comparisons were made. (LI1.03B—TOC 14: Tracking Expectations)

INTRODUCING THE MODEL

1. Tell students that the model they are about to read compares neat people with sloppy people. Ask them if they were comparing the two, would they try to show how they were similar, different, or both similar and different. Why? (Most students will probably favour different because it would be easier to think of examples.) After some discussion, suggest they read the model to see whether the author compares similarities, differences, or both. (LI1.02P—AR 22: Response to Reading)

2. Activity #1 on page 227 from the Academic Course is appropriate for the Applied Course. (LI1.03B—TOC 14: Tracking Expectations)

INVESTIGATING THE MODEL

1. Ask students to provide three main points that Suzanne Britt uses to persuade the reader that sloppy people are better than neat people. List these on the left-hand side of the board. Then ask students to provide three main ideas Britt uses to convince the reader that neat people are worse than sloppy people. Write these on the right-hand side of the board.

    Tell students that the writer could have taken the opposite point of view: that neat people are better than sloppy people. Ask them to suggest three points she could have used to persuade readers of this position, and three main points to convince us that sloppy people are not as desirable as neat people. Record these in the same manner as above. Possible answers are shown in the table on the following page.

Sample criteria for a comparison:

- is used in descriptive, expository, or persuasive writing to examine two or more subjects

- uses points for comparison based on direct observation, analysis, or research

- contains a thesis sentence that limits scope and reveals purpose

- is usually organized by block method (arranged by subject) or by point-by-point method (arranged by characteristics)

- may include both common elements of topics and distinctions between or among topics

- may not always have conclusions (if part of longer piece of writing)

- has a conclusion that usually summarizes, evaluates, or draws a conclusion if it stands alone

Sloppy People Are Better	Neat People Are Worse
They carry in their mind's eye a heavenly vision, a precise plan ...	They throw out everything.
They save everything.	They only care about results.
They give attention to every detail.	They are vicious with mail.

Neat People Are Better	Sloppy People Are Worse
They prevent accidents (i.e., tripping).	They don't care if others hate their messes.
They know where things are.	They save things that others could use.
They don't waste valuable space.	They risk disease by leaving rotting food around.

After looking at the two lists, point out that people who write comparisons often prepare such lists to help them clarify their positions and to identify their main arguments. This procedure also helps them to identify which of their arguments are strongest and to ensure that they have a balance of arguments to support their position and to criticize the opposing one. Suggest to students that they use this strategy when they write their own comparisons in Writer's Workshop. (LI1.04P—TOC 14: Tracking Expectations)

2. Activity #1 on page 228 from the Academic Course is appropriate for the Applied Course. (LI1.06B—AR 22: Response to Reading)

Answers:

See the Academic Course on pages 228–229 for answers.

Student Book 1.–6. (LI1.04P—AR 22: Response to Reading)

EXTENDING THE MODEL

1.–2. Activities #1–2 on page 229 from the Academic Course is appropriate for the Applied Course.

1. (LGV.02B—SSEC 5: Oral Presentation)

2. (LI1.02P—TOC 14: Tracking Expectations)

3. Good topic sentences help writers to focus their writing. Ask students to choose three examples of effective topic sentences from the model, and to explain why they found them effective. They should be able to state their positions clearly and succinctly in a class discussion. (LI1.04P—AR 22: Response to Reading)

WRITER'S WORKSHOP

1. As an alternative to students choosing their own topic, you could ask them to rewrite "Neat People vs. Sloppy People" from the opposite point of view: Sloppy people are lazier and meaner than neat people. Tell them to use some of the ideas from the chart they developed in activity #1 in the *Teacher's Guide* under Investigating the Model. (WRV.03P—AR 2: Comparison)

2. Activity #2 on pages 229–230 from the Academic Course is appropriate for the Applied Course. (WR1.01P—AR 2: Comparison)

Student Book 1.–6. (WRV.01P—AR 2: Comparison); 7. (WRV.03P—AR 2: Comparison); 8. (WRV.04B—AR 2: Comparison; WRV.05B—AR 2: Comparison)

ORAL LANGUAGE EXTENSION

You may wish to assign a topic for the role-play suggested in the student book to illustrate a poorly functioning group. One possibility is to have students reread the model on their own and pick out three examples of humour that they liked the best. Then have them discuss their individual choices in their groups and role-play coming to a group decision on the three best examples. (LI1.04P—TOC 14: Tracking Expectations)

Student Book (LG2.07P—SSEC 2: Group Work)

GRAMMAR

The activity on page 230 from the Academic Course is appropriate for the Applied Course.

(WR5.05P—TOC 4: Grammar; LG1.05P—TOC 4: Grammar)

Answers:
See the Academic Course on pages 230–231 for answers.

Student Book 1.–2. (WR5.05P—TOC 4: Grammar; LG1.05P—TOC 4: Grammar)

MEDIA LINK

Discuss with students the way newspaper articles are written in inverted pyramid style (most important to least important). Why does a newspaper usually structure its facts this way? (Editors can cut the length of the story and it will still appear as a whole piece.) Given that newspaper articles are organized this way, which method (Block or Point-by-Point) would you be most likely to use if you were writing a comparison for a newspaper? (Point-by-Point) (MDV.01P—AR 21: Response to Media)

If you are not able to obtain sufficient newspapers for each student, have students do the activity in small groups.
Student Book (MD1.02P—AR 21: Response to Media)

MECHANICS

1. Provide students with a list of rules for using colons, semicolons, and dashes. Review each of the rules for each of the punctuation marks. Organize students into groups of four and ask them to scan through newspapers and magazines to find examples of sentences that demonstrate each rule. Have students put two or three examples for each rule on the board. Discuss these together and clarify any misunderstandings. (WR5.15B—TOC 8: Mechanics; LG1.07B—TOC 8: Mechanics)

2. Tell students that you are going to read some sentences to them. They are to write the sentences in their notebooks, and insert the appropriate punctuation. Read each sentence slowly; then repeat it. Take up the answers and have students explain for each sentence why they chose the type of punctuation they did. Clarify any misunderstandings. (WR5.15B—TOC 8: Mechanics; LG1.07B—TOC 8: Mechanics)
   a) Sloppy people are sometimes neat; neat people are never sloppy. (semicolon between two independent clauses)
   b) Sloppy people are sometimes neat, but neat people are never sloppy. (no semicolon with a coordinating conjunction)

MORE ORAL LANGUAGE

Point out to students that every day people appeal to them to accept particular points of view. These appeals come from print, television, and from family and friends. In order to make decisions about things they hear, they must be good critical listeners. Have students work with a partner in the following activity: students take turns reading their comparisons to each other; as one person reads, the other listens carefully for the following: introduction, thesis, topic sentences and examples, and summary or conclusion; each student writes a few notes while listening and afterward completes the notes by filling in important details; students tell each other why they agree or disagree with the thesis and then critique the examples used. (LG2.02P—TOC 7: Listening)

MORE CHALLENGE

Ask students to explain why each of the following sentences is incorrect. Have them rewrite the sentences correctly. (WR5.05P—TOC 4: Grammar; LG1.05P—TOC 4: Grammar)

1. Planes will get you to your destination faster than any other form of transportation. (Faster compares only two things.)
2. Sylvia spoke Spanish more fluently than any student. (More compares two things.)
3. Who played most aggressively, Mark or Ryan? (Most compares three or more.)
4. Of the two students, Shania sang the sweetest. (Sweetest compares three or more things and is an adjective.)
5. Carol swam more faster than Sheena. (You cannot use more with faster.)

MORE MEDIA

Have students work in small groups for the following activity. Examine the front pages of the three newspapers and classify them according to the following categories: good news, bad news, and neutral news. Collect the results from each group and compare them, paper to paper. Then have students rank the items on the front page of each newspaper according to the following: the most important news; the most interesting news; the items that most people would read first; the items that would appeal to older readers; the items that would appeal to younger readers. Have students share their results, and discuss the implications (the most important news is not always the most interesting; newspapers must try to appeal to a variety of readers; newspapers are mostly designed for older readers). (LI2.03P—TOC 14: Tracking Expectations; MD1.03P—AR 21: Response to Media)

Ask students to explain in their own words what is meant by each of the following statements. Some possible answers are given in parentheses. (WR5.15B—TOC 8: Mechanics; LG1.07B—TOC 8: Mechanics)

The colon is not needed very often. (It is used mainly to introduce items or ideas.)

The semicolon is a tricky piece of punctuation. (It is often described as both a strong comma and a weak period because it is used to join and separate parts of a sentence.)

MORE SUPPORT

Indicate to students that some homophones can be made by dropping a silent letter (e.g., wrung, rung). Ask students to write the homophone partner for each of the following words. (WR5.12B—TOC 16: Word Study & Spelling; LG1.07B—TOC 16: Word Study & Spelling)

1. knew	2. knight	3. knit
4. knot	5. two	6. wrack
7. wrap	8. wrest	9. wring
10. write	11. wrote	

c) Someday sloppy people will do the following: alphabetize all their books, go through their wardrobes, and put newspaper clippings in a scrapbook. (colon before a list)

d) Someday sloppy people will do such things as alphabetize all their books, go through their wardrobes, and put newspaper clippings in a scrapbook. (no colon after *such as, including,* or *for example*)

e) My older brother was always sloppy; however, I was always neat. (semicolon to join two independent clauses joined by a transition word)

f) I know I can be sloppy; I will practise every day. (semicolon between two independent clauses)

USAGE & STYLE

The activity on page 232 from the Academic Course is appropriate for the Applied Course.

(WR5.06P—TOC 15: Usage & Style; LG1.05P—TOC 15: Usage & Style)

Answers:
See the Academic Course on page 232 for answers.
Student Book 1.–2. (WR5.06P—TOC 15: Usage & Style; LG1.05P—TOC 15: Usage & Style)

WORD STUDY & SPELLING

Working in pairs and using the list of common homophones on student book page 211, have one student develop a sentence with a homophone in it. Then have the partner identify the homophone in the sentence and spell it. Have students switch roles, carrying out this activity 10 times. (WR5.12B—TOC 16: Word Study & Spelling; LG1.07B—TOC 16: Word Study & Spelling)

Answers:
See the Academic Course on page 233 for answers.

Student Book 1.–2. (WR5.12B—TOC 16: Word Study & Spelling; LG1.07B—TOC 16: Word Study & Spelling)

WORD ORIGINS

See the Academic Course on page 233 for answers.

Student Book (LG1.03B—TOC 16: Word Study & Spelling)

ANSWERS TO EXTRA PRACTICE

See the Academic Course on pages 234–235 for answers.

Grammar
(WR5.05P—TOC 4: Grammar; LG1.05D—TOC 4: Grammar)

Mechanics
(WR5.15B—TOC 8: Mechanics; LG1.07B—TOC 8: Mechanics)

Usage & Style
(WR5.06P—TOC 15: Usage & Style; LG1.05P—TOC 15: Usage & Style)

Word Study & Spelling
(WR5.12B—TOC 16: Word Study & Spelling; LG1.07B—TOC 16: Word Study & Spelling)

GRAMMAR

NAME: _____ **DATE:** _____

Rewrite the following sentences, correcting any errors in the use of the comparative or superlative forms of adjectives or adverbs.

1. Of the four comparisons, this one is the more interesting.

   _____

2. Knowledge about writing forms has become importanter to high school students.

   _____

3. These exercises were completed the most fastest.

   _____

4. Who scored the most baskets during the first half of the game, Leah or Samantha?

   _____

5. This type of shoe is the bestest of all.

   _____

6. Raymond is working slowlier than Jeff.

   _____

7. All of the comparisons were good, but Noah's was better.

   _____

8. Which of these exercises is the more difficult?

   _____

9. Of the six cars tested, this one used the less gas.

   _____

10. Mara is the most friendliest person in our group.

    _____

MECHANICS

NAME: _____ DATE: _____

Decide whether each of the following comparisons requires a colon or a semicolon.

1. In our dance competition, the first place winner gets gold_ second place, silver_ and third place, bronze.

2. Following are the medals which will be awarded at the dance competition_ gold, silver, and bronze.

3. There will be pizza available after the dance_ however, it will cost $2.00 per slice.

4. The star player scored three goals_ the fans went wild.

5. The following foods are needed for the Food Bank_ soup, peanut butter, and cereal.

6. The following cities are experiencing tremendous growth_ Vancouver, British Columbia_ Calgary, Alberta_ Waterloo, Ontario_ and Halifax, Nova Scotia.

7. Not a sound was to be heard_ not a breath was to be taken.

8. I found a knapsack containing the following_ two textbooks, a lunch bag, and a pencil case.

9. I do not plan on attending the practice_ moreover, I am writing a letter to the coach.

10. The problem looks very easy_ in fact, it is quite difficult.

USAGE & STYLE

NAME: _____ DATE: _____

Correct any problems with the way words are used in the following comparisons. Write the correct answers in your notebook.

1. He is much neater then his friends.

   _____

2. I think I am very different than you.

   _____

3. Their approach to the problem is most unique.

   _____

4. Your locker has fewer clutter than mine.

   _____

5. My teacher differed from me on the solution to the problem.

   _____

6. Tell me that your manners and conduct are more different than what they were last week.

   _____

7. There were less peanuts in the jar following the movie.

   _____

8. We cleaned up the mess, put the furniture back in place, than turned down the music.

   _____

9. The colour of her jacket is different with yours.

   _____

10. I differ from Tara's idea about the best use of the funds.

   _____

WORD STUDY & SPELLING

NAME: _____ DATE: _____

Correct any misused words in the following sentences. Write the correct words in your notebook.

1. The sail at the store included some too-for-won items.

   _____

2. I cent the principle a copy of the minutes from our student counsel meeting.

   _____

3. Do you think we should paint the sealing white or blew?

   _____

4. Your not going to bleach your hare read, are you?

   _____

5. The weather is going to bee fowl tomorrow. Plan to ware something warm.

   _____

6. Did you bye some serial at the grocery store when you wear their?

   _____

7. They hoped for piece after the rain of the dictator ended.

   _____

8. Will you please bye me something four my week condition?

   _____

9. We herd that the creak will have its coarse changed. Do you no why this is sew?

   _____

10. The led pale was to heavy to lift. A wooden won wood have bean more practical.

   _____

Academic Expectations

GRADE 9 EXPECTATIONS		DEMONSTRATION OF LEARNING	ASSESSMENT TOOLS
LITERATURE STUDIES AND READING			
Overall (LIV.01D)	• read and demonstrate an understanding of a variety of literary and informational texts, from contemporary and historical periods		
Specific (LI1.02D)	• select and read texts for different purposes, with an emphasis on recognizing the elements of literary genres and the organization of informational materials, collecting and assessing information, responding imaginatively, and exploring human experiences and values	• discuss changes in advertising and speculate on future (Introducing the Unit #1)	• TOC 13: Tracking Expectations
(LI1.04D)	• locate explicit information and ideas in texts to use in developing opinions and interpretations	• give examples from models for use in interpretation (Investigating the Models SB #1–6)	• AR 21: Response to Media
WRITING			
Overall (WRV.01D)	• use a variety of print and electronic sources to gather information and explore ideas for their written work	• find print ads and Web pages to use as models for advertisement and Web page (Writer's Workshop TG) • prepare questions to ask guest speaker in advertising (More Support TG, page 252) • develop ideas for print ad and Web page (Writer's Workshop SB #1–5)	• AR 1: Advertisement • AR 1: Advertisement • AR 1: Advertisement
Overall (WRV.03D)	• use a variety of organizational techniques to present ideas and supporting details logically and coherently in written work	• write copy and format print ad and Web page (Writer's Workshop SB #6–7)	• AR 1: Advertisement
Overall (WRV.04D)	• revise their written work, independently and collaboratively, with a focus on support for ideas and opinions, accuracy, clarity, and unity	• revise print ad and Web page (Writer's Workshop SB #8–9)	• AR 1: Advertisement
Overall (WRV.05D)	• edit and proofread to produce final drafts, using correct grammar, spelling, and punctuation, according to the conventions of standard Canadian English, with the support of print and electronic resources when appropriate	• edit and proofread print ad and Web page (Writer's Workshop SB #9)	• AR 1: Advertisement
Specific (WR5.07B)	• identify and correct sentence fragments, run-on sentences, and comma splices	• identify sentence fragments (Grammar TG #1) • correct sentence fragments (Grammar TG #2) • discuss when sentence fragments are acceptable and when not (Grammar TG #3) • write complete sentences from sentence fragments (Grammar TG #4) • use sentence fragments correctly (Grammar SB #1–4) • write complete sentences, eliminating sentence fragments (EP: Grammar)	• TOC 4: Grammar • TOC 4: Grammar • TOC 4: Grammar • TOC 4: Grammar • TOC 4: Grammar • TOC 4: Grammar
(WR5.11B)	• use knowledge of a wide range of spelling patterns and rules to identify, analyze, and correct spelling errors	• use spelling rules to correct spelling (Word Study & Spelling TG) • think of words to illustrate spelling rules (Word Study & Spelling SB #1–2) • spell words correctly (EP: Word Study & Spelling)	• TOC 16: Word Study & Spelling • TOC 16: Word Study & Spelling • TOC 16: Word Study & Spelling

AR=Assessment Rubric   EP=Extra Practice   SB=Student Book   SSEC=Student Self-Evaluation Checklist   TG=Teacher's Guide   TOC=Teacher Observation Checklist

GRADE 9 EXPECTATIONS		DEMONSTRATION OF LEARNING	ASSESSMENT TOOLS
		LANGUAGE	
Overall (LGV.01D)	• use knowledge of vocabulary and language conventions to speak, write, and read competently using a level of language appropriate to the purpose and audience		
Specific (LG1.02B)	• identify and explain examples of slang, jargon, dialect, and colloquialism, as well as of standard Canadian English, in literary texts and their own oral and written work	• decide what forms of writing are formal or informal (Usage & Style TG #1) • choose examples of dialogue with colloquial language (Usage & Style TG #2) • distinguish between slang and jargon (Usage & Style TG #3) • create class scrapbook of "Varieties of English" (Usage & Style TG #4) • identify standard and nonstandard Canadian English, colloquialisms, and slang (Usage & Style SB #1–5) • write sentences in standard Canadian English; identify examples of colloquialisms, slang, and jargon (EP: Usage & Style)	• TOC 15: Usage & Style • TOC 15: Usage & Style • TOC 15: Usage & Style • TOC 15: Usage & Style • TOC 15: Usage & Style • TOC 15: Usage & Style
(LG1.03B)	• identify words borrowed from other languages and words and terms recently introduced to describe new ideas, inventions, and products, and explain their origins	• think of brand names that have become common nouns or verbs (Word Origins SB)	• TOC 16: Word Study & Spelling
(LG1.06B)	• recognize, describe, and correct sentence errors in oral and written language	• identify sentence fragments (Grammar TG #1) • correct sentence fragments (Grammar TG #2) • discuss when sentence fragments are acceptable and when not (Grammar TG #3) • write complete sentences from sentence fragments (Grammar TG #4) • use sentence fragments correctly (Grammar SB #1–4)	• TOC 4: Grammar • TOC 4: Grammar • TOC 4: Grammar • TOC 4: Grammar • TOC 4: Grammar
Overall (LGV.02B)	• use listening techniques and oral communication skills to participate in classroom discussions and more formal activities, such as storytelling, role playing, and reporting/ presenting, for specific purposes and audiences		
Specific (LG2.06D)	• explain how oral communication skills can contribute to success in all curriculum areas and the world outside the school	• interview people whose jobs involve listening and speaking skills (Oral Language Extension TG) • interview teacher to create radio ad to promote oral communication skills (Oral Language Extension SB)	• TOC 1: Conducting an Interview • TOC 1: Conducting an Interview
		MEDIA STUDIES	
Overall (MDV.01D)	• use knowledge of the elements, intended audiences, and production practices of a variety of media forms to analyze specific media works	• discuss how to use advertisements to find products or services (Introducing the Models TG #3) • discuss effectiveness of models and what they would change (Investigating the Models TG)	• AR 21: Response to Media • AR 21: Response to Media

AR=Assessment Rubric   EP=Extra Practice   SB=Student Book   SSEC=Student Self-Evaluation Checklist   TG=Teacher's Guide   TOC=Teacher Observation Checklist

| --- | --- | --- |
MEDIA STUDIES (continued)		
Specific (MD1.01B) • demonstrate critical thinking skills by identifying the differences between explicit and implicit messages in media works	• compare packaging on milk containers with print ad model (Extending the Models TG #1)	• AR 21: Response to Media
(MD1.02D) • identify how elements of media forms are used in a variety of media works and explain the effects of different treatments	• find examples of advertising techniques (Extending the Models TG #2) • evaluate ads on the basis of visual features (Mechanics TG) • evaluate design and text of models (Mechanics SB #1–4) • explain how design elements have been used in advertising (EP: Mechanics)	• AR 21: Response to Media • TOC 8: Mechanics • TOC 8: Mechanics • TOC 8: Mechanics
(MD1.03D) • compare and explain their own and their peers' reactions to a variety of media works	• explain what made them remember various advertisements (Introducing the Models TG #1) • log exposure to advertising over 24-hour period and evaluate influence (Media Link SB)	• AR 21: Response to Media • AR 21: Response to Media
(MD1.04D) • identify factors that influence media production and distribution and explain the effect of these factors on specific media works	• discuss factors in advertising (Introducing the Unit TG #2) • discuss effects of shopping on the Web (More Challenge TG, page 252) • discuss results of survey of different types of radio stations (More Oral Language TG) • discuss motives for logos on products worn or carried (More Media TG)	• AR 21: Response to Media • AR 21: Response to Media • TOC 2: Conducting Research • AR 21: Response to Media
Overall (MDV.02D) • use knowledge of a variety of media forms, purposes, and audiences to create media works and describe their intended effect		
Specific (MD2.02D) • create media works for different purposes and explain how each has been designed to achieve its particular purpose	• make collage of advertisements they think are particularly effective (Introducing the Models TG #2)	• AR 12: Media Product

AR=Assessment Rubric   EP=Extra Practice   SB=Student Book   SSEC=Student Self-Evaluation Checklist   TG=Teacher's Guide   TOC=Teacher Observation Checklist

INSTRUCTIONAL STRATEGIES FOR THE ACADEMIC COURSE

LEARNING GOALS

- write an advertisement
- identify and correct sentence fragments
- identify design elements
- adapt punctuation for advertisements
- identify and explain examples of slang and colloquialisms
- use knowledge of useful spelling rules

PLANNING INFORMATION

Links to Other Nelson English 9 Resources

Literature & Media 9
See "A Product Advertisement," p. 322 and "Unico," p. 333.

Write Source 2000
Colloquialisms—"Colloquialisms," p. 138; **Design Elements**—"Designing Your Writing," pp. 27–29; **Sentence Fragments**—"Sentence Fragment," p. 86; **Slang**—"Slang," p. 140; **Spelling Rules**—"Improved Spelling," pp. 411–418

INTRODUCING THE UNIT

1. Find an article that gives a brief history of advertising. Read the article to students or give them a hard copy. As a follow-up, ask them how advertising has changed with the invention of new technology (e.g., the printing press, radio, television, computers). Find out what directions they think advertising will take in the future. (LI1.02D—TOC 14: Tracking Expectations)

2. To get students thinking about the media and advertising, write the following statements on the board or on a handout:

   - Advertising is not a medium in itself.
   - Advertising is the driving, often the shaping force, behind most of the media.
   - While advertising is everywhere, at times it seems almost invisible.
   - Advertising is an important business, both for those who create ads and for those who want to sell something.
   - Advertisements are among the most carefully prepared presentations in the media.

   Have a class discussion about the meaning of these statements, or have students discuss them in small groups (one statement per group). Have each group appoint a recorder who will take notes and be responsible for reporting the results of the group discussion to the whole class. (MD1.04D—AR 21: Response to Media)

INTRODUCING THE MODELS

1. Ask students to identify sources of advertisements (e.g., television, radio, magazines, newspapers, billboards, bulletin boards, posters, junk mail, neon signs, bumper stickers, logos on clothing and equipment, Web sites) and list them on the board. Have students jot down in their notebooks one example of each type of advertising that they have seen in the past week (e.g., a poster advertising a company selling diet products). Have students share their examples with the class, and then ask them what made them remember the ads (e.g., colours, visual appeal, dialogue, content, and unique approach). (MD1.03D—AR 21: Response to Media)

2. Ask students to bring to class two examples of advertising that they think are particularly effective. Have some students make a collage of these advertisements on a bulletin board for use during the study of this unit. (MD2.02D—AR 12: Media Product)

3. Ask students to imagine that they want or need each product or service listed below.
   a) stereo system
   b) pair of jeans
   c) food and drinks for a party
   d) mountain bike
   e) fitness classes
   f) CD
   g) book
   h) someone to repair a television

Ask them to answer the following questions about each item:

- Where would you go to find information on the product or service?

- If a product is involved, how would you decide whether to buy one brand or another?

- How would you decide which business (individual, store, or company) would be the best one from which to buy the product or service?

Have students share their answers. (MDV.01D—AR 21: Response to Media)

INVESTIGATING THE MODELS

Have students complete the activities in the student book and then ask them to summarize their views of the two ads by answering these questions: How effective are the ads in communicating their messages? If you had the opportunity to make changes in these ads, what would you change? (MDV.01D—AR 21: Response to Media)

Answers:

1. The purpose of the print ad is to create the idea that your life will be better if you drink milk. The purpose of the Web page is to provide health information which will make readers want to buy milk.

2. The milk ad is probably aimed at both teenagers and adults. The text, "Drink Milk. Love Life." could appeal to a young person or an adult, as would the image of the tennis player. The Web page is aimed at youth. The language ("girls," "guys," "bone-growin'," "bod"), the reasons given that you should drink milk ("bone-growin' nutrients," "get the D without the burn"), and the tone (informal) are all designed for a young audience.

3. The Web page relies more on text, while the print ad relies more on images. Possible answers
   One reason is the underlying approach of the ads: the Web ad uses factual information about health to convince readers to buy milk; the print ad tries to convince readers to buy milk by associating it with an attractive lifestyle. Another reason involves the conventions of these two media. The Web is viewed by readers as a source of information, so their expectation will be to find information even in an ad for a product; on the other hand, the convention in magazines is for the ads to be secondary to the articles and as such, to be visual and not require much reading.

4. The Web page is trying to persuade with factual information presented through the use of diagrams and text. In addition to what is on this page, the Web site offers more information to the reader who can click on any of the following: myths & realities, body benefits, nutrient knowledge, all kinds of milk, and the milk story. The site relies on words much more than graphic presentation. The milk ad with its flowing patterns (the milk, the pitcher, and the tennis player), is meant to make you think of milk as something pleasurable. The emphasis is on the attractive, well-designed image and the appealing colour while the text is limited to four words which echo the message of the image.

   Print ads like the milk ad are usually found in magazines. They need to be powerful enough to draw the reader's eye to them, and the text brief enough that the reader will get the message quickly before moving on. On the other hand, people choose to go to Web sites to find information; therefore, more substantive information can be provided and people will usually take more time to read it.

   The technological advantages of Web pages are that they can use multimedia, they can be updated at any time without major design changes, and they do not necessarily need expensive personnel to develop them. A print ad is limited to a two-dimensional representation on a flat page; it is usually developed by a professional advertising company and is usually limited to one-time use.

> ## CHECKPOINT
>
> Sample criteria for an advertisement:
>
> - is designed to sell a product or service, create an image, provide information, or persuade audience to behave in certain way
>
> - is almost always targeted at a particular audience
>
> - usually relies on words and images to convey message
>
> - is affected by medium in which it appears
>
> - often breaks grammatical rules to increase impact
>
> - promotes product directly or indirectly

5. Possible answers:
   Vitamin D!
   Give you a clue—it starts with M-I-L—OK, OK ...
   Drink Milk. Love Life.

6. The Web ad associates drinking milk with being healthy through getting enough calcium; the print ad associates drinking milk with living "the good life." Students will have varying opinions as to which is more effective.

Student Book 1.–6. (LI1.04D—AR 22: Response to Reading)

EXTENDING THE MODELS

1. Obtain some of the most current packaging available on containers of milk, and have students compare the advertising with the print ad model. Ask students to consider the following in their comparisons: language, visual features, content, and each advertisement as a whole. (MD1.01B—AR 21: Response to Media)

2. Ask students to look through magazines to find one example of each of the following types of advertising claims. (MD1.02D—AR 21: Response to Media)

   - Testimonial: the endorsement of a product by a well-known person or organization
   - Plain Folks: talking down to people in order to appear to be one of them (e.g., Milk Web site)
   - Bandwagon: suggesting that everyone is doing it
   - Snob Appeal: suggesting that your status will improve if you use the product
   - Facts and Figures: implies that statistics prove that the product is a good one
   - Hidden Fears: plays on people's fears and insecurities
   - Repetition: the same word or phrase is used several times
   - Magic Ingredients: implies that the product is scientifically based
   - Weasel Words: uses vague words (e.g., new, improved) to mislead the consumer

WRITER'S WORKSHOP

Make sure that students have plenty of models to refer to for the design and writing of their advertisements. Suggest that they refer to the bulletin board display made in Introducing the Models, activity #2. As further resources, have them find print ads and Web pages that contain content and features similar to what they may like to develop. (WRV.01D—AR 1: Advertisement)

NOTE: You should complete the Mechanics section of this unit on pages 180 to 182 of the student book (identify design elements) before having students complete Writer's Workshop.

Student Book 1.–5. (WRV.01D—AR 1: Advertisement); 6.–7. (WRV.03D—AR 1: Advertisement); 8.–9. (WRV.04D—AR 1: Advertisement); 9. (WRV.05D—AR 1: Advertisement)

ORAL LANGUAGE EXTENSION

In addition to teachers, you could suggest that students interview someone—perhaps a family member—working in other areas where listening and speaking skills are important for good job performance (e.g., sales, counselling, human resources, politics, some areas of law, radio or TV journalism). (LG2.06D—TOC 1: Conducting an Interview)

Student Book (LG2.06D—TOC 1: Conducting an Interview)

MORE SUPPORT

Invite one or more of the following people to your classroom to speak about effective print advertising and Web design: a senior student in your school who plans to go into advertising; a teacher from the Visual Arts or Business Departments in your school; a community college student in advertising; a person responsible for designing ads for a newspaper; a person from an advertising agency; a person in a corporation responsible for advertising. Discuss with students what kinds of questions they should prepare to get the most out of these presentations. (WR1.01D—AR 1: Advertisement)

MORE CHALLENGE

The "cyberspace mall" is a reality. You can now buy books, CDs, appliances, cars, and many other products on the Internet. This form of shopping will expand greatly in the future and the competition among companies to get you to buy from them will be fierce. Assign a small group (or groups) of students to find out what is currently available for purchase on the Internet. Have them examine the Web sites of some of the vendors, and make a list of some of the items you can buy. Ask them to look at the persuasive techniques vendors use in their advertising to convince customers to buy from them; then compare the persuasive techniques of one Web site to another. What effect is Internet shopping having on businesses in your town or city? Will they be able to compete with the discounted prices on the Internet? What does the future hold for people who like to do their shopping from home? Have the group(s) present their findings to the class. (MD1.04D—AR 21: Response to Media)

GRAMMAR

1. Tape record a brief conversation among a group of students (with their knowledge and permission). Prepare a written transcription of the tape, and then identify all the sentence fragments used in the conversation. Select four examples and write them on the board, one for each of the following: one without a subject, one without a verb, one which is a phrase, and one which is a subordinate clause.

   Tell students that the groups of words on the board come from a conversation among students which they will hear shortly. Ask them if the groups of words are sentences. If not, why not? What's missing? Tell students what the formal name for such groups of words is (sentence fragments).

   Play the tape for your students. Ask them to listen carefully for examples of sentence fragments, and to write as many of them as they can in their notebooks. Following the playing of the conversation, distribute the written transcript. Ask students to check their notes, and identify any sentence fragments which they missed.

   Compile a class list of the sentence fragments on the board. Have one student suggest what is missing in each fragment (subject, verb, principal clause) and have other students confirm the answer. If a group of words like the following is given: "Go to your locker," point out that "you" is understood; therefore, the group of words is a sentence. (WR5.07B—TOC 4: Grammar; LG1.06B—TOC 4: Grammar)

2. Ask students to suggest how the fragments in the transcript could be made into sentences. Write some of the answers on the board and discuss why they are appropriate or not appropriate. (WR5.07B—TOC 4: Grammar; LG1.06B—TOC 4: Grammar)

3. Tell students that if they recorded most conversations, they would probably find many examples of sentence fragments. Point out that while this seems quite acceptable in speech, it is not acceptable in writing. Discuss why this is so. (Writing is more formal; therefore, most writing situations have fragments removed. Also sentence fragments in writing can be difficult to understand since they lack context and there is no body language (i.e., shrugs) to help fill in the gaps in meaning. In what situations should sentence fragments not be used in oral language? (more formal situations) (WR5.07B—TOC 4: Grammar; LG1.06B—TOC 4: Grammar)

4. In each of the following, get rid of the sentence fragments by writing one or two good sentences. (WR5.07B—TOC 4: Grammar; LG1.06B—TOC 4: Grammar)

   a) We completed our advertising assignments. By working very late at night.
   b) We listened to many radio programs. Rock, easy-listening, and educational.
   c) We all contributed. Every person in the class.
   d) Since advertisements are designed to sell a particular product or service.
   e) Leer & Associates of Sydney, who is a good advertising agency.
   f) On Monday we read numerous Web sites. Examining every one for content.
   g) We first went to the newspaper facility. Then to the television and radio stations.
   h) The advertising seminar was at the Royal York. An old hotel where many famous people have stayed.
   i) A new advertisement on milk is soon to be released. The date of which will be announced later.
   j) Online shopping is the upcoming trend. Everything from CDs to cars.

Answers:

1. a) S   b) S   c) F
   d) F   e) F   f) F

MORE ORAL LANGUAGE

Divide the class into groups and assign each group one of the following types of radio stations: easy-listening, rock music, all-news, country-and-western, information/culture (e.g., CBC). Tell students to listen to their stations for at least two hours (or an amount of time that suits the program) over a certain period of time. During the two hours, they will focus on answering the following questions:

What portion of the station's programming was devoted to each of the following: advertising, music, news, and host "chatter"?

Was the advertising based more on factual or emotional appeal?

What age group is the station mainly designed to serve? How do you know this?

What kinds of news stories does the station concentrate on?

As a class, design a log suitable for recording the information needed to answer the above questions. Each group is to report its findings orally to the class at the end of the activity. Following the presentations, ask the class whether any conclusions can be drawn from all of the information presented. Discuss the validity of conclusions put forward. (MD1.04D—TOC 2: Conducting Research)

Possible answers
- c) You are looking great!
- d) That film is in a class by itself.
- e) You must have enough Vitamin D to be a healthy person.
- f) What does "fitness for your face" mean?

2. Possible answers
   - a) You deserve the best, so be good to yourself.
   - b) We know that this cream will cleanse your skin deep down.
   - c) If you drink milk, good things will happen.
   - d) If you apply it at night, you will wake up refreshed.
   - e) Do it because you owe it to yourself.

3. Student work.

4. Student work.

Student Book 1.–4. (WR5.07B—TOC 4: Grammar; LG1.06B—TOC 4: Grammar)

MEDIA LINK

This activity is similar to the More Oral Language activity suggested earlier in this guide; however, this activity focuses exclusively on advertising, and involves a variety of sources. If you used the More Oral Language activity, you may wish to delete radio from the list of sources given in the activity. A chart for recording observations similar to that suggested in the Oral Language activity should be developed with the class.

Student Book (MD1.03D—AR 21: Response to Media)

MECHANICS

Collect 10 examples of ads from volunteers that, to a greater and lesser extent, demonstrate the design features outlined in this section. Put them on display around the room. Beside each ad, place a blank sheet of paper. Ask students to do the following:
- circulate around the room looking at each ad for its visual impact
- select the three ads they like best and put a check mark beside them on the blank paper

Count the number of check marks for each ad, and rearrange the ads on the front board from those with the most check marks to those with the least. Beginning with the former, ask students to identify their visual features (e.g., typeface, use of colour) and write these features on the board. Work through all of the ads in the same way, adding different features as they are suggested. (MD1.02D—TOC 8: Mechanics)

Answers:
NOTE: Since answers will vary in activities #1–2, it is important that students share the results of their small group discussions with the whole class.

Possible answers
1. The dominant feature of the Web page is a visual aid, i.e., a chart. The ad also uses different fonts and sizes of type, white space, bold print, some colour, circles, and arrows. The chart is organized with the glass of milk in the centre to focus the message about milk. Everything around it on the rest of the page contributes to the idea that drinking milk contributes to good health.

   In the print ad, the large bold type, the overall design, and the use of colour all work together to convey the basic message of the ad—drinking milk contributes to the enjoyment of life. Students might comment on: the style and colour of the type—thick white letters against dark blue; the capitalization of each word which emphasizes the message; the fluid-like motion in the design of the glass, pitcher, and tennis player; the suggestion of milk in the pitcher which

---

MORE MEDIA

Students are very aware of advertising on things that they wear or carry every day (e.g., T-shirts, jackets, caps, bags). Ask students for examples of some currently popular logos and brand names that they have purchased recently and list them on the board. Discuss their motives in purchasing these items, and the motives of the company in selling them. Use the following questions as prompts. (MD1.04D—AR 21: Response to Media)

- What is the relationship between you and the company?
- Is the extra price for a brand name really worth it?
- Is it the logo which counts or the name associated with the logo?
- What are some examples of logos that were popular but have gone out of favour? How does this happen?
- How can a company maintain its position as having "the thing to buy"?

creates a pleasing impression of the product; and the use of soft colour on a dark background which produces an eye-catching silhouette effect.

2. a) The student book uses all of the features mentioned including different fonts, varying sizes of type, white space, bold and italic type, visual aids (photographs, charts, icons, and headings), colour, boxes, bullets, and underlining.
   b) Special boxes, shading, drawings, arrows, and borders.

3. a) The question mark involves the reader in what is being said and encourages him or her to read on and find the answer.
   b) The exclamation mark catches your attention. It helps to emphasize the importance of Vitamin D.
   c) This use of ellipsis at the end of the statement invites the reader to go further for more information.
   d) The use of commands or imperative sentences catches your attention because they are telling you emphatically to do something.

4. Student work.

Student Book 1.–4. (MD1.02D—TOC 8: Mechanics)

USAGE & STYLE

1. Place the following statement on the board:

   > In one way, the use of language is similar to the use of clothes. We change language to fit the audience and the situation.

   Ask students what is meant by this. (Language can be used for both formal and informal situations. The same can be said of clothes.)

   Draw a continuum like that below on the board. Tell students that you are going to read a list of various forms of writing and speaking, and they are to suggest where the form should be placed on the continuum. They should base their decisions on the level of formality each of the forms might require. Once the forms are on the continuum, ask them if there are any changes they would make in the placement of the items. (LG1.02B—TOC 15: Usage & Style)

   Writing/Speaking

   Informal   Formal

   _____

   Writing: script, brochure, friendly letter, list, report, business letter, diary, thank-you note, notes for a speech

   Speaking: storytelling, report, conversation, role-play, speech, interview, discussion, debate

2. Ask students to read the definition of colloquialisms on page 182 of the student book. Reread the last sentence of the definition. Ask for student volunteers to bring in some selections from scripts, short stories, or novels that contain dialogue with colloquial language and have them read these to the class. (LG1.02B—TOC 15: Usage & Style)

3. Ask students to read the definition of slang on page 183 of the student book, and then the definition of jargon on page 136. Ask them to identify the difference between the two terms. (Slang is a highly informal language used by a particular group of people; jargon is the specialized language, often technical, used by people in various occupations or professions.) (LG1.02B—TOC 15: Usage & Style)

4. Tell students that you would like to develop a class scrapbook entitled "Varieties of English." You will need examples of the following varieties for different sections

of the scrapbook: formal language, informal language, colloquialisms, slang, jargon, idioms, clichés, and dialect. Ask students to bring examples to class. When enough examples have been collected, ask for student volunteers to help put the book together. Display the book for all students to read. (LG1.02B—TOC 15: Usage & Style)

Answers:

NOTE: For the purpose of activity #1, you can consider sentences that are incorrect grammatically as nonstandard Canadian English.

1. a) NS   b) NS   c) S
   d) NS   e) S

2. Possible answers:
   "You get on my nerves sometimes."
   "How's it going, Grant?"
   "Where's the action?"

3.–5. Student work.

Student Book 1.–5. (LG1.02B—TOC 15: Usage & Style)

WORD STUDY & SPELLING

Remind students that there are many rules available for spelling words in English, but there are exceptions to almost every one of them. Some people (e.g., Andrew Carnegie) have attempted to change our spelling system to make it more representative of the sounds of speech, but the general public has not been willing to implement the change. Tell students that it would be impossible for them to learn all the rules of spelling, but there are some rules that they should find useful.

While students have their books closed, write the following words on the board:

| bel<u>ie</u>ve | <u>C</u>elsius | carr<u>y</u> | chang<u>e</u> | <u>ski</u>m |
| de<u>ce</u>it | <u>c</u>at | carr<u>ied</u> | chang<u>ing</u> | ski<u>mm</u>ed |

Tell them that each pair of words demonstrates a rule for spelling, and you have underlined the part of the word the rule applies to. Ask them to write the spelling rule each pair demonstrates.

Following the exercise, ask students to use the rules outlined in the Word Study & Spelling section on pages 183 and 184 to check their answers. The rules are listed in the same order as the word pairs. Discuss any problems or questions students have arising from the use of these rules. (WR5.11B—TOC 16: Word Study & Spelling)

Answers:

1. Possible answers
   a) calcium, create, colony; reality — realities; surprise — surprising; get — getting
      (There may not be examples for all of the rules.)
   b) Student work.

2. Possible answers: protein, weird, flyer

Student Book 1.–2. (WR5.11B—TOC 16: Word Study & Spelling)

WORD ORIGINS

Answers:

Possible answers

Ski-Doo — for snow machine

Jet Ski — for personal watercraft

Walkman — for small cassette and/or radio player with earphones

Gore-Tex — for a water-repellant, breathable fabric

Student Book (LG1.03B—TOC 16: Word Study & Spelling)

Answers to Extra Practice

Grammar

1. (F) We spent two weeks in the Rocky Mountains.

2. (F) The old boat was left to deteriorate.

3. (S) Go to the last house on the corner of Glasgow Street.

4. (F) We camped near the Fraser River on the weekend.

5. (S) Her home is just east of town. It is the first house on the left past the high school.

6. (S) (F) Sam is going to teach me to play tennis as soon as the new courts are built.

7. (S) (F) It is not a problem if you can't make it to the meeting on time.

8. (F) The next time you want to be involved, please call first.

9. (S) (F) Rita likes to read historical fiction books.

10. (F) (S) Phrases that are unattached to any sentence are sentence fragments.

(WR5.07B—TOC 4: Grammar)

Mechanics

Possible answers

1. Type of font (typeface)	2. Size of type
3. Use of white space	4. Bold or italic type
5. Charts or graphs	6. Boxes, bullets, and underlining

Student work.

(MD1.02D—TOC 8: Mechanics)

Usage & Style

Possible answers

1. "People are more satisfied when they look after their own problems."

2. "That was an excellent movie."

3. When she started her car, Wilma was frightened by noises which seemed to come from the muffler and from under the hood.

4. "I wish you were good at getting up in the morning instead of my always trying to get you out of bed."

5. colloquial	6. colloquial
7. jargon	8. slang
9. colloquial	10. jargon

(LG1.02B—TOC 15: Usage & Style)

Word Study & Spelling

1. weird — C	2. hieght — height
3. noticable — noticeable	4. happyness — happiness
5. admireable — admirable	6. commitee — committee
7. usable — C	8. advantageous — C
9. receive — C	10. sleigh — C
11. acheive — achieve	12. suficient — sufficient
13. protein — C	14. sillyness — silliness
15. controled — controlled	16. neighbour — C
17. seiling — ceiling	18. strangly — strangely
19. giggle — C	20. couragous — courageous

(WR5.11B—TOC 16: Word Study & Spelling)

	GRADE 9 EXPECTATIONS	DEMONSTRATION OF LEARNING	ASSESSMENT TOOLS
LITERATURE STUDIES AND READING			
Overall (LIV.01P)	• read and demonstrate an understanding of a variety of literary and informational texts		
Specific (LI1.02P)	• select and read texts for a variety of purposes, with an emphasis on recognizing the elements of literary genres and the organization of informational materials, collecting and using information, extending personal knowledge, and responding imaginatively	• discuss changes in advertising and speculate on future (Introducing the Unit #1)	• TOC 14: Tracking Expectations
(LI1.04P)	• locate and use explicit information and ideas from texts in forming opinions and developing generalizations	• give examples from models for use in interpretation (Investigating the Models SB #1–6)	• AR 21: Response to Media
WRITING			
Overall (WRV.01P)	• use print and electronic sources to gather information and explore ideas for their written work	• find print ads and Web pages to use as models for advertisement and Web page (Writer's Workshop TG #1) • develop ideas for print ad and Web page (Writer's Workshop SB #1–5)	• AR 1: Advertisement • AR 1: Advertisement
Specific (WR1.01P)	• investigate potential topics by asking questions, identifying information needs, and developing research plans to gather data	• formulate questions to gather information for advertisement (Writer's Workshop TG #2)	• AR 1: Advertisement
Overall (WRV.02P)	• identify the literary and informational forms suited to specific purposes and audiences and use the forms appropriately in their own writing, with an emphasis on communicating information accurately		
Specific (WR2.01P)	• identify the purpose for each piece of writing	• design ad with purpose in mind (Writer's Workshop TG #2)	• AR 1: Advertisement
(WR2.02P)	• identify the specific audience for each piece of writing	• design ad for specific audience (Writer's Workshop TG #2)	• AR 1: Advertisement
Overall (WRV.03P)	• use a variety of forms of writing to express themselves, clarify their ideas, and engage the audience's attention, imagination, and interest	• write copy and format print ad and Web page (Writer's Workshop SB #6–7)	• AR 1: Advertisement
Overall (WRV.04B)	• revise their written work, collaboratively and independently, with a focus on support for ideas, accuracy, clarity, and unity	• revise print ad and Web page (Writer's Workshop SB #8–9)	• AR 1: Advertisement
Overall (WRV.05B)	• edit and proofread to produce final drafts, using correct grammar, spelling, and punctuation, according to the conventions of standard Canadian English specified for this course, with the support of print and electronic resources when appropriate	• edit and proofread print ad and Web page (Writer's Workshop SB #9)	• AR 1: Advertisement
Specific (WR5.07B)	• identify and correct sentence fragments, run-on sentences, and comma splices	• identify sentence fragments (Grammar TG #1) • write complete sentences from sentence fragments (Grammar TG #2) • use sentence fragments correctly (Grammar SB #1–4) • write complete sentences eliminating sentence fragments (EP: Grammar)	• TOC 4: Grammar • TOC 4: Grammar • TOC 4: Grammar • TOC 4: Grammar
(WR5.11B)	• use knowledge of a wide range of spelling patterns and rules to identify, analyze, and correct spelling errors	• use spelling rules to correct spelling (Word Study & Spelling TG) • write down words dictated using spelling rules (More Support TG, page 264) • spell words correctly (EP: Word Study & Spelling)	• TOC 16: Word Study & Spelling • TOC 16: Word Study & Spelling • TOC 16: Word Study & Spelling

AR=Assessment Rubric   EP=Extra Practice   SB=Student Book   SSEC=Student Self-Evaluation Checklist   TG=Teacher's Guide   TOC=Teacher Observation Checklist

GRADE 9 EXPECTATIONS		DEMONSTRATION OF LEARNING	ASSESSMENT TOOLS
LANGUAGE			
Overall (LGV.01P)	• use knowledge of vocabulary and language conventions to speak, write, and read clearly and correctly		
Specific (LG1.02B)	• identify and explain examples of slang, jargon, dialect, and colloquialism, as well as of standard Canadian English, in literary texts and their own oral and written work	• decide what forms of writing are formal or informal (Usage & Style TG #1) • create class scrapbook of "Varieties of English" (Usage & Style TG #2) • write sentences in formal standard Canadian English (More Support TG, page 264) • identify standard and nonstandard Canadian English, colloquialisms, and slang (Usage & Style SB #1–5) • write sentences in standard Canadian English; identify examples of colloquialisms, slang, and jargon (EP: Usage & Style)	• TOC 15: Usage & Style • TOC 15: Usage & Style • TOC 15: Usage & Style • TOC 15: Usage & Style • TOC 15: Usage & Style
(LG1.06B)	• recognize, describe, and correct sentence errors in oral and written language	• identify sentence fragments (Grammar TG #1) • write complete sentences from sentence fragments (Grammar TG #2) • use sentence fragments correctly (Grammar SB #1–4)	• TOC 4: Grammar • TOC 4: Grammar • TOC 4: Grammar
Overall (LGV.02B)	• use listening techniques and oral communication skills to participate in classroom discussions and more formal activities, such as storytelling, role playing, and reporting/ presenting, for specific purposes and audiences		
Specific (LG2.03P)	• work with a partner to plan and make oral presentations to a small group, selecting and using vocabulary and methods of delivery to suit audience and purpose	• with a partner, record and play 30-second radio ad (More Oral Language TG)	• SSEC 5: Oral Presentation
(LG2.06P)	• identify examples of the use of oral communication skills in school and the world outside the school	• interview people whose jobs involve listening and speaking skills (Oral Language Extension TG) • interview teacher to create radio ad to promote oral communication skills (Oral Language Extension SB)	• TOC 1: Conducting an Interview • TOC 1: Conducting an Interview
MEDIA STUDIES			
Overall (MDV.01P)	• identify and describe the elements, intended audiences, and production practices of a variety of media forms	• discuss and explain reaction to models (Investigating the Models TG)	• AR 21: Response to Media
Specific (MD1.01B)	• demonstrate critical thinking skills by identifying the differences between explicit and implicit messages in media works	• compare packaging on milk containers with print ad model (Extending the Models TG #2)	• AR 21: Response to Media

AR=Assessment Rubric   EP=Extra Practice   SB=Student Book   SSEC=Student Self-Evaluation Checklist   TG=Teacher's Guide   TOC=Teacher Observation Checklist

GRADE 9 EXPECTATIONS	DEMONSTRATION OF LEARNING	ASSESSMENT TOOLS
MEDIA STUDIES (continued)		
(MD1.02P) • identify and describe the elements used to structure media works in a variety of forms	• evaluate ads on the basis of visual features (Mechanics TG) • evaluate design and text of models (Mechanics SB #1–4) • explain how design elements have been used in advertisement (EP: Mechanics)	• TOC 8: Mechanics • TOC 8: Mechanics • TOC 8: Mechanics
(MD1.03P) • compare the reactions of different people or groups to a variety of media works	• explain what made people remember various advertisements (Introducing the Models TG #1) • log exposure to advertising over 24-hour period and evaluate influence (Media Link SB)	• AR 21: Response to Media • AR 21: Response to Media
(MD1.04P) • identify factors that influence media production, distribution, and advertising	• discuss factors in advertising (Introducing the Unit TG #2) • discuss financial impact of advertising on media • discuss reasons for short- and long-term ads (Extending the Models TG #1) • investigate current shopping sites on the Internet (More Challenge TG, page 263) • discuss motives for logos on products worn or carried (More Media TG)	• AR 21: Response to Media • AR 21: Response to Media • AR 21: Response to Media • AR 21: Response to Media • AR 21: Response to Media
Overall (MDV.02P) • use knowledge of a variety of media forms, purposes, and audiences to create media works		
Specific (MD2.02P) • create media works for different purposes	• make collage of advertisements they think are particularly effective (Introducing the Models TG #2)	• AR 12: Media Product

AR=Assessment Rubric   EP=Extra Practice   SB=Student Book   SSEC=Student Self-Evaluation Checklist   TG=Teacher's Guide   TOC=Teacher Observation Checklist

INSTRUCTIONAL STRATEGIES FOR THE APPLIED COURSE

PLANNING INFORMATION

Links to Other Nelson English 9 Resources

Literature & Media 9
See "A Product Advertisement," p. 322 and "Unico," p. 333.

Write Source 2000
Colloquialisms—"Colloquialisms," p. 138; **Design Elements**—"Designing Your Writing," pp. 27–29; **Sentence Fragments**—"Sentence Fragment," p. 86; **Slang**—"Slang," p. 140; **Spelling Rules**—"Improved Spelling," pp. 411–418

INTRODUCING THE UNIT

1. Activitiy #1 on page 250 from the Academic Course is appropriate for the Applied Course. (LI1.02P—TOC 14: Tracking Expectations)

2. To get students thinking about the media and advertising write the following statements on the board or on a handout. Discuss the meaning of the statements with the whole class or have students discuss them in small groups (one statement per group). With the second option, have the group choose a recorder to take notes and be responsible for reporting the group's discussion to the whole class. (MD1.04P—AR 21: Response to Media)

   • Advertising has changed the landscape of our country.
   • The most important part of the advertising picture is the consumer.
   • Advertising may have both a positive and a negative influence on people.
   • Advertising is a major source of jobs.
   • Advertisers appeal to the most basic human desires.

INTRODUCING THE MODELS

Activities #1–2 on page 250 from the Academic Course are appropriate for the Applied Course.

1. (MD1.03P—AR 21: Response to Media)

2. (MD2.02P—AR 12: Media Product)

3. Ask students if they agree or disagree with the following statement:

   Advertising is necessary to reduce the cost of newspapers, magazines, television programs, and most other media. Without it, consumers would pay a lot more for these things.

   Then ask them to predict what would happen if advertising were banned. (MD1.04P—AR 21: Response to Media)

INVESTIGATING THE MODELS

Ask students give their first impressions of the two models. You can use the following as prompts. (MDV.01P—AR 21: Response to Media)
   • Which advertisement appeals to you the most?
   • Which ad appeals to you the least?
   • What are some reasons for your answers?

Answers:
See the Academic Course on pages 251–252 for answers.
Student Book 1.–6. (LI1.04P—AR 21: Response to Media)

LEARNING GOALS

• write an advertisement
• identify and correct sentence fragments
• identify design elements
• adapt punctuation for advertisements
• identify and explain examples of slang and colloquialisms
• use knowledge of useful spelling rules

CHECKPOINT

Sample criteria for an advertisement:

• is designed to sell a product or service, create an image, provide information, or persuade audience to behave in certain way

• is almost always targeted at a particular audience

• usually relies on words and images to convey message

• is affected by medium in which it appears

• often breaks grammatical rules to increase impact

• promotes product directly or indirectly

The "cyberspace mall" is a reality. You can now buy books, CDs, appliances, cars, and many other products on the Internet. This form of shopping will expand greatly in the years ahead, and the competition among companies to get you to buy from them will be fierce. Have students imagine that they will soon have their own business in their chosen field. They will consider offering consumers their product or service on the Internet. Have them find out as much as they can about current shopping sites on the Internet, and answer the following questions:

- What sort of competition is already selling this product or service on the Internet?
- What kind of site (content and style) would they need to develop to compete with others selling this product or service?
- Where might they go to find someone to design their site?
- What are the pros and cons of having a Web site for a business?

Have students report their findings to the class. (MD1.04P—AR 21: Response to Media)

Ask students to work in pairs to write a 30-second radio advertisement for the Colony Hotel. Before writing their ads, they should discuss whether to base their ad on a factual or on an emotional approach. They should decide on the age of their target audience. Suggest that they may wish to use background music if they are trying to promote a particular mood. Once they have written their messages, students should practise them orally and then record and play them for the class. After each ad is presented, the listeners can critique the presentation stating what they liked, what they didn't like, and why. (LG2.03P—SSEC 5: Oral Presentation)

EXTENDING THE MODELS

1. Point out to students that some ads are effective for a limited amount of time while others may be used for a long time. Ask them which of these two categories the two models fit into. Have them justify their answers. (The second ad could be in use for a relatively long time because there is nothing that will become dated. The first ad on the Web site could become dated because of the use of statistics; in addition, the information available from the other sites at the top of the page might need updating.)

   Ask students for other examples of short- and long-term ads and have them give reasons for their choices. (MD1.04P—AR 21: Response to Media)

NOTE: If you developed a collage of ads on a bulletin board, students could refer to some of these for examples. Also, a series of posters with photographs of celebrities promoting milk was developed for the U.S. market. These were in many teen and sports magazines. They could be cited as examples of ads with a short life span since some of these people may not have been popular six months or a year later.

2. Activity #1 on page 252 from the Academic Course is appropriate for the Applied Course.

   (MD1.01B—AR 21: Response to Media)

WRITER'S WORKSHOP

1. Activity #1 on page 252 from the Academic Course is appropriate for the Applied Course.

   (WRV.01P—AR 1: Advertisement)

NOTE: You should complete the Mechanics section of this unit on pages 180 to 182 of the student book (identify design elements) before having students complete Writer's Workshop.

2. As an alternative to the focus of Writer's Workshop in the student book, you may prefer to have some students design a print or Web page advertisement for the business where they currently have a part-time job, or where they might wish to work in the future. Another option is to design the ad for a place where a member of their immediate or extended family works.

   Before designing the ad, have students make up a list of questions they need to ask. Remind them to use the information they have learned about ads in this unit to help them design their questions. They may have to arrange a meeting with an appropriate person in order to acquire the information they need. (WR1.01P—AR 1: Advertisement; WR2.01P—AR 1: Advertisement; WR2.02P—AR 1: Advertisement)

Student Book 1.–5. (WRV.01P—AR 1: Advertisement); 6.–7. (WRV.03P—AR 1: Advertisement); 8.–9. (WRV.04B—AR 1: Advertisement); 9. (WRV.05B—AR 1: Advertisement)

ORAL LANGUAGE EXTENSION

The activity on page 252 from the Academic Course is appropriate for the Applied Course.

(LG2.06P—TOC 1: Conducting an Interview)

Student Book (LG2.06P—TOC 1: Conducting an Interview)

GRAMMAR

1. Ask students to turn to page 51 in the student book. Have them identify any sentence fragments that exist in the dialogue spoken by Tim printed in capital letters. (HUH? MORE LEAVES? HOWZAT?) Point out that dialogue is another situation where sentence fragments are often found.

   Explain to students that most people use incomplete sentences in their everyday conversations. To illustrate this, you could ask four students to come to the front of the room to have a 30-second conversation on some topic. Tape record the conversation and then play it back to the class. If students hear a sentence fragment, they should raise their hands. Stop the recorder. Ask students to provide you with the sentence fragment, and write these on the board. Ask students to explain why they are sentence fragments. (WR5.07B—TOC 4: Grammar; LG1.06B—TOC 4: Grammar)

2. Activity #4 on page 253 from the Academic Course is appropriate for the Applied Course.

(WR5.07B—TOC 4: Grammar; LG1.06B—TOC 4: Grammar)

Answers:
See the Academic Course on pages 253–254 for answers.

Student Book 1.–4. (WR5.07B—TOC 4: Grammar; LG1.06B—TOC 4: Grammar)

MEDIA LINK

Student Book (MD1.03P—AR 21: Response to Media)

MECHANICS

The activity on page 254 from the Academic Course is appropriate for the Applied Course.

(MD1.02P—TOC 8: Mechanics)

Answers:
See the Academic Course on pages 254–255 for answers.

Student Book 1.–4. (MD1.02P—TOC 8: Mechanics)

USAGE & STYLE

Activities #1 and 4 on pages 255 and 256 from the Academic Course are appropriate for the Applied Course.

1. (LG1.02B—TOC 15: Usage & Style)

2. (LG1.02B—TOC 15: Usage & Style)

Answers:
See the Academic Course on page 256 for answers.

Student Book 1.–5 (LG1.02B—TOC 15: Usage & Style)

WORD STUDY & SPELLING

The activity on page 256 from the Academic Course is appropriate for the Applied course.

(WR5.11B—TOC 16: Word Study & Spelling)

MORE MEDIA

Students are very aware of advertising on things that they wear or carry every day (e.g., T-shirts, jackets, caps, bags). Ask students for examples of some currently popular logos and brand names that they have purchased recently and list them on the board. Discuss their motives in purchasing these items, and the motives of the company in selling them. Use the following questions as prompts.

- Why do you buy clothes and bags with particular logos?
- How does one brand or logo become "the thing to have"?
- How do companies keep your interest in buying their brand?
- Do you think it is fair that companies who produce such popular brands charge more for their products? Why or why not?

Have students bring to class some of the ads for popular brands that they buy or would like to buy. Ask them to identify the techniques used in the ads to persuade them to buy the product. (MD1.04P—AR 21: Response to Media)

MORE SUPPORT

Ask students to rewrite the following sentences in formal standard Canadian English. (LG1.02B—TOC 15: Usage & Style)
1. "I ain't got no way to get home after the game," said Shawn.
2. By the looks of the old ticker it will soon be time to chow down.
3. He always drags on complaining about somethin'. What a sourpuss!
4. "I'm mighty glad to meecha," said the new neighbour.
5. We're meeting the gang at our usual hangout.

Possible answers
1. "I have no way to get home after the game," said Shawn.
2. According to the time on my watch, it will soon be time for dinner.
3. He is always complaining about something. He is not a nice person to be with at times.
4. "I am very pleased to meet you," said the new neighbour.
5. We are meeting our friends at our usual meeting place.

MORE SUPPORT

Dictate the following words and have students write them using the rules presented in this section. (WR5.11B—TOC 16: Word Study & Spelling)

niece	neighbour	shriek
weigh	civil	ceiling
cabin	spying	satisfying
dryer	admiring	unnerving
canning	fatter	

ANSWERS TO EXTRA PRACTICE

See the Academic Course on page 257 for answers.

Grammar
(WR5.07B–TOC 4: Grammar)

Mechanics
(MD1.02P—TOC 8: Mechanics)

Usage & Style
(LG1.02B—TOC 15: Usage & Style)

Word Study & Spelling
(WR5.11B—TOC 16: Word Study & Spelling)

GRAMMAR

NAME: _____   DATE: _____

Identify the following groups of words as sentences (S) or sentence fragments (F). Rewrite the sentence fragments to make them into sentences.

1. Spent two weeks in the Rocky Mountains.

   _____

2. The old boat left to deteriorate.

   _____

3. Go to the last house on the corner of Glasgow Street.

   _____

4. Camped near the Fraser River on the weekend.

   _____

5. Her home is just east of town. It is the first house on the left past the high school.

   _____

6. Sam is going to teach me to play tennis. As soon as the new courts are built.

   _____

7. You can't make it to the meeting on time. No problem.

   _____

8. And so the next time you want to be involved, please call first.

   _____

9. Rita likes to read fiction books. Historical fiction.

   _____

10. Phrases that are unattached to any sentence. These are sentence fragments.

   _____

MECHANICS

NAME: _____ DATE: _____

List six design elements (e.g., colour) that you could consider using in an advertisement to direct your readers' eyes to key information.

1. _____

2. _____

3. _____

4. _____

5. _____

6. _____

Find a magazine advertisement that illustrates as many of the design elements listed above as possible. Explain below how these design elements have been used. Attach the advertisement to this sheet.

_____

_____

_____

_____

_____

_____

_____

_____

USAGE & STYLE

NAME: _____ DATE: _____

Rewrite the following nonstandard Canadian English sentences into standard Canadian English.

1. "Folks does best when they look after their own problems."

   _____

2. "That picture weren't half bad."

   _____

3. Starting her car, Wilma was frightened when she heard noises which seemed to come from the silencer and under the bonnet.

   _____

4. "Well, I'd a heap rather you was good about gettin' up in the morning instead of draggin' yuh out of the sack."

   _____

Identify each of the following as a colloquial expression (C), slang (S), or jargon (J).

5. "Like, what's happenin', man?" _____

6. "She's nothing but a stuffed shirt." _____

7. "Download the information before removing the disk from the hard drive." _____

8. "You think you are going to the concert? Not." _____

9. "Sometimes you really get on my nerves." _____

10. "You have many types of investment alternatives including GICs, stocks, bonds, and mutual funds."

    _____

WORD STUDY & SPELLING

NAME: _____ DATE: _____

Some of the following words are spelled correctly; others are spelled incorrectly. In the space provided after each word, write (C) if the word is spelled correctly. If the word is spelled incorrectly, write it correctly.

1. weird _____

2. hieght _____

3. noticable _____

4. happyness _____

5. admireable _____

6. commitee _____

7. usable _____

8. advantageous _____

9. receive _____

10. sleigh _____

11. acheive _____

12. suficient _____

13. protein _____

14. sillyness _____

15. controled _____

16. neighbour _____

17. seiling _____

18. strangly _____

19. giggle _____

20. couragous _____

Unit 12: Letter to the Editor

Academic Expectations

GRADE 9 EXPECTATIONS	DEMONSTRATION OF LEARNING	ASSESSMENT TOOLS
LITERATURE STUDIES AND READING		
Overall (LIV.01D) • read and demonstrate an understanding of a variety of literary and informational texts, from contemporary and historical periods	• demonstrate understanding of forms of persuasion (Reflect on Persuasive Writing Forms SB #1–2)	• TOC 13: Tracking Expectations
Specific (LI1.03B) • describe a variety of reading strategies and select and use them effectively before, during, and after reading to understand texts	• using titles, predict which letter to the editor will be more controversial (Introducing the Models TG #2)	• TOC 10: Reading Strategies
(LI1.04D) • locate explicit information and ideas in texts to use in developing opinions and interpretations	• give examples from models for use in interpretation (Investigating the Models SB #1–6)	• AR 22: Response to Reading
(LI1.05D) • analyze information, ideas, and elements in texts to make inferences about meaning	• explain why logic is weak in series of statements; rewrite statements (Writer's Workshop TG)	• TOC 13: Tracking Expectations
(LI1.07D) • explain how readers' different backgrounds might influence the way they understand and interpret a text	• analyze level of language in letters to the editor to infer readership (Extending the Models TG #3)	• TOC 13: Tracking Expectations
Overall (LIV.02D) • demonstrate an understanding of the elements of a variety of literary and informational forms, with a focus on plays, short stories, and short essays	• discuss purposes of a letter to the editor (Introducing the Models TG #1) • discuss use of statistics in letters to the editor (Extending the Models TG #1) • identify tone in letters to the editor and discuss whether content fits tone (Extending the Models TG #2) • compare four forms of persuasive writing (Looking Over Persuasive Writing Forms SB #1) • evaluate letters to the editor (Using the Persuasive Writing Forms SB #3)	• TOC 13: Tracking Expectations • TOC 13: Tracking Expectations • TOC 13: Tracking Expectations • TOC 13: Tracking Expectations • TOC 13: Tracking Expectations
Overall (LIV.03B) • identify and explain the effect of specific elements of style in a variety of literary and informational texts		
Specific (LI3.01D) • explain how authors use diction and phrasing to achieve particular effects in their writing	• identify level of language (formal or informal) in letters to the editor (Extending the Models TG #3)	• TOC 13: Tracking Expectations
WRITING		
Overall (WRV.01D) • use a variety of print and electronic sources to gather information and explore ideas for their written work	• gather and organize ideas for letter to the editor (Writer's Workshop SB #1–4)	• AR 11: Letter to the Editor
Specific (WR1.03D) • group and label information and ideas, evaluate the relevance, accuracy, and completeness of the information and ideas; and discard irrelevant material	• create counterarguments in defending a position (More Support TG)	• AR 11: Letter to the Editor
Overall (WRV.03D) • use a variety of organizational techniques to present ideas and supporting details logically and coherently in written work	• write a letter to the editor (Writer's Workshop SB #5) • write a persuasive essay (More Challenge TG) • write a comparison of historical event in textbook and fiction (Using the Persuasive Writing Forms SB #1) • rewrite advertisement for new audience (Using the Persuasive Writing Forms SB #2) • write research report on explicit and implicit messages in television sitcoms or advertisements (Using the Persuasive Writing Forms SB #4)	• AR 11: Letter to the Editor • AR 16: Persuasive Writing • AR 2: Comparison • AR 1: Advertisement • AR 20: Research Report

AR=Assessment Rubric   EP=Extra Practice   SB=Student Book   SSEC=Student Self-Evaluation Checklist   TG=Teacher's Guide   TOC=Teacher Observation Checklist

GRADE 9 EXPECTATIONS		DEMONSTRATION OF LEARNING	ASSESSMENT TOOLS
WRITING (continued)			
Specific (WR3.06D)	• provide an introduction, body, and conclusion in written reports and short essays	• write research report on explicit and implicit messages in television sitcoms or advertisements (Using the Persuasive Writing Forms SB #4)	• AR 20: Research Report
Overall (WRV.04D)	• revise their written work, independently and collaboratively, with a focus on support for ideas and opinions, accuracy, clarity, and unity	• revise letter to the editor (Writer's Workshop SB #6) • revise comparison of historical event in textbook and fiction (Using the Persuasive Writing Forms SB #1) • revise advertisement for new audience (Using the Persuasive Writing Forms SB #2) • revise research report on explicit and implicit messages in television sitcoms or advertisements (Using the Persuasive Writing Forms SB #4)	• AR 11: Letter to the Editor • AR 2: Comparison • AR 1: Advertisement • AR 20: Research Report
Overall (WRV.05D)	• edit and proofread to produce final drafts, using conventions of standard Canadian English, with the support of print and electronic resources when appropriate	• edit and proofread letter to the editor (Writer's Workshop SB #6) • edit and proofread comparison of historical event in textbook and fiction (Using the Persuasive Writing Forms SB #1) • edit and proofread advertisement for new audience (Using the Persuasive Writing Forms SB #2) • edit and proofread research report on explicit and implicit messages in television sitcoms or advertisements (Using the Persuasive Writing Forms SB #4)	• AR 11: Letter to the Editor • AR 2: Comparison • AR 1: Advertisement • AR 20: Research Report
Specific (WR5.04B)	• edit and proofread their own and others' writing, identifying and correcting errors according to the requirements for grammar, usage, spelling, and punctuation	• check business letters for correct format, punctuation, and capitalization (Mechanics TG #1) • develop class list of guidelines for writing letters to the editor (Mechanics TG #2) • list rules for abbreviations in formal writing (Mechanics TG #3) • check format, punctuation, and capitalization in letters to the editor (Mechanics SB #1) • create lists of proofreading strategies (Word Study & Spelling TG #1) • use proofreading strategies (Word Study & Spelling SB #1–2) • correct covering letter (EP: Mechanics) • list proofreading strategies (EP: Word Study & Spelling)	• TOC 8: Mechanics • TOC 8: Mechanics • TOC 8: Mechanics • TOC 8: Mechanics • TOC 16: Word Study & Spelling • TOC 16: Word Study & Spelling • TOC 8: Mechanics • TOC 16: Word Study & Spelling
(WR5.09B)	• make pronouns agree with their antecedents in number and gender	• discuss use of subjective, objective, and possessive pronouns (Grammar TG #1) • use chart to determine case, person, gender, and number of personal pronouns (Grammar TG #2) • give case, person, gender, and number of personal pronouns in model (Grammar TG #3) • make pronouns agree with their antecedents (Grammar TG #4) • correct written work so pronouns agree with antecedents (Grammar SB #1–2) • correct errors in pronoun antecedent agreement (EP: Grammar)	• TOC 4: Grammar • TOC 4: Grammar • TOC 4: Grammar • TOC 4: Grammar • TOC 4: Grammar • TOC 4: Grammar
(WR5.14B)	• use a variety of resources to correct errors in spelling	• list limitations of spell checker (Word Study & Spelling TG #2)	• TOC 16: Word Study & Spelling

AR=Assessment Rubric   EP=Extra Practice   SB=Student Book   SSEC=Student Self-Evaluation Checklist   TG=Teacher's Guide   TOC=Teacher Observation Checklist

GRADE 9 EXPECTATIONS	DEMONSTRATION OF LEARNING	ASSESSMENT TOOLS
LANGUAGE		
Overall (LGV.01D)	• use knowledge of vocabulary and language conventions to speak, write, and read competently using a level of language appropriate to the purpose and audience		
Specific (LG1.03B)	• identify words borrowed from other languages and words and terms recently introduced to describe new ideas, inventions, and products, and explain their origins	• identify words from the Near East (Word Origins SB)	• TOC 16: Word Study & Spelling
(LG1.04B)	• select words and phrases appropriate to informal and formal styles, to suit the purpose and intended audience of oral and written work	• consider being concise in letters (Usage & Style TG #1) • discuss suggestions for making letters stronger (Usage & Style TG #2) • provide examples of forceful writing (Usage & Style SB #1–6) • rewrite sentences making them effective (EP: Usage & Style)	• TOC 15: Usage & Style • TOC 15: Usage & Style • TOC 15: Usage & Style • TOC 15: Usage & Style
(LG1.05D)	• recognize, describe, and use correctly, in oral and written language, the language structures of standard Canadian English and its conventions of grammar and usage, including: – parts of speech: nouns, pronouns, verbs, adverbs, adjectives, conjunctions, prepositions, interjections – agreement between subject and verb, and between pronoun and antecedent	• discuss use of subjective, objective, and possessive pronouns (Grammar TG #1) • use chart to determine case, person, gender, and number of personal pronouns (Grammar TG #2) • give case, person, gender, and number of personal pronouns in model (Grammar TG #3) • make pronouns agree with their antecedents (Grammar TG #4) • correct written work so pronouns agree with antecedents (Grammar SB #1–2) • correct errors in pronoun antecedent agreement (EP: Grammar)	• TOC 4: Grammar • TOC 4: Grammar • TOC 4: Grammar • TOC 4: Grammar • TOC 4: Grammar • TOC 4: Grammar
(LG1.07B)	• recognize, describe, and use correctly, in oral and written language, the conventions of standard Canadian English for spelling, capitalization, and punctuation, including: – spelling: homophones and possessive pronouns and adjectives – capitalization: of proper nouns and in direct quotations, scripts, dialogue, and poetry – punctuation: period, question mark, exclamation mark, comma, dash, apostrophe, colon, quotation marks, parentheses, ellipses	• check business letters for correct format, punctuation, and capitalization (Mechanics TG #1) • develop class list of guidelines for writing letters to the editor (Mechanics TG #2) • list rules for abbreviations in formal writing (Mechanics TG #3) • check format, punctuation, and capitalization in letter to the editor (Mechanics SB #1) • correct covering letter (EP: Mechanics)	• TOC 8: Mechanics • TOC 8: Mechanics • TOC 8: Mechanics • TOC 8: Mechanics • TOC 8: Mechanics
Overall (LGV.02B)	• use listening techniques and oral communication skills to participate in classroom discussions and more formal activities, such as storytelling, role playing, and reporting/ presenting, for specific purposes and audiences	• discuss types of information needed to form an opinion (Introducing the Unit TG #1) • share reasons why they took a particular position on an issue (Introducing the Unit TG #2) • discuss importance of free speech and critical analysis of opinions (Introducing the Unit TG #3)	• TOC 13: Tracking Expectations • TOC 13: Tracking Expectations • TOC 13: Tracking Expectations
Specific (LG2.01D)	• communicate orally in group discussions for different purposes, with a focus on identifying key ideas and supporting details, distinguishing fact from opinion, asking clarifying questions, and following instructions	• give impromptu speeches expressing an opinion (More Oral Language TG)	• TOC 11: Speaking
(LG2.02D)	• communicate in group discussions by sharing the duties of the group, speaking in turn, listening actively, taking notes, paraphrasing key points made by others, exchanging and challenging ideas and information, asking appropriate questions, reconsidering their own ideas and opinions, managing conflict, and respecting the opinions of others	• in groups of three or four, debate issue featured in persuasive speech (Oral Language Extension SB)	• TOC 5: Group Work

AR=Assessment Rubric   EP=Extra Practice   SB=Student Book   SSEC=Student Self-Evaluation Checklist   TG=Teacher's Guide   TOC=Teacher Observation Checklist

GRADE 9 EXPECTATIONS	DEMONSTRATION OF LEARNING	ASSESSMENT TOOLS
LANGUAGE (continued)		
(LG2.03D) • plan and make oral presentations to a small group or the class, selecting and using vocabulary and methods of delivery to suit audience and purpose; gather ideas and information; plan, create, rehearse, revise, and assess presentations such as dramatizations, reports, and speeches	• give a persuasive speech based on their letter to the editor (Oral Language Extension SB)	• TOC 11: Speaking
(LG2.07D) • analyze their own and others' oral presentations to identify strengths and weaknesses, and plan ways to improve their performance	• after hearing speech, give speaker feedback (Oral Language Extension SB)	• SSEC 5: Oral Presentation
MEDIA STUDIES		
Overall (MDV.01D) • use knowledge of the elements, intended audiences, and production practices of a variety of media forms to analyze specific media works		
Specific (MD1.01B) • demonstrate critical thinking skills by identifying the differences between explicit and implicit messages in media works	• compare book covers for different audiences (Using the Persuasive Writing Forms SB #2) • identify differences between explicit and implicit messages in television sitcoms or advertisements (Using the Persuasive Writing Forms SB #4)	• AR 21: Response to Media • AR 21: Response to Media
(MD1.02D) • identify how elements of media forms are used in a variety of media works and explain the effects of different treatments	• analyze editorial cartoons (Media Link SB)	• AR 21: Response to Media
(MD1.03D) • compare and explain their own and their peers' reactions to a variety of media works	• compare reactions to two editorials (newspaper or magazine and radio or television) (More Media TG)	• AR 21: Response to Media
Overall (MDV.02D) • use knowledge of a variety of media forms, purposes, and audiences to create media works and describe their intended effect		
Specific (MD2.01D) • adapt a work of literature to another media form and determine what aspects have been strengthened and/or weakened by the adaptation	• draw cartoon to illustrate point made in letter to the editor (Media Link SB)	• AR 12: Media Product
(MD2.03D) • create media works appropriate to different audiences and explain why a particular design should appeal to a particular audience	• redesign book cover for new audience and explain (Using the Persuasive Writing Forms SB #2)	• AR 12: Media Product

AR=Assessment Rubric   EP=Extra Practice   SB=Student Book   SSEC=Student Self-Evaluation Checklist   TG=Teacher's Guide   TOC=Teacher Observation Checklist

INSTRUCTIONAL STRATEGIES FOR THE ACADEMIC COURSE

PLANNING INFORMATION

Links to Other Nelson English 9 Resources

Literature & Media 9
Letter to the Editor—See "A Mother's Heart Aches" by Carol Cayenne, pp. 166–167.

Write Source 2000
Letters—"Writing Business Letters," pp. 241–250; **Arguments**—"Thinking Through an Argument," pp. 121–122; **Pronoun Agreement**—"Problems with Pronouns," p. 90; **Proofreading**—"Editing and Proofreading," pp. 79–83

LEARNING GOALS

- write a letter to the editor
- make pronouns agree with their antecedents in gender and number
- use correct punctuation, capitalization, and format in letters
- use effective openings
- use strong arguments
- use effective proofreading strategies

INTRODUCING THE UNIT

1. Point out to students that, in our everyday lives, all of us are continually forming opinions about a wide variety of subjects: everything from a new trend in clothing to a decision made by one of our friends. Not only are we forming opinions but we are expressing them to friends, family, teachers, and others in the community. Have students think about the kinds of opinions they form each day and note some of their examples on the board.

   Discuss which kinds of opinions are easy to form and which are more difficult. (Those that have to do with everyday life can be relatively easy but forming opinions about controversial issues can be harder. Discuss with students what kinds of information a person needs to develop a sound opinion on such issues (e.g., facts, statistics, current policy, history of the issue, what those in authority say).

   Point out that as they begin to form opinions on these issues, students will likely find articles in newspapers and magazines that they think are wrong, silly, or taking a position they don't agree with; they may feel they want to express their opinion on the issue at hand. This unit will provide them with information on how to express an opinion in a letter to the editor. (LGV.02B—TOC 13: Tracking Expectations)

2. Ask students to think of a situation when they have had to decide between two opposing opinions. Ask them to think about the position they supported and answer the following questions in point form in their notebooks:

   - Was it difficult to decide which position to support? Why?
   - Did you make this decision yourself or were you influenced by friends, family members, an authority figure, an expert, or anyone else?
   - Was your position based mainly on facts or emotion?
   - If you were asked for your opinion on the same matter again, would you take the same position? Why or why not?

   Ask students who feel comfortable to share some of their thoughts with the rest of the class. (LGV.02B—TOC 13: Tracking Expectations)

3. Discuss why free speech (the right to express an opinion) is important in a democratic society, and why it is equally important for students to learn to analyze critically the persuasive messages, including opinions, bombarding them every day. (LGV.02B—TOC 13: Tracking Expectations)

INTRODUCING THE MODELS

1. Ask students to read the introduction to the unit on page 186 of the student book. Emphasize the five purposes that a letter to the editor may have. For each purpose, ask students to suggest an example of an issue or situation in their own

community that might prompt a letter to the editor. (LIV.02D—TOC 13: Tracking Expectations)

2. Ask students to read the titles of the two letters to the editor in their student books and predict which letter will be the more controversial. Have them share the reasons for their opinions. (LI1.03B—TOC 10: Reading Strategies)

INVESTIGATING THE MODELS

Answers:

1. The purpose of the first model is to express appreciation but also possibly to persuade readers of the value of downtime in families as opposed to organized activities; the purpose of the second model is to persuade readers of the need for action on a political issue.

2. The point of view in the first model is expressed as follows: "It was while doing nothing that my family and I would often end up having the most fun." The general thesis is that some of the best family times are the occasions when members just spend time together and don't do anything that has been organized. The second model's position is found in the following statement: "Unfortunately, he forgot the most important question of all: Was the carpet made from child labour and the exploitation of children?" The general thesis of this letter is that because many imported carpets are made from child labour, Canadian consumers should try to avoid buying them; they should also pressure the government and importers to adopt a system called "Rugmark" which tells consumers that a carpet was not made through the exploitation of children.

3. The main arguments in point form in "The Joy of Just Doing Nothing":
   - while the writer and her sister had a number of organized activities like piano lessons and museum visits when they were growing up, these weren't the most important things their parents gave them
   - what was important were the Sunday afternoons spent together doing things like chatting with her mom while she prepared Sunday dinner; helping to cut up the vegetables; watching baseball games with her dad; and going for casual walks in the park
   - some of the best times happen when you are just "doing nothing"

The main arguments in point form in "Don't Exploit Children":

   - when buying a carpet, the first question to ask is whether it was made with the labour of exploited children
   - thousands of children work in slave-like conditions
   - employers hire children because their small fingers can make the tiny knots that make carpets so attractive to Western consumers
   - children are taken from their families in exchange for small loans
   - they work as bonded labourers and can never escape the system because of the high interest rates charged by unscrupulous factory owners
   - Canada should follow Germany and require that carpets be marked with a tag called "Rugmark" which says they were not made with child labour

Some students might suggest that the second model is more convincing because the examples are stronger and it deals with hard facts; however, other students might argue that the first is equally effective in making its point. They might want to discuss the fact that each of the models has a different purpose. This influences the kinds of examples and tone that the writer uses but doesn't necessarily make one example weaker than the other.

CHECKPOINT

Sample criteria for letter to the editor:

- is used to criticize, correct, persuade, express appreciation, or question
- usually begins by identifying issue and expressing an opinion
- provides detailed arguments to support opinion
- has details that are arranged in effective order
- often has strongest argument near end of letter
- often ends with call to action, a question, or summary of main argument
- is usually written in formal language

4. Possible answer

The strongest example in "The Joy of Just Doing Nothing" is the enjoyment the family felt walking in the park. The author placed this argument in the best possible position (the end of the letter) as it is something most people can relate to and it leaves the reader with a strong impression of good times in the family.

The strongest argument in "Don't Exploit Children" is the example of the young Pakistani boy who escaped from his exploiting employer and was later murdered. The author placed this argument in the best possible position (near the beginning) since it establishes quickly the type of damage being done by those who exploit children in the carpet industry.

5. The first model ends with a summary and some advice: "Looking back, I know that spending time together on those occasions was really important. You don't always have to be out doing something special. Sometimes the special times are already taking place, and you don't even realize it."

The second model ends with a call to action and a question: "Consumers in Canada must be ready to challenge our government and importers on this important question. Wouldn't we all enjoy our carpets a lot more if we knew they were not made from the exploitation and suffering of children?"
Student work.

6. First model: "As a high school student growing up ..."; "'culturally important places'"; "My parents naturally felt the need to try to encourage us ..."; "But these heartfelt efforts ..."; "Sometimes the family would go for a walk ..."; "Looking back, I know that ..."

Second model: The entire letter is written in formal language.

Student Book 1.–5. (LI1.04D—AR 22: Response to Reading)

EXTENDING THE MODELS

1. Explain to students that some writers of letters to the editor use statistics to support their arguments, but that this technique should not be overused. Also, if statistics are used, they must be up-to-date. Have students collect and share some examples of letters with statistics in them. Ask them to comment on the use of this technique in Craig Kielburger's letter and in some of their examples. Do they find the statistics believable? Do they increase the effectiveness of the letter? (LIV.02D—TOC 13: Tracking Expectations)

2. Collect letters to the editor with a variety of tones (e.g., serious, humorous, urgent, angry, sad, light-hearted). Put the list of various tones on the board. Read the letters aloud. For each letter, ask students to identify the tone. Discuss whether the content fits the tone. (LIV.02D—TOC 13: Tracking Expectations)

3. Point out that most magazines have a letters-to-the-editor section. Ask students to collect five letters from different magazines (either print or on the Web), and then to identify the level of language (formal/informal) used in them. Did the level of language used in the letters match the language used in the rest of the magazine, or was it different? What might this tell you about the people who read this magazine? Discuss whether students would feel comfortable writing to a magazine that they read. If not, why not? (LI3.01D—TOC 13: Tracking Expectations; LI1.07D—TOC 13: Tracking Expectations)

WRITER'S WORKSHOP

NOTE: before students write their letters to the editor, you might want to complete the Mechanics section of this unit on pages 195–197 of the student book as it deals with proper format and punctuation for formal letter writing.

Challenge some students to write a persuasive essay in addition to a letter to the editor. Students can use The Writing Process on pages 10–15 of the student book as reference for writing a persuasive essay. Using the model on pages 14–15, point out to students the following characteristics of a persuasive essay:

- usually deals with some debatable subject
- assumes that the reader will hold the opposite point of view
- begins by identifying the issue and expressing an opinion
- anticipates the reader's concerns or arguments and addresses them
- presents supporting details
- relies on logical reasoning
- uses a third-person point of view
- concludes with a logical statement of what the reader should do or think

Topics for their essays might come from the editorial pages of newspapers and magazines. Students may wish to respond to social, political, or ethical issues facing all of society, or young people in particular. (WRV.03D—AR 16: Persuasive Writing)

MORE ORAL LANGUAGE

Point out to students that there may be times when they are expected to respond on the spot to someone who has asked their opinion. In order to practise responding, they are going to deliver some impromptu speeches in small groups.

Emphasize that when they are faced with a situation where a quick response is required, they should organize their answers using a similar framework to that used in a letter to the editor: state your opinion; provide arguments, reasons and/ or examples; provide a conclusion that either restates your opinion or provides a call to action. Listed below are two options for this activity:

1. Divide the class into groups of three, numbering each student 1, 2, or 3. Student 1 asks a question; student 2 answers the question; student 3 evaluates both the question and the response. Give each member of the group an opportunity to play each role.

2. Divide the class into small groups of four or five students. Ask students to think up enough questions for an impromptu-speech box for each group. Distribute the boxes to the groups with questions to be selected at random. Allow students one minute to gather their thoughts and then to give a response to the question drawn.

(LG2.01D—TOC 11: Speaking)

Tell students that they must take a position in the letters they write, avoiding ambivalence in stating their opinions. Indicate to students that one method of checking the strength of their arguments including reasons and examples to back them up, is to put themselves in the position of the reader. What weakness might the reader find in my arguments, reasons, or examples? How might I change them to make them stronger?

Write the statements below on the board or on an overhead transparency. Organize students into pairs and have them explain why the logic in each statement is weak. Then have students rewrite the statements. (LI1.05D—TOC 13: Tracking Expectations)

a) All people who employ young children are criminals. (generalization — can't prove this)
b) Factory owners use children with small fingers to tie the tiny knots because the tiny knots can only be tied by children. (circular argument — same idea)
c) Consumers in Canada haven't pressured our government enough on adopting "Rugmart." This is why children are still lacking nourishment and fresh air. (leap in logic with faulty cause-and-effect relationship)
d) Requiring students to work in factories is like requiring adults to work all night. (faulty analogy and weak logic)
e) Child labour is definitely on the rise in some countries. Last week I heard about a child being required to work at making carpets at the age of four. (misleading evidence — general statement supported with poor example)

Possible answers
a) Some people who employ young children may be committing criminal acts.
b) Factory owners use children to tie the tiny knots because adults' fingers are too big.
c) Consumers in Canada haven't pressured the government enough on adopting "Rugmark," a program which would reduce the sale of carpets made with child labour.
d) Requiring children to work in factories is the same as denying them their childhood.
e) Recent statistics released by the United Nations show that child labour is definitely on the rise in some countries.

Student Book 1.–4. (WRV.01D—AR 11: Letter to the Editor); 5. (WRV.03D—AR 11: Letter to the Editor); 6. (WRV.04D—AR 11: Letter to the Editor; WRV.05D—AR 11: Letter to the Editor)

ORAL LANGUAGE EXTENSION

Make clear to students that this activity is not asking for a fully developed, formal speech; rather, the purpose is to provide them with an opportunity to learn and practise those skills and behaviours which they would require in a more formal speech to a larger audience.

Student Book (LG2.02D—TOC 5: Group Work; LG2.03D—TOC 11: Speaking; LG2.07D—SSEC 5: Oral Presentation)

GRAMMAR

1. Indicate to students that pronouns perform all the same functions as nouns; however, unlike nouns (e.g., Claire), personal pronouns change form (e.g., she, her, hers) as their use in sentences changes. Sometimes, this causes difficulty in writing because the writer is not sure which pronoun to use. Put the following three sentences on the board:

   He watched TV with Emma.
   Claire phoned *him*.
   His favourite players sometimes made mistakes.

Point out that all three pronouns (in italics) in the above sentences refer to the same person, even though the forms are different in each sentence. Indicate that each of the personal pronouns belongs to a different case. The case of a pronoun is determined by how it is used (i.e., its function) in a sentence.

Ask students to look at the following chart to find the name of the case for each of the pronouns. (*He*—nominative or subjective case; *him*—objective case; *his*—possessive case) (WR5.09B—TOC 4: Grammar; LG1.05D—TOC 4: Grammar)

CASE	PERSON	GENDER	NUMBER	
			singular	plural
Nominative/ Subjective pronouns	first second third	masculine feminine neuter	I you he she it	we you they they they
Objective pronouns	first second third	masculine feminine neuter	me you him her it	us you them them them
Possessive pronouns	first second third	masculine feminine neuter	my, mine your, yours his her, hers it	our, ours you, yours their, theirs their, theirs their, theirs

NOTE: You may wish to explain that the pronoun "his" in the third sentence is used as an adjective. You may also wish to explain that possessive pronouns may be used in three ways: before nouns, by themselves, or before gerunds (an *-ing* word that functions as a noun), and that the form of the possessive pronoun may change depending on its use (my, mine). Example sentences are provided below.

This is *my* book.
This book is *mine.*
Take *mine.*
My sleeping late caused me to forget *my* book.

Summarize by saying that in previous units students learned that nouns and personal pronouns could be used as subjects, objects (direct objects, indirect objects, objects of prepositions), or possessives in sentences. When pronouns are used in these ways, we say that they are in the nominative (or subjective) case, objective case, or the possessive case.

2. In the following sentence, ask students these questions: Is "he" in the first, second, or third person? Is "he" masculine, feminine, or neuter? Is "he" singular or plural?

     He watched TV with Emma.

Using "he" as an example, show students how the chart may be used to determine the case, person, gender, and number of a personal pronoun. Select three different pronouns, each in a different case, and ask students to identify the case, person, gender, and number. (WR5.09B—TOC 4: Grammar; LG1.05D—TOC 4: Grammar)

Examples: we (nominative case, first person, plural)
            theirs (possessive case, third person, plural)
            her (objective case or possessive case, third person, feminine, singular)

3. Ask students to reread "The Joy of Doing Nothing" and to pick out all of the personal pronouns. For each pronoun indicate its case, person, gender (if applicable), and number. Ask them to try doing this exercise without using the chart. Then, have them check their answers using the chart. (WR5.09B—TOC 4: Grammar; LG1.05D—TOC 4: Grammar)

Example: me (objective case, first person, singular)

4. Use the following sentences to review some of the difficulties which can arise with agreement of pronouns and their antecedents. Ask students to identify the mistake in each sentence and suggest how to correct it. For example, in the first sentence the pronoun "our" (first person, plural) does not agree with the pronoun "I" (first person, singular). The pronoun "our" should be replaced with the first person, singular pronoun "my." The mistake in each sentence has been underlined. (WR5.09B—TOC 4: Grammar; LG1.05D—TOC 4: Grammar)

a) Last weekend, I attended a picnic in a nearby park at which members of our family were present. (number error — my)

b) Our car stopped on the way to the picnic because she ran out of gas. (gender error — it)

c) One of our friends joined us in the park. They enjoyed the day with us. (number error — he/she)

d) My family and me sometimes just enjoyed doing nothing. (case error — I)

Answers:

1. It seems, according to a recent article (Plaza Bans Teens, September 15) that the owner of Kitgate Plaza, Mr. Solanyi, wants to ban teenagers from the premises because they "create a nuisance." This accusation is simply untrue. My friends and I like to meet at the plaza after school, but we don't "create a nuisance," as the plaza owner claimed. Ask anyone who has visited the plaza while we were there, and he or she will tell you that we are polite and cause no trouble.

So why is Mr. Solanyi afraid of us? What have we done to deserve his distrust? He may not like our style of clothing or our hair; all people are entitled to their own opinions. But that does not mean it is all right to discriminate against my friends and me. It is he who is acting badly, not we.

2. Student work.

Student Book 1.–2. (WR5.09B—TOC 4: Grammar; LG1.05D—TOC 4: Grammar)

MEDIA LINK

If students are not able to locate award-winning cartoons, you may assist by bringing some to class or have them collect cartoons from various newspapers and magazines.

Student Book (MD1.02D—AR 21: Response to Media; MD2.01D—AR 12: Media Product)

MECHANICS

Tell students that they can usually find special instructions for writing letters to the editor on the editorial page of most newspapers or magazines. Indicate that the following instructions are fairly typical of those they will find.

- Letters should include your name, address, and phone number for verification.
- All letters are edited for clarity, style, and length.
- Writers are generally limited to 200 words.
- Only those people whose letters have been chosen for publication will be contacted.
- Copyright remains with the authors, but the publisher and its licensees may freely reproduce their work in print, electronic, or other forms.

MORE MEDIA

Ask students to select two editorials, one from a newspaper or magazine, and one from radio or television (tape recording). Ask them to show/play the editorials to different people (friends, members of their family), and to record the reactions in point form. Have them write a brief report on the results. (MD1.03D—AR 12: Media Product)

NOTE: If students are not able to find an example of an editorial on radio or television, as an alternative, ask them to record interviews of people on radio or television who are responding to a controversial issue (e.g., Should there be more universal testing of high school students? Should there be tougher fines for environmental polluters?).

1. Distribute copies of a business letter to your students, or ask them to bring in, with prior approval, copies of letters which have been received at home. Have them identify the basic parts (heading, salutation, body, closing, and signature), and the required punctuation and capitalization. When taking up the answers, make students aware of the format and punctuation options which exist, including the styles outlined on page 196 of the student book. (WR5.04B—TOC 8: Mechanics; LG1.07B—TOC 8: Mechanics)

2. Ask students to read pages 195 and 196 of the student book. Using the information developed from the activities above and the information in the book, develop a class list of rules to follow when writing letters to the editor. Post the guidelines in the classroom for reference. (WR5.04B—TOC 8: Mechanics; LG1.07B—TOC 8: Mechanics)

3. Point out that abbreviations may be used in informal writing, but not so often in formal writing. Working in groups of four, have students look for abbreviations in the models, the letters to the editor which they brought to school, and in articles in newspapers and magazines. Using these examples from formal writing, have them create a list of rules outlining when the use of abbreviations is appropriate in formal writing. (WR5.04B—TOC 8: Mechanics; LG1.07B—TOC 8: Mechanics)

Answers:

1. Student work.

Student Book 1. (WR5.04B—TOC 8: Mechanics; LG1.07B—TOC 8: Mechanics)

USAGE & STYLE

1. Write the following statement on the board:

   A letter to the editor is a short piece of writing.

   Point out to students that as writers, they must ensure that they "get the most out of every word, sentence, and paragraph" they put down on paper. Ask students what they think this statement means (e.g., get right to the point; avoid wordy sentences; use only the strongest arguments; be concise). Suggest that they should consider these things both at the drafting and the revising stages of their letter-writing. (LG1.04B—TOC 15: Usage & Style)

2. Tell students that the Usage & Style section contains suggestions for making their letters stronger. The first two suggestions in the purple boxes suggest ways to give their openings and closings more punch, while the last two provide suggestions for making their arguments more forceful. Discuss the statements one at a time. Following are some suggestions to use to clarify each statement. (LG1.04B—TOC 15: Usage & Style)

   Make every word count.
   Write each of the stems for the weak examples on the board (e.g., The purpose of this letter....). Discuss why each of the stems is weak. Ask students to look at the letters to the editor brought to class. Have them comment on the effectiveness of the openings.

   Use one or two rhetorical questions to engage your audience.
   Ask students to look for examples of rhetorical questions in the class collection of letters to the editor. Ask them if the questions engaged their attention. Point out that rhetorical questions usually appear in the title, in the opening, or in the conclusion. Ask students to comment on the effectiveness of the rhetorical question at the end of the second model. Point out that the question at the beginning of the model is not rhetorical because an answer would have been expected.

Avoid personal attacks and absolute statements.
Discuss why personal attacks should not be used. (could be sued for defamation of character; newspaper or magazine would probably not print them; readers may not be sympathetic to arguments)

Ask students to write one example of an absolute statement using each of the following: never, always, all, impossible. Have students read some of their absolute statements. Have other members of the class suggest ways the statements could be rewritten to make them acceptable.

Examples: Never trust a door-to-door sales person.
Parents should always believe their children.
All action films are silly.
It is impossible for him to be reelected.

State your position boldly, and back it up with strong statements.
Ask students for examples of redundant phrases (e.g., I think that ..., I for one ...) Emphasize that weak or ineffectual statements have no place in a letter to the editor.

Answers:

1. Possible answers
    The opening of "The Joy of Doing Nothing" is effective. The writer states clearly that she agrees with the position taken by a previous writer, and indicates that the article made her reflect on her "fondest memories of growing up." The tone of the letter (semi-formal) is established in the opening.

    The opening of "Don't Exploit Children" is very effective. The writer quickly gets to the point in correcting the writer of the article he is responding to: "Unfortunately, he forgot the most important question of all ..." This introduction also supports the title of the letter and sets up the arguments to follow.

2. Possible answers
    CAN "DOING NOTHING" REALLY BE FUN?

    WHY ARE CHILDREN BEING EXPLOITED?

3. Student work.

4. Possible answers
    "It was while doing nothing that my family and I would often end up having the most fun." Examples used to back up opinion: chatting with her mom; watching baseball with her dad; talking and walking in a nearby park.

    "Unfortunately, he forgot the most important question of all: Was the carpet made from child labour and the exploitation of children?" Examples used to back up opinion: the story of the young Pakistani boy, Iqbal Masih; the fact that many children work in slave-like conditions in the carpet industry; the fact that children are often turned into bonded labourers, a condition from which they rarely escape.

    "Consumers in Canada must be ready to challenge our government and importers on this important question." Example used to back up opinion: the fact that consumer pressure in Germany led to the adoption of a tag called "Rugmark" that guarantees that the rug was not made through the exploitation of children.

5. Possible answer
    Don't you think year-round schooling would be a good idea? It would make better use of space in classrooms, and result in better retention of what has been learned. These benefits make year-round schooling an option worth considering.

6. Student work.

Student Book 1.–6. (LG1.04B—TOC 15: Usage & Style)

WORD STUDY & SPELLING

1. Ask students why it is sometimes difficult to find errors in their own work when they proofread it. (focusing on content rather than the surface errors; lack of knowledge; carelessness; laziness) Explain why they should first read their writing for content, and then read their writing for surface errors. Also, if they spot what they think is an error, but aren't sure about it, they should use a handbook to find the correct answer.

   Ask students to describe methods they currently use to proofread their writing. List these on the board in point form. Tell students that this section of the unit lists several methods that can be used for proofreading. These methods are not limited to proofreading for spelling errors, but other errors as well. Have students compare their list with the proofreading methods in the student book. (WR5.04B—TOC 16: Word Study & Spelling)

2. Have students review the limitations of a computer spell checker and discuss why using one will not guarantee them word-perfect spelling. (WR5.14B—TOC 16: Word Study & Spelling)

Answers:

1. Student work.

2. Student work.

Student Book 1.–2. (WR5.04B—TOC 16: Word Study & Spelling)

WORD ORIGINS

Answers:

bungalow — a one-storey house; originally from Hindi *bangla* (house) of the Bengal type
calico — a coarse, brightly printed fabric; originally from *Calicut,* a town in India
cheetah — a long-legged, swift-running wild cat of Africa and southwest Asia, with black-spotted tawny fur and nonretractable claws: originally from Hindi *cita*, from Sanskrit *citrakaya* (tiger); from *citra (*bright, speckled); and *kaya* (body)
curry — a spicy dish of oriental, especially Indian, origin; originally from a Tamil word, *kari* (sauce or relish)
pyjamas — loose-fitting night-clothes; from Hindi *paijama* (loose-fitting trousers)
Student Book (LG1.03B—TOC 16: Word Study & Spelling)

ANSWERS TO EXTRA PRACTICE

Grammar

1. As July grew near, each of the girls was making her summer plans.

2. We athletes like to do stretching exercises before participating in strenuous activity.

3. She and I will be going to work at Mountain View Lodge this summer.

4. There are too many students and too few spaces. This situation is unacceptable.

5. Tomorrow, Lana and I are going to the new restaurant.

6. Last night, I attended the school play with my family.

7. This old sweater is my favourite, but I guess it's time to get rid of it.

8. The teacher showed the pronoun chart to us.

9. Neither Sonya nor I is responsible for the mess.

(WR5.09B—TOC 4: Grammar; LG1.05D—TOC 4: Grammar)

Mechanics
Possible answer

123 Sanford Drive
Southampton, ON
N0H 2L0

Dear Mr. Black:

I am writing to express my opinion on Jeff Snyder's article, Students Can Contribute Too (June 3, 2000, p. B9). My letter is attached. I can be reached at 797-0000 after 6 p.m. or by e-mail at ldobson@golden.net.

Yours sincerely,

Lillie Dobson

(WR5.04B—TOC 8: Mechanics; LG1.07B—TOC 8: Mechanics)

Usage & Style
Possible answers
1. Charging a bigger fee for the use of arenas for hockey will result in more young people dropping out of the sport.

2. The editorial written by Jeff Snyder does not include all the facts.

3. Don't Students' Opinions Count?

4. Isn't the Next Step Obvious?

5. Mr. Sams is mistaken if he thinks we are going to be swayed by his opinion.

6. A few students at that school are always getting into trouble.

7. Ms. Richardson doesn't have enough information about this issue.

8. Solutions like that suggested by the writer often don't work.

(LG1.04B—TOC 15: Usage & Style)

Word Study & Spelling
Possible answers
1. Read the piece backward looking at each word individually.

2. Have a classmate or friend read it.

3. Check and double-check statistics and the spelling of people's names.

4. Focus on only one or two possible problems (e.g., capitals, end punctuation).

5. Check carefully for the type of errors you make most often.

(WR5.04B—TOC 16: Word Study & Spelling)

REFLECT AND BUILD ON YOUR LEARNING

REFLECTING ON PERSUASIVE WRITING FORMS

1. Student work.

2. Possible answer

Other persuasive forms include opinion piece, letter of application, letter of recommendation, editorial, resume, persuasive/argumentative essay, brochure/pamphlet, speech, debate, advice column, and proposal.

Example: An editorial states a position on an issue; uses a number of arguments, often including statistics, to support a position; usually ends with a call to action for citizens or with a recommendation to government to change or adopt a particular policy. If you were the editor of a newspaper or magazine, you would write at least some of the editorials in your publication as part of your job.

Student Book 1.–2. (LIV.01D—TOC 13: Tracking Expectations)

LOOKING OVER PERSUASIVE WRITING FORMS

Answers

1. Possible answer

CRITERIA	COMPARISON	ADVERTISEMENT	LETTER TO THE EDITOR	EDITORIAL
Purpose	analyze, differentiate, explain, evaluate, inform, persuade, entertain	sell a product, create an image, promote a company or brand name	criticize, correct, persuade, express appreciation, question	express opinion of editor; persuade, inform, criticize, recommend
Audience	may be specific target or general	may be specific target or may be general	may be specific group or general readership	readership of publication or listeners/viewers in electronic media
Introduction	thesis sentence	may or may not have an introduction	identifies issue and expresses opinion	identifies issue and expresses opinion
Body	uses Block or Point-by-Point method to discuss similarities and differences	uses words and images (explicit and implicit to persuade)	provides detailed arguments	provides arguments to support position
Conclusion	usually a summary statement	may or may not have a conclusion	call to action, question, or summary	issues a call to action or recommends a change or adoption of a new policy especially for government

Student Book. 1. (LIV.02D—TOC 13: Tracking Expectations)

USING THE PERSUASIVE WRITING FORMS

1. Students do not have to be limited to a textbook for their comparisons since particular historical events may not be discussed in available history texts. Therefore, students could research other nonfiction sources. Encourage students to

develop a Venn diagram (page 163 of the student book) to help them with the organization of their comparison.

Student Book 1. (WRV.03D—AR 2: Comparison; WRV.04D—AR 2: Comparison; WRV.05D—AR 2: Comparison)

2. Due to the length of the explanation in the student book, you should ensure that all students understand exactly what the assignment is asking them to do. You may wish to review the differences (audience, images, and language) between the milk ads on pages 173–175 before assigning this activity.

Student Book 2. (MD1.01B—AR 21: Response to Media; MD2.03D—AR 12: Media Product; WRV.03D—AR 1: Advertisement; WRV.04D—AR 1: Advertisement; WRV.05D—AR 1: Advertisement)

3. Remind students that the list of features of letters to the editor are outlined for them on page 189 of the student book. The option of using magazine editorials, as well as newspaper editorials, could be made available to students.

Student Book 3. (LIV.02D—TOC 13: Tracking Expectations)

4. This assignment will be challenging for some students to complete individually. Therefore, you may wish to have students work in groups to write a focus statement, research the topic, and develop an outline including subtopics and supporting details. Then, ask each student to write his or her own draft report based on the outline done by the group and to supplement it with an effective introduction, conclusion, and bibliography. Once drafts are completed, students in the group could work together to check that each report is interesting to readers, is well organized, provides enough facts and examples, and follows the format required for a bibliography. Students could then write their final drafts and share them with members of the group.

Student Book 4. (WRV.03D—AR 20: Research Report; WR3.06D—AR 20: Research Report; WRV.04D—AR 20: Research Report; WR4.04B—SSEC 6: Peer Assessment: Writing; WRV.05D—AR 20: Research Report; MD1.01B—AR 21: Response to Media)

	GRADE 9 EXPECTATIONS	DEMONSTRATION OF LEARNING	ASSESSMENT TOOLS
LITERATURE STUDIES AND READING			
Overall (LIV.01P)	• read and demonstrate an understanding of a variety of literary and informational texts	• demonstrate understanding of forms of persuasion (Reflect on Persuasive Writing Forms SB #1–2)	• TOC 14: Tracking Expectations
Specific (LI1.02P)	• select and read texts for a variety of purposes, with an emphasis on recognizing the elements of literary genres and the organization of informational materials, collecting and using information, extending personal knowledge, and responding imaginatively	• identify fact and opinion in news program (Introducing the Unit TG #1) • suggest additional arguments for models (Extending the Models TG #1)	• TOC 14: Tracking Expectations • TOC 14: Tracking Expectations
(LI1.03B)	• describe a variety of reading strategies and select and use them effectively before, during, and after reading to understand texts	• predict content of model letters from titles and photographs (Introducing the Models TG #1)	• TOC 10: Reading Strategies
(LI1.04P)	• locate and use explicit information and ideas from texts in forming opinions and developing generalizations	• distinguish fact from opinion (Introducing the Unit TG #2) • give examples from models for use in interpretation (Investigating the Models SB #1–6)	• TOC 14: Tracking Expectations • AR 22: Response to Reading
(LI1.05P)	• make inferences based on the information and ideas presented in texts	• explain why logic is weak in series of statements; rewrite statements (Writer's Workshop TG)	• TOC 14: Tracking Expectations
Overall (LIV.02P)	• demonstrate an understanding of the elements of a variety of literary and informational forms, with a focus on plays, short stories, and newspaper and magazine articles	• discuss purposes of a letter to the editor (Introducing the Models TG #2) • discuss use of statistics in letters to the editor (Extending the Models TG #2) • identify tone in letters to the editor and discuss whether content fits tone (Extending the Models TG #2) • compare four forms of persuasive writing (Looking Over Persuasive Writing Forms SB #1) • evaluate letters to the editor (Using the Persuasive Writing Forms SB #3	• TOC 14: Tracking Expectations • TOC 14: Tracking Expectations • TOC 14: Tracking Expectations • TOC 14: Tracking Expectations • TOC 14: Tracking Expectations
WRITING			
Overall (WRV.01P)	• use print and electronic sources to gather information and explore ideas for their written work	• gather and organize ideas for letter to the editor (Writer's Workshop SB #1–4)	• AR 11: Letter to the Editor
Overall (WRV.03P)	• use a variety of forms of writing to express themselves, clarify their ideas, and engage the audience's attention, imagination, and interest	• write a letter to the editor (Writer's Workshop SB #5) • write a comparison of historical event in textbook and fiction (Using the Persuasive Writing Forms SB #1) • rewrite advertisement for new audience (Using the Persuasive Writing Forms SB #2) • write research report on explicit and implicit messages in television sitcoms or advertisements (Using the Persuasive Writing Forms SB #4)	• AR 11: Letter to the Editor • AR 2: Comparison • AR 1: Advertisement • AR 20: Research Report
Specific (WR3.06P)	• provide an introduction, body, and conclusion in written reports	• write research report on explicit and implicit messages in television sitcoms or advertisements (Using the Persuasive Writing Forms SB #4)	• AR 20: Research Report

AR=Assessment Rubric   EP=Extra Practice   SB=Student Book   SSEC=Student Self-Evaluation Checklist   TG=Teacher's Guide   TOC=Teacher Observation Checklist

GRADE 9 EXPECTATIONS	**DEMONSTRATION OF LEARNING**	**ASSESSMENT TOOLS**
WRITING (continued)		
Overall (WRV.04B) • revise their written work, collaboratively and independently, with a focus on support for ideas, accuracy, clarity, and unity	• revise letter to the editor (Writer's Workshop SB #6) • revise comparison of historical event in textbook and fiction (Using the Persuasive Writing Forms SB #1) • revise advertisement for new audience (Using the Persuasive Writing Forms SB #2) • revise research report on explicit and implicit messages in television sitcoms or advertisements (Using the Persuasive Writing Forms SB #4)	• AR 11: Letter to the Editor • AR 2: Comparison • AR 1: Advertisement • AR 20: Research Report
Overall (WRV.05B) • edit and proofread to produce final drafts, using correct grammar, spelling, and punctuation, according to the conventions of standard Canadian English specified for this course, with the support of print and electronic resources when appropriate	• edit and proofread letter to the editor (Writer's Workshop SB #6) • edit and proofread comparison of historical event in textbook and fiction (Using the Persuasive Writing Forms SB #1) • edit and proofread advertisement for new audience (Using the Persuasive Writing Forms SB #2) • edit and proofread research report on explicit and implicit messages in television sitcoms or advertisements (Using the Persuasive Writing Forms SB #4)	• AR 11: Letter to the Editor • AR 2: Comparison • AR 1: Advertisement • AR 20: Research Report
Specific (WR5.04B) • edit and proofread their own and others' writing, identifying and correcting errors according to the requirements for grammar, usage, spelling, and punctuation	• check business letters for correct format, punctuation, and capitalization (Mechanics TG #1) • develop class list of guidelines for writing letters to the editor (Mechanics TG #2) • list rules for abbreviations in formal writing (Mechanics TG #3) • check format, punctuation, and capitalization in letters to the editor (Mechanics SB #1) • create lists of proofreading strategies (Word Study & Spelling TG #1) • use proofreading strategies (Word Study & Spelling SB #1–2) • correct covering letter (EP: Mechanics) • list proofreading strategies (EP: Word Study & Spelling)	• TOC 8: Mechanics • TOC 8: Mechanics • TOC 8: Mechanics • TOC 8: Mechanics • TOC 16: Word Study & Spelling • TOC 16: Word Study & Spelling • TOC 8: Mechanics • TOC 16: Word Study & Spelling
(WR5.09B) • make pronouns agree with their antecedents in number and gender	• discuss use of subjective, objective, and possessive pronouns (Grammar TG #1) • use chart to determine case, person, gender, and number of personal pronouns (Grammar TG #2) • give case, person, gender, and number of personal pronouns in model (Grammar TG #3) • make pronouns agree with their antecedents (Grammar TG #4) • correct written work so pronouns agree with antecedents (Grammar SB #1–2) • identify case of pronouns (More Support TG, page 290) • rewrite sentences using pronouns correctly (More Support TG, page 291) • correct errors in pronoun antecedent (EP: Grammar)	• TOC 4: Grammar • TOC 4: Grammar • TOC 4: Grammar • TOC 4: Grammar • TOC 4: Grammar • TOC 4: Grammar • TOC 4: Grammar • TOC 4: Grammar
(WR5.14B) • use a variety of resources to correct errors in spelling	• list limitations of spell checker (Word Study & Spelling TG #2)	• TOC 16: Word Study & Spelling

AR=Assessment Rubric   EP=Extra Practice   SB=Student Book   SSEC=Student Self-Evaluation Checklist   TG=Teacher's Guide   TOC=Teacher Observation Checklist

GRADE 9 EXPECTATIONS	DEMONSTRATION OF LEARNING	ASSESSMENT TOOLS
LANGUAGE		
Overall (LGV.01P)	• use knowledge of vocabulary and language conventions to speak, write, and read clearly and correctly		
Specific (LG1.03B)	• identify words borrowed from other languages and words and terms recently introduced to describe new ideas, inventions, and products, and explain their origins	• identify words from the Near East (Word Origins SB)	• TOC 16: Word Study & Spelling
(LG1.04B)	• select words and phrases appropriate to informal and formal styles, to suit the purpose and intended audience of oral and written work	• avoid gender bias (More Challenge TG) • consider being concise in letters (Usage & Style TG #1) • discuss suggestions for making letters stronger (Usage & Style TG #2) • provide examples of forceful writing (Usage & Style SB #1–6) • rewrite sentences making them effective (EP: Usage & Style)	• TOC 4: Grammar • TOC 15: Usage & Style • TOC 15: Usage & Style • TOC 15: Usage & Style • TOC 15: Usage & Style
(LG1.05P)	• recognize, describe, and use correctly, in oral and written language, the language structures of standard Canadian English and its conventions of grammar and usage, including: – parts of speech: nouns, pronouns, verbs, adverbs, adjectives, conjunctions, prepositions, interjections – agreement between subject and verb, and between pronoun and antecedent	• discuss use of subjective, objective, and possessive pronouns (Grammar TG #1) • use chart to determine case, person, gender, and number of personal pronouns (Grammar TG #2) • give case, person, gender, and number of personal pronouns in model (Grammar TG #3) • make pronouns agree with their antecedents (Grammar TG #4) • correct written work so pronouns agree with antecedents (Grammar SB #1–2) • identify case of pronouns (More Support TG, page 290) • rewrite sentences using pronouns correctly (More Support TG, page 291) • correct gender bias in pronouns (More Challenge TG) • correct errors in pronoun antecedent agreement (EP: Grammar)	• TOC 4: Grammar • TOC 4: Grammar • TOC 4: Grammar • TOC 4: Grammar • TOC 4: Grammar • TOC 4: Grammar • TOC 4: Grammar • TOC 4: Grammar • TOC 4: Grammar
(LG1.07B)	• recognize, describe, and use correctly, in oral and written language, the conventions of standard Canadian English for spelling, capitalization, and punctuation, including: – spelling: homophones and possessive pronouns and adjectives – capitalization: of proper nouns and in direct quotations, scripts, dialogue, and poetry – punctuation: period, question mark, exclamation mark, comma, dash, apostrophe, colon, quotation marks, parentheses, ellipses	• check business letters for correct format, punctuation, and capitalization (Mechanics TG #1) • develop class list of guidelines for writing letters to the editor (Mechanics TG #2) • list rules for abbreviations in formal writing (Mechanics TG #3) • check format, punctuation, and capitalization in letter to the editor (Mechanics SB #1) • correct covering letter (EP: Mechanics)	• TOC 8: Mechanics • TOC 8: Mechanics • TOC8: Mechanics • TOC 8: Mechanics • TOC 8: Mechanics
Overall (LGV.02B)	• use listening techniques and oral communication skills to participate in classroom discussions and more formal activities, such as storytelling, role playing, and reporting/presenting, for specific purposes and audiences	• discuss types of information needed to form an opinion (Introducing the Unit TG #1)	• TOC 14: Tracking Expectations
Specific (LG2.01P)	• use listening techniques and oral communication skills to participate in group discussions	• in groups of three or four, debate issue featured in persuasive speech (Oral Language Extension SB) • give impromptu speeches expressing an opinion (More Oral Language TG)	• TOC 5: Group Work • TOC 11: Speaking
(LG2.03P)	• work with a partner to plan and make oral presentations to a small group, selecting and using vocabulary and methods of delivery to suit audience and purpose	• give a persuasive speech based on their letter to the editor (Oral Language Extension SB)	• TOC 11: Speaking

AR=Assessment Rubric   EP=Extra Practice   SB=Student Book   SSEC=Student Self-Evaluation Checklist   TG=Teacher's Guide   TOC=Teacher Observation Checklist

GRADE 9 EXPECTATIONS	DEMONSTRATION OF LEARNING	ASSESSMENT TOOLS
LANGUAGE (continued)		
(LG2.07P) • analyze their own and others' oral communication skills, identifying strengths and weaknesses and suggesting ways to improve	• after hearing speech, give speaker feedback (Oral Language Extension SB)	• SSEC 5: Oral Presentation
MEDIA STUDIES		
Overall (MDV.01P) • identify and describe the elements, intended audiences, and production practices of a variety of media forms		
Specific (MD1.01B) • demonstrate critical thinking skills by identifying the differences between explicit and implicit messages in media works	• compare book covers for different audiences (Using the Persuasive Writing Forms SB #2) • identify differences between explicit and implicit messages in television sitcoms or advertisements (Using the Persuasive Writing Forms SB #4)	• AR 21: Response to Media • AR 21: Response to Media
(MD1.02P) • identify and describe the elements used to structure media works in a variety of forms	• analyze editorial cartoons (Media Link SB)	• AR 21: Response to Media
(MD1.03P) • compare the reactions of different people or groups to a variety of media works	• compare reactions to two editorials (newspaper or magazine and radio or television) (More Media TG)	• AR 12: Media Product
Overall (MDV.02P) • use knowledge of a variety of media forms, purposes, and audiences to create media works		
Specific (MD2.01P) • adapt a work of literature for presentation in another media form	• draw cartoon to illustrate point made in letter to the editor (Media Link SB)	• AR 12: Media Product
(MD2.03P) • analyze the characteristics of different audiences and create media works designed specifically for them	• redesign book cover for new audience and explain (Using the Persuasive Writing Forms SB #2)	• AR 12: Media Product

AR=Assessment Rubric   EP=Extra Practice   SB=Student Book   SSEC=Student Self-Evaluation Checklist   TG=Teacher's Guide   TOC=Teacher Observation Checklist

Instructional Strategies for the Applied Course

Planning Information

Links to Other Nelson English 9 Resources

Literature & Media 9
Letter to the Editor—See "A Mother's Heart Aches" by Carol Cayenne, pp. 166–167.

Write Source 2000
Letters—"Writing Business Letters," pp. 241–250; **Arguments**—"Thinking Through an Argument," pp. 121–122; **Pronoun Agreement**—"Problems with Pronouns," p. 90; **Proofreading**—"Editing and Proofreading," pp. 79–83

Introducing the Unit

1. Tape record a segment of a news program that includes comments from various people. Play it for students and ask them to listen for facts and opinions. Have them record these in chart form. When discussing the results, ask them to identify the clues that helped them distinguish facts from opinions. (LI1.02P—TOC 14: Tracking Expectations)

2. Working as a class, ask students for five factual sentences about some event or issue which is currently being discussed in the local school or community. Then, ask students, working in pairs, to rewrite the sentences so that each one expresses an opinion rather than a fact.

   Provide the following sentences as examples:
   Fact: Students will be leaving for summer holidays at the end of June.
   Opinion: Excited students will be charging out of the building at the end of June to begin their long-awaited holidays.

   Have one student from each pair read the factual sentence and the second student read the opinion sentence. Ask the class to identify any key words that were added or changed to make the factual statement into an opinion. Complete the activity by discussing the difference between something that is factual and something that expresses an opinion. (LI1.04P—TOC 14: Tracking Expectations)

3. Activity #1 on page 273 from the Academic Course is appropriate for the Applied Course. (LGV.02B—TOC 14: Tracking Expectations)

Introducing the Models

1. Ask students to read the titles of the models and to look at the photographs accompanying each letter. Ask them to predict the content of each letter based on the titles and the photographs. Record their ideas on the board. Following their reading of the models, have students identify which of their predictions are true. (LI1.03B—TOC 10: Reading Strategies)

2. Activity #1 on pages 273–274 from the Academic Course is appropriate for the Applied Course. (LIV.02P—TOC 14: Tracking Expectations)

Investigating the Models

Answers:
See the Academic Course on pages 274–275 for answers.

Student Book 1.–5. (LI1.04P—AR 22: Response to Reading)

LEARNING GOALS

- write a letter to the editor
- make pronouns agree with their antecedents in gender and number
- use correct punctuation, capitalization, and format in letters
- use effective openings
- use strong arguments
- use effective proofreading strategies

CHECKPOINT

Sample criteria for letter to the editor:

- is used to criticize, correct, persuade, express appreciation, or question
- usually begins by identifying issue and expressing an opinion
- provides detailed arguments to support opinion
- has details that are arranged in effective order
- often has strongest argument near end of letter
- often ends with call to action, a question, or summary of main argument
- is usually written in formal language

---

1. Working in groups of four, ask students to suggest two additional arguments, one for each model, that the authors might have used in their letters to the editor. Have the groups bring their suggestions back to the whole class and discuss which arguments were the strongest and why. (LI1.02P—TOC 14: Tracking Expectations)

2.–3. Activities #1–2 on page 275 from the Academic Course is appropriate for the Applied Course.

2. (LIV.02P—TOC 14: Tracking Expectations)

3. (LIV.02P—TOC 14: Tracking Expectations)

WRITER'S WORKSHOP

The activity on pages 275–276 from the Academic Course is appropriate for the Applied Course.

(LI1.05P—TOC 14: Tracking Expectations)

Student Book 1.–4. (WRV.01P—AR 11: Letter to the Editor); 5. (WRV.03P—AR 11: Letter to the Editor); 6. (WRV.04B—AR 11: Letter to the Editor; WRV.05B—AR 11: Letter to the Editor)

ORAL LANGUAGE EXTENSION

Make clear to students that this activity is not asking for a fully developed, formal speech; rather, the purpose is to provide them with an opportunity to learn and practise those skills and behaviours which they would require in a more formal speech to a larger audience.

Student Book (LG2.01P—TOC 5: Group Work; LG2.03P—TOC 11: Speaking; LG2.07P—SSEC 5: Oral Presentation)

GRAMMAR

The activities on pages 277–278 from the Academic Course are appropriate for the Applied Course.

1.–4. (WR5.09B—TOC 4: Grammar; LG1.05P—TOC 4: Grammar)

Answers:
See the Academic Course on page 278 for answers.

Student Book 1.–2. (WR5.09B—TOC 4: Grammar; LG1.05P—TOC 4: Grammar)

MEDIA LINK

If students are not able to locate award-winning cartoons, you may assist by bringing some to class or have them collect cartoons from various newspapers and magazines.

Student Book (MD1.02P—AR 21: Response to Media; MD2.01P—AR 12: Media Product)

MECHANICS

Tell students that they can usually find special instructions for writing letters to the editor on the editorial page of most newspapers or magazines. Indicate that the following instructions are fairly typical of those they will find.
- Letters should include your name, address, and phone number for verification.
- All letters are edited for clarity, style, and length.
- Writers are generally limited to 200 words.

MORE ORAL LANGUAGE

Point out to students that there may be times when they are expected to respond on the spot to someone who has asked their opinion. In order to practise responding, they are going to deliver some impromptu speeches in small groups.

Emphasize that when they are faced with a situation where a quick response is required, they should organize their answers using a similar framework to that used in a letter to the editor: state your opinion; provide arguments, reasons and/ or examples; provide a conclusion that either restates your opinion or provides a call to action. Listed below are two options for this activity:

1. Divide the class into groups of three, numbering each student 1, 2, or 3. Student 1 asks a question; student 2 answers the question; student 3 evaluates both the question and the response. Give each member of the group an opportunity to play each role.

2. Divide the class into small groups of four or five students. Ask students to think up enough questions for an impromptu-speech box for each group. Distribute the boxes to the groups with questions to be selected at random. Allow students one minute to gather their thoughts and then to give a response to the question drawn.

(LG2.01P—TOC 11: Speaking)

MORE SUPPORT

Ask students to indicate whether the italicized pronoun in each sentence is a subject, object, or possessive. Then, have students indicate the case of each pronoun. (WR5.09B—TOC 4: Grammar; LG1.05P—TOC 4: Grammar)

a) *He* forgot the most important question of all.
b) If you don't believe *me*, check out the article in the local newspaper.
c) I think *my* parents sometimes felt badly that we weren't all out doing something special, but no one really minded.

Answers:

a) he — subject; nominative case
b) me — object; objective case
c) my — possessive; possessive case

- Only those people whose letters have been chosen for publication will be contacted.
- Copyright remains with the authors, but the publisher and its licensees may freely reproduce their work in print, electronic, or other forms.

The activities on pages 279–280 from the Academic Course are appropriate for the Applied Course.

1. (WR5.04B—TOC 8: Mechanics; LG1.07B—TOC 8: Mechanics)

2. (WR5.04B—TOC 8: Mechanics; LG1.07B—TOC 8: Mechanics)

3. (WR5.04B—TOC 8: Mechanics; LG1.07B—TOC 8: Mechanics)

Answers:

See the Academic Course on page 279 for answers.

Student Book 1. (WR5.04B—TOC 8: Mechanics; LG1.07B—TOC 8: Mechanics)

USAGE & STYLE

The activities on pages 279–280 from the Academic Course are appropriate for the Applied Course.

1. (LG1.04B—TOC 15: Usage & Style)

2. (LG1.04B—TOC 15: Usage & Style)

Answers:

See the Academic Course on pages 280–281 for answers.

Student Book 1.–6. (LG1.04B—TOC 15: Usage & Style)

WORD STUDY & SPELLING

The activities on page 281 from the Academic Course are appropriate for the Applied Course.

1. (WR5.04B—TOC 16: Word Study & Spelling)

2. (WR5.14B—TOC 16: Word Study & Spelling)

Answers:

See the Academic Course on page 281 for answers.

Student Book 1.–2. (WR5.04B—TOC 16: Word Study & Spelling)

WORD ORIGINS

Answers:

See the Academic Course on page 281 for answers.

(LG1.03B—TOC 16: Word Study & Spelling)

ANSWERS TO EXTRA PRACTICE

See the Academic Course on pages 281–282 for answers.

Grammar

(WR5.09B—TOC 4: Grammar)

MORE SUPPORT

Ask students to rewrite the following sentences, making sure that the pronouns in each sentence are written in the same person. The improper pronouns have been underlined, and the answers are in parentheses. (WR5.09B—TOC 4: Grammar; LG1.05P—TOC 4: Grammar)

a) We like doing nothing because you can just enjoy one another's company. (we)

b) We would sometimes catch a baseball game on TV and yell in unison if your favourite player made an error. (our)

c) I remember just chatting with our mom in the kitchen as she prepared Sunday dinner and helping us cut up some vegetables. (my, her)

MORE CHALLENGE

1. Use the examples below to point out problems that can arise with gender bias. In each example, explain how gender bias has been avoided by using a neuter pronoun. (LG1.04B—TOC 4: Grammar)

   Biased: A politician can sometimes act against his own best interests.

   Neutral: Politicians can sometimes act against their own best interests.

   Biased: Whoever fails to spend time with her family will regret the decision in the future.

   Neutral: Persons who fail to spend time with their families will regret the decision in the future.

2. Ask students to find a new way to express each of the following to avoid the problem of gender bias. They can change words as well as pronouns where necessary.

   a) Nobody believes a consumer when she says she doesn't need a television.
   b) A politician can't have his cake and eat it too.
   c) Man has yet to understand that doing nothing sometimes is perfectly acceptable.

   Possible answers

   a) Nobody believes consumers when they say they don't need televisions.
   b) Politicians can't have their cake and eat it too.
   c) People have yet to understand that doing nothing sometimes is perfectly acceptable.

Ask students to select two editorials, one from a newspaper or magazine, and one from radio or television (tape recording). Ask them to show/play the editorials to different people (friends, members of their family), and to record the reactions in point form. Have them write a brief report on the results.
(MD1.03P—AR 12: Media Product)

NOTE: If students are not able to find an example of an editorial on radio or television, as an alternative, ask them to record interviews of people on radio or television who are responding to a controversial issue (e.g., Should there be more universal testing of high school students? Should there be tougher fines for environmental polluters?).

Mechanics
(WR5.04B—TOC 8: Mechanics; LG1.07B—TOC 8: Mechanics)

Usage & Style
(LG1.04B—TOC 15: Usage & Style)

Word Study & Spelling
(WR5.04B—TOC 16: Word Study & Spelling)

REFLECT AND BUILD ON YOUR LEARNING

REFLECTING ON PERSUASIVE WRITING FORMS

1. Student work.

2. Possible answer

   Other persuasive forms include opinion piece, letter of application, letter of recommendation, editorial, resume, persuasive/argumentative essay, brochure/pamphlet, speech, debate, advice column, and proposal.

   Example: An editorial states a position on an issue; uses a number of arguments, often including statistics, to support a position; usually ends with a call to action for citizens or with a recommendation to government to change or adopt a particular policy. If you were the editor of a newspaper or magazine, you would write at least some of the editorials in your publication as part of your job.

Student Book 1.–2. (LIV.01P—TOC 14: Tracking Expectations)

LOOKING OVER PERSUASIVE WRITING FORMS

Answers:

1. Possible answer

CRITERIA	COMPARISON	ADVERTISEMENT	LETTER TO THE EDITOR	EDITORIAL
Purpose	analyze, differentiate, explain, evaluate, inform, persuade, entertain	sell a product, create an image, promote a company or brand name	criticize, correct, persuade, express appreciation, question	express opinion of editor; persuade, inform, criticize, recommend
Audience	may be specific target or general	may be specific target or may be general	may be specific group or general readership	readership of publication or listeners/viewers in electronic media
Introduction	thesis sentence	may or may not have an introduction	identifies issue and expresses opinion	identifies issue and expresses opinion
Body	uses Block or Point-by-Point method to discuss similarities and differences	uses words and images (explicit and implicit to persuade)	provides detailed arguments	provides arguments to support position
Conclusion	usually a summary statement	may or may not have a conclusion	call to action, question, or summary	issues a call to action or recommends a change or adoption of a new policy especially for government

Student Book. 1. (LIV.02P—TOC 14: Tracking Expectations)

USING THE PERSUASIVE WRITING FORMS

1. Students do not have to be limited to a textbook for their comparisons since particular historical events may not be discussed in available history texts. Therefore, students could research other nonfiction sources. Encourage students to

develop a Venn diagram (page 163 of the student book) to help them with the organization of their comparison.

Student Book 1. (WRV.03P—AR 2: Comparison; WRV.04B—AR 2: Comparison; WRV.05B—AR 2: Comparison)

2. Due to the length of the explanation in the student book, you should ensure that all students understand exactly what the assignment is asking them to do. You may wish to review the differences (audience, images, and language) between the milk ads on pages 173–175 before assigning this activity.

Student Book 2. (MD1.01B—AR 21: Response to Media; MD2.03P—AR 12: Media Product; WRV.03P—AR 1: Advertisement; WRV.04B—AR 1: Advertisement; WRV.05B—AR 1: Advertisement)

3. Remind students that the list of features of letters to the editor are outlined for them on page 189 of the student book. The option of using magazine editorials, as well as newspaper editorials, could be made available to students.

Student Book 3. (LIV.02P—TOC 13: Tracking Expectations)

4. This assignment will be challenging for some students to complete individually. Therefore, you may wish to have students work in groups to write a focus statement, research the topic, and develop an outline including subtopics and supporting details. Then, ask each student to write his or her own draft report based on the outline done by the group and to supplement it with an effective introduction, conclusion, and bibliography. Once drafts are completed, students in the group could work together to check that each report is interesting to readers, is well organized, provides enough facts and examples, and follows the format required for a bibliography. Students could then write their final drafts and share them with members of the group.

Student Book 4. (WRV.03P—AR 20: Research Report; WR3.06P—AR 20: Research Report; WRV.04B—AR 20: Research Report; WR4.04B—SSEC 6: Peer Assessment: Writing; WRV.05B—AR 20: Research Report; MD1.01B—AR 21: Response to Media)

GRAMMAR

NAME: _____ **DATE:** _____

Rewrite the following sentences, correcting any errors in pronoun antecedent agreement, use of subjective or objective pronouns, vague pronoun reference, and gender bias in pronouns.

1. As July grew near, each of the girls was making their summer plans.

   _____

2. Us athletes like to do stretching exercises before participating in strenuous activity.

   _____

3. Her and I will be going to work at Mountain View Lodge this summer.

   _____

4. There are too many students and too few spaces. This is unacceptable.

   _____

5. Tomorrow, Lana and me are going to the new restaurant.

   _____

6. Last night, I attended the school play with our family.

   _____

7. This old sweater is my favourite, but I guess its time to get rid of her.

   _____

8. The teacher showed the pronoun chart to we.

   _____

9. Neither Sonya nor me are responsible for the mess.

   _____

MECHANICS

NAME: _____ DATE: _____

Rewrite the following covering letter sent to a newspaper with a letter to the editor. Correct any errors in format, punctuation, and spelling, and add any missing information which the editor would require from you.

123 Sanford Dr
Southampton, ON
N0h 2L0

Dear Mr Blck,

Here is a copy of my opinion on one of the editorials, which appeared in your newspaper. I hope you will print it in your paper soon.

Yours truly,

Lillie

USAGE & STYLE

NAME: _____ DATE: _____

Rewrite the following openings for a letter to the editor to make them more effective.

1. This letter will convince you to change your mind on charging a bigger fee for the use of arenas for hockey.

   _____

2. I don't much like the editorial I read by Jeff Snyder.

   _____

Write a rhetorical question which could be used in place of each of the following headings for a letter to the editor.

3. Students Are People Too

   _____

4. The Next Step Is Obvious

   _____

Rewrite the following sentences to avoid personal attacks and absolute statements.

5. Mr. Sams is insane if he thinks we are going to be swayed by his opinion.

   _____

6. Students at that school are always getting into trouble.

   _____

7. Ms. Pretty doesn't have a clue about this issue.

   _____

8. Solutions like that suggested by the writer never work.

   _____

WORD STUDY & SPELLING

NAME: _____ DATE: _____

List in the spaces provided below, five proofreading methods you could use to ensure that your written work has no mechanics or spelling errors in it.

1. _____
   _____
   _____
   _____
   _____

2. _____
   _____
   _____
   _____
   _____

3. _____
   _____
   _____
   _____
   _____

4. _____
   _____
   _____
   _____
   _____

5. _____
   _____
   _____
   _____
   _____

LANGUAGE & WRITING 9

ASSESSMENT TOOLS

Teacher Observation Checklists

1. Conducting an Interview
2. Conducting Research
3. Fiction Writing
4. Grammar
5. Group Work
6. Journal Response
7. Listening
8. Mechanics
9. Nonfiction Writing
10. Reading Strategies
11. Speaking
12. Storyboarding a Video
13. Tracking Expectations (Academic)
14. Tracking Expectations (Applied)
15. Usage & Style
16. Word Study & Spelling

Student Self-Evaluation Checklists

1. Editing/Proofreading
2. Group Work
3. Listening
4. Media Creation
5. Oral Presentation
6. Peer Assessment: Writing
7. Peer Editing
8. Reading Strategies
9. Research
10. Revising
11. Spelling

Assessment Rubrics

1. Advertisement
2. Comparison
3. Conferencing
4. Descriptive Writing
5. Dramatization
6. Event Description
7. Explanation
8. Expository Writing
9. Group Presentation
10. Humorous Personal Narrative
11. Letter to the Editor
12. Media Product
13. Narrative Writing
14. News Article
15. Oral Language
16. Persuasive Writing
17. Poetry
18. Précis
19. Profile
20. Research Report
21. Response to Media
22. Response to Reading
23. Script
24. Short Story

CONDUCTING AN INTERVIEW

NAME: _____

Expectations

Students will:

- use listening techniques and oral communication skills (LG2.01D/*LG2.01P*);
- select words and phrases appropriate to purpose and audience (LG1.04B/*LG1.04B*);
- select and use methods of delivery to suit purpose and audience (LG2.03D/*LG2.03P*; LGV.01B/*LGV.01P*);
- listen actively and ask appropriate questions (LG2.01D/*LG2.01P*);
- identify key ideas, paraphrase key points, and ask clarifying questions (LG2.01D/*LG2.01P*); and
- identify strengths and weaknesses of interviewing technique and plan ways to improve (LG2.07D/*LG2.07P*).

CRITERIA	S	O	N	D	J	F	M	A	M	J
Understanding										
• demonstrates understanding that an interview involves the exchange of ideas and information										
• identifies the purpose of an interview										
• recognizes that questions must be carefully chosen and framed to achieve the purpose										
Thinking										
• frames questions to obtain the desired information										
• identifies responses that require clarification or elaboration										
• identifies strengths and weaknesses of interview content and technique, and identifies ways to improve										
Communication										
• uses appropriate language and tone										
• establishes rapport with the interviewee										
• asks questions to elicit clarification and elaboration										
• shows respect for the opinions and feelings of the interviewee										
Application										
• obtains background information before the interview (if appropriate)										
• prepares questions that focus on the purpose										
• predicts possible responses and prepares follow-up questions										
• listens actively and critically to responses										

Codes:

4 Above Standard
3 At Standard
2 Approaching Standard
1 Below Standard
0 Insufficient Achievement

CONDUCTING RESEARCH

NAME: _____

Expectations

Students will:

- use a variety of print and electronic sources to gather information (WR1.02D/*WR1.02P*);
- investigate potential topics by formulating questions, identifying information needs, and developing research plans (WR1.01D/*WR1.01P*);
- group and label information and ideas; evaluate relevance, accuracy, and completeness of information and ideas (WR1.03D/*WR1.03P*);
- use results of research to develop the content of written work (WR1.04D/*WR1.04P*); and
- present research findings in a form appropriate for audience and purpose (WR2.01D/*WR2.03P*)

CRITERIA	S	O	N	D	J	F	M	A	M	J
Understanding										
• identifies prior knowledge related to the topic										
• demonstrates understanding of how to access information in a variety of forms										
• identifies the purpose and audience for the research										
Thinking										
• narrows topic to a manageable scope										
• generates questions and lists information needs										
• develops a research plan outlining sources to be consulted										
• evaluates information to ensure it is relevant, accurate, and complete										
• organizes ideas effectively										
• uses research to generate own ideas										
Communication										
• presents research in a form appropriate for audience and purpose										
• uses language appropriate for audience and purpose										
Application										
• consults a variety of reference resources to locate and obtain information										
• summarizes information from specific sources										
• uses strategies to organize and label ideas and information (grouping, charting, webbing, etc.)										
• records bibliographic details for sources used										

Codes:

4 Above Standard

3 At Standard

2 Approaching Standard

1 Below Standard

0 Insufficient Achievement

FICTION WRITING

NAME: _____

Expectations

Students will:

- select and use literary forms suited to a variety of purposes and audiences (WR2.01D/*WR2.03P*; LIV.02D/*LIV.02P*);
- use a unifying image, mood, or voice to structure descriptive paragraphs or poems (WR3.01D/*WR3.03P);*
- use changes in time, place, speaker, or point of view to structure narrative paragraphs (WR3.02D/*WR3.04P*);
- adapt and use punctuation suited to requirements of the literary form (WR5.15B/*WR5.15B*; WR5.16B/*WR5.16B*); and
- revise drafts for clarity and unity (WR4.01D/*WR4.01B*; WR4.04B/*WR4.04B*).

CRITERIA	S	O	N	D	J	F	M	A	M	J
Understanding										
• demonstrates understanding of the function of basic elements of fiction (setting, character, plot)										
• demonstrates understanding of basic plot structure										
Thinking										
• chooses a form appropriate for audience and purpose										
• forms a coherent plot with a beginning, middle, and end										
• creates interesting characters										
• creates a clear problem or conflict for the main character(s)										
• develops an effective and appropriate resolution										
Communication										
• uses words and images effectively										
• develops a personal voice in writing										
• develops characters through description, dialogue, and actions										
Application										
• creates an effective title										
• correctly uses the mechanics of presenting dialogue										
• adapts punctuation for form and purpose										
• structures narrative paragraphs appropriately										
• seeks feedback and makes revisions										

Codes:

4 Above Standard

3 At Standard

2 Approaching Standard

1 Below Standard

0 Insufficient Achievement

LANGUAGE & WRITING 9

GRAMMAR

NAME: _____

Expectations

Students will:

- use parts of speech correctly (WR5.05D/*WR5.05P;* LG1.05D/*LG1.05P*);
- construct complete and correct compound and complex sentences (WR5.06D/*WR5.06P;* LG1.05D/*LG1.05P*);
- identify and correct sentence errors (WR5.07B/*WR5.07B;* LG1.06B/*LG1.06B*);
- show subject/verb and pronoun/antecedent agreement (WR5.08B/*WR5.08B;* WR5.09B/*WR5.09B;* LG1.05D/*LG1.05P*); and
- use consistent and appropriate verb tense (WR5.10B/*WR5.10B;* LG1.05D/*LG1.05P*).

CRITERIA	S	O	N	D	J	F	M	A	M	J
Parts of Speech										
• uses parts of speech correctly: nouns, verbs, adverbs, and adjectives										
• uses parts of speech correctly: pronouns, prepositions, conjunctions, and interjections										
• uses subjects and predicates correctly										
• uses direct and indirect objects, transitive and intransitive verbs, and subject complements										
• uses prepositional and participial phrases correctly										
• uses comparative and superlative forms of adjectives and adverbs correctly										
Sentence Structure										
• constructs simple, compound, and complex sentences										
• selects and uses parallel structures										
Sentence Errors										
• recognizes and corrects run-on sentences and comma splices										
• identifies and corrects sentence fragments										
Agreement										
• uses subject-verb agreement correctly										
• makes pronouns agree with their antecedents in gender and number										

Codes:

4 Above Standard
3 At Standard
2 Approaching Standard
1 Below Standard
0 Insufficient Achievement

GROUP WORK

NAME: _____

Expectations

Students will:

- use listening and speaking skills to participate in group discussions (LG2.01D/*LG2.01P*; LG2.02D/*LG2.02P*);
- use techniques of effective listening by restating ideas presented (LG2.02D/*LG2.02P*); and
- analyze their own and others' oral communication skills, identifying strengths and weaknesses and suggesting ways to improve (LG2.07D/*LG2.07P*).

CRITERIA	S	O	N	D	J	F	M	A	M	J
Understanding										
• uses the group discussion to achieve the desired goal or fulfill the assigned task										
• prepares thoroughly in order to participate in a meaningful manner										
• demonstrates an understanding of the importance of the various roles needed to enable the group to function effectively										
Thinking										
• builds effectively on the ideas of others										
• uses group discussion to reconsider ideas and opinions										
• develops creative or innovative approaches for the assigned task										
• reflects on contribution to the group and considers ways of improving future group participation										
Communication										
• listens actively and stays on task										
• encourages others through the use of verbal and nonverbal (e.g., nodding, eye contact) cues										
• asks pertinent questions so that the group achieves its purpose										
• responds appropriately to dissenting opinions										
• speaks clearly and organizes ideas logically										
Application										
• takes notes throughout the discussion										
• participates effectively in a variety of roles within the group (e.g., reporter, recorder, leader)										
• shows interest and involvement throughout the discussion										

Codes:

4 Above Standard
3 At Standard
2 Approaching Standard
1 Below Standard
0 Insufficient Achievement

Journal Response

Name: _____

Expectations

Students will:

- analyze information, ideas, and elements in texts to make inferences (LI1.05D/*LI1.05P*);
- describe information, ideas, opinions, and themes in texts (LI1.01D/*LI1.01P*);
- use an organizational structure suitable to the nature of the journal entry (WR3.03D/*WR3.05P*; WR2.02D/*WR2.04P*); and
- support opinions or interpretations with specific information (LI1.06D/*LI1.06P*).

CRITERIA	S	O	N	D	J	F	M	A	M	J
Understanding										
• demonstrates an understanding of the variety of purposes for which a journal may be used										
• recognizes the role of personal reflection to enrich experiences with texts										
Thinking										
• makes connections among ideas, texts, opinions, prior knowledge, and personal experiences										
• shows evidence of critical thinking by asking relevant questions, drawing conclusions, making inferences, and noting similarities and differences										
Communication										
• expresses and explores feelings, thoughts, and ideas										
• focuses on the topic										
• shows developing fluency as a writer										
• writes clearly and organizes ideas logically										
• uses appropriate voice and level of language										
Application										
• uses journal writing for a variety of purposes										
• completes journal entries regularly										
• writes entries of an appropriate length										
• uses vocabulary and sentence structure appropriate for the grade level										

Codes:

4 Above Standard

3 At Standard

2 Approaching Standard

1 Below Standard

0 Insufficient Achievement

LISTENING

NAME: _____

Expectations
Students will:
- identify key ideas and supporting details; distinguish fact from opinion, follow instructions (LG2.01D/*LG2.01P*); and
- listen actively in group discussions, taking notes and reconsidering their own ideas and opinions (LG2.02D/*LG2.02P*).

CRITERIA	S	O	N	D	J	F	M	A	M	J
Understanding										
• demonstrates understanding of listening as an active process										
• recognizes that there is a purpose for every listening experience										
Thinking										
• identifies the purpose for the listening experience										
• distinguishes fact from opinion										
• identifies organizational structure										
• compares speaker's ideas to own ideas										
• notes relationships between ideas (e.g., cause/effect, problem/solution)										
Communication										
• makes eye contact with the speaker to demonstrate attentiveness										
• uses appropriate gestures and facial expressions to respond to the speaker (e.g., nods in agreement, smiles)										
• shows behaviours that demonstrate respect for the speaker's needs and feelings										
Application										
• prepares for listening by noting purpose and prior knowledge										
• takes notes that reflect understanding of content and organizational structure										
• asks questions that reveal active, critical listening										
• follows oral instructions										

Codes:
4 Above Standard
3 At Standard
2 Approaching Standard
1 Below Standard
0 Insufficient Achievement

MECHANICS

NAME: _____

Expectations

Students will:

- use punctuation correctly, including period, question mark, exclamation mark, comma, dash, apostrophe, colon, quotation marks, parentheses, and ellipses (WR5.15B/*WR5.15B*; LG1.07B/*LG1.07B*);
- adapt punctuation and capitalization for the special requirements of direct quotations, scripts, dialogue, and poetry (WR5.16B/*WR5.16B*); and
- recognize, describe, and use correctly components of sentences (WRV.05D/*WRV.05B*).

CRITERIA	S	O	N	D	J	F	M	A	M	J
Punctuation										
• uses commas correctly										
• punctuates essential and nonessential clauses correctly										
• uses colons, semicolons, and dashes correctly										
Adaptation of Punctuation										
• punctuates and capitalizes dialogue correctly										
• uses punctuation in scripts correctly										
• adapts punctuation for poetry										
• uses ellipses and square brackets in direct quotations										
• learns proper punctuation for definitions										
• adapts punctuation for advertisements										
• uses correct punctuation, capitalization, and format in letters										
Bibliography										
• creates a bibliography following a prescribed style										
Design Elements										
• identifies and uses design elements appropriate for audience and purpose										
Numerical Information										
• presents numerical information using a consistent style										

Codes:

4 Above Standard
3 At Standard
2 Approaching Standard
1 Below Standard
0 Insufficient Achievement

NONFICTION WRITING

NAME: _____

Expectations

Students will:

- use a variety of print and electronic sources to gather information (WR1.02D/*WR1.02P*);
- use informational forms appropriate for audience and purpose (WR2.01D/*WR2.03P*);
- use a variety of organizational techniques to present ideas and support details (WR3.03D/*WRD.05D*; WR3.04D/*WR3.01P*; WR3.05D/*WRD.02P*; WR3.06D/*WR3.06P*);
- use a single controlling idea and connecting words to structure a series of paragraphs (WR3.03D/*WR3.05P*);
- structure expository paragraphs using a topic sentence, supporting sentences, connecting words, and a concluding sentence (WR3.05D/*WR3.02P*);
- provide an introduction, body, and conclusion (WR3.06D/*WR3.06P*);
- identify sources of ideas, information, and quotations (WR5.01D/*WR5.01P*); and
- revise, edit, and proofread written work (WR4.01D/*WR4.01B*; WR5.04B/*WR5.04P*).

CRITERIA	S	O	N	D	J	F	M	A	M	J
Understanding										
• identifies sources and techniques for gathering information										
• identifies and explains a variety of informational forms										
Thinking										
• explains choices of form, content, and language appropriate for purpose and audience										
• identifies controlling idea(s)										
Communication										
• uses a single controlling idea and connecting words to structure a series of paragraphs										
• uses organizational techniques to present a unified and coherent overall structure										
• supports and explains ideas and opinions										
Application										
• uses a variety of sources to obtain information										
• seeks feedback on drafts and revises										
• provides an introduction, body, and conclusion										
• includes a bibliography in appropriate format										
• identifies sources of quoted material										
• proofreads for spelling, grammar, and punctuation										

Codes:

4 Above Standard

3 At Standard

2 Approaching Standard

1 Below Standard

0 Insufficient Achievement

READING STRATEGIES

NAME: _____

Expectation

Students will:

- describe a variety of reading strategies and select and use them effectively before, during, and after reading to understand texts (LI1.03B/*LI1.03B*).

CRITERIA	S	O	N	D	J	F	M	A	M	J
Pre-Reading										
• previews title, headings, diagrams, illustrations, charts, etc., to form a general idea of content										
• previews text to make predictions about content										
• relates prior knowledge and personal experiences to the topic										
• seeks background information										
During Reading										
• monitors comprehension to note difficulties; applies strategies to overcome difficulties										
• reads text in sections; asks questions and makes predictions										
• answers questions and confirms predictions while reading										
• applies understanding of text forms and features										
• visualizes places, people, and events										
• draws pictures or diagrams to aid comprehension while reading										
• makes connections with prior knowledge while reading										
• restates information, ideas, or plot in own words										
• rereads to clarify meaning										
• uses context to predict word meanings; uses dictionary to confirm word meanings										
Post-Reading										
• answers questions and confirms predictions										
• connects new learning to prior knowledge										
• makes a comparison chart to note similarities and differences										
• summarizes information or events										
• records personal responses in a journal										
• draws pictures or diagrams to confirm understanding										
• creates a mind map (web) to organize related ideas										

Codes:

4 Above Standard
3 At Standard
2 Approaching Standard
1 Below Standard
0 Insufficient Achievement

SPEAKING

NAME: _____

Expectations

Students will:

- communicate orally in group discussions for different purposes (LG2.01D/*LG2.01P*);
- communicate in group discussions by speaking in turn, paraphrasing key points made by others, exchanging and challenging ideas and information, and asking appropriate questions (LG2.02D/*LG2.02P*);
- plan and make oral presentations to a small group or the class, selecting and using vocabulary and methods of delivery to suit audience and purpose (LG2.03D/*LG2.03P*);
- use specific examples, facial expressions, gestures, intonation, humour, and visual aids and technology to engage the audience's interest (LG2.04D/*LG2.04P*);
- use strategies to ensure confident delivery in oral presentations (LG2.05D/*LG2.05P*); and
- explain the importance of oral communication skills at school and in the world outside (LG2.06D/*LG2.06P*).

CRITERIA	S	O	N	D	J	F	M	A	M	J
Understanding										
• demonstrates an understanding that communication skills contribute to success at school and beyond										
• recognizes the importance of engaging audience interest										
Thinking										
• identifies purpose and audience for oral work										
• effectively organizes ideas in presentations										
• shows evidence of logical reasoning										
• challenges, builds on, or paraphrases ideas of others in discussion										
Communication										
• uses facial expressions, gestures, and intonation to engage audience and clarify meaning										
• makes eye contact with audience while speaking										
• highlights key points and uses details and examples to support ideas										
• shows respect for others in group discussions										
• uses vocabulary appropriate for the audience										
Application										
• practises with cue cards and relaxation exercises to ensure confident delivery										
• practises with visual aids and technology to smoothly integrate these elements into presentation										
• engages in self- and peer evaluation of presentations and group discussions										
• plans ways to improve performance in presentations and group discussions										

Codes:

4 Above Standard   3 At Standard   2 Approaching Standard   1 Below Standard   0 Insufficient Achievement

LANGUAGE & WRITING 9   Copyright © 2000 Nelson Thomson Learning

STORYBOARDING A VIDEO

NAME: _____

Expectations

Students will:

- adapt a work of literature into another media form (MD2.01D/*MD2.01P*);
- create media works for different purposes and explain how each has been designed to achieve its particular purpose (MD2.02D/*MD2.02P*); and
- create media works appropriate to different audiences and explain why each should appeal to a different audience (MD2.03D/*MD2.03P*).

CRITERIA	S	O	N	D	J	F	M	A	M	J
Understanding										
• explains the purpose of a storyboard										
• identifies elements required in a storyboard										
• demonstrates an understanding of the effects created by specific techniques										
Thinking										
• makes effective creative decisions appropriate for the audience and purpose										
• chooses appropriate techniques for creating specific effects										
• explains how specific creative decisions relate to the audience and purpose										
Communication										
• clearly communicates visual and print information										
• uses appropriate terminology and vocabulary correctly (wide angle, pan, establishing shot, etc.)										
Application										
• includes an appropriate number of frames										
• includes dialogue and appropriate audio instructions										
• specifies camera angles, distances, and movements										
• uses camera techniques effectively										

Codes:

4 Above Standard

3 At Standard

2 Approaching Standard

1 Below Standard

0 Insufficient Achievement

TRACKING EXPECTATIONS (ACADEMIC)

NAME: _____

ACADEMIC EXPECTATIONS	S	O	N	D	J	F	M	A	M	J
Literature Studies and Reading										
Overall **LIV.01D** • read and demonstrate an understanding of a variety of literary and informational texts from contemporary and historical periods										
LI1.01D • describe information, ideas, opinions, and themes in texts they have read during the year from different cultures and historical periods and in a variety of genres										
LI1.02D • select and read texts for different purposes, recognizing the elements of literary genres and the organization of informational materials										
LI1.03D • describe a variety of reading strategies and select and use them effectively before, during, and after reading to understand texts										
LI1.04D • locate explicit information and ideas in texts to use in developing opinions and interpretations										
LI1.05D • analyze information, ideas, and elements in texts to make inferences about meaning										
LI1.06D • use specific evidence from a text to support opinions and judgments										
LI1.07D • explain how readers' different backgrounds might influence the way they understand and interpret a text										
Overall **LI1.08D** • explain how the background of the author might influence the information and ideas in a text										
LIV.02D • demonstrate an understanding of the elements of a variety of literary and informational forms										
LI2.01D • use knowledge of elements of drama, such as plot and subplot to understand and interpret examples of the genre										
LI2.02D • use knowledge of elements of the short story to understand and interpret examples of the genre										
LI2.03D • use knowledge of elements of short essays to understand and interpret examples of the genre										
Overall **LIV.03B** • identify and explain the effect of specific elements of style in a variety of literary and informational texts										
LI3.01D • explain how authors use diction and phrasing to achieve particular effects in their writing										
LI3.02D • explain how authors use stylistic devices to achieve particular effects in their writing										
LI3.03D • explain how authors and editors use design elements to help communicate ideas										
Writing										
Overall **WRV.01D** • use a variety of print and electronic sources to gather information and explore ideas for their written work										
WR1.01D • investigate potential topics by formulating questions, identifying information needs, and developing research plans to gather data										
WR1.02D • locate and summarize information from print and electronic sources										
WR1.03D • group and label information and ideas, evaluate the relevance, accuracy, and completeness of the information and ideas; and discard irrelevant material										
WR1.04D • use the information and ideas generated by research to develop the content of written work										

Codes: 4 Above Standard   3 At Standard   2 Approaching Standard   1 Below Standard   0 Insufficient Achievement

ACADEMIC EXPECTATIONS	S	O	N	D	J	F	M	A	M	J
Writing										
Overall WRV.02D • identify and use the literary and informational forms suited to various purposes and audiences and use the forms appropriately in their own writing, with an emphasis on supporting opinions or interpretations with specific information										
WR2.01D • demonstrate an understanding of literary and informational forms by selecting and using forms of writing appropriate to different purposes and audiences										
WR2.02D • select first or third person and an appropriate level of language to suit the form, purpose, and audience of written work										
Overall WRV.03D • use a variety of organizational techniques to present ideas and supporting details logically and coherently in written work										
WR3.01D • use a unifying image, mood, or voice to structure descriptive paragraphs or poems										
WR3.02D • use changes in time, place, speaker, or point of view to structure narrative paragraphs										
WR3.03D • use a single controlling idea and connecting words to structure a series of paragraphs										
WR3.04D • use key words from questions or prompts to organize ideas, information, and evidence in homework answers										
WR3.05D • structure expository paragraphs using a topic sentence, supporting sentences to develop the topic, connecting words to link the sentences, and a concluding sentence										
WR3.06D • provide an introduction, body, and conclusion in written reports and short essays										
Overall WRV.04D • revise their written work, independently and collaboratively, with a focus on support for ideas and opinions, accuracy, clarity, and unity										
WR4.01D • revise drafts to ensure that ideas are adequately developed with relevant supporting details and to achieve clarity and unity										
WR4.02B • revise drafts to ensure consistency in use of first or third person and use of an appropriate level of language										
WR4.03D • make constructive suggestions to peers										
WR4.04B • consider reactions from teachers, peers, and others in revising and editing written work										
Overall WRV.05D • edit and proofread to produce final drafts, using correct grammar, spelling, and punctuation, according to the conventions of standard Canadian English, with the support of print and electronic resources when appropriate										
WR5.01D • identify sources of ideas, information, and quotations in writing and independent research projects										
WR5.02B • select the publication method or vehicle most accessible or appealing to the intended audience										
WR5.03D • assess their facility with the writing process, documenting their use of different genres and forms in personal and assigned writing and identifying goals for writing improvement and growth										
WR5.04B • edit and proofread their own and others' writing, identifying and correcting errors according to the requirements for grammar, usage, spelling, and punctuation										
WR5.05D • use parts of speech correctly										
WR5.06D • construct complete and correct compound and complex sentences										
WR5.07B • identify and correct sentence fragments, run-on sentences, and comma splices										

Codes: 4 Above Standard   3 At Standard   2 Approaching Standard   1 Below Standard   0 Insufficient Achievement

ACADEMIC EXPECTATIONS		S	O	N	D	J	F	M	A	M	J
Writing											
WR5.08B	• make compound sentences agree with verbs in simple and compound sentences										
WR5.09B	• make pronouns agree with their antecedents in number and gender										
WR5.10B	• use consistent and appropriate verb tense and voice i.e., active and passive for clarity in narrative and expository writing										
WR5.11B	• use knowledge of a wide range of spelling patterns and rules to identify, analyze, and correct spelling errors										
WR5.12B	• use and spell homophones correctly										
WR5.13B	• use the apostrophe correctly when spelling contractions and possessives										
WR5.14B	• use a variety of resources to correct errors in spelling										
WR5.15B	• use punctuation correctly										
WR5.16B	• adapt punctuation and capitalization for the special requirements of direct quotations, scripts, dialogue, and poetry										
Language											
Overall LGV.01D	• use knowledge of vocabulary and language conventions to speak, write, and read competently using a level of language appropriate to the purpose and audience										
LG1.01B	• describe strategies used to expand vocabulary and provide evidence of other vocabulary-building activities										
LG1.02B	• identify and explain examples of slang, jargon, dialect and colloquialism, as well as of standard Canadian English, in literary texts and their own oral and written work										
LG1.03B	• identify words borrowed from other languages and words and terms recently introduced to describe new ideas, inventions, and products, and explain their origins										
LG1.04B	• select words and phrases appropriate to informal and formal styles, to suit the purpose and intended audience of oral and written work										
LG1.05D	• recognize, describe, and use correctly, in oral and written language, the language structures of standard Canadian English and its conventions of grammar and usage										
LG1.06B	• recognize, describe, and correct sentence errors in oral and written language										
LG1.07B	• recognize, describe, and use correctly, in oral and written language, the conventions of standard Canadian English for spelling, capitalization, and punctuation										
Overall LGV.02B	• use listening techniques and oral communication skills to participate in classroom discussions and more formal activities, such as storytelling, role playing, and reporting/presenting, for specific purposes and audiences										
LG2.01D	• communicate orally in group discussions for different purposes, with a focus on identifying key ideas and supporting details, distinguishing fact from opinion, asking clarifying questions, and following instructions										
LG2.02D	• communicate in group discussions by sharing the duties of the group, speaking in turn, listening actively, taking notes, paraphrasing key points made by others, exchanging and challenging ideas and information, asking appropriate questions, reconsidering their own ideas and opinions, managing conflict, and respecting the opinions of others										
LG2.03D	• plan and make oral presentations to a small group or the class; gather ideas and information; plan, create, rehearse, revise, and assess presentations such as dramatizations, reports, and speeches										

Codes: 4 Above Standard   3 At Standard   2 Approaching Standard   1 Below Standard   0 Insufficient Achievement

ACADEMIC EXPECTATIONS		S	O	N	D	J	F	M	A	M	J
Language											
LG2.04D	• use specific examples, facial expressions, gestures, intonation, humour, and visual aids and technology, as appropriate, to engage the audience's interest during oral presentations										
LG2.05D	• practise with cue cards and relaxation exercises to ensure confident delivery in oral presentations										
LG2.06D	• explain how oral communication skills can contribute to success in all curriculum areas and the world outside the school										
LG2.07D	• analyze their own and others' oral presentations to identify strengths and weaknesses, and plan ways to improve their performance										
Media Studies											
Overall MDV.01D	• use knowledge of the elements, intended audiences, and production practices of a variety of media forms to analyze specific media works										
MD1.01B	• demonstrate critical thinking skills by identifying the differences between explicit and implicit messages in media works										
MD1.02D	• identify how elements of media forms are used in a variety of media works and explain the effects of different treatments										
MD1.03D	• compare and explain their own and their peers' reactions to a variety of media works										
MD1.04D	• identify factors that influence media production and distribution and explain the effect of these factors on specific media works										
Overall MDV.02D	• use knowledge of a variety of media forms, purposes, and audiences to create media works and describe their intended effect										
MD2.01D	• adapt a work of literature to another media form and determine what aspects have been strengthened and/or weakened by the adaptation										
MD2.02D	• create media works for different purposes and explain how each has been designed to achieve its particular purpose										
MD2.03D	• create media works appropriate to different audiences and explain why a particular design should appeal to a particular audience										

Codes: 4 Above Standard   3 At Standard   2 Approaching Standard   1 Below Standard   0 Insufficient Achievement

TRACKING EXPECTATIONS (APPLIED)

NAME: _____

APPLIED EXPECTATIONS	S	O	N	D	J	F	M	A	M	J
Literature Studies and Reading										
Overall LIV.01P • read and demonstrate an understanding of a variety of literary and informational texts										
LI1.01P • describe information, ideas, opinions, and themes in texts from a variety of print and electronic sources										
LI1.02P • select and read texts for a variety of purposes, with an emphasis on recognizing the elements of literary genres and the organization of informational materials, collecting and using information, extending personal knowledge, and responding imaginatively										
LI1.03P • describe a variety of reading strategies and select and use them effectively to understand texts										
LI1.04P • locate and use explicit information and ideas from texts in forming opinions and developing generalizations										
LI1.05P • make inferences based on the information and ideas presented in texts										
LI1.06P • use specific references from a text to support opinions and judgments										
LI1.07P • identify how readers' different backgrounds might influence the way they understand and interpret a text										
Overall LIV.02P • demonstrate an understanding of the elements of a variety of literary and informational forms										
LI2.01P • use knowledge of elements of drama to understand and interpret texts in the genre										
LI2.02P • use knowledge of elements of the short story to understand and interpret texts in the genre										
LI2.03P • use knowledge of elements of newspaper and magazine articles, to understand and interpret texts in the genre										
LIV.03B • identify and explain the effect of specific elements of style in a variety of literary and informational texts										
LI3.01P • explain how authors use stylistic devices to achieve intended effects										
LI3.02P • explain how authors choose words and phrases to achieve intended effects										
LI3.03P • explain how authors and editors use design elements to help convey meaning										
Writing										
Overall WRV.01P • use print and electronic sources to gather information and explore ideas for their written work										
WR1.01 • investigate potential topics by asking questions, identifying information needs, and developing research plans to gather data										
WR1.02P • locate and record information and ideas from print and electronic sources										
WR1.03P • sort and group information and ideas, assess their relevance and accuracy, and discard irrelevant material										
WR1.04P • use the information and ideas generated by research to explore topics for written work										
Overall WRV.02P • identify the literary and informational forms suited to specific purposes and audiences and use the forms appropriately in their own writing										

Codes: 4 Above Standard   3 At Standard   2 Approaching Standard   1 Below Standard   0 Insufficient Achievement

LANGUAGE & WRITING 9

APPLIED EXPECTATIONS		S	O	N	D	J	F	M	A	M	J
Writing											
WR2.01P	• identify the purpose for each piece of writing										
WR2.02P	• identify the specific audience for each piece of writing										
WR2.03P	• demonstrate an understanding of literary and informational forms of writing by selecting a form appropriate to the specific purpose and audience										
WR2.04P	• use the third-person singular and an appropriate level of language in expository forms requiring objectivity										
Overall WRV.03P	• use a variety of forms of writing to express themselves, clarify their ideas, and engage the audience's attention, imagination, and interest										
WR3.01P	• use key words in questions or prompts to organize information and ideas in homework answers										
WR3.02P	• structure expository paragraphs using a topic sentence, supporting sentences to develop the topic, connecting words to link the sentences, and a concluding sentence										
WR3.03P	• use a unifying image, emotion, or sensation to structure descriptive paragraphs or poems										
WR3.04P	• use changes in time, place, or speaker to structure narrative paragraphs										
WR3.05P	• use a single controlling idea to structure a series of paragraphs										
WR3.06P	• provide an introduction, body, and conclusion in written reports										
WR3.07P	• present directions, instructions, and reports of investigations in a logical order										
Overall WRV.04P	• revise their written work, collaboratively and independently, with a focus on support for ideas, accuracy, clarity, and unity										
WR4.01P	• revise drafts to ensure that ideas are adequately developed with supporting details, and to achieve clarity and unity										
WR4.02B	• revise drafts to ensure consistency in use of first or third person and use of an appropriate level of language										
WR4.03P	• make constructive suggestions to peers, using prompts, checklists, open-ended statements, and questions										
WR4.04B	• consider reactions from teachers, peers, and others in revising and editing written work										
Overall WRV.05P	• edit and proofread to produce final drafts, using correct grammar, spelling, and punctuation, according to the conventions of standard Canadian English specified for this course										
WR5.01P	• identify sources of ideas, information, and quotations in written work										
WR5.02B	• select the publication method or vehicle most accessible or appealing to the intended audience										
WR5.03P	• provide documentation showing their use of the writing process										
WR5.04B	• edit and proofread their own and others' writing										
WR5.05P	• identify and use parts of speech correctly										
WR5.06P	• construct complete and correct compound and complex sentences										
WR5.07B	• identify and correct sentence fragments, run-on sentences, and comma splices										
WR5.08B	• make compound subjects agree with verbs in simple and compound sentences										
WR5.09B	• make pronouns agree with their antecedents in number and gender										
WR5.10B	• use consistent and appropriate verb tense and voice for clarity in narrative and expository writing										

Codes: 4 Above Standard   3 At Standard   2 Approaching Standard   1 Below Standard   0 Insufficient Achievement

APPLIED EXPECTATIONS	S	O	N	D	J	F	M	A	M	J
Writing										
WR5.11B • use knowledge of a wide range of spelling patterns and rules to identify, analyze, and correct spelling errors										
WR5.12B • use and spell homophones correctly										
WR5.13B • use the apostrophe correctly when spelling contractions and possessives										
WR5.14B • use a variety of resources to correct errors in spelling										
WR5.15B • use punctuation correctly										
WR5.16B • adapt punctuation and capitalization for the special requirements of direct quotations, scripts, dialogue, and poetry										
Language										
Overall LGV.01P • use knowledge of vocabulary and language conventions to speak, write, and read clearly and correctly										
LG1.01B • describe strategies used to expand vocabulary and provide evidence of other vocabulary-building activities										
LG1.02B • identify and explain examples of slang, jargon, dialect, and colloquialism, as well as of standard Canadian English										
LG1.03B • identify words borrowed from other languages, and words and terms recently introduced to describe new ideas, inventions, and products, and explain their origins										
LG1.04B • select words and phrases to suit the purpose and intended audience of oral and written work										
LG1.05P • recognize, describe, and use correctly, in oral and written language, the language structures of standard Canadian English and its conventions of grammar and usage										
LG1.06B • recognize, describe, and correct sentence errors in oral and written language										
LG1.07B • recognize, describe, and use correctly, in oral and written language, the conventions of standard Canadian English for spelling, capitalization, and punctuation										
Overall LGV.02B • use listening techniques and oral communication skills to participate in classroom discussions and more formal activities										
LG2.01P • use listening techniques and oral communication skills to participate in group discussions										
LG2.02P • use techniques of effective listening and demonstrate an understanding of oral presentations by restating the main ideas presented and identifying the strengths and weaknesses of presentations										
LG2.03P • work with a partner to plan and make oral presentations to a small group										
LG2.04P • use eye contact, specific examples, humour, and visual aids and technology, as appropriate, to engage the audience's interest during oral presentations										
LG2.05P • practise with cue cards, use breathing exercises, and rehearse with peers to ensure confident delivery in oral presentations										
LG2.06P • identify examples of the use of oral communication skills in school and the world outside the school										
LG2.07P • analyze their own and others' oral communication skills										

Codes: 4 Above Standard   3 At Standard   2 Approaching Standard   1 Below Standard   0 Insufficient Achievement

LANGUAGE & WRITING 9

APPLIED EXPECTATIONS		S	O	N	D	J	F	M	A	M	J
Media Studies											
MDV.01P	• identify and describe the elements, intended audiences, and production practices of a variety of media forms										
MD1.01B	• demonstrate critical thinking skills by identifying the differences between explicit and implicit messages in media works										
MD1.02P	• identify and describe the elements used to structure media works in a variety of forms										
MD1.03P	• compare the reactions of different people or groups to a variety of media works										
MD1.04P	• identify factors that influence media production, distribution, and advertising										
Overall MDV.02P	• use knowledge of a variety of media forms, purposes, and audiences to create media works										
MD2.01P	• adapt a work of literature for presentation in another media form										
MD2.02P	• create media works for different purposes										
MD2.03P	• analyze the characteristics of different audiences and create media works designed specifically for them										

Codes:　4 Above Standard　　3 At Standard　　2 Approaching Standard　　1 Below Standard　　0 Insufficient Achievement

　　　LANGUAGE & WRITING 9

USAGE & STYLE

NAME: _____

Expectations

Students will:

- use consistent and appropriate verb tense and voice (i.e., active and passive) for clarity in narrative and expository writing (WR5.10B/*WR5.10B*; LG1.05D/*LG1.05P*);
- identify and explain examples of slang, jargon, dialect, and colloquialisms (LG1.02B/*LG1.02B*); and
- select words and phrases appropriate to informal and formal styles, to suit the purpose and intended audience of oral and written work (LG1.04B/*LG1.04B*).

CRITERIA	S	O	N	D	J	F	M	A	M	J
Verb Tense and Voice										
• uses consistent and appropriate verb tense and voice										
Vocabulary										
• identifies examples of dialect, slang, jargon, and colloquialisms										
Elements of Style										
• understands how authors use stylistic devices to achieve particular effects										
• identifies elements of foreshadowing in short stories										
• uses effective openings										
• uses strong arguments										
• uses precise and interesting nouns, verbs, and modifiers										
Sentence Structure										
• selects first or third person to suit the form, purpose, and audience										
• uses transitions to connect ideas										
• recognizes and corrects errors in comparison sentences										
• identifies and corrects misplaced/dangling modifiers										

Codes:

4 Above Standard
3 At Standard
2 Approaching Standard
1 Below Standard
0 Insufficient Achievement

WORD STUDY & SPELLING

NAME: _____

Expectations

Students will:

- describe strategies used to expand vocabulary and provide evidence of other vocabulary-building activities (LG1.01B/*LG1.01B*);
- identify words borrowed from other languages and words and terms recently introduced to describe new ideas, inventions, and products, and explain their origins (LG1.03B/*LG1.03B*);
- use knowledge of vocabulary to speak, write, and read competently (LGV.01B/*LGV.01P*);
- use knowledge of a wide range of spelling patterns and rules to identify, analyze, and correct spelling errors (WR5.11B/*WR5.11B*); and
- use and spell homophones correctly (WR5.12B/*WR5.12B*).

CRITERIA	S	O	N	D	J	F	M	A	M	J
Word Origins										
• identifies words borrowed from other languages										
• explains how words change over time										
• explains the origin of words and terms used to describe new ideas, inventions, and products										
Vocabulary Expansion										
• explores how prefixes affect the spelling of a word										
• expands vocabulary by using suffixes										
• recognizes Greek and Latin root words										
• creates personal and class dictionaries of newly encountered words										
Spelling										
• uses spelling strategies to correct spelling errors										
• describes the conventions of standard Canadian English spelling										
• applies spelling rules										
• uses a dictionary and thesaurus to find word replacements										
• uses apostrophes for possessives										
• uses effective proofreading strategies										

Codes:

4 Above Standard
3 At Standard
2 Approaching Standard
1 Below Standard
0 Insufficient Achievement

EDITING/PROOFREADING

NAME: _____ DATE: _____

SELECTION: _____

	Yes	Sometimes	No

Grammar and Usage

Did I:

	Yes	Sometimes	No
• use first or third person consistently (first person = I; third person = he/she/they)?	☐	☐	☐
• check to ensure that all sentences are complete, and that there are no run-on sentences or comma splices?	☐	☐	☐
• check for agreement between subjects and verbs, and between pronouns and their antecedents?	☐	☐	☐
• use verb tenses (i.e., past, present, future) consistently and appropriately?	☐	☐	☐

Spelling and Punctuation

Did I:

	Yes	Sometimes	No
• use a dictionary to check word spellings?	☐	☐	☐
• check the spelling of names and places?	☐	☐	☐
• use apostrophes for contractions and possessives?	☐	☐	☐
• check for proper punctuation at the end of each sentence?	☐	☐	☐
• use punctuation marks where needed (e.g., comma, quotation marks, dash, colon, parentheses, ellipses)?	☐	☐	☐

Proofreading Strategies

Did I:

	Yes	Sometimes	No
• read my writing out loud?	☐	☐	☐
• check for spelling errors by reading my work backward?	☐	☐	☐
• use a printout to proofread my writing (if done on a computer)?	☐	☐	☐
• use a resource to help me with my proofreading questions (e.g., a writing handbook or style guide)?	☐	☐	☐

Summary Reflections

When I proofread, I'm confident about checking for problems such as _____

_____

I'd like to be more confident about checking for problems such as _____

_____

I can become a more confident proofreader by _____

_____

LANGUAGE & WRITING 9

GROUP WORK

NAME: _____   DATE: _____

	Yes	Sometimes	No

Our Work as a Group

Did we:

- assign different roles or responsibilities to each member of the group? ☐ ☐ ☐
- understand and agree on the roles or responsibilities of each member of the group? ☐ ☐ ☐
- all come prepared to meetings and discussions? ☐ ☐ ☐
- stay focused on the topic or task and not waste time? ☐ ☐ ☐
- ensure that everyone in the group participated in meetings and discussions? ☐ ☐ ☐
- remain polite and helpful to each other? ☐ ☐ ☐
- find ways to solve conflicts and differences of opinions? ☐ ☐ ☐
- show respect for each other's opinions even when they differed from those of others in the group? ☐ ☐ ☐
- discuss and resolve any problems related to the way we were working as a group? ☐ ☐ ☐
- discuss how our group worked well and how we could have been more effective, at the end of the task or discussion? ☐ ☐ ☐

My Participation in the Group

Did I:

- understand my role or responsibility or ask for clarification if I did not? ☐ ☐ ☐
- come prepared to each meeting or discussion? ☐ ☐ ☐
- help the group stay focused on the task or topic? ☐ ☐ ☐
- ask questions, contribute ideas and opinions, make compromises, and accept that the group might not agree with all my ideas? ☐ ☐ ☐
- remain polite to other members of the group? ☐ ☐ ☐
- support other members of the group by saying things like "Good idea" or "Good work"? ☐ ☐ ☐

Summary Reflection

The next time I participate in a group, I'm going to work on _____

_____

_____

_____

_____

LISTENING

NAME: _____   DATE: _____

SPEAKER: _____   TOPIC: _____

	Yes	Sometimes	No

Before Listening

Did I:

- think about my purpose for listening? (For example, Why is this information important to me? What do I need to do with this information?)   ☐ ☐ ☐

- brainstorm a point-form list of what I already knew about the topic?   ☐ ☐ ☐

- prepare a list of questions about the topic that I thought the speaker would answer?   ☐ ☐ ☐

During Listening

Did I:

- watch the face of the person speaking?   ☐ ☐ ☐
- listen for clues about how the speaker organized his/her information? (For example, did the speaker identify main points, sub-topics, or issues; discuss problems and solutions; or describe causes and effects?)   ☐ ☐ ☐

- try to visualize the scenes, events, and descriptions the speaker talked about?   ☐ ☐ ☐

- ask myself questions about what I was hearing?   ☐ ☐ ☐

- try to tell the difference between facts and opinions in the speaker's message?   ☐ ☐ ☐
- take notes as I listened to the speaker? (e.g., sketched diagrams, listed key words and details, used circles and arrows to connect related ideas)?   ☐ ☐ ☐

After Listening

Did I:

- revise or rewrite my notes to make them clear, organize the ideas, and add additional details I remembered?   ☐ ☐ ☐
- make notes about information that wasn't clear to me, and ask the speaker or other listeners to clarify ideas?   ☐ ☐ ☐
- make a list of questions I had and then make a note about ways I could find answers to my questions?   ☐ ☐ ☐

Summary Reflections

When I listen to a speaker, I'm good at _____

_____

I can improve my listening skills by _____

_____

_____

MEDIA CREATION

NAME: _____ DATE: _____

MEDIA PRODUCT: _____

	Yes	Sometimes	No

Planning

Did I:

- identify the purpose and audience of my product?

- identify the main message I wanted to communicate?

- find effective examples of the type of product I wanted to create to use as models?
- make decisions about how to use conventions appropriate for the medium I was using (e.g., camera angles for a video, navigation bar for a Web site)?
- plan how I would use language and images to communicate with my audience (e.g., matching images and audio script in a multimedia presentation, deciding what would be communicated through dialogue and through visuals for a video)

- assess my project to ensure that it was manageable in size and complexity?

- identify all materials, equipment, and outside expertise I would require?
- complete preparation stages appropriate for my product (e.g., rough sketches for art, storyboard for a video, tree diagram for Web site navigation)?
- review planned techniques and content to ensure that they related to my purpose and audience?

Creating

Did I:

- keep my purpose and audience in mind during the creation process?
- use techniques to communicate my message effectively (e.g., using larger type to identify headings and emphasize important information, using persuasive techniques in copy for a print ad, or using camera techniques to heighten drama in a video)?
- find ways to create visual appeal for my audience (e.g., including graphics on a Web site or interesting images in a multimedia presentation)?

Revising

Did I:

- look for ways to strengthen the connection of my work to its purpose and audience (e.g., made a Web site easier to navigate, or reorganized images in a multimedia presentation to use contrast to emphasize my message)?

- ask others for feedback and consider their responses?

Summary Reflections

When I created this product, my intended audience was _____ and my purpose was to _____

I designed this product to achieve this purpose by _____

The next time I create a similar product, I would _____

ORAL PRESENTATION

NAME: _____ DATE: _____

PRESENTATION TOPIC: _____

	Yes	Sometimes	No
Before the Presentation			
Did I:			
• identify and focus my topic?	☐	☐	☐
• make notes about information I needed to find and where I might find it?	☐	☐	☐
• plan and prepare visual aids and/or technology to illustrate and explain my ideas and keep my audience interested?	☐	☐	☐
• gather and organize information, paying attention to the best order for presenting ideas and the time limit for my presentation?	☐	☐	☐
• ensure that the presentation emphasized the main points and included examples, explanations, and supporting details where appropriate?	☐	☐	☐
• make brief notes on index or cue cards to remind myself of what I wanted to say and in what order?	☐	☐	☐
• try to use language appropriate for my audience and purpose?	☐	☐	☐
• rehearse my presentation to make sure I knew my material?	☐	☐	☐
• use a tape recorder to identify how I could improve my presentation, or rehearse my presentation in front of a friend and ask for feedback?	☐	☐	☐
• use relaxation techniques prior to making my presentation (e.g., taking slow, deep breaths or using mental visualization)?	☐	☐	☐
During the Presentation			
Did I:			
• speak in a clear, audible, and confident voice, taking care not to speak too quickly?	☐	☐	☐
• vary the pitch of my voice and use gestures, facial expressions, and humour (if appropriate) to hold the audience's interest?	☐	☐	☐
• make eye contact with members of the audience?	☐	☐	☐
• use visual aids and/or technology in a way that did not interrupt the flow of my presentation?	☐	☐	☐
After the Presentation			
Did I:			
• ask members of the audience for feedback?	☐	☐	☐

Summary Reflections

When I make a presentation to a group, I am confident at _____

I'd like to be more confident at _____

I can improve my oral presentation skills by _____

_____

PEER ASSESSMENT: WRITING

SELECTION TITLE: _____ AUTHOR: _____

ASSESSMENT BY: _____ DATE: _____

	Yes	Sometimes	No
General			
• The purpose of the selection is clear; the language and approach are appropriate for the intended audience.	☐	☐	☐
• All parts of the selection are related to the author's purpose.	☐	☐	☐
• The writing attracts and maintains the reader's interest.	☐	☐	☐
• The selection is free of inappropriate stereotypes and gender bias.	☐	☐	☐
Nonfiction			
• The title gives a clear idea of the subject.	☐	☐	☐
• The main ideas are clearly stated.	☐	☐	☐
• The ideas are presented in an order that is logical and effective.	☐	☐	☐
• Details, examples, and explanations support ideas and develop paragraphs.	☐	☐	☐
• Writing techniques have been used to hold the reader's interest and to clarify ideas (e.g., rhetorical questions, comparison/contrast, problems/solutions).	☐	☐	☐
• The selection includes an effective introduction and conclusion.	☐	☐	☐
• Quotation marks are used to identify words and phrases taken directly from a source and the sources of quotations have been identified.	☐	☐	☐
• The bibliography identifies all sources used and has been organized in the appropriate format.	☐	☐	☐
Fiction			
• The title is effective.	☐	☐	☐
• The setting is clear.	☐	☐	☐
• Details have been provided to develop characters (e.g., physical descriptions, actions, dialogue).	☐	☐	☐
• The plot includes rising action, climax, and a satisfying resolution.	☐	☐	☐
• Dialogue sounds natural and has been used effectively.	☐	☐	☐
• Techniques have been used to make the writing more effective (e.g., sensory descriptions, interesting verbs, similes, metaphors, contrast).	☐	☐	☐

Overall Comments

Generally, what I liked most about this selection is _____

Specific things I liked about this selection include: _____

My suggestions for improving this selection are: _____

PEER EDITING

SELECTION TITLE: _____ **AUTHOR:** _____

EDITED BY: _____ **DATE:** _____

	Yes	Sometimes	No
General			
• Main ideas are clearly stated and appear in a logical order; ideas are supported by details, explanations, and/or examples (for nonfiction).	☐	☐	☐
• First or third person is used consistently.	☐	☐	☐
• Paragraphs are used appropriately (for a new speaker, a new topic, or a change in time or place).	☐	☐	☐
• Language is appropriate for the purpose and audience.	☐	☐	☐
• Sources of information and quotations are identified (for nonfiction).	☐	☐	☐
• Used correct grammar and sentence structure.	☐	☐	☐
• Used appropriate verb tenses; subjects and verbs agree.	☐	☐	☐
• Used apostrophes for contractions and possessives.	☐	☐	☐
• Used correct spelling.	☐	☐	☐
• Used correct punctuation marks.	☐	☐	☐

Feedback

From an editorial perspective, this selection is strong in the following areas: _____

_____

_____

Suggested areas for improvement include: _____

_____

_____

_____

_____

_____

_____

_____

_____

_____

_____

READING STRATEGIES

NAME: _____ **DATE:** _____

	Yes	Sometimes	No

Before Reading

Did I:

	Yes	Sometimes	No
• read the title?	☐	☐	☐
• read the headings?	☐	☐	☐
• preview text features (e.g., pictures, diagrams, italicized words)?	☐	☐	☐
• predict what the selection was about?	☐	☐	☐
• think about what I already knew about the topic?	☐	☐	☐
• ask myself questions about the topic?	☐	☐	☐
• skim the selection?	☐	☐	☐
• understand my reason for reading?	☐	☐	☐

During Reading

Did I:

	Yes	Sometimes	No
• look for the main ideas?	☐	☐	☐
• take jot notes?	☐	☐	☐
• draw diagrams and maps outlining the main ideas and important details?	☐	☐	☐
• confirm what I already knew about the topic?	☐	☐	☐

During Reading (continued)

Did I:

	Yes	Sometimes	No
• look for answers to my questions?	☐	☐	☐
• summarize the main ideas?	☐	☐	☐
• stop to ask myself questions?	☐	☐	☐
• use context clues to figure out words I did not know?	☐	☐	☐
• confirm my predictions?	☐	☐	☐
• make personal connections?	☐	☐	☐
• re-read sections that I did not understand?	☐	☐	☐

After Reading

Did I:

	Yes	Sometimes	No
• think about what I had learned?	☐	☐	☐
• summarize the main ideas?	☐	☐	☐
• discuss ideas from the selection with someone else?	☐	☐	☐
• look for more information on the topic of the selection?	☐	☐	☐
• sketch or write about the information?	☐	☐	☐

Summary Reflections

The strategy/strategies that I find most helpful in reading and understanding texts is/are _____

_____

_____

_____

The strategies I plan to use next time I read include: _____

_____

_____

_____

_____

RESEARCH

NAME: _____ DATE: _____

RESEARCH TOPIC: _____

	Yes	Sometimes	No

Planning

Did I:

- narrow my selected topic down to make it manageable? ☐ ☐ ☐

- consider the purpose and audience for my research topic? ☐ ☐ ☐
- decide on a presentation format that would work well with my topic, purpose, and audience? ☐ ☐ ☐
- think about how my presentation format would relate to the content (e.g., an oral presentation might require audio/visual aids)? ☐ ☐ ☐
- use a strategy such as charting or webbing to organize what I knew about the topic, identify questions I had about the topic, and record resources I could use to find out more information? ☐ ☐ ☐

Researching

Did I:

- use resources to help me locate information about the topic, such as people (teachers, librarians, friends, family), computer or card catalogues, periodical indexes, and Internet search engines? ☐ ☐ ☐
- consult a variety of resources, such as encyclopedias, books, magazines, newspapers, vertical files, CD-ROMs, Web sites, documentaries, and TV shows? ☐ ☐ ☐
- make point-form notes about the information I found that was relevant to my topic? ☐ ☐ ☐
- use quotation marks when I used an author's exact words and make a note about the page number and source of the quotation? ☐ ☐ ☐
- record details about each resource used for my bibliography? ☐ ☐ ☐

Planning

Did I:

- organize my research notes into subtopics, and put the subtopics into a logical order to develop an outline? ☐ ☐ ☐
- look at my notes for each subtopic and try to come up with my own ideas (e.g., conclusions, causes and effects, problems and solutions, similarities and differences)? ☐ ☐ ☐

Continued

LANGUAGE & WRITING 9

	Yes	Sometimes	No

Writing

Did I:

- structure my report using an introduction, body, and conclusion? ☐ ☐ ☐
- use different paragraphs or sections for each main idea stated in my introduction, and develop each idea with supporting details such as facts, examples, and reasons? ☐ ☐ ☐
- prepare a bibliography? ☐ ☐ ☐
- ask someone to give feedback on my first draft? ☐ ☐ ☐
- make revisions and proofread my final draft? ☐ ☐ ☐

Summary Reflections

When I prepared this research report, my purpose was to _____

_____

_____

I am pleased with the way _____

Based on my experiences with this report, the next time I prepare a research report, I will _____

_____

_____

_____

_____

_____

_____

_____

_____

_____

_____

_____

REVISING

SELECTION: _____

NAME: _____ **DATE:** _____

	Yes	Sometimes	No
Focus of Writing			
• Does my writing have a clear focus on my purpose and my main point or idea?	☐	☐	☐
• Have I written using a tone and vocabulary that is appropriate for my audience?	☐	☐	☐
Organization of Ideas			
• Is my method of organization clear and easy to follow?	☐	☐	☐
• Do I need to reorder any parts to fit my organizational structure or to make the order of ideas more logical?	☐	☐	☐
• Have I cut all information that is not relevant to my purpose/topic?	☐	☐	☐
• Do I need to add information to better achieve my purpose?	☐	☐	☐
• Do I need to add details to sentences that are too general or vague?	☐	☐	☐
• Have I included information and examples to support my ideas and opinions?	☐	☐	☐
Clarity			
• Do I need to rewrite any parts to make ideas or explanations clearer?	☐	☐	☐
• Have I used techniques to make my beginning and closing interesting and effective?	☐	☐	☐
Accuracy			
• Have I checked to make sure that all my information (names, dates, facts, figures, etc.) is accurate?	☐	☐	☐
• Have I asked someone to give me feedback on how to improve my writing?	☐	☐	☐

Summary Reflections

When I revise my work, I'm confident about checking for _____

_____

_____

I can become more proficient at revising my work by _____

_____

_____

_____

_____

LANGUAGE & WRITING 9

SPELLING

NAME: _____ DATE: _____

SELECTION TITLE: _____

	Yes	Sometimes	No

Did I:

- check my use of homophones (words that sound the same but are spelled differently, such as *there/their/they're*) to ensure that I have used the correct words? ☐ ☐ ☐

- check the spelling of words with double letters (e.g., *committee, embarrass, travelling*)? ☐ ☐ ☐

- check the spelling of words with *ie* or *ei* (e.g., *receive, neighbour, chief, relief*)? ☐ ☐ ☐

- check the spelling of hyphenated words (e.g., as *self-evaluation, pre-empt, re-examine*)? ☐ ☐ ☐

- confirm the spelling of names, places, and titles? ☐ ☐ ☐

- use Canadian spellings of words (e.g., *colour, honour, practise, favourite, labelling, catalogue*)? ☐ ☐ ☐

- check the spelling of words with silent letters (e.g., *psychology, climb, knock*) ☐ ☐ ☐

- check the spelling of words with endings that sound the same, such as *-ant/-ent* (*pleasant, garment*); *-ible/-able* (*responsible, comfortable*); *-tion/-sion* (*combination, invasion*)? ☐ ☐ ☐

- listen for each syllable in long words to ensure I didn't leave out any letters? ☐ ☐ ☐

- use a spell-check program for writing I did on a computer? ☐ ☐ ☐

- use a dictionary to check words that didn't look right or that I was not sure how to spell? ☐ ☐ ☐

- ask someone to check my writing for spelling errors? ☐ ☐ ☐

- record any words I misspelled in my learning log? ☐ ☐ ☐

Summary Reflections

The spelling strategies I'm most confident at include _____

_____

_____

I need to work on checking for _____

_____

_____

_____

ADVERTISEMENT

NAME: _____ DATE: _____

Categories	Below Level	LEVELS OF ACHIEVEMENT*			
		50–59% Level 1	60–69% Level 2	70–79% Level 3	80–100% Level 4
Knowledge/ Understanding	*The student:*				
• knowledge of the forms and purposes of advertisements	• shows very limited knowledge of the forms and purposes of advertisements	• shows limited knowledge of the forms and purposes of advertisements	• shows some knowledge of the forms and purposes of advertisements	• shows considerable knowledge of the forms and purposes of advertisements	• shows thorough knowledge of the forms and purposes of advertisements
• understanding of the relationship between an advertisement and its medium	• shows very limited understanding of the relationship between an advertisement and its medium	• shows limited understanding of the relationship between an advertisement and its medium	• shows some understanding of the relationship between an advertisement and its medium	• shows considerable understanding of the relationship between an advertisement and its medium	• shows thorough understanding of the relationship between an advertisement and its medium
• understanding of the uses and effects of aesthetic elements in advertisements	• shows very limited understanding of the uses and effects of aesthetic elements	• shows limited understanding of the uses and effects of aesthetic elements	• shows some understanding of the uses and effects of aesthetic elements	• shows considerable understanding of the uses and effects of aesthetic elements	• shows thorough understanding of the uses and effects of aesthetic elements
Thinking/Inquiry	*The student:*				
• analysis of the text and images of an advertisement	• analyzes an advertisement with very limited effectiveness	• analyzes an advertisement with limited effectiveness	• analyzes an advertisement with some effectiveness	• analyzes an advertisement with considerable effectiveness	• analyzes an advertisement with a high degree of effectiveness
• planning an advertisement	• uses a storyboard to plan an advertisement with very limited effectiveness	• uses a storyboard to plan an advertisement with limited effectiveness	• uses a storyboard to plan an advertisement with some effectiveness	• uses a storyboard to plan an advertisement with considerable effectiveness	• uses a storyboard to plan an advertisement with a high degree of effectiveness
Communication	*The student:*				
• communication of ideas and information in an advertisement	• communicates ideas and information with very limited clarity	• communicates ideas and information with limited clarity	• communicates ideas and information with some clarity	• communicates ideas and information with considerable clarity	• communicates ideas and information with a high degree of clarity
• communication to an audience for a purpose	• communicates with a very limited sense of audience and purpose	• communicates with a limited sense of audience and purpose	• communicates with some sense of audience and purpose	• communicates with a clear sense of audience and purpose	• communicates with a strong sense of audience and purpose
• use of the advertisement form(s)	• shows very limited command of the advertisement form(s)	• shows limited command of the advertisement form(s)	• shows some command of the advertisement form(s)	• shows considerable command of the advertisement form(s)	• shows extensive command of the advertisement form(s)
Application	*The student:*				
• application of appropriate language conventions in an advertisement	• uses appropriate language conventions with very limited accuracy and effectiveness	• uses appropriate language conventions with limited accuracy and effectiveness	• uses appropriate language conventions with some accuracy and effectiveness	• uses appropriate language conventions with considerable accuracy and effectiveness	• uses appropriate language conventions with a high degree of accuracy and effectiveness
• application of media conventions and techniques	• uses media conventions and techniques with very limited effectiveness	• uses media conventions and techniques with limited effectiveness	• uses media conventions and techniques with some effectiveness	• uses media conventions and techniques with considerable effectiveness	• uses media conventions and techniques with a high degree of effectiveness
• application of the writing process for an advertisement	• uses the writing process with very limited effectiveness	• uses the writing process with limited effectiveness	• uses the writing process with some effectiveness	• uses the writing process with considerable effectiveness	• uses the writing process with a high degree of effectiveness
• making connections among purpose, target audience, and medium	• makes connections with very limited effectiveness	• makes connections with limited effectiveness	• makes connections with some effectiveness	• makes connections with considerable effectiveness	• makes connections with a high degree of effectiveness
• application of technology for an advertisement	• uses technology with very limited appropriateness and effectiveness	• uses technology with limited appropriateness and effectiveness	• uses technology with some appropriateness and effectiveness	• uses technology with considerable appropriateness and effectiveness	• uses technology with a high degree of appropriateness and effectiveness

* For a description of the levels of student achievement, please see The Achievement Chart for English, *The Ontario Curriculum Grades 9 and 10*, pp.46–49.

COMPARISON

NAME: _____ DATE: _____

Categories	Below Level 1	50–59% Level 1	60–69% Level 2	70–79% Level 3	80–100% Level 4
		LEVELS OF ACHIEVEMENT*			
Knowledge/ Understanding	*The student:*				
• knowledge of the form and purpose of a comparison	• shows very limited knowledge of the form and purpose of a comparison	• shows limited knowledge of the form and purpose of a comparison	• shows some knowledge of the form and purpose of a comparison	• shows considerable knowledge of the form and purpose of a comparison	• shows thorough knowledge of the form and purpose of a comparison
• understanding of the relationships among facts, ideas, concepts, and themes	• shows very limited understanding of the relationships among facts, ideas, concepts, and themes	• shows limited understanding of the relationships among facts, ideas, concepts, and themes	• shows some understanding of the relationships among facts, ideas, concepts, and themes	• shows considerable understanding of the relationships among facts, ideas, concepts, and themes	• shows thorough understanding of the relationships among facts, ideas, concepts, and themes
Thinking/Inquiry	*The student:*				
• critical thinking skills	• uses critical thinking skills to make a comparison with very limited effectiveness	• uses critical thinking skills to make a comparison with limited effectiveness	• uses critical thinking skills to make a comparison with some effectiveness	• uses critical thinking skills to make a comparison with considerable effectiveness	• uses critical thinking skills to make a comparison with a high degree of effectiveness
Communication	*The student:*				
• communication of information and ideas	• communicates information and ideas with very limited clarity	• communicates information and ideas with limited clarity	• communicates information and ideas with some clarity	• communicates information and ideas with considerable clarity	• communicates information and ideas with a high degree of clarity
• communication to an audience for a purpose	• communicates with a very limited sense of audience and purpose	• communicates with a limited sense of audience and purpose	• communicates with some sense of audience and purpose	• communicates with a clear sense of audience and purpose	• communicates with a strong sense of audience and purpose
• use of the comparison form	• shows very limited command of the comparison form	• shows limited command of the comparison form	• shows some command of the comparison form	• shows considerable command of the comparison form	• shows extensive command of the comparison form
Application	*The student:*				
• application of language conventions	• uses language conventions with very limited accuracy and effectiveness	• uses language conventions with limited accuracy and effectiveness	• uses language conventions with some accuracy and effectiveness	• uses language conventions with considerable accuracy and effectiveness	• uses language conventions with a high degree of accuracy and effectiveness
• application of degrees of comparison for adjectives and adverbs	• uses degrees of comparison for adjectives and adverbs with very limited accuracy and effectiveness	• uses degrees of comparison for adjectives and adverbs with limited accuracy and effectiveness	• uses degrees of comparison for adjectives and adverbs with some accuracy and effectiveness	• uses degrees of comparison for adjectives and adverbs with considerable accuracy and effectiveness	• uses degrees of comparison for adjectives and adverbs accurately and effectively all or almost all of the time
• application of the writing process	• uses the writing process with very limited effectiveness	• uses the writing process with limited effectiveness	• uses the writing process with some effectiveness	• uses the writing process with considerable effectiveness	• uses the writing process with a high degree of effectiveness

* For a description of the levels of student achievement, please see The Achievement Chart for English, *The Ontario Curriculum Grades 9 and 10*, pp.46–49.

CONFERENCING

NAME: _____   DATE: _____

Categories	Below Level 1	LEVELS OF ACHIEVEMENT*			
		50–59% Level 1	60–69% Level 2	70–79% Level 3	80–100% Level 4
Knowledge/ Understanding	*The student:*				
• knowledge of the writing form(s)	• shows very limited knowledge of the writing form(s)	• shows limited knowledge of the writing form(s)	• shows some knowledge of the writing form(s)	• shows considerable knowledge of the writing form(s)	• shows thorough knowledge of the writing form(s)
• understanding of information, ideas, concepts, and themes	• shows very limited understanding of information, ideas, concepts, and themes	• shows limited understanding of information, ideas, concepts, and themes	• shows some understanding of information, ideas, concepts, and themes	• shows considerable understanding of information, ideas, concepts, and themes	• shows thorough and insightful understanding of information, ideas, concepts, and themes
• understanding of the use and effects of stylistic devices	• shows very limited understanding of the use and effects of stylistic devices	• shows limited understanding of the use and effects of stylistic devices	• shows some understanding of the use and effects of stylistic devices	• shows considerable understanding of the use and effects of stylistic devices	• shows thorough and insightful understanding of the use and effects of stylistic devices
Thinking/Inquiry	*The student:*				
• critical and creative thinking skills	• uses critical and creative thinking skills with very limited effectiveness	• uses critical and creative thinking skills with limited effectiveness	• uses critical and creative thinking skills with some effectiveness	• uses critical and creative thinking skills with considerable effectiveness	• uses critical and creative thinking skills with a high degree of effectiveness
• inquiry skills	• uses inquiry skills with very limited effectiveness	• uses inquiry skills with limited effectiveness	• uses inquiry skills with some effectiveness	• uses inquiry skills with considerable effectiveness	• uses inquiry skills with a high degree of effectiveness
Communication	*The student:*				
• communication of information and ideas	• communicates information and ideas with very limited clarity	• communicates information and ideas with limited clarity	• communicates information and ideas with some clarity	• communicates information and ideas with considerable clarity	• communicates information and ideas with a high degree of clarity
• communication to an audience for a purpose	• communicates with a very limited sense of audience and purpose	• communicates with a limited sense of audience and purpose	• communicates with some sense of audience and purpose	• communicates with a clear sense of audience and purpose	• communicates with a strong sense of audience and purpose
• use of the writing form(s)	• shows very limited command of the writing form(s)	• shows limited command of the writing form(s)	• shows some command of the writing form(s)	• shows considerable command of the writing form(s)	• shows extensive command of the writing form(s)
Application	*The student:*				
• application of language conventions	• uses language conventions with very limited accuracy and effectiveness	• uses language conventions with limited accuracy and effectiveness	• uses language conventions with some accuracy and effectiveness	• uses language conventions with considerable accuracy and effectiveness	• uses language conventions with a high degree of accuracy and effectiveness
• application of the writing process	• uses the writing process with very limited effectiveness	• uses the writing process with limited effectiveness	• uses the writing process with some effectiveness	• uses the writing process with considerable effectiveness	• uses the writing process with a high degree of effectiveness

* For a description of the levels of student achievement, please see The Achievement Chart for English, *The Ontario Curriculum Grades 9 and 10*, pp.46–49.

DESCRIPTIVE WRITING

NAME: _____ DATE: _____

Categories	Below Level 1	50–59% Level 1	60–69% Level 2	70–79% Level 3	80–100% Level 4
LEVELS OF ACHIEVEMENT*					
Knowledge/ Understanding	*The student:*				
• knowledge of elements of descriptive writing	• shows very limited knowledge of elements of descriptive writing	• shows limited knowledge of elements of descriptive writing	• shows some knowledge of elements of descriptive writing	shows considerable knowledge of elements of descriptive writing	• shows thorough knowledge of elements of descriptive writing
• understanding of ideas and theme	• shows very limited understanding of ideas and theme	• shows limited understanding of ideas and theme	• shows some understanding of ideas and theme	• shows considerable understanding of ideas and theme	• shows thorough and insightful understanding of ideas and theme
• understanding of the uses and effects of diction and stylistic devices	• shows very limited understanding of the uses and effects of diction and stylistic devices	• shows limited understanding of the uses and effects of diction and stylistic devices	• shows some understanding of the uses and effects of diction and stylistic devices	• shows considerable understanding of the uses and effects of diction and stylistic devices	• shows thorough and insightful understanding of the uses and effects of diction and stylistic devices
Thinking/Inquiry	*The student:*				
• critical thinking skills	• uses critical thinking skills to select descriptive details with very limited effectiveness	• uses critical thinking skills to select descriptive details with limited effectiveness	• uses critical thinking skills to select descriptive details with some effectiveness	• uses critical thinking skills to select descriptive details with considerable effectiveness	• uses critical thinking skills to select descriptive details with a high degree of effectiveness
• creative thinking skills	• uses creative thinking skills to convey a dominant impression with very limited effectiveness	• uses creative thinking skills to convey a dominant impression with limited effectiveness	• uses creative thinking skills to convey a dominant impression with some effectiveness	• uses creative thinking skills to convey a dominant impression with considerable effectiveness	• uses creative thinking skills to convey a dominant impression with a high degree of effectiveness
Communication	*The student:*				
• communication of ideas and theme	• communicates ideas and theme with very limited clarity and organization	• communicates ideas and theme with limited clarity and organization	• communicates ideas and theme with some clarity and organization	• communicates ideas and theme with considerable clarity and organization	• communicates ideas and theme with a high degree of clarity and organization
• communication to an audience for a purpose	• communicates with a very limited sense of audience and purpose	• communicates with a limited sense of audience and purpose	• communicates with some sense of audience and purpose	• communicates with a clear sense of audience and purpose	• communicates with a strong sense of audience and purpose
• use of elements of descriptive writing	• shows very limited command of elements of descriptive writing	• shows limited command of elements of descriptive writing	• shows some command of elements of descriptive writing	• shows considerable command of elements of descriptive writing	• shows extensive command of elements of descriptive writing
Application	*The student:*				
• application of language conventions	• uses language conventions with very limited accuracy and effectiveness	• uses language conventions with limited accuracy and effectiveness	• uses language conventions with some accuracy and effectiveness	• uses language conventions with considerable accuracy and effectiveness	• uses language conventions with a high degree of accuracy and effectiveness
• application of the writing process	• uses the writing process with very limited effectiveness	• uses the writing process with limited effectiveness	• uses the writing process with some effectiveness	• uses the writing process with considerable effectiveness	• uses the writing process with a high degree of effectiveness
• application of diction and stylistic devices	• uses diction and stylistic devices with very limited effectiveness	• uses diction and stylistic devices with limited effectiveness	• uses diction and stylistic devices with some effectiveness	• uses diction and stylistic devices with considerable effectiveness	• uses diction and stylistic devices with a high degree of effectiveness

* For a description of the levels of student achievement, please see The Achievement Chart for English, *The Ontario Curriculum Grades 9 and 10*, pp.46–49.

DRAMATIZATION

NAME: _____ DATE: _____

Categories	Below Level 1	LEVELS OF ACHIEVEMENT*			
		50–59% Level 1	60–69% Level 2	70–79% Level 3	80–100% Level 4
Knowledge/ Understanding	*The student:*				
• knowledge of the dramatic form	• shows very limited knowledge of the dramatic form	• shows limited knowledge of the dramatic form	• shows some knowledge of the dramatic form	• shows considerable knowledge of the dramatic form	• shows thorough knowledge of the dramatic form
• understanding of information and ideas	• shows very limited understanding of information and ideas	• shows limited understanding of information and ideas	• shows some understanding of information and ideas	• shows considerable understanding of information and ideas	• shows thorough and insightful understanding of information and ideas
• understanding of the uses and effect of dramatic elements	• shows very limited understanding of the uses and effect of dramatic elements	• shows limited understanding of the uses and effect of dramatic elements	• shows some understanding of the uses and effect of dramatic elements	• shows considerable understanding of the uses and effect of dramatic elements	• shows thorough and insightful understanding of the uses and effect of dramatic elements
Thinking/Inquiry	*The student:*				
• creative thinking skills	• uses creative thinking skills (in preparing and presenting the dramatization) with very limited effectiveness	• uses creative thinking skills (in preparing and presenting the dramatization) with limited effectiveness	• uses creative thinking skills (in preparing and presenting the dramatization) with some effectiveness	• uses creative thinking skills (in preparing and presenting the dramatization) with considerable effectiveness	• uses creative thinking skills (in preparing and presenting the dramatization) with a high degree of effectiveness
Communication	*The student:*				
• communication of information and ideas	• communicates information and ideas with very limited clarity	• communicates information and ideas with limited clarity	• communicates information and ideas with some clarity	• communicates information and ideas with considerable clarity	• communicates information and ideas with a high degree of clarity
• communication to an audience for a purpose	• communicates with a very limited sense of audience and purpose	• communicates with a limited sense of audience and purpose	• communicates with some sense of audience and purpose	• communicates with a clear sense of audience and purpose	• communicates with a strong sense of audience and purpose
• use of the dramatic form	• shows very limited command of the dramatic form	• shows limited command of the dramatic form	• shows some command of the dramatic form	• shows considerable command of the dramatic form	• shows extensive command of the dramatic form
Application	*The student:*				
• application of language conventions	• uses language conventions with very limited accuracy and effectiveness	• uses language conventions with limited accuracy and effectiveness	• uses language conventions with some accuracy and effectiveness	• uses language conventions with considerable accuracy and effectiveness	• uses language conventions with a high degree of accuracy and effectiveness
• application of oral communication conventions and techniques	• uses oral communication conventions and techniques with very limited effectiveness	• uses oral communication conventions and techniques with limited effectiveness	• uses oral communication conventions and techniques with some effectiveness	• uses oral communication conventions and techniques with considerable effectiveness	• uses oral communication conventions and techniques with a high degree of effectiveness

* For a description of the levels of student achievement, please see The Achievement Chart for English, *The Ontario Curriculum Grades 9 and 10*, pp.46–49.

EVENT DESCRIPTION

NAME: _____   DATE: _____

		LEVELS OF ACHIEVEMENT*			
Categories	**Below Level 1**	**50–59% Level 1**	**60–69% Level 2**	**70–79% Level 3**	**80–100% Level 4**
Knowledge/ Understanding	*The student:*				
• knowledge of the event description form	• shows very limited knowledge of the event description form	• shows limited knowledge of the event description form	• shows some knowledge of the event description form	• shows considerable knowledge of the event description form	• shows thorough knowledge of the event description form
• understanding of relationships between facts and ideas in the event description	• shows very limited understanding of relationships between facts and ideas	• shows limited understanding of relationships between facts and ideas	• shows some understanding of relationships between facts and ideas	• shows considerable understanding of relationships between facts and ideas	• shows thorough and insightful understanding of relationships between facts and ideas
Thinking/Inquiry	*The student:*				
• creative thinking skills	• uses sensory details with very limited effectiveness	• uses sensory details with limited effectiveness	• uses sensory details with some effectiveness	• uses sensory details with considerable effectiveness	• uses sensory details with a high degree of effectiveness
• drawing conclusions about the significance of the event	• draws conclusions about the significance of the event with very limited clarity	• draws conclusions about the significance of the event with limited clarity	• draws conclusions about the significance of the event with some clarity	• draws conclusions about the significance of the event with considerable clarity	• draws conclusions about the significance of the event with a high degree of clarity
Communication	*The student:*				
• communication of information and impressions	• communicates information and impressions with very limited accuracy and clarity	• communicates information and impressions with limited accuracy and clarity	• communicates information and impressions with some accuracy and clarity	• communicates information and impressions with considerable accuracy and clarity	• communicates information and impressions with a high degree of accuracy and clarity
• communication to an audience for a purpose	• communicates with a very limited sense of audience and purpose	• communicates with a limited sense of audience and purpose	• communicates with some sense of audience and purpose	• communicates with a clear sense of audience and purpose	• communicates with a strong sense of audience and purpose
• use of the event description form	• shows very limited command of the event description form	• shows limited command of the event description form	• shows some command of the event description form	• shows considerable command of the event description form	• shows extensive command of the event description form
Application	*The student:*				
• application of language conventions	• uses language conventions with very limited accuracy and effectiveness	• uses language conventions with limited accuracy and effectiveness	• uses language conventions with some accuracy and effectiveness	• uses language conventions with considerable accuracy and effectiveness	• uses language conventions with a high degree of accuracy and effectiveness
• application of the writing process	• uses the writing process with very limited effectiveness	• uses the writing process with limited effectiveness	• uses the writing process with some effectiveness	• uses the writing process with considerable effectiveness	• uses the writing process with a high degree of effectiveness

* For a description of the levels of student achievement, please see The Achievement Chart for English, *The Ontario Curriculum Grades 9 and 10*, pp.46–49.

EXPLANATION

NAME: _____ DATE: _____

Categories	Below Level 1	50–59% Level 1	60–69% Level 2	70–79% Level 3	80–100% Level 4
			LEVELS OF ACHIEVEMENT*		
Knowledge/ Understanding	*The student:*				
• knowledge of the explanation form	• shows very limited knowledge of the explanation form	• shows limited knowledge of the explanation form	• shows some knowledge of the explanation form	• shows considerable knowledge of the explanation form	• shows thorough knowledge of the explanation form
• understanding of cause-and-effect relationships	• shows very limited understanding of cause-and-effect relationships	• shows limited understanding of cause-and-effect relationships	• shows some understanding of cause-and-effect relationships	• shows considerable understanding of cause-and-effect relationships	• shows thorough and insightful understanding of cause-and-effect relationships
Thinking/Inquiry	*The student:*				
• critical thinking skills	• uses critical thinking skills to create analogies and link ideas with very limited effectiveness	• uses critical thinking skills to create analogies and link ideas with limited effectiveness	• uses critical thinking skills to create analogies and link ideas with some effectiveness	• uses critical thinking skills to create analogies and link ideas with considerable effectiveness	• uses critical thinking skills to create analogies and link ideas with a high degree of effectiveness
• inquiry skills	• uses inquiry skills to gather information with very limited effectiveness	• uses inquiry skills to gather information with limited effectiveness	• uses inquiry skills to gather information with some effectiveness	• uses inquiry skills to gather information with considerable effectiveness	• uses inquiry skills to gather information with a high degree of effectiveness
Communication	*The student:*				
• communication of information and ideas	• communicates information and ideas with very limited clarity and organization	• communicates information and ideas with limited clarity and organization	• communicates information and ideas with some clarity and organization	• communicates information and ideas with considerable clarity and organization	• communicates information and ideas with a high degree of clarity and organization
• communication to an audience for a purpose	• communicates with a very limited sense of audience and purpose	• communicates with a limited sense of audience and purpose	• communicates with some sense of audience and purpose	• communicates with a clear sense of audience and purpose	• communicates with a strong sense of audience and purpose
• use of the explanation form	• shows very limited command of the explanation form	• shows limited command of the explanation form	• shows some command of the explanation form	• shows considerable command of the explanation form	• shows extensive command of the explanation form
Application	*The student:*				
• application of language conventions	• uses language conventions with very limited accuracy and effectiveness	• uses language conventions with limited accuracy and effectiveness	• uses language conventions with some accuracy and effectiveness	• uses language conventions with considerable accuracy and effectiveness	• uses language conventions with a high degree of accuracy and effectiveness
• application of the writing process	• uses the writing process with very limited effectiveness	• uses the writing process with limited effectiveness	• uses the writing process with some effectiveness	• uses the writing process with considerable effectiveness	• uses the writing process with a high degree of effectiveness
• application of visual aids (e.g., tables, charts, illustrations)	• uses visual aids to support the explanation with very limited effectiveness	• uses visual aids to support the explanation with limited effectiveness	• uses visual aids to support the explanation with some effectiveness	• uses visual aids to support the explanation with considerable effectiveness	• uses visual aids to support the explanation with a high degree of effectiveness

* For a description of the levels of student achievement, please see The Achievement Chart for English, *The Ontario Curriculum Grades 9 and 10*, pp.46–49.

EXPOSITORY WRITING

NAME: _____ DATE: _____

Categories	LEVELS OF ACHIEVEMENT*				
	Below Level 1	50–59% Level 1	60–69% Level 2	70–79% Level 3	80–100% Level 4
Knowledge/ Understanding	*The student:*				
• knowledge of the elements of expository writing	• shows very limited knowledge of the elements of expository writing	• shows limited knowledge of the elements of expository writing	• shows some knowledge of the elements of expository writing	• shows considerable knowledge of the elements of expository writing	• shows thorough knowledge of the elements of expository writing
• understanding of information and ideas	• shows very limited understanding of information and ideas	• shows limited understanding of information and ideas	• shows some understanding of information and ideas	• shows considerable understanding of information and ideas	• shows thorough and insightful understanding of information and ideas
• understanding of the relationship between facts and ideas	• shows very limited understanding of the relationship between facts and ideas	• shows limited understanding of the relationship between facts and ideas	• shows some understanding of the relationship between facts and ideas	• shows considerable understanding of the relationship between facts and ideas	• shows thorough and insightful understanding of the relationship between facts and ideas
Thinking/Inquiry	*The student:*				
• critical thinking skills	• uses critical thinking skills in producing expository writing with very limited effectiveness	• uses critical thinking skills in producing expository writing with limited effectiveness	• uses critical thinking skills in producing expository writing with some effectiveness	• uses critical thinking skills in producing expository writing with considerable effectiveness	• uses critical thinking skills in producing expository writing with a high degree of effectiveness
• inquiry skills	• uses inquiry skills to gather information with very limited effectiveness	• uses inquiry skills to gather information with limited effectiveness	• uses inquiry skills to gather information with some effectiveness	• uses inquiry skills to gather information with considerable effectiveness	• uses inquiry skills to gather information with a high degree of effectiveness
Communication	*The student:*				
• communication of information and ideas	• communicates information and ideas with very limited clarity and organization	• communicates information and ideas with limited clarity and organization	• communicates information and ideas with some clarity and organization	• communicates information and ideas with considerable clarity and organization	• communicates information and ideas with a high degree of clarity and organization
• communication to an audience for a purpose	• communicates with a very limited sense of audience and purpose	• communicates with a limited sense of audience and purpose	• communicates with some sense of audience and purpose	• communicates with a clear sense of audience and purpose	• communicates with a strong sense of audience and purpose
• use of elements of expository writing	• shows very limited command of elements of expository writing	• shows limited command of elements of expository writing	• shows some command of elements of expository writing	• shows considerable command of elements of expository writing	• shows extensive command of elements of expository writing
Application	*The student:*				
• application of language conventions	• uses language conventions with very limited accuracy and effectiveness	• uses language conventions with limited accuracy and effectiveness	• uses language conventions with some accuracy and effectiveness	• uses language conventions with considerable accuracy and effectiveness	• uses language conventions with a high degree of accuracy and effectiveness
• application of the writing process	• uses the writing process with very limited effectiveness	• uses the writing process with limited effectiveness	• uses the writing process with some effectiveness	• uses the writing process with considerable effectiveness	• uses the writing process with a high degree of effectiveness

* For a description of the levels of student achievement, please see The Achievement Chart for English, *The Ontario Curriculum Grades 9 and 10*, pp.46–49.

GROUP PRESENTATION

NAME: _____ DATE: _____

Categories	Below Level 1	LEVELS OF ACHIEVEMENT*			
		50–59% Level 1	60–69% Level 2	70–79% Level 3	80–100% Level 4
Knowledge/ Understanding	*The student:*				
• knowledge of the conventions of a group presentation	• shows very limited knowledge of the conventions of a group presentation	• shows limited knowledge of the conventions of a group presentation	• shows some knowledge of the conventions of a group presentation	• shows considerable knowledge of the conventions of a group presentation	• shows thorough knowledge of the conventions of a group presentation
• understanding of information and ideas	• shows very limited understanding of information and ideas	• shows limited understanding of information and ideas	• shows some understanding of information and ideas	• shows considerable understanding of information and ideas	• shows thorough and insightful understanding of information and ideas
Thinking/Inquiry	*The student:*				
• critical thinking skills	• uses critical thinking skills (in preparing and presenting) with very limited effectiveness	• uses critical thinking skills (in preparing and presenting) with limited effectiveness	• uses critical thinking skills (in preparing and presenting) with some effectiveness	• uses critical thinking skills (in preparing and presenting) with considerable effectiveness	• uses critical thinking skills (in preparing and presenting) with a high degree of effectiveness
• inquiry skills	• uses inquiry skills in preparing with very limited effectiveness	• uses inquiry skills in preparing with limited effectiveness	• uses inquiry skills in preparing with some effectiveness	• uses inquiry skills in preparing with considerable effectiveness	• uses inquiry skills in preparing with a high degree of effectiveness
Communication	*The student:*				
• communication of information and ideas	• communicates information and ideas with very limited clarity	• communicates information and ideas with limited clarity	• communicates information and ideas with some clarity	• communicates information and ideas with considerable clarity	• communicates information and ideas with a high degree of clarity
• communication to an audience for a purpose	• communicates with a very limited sense of audience and purpose	• communicates with a limited sense of audience and purpose	• communicates with some sense of audience and purpose	• communicates with a clear sense of audience and purpose	• communicates with a strong sense of audience and purpose
Application	*The student:*				
• application of language conventions	• uses language conventions with very limited accuracy and effectiveness	• uses language conventions with limited accuracy and effectiveness	• uses language conventions with some accuracy and effectiveness	• uses language conventions with considerable accuracy and effectiveness	• uses language conventions with a high degree of accuracy and effectiveness
• application of oral communication conventions and techniques	• uses oral communication conventions and techniques with very limited effectiveness	• uses oral communication conventions and techniques with limited effectiveness	• uses oral communication conventions and techniques with some effectiveness	• uses oral communication conventions and techniques with considerable effectiveness	• uses oral communication conventions and techniques with a high degree of effectiveness
• application of technology	• uses appropriate visual aids and technology with very limited effectiveness	• uses appropriate visual aids and technology with limited effectiveness	• uses appropriate visual aids and technology with some effectiveness	• uses appropriate visual aids and technology with considerable effectiveness	• uses appropriate visual aids and technology with a high degree of effectiveness

* For a description of the levels of student achievement, please see The Achievement Chart for English, *The Ontario Curriculum Grades 9 and 10*, pp.46–49.

HUMOROUS PERSONAL NARRATIVE

NAME: _____   DATE: _____

Categories	LEVELS OF ACHIEVEMENT*				
	Below Level 1	50–59% Level 1	60–69% Level 2	70–79% Level 3	80–100% Level 4
Knowledge/ Understanding	*The student:*				
• knowledge of the personal narrative form	• shows very limited knowledge of the personal narrative form	• shows limited knowledge of the personal narrative form	• shows some knowledge of the personal narrative form	• shows considerable knowledge of the personal narrative form	• shows thorough knowledge of the personal narrative form
• understanding of information, ideas, and theme	• shows very limited understanding of information, ideas, and theme	• shows limited understanding of information, ideas, and theme	• shows some understanding of information, ideas, and theme	• shows considerable understanding of information, ideas, and theme	• shows thorough and insightful understanding of information, ideas, and theme
• understanding of the uses and effect of first-person point of view and organizational pattern	• shows very limited understanding of first-person point of view and organizational pattern (e.g., chronological)	• shows limited understanding of first-person point of view and organizational pattern (e.g., chronological)	• shows some understanding of first-person point of view and organizational pattern (e.g., chronological)	• shows considerable understanding of first-person point of view and organizational pattern (e.g., chronological)	• shows thorough and insightful understanding of first-person point of view and organizational pattern (e.g., chronological)
Thinking/Inquiry	*The student:*				
• creative thinking skills	• creates humour in the personal narrative with very limited effectiveness	• creates humour in the personal narrative with limited effectiveness	• creates humour in the personal narrative with some effectiveness	• creates humour in the personal narrative with considerable effectiveness	• creates humour in the personal narrative with a high degree of effectiveness
Communication	*The student:*				
• communication of information, ideas, and theme	• communicates information, ideas, and theme with very limited clarity	• communicates information, ideas, and theme with limited clarity	• communicates information, ideas, and theme with some clarity	• communicates information, ideas, and theme with considerable clarity	• communicates information, ideas, and theme with a high degree of clarity
• communication to an audience for a specific purpose	• communicates with a very limited sense of audience and specific purpose	• communicates with a limited sense of audience and specific purpose	• communicates with some sense of audience and specific purpose	• communicates with a clear sense of audience and specific purpose	• communicates with a strong sense of audience and specific purpose
• use of the personal narrative form	• shows very limited command of the personal narrative form	• shows limited command of the personal narrative form	• shows some command of the personal narrative form	• shows considerable command of the personal narrative form	• shows extensive command of the personal narrative form
Application	*The student:*				
• application of language conventions	• uses language conventions with very limited accuracy and effectiveness	• uses language conventions with limited accuracy and effectiveness	• uses language conventions with some accuracy and effectiveness	• uses language conventions with considerable accuracy and effectiveness	• uses language conventions with a high degree of accuracy and effectiveness
• application of the writing process	• uses the writing process with very limited effectiveness	• uses the writing process with limited effectiveness	• uses the writing process with some effectiveness	• uses the writing process with considerable effectiveness	• uses the writing process with a high degree of effectiveness

* For a description of the levels of student achievement, please see The Achievement Chart for English, *The Ontario Curriculum Grades 9 and 10*, pp.46–49.

LETTER TO THE EDITOR

NAME: _____ DATE: _____

Categories	LEVELS OF ACHIEVEMENT*				
	Below Level 1	50–59% Level 1	60–69% Level 2	70–79% Level 3	80–100% Level 4
Knowledge/ Understanding	**The student:**				
• knowledge of the form of the letter to the editor	• shows very limited knowledge of the form of the letter to the editor	• shows limited knowledge of the form of the letter to the editor	• shows some knowledge of the form of the letter to the editor	• shows considerable knowledge of the form of the letter to the editor	• shows thorough knowledge of the form of the letter to the editor
• understanding of information, ideas, and issues	• shows very limited understanding of information, ideas, and issues	• shows limited understanding of information, ideas, and issues	• shows some understanding of information, ideas, and issues	• shows considerable understanding of information, ideas, and issues	• shows thorough and insightful understanding of information, ideas, and issues
• understanding of the relationship between fact and opinion	• shows very limited understanding of the relationship between fact and opinion	• shows limited understanding of the relationship between fact and opinion	• shows some understanding of the relationship between fact and opinion	• shows considerable understanding of the relationship between fact and opinion	• shows thorough and insightful understanding of the relationship between fact and opinion
Thinking/Inquiry	**The student:**				
• critical thinking skills	• uses critical thinking skills to identify key ideas and issues and to form an opinion with very limited effectiveness	• uses critical thinking skills to identify key ideas and issues and to form an opinion with limited effectiveness	• uses critical thinking skills to identify key ideas and issues and to form an opinion with some effectiveness	• uses critical thinking skills to identify key ideas and issues and to form an opinion with considerable effectiveness	• uses critical thinking skills to identify key ideas and issues and to form an opinion with a high degree of effectiveness
• inquiry skills	• uses inquiry skills to gather and select information to support an opinion with very limited effectiveness	• uses inquiry skills to gather and select information to support an opinion with limited effectiveness	• uses inquiry skills to gather and select information to support an opinion with some effectiveness	• uses inquiry skills to gather and select information to support an opinion with considerable effectiveness	• uses inquiry skills to gather and select information to support an opinion with a high degree of effectiveness
Communication	**The student:**				
• communication of information, ideas, and opinions in a letter to the editor	• communicates information, ideas, and opinions with very limited clarity	• communicates information, ideas, and opinions with limited clarity	• communicates information, ideas, and opinions with some clarity	• communicates information, ideas, and opinions with considerable clarity	• communicates information, ideas, and opinions with a high degree of clarity
• communication to an audience for a purpose	• communicates with a very limited sense of audience and purpose	• communicates with a limited sense of audience and purpose	• communicates with some sense of audience and purpose	• communicates with a clear sense of audience and purpose	• communicates with a strong sense of audience and purpose
Application	**The student:**				
• use of the letter to the editor form	• shows very limited command of the form of the letter to the editor	• shows limited command of the form of the letter to the editor	• shows some command of the form of the letter to the editor	• shows considerable command of the form of the letter to the editor	• shows extensive command of the form of the letter to the editor
• application of language conventions	• uses language conventions with very limited accuracy and effectiveness	• uses language conventions with limited accuracy and effectiveness	• uses language conventions with some accuracy and effectiveness	• uses language conventions with considerable accuracy and effectiveness	• uses language conventions with a high degree of accuracy and effectiveness
• application of the writing process	• uses the writing process with very limited effectiveness	• uses the writing process with limited effectiveness	• uses the writing process with some effectiveness	• uses the writing process with considerable effectiveness	• uses the writing process with a high degree of effectiveness
• making connections between English and the world outside the school	• makes connections with very limited effectiveness	• makes connections with limited effectiveness	• makes connections with some effectiveness	• makes connections with considerable effectiveness	• makes connections with a high degree of effectiveness

* For a description of the levels of student achievement, please see The Achievement Chart for English, *The Ontario Curriculum Grades 9 and 10*, pp.46–49.

MEDIA PRODUCT

NAME: _____ DATE: _____

Categories	Below Level 1	50–59% Level 1	60–69% Level 2	70–79% Level 3	80–100% Level 4
			LEVELS OF ACHIEVEMENT*		
Knowledge/ Understanding	*The student:*				
• knowledge of media form, conventions, and terminology	• shows very limited knowledge of media form, conventions, and terminology	• shows limited knowledge of media form, conventions, and terminology	• shows some knowledge of media form, conventions, and terminology	• shows considerable knowledge of media form, conventions, and terminology	• shows thorough knowledge of media form, conventions, and terminology
• understanding of relationships among facts, ideas, concepts, and themes	• shows very limited understanding of relationships among facts, ideas, concepts, and themes	• shows limited understanding of relationships among facts, ideas, concepts, and themes	• shows some understanding of relationships among facts, ideas, concepts, and themes	• shows considerable understanding of relationships among facts, ideas, concepts, and themes	• shows thorough understanding of relationships among facts, ideas, concepts, and themes
• understanding of the uses and effects of aesthetic elements in a media product	• shows very limited understanding of the uses and effects of aesthetic elements in a media product	• shows limited understanding of the uses and effects of aesthetic elements in a media product	• shows some understanding of the uses and effects of aesthetic elements in a media product	• shows considerable understanding of the uses and effects of aesthetic elements in a media product	• shows thorough understanding of the uses and effects of aesthetic elements in a media product
Thinking/Inquiry	*The student:*				
• analysis of a media product	• analyzes a media product with very limited effectiveness	• analyzes a media product with limited effectiveness	• analyzes a media product with some effectiveness	• analyzes a media product with considerable	effectiveness
• planning a media product	• plans a media product with very limited effectiveness	• plans a media product with limited effectiveness	• plans a media product with some effectiveness	• plans a media product with considerable effectiveness	• plans a media product with a high degree of effectiveness
Communication	*The student:*				
• communication of media messages	• communicates media messages with very limited clarity	• communicates media messages with limited clarity	• communicates media messages with some clarity	• communicates media messages with considerable clarity	• communicates media messages with a high degree of clarity
• communication to an audience for a purpose	• communicates with a very limited sense of audience and purpose	• communicates with a limited sense of audience and purpose	• communicates with some sense of audience and purpose	• communicates with a clear sense of audience and purpose	• communicates with a strong sense of audience and purpose
• use of the media form	• shows very limited command of the media form	• shows limited command of the media form	• shows some command of the media form	• shows considerable command of the media form	• shows extensive command of the media form
Application	*The student:*				
• application of language conventions in a media product	• uses language conventions with very limited accuracy and effectiveness	• uses language conventions with limited accuracy and effectiveness	• uses language conventions with some accuracy and effectiveness	• uses language conventions with considerable accuracy and effectiveness	• uses language conventions with a high degree of accuracy and effectiveness
• application of media conventions and techniques	• uses media conventions and techniques with very limited effectiveness	• uses media conventions and techniques with limited effectiveness	• uses media conventions and techniques with some effectiveness	• uses media conventions and techniques with con-siderable effectiveness	• uses media conventions and techniques with a high degree of effectiveness
• application of the writing process for a media product	• uses the writing process with very limited effectiveness	• uses the writing process with limited effectiveness	• uses the writing process with some effectiveness	• uses the writing process with considerable effectiveness	• uses the writing process with a high degree of effectiveness
• application of technology for a media product	• uses technology with very limited appropriateness and effectiveness	• uses technology with limited appropriateness and effectiveness	• uses technology with some appropriateness and effectiveness	• uses appropriate technology with considerable effectiveness	• uses appropriate technology with a high degree of effectiveness
• making critical connections between media products	• makes critical connections with very limited effectiveness	• makes critical connections with limited effectiveness	• makes critical connections with some effectiveness	• makes critical connections with considerable effectiveness	• makes critical connections with a high degree of effectiveness

* For a description of the levels of student achievement, please see The Achievement Chart for English, *The Ontario Curriculum Grades 9 and 10*, pp.46–49.

NARRATIVE WRITING

NAME: _____ DATE: _____

Categories	Below Level 1	50–59% Level 1	60–69% Level 2	70–79% Level 3	80–100% Level 4
		LEVELS OF ACHIEVEMENT*			
Knowledge/ Understanding	*The student:*				
• knowledge of the narrative genre	• shows very limited knowledge of the narrative genre	• shows limited knowledge of the narrative genre	• shows some knowledge of the narrative genre	• shows considerable knowledge of the narrative genre	• shows thorough knowledge of the narrative genre
• understanding of ideas and theme	• shows very limited understanding of ideas and theme	• shows limited understanding of ideas and theme	• shows some understanding of ideas and theme	• shows considerable understanding of ideas and theme	• shows thorough and insightful understanding of ideas and theme
• understanding of the uses and effect of stylistic devices and point of view	• shows very limited understanding of stylistic devices and point of view	• shows limited understanding of stylistic devices and point of view	• shows some understanding of stylistic devices and point of view	• shows considerable understanding of stylistic devices and point of view	• shows thorough and insightful understanding of stylistic devices and point of view
Thinking/Inquiry	*The student:*				
• creative thinking skills	• uses creative thinking skills (in planning and writing the narrative) with very limited effectiveness	• uses creative thinking skills (in planning and writing the narrative) with limited effectiveness	• uses creative thinking skills (in planning and writing the narrative) with some effectiveness	• uses creative thinking skills (in planning and writing the narrative) with considerable effectiveness	• uses creative thinking skills (in planning and writing the narrative) with a high degree of effectiveness
Communication	*The student:*				
• communication of ideas and theme	• communicates ideas and theme with very limited clarity	• communicates ideas and theme with limited clarity	• communicates ideas and theme with some clarity	• communicates ideas and theme with considerable clarity	• communicates ideas and theme with a high degree of clarity
• communication to an audience for a purpose	• communicates with a very limited sense of audience and purpose	• communicates with a limited sense of audience and purpose	• communicates with some sense of audience and purpose	• communicates with a clear sense of audience and purpose	• communicates with a strong sense of audience and purpose
• use of the elements of the narrative form	• shows very limited command of the elements of the narrative form	• shows limited command of the elements of the narrative form	• shows some command of the elements of the narrative form	• shows considerable command of the elements of the narrative form	• shows extensive command of the elements of the narrative form
Application	*The student:*				
• application of language conventions	• uses language conventions with very limited accuracy and effectiveness	• uses language conventions with limited accuracy and effectiveness	• uses language conventions with some accuracy and effectiveness	• uses language conventions with considerable accuracy and effectiveness	• uses language conventions with a high degree of accuracy and effectiveness
• application of the writing process	• uses the writing process with very limited effectiveness	• uses the writing process with limited effectiveness	• uses the writing process with some effectiveness	• uses the writing process with considerable effectiveness	• uses the writing process with a high degree of effectiveness

* For a description of the levels of student achievement, please see The Achievement Chart for English, *The Ontario Curriculum Grades 9 and 10*, pp.46–49.

LANGUAGE & WRITING 9

NEWS ARTICLE

NAME: _____ DATE: _____

		LEVELS OF ACHIEVEMENT*			
Categories	**Below Level 1**	**50–59% Level 1**	**60–69% Level 2**	**70–79% Level 3**	**80–100% Level 4**
Knowledge/ Understanding	*The student:*				
• knowledge of newspaper terminology	• shows very limited knowledge of newspaper terminology	• shows limited knowledge of newspaper terminology	• shows some knowledge of newspaper terminology	• shows considerable knowledge of newspaper terminology	• shows thorough knowledge of newspaper terminology
• understanding of the 5 W's	• shows very limited understanding of the 5 W's	• shows limited understanding of the 5 W's	• shows some understanding of the 5 W's	• shows considerable understanding of the 5 W's	• shows thorough understanding of the 5 W's
• understanding of the concept that media construct reality	• shows very limited understanding of the concept that media construct reality	• shows limited understanding of the concept that media construct reality	• shows some understanding of the concept that media construct reality	• shows considerable understanding of the concept that media construct reality	• shows thorough understanding of the concept that media construct reality
• understanding of the relationship between facts and ideas	• shows very limited understanding of the relationship between facts and ideas	• shows limited understanding of the relationship between facts and ideas	• shows some understanding of the relationship between facts and ideas	• shows considerable understanding of the relationship between facts and ideas	• shows a high degree of understanding of the relationship between facts and ideas
Thinking/Inquiry	*The student:*				
• analyzing information	• analyzes information with very limited effectiveness	• analyzes information with limited effectiveness	• analyzes information with some effectiveness	• analyzes information with considerable effectiveness	• analyzes information with a high degree of effectiveness
• drawing conclusions	• draws conclusions with very limited effectiveness	• draws conclusions with limited effectiveness	• draws conclusions with some effectiveness	• draws conclusions with considerable effectiveness	• draws conclusions with a high degree of effectiveness
Communication	*The student:*				
• communication of information and ideas	• communicates information and ideas with very limited clarity and organization	• communicates information and ideas with limited clarity and organization	• communicates information and ideas with some clarity and organization	• communicates information and ideas with considerable clarity and organization	• communicates information and ideas with a high degree of clarity and organization
• communication to an audience for a purpose	• communicates with a very limited sense of audience and purpose	• communicates with a limited sense of audience and purpose	• communicates with some sense of audience and purpose	• communicates with a clear sense of audience and purpose	• communicates with a strong sense of audience and purpose
• use of the news article form	• shows a very limited command of the news article form	• shows a limited command of the news article form	• shows some command of the news article form	• shows considerable command of the news article form	• shows extensive command of the news article form
Application	*The student:*				
• application of language conventions	• uses language conventions with very limited accuracy and effectiveness	• uses language conventions with limited accuracy and effectiveness	• uses language conventions with some accuracy and effectiveness	• uses language conventions with considerable accuracy and effectiveness	• uses language conventions with a high degree of accuracy and effectiveness
• application of the writing process	• uses the writing process with very limited effectiveness	• uses the writing process with limited effectiveness	• uses the writing process with some effectiveness	• uses the writing process with considerable effectiveness	• uses the writing process with a high degree of effectiveness
• application of newspaper conventions	• uses newspaper conventions with very limited appropriateness and effectiveness	• uses newspaper conventions with limited appropriateness and effectiveness	• uses newspaper conventions with some appropriateness and effectiveness	• uses appropriate newspaper conventions with considerable effectiveness	• uses appropriate newspaper conventions with a high degree of effectiveness
• making connections between English and the world outside the school	• makes connections with very limited effectiveness	• makes connections with limited effectiveness	• makes connections with some effectiveness	• makes connections with considerable effectiveness	• makes connections with a high degree of effectiveness

* For a description of the levels of student achievement, please see The Achievement Chart for English, *The Ontario Curriculum Grades 9 and 10*, pp.46–49.

ORAL LANGUAGE

NAME: _____ DATE: _____

		LEVELS OF ACHIEVEMENT*			
Categories	**Below Level 1**	**50–59% Level 1**	**60–69% Level 2**	**70–79% Level 3**	**80–100% Level 4**
Knowledge/ Understanding	*The student:*				
• knowledge of the oral language form (e.g., debate, storytelling, oral report, etc.)	• shows very limited knowledge of the oral language form	• shows limited knowledge of the oral language form	• shows some knowledge of the oral language form	• shows considerable knowledge of the oral language form	• shows thorough knowledge of the oral language form
• understanding of information and ideas	• shows very limited understanding of information and ideas	• shows limited understanding of information and ideas	• shows some understanding of information and ideas	• shows considerable understanding of information and ideas	• shows thorough and insightful understanding of
Thinking/Inquiry	*The student:*				
information and ideas • critical and creative thinking skills	• uses critical and creative thinking skills (in preparing and presenting) with very limited effectiveness	• uses critical and creative thinking skills (in preparing and presenting) with limited effectiveness	• uses critical and creative thinking skills (in preparing and presenting) with some effectiveness	• uses critical and creative thinking skills (in preparing and presenting) with considerable effectiveness	• uses critical and creative thinking skills (in preparing and presenting) with a high degree of effectiveness
• inquiry skills	• uses inquiry skills in preparing with very limited effectiveness	• uses inquiry skills in preparing with limited effectiveness	• uses inquiry skills in preparing with some effectiveness	• uses inquiry skills in preparing with considerable effectiveness	• uses inquiry skills in preparing with a high degree of effectiveness
Communication	*The student:*				
• communication of information and ideas	• communicates information and ideas with very limited clarity	• communicates information and ideas with limited clarity	• communicates information and ideas with some clarity	• communicates information and ideas with considerable clarity	• communicates information and ideas with a high degree of clarity
• communication to an audience for a purpose	• communicates with a very limited sense of audience and purpose	• communicates with a limited sense of audience and purpose	• communicates with some sense of audience and purpose	• communicates with a clear sense of audience and purpose	• communicates with a strong sense of audience and purpose
• use of the oral language form	• shows very limited command of the oral language form	• shows limited command of the oral language form	• shows some command of the oral language form	• shows considerable command of the oral language form	• shows extensive command of the oral language form
Application	*The student:*				
• application of language conventions	• uses language conventions with very limited accuracy and effectiveness	• uses language conventions with limited accuracy and effectiveness	• uses language conventions with some accuracy and effectiveness	• uses language conventions with considerable accuracy and effectiveness	• uses language conventions with a high degree of accuracy and effectiveness
• application of oral communication conventions and techniques	• uses oral communication conventions and techniques with very limited effectiveness	• uses oral communication conventions and techniques with limited effectiveness	• uses oral communication conventions and techniques with some effectiveness	• uses oral communication conventions and techniques with considerable effectiveness	• uses oral communication conventions and techniques with a high degree of effectiveness
• application of technology	• uses appropriate visual aids and technology with very limited effectiveness	• uses appropriate visual aids and technology with limited effectiveness	• uses appropriate visual aids and technology with some effectiveness	• uses appropriate visual aids and technology with considerable effectiveness	• uses appropriate visual aids and technology with a high degree of effectiveness

* For a description of the levels of student achievement, please see The Achievement Chart for English, *The Ontario Curriculum Grades 9 and 10*, pp.46–49.

PERSUASIVE WRITING

NAME: _____ DATE: _____

Categories	Below Level 1	50–59% Level 1	60–69% Level 2	70–79% Level 3	80–100% Level 4
		LEVELS OF ACHIEVEMENT*			
Knowledge/ Understanding	*The student:*				
• knowledge of the elements and techniques of persuasive writing	• shows very limited knowledge of the elements and techniques of persuasive writing	• shows limited knowledge of the elements and techniques of persuasive writing	• shows some knowledge of the elements and techniques of persuasive writing	• shows considerable knowledge of the elements and techniques of persuasive writing	• shows thorough knowledge of the elements and techniques of persuasive writing
• understanding of information, ideas, concepts, and themes	• shows very limited understanding of information, ideas, concepts, and themes	• shows limited understanding of information, ideas, concepts, and themes	• shows some understanding of information, ideas, concepts, and themes	• shows considerable understanding of information, ideas, concepts, and themes	• shows thorough and insightful understanding of information, ideas, concepts, and themes
• understanding of the uses and effects of diction and stylistic devices	• shows very limited understanding of the uses and effects of diction and stylistic devices	• shows limited understanding of the uses and effects of diction and stylistic devices	• shows some understanding of the uses and effects of diction and stylistic devices	• shows considerable understanding of the uses and effects of diction and stylistic devices	• shows thorough and insightful understanding of the uses and effects of diction and stylistic devices
Thinking/Inquiry	*The student:*				
• critical thinking skills	• uses critical thinking skills to formulate a controlling idea with very limited effectiveness	• uses critical thinking skills to formulate a controlling idea with limited effectiveness	• uses critical thinking skills to formulate a controlling idea with some effectiveness	• uses critical thinking skills to formulate a controlling idea with considerable effectiveness	• uses critical thinking skills to formulate a controlling idea with a high degree of effectiveness
• inquiry skills	• uses inquiry skills to gather and select information to support the controlling idea with very limited effectiveness	• uses inquiry skills to gather and select information to support the controlling idea with limited effectiveness	• uses inquiry skills to gather and select information to support the controlling idea with some effectiveness	• uses inquiry skills to gather and select information to support the controlling idea with considerable effectiveness	• uses inquiry skills to gather and select information to support the controlling idea with a high degree of effectiveness
Communication	*The student:*				
• communication of information and ideas	• communicates information and ideas with very limited clarity	• communicates information and ideas with limited clarity	• communicates information and ideas with some clarity	• communicates information and ideas with considerable clarity	• communicates information and ideas with a high degree of clarity
• communication to an audience for a purpose	• communicates with a very limited sense of audience and purpose	• communicates with a limited sense of audience and purpose	• communicates with some sense of audience and purpose	• communicates with a clear sense of audience and purpose	• communicates with a strong sense of audience and purpose
• use of the elements of persuasive writing	• shows very limited command of elements of persuasive writing	• shows limited command of elements of persuasive writing	• shows some command of the elements of persuasive writing	• shows considerable command of elements of persuasive writing	• shows extensive command of elements of persuasive writing
Application	*The student:*				
• application of language conventions	• uses language conventions with very limited accuracy and effectiveness	• uses language conventions with limited accuracy and effectiveness	• uses language conventions with some accuracy and effectiveness	• uses language conventions with considerable accuracy and effectiveness	• uses language conventions with a high degree of accuracy and effectiveness
• application of the writing process	• uses the writing process with very limited effectiveness	• uses the writing process with limited effectiveness	• uses the writing process with some effectiveness	• uses the writing process with considerable effectiveness	• uses the writing process with a high degree of effectiveness
• application of techniques of persuasion	• uses techniques of persuasion with very limited effectiveness	• uses techniques of persuasion with limited effectiveness	• uses techniques of persuasion with some effectiveness	• uses techniques of persuasion with considerable effectiveness	• uses techniques of persuasion with a high degree of effectiveness

* For a description of the levels of student achievement, please see The Achievement Chart for English, *The Ontario Curriculum Grades 9 and 10*, pp.46–49.

POETRY

NAME: _____ DATE: _____

Categories	Below Level 1	50–59% Level 1	60–69% Level 2	70–79% Level 3	80–100% Level 4
		LEVELS OF ACHIEVEMENT*			
Knowledge/ Understanding	*The student:*				
• knowledge of the poetic form	• shows very limited knowledge of the poetic form	• shows limited knowledge of the poetic form	• shows some knowledge of the poetic form	• shows considerable knowledge of the poetic form	• shows thorough knowledge of the poetic form
• understanding of theme	• shows very limited understanding of the theme	• shows limited understanding of the theme	• shows some understanding of the theme	• shows considerable understanding of the theme	• shows thorough and insightful understanding of the theme
Thinking/Inquiry	*The student:*				
• creative thinking skills	• uses creative thinking skills (in planning and writing the poem) with very limited effectiveness	• uses creative thinking skills (in planning and writing the poem) with limited effectiveness	• uses creative thinking skills (in planning and writing the poem) with some effectiveness	• uses creative thinking skills (in planning and writing the poem) with considerable effectiveness	• uses creative thinking skills (in planning and writing the poem) with a high degree of effectiveness
Communication	*The student:*				
• communication of theme	• communicates the theme with very limited clarity	• communicates the theme with limited clarity	• communicates the theme with some clarity	• communicates the theme with considerable clarity	• communicates the theme with a high degree of clarity
• communication to an audience for a purpose	• communicates with a very limited sense of audience and purpose	• communicates with a limited sense of audience and purpose	• communicates with some sense of audience and purpose	• communicates with a clear sense of audience and purpose	• communicates with a strong sense of audience and purpose
• use of the poetic form	• shows very limited command of the poetic form	• shows limited command of the poetic form	• shows some command of the poetic form	• shows considerable command of the poetic form	• shows extensive command of the poetic form
Application	*The student:*				
• application of language conventions	• uses language conventions with very limited accuracy and effectiveness	• uses language conventions with limited accuracy and effectiveness	• uses language conventions with some accuracy and effectiveness	• uses language conventions with considerable accuracy and effectiveness	• uses language conventions with a high degree of accuracy and effectiveness
• application of the writing process	• uses the writing process with very limited competence	• uses the writing process with limited competence	• uses the writing process with some competence	• uses the writing process with considerable competence	• uses the writing process with a high degree of competence

* For a description of the levels of student achievement, please see The Achievement Chart for English, *The Ontario Curriculum Grades 9 and 10*, pp.46–49.

PRÉCIS

NAME: _____ **DATE:** _____

Categories	Below Level 1	50–59% Level 1	60–69% Level 2	70–79% Level 3	80–100% Level 4
		LEVELS OF ACHIEVEMENT*			
Knowledge/ Understanding	*The student:*				
• knowledge of the form and conventions of the précis	• shows very limited knowledge of the form and conventions of the précis	• shows limited knowledge of the form and conventions of the précis	• shows some knowledge of the form and conventions of the précis	• shows considerable knowledge of the form and conventions of the précis	• shows thorough knowledge of the form and conventions of the précis
• understanding of information and ideas in the original text	• shows very limited understanding of information and ideas in the original text	• shows limited understanding of information and ideas in the original text	• shows some understanding of information and ideas in the original text	• shows considerable understanding of information and ideas in the original text	• shows thorough understanding of information and ideas in the original text
Thinking/Inquiry	*The student:*				
• critical thinking skills: selection of significant information and ideas	• uses critical thinking skills to select significant information and ideas with very limited effectiveness	• uses critical thinking skills to select significant information and ideas with limited effectiveness	• uses critical thinking skills to select significant information and ideas with some effectiveness	• uses critical thinking skills to select significant information and ideas with considerable effectiveness	• uses critical thinking skills to select significant information and ideas with a high degree of effectiveness
• critical thinking skills: elimination of insignificant information and ideas	• uses critical thinking skills to eliminate insignificant information and ideas with very limited effectiveness	• uses critical thinking skills to eliminate insignificant information and ideas with limited effectiveness	• uses critical thinking skills to eliminate insignificant information and ideas with some effectiveness	• uses critical thinking skills to eliminate insignificant information and ideas with considerable effectiveness	• uses critical thinking skills to eliminate insignificant information and ideas with a high degree of effectiveness
Communication	*The student:*				
• communication of key information and ideas	• communicates key information and ideas with very limited unity	• communicates key information and ideas with limited unity	• communicates key information and ideas with some unity	• communicates key information and ideas with considerable unity	• communicates key information and ideas with a high degree of unity
Application	*The student:*				
• application of language conventions	• uses language conventions with very limited accuracy and effectiveness	• uses language conventions with limited accuracy and effectiveness	• uses language conventions with some accuracy and effectiveness	• uses language conventions with considerable accuracy and effectiveness	• uses language conventions with a high degree of accuracy and effectiveness
• application of the writing process	• uses the writing process with very limited effectiveness	• uses the writing process with limited effectiveness	• uses the writing process with some effectiveness	• uses the writing process with considerable effectiveness	• uses the writing process with a high degree of effectiveness

* For a description of the levels of student achievement, please see The Achievement Chart for English, *The Ontario Curriculum Grades 9 and 10*, pp.46–49.

PROFILE

NAME: _____ DATE: _____

Categories	Below Level 1	50–59% Level 1	60–69% Level 2	70–79% Level 3	80–100% Level 4
		LEVELS OF ACHIEVEMENT*			
Knowledge/ Understanding	*The student:*				
• knowledge of the profile form	• shows very limited knowledge of the profile form	• shows limited knowledge of the profile form	• shows some knowledge of the profile form	• shows considerable knowledge of the profile form	• shows thorough knowledge of the profile form
• understanding of information and ideas	• shows very limited understanding of information and ideas	• shows limited understanding of information and ideas	• shows some understanding of information and ideas	• shows considerable understanding of information and ideas	• shows thorough and insightful understanding of information and ideas
Thinking/Inquiry	*The student:*				
• critical thinking skills	• uses critical thinking skills to identify and support key points about the subject with very limited effectiveness	• uses critical thinking skills to identify and support key points about the subject with limited effectiveness	• uses critical thinking skills to identify and support key points about the subject with some effectiveness	• uses critical thinking skills to identify and support key points about the subject with considerable effectiveness	• uses critical thinking skills to identify and support key points about the subject with a high degree of effectiveness
Communication	*The student:*				
• communication of key information and ideas	• communicates the subject's key qualities or experiences with very limited clarity	• communicates the subject's key qualities or experiences with limited clarity	• communicates the subject's key qualities or experiences with some clarity	• communicates the subject's key qualities or experiences with considerable clarity	• communicates the subject's key qualities or experiences with a high degree of clarity
• communication to an audience for a purpose	• communicates with a very limited sense of audience and purpose	• communicates with a limited sense of audience and purpose	• communicates with some sense of audience and purpose	• communicates with a clear sense of audience and purpose	• communicates with a strong sense of audience and purpose
• use of the profile form	• shows very limited command of the profile form	• shows limited command of the profile form	• shows some command of the profile form	• shows considerable command of the profile form	• shows extensive command of the profile form
Application	*The student:*				
• application of language conventions	• uses language conventions with very limited accuracy and effectiveness	• uses language conventions with limited accuracy and effectiveness	• uses language conventions with some accuracy and effectiveness	• uses language conventions with considerable accuracy and effectiveness	• uses language conventions with a high degree of accuracy and effectiveness
• application of the writing process	• uses the writing process with very limited effectiveness	• uses the writing process with limited effectiveness	• uses the writing process with some effectiveness	• uses the writing process with considerable effectiveness	• uses the writing process with a high degree of effectiveness

* For a description of the levels of student achievement, please see The Achievement Chart for English, *The Ontario Curriculum Grades 9 and 10*, pp.46–49.

RESEARCH REPORT

NAME: _____ DATE: _____

Categories	Below Level 1	LEVELS OF ACHIEVEMENT*			
		50–59% Level 1	60–69% Level 2	70–79% Level 3	80–100% Level 4
Knowledge/ Understanding	*The student:*				
• knowledge of the research report form	• shows very limited knowledge of the research report form	• shows limited knowledge of the research report form	• shows some knowledge of the research report form	• shows considerable knowledge of the research report form	• shows thorough knowledge of the research report form
• understanding of the relationship between facts and ideas	• shows very limited understanding of the relationship between facts and ideas	• shows limited understanding of the relationship between facts and ideas	• shows some understanding of the relationship between facts and ideas	• shows considerable understanding of the relationship between facts and ideas	• shows thorough and insightful understanding of the relationship between facts and ideas
Thinking/Inquiry	*The student:*				
• critical thinking skills	• selects relevant and accurate information with very limited effectiveness	• selects relevant and accurate information with limited effectiveness	• selects relevant and accurate information with some effectiveness	• selects relevant and accurate information with considerable effectiveness	• selects relevant and accurate information with a high degree of effectiveness
Communication	*The student:*				
• communication of information and ideas	• communicates information and ideas by organizing subtopics with very limited effectiveness	• communicates information and ideas by organizing subtopics with limited effectiveness	• communicates information and ideas by organizing subtopics with some effectiveness	• communicates information and ideas by organizing subtopics with considerable effectiveness	• communicates information and ideas by organizing subtopics with a high degree of effectiveness
• communication to an audience for a purpose	• communicates with a very limited sense of audience and purpose	• communicates with a limited sense of audience and purpose	• communicates with some sense of audience and purpose	• communicates with a clear sense of audience and purpose	• communicates with a strong sense of audience and purpose
Application	*The student:*				
• application of language conventions	• uses language conventions with very limited accuracy and effectiveness	• uses language conventions with limited accuracy and effectiveness	• uses language conventions with some accuracy and effectiveness	• uses language conventions with considerable accuracy and effectiveness	• uses language conventions with a high degree of accuracy and effectiveness
• application of the writing process	• uses the writing process with very limited effectiveness	• uses the writing process with limited effectiveness	• uses the writing process with some effectiveness	• uses the writing process with considerable effectiveness	• uses the writing process with a high degree of effectiveness
• documentation of sources	• uses citations and references with very limited accuracy and completeness	• uses citations and references with limited accuracy and completeness	• uses citations and references with some accuracy and completeness	• uses citations and references with considerable accuracy and completeness	• uses citations and references with extensive accuracy and completeness

* For a description of the levels of student achievement, please see The Achievement Chart for English, *The Ontario Curriculum Grades 9 and 10*, pp.46–49.

RESPONSE TO MEDIA

NAME: _____ **DATE:** _____

Categories	Below Level 1	50–59% Level 1	60–69% Level 2	70–79% Level 3	80–100% Level 4
		LEVELS OF ACHIEVEMENT*			
Knowledge/ Understanding	*The student:*				
• knowledge of media conventions	• shows very limited knowledge of media conventions	• shows limited knowledge of media conventions	• shows some knowledge of media conventions	• shows considerable knowledge of media conventions	• shows thorough knowledge of media conventions
• knowledge of factors that influence media production	• shows very limited knowledge of factors that influence media production	• shows limited knowledge of factors that influence media production	• shows some knowledge of factors that influence media production	• shows considerable knowledge of factors that influence media production	• shows thorough knowledge of factors that influence media production
• understanding of the concept of audience	• shows very limited understanding of the concept of audience	• shows limited understanding of the concept of audience	• shows some understanding of the concept of audience	• shows considerable understanding of the concept of audience	• shows thorough understanding of the concept of audience
• understanding of the uses and effects of aesthetic elements in media works	• shows very limited understanding of the uses and effects of aesthetic elements	• shows limited understanding of the uses and effects of aesthetic elements	• shows some understanding of the uses and effects of aesthetic elements	• shows considerable understanding of the uses and effects of aesthetic elements	• shows thorough understanding of the uses and effects of aesthetic elements
Thinking/Inquiry	*The student:*				
• identifying media messages	• identifies media messages with very limited effectiveness	• identifies media messages with limited effectiveness	• identifies media messages with some effectiveness	• identifies media messages with considerable effectiveness	• identifies media messages with a high degree of effectiveness
• drawing conclusions about target audience	• draws conclusions about target audience with very limited effectiveness	• draws conclusions about target audience with limited effectiveness	• draws conclusions about target audience with some effectiveness	• draws conclusions about target audience with considerable effectiveness	• draws conclusions about target audience with a high degree of effectiveness
• assessing peer media products	• peer-assesses with very limited effectiveness	• peer-assesses with limited effectiveness	• peer-assesses with some effectiveness	• peer-assesses with considerable effectiveness	• peer-assesses with a high degree of effectiveness
Communication	*The student:*				
• communication of information and ideas	• communicates information and ideas with very limited clarity	• communicates information and ideas with limited clarity	• communicates information and ideas with some clarity	• communicates information and ideas with considerable clarity	• communicates information and ideas with a high degree of clarity
• communication to an audience for a purpose	• communicates with a very limited sense of audience and purpose	• communicates with a limited sense of audience and purpose	• communicates with some sense of audience and purpose	• communicates with a clear sense of audience and purpose	• communicates with a strong sense of audience and purpose
Application	*The student:*				
• application of language conventions	• uses language conventions with very limited accuracy and effectiveness	• uses language conventions with limited accuracy and effectiveness	• uses language conventions with some accuracy and effectiveness	• uses language conventions with considerable accuracy and effectiveness	• uses language conventions with a high degree of accuracy and effectiveness
• application of oral communication conventions and techniques	• uses oral communication conventions and techniques with very limited effectiveness	• uses oral communication conventions and techniques with limited effectiveness	• uses oral communication conventions and techniques with some effectiveness	• uses oral communication conventions and techniques with considerable effectiveness	• uses oral communication conventions and techniques with a high degree of effectiveness
• application of writing process in media response	• uses writing process with very limited effectiveness	• uses writing process with limited effectiveness	• uses writing process with some effectiveness	• uses writing process with considerable effectiveness	• uses writing process with a high degree of effectiveness
• making connections between personal experience and media works	• makes connections with very limited effectiveness	• makes connections with limited effectiveness	• makes connections with some effectiveness	• makes connections with considerable effectiveness	• makes connections with a high degree of effectiveness

* For a description of the levels of student achievement, please see The Achievement Chart for English, *The Ontario Curriculum Grades 9 and 10*, pp.46–49.

RESPONSE TO READING

NAME: _____   DATE: _____

Categories	Below Level 1	LEVELS OF ACHIEVEMENT*			
		50–59% Level 1	60–69% Level 2	70–79% Level 3	80–100% Level 4
Knowledge/ Understanding	*The student:*				
• knowledge of the content and form of a text	• shows very limited knowledge of the content and form of a text	• shows limited knowledge of the content and form of a text	• shows some knowledge of the content and form of a text	• shows considerable knowledge of the content and form of a text	• shows thorough knowledge of the content and form of a text
• understanding of the explicit meaning of a text	• shows very limited understanding of the explicit meaning of a text	• shows limited understanding of the explicit meaning of a text	• shows some understanding of the explicit meaning of a text	• shows considerable understanding of the explicit meaning of a text	• shows thorough and insightful understanding of the explicit meaning of a text
• understanding of the elements and effects of style in a text	• shows very limited understanding of the elements and effects of style in a text	• shows limited understanding of the elements and effects of style in a text	• shows some understanding of the elements and effects of style in a text	• shows considerable understanding of the elements and effects of style in a text	• shows thorough and insightful understanding of the elements and effects of style in a text
Thinking/Inquiry	*The student:*				
• critical thinking skills	• infers the implicit meaning of a text with very limited effectiveness	• infers the implicit meaning of a text with limited effectiveness	• infers the implicit meaning of a text with some effectiveness	• infers the implicit meaning of a text with considerable effectiveness	• infers the implicit meaning of a text with a high degree of effectiveness
Communication	*The student:*				
• communication of response to information and ideas	• communicates response to information and ideas with very limited clarity	• communicates response to information and ideas with limited clarity	• communicates response to information and ideas with some clarity	• communicates response to information and ideas with considerable clarity	• communicates response to information and ideas with a high degree of clarity
Application	*The student:*				
• application of language conventions	• uses language conventions with very limited accuracy and effectiveness	• uses language conventions with limited accuracy and effectiveness	• uses language conventions with some accuracy and effectiveness	• uses language conventions with considerable accuracy and effectiveness	• uses language conventions with a high degree of accuracy and effectiveness
• application of reading strategies	• uses reading strategies with very limited effectiveness	• uses reading strategies with limited effectiveness	• uses reading strategies with some effectiveness	• uses reading strategies considerable effectiveness	• uses reading strategies with a high degree of effectiveness
• application of the writing process, or the conventions and techniques of oral communication or media	• uses the writing process, or the conventions and techniques of oral communication or media with very limited effectiveness	• uses the writing process, or the conventions and techniques of oral communication or media with limited effectiveness	• uses the writing process, or the conventions and techniques of oral communication or media with some effectiveness	• uses the writing process, or the conventions and techniques of oral communication or media with considerable effectiveness	• uses the writing process, or the conventions and techniques of oral communication or media with a high degree of effectiveness
• making connections with other texts	• makes connections with other texts with very limited effectiveness	• makes connections with other texts with limited effectiveness	• makes connections with other texts with some effectiveness	• makes connections with other texts with considerable effectiveness	• makes connections with other texts with a high degree of effectiveness

* For a description of the levels of student achievement, please see The Achievement Chart for English, *The Ontario Curriculum Grades 9 and 10*, pp.46–49.

SCRIPT

NAME: _____ DATE: _____

Categories	Below Level 1	LEVELS OF ACHIEVEMENT*			
		50–59% Level 1	60–69% Level 2	70–79% Level 3	80–100% Level 4
Knowledge/ Understanding	*The student:*				
• knowledge of the elements of drama	• shows very limited knowledge of the elements of drama	• shows limited knowledge of the elements of drama	• shows some knowledge of the elements of drama	• shows considerable knowledge of the elements of drama	• shows thorough knowledge of the elements of drama
• understanding of ideas, concepts, and theme	• shows very limited understanding of ideas, concepts, and theme	• shows limited understanding of ideas, concepts, and theme	• shows some understanding of ideas, concepts, and theme	• shows considerable understanding of ideas, concepts, and theme	• shows thorough and insightful understanding of ideas, concepts, and theme
• understanding of the uses and effect of dialogue and dramatic action	• shows very limited understanding of dialogue and dramatic action	• shows limited understanding of dialogue and dramatic action	• shows some understanding of dialogue and dramatic action	• shows considerable understanding of dialogue and dramatic action	• shows thorough and insightful understanding of dialogue and dramatic action
Thinking/Inquiry	*The student:*				
• creative thinking skills	• uses creative thinking skills (in planning and writing the script) with very limited effectiveness	• uses creative thinking skills (in planning and writing the script) with limited effectiveness	• uses creative thinking skills (in planning and writing the script) with some effectiveness	• uses creative thinking skills (in planning and writing the script) with considerable effectiveness	• uses creative thinking skills (in planning and writing the script) with a high degree of effectiveness
Communication	*The student:*				
• communication of ideas and theme	• communicates ideas and theme with very limited clarity	• communicates ideas and theme with limited clarity	• communicates ideas and theme with some clarity	• communicates ideas and theme with considerable clarity	• communicates ideas and theme with a high degree of clarity
• communication to an audience for a purpose	• communicates with very limited sense of audience and purpose	• communicates with limited sense of audience and purpose	• communicates with some sense of audience and purpose	• communicates with a clear sense of audience and purpose	• communicates with a strong sense of audience and purpose
• use of the script form	• shows very limited command of the script form	• shows limited command of the script form	• shows some command of the script form	• shows considerable command of the script form	• shows extensive command of the script form
Application	*The student:*				
• application of language conventions	• uses language conventions with very limited accuracy and effectiveness	• uses language conventions with limited accuracy and effectiveness	• uses language conventions with some accuracy and effectiveness	• uses language conventions with considerable accuracy and effectiveness	• uses language conventions with a high degree of accuracy and effectiveness
• application of the writing process	• uses the writing process with very limited effectiveness	• uses the writing process with limited effectiveness	• uses the writing process with some effectiveness	• uses the writing process with considerable effectiveness	• uses the writing process with a high degree of effectiveness

* For a description of the levels of student achievement, please see The Achievement Chart for English, *The Ontario Curriculum Grades 9 and 10*, pp.46–49.

SHORT STORY

NAME: _____   DATE: _____

Categories	Below Level 1	50–59% Level 1	60–69% Level 2	70–79% Level 3	80–100% Level 4
LEVELS OF ACHIEVEMENT* (spanning)					
Knowledge/ Understanding	*The student:*				
• knowledge of the elements of the short story form	• shows very limited knowledge of the elements of the short story form	• shows limited knowledge of the elements of the short story form	• shows some knowledge of the elements of the short story form	• shows considerable knowledge of the elements of the short story form	• shows thorough knowledge of the elements of the short story form
• understanding of ideas and theme	• shows very limited understanding of ideas and theme	• shows limited understanding of ideas and theme	• shows some understanding of ideas and theme	• shows considerable understanding of ideas and theme	• shows thorough and insightful understanding of ideas and theme
• understanding of the uses and effect of stylistic devices and point of view	• shows very limited understanding of stylistic devices and point of view	• shows limited understanding of stylistic devices and point of view	• shows some understanding of stylistic devices and point of view	• shows considerable understanding of stylistic devices and point of view	• shows thorough and insightful understanding of stylistic devices and point of view
Thinking/Inquiry	*The student:*				
• creative thinking skills	• uses creative thinking skills (in planning and writing the short story) with very limited effectiveness	• uses creative thinking skills (in planning and writing the short story) with limited effectiveness	• uses creative thinking skills (in planning and writing the short story) with some effectiveness	• uses creative thinking skills (in planning and writing the short story) with considerable effectiveness	• uses creative thinking skills (in planning and writing the short story) with a high degree of effectiveness
Communication	*The student:*				
• communication of ideas and theme	• communicates ideas and theme with very limited clarity	• communicates ideas and theme with limited clarity	• communicates ideas and theme with some clarity	• communicates ideas and theme with considerable clarity	• communicates ideas and theme with a high degree of clarity
• communication to an audience for a purpose	• communicates with a very limited sense of audience and purpose	• communicates with a limited sense of audience and purpose	• communicates with some sense of audience and purpose	• communicates with a clear sense of audience and purpose	• communicates with a strong sense of audience and purpose
• use of the elements of the short story form	• shows very limited command of the elements of the short story form	• shows limited command of the elements of the short story form	• shows some command of the elements of the short story form	• shows considerable command of the elements of the short story form	• shows extensive command of the elements of the short story form
Application	*The student:*				
• application of the writing process	• uses the writing process with very limited effectiveness	• uses the writing process with limited effectiveness	• uses the writing process with some effectiveness	• uses the writing process with considerable effectiveness	• uses the writing process with a high degree of effectiveness
• application of language conventions	• uses language conventions with very limited accuracy and effectiveness	• uses language conventions with limited accuracy and effectiveness	• uses language conventions with some accuracy and effectiveness	• uses language conventions with considerable accuracy and effectiveness	• uses language conventions with a high degree of accuracy and effectiveness

* For a description of the levels of student achievement, please see The Achievement Chart for English, *The Ontario Curriculum Grades 9 and 10*, pp.46–49.

GRADE 9 ACADEMIC CURRICULUM EXPECTATIONS	UNIT
LITERATURE STUDIES AND READING	
Overall (LIV.01D) • read and demonstrate an understanding of a variety of literary and informational texts, from contemporary and historical periods	**Unit 1:** Humorous Personal Narrative **Unit 2:** Short Story **Narration:** Reflect and Build on Your Learning **Unit 4:** Poetry **Description:** Reflect and Build on Your Learning **Exposition:** Reflect and Build on Your Learning **Persuasion:** Reflect and Build on Your Learning
Specific (LI1.01D) • describe information, ideas, opinions, and themes in print and electronic texts they have read during the year from different cultures and historical periods and in a variety of genres, including novels, short stories, plays, poems, biographies, short essays, and articles from newspapers, magazines, and encyclopedias	**Unit 2:** Short Story **Unit 4:** Poetry **Unit 5:** Profile **Unit 6:** Event Description **Unit 7:** Explanation
(LI1.02D) • select and read texts for different purposes, with an emphasis on recognizing the elements of literary genres and the organization of informational materials, collecting and assessing information, responding imaginatively, and exploring human experiences and values	**Unit 1:** Humorous Personal Narrative **Unit 2:** Short Story **Unit 3:** Script **Unit 4:** Poetry **Unit 6:** Event Description **Unit 8:** Précis **Unit 9:** Research Report **Unit 10:** Comparison **Unit 11:** Advertisement
(LI1.03B) • describe a variety of reading strategies and select and use them effectively before, during, and after reading to understand texts	**Unit 2:** Short Story **Unit 6:** Event Description **Unit 7:** Explanation **Unit 8:** Précis **Unit 9:** Research Report **Unit 10:** Comparison **Unit 12:** Letter to the Editor
(LI1.04D) • locate explicit information and ideas in texts to use in developing opinions and interpretations	**Unit 6:** Event Description **Unit 7:** Explanation **Unit 8:** Précis **Unit 9:** Research Report **Unit 10:** Comparison **Unit 11:** Advertisement **Unit 12:** Letter to the Editor
(LI1.05D) • analyze information, ideas, and elements in texts to make inferences about meaning	**Unit 1:** Humorous Personal Narrative **Unit 3:** Script **Unit 8:** Précis **Unit 10:** Comparison **Unit 12:** Letter to the Editor
(LI1.06D) • use specific evidence from a text to support opinions and judgments	**Unit 3:** Script **Unit 6:** Event Description **Unit 7:** Explanation **Unit 9:** Research Report **Unit 10:** Comparison
(LI1.07D) • explain how readers' different backgrounds might influence the way they understand and interpret a text	**Unit 2:** Short Story **Unit 10:** Comparison **Unit 12:** Letter to the Editor
(LI1.08D) • explain how the background of the author might influence the information and ideas in a text	**Unit 1:** Humorous Personal Narrative **Unit 4:** Poetry

LITERATURE STUDIES AND READING (continued)

Overall (LIV.02D)	• demonstrate an understanding of the elements of a variety of literary and informational forms, with a focus on plays, short stories, and short essays	**Unit 1:** Humorous Personal Narrative **Unit 2:** Short Story **Narration:** Reflect and Build on Your Learning **Unit 5:** Profile **Unit 6:** Event Description **Description:** Reflect and Build on Your Learning **Unit 7:** Explanation **Unit 8:** Précis **Unit 9:** Research Report **Exposition:** Reflect and Build on Your Learning **Unit 10:** Comparison **Unit 12:** Letter to the Editor **Persuasion:** Reflect and Build on Your Learning
Specific (LI2.01D)	• use knowledge of elements of drama, such as plot and subplot, character portrayal, conflict, dramatic structure, dramatic purpose, dramatic irony, dialogue, and stage directions, to understand and interpret examples of the genre	**Unit 3:** Script
(LI2.02D)	• use knowledge of elements of the short story, such as plot, characterization, setting, conflict, theme, mood, and point of view, to understand and interpret examples of the genre	**Unit 2:** Short Story **Unit 8:** Précis
(LI2.03D)	• use knowledge of elements of short essays, such as introductions, thesis statements, topic sentences, supporting details, connecting words, and conclusions, to understand and interpret examples of the genre	**Narration:** Reflect and Build on Your Learning
Overall (LIV.03B)	• identify and explain the effect of specific elements of style in a variety of literary and informational texts	**Unit 1:** Humorous Personal Narrative **Unit 2:** Short Story
Specific (LI3.01D)	• explain how authors use diction and phrasing to achieve particular effects in their writing	**Unit 6:** Event Description **Unit 12:** Letter to the Editor
(LI3.02D)	• explain how authors use stylistic devices, such as simile, metaphor, personification, imagery, foreshadowing, onomatopoeia, oxymoron, alliteration, and symbol, to achieve particular effects in their writing	**Unit 2:** Short Story **Unit 4:** Poetry
(LI3.03D)	• explain how authors and editors use design elements to help communicate ideas	**Unit 3:** Script **Unit 4:** Poetry **Unit 8:** Précis **Unit 9:** Research Report

WRITING

Overall (WRV.01D)	• use a variety of print and electronic sources to gather information and explore ideas for their written work	**Unit 1:** Humorous Personal Narrative **Unit 2:** Short Story **Unit 3:** Script **Unit 4:** Poetry **Unit 5:** Profile **Unit 6:** Event Description **Unit 7:** Explanation **Unit 8:** Précis **Unit 9:** Research Report **Unit 10:** Comparison **Unit 11:** Advertisement **Unit 12:** Letter to the Editor
Specific (WR1.01D)	• investigate potential topics by formulating questions, identifying information needs, and developing research plans to gather data	**Unit 1:** Humorous Personal Narrative **Unit 3:** Script **Narration:** Reflect and Build on Your Learning **Unit 5:** Profile **Unit 6:** Event Description **Unit 7:** Explanation **Unit 9:** Research Report **Unit 10:** Comparison

	WRITING (continued)	
(WR1.02D)	• locate and summarize information from print and electronic sources, including vertical files, periodicals, dictionaries, encyclopedias, electronic newsgroups, e-mail messages, and electronic databases	**Unit 1:** Humorous Personal Narrative **Unit 2:** Short Story **Unit 3:** Script **Unit 5:** Profile
(WR1.03D)	• group and label information and ideas; evaluate the relevance, accuracy, and completeness of the information and ideas; and discard irrelevant material	**Unit 2:** Short Story **Unit 5:** Profile **Unit 6:** Event Description **Unit 7:** Explanation **Unit 10:** Comparison **Unit 12:** Letter to the Editor
(WR1.04D)	• use the information and ideas generated by research to develop the content of written work	**Unit 3:** Script
Overall (WRV.02D)	• identify the literary and informational forms suited to various purposes and audiences and use the forms appropriately in their own writing, with an emphasis on supporting opinions or interpretations with specific information	**Unit 9:** Research Report
Specific (WR2.01D)	• demonstrate an understanding of literary and informational forms, such as myths, poems, short stories, scripts, advertisements, formal letters, reviews, and supported opinion essays, by selecting and using forms of writing appropriate to different purposes and audiences	**Unit 1:** Humorous Personal Narrative **Unit 2:** Short Story **Unit 3:** Script **Unit 4:** Poetry **Unit 5:** Profile **Unit 6:** Event Description
(WR2.02D)	• select first or third person and an appropriate level of language to suit the form, purpose, and audience of written work	**Unit 2:** Short Story
Overall (WRV.03D)	• use a variety of organizational techniques to present ideas and supporting details logically and coherently in written work	**Unit 1:** Humorous Personal Narrative **Unit 2:** Short Story **Unit 3:** Script **Narration:** Reflect and Build on Your Learning **Unit 4:** Poetry **Unit 5:** Profile **Unit 6:** Event Description **Description:** Reflect and Build on Your Learning **Unit 7:** Explanation **Unit 8:** Précis **Unit 9:** Research Report **Exposition:** Reflect and Build on Your Learning **Unit 10:** Comparison **Unit 11:** Advertisement **Unit 12:** Letter to the Editor **Persuasion:** Reflect and Build on Your Learning
Specific (WR3.01D)	• use a unifying image, mood, or voice to structure descriptive paragraphs or poems	**Unit 6:** Event Description
(WR3.02D)	• use changes in time, place, speaker, or point of view to structure narrative paragraphs	**Unit 5:** Profile
(WR3.03D)	• use a single controlling idea and connecting words to structure a series of paragraphs	**Unit 9:** Research Report
(WR3.04D)	• use key words from questions or prompts to organize ideas, information, and evidence in homework answers	**Exposition:** Reflect and Build on Your Learning
(WR3.05D)	• structure expository paragraphs using a topic sentence, supporting sentences to develop the topic, connecting words to link the sentences, and a concluding sentence	**Narration:** Reflect and Build on Your Learning **Exposition:** Reflect and Build on Your Learning

	WRITING (continued)	
(WR3.06D)	• provide an introduction, body, and conclusion in written reports and short essays	**Persuasion:** Reflect and Build on Your Learning
Overall (WRV.04D)	• revise their written work, independently and collaboratively, with a focus on support for ideas and opinions, accuracy, clarity, and unity	**Unit 1:** Humorous Personal Narrative **Unit 2:** Short Story **Unit 3:** Script **Narration:** Reflect and Build on Your Learning **Unit 4:** Poetry **Unit 5:** Profile **Unit 6:** Event Description **Description:** Reflect and Build on Your Learning **Unit 7:** Explanation **Unit 8:** Précis **Unit 9:** Research Report **Exposition:** Reflect and Build on Your Learning **Unit 10:** Comparison **Unit 11:** Advertisement **Unit 12:** Letter to the Editor **Persuasion:** Reflect and Build on Your Learning
Specific (WR4.01D)	• revise drafts to ensure that ideas are adequately developed with relevant supporting details and to achieve clarity and unity	**Unit 1:** Humorous Personal Narrative
(WR4.02B)	• revise drafts to ensure consistency in use of first or third person and use of an appropriate level of language	**Unit 5:** Profile
(WR4.03D)	• make constructive suggestions to peers	**Unit 2:** Short Story **Unit 3:** Script
(WR4.04B)	• consider reactions from teachers, peers, and others in revising and editing written work	**Unit 3:** Script
Overall (WRV.05D)	• edit and proofread to produce final drafts, using correct grammar, spelling, and punctuation, according to the conventions of standard Canadian English, with the support of print and electronic resources when appropriate	**Unit 1:** Humorous Personal Narrative **Unit 2:** Short Story **Unit 3:** Script **Narration:** Reflect and Build on Your Learning **Unit 4:** Poetry **Unit 5:** Profile **Unit 6:** Event Description **Description:** Reflect and Build on Your Learning **Unit 7:** Explanation **Unit 8:** Précis **Unit 9:** Research Report **Exposition:** Reflect and Build on Your Learning **Unit 10:** Comparison **Unit 11:** Advertisement **Unit 12:** Letter to the Editor **Persuasion:** Reflect and Build on Your Learning
Specific (WR5.01D)	• identify sources of ideas, information, and quotations in writing and independent research projects	**Unit 9:** Research Report
(WR5.02B)	• select the publication method or vehicle most accessible or appealing to the intended audience	**Unit 1:** Humorous Personal Narrative **Unit 7:** Explanation
(WR5.03D)	• assess their facility with the writing process, documenting their use of different genres and forms in personal and assigned writing and identifying goals for writing improvement and growth	**Unit 1:** Humorous Personal Narrative **Unit 5:** Profile
(WR5.04B)	• edit and proofread their own and others' writing, identifying and correcting errors according to the requirements for grammar, usage, spelling, and punctuation listed below:	**Unit 6:** Event Description **Unit 12:** Letter to the Editor
(WR5.05D)	• use parts of speech correctly: nouns, pronouns, verbs, adverbs, adjectives, conjunctions, prepositions, and interjections	**Unit 1:** Humorous Personal Narrative **Unit 2:** Short Story **Unit 9:** Research Report **Unit 10:** Comparison

GRADE 9 ACADEMIC CURRICULUM EXPECTATIONS	UNIT
WRITING (continued)	
(WR5.06D) • construct complete and correct compound and complex sentences, using the following sentence components as required: subject, predicate, object, subject complement; main and subordinate clauses; prepositional and participial phrases	**Unit 3:** Script **Unit 4:** Poetry **Unit 5:** Profile **Unit 6:** Event Description **Unit 7:** Explanation **Unit 8:** Précis **Unit 10:** Comparison
(WR5.07B) • identify and correct sentence fragments, run-on sentences, and comma splices	**Unit 8:** Précis **Unit 11:** Advertisement
(WR5.08B) • make compound subjects agree with verbs in simple and compound sentences	**Unit 9:** Research Report
(WR5.09B) • make pronouns agree with their antecedents in number and gender	**Unit 12:** Letter to the Editor
(WR5.10B) • use consistent and appropriate verb tense and voice for clarity in narrative and expository writing	**Unit 1:** Humorous Personal Narrative **Unit 7:** Explanation
(WR5.11B) • use knowledge of a wide range of spelling patterns and rules to identify, analyze, and correct spelling errors	**Unit 3:** Script **Unit 6:** Event Description **Unit 11:** Advertisement
(WR5.12B) • use and spell homophones correctly	**Unit 10:** Comparison
(WR5.13B) • use the apostrophe correctly when spelling contractions and possessives	**Unit 9:** Research Report
(WR5.14B) • use a variety of resources to correct errors in spelling	**Unit 12:** Letter to the Editor
(WR5.15B) • use punctuation correctly, including period, question mark, exclamation mark, comma, dash, apostrophe, colon, quotation marks, parentheses, and ellipses	**Unit 1:** Humorous Personal Narrative **Unit 7:** Explanation **Unit 10:** Comparison
(WR5.16B) • adapt punctuation and capitalization for the special requirements of direct quotations, scripts, dialogue, and poetry	**Unit 2:** Short Story **Unit 3:** Script **Unit 4:** Poetry **Unit 5:** Profile
LANGUAGE	
Overall (LGV.01D) • use knowledge of vocabulary and language conventions to speak, write, and read competently using a level of language appropriate to the purpose and audience	**Unit 8:** Précis
Specific (LG1.01B) • describe strategies used to expand vocabulary and provide evidence of other vocabulary-building activities	**Unit 4:** Poetry **Unit 5:** Profile **Unit 6:** Event Description **Unit 7:** Explanation **Unit 8:** Précis
(LG1.02B) • identify and explain examples of slang, jargon, dialect, and colloquialism, as well as of standard Canadian English, in literary texts and their own oral and written work	**Unit 2:** Short Story **Unit 3:** Script **Narration:** Reflect and Build on Your Learning **Unit 8:** Précis **Unit 11:** Advertisement
(LG1.03B) • identify words borrowed from other languages and words and terms recently introduced to describe new ideas, inventions, and products, and explain their origins	**Unit 1:** Humorous Personal Narrative **Unit 2:** Short Story **Unit 3:** Script **Narration:** Reflect and Build on Your Learning **Unit 5:** Profile **Unit 6:** Event Description **Unit 7:** Explanation **Unit 8:** Précis **Unit 9:** Research Report **Unit 10:** Comparison **Unit 11:** Advertisement **Unit 12:** Letter to the Editor

	LANGUAGE (continued)	
(LG1.04B)	• select words and phrases appropriate to informal and formal styles, to suit the purpose and intended audience of oral and written work	**Unit 3:** Script **Unit 6:** Event Description **Unit 12:** Letter to the Editor
(LG1.05D)	• recognize, describe, and use correctly, in oral and written language, the language structures of standard Canadian English and its conventions of grammar and usage, including: – parts of speech: nouns, pronouns, verbs, adverbs, adjectives, conjunctions, prepositions, interjections	**Unit 1:** Humorous Personal Narrative **Unit 2:** Short Story **Unit 3:** Script **Unit 9:** Research Report **Unit 10:** Comparison **Unit 12:** Letter to the Editor
	– simple, compound, and complex sentences	**Unit 5:** Profile
	– components of sentences: subject, predicate, object, subject complement, prepositional and participial phrases, main and subordinate clauses	**Unit 3:** Script **Unit 4:** Poetry **Unit 6:** Event Description **Unit 7:** Explanation **Unit 8:** Précis **Unit 10:** Comparison
	– agreement between subject and verb, and between pronoun and antecedent	**Unit 9:** Research Report **Unit 12:** Letter to the Editor
	– consistency of verb tense and voice	**Unit 1:** Humorous Personal Narrative **Unit 7:** Explanation
(LG1.06B)	• recognize, describe, and correct sentence errors in oral and written language	**Unit 8:** Précis **Unit 11:** Advertisement
(LG1.07B)	• recognize, describe, and use correctly, in oral and written language, the conventions of standard Canadian English for spelling, capitalization, and punctuation, including: – spelling: homophones and possessive pronouns and adjectives	**Unit 10:** Comparison **Unit 12:** Letter to the Editor
	– capitalization: of proper nouns and in direct quotations, scripts, dialogue, and poetry	**Unit 2:** Short Story **Unit 12:** Letter to the Editor
	– punctuation: period, question mark, exclamation mark, comma, dash, apostrophe, colon, quotation marks, parentheses, ellipses	**Unit 1:** Humorous Personal Narrative **Unit 2:** Short Story **Unit 7:** Explanation **Unit 9:** Research Report **Unit 10:** Comparison **Unit 12:** Letter to the Editor
Overall (LGV.02B)	• use listening techniques and oral communication skills to participate in classroom discussions and more formal activities, such as storytelling, role playing, and reporting/presenting, for specific purposes and audiences	**Unit 1:** Humorous Personal Narrative **Unit 2:** Short Story **Unit 5:** Profile **Description:** Reflect and Build on Your Learning **Unit 8:** Précis **Unit 10:** Comparison **Unit 12:** Letter to the Editor
Specific (LG2.01D)	• communicate orally in group discussions for different purposes, with a focus on identifying key ideas and supporting details, distinguishing fact from opinion, asking clarifying questions, and following instructions	**Unit 2:** Short Story **Unit 3:** Script **Narration:** Reflect and Build on Your Learning **Unit 6:** Event Description **Unit 9:** Research Report **Unit 10:** Comparison **Unit 12:** Letter to the Editor
(LG2.02D)	• communicate in group discussions by sharing the duties of the group, speaking in turn, listening actively, taking notes, paraphrasing key points made by others, exchanging and challenging ideas and information, asking appropriate questions, reconsidering their own ideas and opinions, managing conflict, and respecting the opinions of others	**Unit 2:** Short Story **Unit 6:** Event Description **Unit 8:** Précis **Unit 12:** Letter to the Editor

GRADE 9 ACADEMIC CURRICULUM EXPECTATIONS	UNIT
LANGUAGE (continued)	
(LG2.03D) • plan and make oral presentations to a small group or the class, selecting and using vocabulary and methods of delivery to suit audience and purpose	**Unit 1:** Humorous Personal Narrative **Narration:** Reflect and Build on Your Learning **Unit 4:** Poetry **Unit 5:** Profile **Unit 6:** Event Description **Unit 7:** Explanation **Unit 8:** Précis **Unit 9:** Research Report **Unit 12:** Letter to the Editor
(LG2.04D) • use specific examples, facial expressions, gestures, intonation, humour, and visual aids and technology, as appropriate, to engage the audience's interest during oral presentations	**Unit 4:** Poetry **Unit 7:** Explanation
(LG2.05D) • practise with cue cards and relaxation exercises (and with visual aids and technology, if used) to ensure confident delivery in oral presentations	**Unit 3:** Script **Unit 6:** Event Description **Unit 9:** Research Report
(LG2.06D) • explain how oral communication skills can contribute to success in all curriculum areas and the world outside the school	**Unit 5:** Profile **Unit 11:** Advertisement
(LG2.07D) • analyze their own and others' oral presentations to identify strengths and weaknesses, and plan ways to improve their performance	**Unit 1:** Humorous Personal Narrative **Unit 8:** Précis **Unit 10:** Comparison **Unit 12:** Letter to the Editor
MEDIA STUDIES	
Overall (MDV.01D) • use knowledge of the elements, intended audiences, and production practices of a variety of media forms to analyze specific media works	**Unit 1:** Humorous Personal Narrative **Unit 2:** Short Story **Narration:** Reflect and Build on Your Learning **Unit 4:** Poetry **Unit 5:** Profile **Unit 6:** Event Description **Unit 7:** Explanation **Unit 10:** Comparison **Unit 11:** Advertisement
Specific (MD1.01B) • demonstrate critical thinking skills by identifying the differences between explicit and implicit messages in media works	**Unit 1:** Humorous Personal Narrative **Unit 11:** Advertisement **Unit 12:** Letter to the Editor **Persuasion:** Reflect and Build on Your Learning
(MD1.02D) • identify how elements of media forms are used in a variety of media works and explain the effects of different treatments	**Unit 1:** Humorous Personal Narrative **Unit 3:** Script **Unit 5:** Profile **Unit 6:** Event Description **Unit 7:** Explanation **Unit 9:** Research Report **Unit 10:** Comparison **Unit 11:** Advertisement **Unit 12:** Letter to the Editor
(MD1.03D) • compare and explain their own and their peers' reactions to a variety of media works	**Unit 10:** Comparison **Unit 11:** Advertisement **Unit 12:** Letter to the Editor
(MD1.04D) • identify factors that influence media production and distribution and explain the effect of these factors on specific media works	**Unit 11:** Advertisement
Overall (MDV.02D) • use knowledge of a variety of media forms, purposes, and audiences to create media works and describe their intended effect	**Unit 5:** Profile **Unit 6:** Event Description **Description:** Reflect and Build on Your Learning **Unit 8:** Précis

	MEDIA STUDIES (continued)	
Specific (MD2.01D)	• adapt a work of literature to another media form and determine what aspects have been strengthened and/or weakened by the adaptation	**Unit 2:** Short Story **Unit 3:** Script **Unit 4:** Poetry **Unit 9:** Research Report **Unit 12:** Letter to the Editor
(MD2.02D)	• create media works for different purposes and explain how each has been designed to achieve its particular purpose	**Unit 2:** Short Story **Unit 5:** Profile **Unit 6:** Event Description **Unit 8:** Précis **Unit 11:** Advertisement
(MD2.03D)	• create media works appropriate to different audiences and explain why a particular design should appeal to a particular audience	**Persuasion:** Reflect and Build on Your Learning

GRADE 9 APPLIED CURRICULUM EXPECTATIONS	UNIT
LITERATURE STUDIES AND READING	
Overall (LIV.01P)	• read and demonstrate an understanding of a variety of literary and informational texts	**Unit 1:** Humorous Personal Narrative **Unit 2:** Short Story **Narration:** Reflect and Build on Your Learning **Unit 4:** Poetry **Description:** Reflect and Build on Your Learning **Exposition:** Reflect and Build on Your Learning **Persuasion:** Reflect and Build on Your Learning
Specific (LI1.01P)	• describe information, ideas, opinions, and themes in texts they have read during the year from a variety of print and electronic sources, including biographies, short stories, poems, plays, novels, brochures, and articles from newspapers, magazines, and encyclopedias	**Unit 2:** Short Story **Unit 4:** Poetry **Unit 5:** Profile **Unit 6:** Event Description **Unit 7:** Explanation
(LI1.02P)	• select and read texts for a variety of purposes, with an emphasis on recognizing the elements of literary genres and the organization of informational materials, collecting and using information, extending personal knowledge, and responding imaginatively	**Unit 2:** Short Story **Unit 3:** Script **Unit 4:** Poetry **Unit 6:** Event Description **Unit 8:** Précis **Unit 9:** Research Report **Unit 10:** Comparison **Unit 11:** Advertisement **Unit 12:** Letter to the Editor
(LI1.03B)	• describe a variety of reading strategies and select and use them effectively before, during, and after reading to understand texts	**Unit 2:** Short Story **Unit 4:** Poetry **Unit 6:** Event Description **Unit 7:** Explanation **Unit 8:** Précis **Unit 9:** Research Report **Unit 10:** Comparison **Unit 12:** Letter to the Editor
(LI1.04P)	• locate and use explicit information and ideas from texts in forming opinions and developing generalizations	**Unit 6:** Event Description **Unit 7:** Explanation **Unit 8:** Précis **Unit 9:** Research Report **Unit 10:** Comparison **Unit 11:** Advertisement **Unit 12:** Letter to the Editor
(LI1.05P)	• make inferences based on the information and ideas presented in texts	**Unit 1:** Humorous Personal Narrative **Unit 3:** Script **Unit 8:** Précis **Unit 12:** Letter to the Editor
(LI1.06B)	• use specific references from a text to support opinions and judgments	**Unit 3:** Script **Unit 4:** Poetry **Unit 6:** Event Description **Unit 7:** Explanation **Unit 10:** Comparison
(LI1.07P)	• identify how readers' different backgrounds might influence the way they understand and interpret a text	**Unit 2:** Short Story

GRADE 9 APPLIED CURRICULUM EXPECTATIONS		UNIT
LITERATURE STUDIES AND READING (continued)		
Overall (LIV.02P)	• demonstrate an understanding of the elements of a variety of literary and informational forms, with a focus on plays, short stories, and newspaper and magazine articles	**Unit 1:** Humorous Personal Narrative **Unit 2:** Short Story **Narration:** Reflect and Build on Your Learning **Unit 5:** Profile **Unit 6:** Event Description **Description:** Reflect and Build on Your Learning **Unit 7:** Explanation **Unit 8:** Précis **Unit 9:** Research Report **Exposition:** Reflect and Build on Your Learning **Unit 12:** Letter to the Editor **Persuasion:** Reflect and Build on Your Learning
Specific (LI2.01P)	• use knowledge of elements of drama, such as plot and subplot, character development and revelation, conflict, dialogue, and stage directions, to understand and interpret examples of the genre	**Unit 3:** Script
(LI2.02P)	• use knowledge of elements of the short story, such as plot, character, setting, conflict, theme, and atmosphere, to understand and interpret texts in the genre	**Unit 2:** Short Story **Unit 8:** Précis
(LI2.03P)	• use knowledge of elements of newspaper and magazine articles, such as headlines, leads, the 5 W's (who, what, where, when, and why), titles, subtitles, and photographs, to understand and interpret texts in the genre	**Unit 10:** Comparison
Overall (LIV.03B)	• identify and explain the effect of specific elements of style in a variety of literary and informational texts	**Unit 1:** Humorous Personal Narrative
Specific (LI3.01P)	• explain how authors use stylistic devices, such as simile, metaphor, personification, imagery, and foreshadowing, to achieve intended effects	**Unit 2:** Short Story
(LI3.02P)	• explain how authors choose words and phrases to achieve intended effects	**Unit 4:** Poetry **Unit 6:** Event Description
(LI3.03P)	• explain how authors and editors use design elements to help convey meaning	**Unit 3:** Script **Unit 4:** Poetry **Unit 8:** Précis **Unit 9:** Research Report
WRITING		
Overall (WRV.01P)	• use print and electronic sources to gather information and explore ideas for their written work	**Unit 1:** Humorous Personal Narrative **Unit 2:** Short Story **Unit 3:** Script **Unit 4:** Poetry **Unit 5:** Profile **Unit 6:** Event Description **Unit 7:** Explanation **Unit 8:** Précis **Unit 9:** Research Report **Unit 10:** Comparison **Unit 11:** Advertisement **Unit 12:** Letter to the Editor
Specific (WR1.01P)	• investigate potential topics by asking questions, identifying information needs, and developing research plans to gather data	**Unit 1:** Humorous Personal Narrative **Unit 2:** Short Story **Narration:** Reflect and Build on Your Learning **Unit 5:** Profile **Unit 6:** Event Description **Unit 7:** Explanation **Unit 10:** Comparison **Unit 11:** Advertisement
(WR1.02P)	• locate and record information and ideas from print and electronic sources, including newspapers and magazines, dictionaries, vertical files, and electronic databases	**Unit 1:** Humorous Personal Narrative **Unit 2:** Short Story **Unit 3:** Script **Unit 5:** Profile

GRADE 9 APPLIED CURRICULUM EXPECTATIONS		UNIT
	WRITING (continued)	
(WR1.03P)	• sort and group information and ideas; assess their relevance and accuracy, and discard irrelevant material	**Unit 2:** Short Story **Unit 5:** Profile **Unit 6:** Event Description **Unit 7:** Explanation
(WR1.04P)	• use the information and ideas generated by research to explore topics for written work	**Unit 5:** Profile
Overall (WRV.02P)	• identify the literary and informational forms suited to specific purposes and audiences and use the forms appropriately in their own writing, with an emphasis on communicating information accurately	**Unit 7:** Explanation
Specific (WR2.01P)	• identify the purpose for each piece of writing	**Unit 11:** Advertisement
(WR2.02P)	• identify the specific audience for each piece of writing	**Unit 11:** Advertisement
(WR2.03P)	• demonstrate an understanding of literary and informational forms of writing, such as letters, personal narratives, short stories, answers to homework questions, summaries, and reports on research topics, by selecting a form appropriate to the specific purpose and audience for each piece of writing	**Unit 3:** Script **Narration:** Reflect and Build on Your Learning **Unit 4:** Poetry **Unit 5:** Profile **Unit 6:** Event Description
(WR2.04P)	• use the third-person singular and an appropriate level of language in expository forms requiring objectivity	**Unit 8:** Précis
Overall (WRV.03P)	• use a variety of forms of writing to express themselves, clarify their ideas, and engage the audience's attention, imagination, and interest	**Unit 1:** Humorous Personal Narrative **Unit 2:** Short Story **Unit 3:** Script **Narration:** Reflect and Build on Your Learning **Unit 4:** Poetry **Unit 5:** Profile **Unit 6:** Event Description **Description:** Reflect and Build on Your Learning **Unit 7:** Explanation **Unit 8:** Précis **Unit 9:** Research Report **Exposition:** Reflect and Build on Your Learning **Unit 10:** Comparison **Unit 11:** Advertisement **Unit 12:** Letter to the Editor **Persuasion:** Reflect and Build on Your Learning
Specific (WR3.01P)	• use key words in questions or prompts to organize information and ideas in homework answers	**Exposition:** Reflect and Build on Your Learning
(WR3.02P)	• structure expository paragraphs using a topic sentence, supporting sentences to develop the topic, connecting words to link the sentences, and a concluding sentence	**Narration:** Reflect and Build on Your Learning **Exposition:** Reflect and Build on Your Learning
(WR3.03P)	• use a unifying image, emotion, or sensation to structure descriptive paragraphs or poems	**Unit 6:** Event Description
(WR3.04P)	• use changes in time, place, or speaker to structure narrative paragraphs	**Unit 2:** Short Story
(WR3.05P)	• use a single controlling idea to structure a series of paragraphs	**Unit 9:** Research Report
(WR3.06P)	• provide an introduction, body, and conclusion in written reports	**Persuasion:** Reflect and Build on Your Learning
(WR3.07P)	• present direction, instructions, and reports of investigations in a logical order, using an organizational pattern such as examples, chronological order, or comparison	**Exposition:** Reflect and Build on Your Learning

GRADE 9 APPLIED CURRICULUM EXPECTATIONS	UNIT
WRITING (continued)	

Overall (WRV.04B)	• revise their written work, collaboratively and independently, with a focus on support for ideas, accuracy, clarity, and unity	**Unit 1:** Humorous Personal Narrative **Unit 2:** Short Story **Unit 3:** Script **Narration:** Reflect and Build on Your Learning **Unit 4:** Poetry **Unit 5:** Profile **Unit 6:** Event Description **Description:** Reflect and Build on Your Learning **Unit 7:** Explanation **Unit 8:** Précis **Unit 9:** Research Report **Exposition:** Reflect and Build on Your Learning **Unit 10:** Comparison **Unit 11:** Advertisement **Unit 12:** Letter to the Editor **Persuasion:** Reflect and Build on Your Learning
Specific (WR4.01P)	• revise drafts to ensure that ideas are adequately developed with supporting details, and to achieve clarity and unity	**Unit 6:** Event Description
(WR4.02B)	• revise drafts to ensure consistency in use of first or third person and use of an appropriate level of language	**Unit 5:** Profile
(WR4.03P)	• make constructive suggestions to peers, using prompts, checklists, open-ended statements, and questions	**Unit 2:** Short Story **Unit 3:** Script
(WR4.04B)	• consider reactions from teachers, peers, and others in revising and editing written work	**Unit 3:** Script
Overall (WRV.05B)	• edit and proofread to produce final drafts, using correct grammar, spelling, and punctuation, according to the conventions of standard Canadian English specified for this course, with the support of print and electronic resources when appropriate	**Unit 1:** Humorous Personal Narrative **Unit 2:** Short Story **Unit 3:** Script **Narration:** Reflect and Build on Your Learning **Unit 4:** Poetry **Unit 5:** Profile **Unit 6:** Event Description **Description:** Reflect and Build on Your Learning **Unit 7:** Explanation **Unit 8:** Précis **Unit 9:** Research Report **Exposition:** Reflect and Build on Your Learning **Unit 10:** Comparison **Unit 11:** Advertisement **Unit 12:** Letter to the Editor **Persuasion:** Reflect and Build on Your Learning
Specific (WR5.01P)	• identify sources of ideas, information, and quotations in written work	**Unit 9:** Research Report
(WR5.02B)	• select the publication method or vehicle most accessible or appealing to the intended audience	**Unit 1:** Humorous Personal Narrative **Unit 7:** Explanation
(WR5.03P)	• provide documentation showing their use of the writing process	**Unit 1:** Humorous Personal Narrative **Unit 5:** Profile
(WR5.04B)	• edit and proofread their own and others' writing, identifying and correcting errors according to the requirements for grammar, usage, spelling, and punctuation listed below:	**Unit 6:** Event Description **Unit 12:** Letter to the Editor
(WR5.05P)	• identify and use parts of speech correctly: nouns, pronouns, verbs, adverbs, adjectives, conjunctions, prepositions, and interjections	**Unit 1:** Humorous Personal Narrative **Unit 2:** Short Story **Unit 10:** Comparison

GRADE 9 APPLIED CURRICULUM EXPECTATIONS	UNIT
WRITING (continued)	
(WR5.06P) • construct complete and correct compound and complex sentences, using the following sentence components as required: subject, predicate, object, subject complement; main and subordinate clauses; prepositional phrases	**Unit 3:** Script **Unit 4:** Poetry **Unit 5:** Profile **Unit 6:** Event Description **Unit 7:** Explanation **Unit 8:** Précis **Unit 9:** Research Report **Unit 10:** Comparison
(WR5.07B) • identify and correct sentence fragments, run-on sentences, and comma splices	**Unit 8:** Précis **Unit 11:** Advertisement
(WR5.08B) • make compound subjects agree with verbs in simple and compound sentences	**Unit 9:** Research Report
(WR5.09B) • make pronouns agree with their antecedents in number and gender	**Unit 12:** Letter to the Editor
(WR5.10B) • use consistent and appropriate verb tense and voice (i.e., active and passive) for clarity in narrative and expository writing	**Unit 1:** Humorous Personal Narrative **Unit 7:** Explanation
(WR5.11B) • use knowledge of a wide range of spelling patterns and rules to identify, analyze, and correct spelling errors	**Unit 3:** Script **Unit 6:** Event Description **Unit 11:** Advertisement
(WR5.12B) • use and spell homophones correctly	**Unit 10:** Comparison
(WR5.13B) • use the apostrophe correctly when spelling contractions and possessives	**Unit 9:** Research Report
(WR5.14B) • use a variety of resources to correct errors in spelling	**Unit 12:** Letter to the Editor
(WR5.15B) • use punctuation correctly, including period, question mark, exclamation mark, comma, dash, apostrophe, colon, quotation marks, parentheses, and ellipses	**Unit 1:** Humorous Personal Narrative **Unit 7:** Explanation **Unit 10:** Comparison
(WR5.16B) • adapt punctuation and capitalization for the special requirements of direct quotations, scripts, dialogue, and poetry	**Unit 2:** Short Story **Unit 3:** Script **Unit 4:** Poetry **Unit 5:** Profile
LANGUAGE	
Overall (LGV.01P) • use knowledge of vocabulary and language conventions to speak, write, and read clearly and correctly	**Unit 8:** Précis
Specific (LG1.01B) • describe strategies used to expand vocabulary and provide evidence of other vocabulary-building activities	**Unit 4:** Poetry **Unit 5:** Profile **Unit 6:** Event Description **Unit 7:** Explanation **Unit 8:** Précis
(LG1.02B) • identify and explain examples of slang, jargon, dialect, and colloquialism, as well as of standard Canadian English, in literary texts and their own oral and written work	**Unit 2:** Short Story **Unit 3:** Script **Narration:** Reflect and Build on Your Learning **Unit 8:** Précis **Unit 11:** Advertisement
(LG1.03B) • identify words borrowed from other languages and words and terms recently introduced to describe new ideas, inventions, and products, and explain their origins	**Unit 1:** Humorous Personal Narrative **Unit 2:** Short Story **Unit 3:** Script **Narration:** Reflect and Build on Your Learning **Unit 5:** Profile **Unit 6:** Event Description **Unit 7:** Explanation **Unit 8:** Précis **Unit 9:** Research Report **Unit 10:** Comparison **Unit 12:** Letter to the Editor

GRADE 9 APPLIED CURRICULUM EXPECTATIONS	UNIT
LANGUAGE (continued)	
(LG1.04B) • select words and phrases appropriate to informal and formal styles, to suit the purpose and intended audience of oral and written work	**Unit 3:** Script **Unit 6:** Event Description **Unit 12:** Letter to the Editor
(LG1.05P) • recognize, describe, and use correctly, in oral and written language, the language structures of standard Canadian English and its conventions of grammar and usage, including: – parts of speech: nouns, pronouns, verbs, adverbs, adjectives, conjunctions, prepositions, interjections	**Unit 1:** Humorous Personal Narrative **Unit 2:** Short Story **Unit 3:** Script **Unit 9:** Research Report **Unit 10:** Comparison **Unit 12:** Letter to the Editor
– simple, compound, and complex sentences	**Unit 5:** Profile
– components of sentences: subject, predicate, object, subject complement, prepositional phrases, main and subordinate clauses	**Unit 3:** Script **Unit 4:** Poetry **Unit 6:** Event Description **Unit 7:** Explanation **Unit 8:** Précis **Unit 10:** Comparison
– agreement between subject and verb, and between pronoun and antecedent	**Unit 9:** Research Report **Unit 12:** Letter to the Editor
– consistency of verb tense and voice	**Unit 1:** Humorous Personal Narrative **Unit 7:** Explanation
(LG1.06B) • recognize, describe, and correct sentence errors in oral and written language	**Unit 8:** Précis **Unit 11:** Advertisement
(LG1.07B) • recognize, describe, and use correctly, in oral and written language, the conventions of standard Canadian English for spelling, capitalization, and punctuation, including: – spelling: homophones and possessive pronouns and adjectives	**Unit 10:** Comparison **Unit 12:** Letter to the Editor
– capitalization: of proper nouns and in direct quotations, scripts, dialogue, and poetry	**Unit 2:** Short Story **Unit 12:** Letter to the Editor
– punctuation: period, question mark, exclamation mark, comma, dash, apostrophe, colon, quotation marks, parentheses, ellipses	**Unit 1:** Humorous Personal Narrative **Unit 2:** Short Story **Unit 7:** Explanation **Unit 9:** Research Report **Unit 10:** Comparison **Unit 12:** Letter to the Editor
Overall (LGV.02B) • use listening techniques and oral communication skills to participate in classroom discussions and more formal activities, such as storytelling, role playing, and reporting/presenting, for specific purposes and audiences	**Unit 1:** Humorous Personal Narrative **Unit 3:** Script **Narration:** Reflect and Build on Your Learning **Unit 4:** Poetry **Unit 5:** Profile **Description:** Reflect and Build on Your Learning **Unit 10:** Comparison **Unit 12:** Letter to the Editor
Specific (LG2.01P) • use listening techniques and oral communication skills to participate in group discussions	**Unit 2:** Short Story **Unit 3:** Script **Narration:** Reflect and Build on Your Learning **Unit 6:** Event Description **Unit 9:** Research Report **Unit 12:** Letter to the Editor
(LG2.02P) • use techniques of effective listening and demonstrate an understanding of oral presentations by restating the main ideas presented and identifying the strengths and weaknesses of presentations	**Unit 8:** Précis

GRADE 9 APPLIED CURRICULUM EXPECTATIONS	UNIT
LANGUAGE (continued)	
(LG2.03P) • work with a partner to plan and make oral presentations to a small group, selecting and using vocabulary and methods of delivery to suit audience and purpose	**Unit 1:** Humorous Personal Narrative **Unit 4:** Poetry **Unit 6:** Event Description **Unit 7:** Explanation **Unit 8:** Précis **Unit 9:** Research Report **Unit 10:** Comparison **Unit 11:** Advertisement **Unit 12:** Letter to the Editor
(LG2.04P) • use eye contact, specific examples, humour, and visual aids and technology, as appropriate, to engage the audience's interest during oral presentations	**Unit 5:** Profile
(LG2.05P) • practise with cue cards, use breathing exercises, and rehearse with peers (and with visual aids and technology, if used), to ensure confident delivery in oral presentations	**Unit 3:** Script **Unit 6:** Event Description **Unit 9:** Research Report
(LG2.06P) • identify examples of the use of oral communication skills in school and the world outside the school	**Unit 11:** Advertisement
(LG2.07D) • analyze their own and others' oral communication skills, identifying strengths and weaknesses and suggesting ways to improve	**Unit 8:** Précis **Unit 10:** Comparison **Unit 12:** Letter to the Editor
MEDIA STUDIES	
Overall (MDV.01P) • identify and describe the elements, intended audiences, and production practices of a variety of media forms	**Unit 1:** Humorous Personal Narrative **Unit 2:** Short Story **Narration:** Reflect and Build on Your Learning **Unit 4:** Poetry **Unit 5:** Profile **Unit 6:** Event Description **Unit 7:** Explanation **Unit 10:** Comparison **Unit 11:** Advertisement
Specific (MD1.01B) • demonstrate critical thinking skills by identifying the differences between explicit and implicit messages in media works	**Unit 1:** Humorous Personal Narrative **Unit 11:** Advertisement **Persuasion:** Reflect and Build on Your Learning
(MD1.02P) • identify and describe the elements used to structure media works in a variety of forms	**Unit 1:** Humorous Personal Narrative **Unit 3:** Script **Unit 5:** Profile **Unit 6:** Event Description **Unit 7:** Explanation **Unit 9:** Research Report **Unit 10:** Comparison **Unit 11:** Advertisement **Unit 12:** Letter to the Editor
(MD1.03P) • compare the reactions of different people or groups to a variety of media works	**Unit 2:** Short Story **Unit 10:** Comparison **Unit 11:** Advertisement **Unit 12:** Letter to the Editor
(MD1.04P) • identify factors that influence media production, distribution, and advertising	**Unit 11:** Advertisement
Overall (MDV.02P) • use knowledge of a variety of media forms, purposes, and audiences to create media works	**Unit 2:** Short Story **Unit 4:** Poetry **Unit 5:** Profile **Unit 6:** Event Description **Description:** Reflect and Build on Your Learning **Unit 8:** Précis

GRADE 9 APPLIED CURRICULUM EXPECTATIONS		UNIT
MEDIA STUDIES (continued)		
Specific (MD2.01P)	• adapt a work of literature for presentation in another media form	**Unit 2:** Short Story **Unit 3:** Script **Unit 4:** Poetry **Unit 9:** Research Report **Unit 12:** Letter to the Editor
(MD2.02P)	• create media works for different purposes	**Unit 2:** Short Story **Unit 4:** Poetry **Unit 6:** Event Description **Unit 8:** Précis **Unit 11:** Advertisement
(MD2.03P)	• analyze the characteristics of different audiences and create media works designed specifically for them	**Persuasion:** Reflect and Build on Your Learning